SHAKESPEAREAN TRAGEDY

Longman Critical Readers

General Editor:

Stan Smith, Professor of English, University of Dundee
Published titles:

K. M. Newton, *George Eliot*

Mary Eagleton, *Feminist Literary Criticism*

Gary Waller, *Shakespeare's Comedies*

John Drakakis, *Shakespearean Tragedy*

Richard Wilson and Richard Dutton, *New Historicism and Renaissance Drama*

Peter Brooker, *Modernism/Postmodernism*

Peter Widdowson, *D. H. Lawrence*

Rachel Bowlby, *Virginia Woolf*

Francis Mulhern, *Contemporary Marxist Literary Criticism*

Annabel Patterson, *John Milton*

Cynthia Chase, *Romanticism*

Michael O'Neill, *Shelley*

Stephanie Trigg, *Medieval English Poetry*

Antony Easthope, *Contemporary Film Theory*

Terry Eagleton, *Ideology*

Maud Ellmann, *Psychoanalytic Literary Criticism*

Andrew Bennett, *Readers and Reading*

Mark Currie, *Metafiction*

Brean Hammond, *Pope*

Graham Holderness, Bryan Loughrey, Andrew Murphy, *Shakespeare: Roman Plays*

Lynn Pykett, *Fin de Siècle Fiction*

Rebecca Stott, *Tennyson*

Steven Connor, *Charles Dickens*

Andrew Hadfield, *Edmund Spenser*

SHAKESPEAREAN TRAGEDY

Edited and Introduced by

John Drakakis

Longman

An imprint of Pearson Education

Harlow, England · London · New York · Reading, Massachusetts · San Francisco
Toronto · Don Mills, Ontario · Sydney · Tokyo · Singapore · Hong Kong · Seoul
Taipei · Cape Town · Madrid · Mexico City · Amsterdam · Munich · Paris · Milan

Pearson Education Limited
Edinburgh Gate, Harlow,
Essex CM 20 2JE, England
and Associated Companies throughout the world.

Visit us on the World Wide Web at:
http://www.pearsoneduc.com

First published 1992

British Library Cataloguing-in-Publication Data
Shakespearean tragedy. – (Longman critical readers)
    I. Drakakis, John II. Series 822.3

    ISBN 0–582–05115–0
    ISBN 0–582–05114–2 pbk

Library of Congress Cataloging-in-Publication Data
Shakespearean tragedy / edited and introduced by John Drakakis
        p. cm. – (Longman critical readers)
    Includes bibliographical references and index.
        ISBN 0–582–05115–0.—ISBN 0–582–05114–2 (pbk.)
        1. Shakespeare, William, 1564–1616–Tragedies.   2. Tragedy
    I. Drakakis, John. II. Series.
    PR2983.S448 1992   91–3194
    822.3' 3– –dc20   CIP

Set in 9 / 11½pt Palatino

Produced by Pearson Education Asia (Pte) Ltd.
Printed and bound by Antony Rowe Ltd, Eastbourne

Transferred to digital print on demand, 2003

Contents

Contents

General Editors' Preface

The outlines of contemporary critical theory are now often taught as a standard feature of a degree in literary studies. The development of particular theories has seen a thorough transformation of literary criticism. For example, Marxist and Foucauldian theories have revolutionized Shakespeare studies, and 'deconstruction' has led to a complete reassessment of Romantic poetry. Feminist criticism has left scarcely any period of literature unaffected by its searching critiques. Teachers of literary studies can no longer fall back on a standardized, received, methodology.

Lecturers and teachers are now urgently looking for guidance in a rapidly changing critical environment. They need help in understanding the latest revisions in literary theory, and especially in grasping the practical effects of the new theories in the form of theoretically sensitized new readings. A number of volumes in the series anthologize important essays on particular theories. However, in order to grasp the full implications and possible uses of particular theories it is essential to see them put to work. This series provides substantial volumes of new readings, presented in an accessible form and with a significant amount of editorial guidance.

Each volume includes a substantial introduction which explores the theoretical issues and conflicts embodied in the essays selected and locates areas of disagreement between positions. The pluralism of theories has to be put on the agenda of literary studies. We can no longer pretend that we all tacitly accept the same practices in literary studies. Neither is a *laissez-faire* attitude any longer tenable. Literature departments need to go beyond the mere toleration of theoretical differences: it is not enough merely to agree to differ; they need actually to 'stage' the differences openly. The volumes in this series all attempt to dramatize the differences, not necessarily with a view to resolving them but in order to foreground the choices presented by different theories or to argue for a particular route through the impasses the differences present.

The theory 'revolution' has had real effects. It has loosened the grip of traditional empiricist and romantic assumptions about language and literature. It is not always clear what is being proposed as the new agenda for literary studies, and indeed the very notion of 'literature' is questioned by the post-structuralist strain in theory. However, the uncertainties and obscurities of contemporary theories appear much less worrying when we see what the best critics have been able to do with them in practice. This series aims to disseminate the best of recent criticism, and to show that it is possible to re-read the canonical texts of literature in new and challenging ways.

RAMAN SELDEN AND STAN SMITH

The Publishers and fellow Series Editor regret to record that Raman Selden died after a short illness in May 1991 at the age of fifty-three. Ray Selden was a fine scholar and a lovely man. All those he has worked with will remember him with much affection and respect.

Acknowledgements

We are grateful to the following for permission to reproduce copyright material:

Associated University Presses for the chapter 'Anger's My Meat' by Janet Adelmen from *Shakespeare: Pattern of Excelling Nature* edited by David Bevington & Jay L. Halio (1978); Basil Blackwell Ltd for a chapter from *William Shakespeare* by Terry Eagleton (1986); Cambridge University Press for an extract from *The Tragic Effect* by André Green, translated by Alan Sheridan (1979); Columbia University Press for the essay 'Romeo & Juliet: love-hatred in the couple' from *Tales of Love* by Julia Kristeva, translated by Leon S. Roudiez, copyright © Columbia University Press; Cornell University Press for an extract from *Drama of a Nation: Public Theater in Renaissance England & Spain* by Walter Cohen, copyright © 1985 by Cornell University; Harvester-Wheatsheaf, a division of Simon & Schuster International, University of Chicago Press & the author, Jonathan Dollimore, for the chapter 'King Lear (c. 1605–6) and Essentialist Humanism' from *Radical Tragedy: Religion, Ideology & Power in the Drama of Shakespeare & his Contemporaries* (first edition, Harvester Press 1984; second edition Havester-Wheatsheaf 1989), copyright © Jonathan Dollimore 1984, 1989; Harvester-Wheatsheaf, a division of Simon & Schuster International, University of Georgia Press & the author, Malcolm Evans, for an extract from the section 'Star Wars' from *Signifying Nothing: Truth's True Contents in Shakespeare's Text* (first edition, Harvester Press 1986; second edition, Harvester-Wheatsheaf 1989), copyright © Malcolm Evans 1986, 1989; The Johns Hopkins University Press & the author, Robert Weimann, for an extract from *Shakespeare & the Popular Tradition in the Theater* edited by Robert Schwartz; Media Presse Edizioni for the essay 'The Breakdown of Medieval Hierarchy in *King Lear*' by Alessandro Serpieri, translated by Sandra Payne, from *Il Piccolo Hans* No. 19 (July–Sept, 1978); Random Century Group & the author's agent for an extract from *Shakespeare's Division of Experience* by Marilyn French (Jonathan Cape Ltd, 1982), copyright © 1981 by Marilyn French; Routledge, a division of Routledge, Chapman & Hall Ltd, for an extract from the chapter 'Finding a Place' from *The Subject of Tragedy* by Catherine Belsey (Methuen & Co. 1985); the chapter 'A Sea Shell' from *That Shakespearian Rag* by Terence Hawkes (Methuen & Co. 1986) & the essay 'Representing Ophelia' by Elaine Showalter from *Shakespeare & the*

Acknowledgements

Question of Theory edited by Patricia Parker & Geoffrey Hartman (Methuen & Co.); University of Chicago Press & the author, Stephen Greenblatt, for the chapter 'The Improvisation of Power' from *Renaissance Self-Fashioning* (1984); Verso, the imprint of New Left Books Ltd, for the essay 'The Great Eclipse: Tragic Form as Deconsecration of Sovereignty' from *Signs Taken for Wonders* by Franco Moretti, translated by S. Fischer, D. Forgacs & D. Miller (1983).

I also wish to record my thanks to Ray Selden for the scrupulous and helpful way in which he has nursed this project through from its inception. I have benefited enormously from his comments on my Introduction.

JD

For Christine, Alexia and Helena

1 Introduction

All discussion of tragedy, whether it be Shakespearean or any other, sooner or later, returns to Aristotle, and, to the general and problematic source of tragic conflict, but also, more specifically, to the question of the affective power of tragedy. For example, what is it in *Titus Andronicus*, or *Romeo and Juliet, Julius Caesar, Hamlet*, or *Othello, King Lear*, or *Macbeth, Antony and Cleopatra* or *Coriolanus*, that continues to affect us, long after the historical specificity of these plays has been obscured? Moreover, what is it, other than the covert imposition of a standard of taste, combined with a series of assumptions about personal artistic development, that insists upon a distinction between 'major' and 'minor' tragedies, and other plays, such as, *Richard III*, or *Richard II*, which are designated 'history' plays? Lilly B. Campbell, for example, distinguishes between the history play as 'a literary medium for history', concerning itself with *politics* defined here as a preoccupation with questions and relations of state, government, and power, and tragedy as a matter of *ethics*, concerned with questions of human conduct, although her argument shows some discomfort with this distinction.[1] Such a generic division is only valid if we accept a reductively constitutional notion of 'history', or if we are content to focus on human conduct as a universal phenomenon. In addition to the imposition of generic distinctions which have the effect of homogenising these texts, such practices function to limit enquiry. Can we regard all of these texts simply as antiquarian documents, remnants of a world we have lost, or do we, through the constitutive agencies of academic criticism, reformulate them as *universally* applicable texts? To put the issue another way, do these plays *mean* in some objective sense, or do we confer meaning on them through a complex process of cultural inscription?

1

Tragedy and metaphysics

In many respects the theory of tragedy obscures these considerations, and directs us to other questions which have their roots in a familiar Aristotelian model. Questions such as: is the source of tragic experience itself metaphysical or anthropological, and how is it possible to assert that the theatrical representation of death and catastrophe, such as we find in Shakespearean tragedy, can produce the kind of pleasure in the spectator which transcends the limits of history; moreover, what kind of emotional and psychological economy would be required in order for the catharsis of which Aristotle speaks to be properly effective? That tragedy involves what we might call a narrative of violence, is axiomatic, although it must be emphasised that what George Steiner describes as the re-enactment of 'private anguish on a public stage',[2] would appear to address a particular and problematical vision of the place of the human in a metaphysical order. To this extent, tragedy as a dramatic form may be said to fulfill a cognitive function in so far as it offers us a knowledge of ourselves, even though Steiner asserts from the outset that 'The tragic personage is broken by forces which can neither be fully understood nor overcome by rational prudence.'[3] In this respect Steiner shares with Georg Lukacs the view that tragedy fulfills a revelatory function where the object is the *essence* of man; Lukacs observes: 'Tragedy can extend only in one direction: upwards. It begins at the moment when enigmatic forces have distilled the essence from a man, have forced him to become essential; and the progress of tragedy consists in his essential, true nature becoming more and more manifest.'[4] And yet, later in his analysis, and to some extent less obviously so than Lukacs, Steiner can refer to the irreducibly *social* nature of drama, and the fact that its conditions cannot be separated 'from that of the audience, or, in a larger yet strict sense, from that of the social and political community'.[5] This division between the social and political, and, by implication the anthropological, on the one hand, and the incomprehensibly metaphysical on the other, remains unresolved in Steiner's general argument. Indeed, his argument oscillates uncomfortably between the notion of history as contingency and that of a non-Christian essentialism, while at the same time preserving the view that tragedy is both a ritual and a *religious* experience.[6] The result is that he is forced to conclude that while 'the tragic theatre is an expression of the prerational phase in history', which is 'founded on the assumption that there are in nature and the psyche occult, uncontrollable forces able to madden or destroy the mind',[7] he insists that 'Tragedy is that form of art which requires the intolerable burden of God's presence.'[8] In certain respects Steiner's argument echoes that of Lukacs, who insists that, 'God must leave the stage, but must yet remain a spectator; that is the historical possibility of tragic epochs.'[9] It is in the audience's sharing of the consequences of this 'intolerable burden', that the possibility of empathy resides, but this leads to a further question: is the empathy which the spectator might feel for the suffering of the tragic hero a genuine indentification with both situation and character – something that we might describe as 'natural' – or is this an index of the covertly political management of human feeling whose roots lie in *ideology*? That is, in a material practice which functions to resolve social contradictions in order to produce a consensual view of 'reality'. For both Steiner and Lukacs, tragedy yields a knowledge of 'self'; in Steiner's case it offers 'a terrible stark insight into human life. Yet in the very excess of his suffering lies man's claim to dignity';[10] in Lukacs' case we are told that 'The essence of these great moments is the pure experience of self.'[11] Clearly his alternation between the metaphysical and the anthropological, along with the refusal to contemplate the involvement of either with the ideological, results, for Steiner, in the maintenance of what we may identify as an artificial separation of these two spheres of activity. Moreover, his insistence that the precondition for tragedy is 'an organic community' of the sort that persisted up until the seventeenth century subscribes uncritically to the Tillyardian fallacy.[12] It does not explain, except in terms of mystery and exhaustion, the *pleasure* which tragedy produces. Nor, indeed, does the argument concerned with the construction of self move beyond the terms of platonism in its repeated emphasis upon human essence. Steiner has nothing to say about the relationship between tragedy and 'subjection', since he assumes that 'In Athens, in Shakespeare's England, and at Versailles, the hierarchies of worldly power were stable and manifest. The wheel of social life spun around the aristocratic life or centre. From it, spokes of order and degree led to the outward rim of the common man.'[13] Here it is only the privileged subject of power who is permitted to encounter a metaphysical order whose contours are already given. This raises the question of the relationship between tragedy as a cautionary narrative since the fate of the aristocratic subject of power 'has tragic revelance because it is public'[14] and the pleasure derived from it in the theatre.

Freud and the pleasure of tragedy

In purely structural terms the association of pleasure with tragedy may be explained in terms of the pleasure/unpleasure differential identified by Freud, whereby in the economy of primary mental processes psychic activity is directed towards pleasure while at the same time drawing back 'from any event which might arouse unpleasure'.[15] Later, in *Beyond The Pleasure Principle*, Freud opposes the 'pleasure principle' to the 'reality principle', where the latter involves the postponement of satisfaction, 'the abandonment of a number of possibilities of gaining satisfaction and the temporary toleration of unpleasure as a step on the long indirect road to pleasure'.[16]

Freud links this economy of pleasure with aesthetics, and subsequently, with dramatic form itself, in his suggestions that where the final outcome of a situation involves a 'yield of pleasure', then the issue should be examined within the framework of 'some system of aesthetics with an economic approach to its subject matter'.[17] In his essay 'Psychopathic Characters on the Stage', the dramatic function of the hero is linked to the origin of drama in sacrificial rites, where the sacrifice itself is shown to appease 'as it were, a rising rebellion against the divine regulation of the universe, which is responsible for the existence of suffering'.[18] Initially, and what is increasingly formulated at an allegorical level, the challenge to divinity serves to shift the tragic conflict away from the plane of metaphysics and into the realm of 'social' struggle. It is from there that Freud moves, not into the area of objective historical struggle, but rather into what he calls the 'drama of character';[19] in this sphere 'the struggle that causes the suffering is fought out in the hero's mind itself – a struggle between different impulses, and one which must have its end in the extinction, not of the hero, but of one of his impulses; it must end, that is to say, in a renunciation'.[20] Freud's driving of the scene of tragedy into the realm of the psychological permits a reconstitution of the conflict in terms of an opposition between 'repressed material' and consciousness,[21] which serves to relocate the tragic struggle at the primal scene of triangulated Oedipal desire. In this context, objective social and historical relations which are implicit in Freud's own theory of tragedy, and within which 'divinity' is equated with patriarchal law, are readmitted as the constituent elements of an allegory of that dialectical conflict between consciousness and the unconscious. Here the latter is the repository of repressed primal impulses always threatening to erupt into the otherwise stable symbolic order. Thus, for Freud *Hamlet* charts the emergence of repressed psychic material in a displaced form, and the dramatist's function is to 'induce the same illness in us' as spectators, who follow its course along with the tragic protagonist.[22] In this way the audience is collectively encouraged to *identify* with the tragic hero, to move through the same experience as a figure such as Hamlet, in order to reach a point where the working out of the character's neurosis onstage produces a catharsis in the spectators through which tension is relieved. The pleasure derived from this experience is, therefore, that combination of *plaisir* and *jouissance* associated by Roland Barthes with the celebration of cultural identity, and what Stephen Heath has called 'a homogenizing movement of the ego', on the one hand, and that 'radically violent pleasure (*jouissance*) which shatters – dissipates, loses – that cultural identity, that ego'[23] on the other. In this context we might say that tragedy both reaffirms subjection, through a celebration of identity, but at the same time it challenges authority, in a manner which Barthes prescribes for all texts: 'The text is (should be) that uninhibited person who shows his behind to the *Political Father*.'[24] In certain respects, and despite the fact that Elizabethan and Jacobean culture was clearly pre-Freudian, the identification of pleasure with a challenge to authority locates with some precision the geographical and political space occupied by the public theatre during this period. Indeed, following on from this we may conclude that tragedy as a *form* emerges historically only when there exists a conflict between identity and authority, in which the issues at stake involve both a violation of established forms of personal and social identity, and an affirmation of what it means to be 'human': in short in precisely the opposite conditions to those which both Steiner and E.M.W. Tillyard outline. Both concerns are articulated in terms of a teleology which, strictly speaking, obscures actual historical causation, although, of course, it is possible to recover that history through an understanding of the text as *symptom*.

Aristotle and tragedy

The concept of tragedy as a violation of order, whether that order is conceived in personal, psychological terms, or in objective public and political terms, is one which functions as a focal point for a number of theories of tragedy, and has long been a familiar way of understanding Shakespearean tragedy. In Aristotle's *Poetics* both the role of the tragic protagonist, and the affective power of the tragic experience itself, centre on a challenge to authority whose power is made manifest in and through conflict, and the result is a return to a position of equilibrium which balances gain and loss in the moment of the reassertion of order. In response to the Platonic dismissal of tragic art as 'a form of play, not to be taken seriously',[25] Aristotle sought to provide a rationale whereby 'pity' and 'fear' could be aroused in order 'to provide an outlet for such emotions'.[26] Moreover, Aristotle goes on to provide an *aesthetic* connection between tragedy and 'order': 'Beauty depends on two conditions – size and order',[27] which he later reinforces with a statement about the integrated nature of the tragic action: 'the story, as an imitation of action, must represent one action, a complete whole; and it must connect with various incidents in such a way that the whole will be disjoined and dislocated if any one of them is transposed or removed.'[28] But Aristotle's concern to ensure that the kinds of statements that poetry makes 'are of the nature rather of universals, whereas those of history are particulars',[29] effectively diverts our attention from a social hierarchy inscribed in the tragic experience itself. According to Aristotle, 'pity', is to be reserved 'for undeserved misfortune', whereas 'fear' is 'for the misfortune of a man *like ourselves*' (my italics).[30] But in addition to the confining of tragedy to 'so few families',[31] he also suggests that in the tragic character there should be an element of 'goodness' possible in all types of person, 'even in a woman or a slave, though the one is of course an inferior and the other a worthless being'.[32] It is in his comments about 'character' that the Bradleyan conception of character as origin, as opposed to that of character as agency, is to be found, although as we shall see, Bradley's theory of tragedy, which received its specific application in his book, *Shakespearean Tragedy* (1904), contains a strong Hegelian strand.[33] But as Augusto Boal has observed, for Aristotle 'Tragedy imitates those actions of man which have the good as their goal', and that 'the highest good is the political one, and the political good is justice'.[34] In other words, the suggestion advanced by Lilly B. Campbell whereby the generic distinction between 'history' and 'tragedy' is dependent upon the separation of politics from ethics[35] is asserted to be an artificial division between two spheres of social and personal activity inextricably linked together at a deep structural level. Moreover, he goes on to comment that Aristotle accepts as 'just' '*already existing* inequalities',[36] and that the institution that expresses both 'the political good' and 'justice' is the Law. Boal then proceeds to ask how those aware of inequality can be made to remain passive, and his reply is, 'Through the many forms of repression: politics, bureaucracy, habits, customs – and Greek tragedy.'[37] It is in precisely this mechanism of repression that Boal inscribes the Aristotelian concept of *catharsis*, an effect of tragedy, which is none other than a displaced form of political control, and which results in passivity. He concludes, 'Tragedy, in all its qualitative and quantitative aspects, exists as a function of the effect it seeks, catharsis',[38] and in Aristotle's *Poetics* this is, above all, a matter of the conjuncture of aesthetics and ideology, whose primary strategic function is to remove that excess which 'threatens the individual's equilibrium, and consequently that of society.'[39]

It is Boal's contention that the invention of the figure of the tragic protagonist effectively 'aristocratised' the theatre, and he goes on to suggest that 'The tragic hero appears when the State begins to utilize the theater for political purposes.'[40] In its constant return to a position of equilibrium, tragedy may be said to reinforce artistically the desirability of political order. Within this context, Boal's suggestion that the idea of *hamartia* as a characteristic flaw that 'can and must be destroyed so that the whole of the character's ethos may conform to the ethos of the society',[41] leads logically to an account which emphasises the reactionary nature of tragedy itself. Whether the tragic hero comes to accept his error, and to know it (*anagnorisis*), or whether that self-knowledge is transferred to the audience who experience vicariously the danger of transgression and the consequences which it poses, the result is, for Boal, an aesthetic experience which is 'the most perfect artistic form of coercion'.[42] He then concludes that tragedy can never be used as a revolutionary weapon, because it is concerned to 'eliminate all that is not commonly accepted, including the revolution, before it takes place'.[43] Boal seeks to challenge the political uses of tragedy, in an attempt to return the genre to an originary theatrical freedom. But, as George Thompson once pointed out in his extraordinary study of the origins of tragic drama, *Aeschylus and Athens* (1941), 'The historian of the past is a citizen of the present.'[44] Boal's reading of the coercive power of tragedy, which is, in fact, a reading more properly addressed to the *uses* of tragedy, presupposes, as does Brecht, to some extent, an already existing structure of political domination from which particular artistic forms require to be liberated. This association of tragedy with other rituals of political domination has led in certain respects to an emphasis which is currently associated with certain strands of New Historicist thinking, whereby a partial reading of Foucault can produce a formula in which it is argued that 'stagecraft collaborates with statecraft in producing spectacles of power'.[45] Of course, we may ask why such spectacles were considered necessary, but what is obscured in such a position is the irreducibly *dialectical* nature of tragedy where, to paraphrase Thompson, opposition between different social groups served to create a tension which called into question traditional structures and assumptions.[46] Thompson detects in classical Greece a growing discontinuity between forms of social mobility, and the sorts of political power attendant upon them, on the one hand, and the precarious consequences of that mobility which can result in destruction as well as success, on the other.[47] Indeed, his formulation of the notion that drama is the space where a ritual experience is contested, provides a useful historical perspective which aligns tragedy with the artistic form in which that contestation is cast, and with the political form in which a *democratic* impulse is articulated. Indeed, as Walter Benjamin has observed, the atonement which the representative figure of the tragic hero undergoes, may bring about a restoration of Law, but it also undermines it at the same time; here atonement 'is designed not only to bring about the restoration but above all the undermining of an ancient body of laws in the linguistic constitution of the renewed community'.[48] For historical purposes, however, we should be careful not to confuse the present trajectory of that democratic impulse, which in this context is structural, with what, for example, in Renaissance England, was still an uncertain future.

Nietzsche on tragedy

Nietzsche's *The Birth of Tragedy* breaks distinctively with Aristotelian theory. He argues:

What distinguishes the Aryan conception is an exalted notion of active sin as the properly Promethean virtue; this notion provides us with the ethical substratum of pessimistic tragedy, which comes to be seen as a justification of human ills, that is to say of human guilt as well as the suffering purchased by that guilt.The tragedy at the heart of things, which the thoughtful Aryan is not disposed to quibble away, the contrariety at the centre of the universe, is seen by him as an interpenetration of several worlds, as for instance a divine and a human, each individually in the right but each, as it encroaches upon the other, having to suffer for its individuality. The individual in the course of his heroic striving towards universality, de-individuation, comes up against that primordial contradiction and learns both to sin and to suffer. The Aryan actions assign to crime the male, the Semites to sin the female gender; and it is quite consistent with these notions that the original act of *hubris* should be attributed to a man, original sin to a woman.[49]

Nietzsche's problematical definition would appear, on the surface, to offer a dialectical account in which the Apollonian *'principium individuationis'* is brought into conflict with the Dionysiac urge to dissolve the *illusion* of self and of empirical reality in a non-differentiating universality. In fact, his assertion that tragedy is 'a supreme form of art', and a 'sublime aesthetic play',[50] emphasises the irreducibly *aesthetic* dimension of human experience in which suffering, shorn of guilt, is the means of access to a 'higher delight'.[51] Indeed, as Gilles Deleuze has argued, for Nietzsche, tragedy is a form of joyful affirmation, 'pure and multiple positivity, dynamic gaiety', a means of affirming 'chance and the necessity of chance; because it affirms multiplicity and the unity of multiplicity', to be set against a 'Christian and dialectic pathos' which is fundamentally nihilistic.[52] In this respect Nietzsche's anti-rationalism anticipates certain strands of current post-modernist thinking. His affirmation of pure Will, drawn into alignment with a 'national character',[53] as the means of giving 'to quotidian experience the stamp of the eternal', becomes the agency of a reaffirmation of the power of myth, which is destroyed when 'a nation begins to view itself historically and to demolish the mythical bulwarks that surround it'.[54] Thus for Nietzsche 'multiple positivity' is aligned with metaphysics in such a way as to celebrate power, as against the Aristotelian formula which balances gain and loss through what is, nonetheless a corrective exposure to suffering. For Nietzsche, transgression is a breaking through the rational Apollonian images which structure empirical reality in a quest for power which, as Terry Eagleton has recently observed, 'is ultimately disinterested', bearing 'its ends entirely within itself, positing them as mere points of resistance essential to its own self-actualizing'.[55] Moreover, Nietzsche is also important as a source of the critique of enlightenment rationalism that lies behind the work of Foucault, and postmodernism generally. A more traditional reading of tragic experience posits the tragic hero as a breaker of laws 'in order to express the full dimension of human existence'.[56] That 'full dimension' does not involve a quasi-Nietzschean dismissal of the fictional nature of empirical reality, and of the laws that structure it, so much as reaffirmation through transgression of those boundaries in and through which the human is defined.

Hegel and Bradley on tragedy

These themes have dogged the analysis of Shakespearean tragedy, and some attempt at a resolution of some of them occurs in A.C. Bradley's celebrated revision of 'Hegel's Theory of Tragedy'.[57] I have commented elsewhere on the manner in which Bradley sought to resituate the Hegelian opposition between the urge for self-determination of the tragic hero in the face of 'the determinatedness of his character'[58] wholly within his character. It must, however, be said that in his essay, which precedes *Shakespearean Tragedy* (1904) by some three years, Bradley wished to retain the Hegelian metaphysical notion of tragedy as 'itself a conflict of the spirit',[59] although this divided spirit, which he labels 'ethical substance' conducts a tragic rather than a moral war: 'not so much the war of good with evil as the war of good with good',[60] and is also now reduced to the formula: 'character in action'.[61] What is significant about Bradley's essay is his essentialist emphasis upon tragedy as 'a conflict of the spirit',[62] while at the same time seeking to enlarge its moral perspective; he observes:

> If we omit all reference to ethical or substantial powers and interests, what have we left? We have the more general idea – to use again a formula not Hegel's own – that tragedy portrays a self-division and self waste of spirit, or a division of spirit involving conflict and waste. It is implied in this that on *both* sides in the conflict there is a spiritual value. The same idea may be expressed (again, I think not in Hegel's own words) by saying that the tragic conflict is one not merely of good with evil, but also, and more essentially, of good with good. Only, in saying this, we must be careful to observe that 'good' here means anything that has spiritual value, not moral goodness alone, and that 'evil' has a similar wide sense.[63]

What Bradley does is to internalise and humanise the Hegelian relation between 'substance as the universal essence and End', or truth and wholeness as a general process of coming to self-consciousness, on the one hand, and *'individualised* reality', which resists incorporation into the larger totality of 'substance', on the other. In Bradley's revised formulation individual 'Action' exposes the internal division of 'substance' which produces tragic conflict,[64] and this allows him to reconstitute these difficult Hegelian categories as the ingredients of an internal psychological conflict which draws towards a catastrophe which he can then describe as 'the violent self-restitution of the divided spiritual unity'.[65] In his discussion of *Macbeth* in this essay, Bradley appears to be aware of the drift of his argument towards discussion of 'personality'. Indeed, after establishing and itemising the presence of not just 'moral goodness', but 'good' in the character of Macbeth, he adds a telling footnote to his discussion which offers some indication of the extent to which he has appropriated and domesticated a series of more abstract idealist Hegelian concepts:

> Our interest in Macbeth may be called interest in a 'personality'; but it is not an interest in some bare form of self-consciousness, nor yet in a person in the legal sense, but in a personality full of matter. This matter is not an ethical or universal end, but it must in a sense be universal – human nature in a particular form – or it would not excite the horror, sympathy, and admiration it does. Nor again, could it excite these feelings if it were not composed largely of qualities on which we set a high value.[66]

Here Bradley can be seen decanting Hegelian dialectics from the definition of tragic conflict as a precondition of smuggling in, significantly in a footnote, a recognisably liberal conception of 'human nature'. Also, at the same time, he dehistoricises and relegates to the realm of contingency all of those institutions, e.g. the family and state, on which 'we' set a high value,[67] through which it is assumed that 'human nature' articulates its essential liberal self. Moreover, the extent to which Bradley's tragic hero becomes the liberal bourgeois subject can be gauged from his later suggestion in *Shakespearean Tragedy* that the concentration in these plays on 'the inward struggle emphasises the fact that this action is essentially the expression of character';[68] this manoeuvre is, of course, anticipated in the earlier essay, in Bradley's concern to insert into Hegel's theory a category that he alleges the latter underrates: 'the action in tragedy of what may be called by a rough distinction moral evil rather than defect'.[69] Clearly, if the focus of tragedy is on human nature and morality, then it is not difficult to see why the wastage to which Bradley refers exerts such an impact upon his argument. For him the tragic hero is an exemplary human being who, having violated a moral imperative whose origins are concealed from us, elicits the contradictory response of admiration and disapproval. In this way tragedy becomes linked inexplicably with both the individual and the moral order, but without the need to explain either except by reference to an undefined 'human nature'. But while he later goes on to say that the 'tragic fact' remains 'something piteous, fearful and mysterious', he confirms the suspicions of Augusto Boal that tragedy may itself be a means of coercion in his conclusion that 'the representation of it does not leave us crushed, rebellious or desperate'.[70]

As in the case of Steiner, Bradley's view of tragedy is religious, but non-Christian, with its emphasis upon the way that forms of 'power, intelligence, life and glory which astound us and seem to call for our worship' persist in 'devouring one another and destroying themselves, often with great pain, as though they came into being for no other end'.[71] This moment of destruction answers what Bradley calls 'a moral necessity',[72] but he is unhappy that the kind of sympathy which a tragic hero elicits renders the notion of 'justice' as a term to describe a form of punishment inappropriate. He argues, 'We might not object to the statement that Lear deserved to suffer for his folly, selfishness and tyranny; but to assert that he deserved to suffer what he did suffer is to do violence not merely to language but to any healthy moral sense.'[73] Though as an audience we do not *judge*, according to Bradley, he remains firmly of the view that 'the ultimate power in the tragic world is a moral order', one that 'does not show itself indifferent to good and evil, or equally favourable or unfavourable to both, but shows itself akin to good and alien from evil'.[74] For Bradley it is 'chiefly evil that disturbs the order of the world', and that evil, conceived in manichean terms as a permanent fact of existence, is described in the following way:

Again, if we confine our attention to the hero, and to those cases where the gross and palpable evil is not in him but elsewhere, we find that the comparatively innocent hero still shows some marked imperfection or defect – irresolution, precipitancy, pride, credulousness, excessive simplicity, excessive susceptibility to sexual emotions, and the like. These defects or imperfections are certainly, in the wide sense of the word, evil, and they contribute decisively to the conflict and catastrophe. And the inference is again obvious. The ultimate power which shows itself disturbed by this evil and reacts against it, must have nature alien to it. Indeed its reaction is so vehement and 'relentless' that it would seem to be bent on nothing short of good in perfection, and to be ruthless in its demand for it.[75]

Despite subsequent reactions against Bradley's characterological criticism, his neo-Aristotelian concern to preserve the relationship between the art of tragedy and the assertion of a moral order, has remained a key feature of Shakespearean criticism in the twentieth century, and has been extended to the field of Jacobean tragedy also.[76] For example, Irving Ribner's *Patterns in Shakespearean Tragedy* (1960), while resisting the characterological concern with 'the psychological problems of individual personality',[77] asserts from the outset that 'Tragedy is an exploration of man's relation to the forces of evil in the world'; but also Shakespeare's own output is said to constitute a 'development' which is, in effect, 'a growth in moral vision.'[78] The ease with which the dramatic and ethical concerns of individual tragedies may in some way be identified with the artist's own personal quest for order, raises fundamental questions of authority, and intentionality, aside from questions of belief. Thus, the 'religious ritual' which Ribner recognises as the pre-history of tragedy is displaced firstly onto the artistic psyche, before being projected into dramatic form in a public arena. The resultant definition which he evolves retains in equivocal form the very appeal to a characterological perspective to which he expressed an earlier opposition: 'Tragedy must impose upon the raw material of human experience a pattern in which the relation of human suffering to human joy becomes apparent, and out of this must come the feeling of reconciliation with which every one of Shakespeare's tragedies ends, and which critics of the most divergent views have recognized.'[79] Ribner's causal alignment of action, damnation, and knowledge, where suffering is the price paid for approaching the knowledge that the universe is secretly purposive, reaffirms the gender-specific nature of tragedy as a form of masculine action inscribed within what is essentially a patriarchal system of values. The question of how such a moral universe may be *produced*, or of the reasons why certain moral values are assigned to particular actions, is never explored, but rather buried in the mystery of religious belief.

Tragedy and the social order

Thus far, the argument has been concerned primarily with the teleological emphasis which traditional Shakespeare criticism has given to tragic form. That is to say, with the *experience* of tragedy as means of coming to terms with human identity within a larger metaphysical order, and with a series of permanent 'truths' accessible only through the suffering of the tragic hero. However, in addition to revealing 'human' potential, such a view of tragedy also discloses the extent to which that potential is necessarily *contained*, an issue which as we observed, is central to Augusto Boal's critique of Aristotle. It is also an issue which figures prominently in New Historicist accounts of Renaissance drama, in which 'power', now a social and material phenomenon rather than a metaphysical force, *displays* itself in the theatre, compelling an orientation of individuals to its strategies, and, as a consequence, producing a series of social identities. The transition here is from the notion of a metaphysical order, characteristic in the work of Bradley and Ribner, to a *structural* account of social relations and the way in which this is articulated in tragedy. We should distinguish here between the organic structuralism of a theoretician such as Lucien

Goldmann, for whom tragedy is both an expression of 'a deep crisis in the relationship between his social and spiritual world',[80] and a 'world vision' comprising 'the intellectual and social life' of a particular social group whose thoughts and feelings may be seen as 'an expression of their economic and social life',[81] and what has more recently been identified as the *discontinuous* experience of Renaissance tragedy generally. Goldmann himself associates Shakespeare with a classicism one of whose constituent features is 'the idea of a union between man and the world, and thus by implication the idea of immanence'.[82] That idea of a union between man and world has always figured prominently in Shakespeare criticism from E.M.W. Tillyard onwards, but in recent years it has been suggested that this fundamental notion of immanence is precisely what has come under scrutiny in the tragedies of Shakespeare and his contemporaries. This unity of man and world has been identified as an *ideology*, that is, as the primary political means through which human beings live their social relations. The question then arises: what are the social and cultural pressures brought to bear upon individual human experience which give it coherence, and what happens when a discontinuity arises between social practices and the ideologies which are designed to guarantee that coherence? The moment that this 'order' is subjected to scrutiny as something which is *produced*, then tragedy becomes the means of locating and registering radical discontinuities between ideology and social praxis, which, for the society within which Shakespeare's tragedies were produced, involved a radical conflict between theology and history.

At the level of ideas, Elizabethan and Jacobean tragedy arises out of a challenge to Christianity. Clifford Leech has observed that in plays such as *Othello* and *King Lear* 'Not only are great evil and suffering presented ... but there is no comprehensible scheme of rewards and punishments suggested.'[83] Moreover, he goes on to observe that 'the tragic picture is incompatible with the Christian faith'.[84] But tragedy also points to a disruption at the level of ideology, that is to say, at that place where the symbolic order – of which, in this case, Christianity is the most powerful constitutive discourse – is no longer able to contain those contradictions which arise in real social relations.

Perhaps the best way into this issue is to consider the relationship between tragic suffering, and the knowledge which it is alleged is revealed as a consequence of that suffering. In his short book *Tragedy* (1969) Clifford Leech suggests that 'through sacrifice man has the opportunity of growing',[85] and he proceeds from there to argue that tragedy itself is a sophisticated and displaced form of the ritual sacrifice of the scapegoat, although this primitive element may be one of which we are barely conscious. He argues that 'in rational terms, we know that no man's death purges us, but, insofar as we sense that a vicarious purging gives us relief, we rebel against it. For a moment we may accept the scapegoat ritual, but in our hearts we feel shame at our acceptance.'[86] In certain respects this resembles Northop Frye's suggestion that an artistic correspondence to the mimetic ritual of killing and eating the scapegoat takes place in tragedy, 'a vision of death which draws the survivors into a new unity', and where the fall of the tragic hero makes visible for a moment, 'a greater world beyond ... but there is also a sense of the mystery and remoteness of that world'.[87] This communal knowledge, albeit mysterious, and in a sense unrealisable in practice, is an extension of the recognition by the tragic hero himself of 'the determined shape of the life he has created for himself, with an implicit comparison with the uncreated potential life he has forsaken'.[88] For Frye, and indeed, for most commentators on tragedy from Hegel onwards, what he calls 'the total *mythos* of tragedy'[89] is binary. Although whereas for Bradley the opposition was located internally within the *spirit* of the tragic hero, for Frye the dialectic is external and structural, involving an originary act and a counterbalancing movement, both of which are rooted in myth as a form of prehistory regulated by the natural movement of the seasons. It need hardly be said that myth is both permanent and invariant. What that myth occludes is a history of which it is the symbolic articulation, a history which, as Alain Robbe-Grillet has argued, is an invention of humanism:

> *Tragedy* may here be defined as an attempt to reclaim the distance that exists between man and things, and give it a new kind of value, so that in effect it becomes an ordeal where victory consists in being vanquished. Tragedy, then, figures as the cultural invention of humanism in its attempt to allow nothing to escape it. Since the harmony between man and things has finally been denounced, the humanist saves his empire by immediately setting up a new form of solidarity, the divorce in itself becoming a major road to redemption.[90]

It is this 'sublimation of a disparity' that Robbe-Grillet rejects, since, he argues, 'when tragedy tries to make us love our misery, we forget all about trying to find a remedy for it'.[91] Moreover, the materialist and existential challenge to humanism that he poses takes the form of the rejection of tragedy as a concept 'that leads to the belief that men, or ideas, (or both), have a profound, and superior nature', and also to the rejection of 'any pre-established order'.[92]

Frye's association of tragedy with the rhythms of nature masks a crucial distinction between an essentialist account of cosmic order, and conceptions of order and disorder which are irreducibly cultural. Or to put the matter another way, there is a danger here of mistaking the metaphor for its origins, and it is this process which, in its secular manifestation as 'human nature' that Robbe-Grillet takes such exception to. But it is, nonetheless, the case that some elements of an anthropological account of tragedy as ritual can provide a useful bridge between essentialist and materialist readings.

Tragedy and violence

Let us return to the notion of *violence*, since this is one element that Bradley and his successors identify as an indispensable feature of tragedy in general and Shakespearean tragedy in particular. It is, perhaps, an obvious point to make, but the *staging* of violence in the public theatre is both a displacement and a transference of a violence which existed not very far beneath the surface of Elizabethan society itself. We might, therefore, regard the sacrifice which is part of the tragic denouement as a particular kind of ritual activity, which René Girard describes as 'an act of violence without risk of vengeance',[93] whose function is 'to quell violence within the community and to prevent conflicts from erupting'.[94] Significantly, Girard regards the act of revenge, which is a feature of a large number of Elizabethan and Jacobean tragedies, and which figures in a number of Shakespearean tragedies, as a form of reprisal which elicits further violence, generating a process of repetition which 'puts the very existence of a society in jeopardy'.[95] In this context sacrifice becomes a ritual of containment, a means of 'prevention in the struggle against violence',[96] where violence itself is the irreducible content of the sacred. But, of course, that structural process is necessary only in time of crisis, and Girard goes out of his way to reject the manichean frame of reference of Romantic provenance, whereby tragedy is perceived in accordance with the struggle between the permanent categories of good and evil. Rather he sees the crisis in terms of a distinction between the 'pure' and the 'impure', the structuring motif of those distinctions through which both the cultural order and individual identity are differentially defined:

> The sacrificial crisis can be defined, therefore, as a crisis of distinctions – that is, a crisis affecting the cultural order. This cultural order is nothing more than a regulated system of distinctions in which the differences among individuals are used to establish their 'identity' and their mutual relationships.[97]

In certain respects Girard's notion of violence as the irreducible content of the sacred,[98] concerned as it is with the destruction of differences, recalls those characteristics which Nietzsche attributes to the Dionysiac state.[99] For Girard tragedy is the theatrical representation of a mythological conflict which replays at the symbolic level the confrontation between a socially produced differentially constructed order on the one hand, and an irreducibly natural and terrifying violence which threatens to engulf it. The mythological conflict itself is described as 'the retrospective transfiguration of sacrificial crises, the reinterpretation of these crises in the light of the cultural order that has arisen from them'.[100] It is the repetition of these crises through the process of reinterpretation that leads to a partial deconstruction of the myths themselves, to the point where he can suggest that 'the term desymbolism is more appropriate to tragedy than symbolism'.[101]

For Girard the notion of *difference* proposed by ethnological structuralists as the irreducible structuring mechanism of all cultural meaning is of limited value. In fact, his identification of the area of 'the sacred' as a category beyond structure risks according to it a metaphysical significance susceptible to Derrida's injunction that this 'centre', 'while governing the structure, escapes structurality'.[102] This is because, for him, 'The sacred concerns itself above all with the destruction of differences, and this nondifference cannot appear as such in the structure.'[103] Indeed, Girard takes the view that it is 'the collapse of the cultural structure of a society' that leads to the 'reciprocal violence' that we associate with tragedy.[104] While at one level this approach may be readily identified as materialist, the suggestion that beneath the cultural order there exists a primitive violence which it is the function of sacrifice to appease, returns us to the non-dialectical opposition between Dionysiac and Apollonian that we observed earlier in Nietzsche's *The Birth of Tragedy*. For Girard, culture is an order imposed on primitive nature, in which the social formation produces and reproduces itself through the generation of myths, and which is held in place through fear and through sacrifice. But what is missing from his analysis is a proper sense of the historical and social conditions under which crisis is produced as a series of disjunctions between different interests. It is, perhaps, of little more than aphoristic value to suggest that 'Tragedy envelops all human relationships in a single tragic antagonism'[105] when there is no clear statement of specific disruption at the level of *ideology* which can account for these antagonisms. Thus, while Girard can offer an important advance at the level of anthropology of tragedy, and in particular suggest ways of articulating the sacrificial violence which is one of its essential features, the allusion to non-differentiating violence beneath the level of human culture threatens to return the argument to essentialism, albeit to an essentialism which is to be distinguished from other essentialisms. That tragedy displaces, and condenses violence, and that it focuses on a surrogate victim, be it an outsider who is not fully integrated into the society, or the figure of the king whose position at the centre is the very thing ' that serves to isolate him from his fellow men, to render him casteless'[106] is a view that is unexceptionable. Similarly, the resistance to the view that tragedy as a dramatic form isolated the victim as *pharmakos*, both poison and antidote,[107] which seeks to adapt human experience to seasonal rites, as in the case of critics such as Northrop Frye, may be regarded as anachronistic. But Clifford Leech has reminded us that 'Tragedy is a form of writing, not of living',[108] a means of inscription which affects every level of cultural life both personal and public. And it is from this point that much of the new work in the area of Shakespearean tragedy has come.

Tragedy and the pharmakos

In the light of Leech's observation, it is worth pausing briefly over the question of tragedy and the Platonic *pharmakon*. In his essay 'Plato's Pharmacy', Jacques Derrida observes that the *pharmakon* is a double-edge remedy which 'can never be simply beneficial'; indeed, he notes that 'the beneficial essence or virtue of a *pharmakon* does not prevent it from hurting'.[109] The subject of discussion in Plato is none other than writing itself, held to be at one level 'a remedy, a beneficial drug', but at another 'a harmful substance, a philter of forgetfulness'.[110] This ambivalence constitutes the *pharmakon* as 'the movement, the locus, and the play: (the production of) difference. It is the difference of difference.'[111] For Derrida, the *pharmakos* becomes a composite figure – wizard, magician, poisoner – who is likened to a scapegoat, engaged in a particular kind of ritual which we may associate closely with tragedy itself: 'The *evil* and the *outside*, the expulsion of the evil, its exclusion out of the body (and out) of the city – these are the two major senses of the character and of the ritual.'[112] The result is a process of explusion of a force which menaces from below, and against which order and hierarchy differentially define themselves. It is significant that both in Plato and in Derrida the body itself becomes a metaphor for the community, engaged in an act of violent expulsion which serves to disinfect its very being:

> The city's *body* thus reconstitutes its unity, closes around the security of its inner courts, gives back to itself the word that links it with itself within the confines of the agora, by violently excluding from its territory the representative of an external threat or aggression. That representative represents the otherness of the evil that comes to affect or infect the inside by unpredictably breaking into it. Yet the representative of the outside is nonetheless *constituted*, regularly granted its place by the community, chosen, kept, fed, etc., in the very heart of the inside …. The ceremony of the *pharmakos* is thus played out on the boundary line between inside and outside, which it has as its function ceaselessly to trace and retrace.[113]

It is precisely this process that, as we saw, Girard sought to chart in terms of the violence which this ritual generated, but it is also useful as a means of augmenting the account of the place and function of the Elizabethan public theatre during the time of Shakespeare. What Derrida and Girard provide is a structural account of the tragic conflict itself which enables us to read specific tragedies in terms of their semiotic representation of the conflict between 'inside' and 'outside', metaphysically santioned order and those material historical forces which challenge its hierarchical structures. To this extent, Shakespearean tragedy is not just a form of writing, but a form of *representation*: a representation of all of those symbolic structures through which order articulates itself. But in addition to its *producing* its 'other', interestingly as a demonic challenge which requires to be contained, the process also offers opportunities for resistance. In the latter case the process involves a subsequent transformation of symbolic structures as the ideologies which hold them in place are no longer able to disguise the material contradictions which the confrontation throws up. In this respect tragedy retains its ambivalence in that it uncovers the very contradictions that it sets out aesthetically to domesticate, and those contradictions are located at *both* the personal and the public levels of communal experience.

At the root of much recent radical criticism of Shakespearean tragedy is a shift from a semantic account of literary texts which denies the *constitutive* role of writing itself in favour of a view of language as an indication or an expression of the inner thoughts of 'characters', or even of the dramatist himself, to a semiotic account. What is at stake here is a distinction between what Jurgen Habermas has recently called, on the one hand, the positing 'as originary the subjectivity of sense-giving acts' as opposed to 'the linguistically created intersubjectivity of mutual understanding' on the other.[114] Traditionally Shakespearean critics have preferred to ascribe to Shakespearean texts values of 'timelessness', 'universality', or 'organic unity', presupposing that they are the product of a transcendent guiding intelligence, and thereby placing both writer and texts in an eternal present. In this realm such texts, and, indeed, the writer himself, are divested of their historical particularity, and have come to be regarded as the transparent vehicles through which Shakespeare the dramatist unfolds his 'mind' to us. At one level, a good deal of the criticism which emanates from this idealist and essentialist perspective is little more than a form of ventriloquism, which signals its own inferiority, while at the same time seeking to efface its own mediational role through the articulation of what Catherine Belsey has described as 'a choric elegy for lost presence'.[115] This deisre to return to the paradise of the text's or the author's self-presence is little more than a positive acknowledgement of a vaguely post-lapsarian imperfection, replete with its own implicit denial of the manifold overdeterminations of a material history. At another, less obvious level, this perception of the text as the unproblematically transparent vehicle of an immutable 'essence' serves to reconstitute Shakespeare as 'authority' and 'living monument'. In this guise the Bard is a permanent, transcendent court of appeal whose presence is approachable yet mysterious. He is, in addition, the means through which attention may be diverted away from the pressing political concerns of quotidian reality, both at the level of these texts' own interventions at particular historical moments, and at the level of their subsequent reconstitution through the mediating agency of criticism and scholarship. It is such agencies which arrange the Shakespeare *oeuvre* into a hierarchy of generic forms, placing tragedy at the apex of the dramatist's achievement. Such criticism, which rests self-satisfied upon extraordinarily vacuous assertions that 'Shakespeare is free',[116] or that a free-floating liberal humanist detachment is a precondition for any critical activity, has yet to grapple productively with, among other things, the Foucauldian perception of an 'author' whose function is that of characterising 'the existence, circulation, and operation of certain discourses within a society'.[117] That is to say, the name 'Shakespeare' does not constitute 'a pure and simple reference'; indeed, it is, as an authorial description, 'more a gesture, a finger pointed at someone; it is, to a certain extent, the equivalent of a description'.[118] Foucault goes on to argue that 'the name of author is not precisely a proper name among others',[119] but is more a means of drawing attention to what he calls 'the existence of certain groups of discourse', while at the same time referring to 'the status of this discourse within a society and culture'.[120] In many respects, of course, we can see how tragedy might constitute part of that discourse, although further investigation would be required to determine precisely what the historically specific constituents of that discourse might be. Though Foucault's definition of the 'author function' raises a further set of methodological and theoretical problems, it does accord a degree of specificity to Roland Barthes' rejection of the literary text as the vehicle through which the author's self-presence is recoverable. 'We know', says Barthes: 'that a text is not a line of words releasing a single theological meaning (the "message" of the author–God) but a multi-dimensional space in which a variety of writings, none of them original, blend and clash. The text is a tissue of quotations drawn from the innumerable centres of culture.'[121]

It is not necessary to drive this perception to Barthes' conclusion in the concept of an open-ended text, one which refuses signification, where 'writing ceaselessly posits meaning ceaselessly to evaporate it, carrying out a systematic exemption of meaning'.[122] This unfettered free play of the signifier places a critique of the text's own ideological investments beyond reach, and its first casualty is a politics of meaning, something which is crucial to an understanding of the conflicts involved in tragedy itself. Attention should rather be drawn to what in Shakespeare's case was an intrinsically collaborative enterprise, the production under determinate circumstances, and with a series of generic models to guide the process, of a dramatic text. Viewed from this perspective, the ascription of the independent authorial 'voice' of 'Shakespeare' to these texts is tantamount to a collusion with an unstated romantic theory of composition, implying a fully conscious writer occupying a transcendent position in relation to his writing, for which the historical evidence is sparse if it exists at all.

Materialist tragedy

In his book *Modern Tragedy* (1966), Raymond Williams argues that the theory of tragedy has traditionally concerned itself with what he calls 'a single and permanent kind of fact' as the chief assumption upon which definitions of tragedy are based. This is, he argues: 'The assumption of a permanent, universal and essentially unchanging human nature (an assumption taken over from one kind of Christianity to ritual anthropology and the general theory of psychoanalysis). Given such an assumption we have to explain tragedy in terms of this unchanging human nature or certain of its faculties.'[123]

This is precisely the assumption that underlies some of the theories of tragedy that have already been outlined earlier. But once it is dislodged then it becomes possible to evolve a different definition; tragedy then becomes: 'not a single and permanent kind of fact, but a series of experiences and conventions and institutions. It is not a case of interpreting this series by reference to a permanent and unchanging human nature. Rather, the varieties of tragic experience are to be interpreted by reference to the changing conventions and institutions.' [124] The accepted view of tragedy that Williams decribes produces, he argues, a correspondence between individual experience, and a universal order, where that latter is unchanging and where man learns through the experience of an *unsuccessful* challenge to know his place. Thus, for Williams, the traditional conception of tragedy, which has underpinned much of the criticism of Shakespearean texts involves, 'a kind of putting experience to the order, for ratification and containment'.[125]

As we observed earlier in the case of Irving Ribner, a metaphysical reading of the ethos of Shakespearean tragedy, replete with a supporting Christian morality, might bear this out, and might easily be extended beyond Shakespeare to the whole sphere of Elizabethan and Jacobean tragedy. Paradoxically, the violence which this reading tacitly condones is regarded by critics such as George Steiner and E.M.W. Tillyard, not as an instrument through which cultural crisis is signalled, but as a confident expression of the moral strength of the order itself. Indeed, in his chapter on 'Sin' in *The Elizabethan World Picture* (1943) Tillyard can assert confidently: 'all the violence of Elizabethan drama has nothing to do with the dissolution of moral standards; on the contrary, it can afford to indulge itself just because those standards were so powerful'.[126] In an earlier chapter entitled 'Order', Tillyard could, with equal confidence, assert that the statement of order contained in Edmund Spenser's *Hymn of Love* was a description of 'what must have been common to all Elizabethans of even modest intelligence'.[127] Rather naively, Tillyard assumes that such statements as those in Spenser's poem, or in Sir Thomas Elyot's *The Book of the Governor* (1534), or in Richard Hooker's *The Laws of Ecclesiastical Polity* (1593–97), or in Ulysses' 'order' speech in *Troilus and Cressida* (1602), are all simple statements of fact, and they replicate directly what the Elizabethans thought.

Of course, we have now become aware that Tillyard's observations refer only in part to the object of his enquiry, and are, in fact, selectively displaced forms of a more pressing, contemporary concern. Methodologically speaking, the approach is similar in its essentialist concerns to that of a critic such as L.C. Knights, who some ten years earlier could distil the action of a tragedy such as *Macbeth* into a single statement: 'I have called Macbeth a statement of evil; but it is a statement not of a philosophy but of ordered emotion.'[128] This statement, or 'theme' is the structural motif which underpins an 'ordered' but emotionally charged referential language through whose transparent surface the sensitive and intelligent reader is able to glimpse an originary universal idea. While this may not be a statement of philosophy, it is clearly informed by a philosophical position which Tillyard shares, and which can be traced back to Plato and Aristotle.

But if, as Rosalind Coward and John Ellis have argued, 'text and context are seen as mutually determining, caught in the same process of production',[129] then questions of authority, as well as questions of the inter-relationship between writer, language and the social formation require radical revision. From this perspective a writer such as Shakespeare is deeply implicated in those linguistic structures which *actively* determine his subject position. Moreover, if thought, language, and social process are mutually interdependent, then meaning itself cannot be a simple question of reference – the establishment of an equivalence between 'symbol' and 'thing' – but must be a construction in language. It therefore follows that the mechanisms deployed in the construction of language, and the selection of certain possibilities from within those governed by the system as a whole which takes place in the act of reading, are those which, in principle, determine the ways in which particular communities make sense of the world. In other words, the means of establishing a hierarchy of values at the conceptual level correspond to a process of differentiation at the material level of the construction of the signifier. Indeed, as Ferdinand de Saussure observed in his *Course in General Linguistics*, 'A linguistic system is a series of phonetic differences matched with a series of conceptual differences.'[130] For Saussure, whose work lies behind much recent radical criticism, *difference* is a principle which is at the structural base of all meaning: 'In language itself, there are only differences'.[131] However, Saussure does not at any point in his analysis raise the question of the function of ideology, so that the social determinants of the manner in which a hierarchy of values and meanings may be established never gets taken beyond the level of formalistic explanation.

The advent of Saussurean linguistics resulted in what Perry Anderson has called a transposition of 'linguistic models to historical processes',[132] and it is what follows from this that has had so crucial an effect on the resurgence of interest in the Renaissance. Indeed, the shift from the kind of literary history and the history of ideas, that characterised the explicit elements of Tillyard's thesis, to a position where the concept of 'history' as a monologic totalising narrative now became problematical, opened the way for a series of new approaches. Louis Montrose has recently charted the development of what he calls 'the newer historical criticism', with its 'refusal of unproblematized distinctions between "literature" and "history", between "text" and "context"'. Here, he argues, 'the collective project is to resituate canonical literary texts among the multiple forms of writing, and in relation to the non-discursive practices and institutions, of the social formation in which those texts have been produced – while, at the same time, recognising that this project of historical resituation is necessarily the textual construction of critics who are themselves historical subjects'.[133] This new emphasis on what Montrose calls 'the *textuality of history*'[134] and upon a range of discursive practices which are culture-specific draws much of its theoretical inspiration from the work of Michel Foucault, and subsequently Hayden White. Against the term 'history' Foucault proposes the term 'archaeology' to denote a departure from the concept of a continuous or progressive 'history', with its own rational teleology. There is, for Foucault, only a discreet series of discourses which determine forms of intellectual enquiry and linguistic representation, and it is within these fundamentally discontinous discursive practices, as I suggested earlier, that the figure of the 'author' is inscribed. As Foucault argues:

'My aim is most decidedly not to use the categories of cultural totalities (whether world views, ideal types, the particular spirit of an age) in order to impose on history, despite itself, the forms of structural analysis. The series described, the limits fixed, the comparisons and correlations made are based not on the old philosophies of history, but are intended to question teleologies and totalizations.'[135]

For Foucault, who possesses discourse possesses power, and 'authority', which is connected to 'desire', involves *the rules and processes of appropriation* of discourse'.[136] Also, for Foucault what he calls 'the archive', rather than 'history' is a kind of 'unconscious' whose structure is far removed from any form of continuous narrative:

> But it deprives us of our continuities; it dissipates that temporal identity in which we are pleased to look at ourselves when we wish to exorcise the discontinuities of history; it breaks the thread of transcendental teleologies; and where anthropological thought once questioned man's being or subjectivity, it now burst open the other, and the outside. In this sense, the diagnosis does not establish the fact of our identity by the play of distinctions. It establishes that we are difference, that our reason is the difference of discourses, our history the difference of times, our selves the difference of masks. That difference, far from being the forgotten and recovered origin, is the dispersion that we are and make.[137]

Foucault's concern with a discontinuous history – a characteristically post-structuralist strategy of fragmentation, that has now become part of the movement of post-modernism – and particularly with questions of discourse, knowledge, and power, has been enthusiastically developed by the kind of American 'New Historicism' which Louis Montrose describes, and whose major exponent is Stephen Greenblatt. Even though there has been a positive response to the Foucauldian focusing of power in discursive structures, for example, madness, the penal system, sexuality and medicine, what New Historicist work tends to play down in this analysis is the precise *political* nature of those social conflicts, antagonisms, and contradictions which underpin particular discourses. In his *History of Sexuality Volume I*, Foucault takes great care to insist upon the materiality of power, suggesting that it 'must be understood in the first instance as the multiplicity of force relations immanent in a sphere in which they operate and which constitute their own organization'.[138] It is, he goes on to argue, 'the name that one attributes to a complex strategical situation in a particular society'[139] suggesting that 'Relations of power are not in a position of exteriority with respect to other types of relationships (economic processes, knowledge relationships,sexual relations), but are immanent in the latter.'[140] Foucault insists that what he calls 'relations of power' fullfill a *constitutive* function; that is that they cannot be collapsed into an idealised concept of power. Indeed, he insists that power in any society exists *only* in and through *relationships* and cannot therefore be essentialised; moreover, their existence, he argues, 'depends on a multiplicity of points of resistance: these play the role of adversary, target, support, or handle in power relation'.[141] It is Foucault's contention that there is no unitary narrative of resistance, but rather that 'there is a plurality of resistances, each of them a special case',[142] but again, he insists that resistance, far from being simply a *reaction* to power is a constituent element of it, manifest in the specificity of material social practice. Because such resistance is what he identifies as disturbances in the even relations of power, 'the odd term in relations of power',[143] then it is distributed irregularly throughout the social formation. For Foucault 'great radical ruptures' occur only occasionally, but generally the situation that confronts us is one of 'mobile and transitory points of resistance, producing cleavages in a society that shift about, fracturing unities and effecting regroupings, furrowing across individuals themselves, cutting them up and remoulding them, marking off irreducible regions in them, in their bodies and minds'.[144] Thus, irregularity, discontinuity, pluralism is the norm, and by implication, tragedy as an artistic inscription of the principle of discontinuity, discloses precisely the political contours of those power relations that Foucault outlines. Moreover, it leads us away from the Renaissance as the narrative precursor of the English Revolution, and into a more complex set of social and cultural interactions that cannot be made to disclose a *telos* of history in any unproblematic way.

For Jonathan Dollimore these discontinuities 'serve a social and political realism',[145] a means of disclosing a materialist 'reality' within which causal relationships can be explained. Taking Brecht's theoretical writings as a starting point, Dollimore proceeds to argue that recent Marxist critics have begun to attend closely 'to the way that literature becomes internally dissonant because of its relationship to social process, actual historical struggle and ideological contradiction'.[146] In the case of the tragedies of Shakespeare and his contemporaries, this internal dissonance arises directly out of the sceptical theatrical representation of the concept of divine authority: 'In the Renaissance God was in trouble',[147] rather than from its reaffirmation. Thus, instead of suffering *disclosing* a covert metaphysical order, what was represented in the theatre were the conditions under which that order was *produced*. Moreover, Dollimore argues, because of the way that 'man' was conceptualised as a dependent creation of God, to deconstruct providence was also, necessarily and inevitably to 'decentre' man.[148] In formal artistic terms the conflict might be described as being between a 'didactic mimesis', that is, an imitation of an *ideal* reality, an immanent design of prescriptive force, behind the appearance of social and cultural forms, and a 'realist mimesis' which ascribed to those symbolic forms a *material* existence. In this context such forms are identified as artistic productions constituted in and through historical discontinuities, open to examination and analysis, and which are themselves subject to empirical verification.[149] In theoretical terms it is also the difference between a critical practice committed to the location of universal truths inside literary texts, on the one hand, and forms of textual analysis which seek to read those texts as cultural productions within a much more divergent social process, on the other.

The questioning of providential design which Dollimore regards as a crucial element of crisis in the culture which produced Shakespeare, was supplemented by the questioning of other social institutions through which the conflicting interests of an increasingly heterogeneous society were articulated. Land enclosure, increased social mobility, economic speculation, aristocratic debt and the consequent fragmentation of estates, the friction between social classes, familial tension, the challenging of gender stereotypes, were all contributory factors to this crisis, although it would be misleading to suggest that the nature of the conflict within each of these spheres of cultural activity was merely an instantiation of a process that was somehow unified at a deep structural level. Many of the social discontinuities to which Dollimore refers arose precisely because there was no clear correspondence between these interrelated but relatively autonomous cultural practices in their historical specificity,and thus it would be a mistake to regard the narrative of crisis as one of uniform development or progress. Moreover, the role of the public theatre in articulating these problems also requires to be borne in mind. An institution that was georaphically located on the margins of a volatile urban society,[150] and which attracted audiences from right across the social spectrum, was extremely well placed to mediate the various crises of representation that could be detected in the relatively autonomous spheres of Elizabethan and Jacobean cultural life. It is still a matter of keen debate as to whether the Elizabethan public theatre simply consolidated the dominant order through its representations, or whether it fulfilled a more subversive function, and , if so, to what extent it was possible to contain that subversion. Moreover, it is also a matter of debate whether a theatre such as the *Globe*, which, in purely iconographical terms replicated that providential design which many traditional critics have detected beneath the surface of Shakespeare's plays, simply recirculated a dominant ideology in its staging of state power, or whether it represented ideology from a perspective which facilitated the disclosure of contradiction. A third, more complex position is also possible, whereby the theatre may be seen as a *producer* of ideology, proposing at the level of aesthetics, solutions to those cultural tensions whose social reality it undertook to negotiate. In other words, the Elizabethan theatre might be thought of as an institution which constructed meanings and values, which proposed fictional solutions, fulfilling a function whereby signification generally could be seen as an inextricable part of material life itself.[151] It is, of course, possible that the Elizabethan public theatre fulfilled all three functions, and that an evaluation of its extraordinarily diverse output must take these constant shifts of emphasis (which were themselves responses to a range of social pressures) fully into a account.

However, Dollimore's work on subjectivity at a historically specific level, along with that of Michel Foucault at the theoretical level, proffers a multi-faceted challenge to the traditional humanist notion of the liberal autonomous subject. In turn, this impinges directly upon certain aspects of Shakespearean tragedy in a new focusing upon the tragic protagonist as 'subject', that is to say the focus of specific constitutive material forces which shape individuality and identity. The pluralising of 'history', has made it possible to investigate alternative 'histories', narratives which deal with groups marginalised or occluded from power structures, whose own subjectivities are inscribed within a range of ideologies. Jacques Lacan's re-reading of Freud has drawn attention to the divisions within subjectivity (in this case, a revision of the Freudian structuring dialectic of the 'conscious' and the 'unconscious') and the resultant 'decentring' has posed a serious challenge to the ideology of humanism, and by implication, to one crucial aspect of the traditional concern with the genre of tragedy. The proposition that the human subject is 'split' has provoked a whole new series of debates about the *position* of 'individuals' within the social formation itself, and as Dollimore has recently reminded us, drama is the place 'in which we see these things operating at all levels simultaneously – the psychic, the private, the familial, the public'.[152] Dollimore's position is part of a wider commitment to 'Cultural Materialism', whereby an art form such as Shakespearean tragedy may be located within the larger social processes of 'consolidation subversion, containment' at work in Elizabethan and Jacobean society.[153] It is his general contention here, and elsewhere, that the *positive* representation of hitherto marginalised or occluded groups in the corpus of Elizabethan and Jacobean tragedy is not an accurate description of what takes place there. Rather, representation is itself subject to a complex web of constraining social mechanisms which the process of conflict discloses. Moreover, the contestations that take place often result in the transformation of dominant discourses, and hence offer opportunities for resistance.[154] What Dollimore proposes, therefore, is a more dynamic role for the tragedy of the period in shaping resistance at the same time that it articulates the dominant structures of Elizabethan and Jacobean society. In giving this conflict a class- and gender-specific location, Cultural Materialism represents a significant advance on its less overtly political transatlantic New Historicist counterpart, although the latter is, in the hands of its most sophisticated practitioner, Stephen Greenblatt, equally aware of the larger structural mechanisms of both containment *and* resistance.

Moreover, with the advent of feminism the humanist autonomous self can no longer be conceived outside the structures of gender, and this has led to a radical revaluation of those institutions, such as patriarchy, through which the categories of masculine and feminine are mediated during the Renaissance. What for Lacan, and to some extent Foucault was a dialectic of 'desire', becomes within feminism generally, and Cultural Materialism, a more complex preoccupation with the explicitly *political* investments made in those institutions designed to secure domination and subjection. For example, in her book *The Subject of Tragedy*, Catherine Belsey argues that, 'To be a subject is to have access to signifying practice, to identify with the "I" who speaks. In so far as signifying practice always precedes the individual, is always learned , the subject is a subjected being, an effect of the meanings it seems to possess.'[155] This has led to the notion of literature as one of a number of discourses, possibly the most important because of its capacity to propose alternatives, through which *representation* of the conflicts between these complex forces is effected. In other words, it is not the alleged *reflective* power of literature or drama which are important, but what Belsey describes as their capacity to disclose 'the meaning and the contests for meaning' within particular cultural institutions, such as marriage.[156] Applied specifically to the realm of Shakespearean tragedy, the resultant questions of gender, politics, ideology and the increasing fragmentation of the subject, can be seen to emerge through the focus upon a crisis which is both personal and public.

The following selection seeks to provide an overview of the range of new work being undertaken in the field of Shakespearean tragedy. It must be emphasised that Shakespearean texts can never be isolated from the context in which they are embedded historically, although a full recovery of the conditions of their production is bound to be, at best, a speculative enterprise. The book begins with two examples of semiotic analysis, both based upon the assumption that literary discourse operates necessarily as part of the larger framework of a system of linguistic signs within which historical concerns are themselves inscribed. Moretti's concern throughout his book *Signs Taken For Wonders* is very much an extension of the original Saussurian postulation of 'a science *which studies the role of signs as part of social life*', a 'semiology' whose purview is 'the nature of signs and the laws governing them'.[157] Whereas Saussure was primarily concerned with the formal relations between the constituent elements of the linguistic sign, and beyond that the internal structures of the system of language as a whole, Moretti extends this concern into the sphere of the sociological, and particularly into the area of the one most potent *symbol* of authority during late sixteenth- and early seventeenth-century English cultural life, sovereignty. He argues that Elizabethan and Jacobean tragedy was decisive in the process of demystifying this symbol, and was instrumental in disclosing the contours of absolutism. He suggests that 'Tragedy, then, stages not the institutions of absolutism, but its culture, its values, its ideology'; and he proceeds, through a range of dramatic and non-dramatic texts to show that while absolutism seeks to construct its own ideal, tragedy 'performs the degradation of the cultural image of the sovereign'.

Although Moretti resists the temptation to regard English tragedy as a means of anticipating the execution of Charles I in 1649, the overall implication of his argument is that history moves from one epoch to another, with the feudal epoch giving way to its recognisably modern successor. To this extent history is shown to retain a teleology which is manifested in the succession from one period to another. It is this notion of periodisation which similarly informs Alessandro Serpieri's textual analysis of *King Lear*. For Serpieri, the opening scene of the play generates a series of oppositions through which the ensuing dramatic narrative is differentially structured, and he pursues these *differences* in the text's rhetorical organisation.

Although both Moretti and Serpieri are concerned with formal questions of structure, both emphasise the notion of text as a material practice within which larger social movements and issues are inscribed. In his book *Drama of A Nation*, Walter Cohen extends this concern to include a comparison between English and Spanish drama during the Renaissance. It is argued that Shakespearean drama in general, and Shakespearean tragedy in particular, occurs at a specific historical moment and is marked by a convergence of popular and aristocratic traditions. In addition to staging the absolutism of which Moretti and Serpieri speak, the plays also proffer what Annabel Patterson has recently described as 'a self-conscious speaking from below'.[158] Cohen situates this convergence of dissonant voices within the larger framework of the transition from feudalism to capitalism, and suggests that what we observe in the tragedies of this period is a representation of what he calls 'A transitional reorganization brought about by a class that could never entirely control the social and economic forces that threatened its hegemony.'[159] Within this context absolutism becomes the means of preserving feudal power, leading, within the sphere of tragedy to a confrontation between absolutism and capitalism.[160] However, Cohen's argument that the shift in the Shakespeare *oeuvre* from 'history play' to tragedy represents a movement from a dramatic form which 'pits feudalism against absolutism', to one which opposes 'absolutism against capitalism', reopens the issue of generic constraint that we observed earlier in relation to the arguments advanced by Lilly B. Campbell. However, Cohen firmly resists the simplistic view that the political and social richness of Shakespearean tragedy aligned the theatre merely as an instrument of state, and he regards the fundamental conflict in these plays in terms of an opposition between residual and emergent elements within ideology itself. Cohen's general argument gains considerably from a comparative dimension, while at the same time remaining within a series of recognisably materialist coordinates, especially the identification of the late sixteenth century as an important moment in the transition from feudalism to capitalism. What concerns him particularly is the question of the structural relationship between dramatic form and the larger professional and historical movements within which its concerns are inscribed. But his suggestion that Elizabethan drama derived its primary influence from the tradition of popular dramaturgy raises the larger question, which has occupied a number of materialist critics, of the space which the popular voice occupies within Shakespearean tragedy.

This important issue is fully addressed in Robert Weimann's *Shakespeare and the Popular Tradition in the Theatre*, a book which preceded Cohen's, but which develops a number of the issues to which the latter refers. Some of Weimann's more recent work has led him to engage more precisely than he does in this book with post-structuralist accounts of Shakespearean tragedy, particularly with questions of representation, and of the convergence of text and history.[161] Here his concern is with the representational capacities of the popular Renaissance stage to generate a range of oppositional meanings which both extend the possibilities of dramatic form in a purely formal manner, but which also embrace certain historical concerns objectively extant in the political antagonisms which structure society itself. Fundamental to Weimann's argument is the theatrical distinction between 'platea' and 'locus', between 'neutral, undifferentiated "place" and symbolic location' on the Elizabethan stage. This, Weimann argues, enabled the performance itself to move relatively freely from the creation of dramatic illusion to what he calls 'the process of consciousness shared by the audience', 'non-illusionistic effects' which functioned as a means of interrogating and criticising social hierarchies which occupied a symbolic location on the stage itself. Here performance itself is shown to be an indispensable part of the dialectical production of meaning, where distance from, or proximity to, the theatre audience contributes centrally to this process. It is Weimann's contention that poetic and theatrical technique serves, 'in Shakespeare, as a mode and a medium of perceiving and comprehending the world as a temporal, spatial, and social experience'; that is to say, dramatic art is a *medium* through which a determinate social history is filtered. Although his idea of 'mode' suggests that drama may also fulfill a *constitutive* function, an issue of crucial importance in the distinction between orthodox and post-structuralist materialist accounts of the Shakespearean text.

In the writing of Weimann and Cohen, the question of 'history' as a product of Enlightenment rationalism is given a much sharper focus than in structural and semiotic accounts of the Shakespearean text, although in the latter it is assumed rather than explicit. Saussurian structuralism depends upon the assumption that a linguistic structure, *langue*, is, by definition, *without* history, since the relationships between its elements are capable of being analysed only at a synchronic level, but that it enters history and is capable of diachronic analysis, when in use by individual speakers of the language as *parole*. A number of critics have observed the ahistorical impetus of structuralism, but more recently there have been a number of objections from post-structuralists to the single narrative of history proposed by classical Marxism, and still present, though in a very sophisticated form in the work of Weimann and Cohen. Against such universalist readings of 'History', and following the Foucauldian analysis of discontinuity, New Historicism of the kind represented by Stephen Greenblatt, focuses upon what Frank Lentriccia describes as a plurality of 'histories' exemplified by 'forces of heterogeneity, contradiction, fragmentation, and difference'.[162] We see in this an amalgamation of terminology associated both with structuralism and with Marxism, although what characterises New Historicism is a certain theoretical indeterminacy. In his book *Renaissance Self-fashioning From More To Shakespeare* Stephen Greenblatt argues that 'in the sixteenth century there were both selves and a sense that they could be fashioned'.[163] The notion of the 'self' accords with the post-structuralist notion of 'the subject', who is both an initiator of action, and who is also inscribed as the object of a range of social and cultural practices and constraints; a self which, as Greenblatt puts it, comprises 'a sense of personal order, a characteristic mode of address to the world, a structure of bounded desires'.[164] This is, of course, a very different notion from the Bradleyan conception of 'character', as free autonomous agent. Indeed, one of the constituent influences upon the self is, for Greenblatt, 'power': not a hypostasised force or an unchanging essence, but a Foucauldian *process*, a determinate series of cultural practices through which particular interests are pursued. For Greenblatt the roles which the self occupies in the social formation are continually negotiable, permitting forms of 'improvisation' whose paths can be traced through a range of cultural phenomena. The plural 'self', capable of transformation, functions to dislocate the elements of ideology which are themselves expressly designed to occlude contradiction. It should be added that in holding on to the concept of 'improvisation' Greenblatt retains a residual commitment to an increasingly uneasy version of personal autonomy which distinguishes his perception of subjectivity from Dollimore's materialist notion of the overdetermined, decentred self. Greenblatt's method is to locate the text of a tragedy such as *Othello* within the synchronic relations between particular constitutive elements of late Renaissance culture, arguing that the tragedy is constructed out of a symbolic interplay of 'violence, sexual anxiety and improvisation'. He is not concerned to locate some central 'truth' in Shakespearean texts, rather he insists 'the truth is radically unstable and yet constantly stabilized', where authority itself is constantly in danger of subversive undermining, and where the force for that potential subversion is to be found in a social process exemplified by the 'living theater' with its 'unsettling repetitions, committed to the shifting voices and audiences, with their shifting aesthetic assumptions and historical imperatives'.

Characteristic of New Historicism is what Louis Montrose describes both as 'the *historicity of texts*', and '*the textuality of history*',[165] which is another way of resisting essentialist notions of truth or of man, while at the same time insisting that the practice of history is a process of production. The location of the Shakespearean text within this dynamic focuses it for us as a relatively autonomous cultural production, replete with its own rules, but related to other forms of cultural production, other texts, circulating in society at a particular historical moment. Within this model the scholar or critic becomes a resourceful, but at times unselfconscious, means of disclosing deep structural relations between a variety of diverse texts as models of the ways in which the discourses of power operate. The theoretical *aporias* or doubts that are sometimes revealed in New Historicism, though they are by no means as easy to separate from an ebullient style in the work of Greenblatt or Montrose as they might be in that of some of their followers, are supplied by Cultural Materialism, its more openly politicised British equivalent. Jonathan Dollimore's book *Radical Tragedy: Religion, Ideology and Power in the Drama of Shakespeare and his Contemporaries* sets out both to challenge the mythographical isolation of Shakespeare as a cultural monument in and through a criticism saturated in ideology, while at the same time attempting to resituate Shakespearean tragedy in a range of troubled contemporary Renaissance discourses of religion and power. Dollimore poses along with New Historicism, a challenge to essentialist humanism, but in a stong reading of Foucault he too resists the temptation to hypostasise power. In the Renaissance 'man' is decentred, a plural subject, but there are also opportunities for resistance, and it is one of the main features of Cultural Materialism as it has developed, that particular forms of resistance are to be found in the dramatic texts of Shakespeare and his contemporaries, and in the theatres for which they wrote, capable of challenging and transforming the social order itself. Implicit in Dollimore's position is a cautious commitment to the proposition that Art itself can be a political weapon, although its resistances are disclosed at the level of *reading* rather than at the more problematical level of an authorial intention. In a subsequent and succinct manifesto of Cultural Materialism, Dollimore observes that the effectiveness of a genre such as tragedy is 'both decided and assessed in the practice of signification', as opposed to the traditional view which emphasises its capacity to transcend 'the historical moment of inception' as a means of 'representing universal truths'.[166] He does not contest the view that tragedy contains universal statements, but he insists that 'they were also resolutely political especially those which defined it as a representation of tyranny'.[167] Indeed, in his contrast of the work of George Steiner with that of the late J.W. Lever, Dollimore insists that the latter views suffering 'as contingent rather than necessary, the effect of social and historical forces focussed in state power'; but he goes on immediately to suggest that 'Though terrifyingly destructive, these forces are not irresistible in the sense of being cosmically or divinely destined.'[168] This view draws in part upon the Brechtian critique of humanist tragedy, but it may also be aligned with Augusto Boal's radical dismantling of Aristotle's *Poetics* that we observed earlier.

If the essential humanist core which the suffering of tragedy is said to disclose is, in fact, divided; and if the radical decentring which results exposes the material social and cultural institutions within which the 'self' is inscribed, and through which it is constituted; then private life may be said to 'include, and often actively reproduce, the exploitation, repression and oppression visible in the public realm'.[169] In this formulation Cultural Materialism straddles the New Historicist preoccupation with power, and the materialist concern with all forms of social being which determine social consciousness. One such area elides the question of 'subjectivity' with relations of gender, and is the explicit concern of feminism.

Catherine Belsey's book, *The Subject of Tragedy*, like Dollimore's, is a seminal text in this respect in that it focuses on the related questions of subjectivity, subjection, identity and difference in the tragedies of Shakespeare and his contemporaries. Again, a distinction must be drawn between a British and North American context, in so far as the feminism which Belsey espouses eschews the notion of a feminine *essence*. Rather she describes an identity which is constructed differentially in and through a range of social institutions, such as marriage and the family, as well as in a range of dramatic and non-dramatic, Shakespearean and non-Shakespearean texts. One of Belsey's main aims in her book is :

> to demonstrate, by placing woman side by side with man, that at the moment when the modern subject was in the process of construction, the 'common-gender noun' largely failed to include women in the range of its meanings. Man is the subject of liberal humanism. Woman has meaning in relation to man. And yet the instability which is the result of this asymmetry is the ground of protest, resistance, feminism.[170]

What Belsey emphasises throughout is a 'sexual politics', which, in the case of the writings of Shakespeare and his contemporaries, is concerned to analyse masculine representations of woman in male-authored texts and the ideologies which are designed to occlude contradiction and hence minimise the possibilities of resistance. *The Subject of Tragedy* is part of a larger project which seeks to focus on the ways in which gendered subjects are drawn into a complicity with liberal humanism which occludes difference in order to transform it into a 'truth' whose masculine, rationalist images women are invited voluntarily to live as subjection. This irreducibly materialist version of feminism may be contrasted in certain respects with that which Marilyn French's *Shakespeare's Division of*

Experience discloses. The very gender categories which Belsey establishes as being based upon relations of *difference* become for French positive terms, with the result that she ascribes certain essential features to 'masculinity' and 'femininity' respectively. Thus, for French dramatic genres are gender-inflected, comedy being 'a feminine mode' with its wider social concern and its desire for harmonious integration through 'felicity and procreation', whereas tragedy is 'masculine' in its preoccupation with the individual in conflict. Moreover, French proceeds to argue that tragedy is modelled on the experience of birth, in so far as it concerns an anguish which results from the hero's paradoxical position 'of being part of a culture, even expressing to a high degree some of its values, and yet increasingly rejecting or being rejected by it'. In the course of this conflict the protagonist discovers an identity in which the feminine must have a place *if* genuine harmony is to be restored.

What French seeks to establish is a *positive* account of what she calls 'the feminine principle', one which inadvertently dispenses with the constitutive notion of 'difference', and one which is ultimately aligned with an authorial intention. In this respect, she fails to disengage from an essentialist perspective, since her implied notion of female subjectivity is one which depends upon an adherence to a fundamentally liberal feminine principle which is all but autonomous. By comparison, Elaine Showalter's emphasis on the issue of 'representation' foregrounds what she calls the 'responsibility' of feminist criticism in relation to theatrical and critical representations of the character of Ophelia. For her the solution is not the liberation of Ophelia from the text of the play, or the uncovering of a narrative which reduces her to 'a metaphor of male experience', but 'rather a *history* of her representation'. The focus on Ophelia's madness raises questions of a psychiatric nature, but Showalter wants to conflate them with questions concerned with 'cultural representation'. Thus, in aligning herself with the representational features of cultural history rather than with the project to excavate an essentialist feminity, Showalter moves much closer to the British *rapprochement* between feminism and materialism which characterises the work of British writers such as Catherine Belsey.

If materialist feminism is concerned to show that questions of gender and sexuality are constitutive within the whole sphere of social relations, then it must, as Jonathan Dollimore has argued, 'disclose the complexities which its ideological representation must disavow'.[171] In the sphere of Shakespearean tragedy this involves both a study of the relationship between questions of gender and dramatic form, but also, a focus on the subject-in-process, which entails an investigation of the convergence of subjectivity and language in the unconscious. This is a sphere which is, quite properly, the concern of psychoanalysis. In his re-reading of Freud, Jacques Lacan insists upon the materiality of language: 'It is the world of words which creates the world of things.'[172] Moreover, he also insists that both the gendered human subject and the unconscious are brought into existence through those differential mechanisms which serve to structure language. Thus, it is in language that the subject comes to recognise her/himself as an 'imaginary' unity, but, because it is constructed from *differences*, it is also a material process of coming-into-being, which leaves traces of that radical 'decentring' whose origins reside in the quasilinguistic structure of the unconscious itself. Lacan argues that what 'resounds' in 'Man' are representations of an 'other scene', the unconscious, where what he calls the 'materially unstable elements' of language itself are located *prior* to their formation as a fantasy of coherence. It is in the unconscious that desire is structured, both as a need requiring satisfaction *and* as a demand for love; and the signifier which structures desire is 'the Phallus', a term which designates a relation, and hence a division in and through which sexual difference is constituted. It is only when this difference is projected into the social sphere that it is exposed to the pressures of ideology which seek to eradicate its division. Applied to Shakespearean tragedy, the imaginary order which the text constructs and reconstructs can be read symptomatically for what it can disclose of the workings of the unconscious itself.

It is in this context that we might view Jacques Lacan's difficult essay on 'Desire and the Interpretation of Desire in *Hamlet*'.[173] In the early part of his essay Lacan locates the figure of Ophelia as the focus of what he takes to be 'the tragedy of desire as it appears in *Hamlet*'. For Lacan, Ophelia becomes 'one of the innermost elements in Hamlet's drama, the drama of Hamlet as the man who has lost the way of his desire'. Although the central figure in the play is Hamlet himself, Lacan argues that the action 'is dominated by the Mother as Other, i.e. the primordial subject of the demand'. He asks the question: 'What does Hamlet lack?', but he identifies the uncertainty in the play as the result of Hamlet's not knowing what he wants. Lacan focuses his discussion around the question of mourning in the play, the expression of sorrow for a loss which generates desire. In this respect both the death of Hamlet's father and of Ophelia leave a gap in the fabric of the real – what Lacan calls 'a hole in the real' – that can only be filled by a signifier which is itself 'essentially the veiled phallus'. Here 'the real' is not to be confused with knowable 'reality', but is to be distinguished from the 'symbolic' and the 'imaginary', where the latter two refer to an order constructed from differences through which their value and meaning are produced, and to those images out of which lived reality is itself constructed; thus the 'symbolic' constitutes an order, which, as Julia Kristeva has observed, contains 'what is forbidden, distinguishable, thinkable', while the 'imaginary' is 'what the Self imagines in order to sustain and expand itself'.[174] For Lacan the act of mourning seeks to rectify the disturbance produced by 'the inadequacy of the signifying elements to cope with the hole that has been created in existence'. In other words, mourning itself represents both a challenge to, and a disturbance in, 'the system of signifiers in their totality', that is, in the symbolic order, which the drama, and the rituals it enacts, is required to address and resolve. Thus *Hamlet* is preoccupied with a violation of law, an issue which Julia Kristeva takes up in a slightly different context in relation to *Romeo and Juliet*. Psychoanalytical criticism generally returns to the process whereby a human subject derives her/his identity, and concludes that that subjectivity is always *divided* or decentred. André Green's analysis of *Othello*, which takes the discussion back to the issue of triangulated Oedipal desire with its emphasis upon the close relationship between matriarchal and patriarchal imperatives, focuses on precisely these issues, as indeed does Janet Adelman's account of *Coriolanus*. It is important to notice that a number of materialist approaches borrow some elements of Lacanian psychoanalysis, particularly those concerned with the internal division of the subject, and the notion that it is in and through language that the subject enters the social order, although, of course, these details are deployed differently, and they deviate from the Oedipal model that such analysis has derived from Frued.

In a technical sense psychoanalytical criticism, along with deconstruction, feminism and the various forms of materialist criticism, can properly be said to be post-structuralist in so far as they proceed, and follow on, from a Saussurian account of the primarily linguistic structure of reality. The questioning of the epistemological foundation of Shakespearean tragedy is, in certain respects, part of a larger project which substitutes the constitutive power of signifying practice for an essentialist commitment to a purely ontological view of language. It is this latter which, to use Derrida's own terminology, conceives of structure 'on the basis of a full presence which is beyond play'.[175] One version of the alternative to this would be the notion of a radical indeterminacy as the *terminus ad quem* of all critical practice. But despite the fact that hitherto Shakespearean tragedy was regarded as the repository of metaphysical 'truth', the alternative of an entirely *free* play is one which has raised further questions. It is, of course, in the interests of various types of materialist criticism to issue a radical challenge to the notion of an ontologically sanctioned authoritative account of the meaning of a Shakespearean text,but some of the most recent examples of criticism of the tragedies have drawn attention to the various ways in which determinate histories imposed limits upon the process of generating meaning. In focusing upon the *textuality* of *King Lear*, Malcolm Evans draws attention to the ways in which discursive practice and the process of representation fragments in the face of social crisis, where not only identity, but meaning itself becomes problematical. Here, deconstruction as a strategic weapon for locating the means whereby an authoritative order imposes itself upon a socially heterogeneous reality is shown to proceed beyond what Evans calls 'delirium and indeterminacy' to a more egalitarian world: 'a vision of a better world, already in prospect at its own moment of levelling and familiarity'. For Evans, the extension of the play of signification which follows from the absence of a transcendent centre points towards an 'abyss' which, he argues, 'is familiar in the topography of Elizabethan and Jacobean drama'. Released from an ontologically sanctioned conception of 'truth', the Shakespearean text *produces* subjects and 'the relations that shape utterance', at the same time that it reveals the impossibility of any final closure. In a way which offers glimpses of other possibilities the text is always *festive* in its capacity to indicate that the situation can always be otherwise. In his emphasis upon the Bakhtinian carnivalesque Evans shares some of the concerns of Robert Weimann, although he is more explicitly concerned about the aesthetic and ideological manoeuvres that a text such as *King Lear* deploys in order to occlude those discourses which might shatter its pretensions to ontological stability. Indeed, he brilliantly conflates a range of materialist positions, to produce a multidimensional approach to Shakespearean texts which resituates them historically, while at the same time reading them through their subsequent reception. For Evans, a text such as *King Lear* offers the prospect of no naive utopian vision; but in its methodological unpicking of ideologies it formulates at the level of carnival a series of articulations of the metaphorical forms which subsequent histories themselves take. Evan's is a complex theory of cultural resistances, involving the location in a text such as *King Lear* of that which escapes containment, but which always returns to challenge the dominant hierarchies of structure.

It is around some of these issues that Terry Eagleton's concerns focus. Here again, the issue of 'play' is subjected to a careful scrutiny from the perspective of determinate histories themselves. And it is around this issue that a number of debates have arisen, especially in relation to the conflict betwen the radical indeterminacy of the text, resistant to all forms of constraint, and a historical necessity that sets limits to that indeterminacy.[176] Eagleton returns the discussion to the materiality of language itself and its implication in historical process. Eagleton, like Evans, locates 'excess' in language itself 'which constantly outruns the confines of the body', but it is two-edged: it is both the instrument of control and the means of liberation. Indeed, this is the source of a fundamental contradiction whereby language is both the 'very index and medium' the human propensity 'to surpass itself', and yet that capacity is offered in a play such as *King Lear* as a 'natural' human activity. Tragedy arises for Eagleton when a play such as *King Lear* 'stares this contradiction full in the face, aware that no poetic symbolism is adequate to resolve it'. Taking in *Timon of Athens* and *Antony and Cleopatra*, he also seeks to locate the process in these plays of ascribing value in the face of a decline of an aristocracy which can be shown to be 'living towards death'. All of these plays disclose contradictions that no poetry can adequately resolve, and in challenging this structural matter within the texts, Eagleton is also challenging a critical practice which ascribes a hierarchy of values to language itself, thereby making meaning under the guise of discovering it.

Finally, and as a necessary corrective to the capacities of criticism as an institution which *makes* meaning, Terence Hawkes's provocative account discloses a series of personal preoccupations which surface as symptoms in Bradley's own criticism of Shakespearean tragedy. Utilising many of the strategies which are evident in the critical positions represented throughout this anthology, Hawkes finally prizes the text-as-object away from the figure of the critic as dispassionate observer. This serves as a necessary reminder that criticism itself *makes* texts and under determinate historical conditions, so that a genre such as Shakespearean tragedy is itself the product of a critical narrative which formulates the object of its enquiry in terms of a selective retrospect. In the same way that texts disclose historical intersubjective relations, so critics are themselves subjects constructed in the differential mechanisms of a range of cognate histories. Blowing the gaff on Bradley effectively drives a wedge between the privileged disciplinary limits which literary criticism imposes upon itself, and relocates its concerns necessarily within the larger framework of cultural studies. To this extent we may conclude that 'Shakespearean tragedy', with its rigid generic boundaries, and internal hierarchy of texts is a category which signally fails to encompass those plays to which it nominally refers. The following selection of essays is designed to provide a series of methodologies for dismantling this category, as a precondition for returning these plays to the complex fields of representation which they continue to inhabit.

Notes

1. LILLY B. CAMPBELL, *Shakespeare's Histories: Mirrors of Elizabethan Policy* (London, 1964), pp. 13–16.

2. Op. cit., p. 3.

3. Ibid., p. 8.

4. GEORG LUKACS, 'The Metaphysics of Tragedy', *Soul and Form*, trans. Anna Bostock (London, 1974), p. 155. See also LUCIEN GOLDMANN, *The Hidden God: A Study of Tragic Vision in the Pensées of Pascal and The Tragedies of Racine*, trans. Philip Thody (reprinted London, 1977), pp. 55–6.

5. Ibid., p. 113.

6. Cf. JONATHAN DOLLIMORE, *Radical Tragedy: Religion, Ideology, and Power in The Drama of Shakespeare and His Contemporaries*, 2nd. edn (London, 1989), pp. xvi–xvii.

7. Ibid., p. 342.

8. Ibid., p. 353.

9. GEORG LUKACS, op. cit., p. 154.

10. Op. cit., p. 9.

11. Op. cit., p. 156.

12. Op. cit., pp. 196–7.

13. Ibid., p. 194.

14. Ibid., p. 195.

15. SIGMUND FREUD, 'Two Principles of Mental Functioning', *On Metapsychology: The Theory of Psychoanalysis*, The Pelican Freud Library, vol. 11, ed. Angela Richards (Harmondsworth, 1984), p. 36. See also, later, *Beyond The Pleasure Principle*, pp. 275–81.

16. Ibid., p. 278.

17. Ibid., p. 287.

18. SIGMUND FREUD, *Art and Literature*, The Pelican Freud Library, vol. 14 (Harmondsworth, 1985), p. 123. See also,'Totem and Taboo', in Sigmund Freud, *The Origins of Religion*, The Pelican Freud Library, vol. 13 (Harmondsworth, 1985), p. 218:

> The hero of tragedy must suffer; to this day that remains the essence of a tragedy. He had to bear the burden of what was known as 'tragic guilt'; the basis of that guilt is not always easy to find, for in the light of our everyday life it is no guilt at all. As a rule it lay in rebellion against some divine or human authority; and the Chorus accompanied the Hero with feelings of sympathy, sought to hold him back, to warn him and to sober him, and mourned over him when he had met with what was felt as the merited punishment for his rash undertaking.

See in addition, SIGMUND FREUD, *The Interpretation of Dreams*, The Pelican Freud Library, vol. 4 (Harmondsworth, 1975), pp. 363–4, for comments on *Oedipus Rex*, and particularly for the idea that the lesson which the spectator learns from tragedy is, 'submission to the divine will and realization of his own impotence'.

19. Ibid., p. 124.

20. Ibid., p. 125.

21. Ibid., p. 126.

22. FREUD, 'Psychopathic Stage Characters', op. cit., p. 127.

23. ROLAND BARTHES, *Image, Music, Text*, trans. Stephen Heath (Glasgow, 1977), p. 9. See also ROLAND BARTHES, *The Pleasure of The Text*, trans. Richard Miller (New York, 1975), pp. 52–5. For a further analysis of *jouissance*, see *Feminine Sexuality: Jaques Lacan and the Ecole Freudienne*, ed. Juliet Mitchell and Jacqueline Rose (London, 1982), pp. 137–48.

24. BARTHES, *The Pleasure of The Text*, p. 53.

25. PLATO, *The Republic*, trans. F.M. Cornford (Oxford, 1961), p. 325.

26. ARISTOTLE, *The Poetics*, ed. J. Warrington (London, 1963), p. 12.

27. Ibid., p. 15.

28. Ibid., p. 17.

29. Ibid.

30. Ibid., pp. 21–2.

31. Ibid., p. 25.

32. Ibid., p. 26.

33. Ibid. Aristotle comments: 'whenever such and such a personage says or does such-and-such a thing it shall be the probable or necessary result of his character, and whenever such-and-such an incident follows upon such-and-such another it shall do so as the necessary or probable consequence thereof'.

34. AUGUSTO BOAL, *Theater of The Oppressed* (London, 1979), p. 21.

35. CAMPBELL, op. cit., p. 16.

36. Ibid., p. 23. See also G.E.M. DE STE CROIX, *The Class Struggle in The Ancient Greek World* (London, 1983), pp. 140ff and also pp. 416ff. for an analysis of the slave culture of ancient Athens, which provides a useful focus for any theory of the preservation of the equilibrium of emotion.

37. Ibid., p. 25.

38. Ibid., p. 27.

39. Ibid., p. 32.

40. Ibid., p. 33.

41. Ibid., p. 34.

42. Ibid., p. 39.

43. Ibid., p. 47. See also p. 54 where Boal refers to the fact that tragedy emerged from within a society that was politically organised along the lines of an 'imperialistic democracy'.

44. GEORGE THOMPSON, *Aeschylus and Athens* (reprinted London, 1980), p. 2.

45. LEONARD TENNENHOUSE, *Power on Display: The Politics of Shakespeare's Genres* (New York and London, 1986), p. 15.

46. THOMPSON, op. cit., p. 76.

47. Ibid., p. 86. Later in his argument Thompson goes on to distinguish between the Classical Greek model of tragic experience, and the history of the evolution of tragic drama in England. In the secularising of Dionysiac ritual in fifth-century Greece, it continued to retain its link with religious practice. By contrast, in Renaissance England, where, 'the Church stood for the feudal nobility, and its liturgy, as the ritual of a ruling class' the liturgy had become stabilised and hence was inimical to change. For Thompson, what he calls 'the impulse to dramatization', which he associates with the peasant activity of seeking to transform liturgical practice into 'mimetic magic', proceeded in the face of ecclesiastical opposition, so that 'when these plays were taken over by the bourgeoisie, the rivals of the feudal nobility, the drama was developed in conscious opposition to religious ritual, of which it rapidly became entirely independent' (p. 186).

48. WALTER BENJAMIN, *The Origins of German Tragic Drama*, trans. John Osborne (London, 1985), p. 115.

49. FRIEDRICH NIETZSCHE, *The Birth of Tragedy and The Genealogy of Morals*, trans. Francis Golffing (New York, 1956), p. 64.

50. Ibid., p. 134.

51. Ibid., p. 126. See also WALTER BENJAMIN, op. cit., p. 103, for a stringent critique of Nietzschean aestheticism; Benjamin observes: 'Where art so firmly occupies the centre of existence as to make man one of its manifestations instead of recognizing him above all as its basis, to see man's existence as the eternal subject of its own creations instead of recognizing him as its own creator, then all sane reflection is at an end'.

52. GILLES DELEUZE, *Nietzsche and Philosophy*, trans. Hugh Tomlinson (London, 1983), p. 36. But see also, PAUL DE MAN, *Allegories of Reading: Figural Language in Rousseau, Nietzsche, Rilke and Proust* (New Haven and London, 1979), pp. 90–102 for a more troubled account of *The Birth of Tragedy*.

53. Op. cit., p. 138.

54. Ibid., p. 139.

55. TERRY EAGLETON, *The Ideology of The Aesthetic* (Oxford 1990), p. 247.

56. REINHOLD NIEBUHR, *Beyond Tragedy* (New York, 1965), p. 164.

57. A.C. BRADLEY, *Oxford Lectures on Poetry* (reprinted, London, 1965), pp. 69–95.

58. ANNE and HENRY PAOLUCCI, *Hegel on Tragedy* (New York and London), p. 294. See also JOHN DRAKAKIS (ed.), *Alternative Shakespeares* (London, 1985), pp. 6–8.

59. Op. cit., p. 71.

60. Ibid.

61. A.C. BRADLEY, *Shakespearean Tragedy* (London, 1904), p. 7.

62. Ibid.

63. Ibid., p. 86.

64. HEGEL, *The Phenomenology of Spirit*, trans. A.V. Miller (Oxford, 1977), p. 266.

65. 'Hegel's Theory of Tragedy', p. 91.

66. Ibid., p. 88, 1n.

67. Ibid., p. 86.

68. Op. cit., p. 13.

69. Op. cit., p. 84.

70. *Shakespearean Tragedy*, p. 18.

71. *Shakespearean Tragedy*, p. 16.

72. Ibid., p. 22.

73. Ibid., p. 23.

74. Ibid.

75. Ibid., p. 25. See also ARISTOTLE, *The Nicomachean Ethics*, trans. J.A.K. Thompson

(Harmondsworth, 1977), p. 251 where the 'good' is associated with 'processes that restore us to our natural state' and where the natural state is one which 'has no deficiency'.

76. Cf. L.C. KNIGHTS, *Some Shakespearean Themes and An Approach To Hamlet* (Harmondsworth, 1966), p. 121, where Knights says of the ending of *Macbeth*: 'It is a fitting close for a play in which moral law has been made present to us not as a convention or command but as the law of life itself, as that which makes for life, and through which alone man can ground himself on, and therefore in his measure know reality.' See also, IAN JACK, 'The Case of John Webster', *Scrutiny*, vol. 16, (1949), ROBERT ORNSTEIN, *The Moral Vision of Jacobean Tragedy* (Madison and Milwaukee, 1965), and IRVING RIBNER, *Jacobean Tragedy: The Quest For Moral Order* (London, 1962).

77. IRVING RIBNER, *Patterns in Shakespearean Tragedy* (London, 1969), p. 4.

78. Ibid., p. 1.

79. Ibid., p. 9.

80. LUCIEN GOLDMANN, *The Hidden God*, trans. Philip Thody (London, 1964), p. 41.

81. Ibid., p. 99.

82. Ibid., p. 42.

83. CLIFFORD LEECH, *Shakespeare's Tragedies and Other Studies in Seventeenth Century Drama* (London, 1965), p. 9. Cf. also, NORTHROP FRYE, *Anatomy of Criticism* (Princeton, New Jersey, 1971), pp. 210–11.

84. Ibid., p. 18.

85. CLIFFORD LEECH, *Tragedy* (London, 1969), p. 12.

86. Ibid., p. 54.

87. NORTHROP FRYE, op. cit., p. 215.

88. Ibid., p. 212.

89. Ibid., p. 209.

90. ALAIN ROBBE-GRILLET, 'Nature, Humanism and Tragedy (1958)', *Snapshots and Towards a New Novel* (London, 1965), p. 83.

91. Ibid., p. 84.

92. Ibid., p. 93.

93. RENÉ GIRARD, *Violence and The Sacred*, trans. Patrick Gregory (Baltimore and London), p. 13.

94. Ibid., p. 14.

95. Ibid.

96. Ibid., p. 17.

97. Ibid., p. 49.

98. Ibid., p. 258.

99. Ibid., p. 127.

100. Ibid., p. 64.

101. Ibid., p. 65.

102. JACQUES DERRIDA, 'Structure, Sign and Play in the Discourse of the Human Sciences', *Writing and Difference*, trans. Alan Bass (London, 1978), p. 279.

103. Ibid., p. 241.

104. Ibid., p. 52.

105. Ibid., p. 65.

106. Ibid., p. 12.

107. Ibid., pp. 95–6.

108. CLIFFORD LEECH, *Tragedy*, p. 68.

109. JACQUES DERRIDA, *Dissemination*, trans. Barbara Johnson (London, 1981), p. 99.

110. Ibid., p. 126. The focus of the discussion is Plato's *Phaedrus* which contains the story about the origin of writing.

111. Ibid., p. 127.

112. Ibid., p. 130.

113. Ibid., p. 133.

114. JURGEN HABERMAS, *The Philosophical Discourse of Modernity*, trans. Frederick G. Lawrence (Oxford, 1990), p. 169.

115. CATHERINE BELSEY, *The Subject of Tragedy* (London, 1985), p. 53.

116. INGA STINA EWBANK, 'Shakespearean Constructs', *TLS*, no.4334 (25 April 1986), p. 452. Ewbank assumes oddly that within the realm of theory and quarry is, 'the search for some unified knowledge of Shakespearean drama' which she regards as futile. She concludes that 'perhaps the best recipe ... is a mixture of scepticism and fideism' – a stance which, it is assumed, guarantees critical objectivity and detachment. What this does, in fact, is to displace the assumed transcendence of the author onto the critic.

117. MICHEL FOUCAULT, *Language, Counter-memory, Practice* (Oxford, 1977), p. 124.

118. Ibid., p. 121.

119. Ibid., p. 122.

120. Ibid., p. 123.

121. ROLAND BARTHES, *Image, Music, Text*, trans. Stephen Heath (Glasgow, 1977), p. 146.

122. Ibid., p. 147.

123. RAYMOND WILLIAMS, *Modern Tragedy* (London, 1966), p. 45.

124. Ibid., pp. 45–6.

125. Ibid., p. 52.

126. E.M.W. TILLYARD, *The Elizabethan World Picture* (London 1943), p. 18.

127. Ibid., p. 10.

128. L.C. KNIGHTS, *Explorations* (Harmondsworth, 1964), p. 41.

129. ROSALIND COWARD and JOHN ELLIS, *Language and Materialism* (London, 1977), p. 62.

130. FERDINAND DE SAUSSURE, *A Course in General Lingusitics*, trans. Roy Harris (London, 1983), p. 118

131. Ibid.

132. PERRY ANDERSON, *In the Tracks of Historical Materialism* (London, 1983), p. 45.

133. LOUIS ADRIAN MONTROSE, 'Renaissance Literary Studies and the Subject of History', *English Literary Renaissance*, **16**, no. 1 (Winter 1986), p. 6.

134. Ibid., p. 8.

135. MICHEL FOUCAULT, *The Archaeology of Knowledge*, trans. A.M. Sheridan Smith (London, 1972), pp. 15–16.

136. Ibid., p. 68.

137. Ibid., p. 131.

138. MICHEL FOUCAULT, *The History of Sexuality, Volume I*, trans. Robert Hurley (Harmondsworth, 1981), p. 92.

139. Ibid., p. 93.

140. Ibid., p. 94.

141. Ibid., p. 95.

142. Ibid., p. 96.

143. Ibid.

144. Ibid.

145. JONATHAN DOLLIMORE, *Radical Tragedy*, p. 63.

146. Ibid., p. 68.

147. Ibid., p. xxix.

148. Ibid.

149. Ibid., pp. 73–82.

150. Cf. STEPHEN MULLANEY, *The Place of the Stage: License, Play and Power in Renaissance England* (Chicago and London, 1988), pp. 49ff.

151. See RAYMOND WILLIAMS, *Marxism and Literature*, p. 99 for a general discussion of the concept of 'mediation'.

152. JONATHAN DOLLIMORE, *Radical Tragedy*, 2nd edn, p. xxvii.

153. JONATHAN DOLLIMORE and ALAN SINFIELD (eds), *Political Shakespeare: New Essays in Cultural Materialism* (Manchester, 1985), pp. 10ff.

154. Ibid., p. 12.

155. CATHERINE BELSEY, *The Subject of Tragedy* (London, 1985), p. 5

156. Ibid., p. 4.

157. FERDINAND DE SAUSSURE, *Course in General Linguistics*, trans. Roy Harris (London, 1983), p. 15. See also, TERENCE HAWKES, *Structuralism and Semiotics* (London, 1977) for a full account of this general area of study.

158. ANNABEL PATTERSON, *Shakespeare and the Popular Voice* (Oxford, 1989), p. 34.

159. WALTER COHEN, *Drama of a Nation: Public Theater in Renaissance England and Spain* (Ithaca and London, 1985), p. 83.

160. Cf. RAYMOND WILLIAMS, *Marxism and Literature*, pp. 121ff and JONATHAN DOLLIMORE, *Radical Tragedy*, p. 7, for the analysis of ideology as containing dominant, residual and emergent elements.

161. Cf. ROBERT WEIMANN, 'Towards a literary theory of ideology: mimesis, representation, authority', Jean E. Howard and Marion F. O'Connor (eds), *Shakespeare Reproduced: the Text in History and Ideology* (London, 1987), pp. 265ff. See also my review of this volume in *Shakespeare Quarterly*, **40**, no. 3 (Fall, 1989), pp. 342–5.

162. FRANK LENTRICCIA, *After The New Criticism* (London, 1983), p. xiv.

163. STEPHEN GREENBLATT, *Renaissance Self-Fashioning from More to Shakespeare* (Chicago and London, 1980), p. 1.

164. Ibid.

165. LOUIS ADRIAN MONTROSE, 'Reniassance Literary Studies and the Subject of History', *English Literary Renaissance*, **16**, no. 1 (Winter 1986), p. 8.

166. JONATHAN DOLLIMORE and ALAN SINFIELD (eds)., *Political Shakespeare: New Essays in Cultural Materialism* (Manchester, 1985), p. 9. See also the Introduction to Jonathan Dollimore, *Radical Tragedy: Religion, Ideology and Power in the Drama of Shakespeare and his Contemporaries*, 2nd edn (New York and London, 1989) for a fuller exposition of the relationship between New Historicism, Cultural Materialism and feminism, and between essentialist and materialist notions of tragedy.

167. Ibid.

168. *Radical Tragedy*, 2nd edn, p. xviii.

169. Ibid., p. xxvii.

170. CATHERINE BELSEY, *op. cit.*, p. ix.

171. DOLLIMORE, *Radical Tragedy*, 2nd edn, p. xxxiv.

172. JACQUES LACAN, *Ecrits: a Selection*, trans. Alan Sheridan (London, 1980), p. 65.

173. JACQUES LACAN, 'Desire and the Interpretation of Desire in *Hamlet*', *Literature and Psychoanalysis: the Question of Reading Otherwise*, ed. Shoshana Felman (Baltimore and London, 1982), pp. 11–52.

174. JULIA KRISTEVA, *Tales of Love*, trans. Leon Roudiez (New York, 1987), p. 7.

175. JACQUES DERRIDA, 'Structure, Sign and Play in the Discourse of the Human Sciences', *Writing and Difference*, trans. Alan Bass (London, 1978), p. 279.

176. See GRAHAM HOLDERNESS, NICK POTTER and JOHN TURNER, *Shakespeare: the Play of History* (London, 1988). See especially, JOHN TURNER '*Macbeth*' where it is argued that the effectiveness of tragic catharsis is invested with political expediency, and which charts the move into 'a world where the erosion of the sacred has removed restraints upon violence and made its eruption ever more likely' (p. 148). The play investigates what Turner calls 'a world ... destroyed by contradictions in its material base, its patriarchalism and its heroic aristocratic code' (Ibid.).

2 Semiotics

Franco Moretti The Great Eclipse: Tragic Form as the Deconsecration of Sovereignty*

Franco Moretti is Professor of English at the University of Salerno in Italy. The book from which this extract is taken, *Signs Taken For Wonders: Essays in the Sociology of Literary Forms*, was published in 1983. Underlying Moretti's general thesis is the suggestion that the function of 'rhetoric' is 'to enlist support for a *particular* system of values' (p. 3), and that 'Rhetorical figures, and the larger combinations which organise long narratives, are thus of a piece with the deep, buried, invisible presuppositions of every world view' (p. 6). Following in part the Hungarian critic Georg Lukacs, Moretti emphasises the relationship between literary *form* and social reality, and suggests that a literary history 'able to rewrite itself as a sociology of symbolic forms, a history of cultural conventions', does have a place in 'the context of a total history of society' (p. 19). Moretti resists the general notion that a particular historical period is best identified through individual exemplary literary forms; rather it is characterised by what he calls 'a kind of parallelogram of rhetorical forces, with its dominant, its imbalances, its conflicts and its division of tasks' (p. 26). While, on the one hand he proposes that one of the primary functions of literature 'is to secure *consent*' (p. 27), he suggests that in the case of Elizabethan and Jacobean tragedy the opposite is true. Indeed, he argues that this form 'more radically than any other cultural phenomenon of the same period' served to discredit 'the values of absolute monarchy, thereby paving the way, with wholly destructive means, for the English revolution of the seventeenth century' (ibid.). He perceives the conflict of tragedy as being between a dominant ideology still committed to presenting as an organic whole, and a historical necessity which foregrounds a radical conflict of interests between different social groups. It is this 'unrepeatable historical

---

*Reprinted from *Signs Taken For Wonders* (London: Verso, 1983), pp. 42–82.

conjuncture' (p. 28) which, Moretti argues, produces tragedy, and to this extent its signifying practices articulate a radical discontinuity which can anticipate as well as mediate larger social conflict.

'That thence the *Royal Actor* born / *The Tragick Scaffold* might adorn: / While round the armed Bands / Did clap their bloody hands. / He nothing common did or mean / Upon that memorable Scene.'[1] Marvell's celebration of Cromwell represents the execution of Charles I as a theatrical spectacle – specifically, as a tragedy. The argument of this essay is that there are excellent reasons why this should be appropriate: Elizabethan and Jacobean tragedy was in fact one of the decisive influences in the creation of a 'public' that for the first time in history assumed the right to bring a king to justice. To acknowledge this profound historical significance, however, is not to say that English Renaissance tragedy is a 'Puritan' or 'bourgeois' or 'revolutionary' cultural form. On the contrary, there is little in English tragedy that anticipates the new age opened up by the stroke of an axe at Whitehall on 30 January 1649. Yet new ages are not brought into being merely through the development of new ideas: the dissolution or overthrowing of old ideas plays an equal part in their emergence. And in the case at hand, historians are agreed that this is indeed the decisive phenomenon.[2] In the pages that follow, therefore, I shall attempt to indicate the elements essential to a definition of tragic form, and to demonstrate that the historical 'task' effectively accomplished by this form was precisely the destruction of the fundamental paradigm of the dominant culture. Tragedy disentitled the absolute monarch to all ethical and rational legitimation. Having deconsecrated the king, tragedy made it possible to decapitate him.

1 'Meantime, we shall express our darker purpose'

Let us begin with the work that initiates English tragedy: *Gorboduc*, written by Thomas Norton and Thomas Sackville in 1562. The play tells the story of a king who abdicates and divides his kingdom between his two sons, Ferrex and Porrex. The latter murders his brother to seize entire control of the realm, but he in turn is murdered by his mother. At this point, the people rise up and kill both king and queen. The nobles, assembled in parliament, put down the rebellion, and although the Duke of Albany betrays their common enterprise to secure the throne for himself, the play concludes with the clear suggestion that the aristocracy-in-arms will put down the rebellion.

The bare logic of events in the play is rich in implications. One is that tragedy presents a universe in which *everything has its origin in the decision of the king*. Tragedy thus pays the monarch an ambiguous homage. If the general culture of absolutism qualified the sovereign power it conferred upon the king with countless hesitations and uncertainties (representatively summed up in Bodin),[3] tragedy surrenders such power to him wholly and without the slightest reserve. In the world of tragedy the monarch is truly *absolute*. I do not mean, either there or in what follows, that tragedy presents the absolute monarch as he really was. It would be a frustrating task indeed to seek a realistic representation of the absolutist political system in the works of English tragedy. The strength (or weakness) of absolutism did not lie in the person of the king, but rather in a system of collective institutions such as a functioning bureaucracy, a sound fiscal system, a permanent army, and an efficient juridical unification: to the point that, as Immanuel Wallerstein has written, it would be more exact to call this system 'statism'.[4] It is also true, however, that the king acted as the summa and symbol of this new system of power in the context of its own political theory, which argued for an increase of power not for the state but for the king. Tragedy, then, stages not the institutions of absolutism, but its culture, its values, its ideology. This fact by no means impairs the capacity of tragedy to perform its task of radical dissolution. On the contrary, profound historical reasons operate in the case of absolutism to make the conflict of ideas (understood as the cultural process by which power is legitimated) a decisive matter. The first of these is specifically English: the numerous structural weaknesses of the crown made it difficult to establish an absolute monarchy *de facto*. All the more reason, then, that the attempt to construct one had to rely on elements of an ideal character. The arguments of James I on the divine right of kings, Carl Schmitt observes, merely masked the dearth of hopes and prospects for his actual position.[5] When, therefore, as we shall see, tragedy performs the degradation of the cultural image of the sovereign, it deprives the monarchy of its central bastion, its ultimate weapon. There is a second, more wide-ranging reason for the crucial pertinence of the ideological field here. In the political system of absolutism, the relation between culture and power differs considerably from that obtaining in other kinds of society, capitalism in particular. In the latter, social power finds its legitimacy from the very beginning in the simple fact that it exists. The property spoken of by the philosophy of natural right – typically posited prior to the social contract – is a real datum. It exists and that suffices. It has no more meaning than the world of nature after the 'disenchantment' effected by seventeenth-century physics. For the philosophy of natural right – which is the real site of origin for the distinction between 'structure' and 'superstructure' – culture is ultimately a latecomer whose function consists in preserving the fundamental given of property. ('The Regulating and

Preserving of Property' is not accidentally the classic formula that, at the beginning of Locke's Second Treatise, defines the tasks and limits of political power.) With absolutism the reverse is true. Here the legitimacy of social power derives from a form of divine investiture. Power is founded in a transcendent design, in an intentional and significant order. Accordingly, political relations have the right to exist only in so far as they *reproduce that order symbolically*. In a word, if bourgeois property can have a meaning because it exists, absolute monarchy can exist because it has a meaning. What occurs in the sphere of absolutist culture is not confined to the heights of the superstructure; it informs the base itself, the condition of existence of political rule. Hence, the cultural conflicts and modifications of the age of absolutism bear directly on the politics of this world, in whose collapse tragedy – generally neglected whenever this problem is being considered – is one of the decisive phenomena.

Sovereignty is a power that, having its origin *in itself*, is thereby released from any control; it is 'self-determined', as Hegel will say. Sovereignty is a *universal* power, reaching and defining every part of the body politic, whose destiny is therefore enveloped within it. Both attributes profoundly inform the structure of *Gorboduc*. Universal, the decision of the king will gradually affect his person, his family, the nobility, the people, and all society: in event after event, the royal act resonates over the entire political body. Self-determining, the king is the only character really free to choose and therefore to *act* in the proper sense of the word. He is the primary and, in a certain sense, the only real actor in modern tragedy. As Kierkegaard put it in his reflections on the difference between ancient and modern tragedy: in the ancient world,

> even if the individual moved freely, he still rested in the substantial categories of state, family, and destiny. This substantial category is exactly the fatalistic element in Greek tragedy, and its exact peculiarity. The hero's destruction is, therefore, not only a result of his own deeds, but is also a suffering, whereas in modern tragedy, the hero's destruction is really not suffering, but is action .... Our age has lost all the substantial categories of family, state, and race. It must leave the individual entirely to himself, so that in a stricter sense he becomes his own creator.[6]

There remains only to add that the chief example of this 'individual' freed from 'substantial categories' *within* society (and not outside it, banished like a vagabond or leper) is furnished by the absolute sovereign, who is literally *absolutus*, that is, released, free. Tragedy could re-emerge only in the late sixteenth century, when the figure of the new prince had entered the stage of history. Without the absolute sovereign, modern tragedy would not have been possible.

With these premises established, let us return to *Gorboduc*. Here the attributes that the king would arrogate to himself are readily given over to him. But the gift is poisoned. Precisely what makes Gorboduc a sovereign – universality and self-determination – also proclaims him, in accordance with a paradigm that remains unchanged through the development of English tragedy, a *tyrant*.[7] The key to the metamorphosis comes early in the play when Gorboduc declares to his counsellors his intention of abdicating. Though the latter attempt to dissuade him with various 'rational' arguments ('Only I mean to show by certain rules, / Which kind hath graft within the mind of man'),[8] Gorboduc never bothers in the least to confute them. He is king not because he can reason and persuade, but simply by virtue of the fact that he *decides*. And he decides in a 'self-determined' way, that is, without having to worry about adducing 'motivations' or 'causes', on which he remains rigorously silent. We inevitably encounter the problem of *decision*, an obligatory one for the history of political theory and of absolute power in particular. As we have already hinted, it is here that the fundamental attribute of the monarch resides: according to Carl Schmitt's definition, sovereign authority is that which decides on 'the state of exception'.[9] This power of decision incarnates itself in dictatorship, which aims to put an end to the state of exception and which, when it succeeds in this, imposes itself on the basis of a permanent and no longer merely occasional sovereignty.[10] It is particularly striking that, from *Gorboduc* forward, English tragedy offers us a dynamic of events diametrically opposed to that described by Schmitt for the case of dictatorship. In tragedy, dictatorship (which, we recall from Benjamin, 'demands the completion of the image of the sovereign, as tyrant') is not the means to end a state of exception, but rather, on the contrary, what provokes it, what initiates civil war. In other words, the force that the king manifests in his decision proclaims him not only a tyrant, but incapable of governing as well. As a consequence, the exercise of sovereignty leads to complete anarchy, as though the two were one and the same. With effects that we will later need to register, tragedy represents absolutism as an irresolvable paradox.

In *Gorboduc*, I have claimed, the king appears as a tyrant, but, at first glance, the contrary seems true, for how can one be a tyrant if, like Gorboduc, one abdicates one's throne? The contradiction is only apparent. The principal characteristic of Gorboduc's abdication lies rather in its form than in its content, and in the fact that it manifests itself as a sovereign decision, an act of free will. In Elizabethan terms, the conflict in the abdication scene (I, ii) occurs between the *will* of Gorboduc and the *reason* of his counsellors. Both terms are crucial in sixteenth-century ethical–political treatises, which locate the difference between king and tyrant precisely in the relationship that is instituted between will and reason. Lydgate's Aristotle had already harped on the point: 'To

Alysaunder he wrote in trouthe / That he shold alwaye be governed by
reason.'[11] 'Obstinacie', writes Thomas Elyot, 'is an affection immoueable,
fixed to wille, abandonynge reason .... By it many a valyaunt capitayne
and noble prince haue nat onely fallen them selfes, but also brought all
their contrayes in daungeour and often tymes to subuercion and ruyne.'[12]
'Wo to him whose will hath wisedomes place', laments Richard II in *The
Mirror for Magistrates;*[13] and Hooker, the great codifier of Elizabethan
ideology, says: 'Two principal fountains there are of human action,
knowledge and will ... ; the will ... differeth greatly from that inferior
natural desire which we call appetite. The object of appetite is whatsoever
sensible good may be wished for; the object of will is that good which
reason doth lead us to seek.'[14] Finally, we read in *The Mirrour of Policie* at
the turn of the century: '[To live under a monarchy] is verie dangerous, and
to be feared (considering the frailetie of man, and the great libertie that
kings haue to doe what they list, whether it bee good or euil, and the great
power that they haue to execute what so their will leadeth them unto).'[15] In
short, as the last quotation makes clear, in the case of the king, will is
power, the power to act. And, significantly, nothing ensures that such a
power to act will be subordinated to the dictates of reason, since, on the
contrary, absolutism aspires to emancipate such power entirely. In the
'autonomy of politics', Elizabethan organicism articulates *the principle of
tyranny*. Hooker's consoling distinction between appetite and will is
founded on the precedence and control accorded to reason, but once this
ceases to be granted, the two forms of will become indistinguishable:
'Tyrannicall power is put into the hands of one alone who ... tyrannizeth
according to his disordinate will, ... according to his sensuall appetite and
will.'[16] Appetite and will are now placed on the same level. The 'too sullied
flesh' triumphs over 'godlike reason': the tyrant subjugates the sovereign.

With *Gorboduc*, the old ethical conflict between will and reason is
transformed into a political clash between executive power and
consultative privilege, between Gorboduc and his counsellors, the
sovereign and the aristocracy. The terms of the conflict are fully consonant
with the system of correspondences that flourished in England around the
middle of the sixteenth century. The king was the 'heart' of the body
politic, the source of action, while the nobility were the 'eyes', or the organs
of sense and intellection.[17] But what was a functional distinction in this
'world picture', a collaboration between different organs for the benefit of
the whole, has in *Gorboduc* become a contest. The first movement of the
first English tragedy is thus to *sever* the connection that sustained the
dominant culture. At bottom, English tragedy is nothing less than the
negation and dismantling of the Elizabethan world picture.

'The Elizabethan world picture', of course, is first and foremost an
historiographical hypothesis. It was advanced independently at roughly
the same time by Theodore Spencer in 1942,[18] and in 1943 by E.M.W.

Tillyard, who 'invented' the term. Also in 1943, Leo Spitzer was writing *Classical and Christian Ideas of World Harmony*, in which he extended a similar argument to all of Western Europe.[19] The argument is basically as follows: European culture is based on the encounter between Platonism and Christianity, the fusion of which dominated it up to the scientific 'disenchantment' of the seventeenth and eighteenth centuries. These are basically, therefore, the only two periods in European culture: the period that extends from antiquity through the Middle Ages to the Renaissance, and the modern period. In all its variations, this argument denies the historical and cultural specificity of the age of absolutism – a denial all the more easily accomplished in the case of England where the existence of such an age was briefer and more precarious than elsewhere. Thus, Tillyard: 'Coming to the [Elizabethan] world picture itself, one can say dogmatically that it was still solidly theocentric, and that it was a simplified version of a much more complicated medieval picture.' In this perspective, the only truly distinctive feature of Elizabethan culture becomes its capacity to integrate some modern elements into the already established medieval totality – its capacity, in short, for 'compromise'.

> Though the general medieval picture of the world survived in outline into the Elizabethan age, its existence was by then precarious. There had been Macchiavelli, to whom the idea of a universe divinely ordered throughout was repugnant …. The greatness of the Elizabethan age was that it contained so much of new without bursting the noble form of the old order. It is here that the Queen herself comes in. Somehow the Tudors had inserted themselves into the constitution of the medieval universe. They were part of the pattern and they had made themselves indispensable.[20]

However well the theory of the Elizabethan world picture explains other phenomena, it fails to grasp the most important fact of the age. For cultural production proceeds by strange leaps and condensations; and in the period of English absolutism, this production is concentrated in the drama-within-the-drama, in tragedy. Had this drama not existed, Elizabethan culture would scarcely have assumed the importance it has for us, and for the very reasons Tillyard gives; because it would not have presented its own distinctive features, such as would make it a specific object of study different from others. If one claims to speak of Elizabethan culture, therefore, one must speak of its tragedy, but this is precisely what the theory of the Elizabethan world picture prevents us from doing. To be sure, the theory takes up the subject of tragedy, but only to assign to it the curious function of confirming its own scheme *a contrario*. The tragic negation, it is argued, goes to show the solidity of medieval organicism, and the need for radical destruction confirms the power of what is to be destroyed. It is as though it were argued that in strangling Desdemona, Othello paid tribute to her importance. No doubt he does, but he strangles her all the same, and similarly, tragedy, in its destruction of the medieval world picture, recognizes its importance, but destroys it nonetheless. And it is on the dynamic of destruction that we need to focus, not on the handsome edifice that, by the end of the fifth act, has been reduced to rubble. This dynamic, as we have seen, originates in the decision of the king – or rather in the fact that the king acts as an *absolute sovereign*. Tillyard is certainly correct to notice the many glorifications of Elizabeth that 'insert' her 'within the constitution of the medieval universe'. But this is only to say that these do not recognize her new, actual function. Only tragedy looks the new prince straight in the face, taking his absolutist claims at their word and systematically elaborating them. Alone in the Elizabethan period, tragedy is truly modern, truly rigorous.

Let us once more return to *Gorboduc* and the conflict there between kingly power and aristocratic reason. By virtue of his action, the king causes the dissolution of the entire body politic. Absolutism thus reveals its full force, which is revealed in turn, however, as a social catastrophe. *Gorboduc* will prove typical of English tragedy, but only in the kind of story it tells and the kind of logic it gives to events. What is still missing is the other essential characteristic of tragedy, its particular form of *reflection* on events. In *Gorboduc*, will emancipates itself from reason, action from speech; and the autonomy of sovereign action, primed by the inscrutable will of the monarch, gives rise to the succession of actions that makes up the story. Yet if reason has been defeated by the will of the king, it has hardly been destroyed. In the last scene of the play, Eubulus, the spokesman for the ideology of the body politic and the most ample exponent of the Elizabethan world picture, reproduces the same arguments rejected by Gorboduc at the beginning. The Elizabethan cultural establishment has stood the brunt of the dramatic action, which, moreover, fully confirms its validity: Eubulus had foreseen it all from the start. Appropriately, the values of this establishment return to the field, enriched and, this time, armed, themselves endowed with the force that in the beginning had been the monopoly of the king. The parliament-in-arms at the end of *Gorboduc* can once again intervene in the course of events and, closing the tragic scission, bring the tragedy to a conclusion. It has reunited force and reason, submitting the former to the latter. Offering us only a limited absolutism, *Gorboduc* is never more than a half-tragedy. The restoration of reason and the restoration of the aristocracy imply one another. If the values of the Elizabethan world picture survive, this is because their political exponents survive as well. Just as the progress of absolutism will eliminate the latter, so too the progress of tragic form – in its development, a shining mirror of the 'crisis of the aristocracy' will render impossible a closure in which reason, not only uninjured but armed, reconquers the stage. We encounter the evidence half a century later, when Shakespeare rewrites *Gorboduc* and calls it *King Lear*.

Although much more complex, the plot of *King Lear* is based on the same assumptions we saw operating in *Gorboduc*. To divide the kingdom is to act against all reason, and in the void that is thereby engendered the destructive force of the selfish 'nature' of Edmund, Goneril, and Regan can be freed. Certain conventions, however, are clearer here than in *Gorboduc*, particularly the apparently paradoxical fact that abdication is a tyrannical act. The decision to abdicate, which in Gorboduc was 'purpose' *tout court*, becomes Lear's 'darker purpose': obscure, inscrutable, arbitrary, and exhibited as such. Moreover, the simple and slight reason Lear adduces for abdicating – the weight of his old age – clearly suggests that he has betrayed his political and public function to the advantage of this physical and private person. Like Claudius or Macbeth, albeit in different form, Lear thus yields to 'fallen nature', and this yielding points to the transformation of the king into a tyrant. The entire abdication scene is dominated by Lear's arrogant absolutism. Unlike Gorboduc, Lear does not stop at simply rejecting the advice of his counsellor Kent; he banishes him from the kingdom under pain of death. What gratifies him in the speeches of Goneril and Regan is the abyss they excavate between himself and them, the unlimited dependence they declare.[21] Conversely, what infuriates him in Cordelia is her untainted feudal spririt: 'I love your Majesty / According to my bond; no more nor less' (I,i,92–3).[22] Cordelia still inhabits a world of reciprocal obligation, of feudal rights and duties, whereas Lear aspires to absolute omnipotence. His 'madness' is in large part the inevitable issue of this aspiration, not its overthrow. Thus, in III, ii, at the height of the storm, he shouts out his absurd orders to the forces of nature ('Blow, winds, and crack your cheeks!'). Or again, in III, iv, he sets himself up in supreme judgement over all daughters. Or again, finally, in the last scene, he can do no better than cover with insults those who have tried to help him, glorifying his own powers: 'A plague upon you murderers, traitors all! / *I* might have sav'd her, now she's gone for ever! / ... / *I* kill'd the slave that was a-hanging thee' (V, iii, 269–70, 274, my italics). Thus, as Benjamin has claimed, madness appears as the definitive sign of the sovereign degeneration.[23]

As *Lear* heightens the absolutist claims made in *Gorboduc*, it simultaneously diminished the counterclaims of the aristocracy. Certainly, *King Lear* quite teems with loyal nobles – Kent, Gloucester, Albany, Edgar, not to mention the numerous Gentlemen who pass on stage simply to attest their fidelity to the old king. What has been lost is not the number of faithful nobles, but their function. They are no longer allowed, as Eubulus was in *Gorboduc*, to inscribe events within an organic and rational framework of political meaning. In the first scene of the tragedy, Kent opposes Lear merely to defend the rights of Cordelia (with whom he shares a feudal ethic), not in the name of the higher interests of the kingdom. Nor as he takes his leave from the court, does he reveal any ability to foresee future consequences. The very service he will later offer to Lear is inspired by fidelity to a person rather than to a political institution. When Gloucester, for his part, tries to give an account of conditions at the start of the play, he has recourse to what already appeared to the Elizabethan audience an empty superstition, 'the excellent foppery of the world': 'These late eclipses in the sun and moon portend no good to us .... Love cools, friendship falls off, brothers divide: in cities, mutinies; in countries, discord; in palaces, treason; and the bond crack'd twixt son and father' (I, ii, 107–8, 110–14). But the clearest instance of the nobility's inadequacy comes in the speech with which Edgar concludes the play:

> The weight of this sad time we must obey;
> Speak what we feel, not what we ought to say.
> The oldest hath borne most; we that are young
> Shall never see so much, nor live so long.

> (V, iii, 323–6)

It should not seem strange that the extraordinary dramatic efficacy of these lines consists in their chilling stupidity, in the drastic banalization they impose on the play. In the very work that has unhinged our trust in the meaning of words, there reappears the obtuse assurance of sing-song proverb and of dead metaphor: 'the weight of time', 'see so much', 'live so long'. The story that has involved the downfall of a kingdom and a pair of families (not to mention, one imagines, a good number of French and English soldiers) is summed up as a 'sad time'. Though *King Lear* has denied the transparency of feelings in language, Edmund now urges us to 'speak what we feel'. 'Old' and 'young', categories which the play has deprived of all interpretive value, are now exhumed as though they might explain something. And finally, to put the seal on all, four impeccably rhymed little verses, bright with monosyllables, come to conclude a work in which a tormented prose has invaded the terrain of rhythmic decorum. The speech of Edgar is the most extraordinary – and appropriate – of anticlimaxes. Its blind mediocrity indicates the chasm that has opened up between facts and words, or more accurately, between referents and signifieds. The close of *King Lear* makes clear that no one is any longer capable of giving meaning to the tragic process; no speech is equal to it, and there precisely lies the tragedy.[24] One notes here the historical caesura that divides *Gorboduc* and *Lear*. In *Gorboduc*, reason though momentarily routed by the decisive power of the king, nonetheless succeeded in foreseeing and bestowing a meaning upon the sequence of actions. It always remained a pole in the drama, endowed with its own representatives, and it emerged from its trial enriched and surer of itself.

By the end, it was equipped to begin putting the world again to rights. In *Lear*, what scant reason remains has been not only defeated, but derided and dissolved by the course of events. If at the end it is allowed the last word, this is only by virtue of that archaic, semimiraculous duel between Gloucester's two sons; and if it returns on stage, it is only with the object of confounding us with the poverty of its reflection.

Before examining the consequences of what has just been said, let us briefly consider the semantic modifications to which the term 'tragedy' is subject in the course of only a few decades. Speaking of the Prologue to Chaucer's *Monk's Tale*, George Steiner observes that the meaning of tragedy for the high Middle Ages does not imply dramatic form. 'A tragedy is a narrative recounting the life of some ancient or eminent personage who suffered a decline of fortune toward a disastrous end.'[25] Tragedy is largely synonymous with misfortune or death, and it keeps this sense not only in the *Mirror for Magistrates*, but even in *Arden of Faversham* (1590?: 'And train thy master to his tragedy')[26] and Kyd's *Spanish Tragedy* (1590?: 'This very sword ... / Shall be the worker of thy tragedy').[27] In this perspective, the prince is more important for what he is than for what he does. If his fall is the most clamorous, this is for 'quantitative' reasons, as it were, rather than reasons inherent in his specific political function. *Gorboduc* represents a second moment, in which tragedy, ceasing to be the story of a king opposed by fate, becomes the story of a tyrant. This new sense of tragedy is found in Elyot: 'in redyng tragoedies, [a man shall] execrate and abhorre the intollerable life of tyrantes'; in Sidney: 'the high and excellent Tragedy ... maketh Kinges feare to be Tyrants, and Tyrants manifest their tirannicall humours'; in Puttenham:

> [Princes'] infamous life and tyrannies were layd open to all the world, their wickedness reproched, their follies and extreme insolences derided, and their miserable ends painted out in playes and pageants, to shew the mutabilitie of fortune, and the just punishment of God in reuenge of a vicious and euill life.[28]

Tragedy now is the story of a tyrant who unmoors action from the hold of reason. Yet if *Gorboduc* and the sixteenth-century treatises privilege this sense of tragedy, it is always with a view to reinforcing the status of reason. Tragedy with them becomes a supremely educational aesthetic form. A last indication of this comes from a dramatic function we have not yet considered. Every act of *Gorboduc* opens with a dumb show and closes with a chorus. On the one hand, the dumb show allegorically stages what will happen in the act proper, and the allegory is so codified, even proverbial, that it will immediately be understood. On the other, the chorus sums up what has happened in the act and emphasizes its significance. Thus, even though the sovereign's decision unchains action from reason, such action continues to occur in the temporal and semantic context established by reason. The moral precedes the tale, and the general model anticipates the particular case. With *Gorboduc*, tragedy takes shape thanks to the insertion of the sovereign at its origin, but this development takes place only within a rigidly circumscribed dramatic structure still possessing certain characteristics that will remain immune from the catastrophe, delimit it, bestow sense on it, and resolve it. Finally, with the destructive power of *King Lear*, tragedy enters a third phase of evolution, in which those 'pales and forts of reason' of which Hamlet was already doubtful are unremittingly struck down. Neither characters nor other dramatic elements succeed in giving significance to the tragic plot: 'th'election lights / On Fortinbras, he has my dying voice. / So tell him, with th'occurrents more and less / Which have solicited – the rest is silence' (*Hamlet*, V, ii, 355–8). 'Th'occurrents more and less': this, for Hamlet, is all one can say at the end of his tragedy. With the mediocre conscientiousness that characterizes him, Horatio will tell Fortinbras 'of carnal, bloody, and unnatural acts, / Of accidental judgements, casual slaughters, / Of deaths put on by cunning and [forc'd] cause, / And in this upshot, purposes mistood / Fall'n on th'inventors' head' (V, ii, 381–5). In short, he will offer him a plot summary. But what of the 'rest', which is nothing if not the meaning of what has happened? On that falls Hamlet's prohibition: let no one presume to confer meaning on it.

From the last observation, it should be clear that the concept of tragedy I am attempting to delineate here can only be a *structural* concept, capable of simultaneously defining a syntagmatic axis (plot) and a paradigmatic axis (values), and of clarifying the unique relation that obtains between them in tragedy. This is to say that the 'tragic – an expression that always refers to a single dimension of the problem, usually (even in Nietzsche) to the content of actions' – does not exist as a possible situation in human history, whether real or imaginary. Only *tragedy* exists – that is, a particular form of *representing* that history: a rigorously asymmetrical structure marked by a constitutive lack. Fully realized tragedy is the parable of the degeneration of the sovereign inserted in a context that *can no longer understand* it. It is a text that lacks an adequate interpretive function and in which the final 'judgement' must be enormously poorer than that on which it is passed. From Hegel forward, this inadequation has been attributed to the disappearance of the chorus and, along with it, of what Hegel called 'a higher moral consciousness, aware of substantial issues, warning against false conflicts, and weighing the outcome'.[29] Whether the chorus of ancient tragedy really functioned as Hegel claims (a question open to considerable debate), in modern tragedy at any rate, the chorus, still existing in *Gorboduc* where it coincided at the end of the play with the aristocracy-in-arms, is missing. With it disappears a universal, 'higher' point of view. Or more exactly this consciousness is no longer a property of those characters who hold the tragic stage, and who are various facets of the dominant class of the time. In modern tragedy, this class appears suddenly *incapable of understanding* the course and sense of history. It has nothing to teach those who are watching and who thus find themselves deprived of that spiritual guidance to which they have been accustomed, precisely when the events they watch make such guidance absolutely necessary. The spectators are literally constrained *to think for themselves*: for the first time, nothing and nobody show them the way. For millenia, 'ideas' had been validated not by their 'intrinsic truth' (a modern scientific criterion), but by the 'authority' of those who proffered them. With modern tragedy, the principle of authority is dissolved, and with it vanishes the chief obstacle to the existence of that *rational public* that others, in other ways, will take charge of forming fully.

2 'A tale told by an idiot, signifying nothing'

For us the concept of theatre refers directly to aesthetic activity, but for the Elizabethans it was before all else connected with a system of political relationships. 'The world's a Theater, the earth a Stage, / Which God, and nature doth with Actors fill, / Kings have their entrance in due equipage, / And some their parts play well and others ill / .... All men haue parts, and each man acts his owne.'[30] The idea that the world is a theatre where men simply play a role is truly meaningful only in the context of a feudal 'status society', whose fundamental characteristics, according to Macpherson's reconstruction, consist in the fact that 'the productive and regulative work of the society is authoritatively allocated to groups, ranks, classes, or persons' each of which 'is confined to a way of workng, and is given and permitted only to have a scale of reward, appropriate to the performance of its or his function'.[31] The significance of the stratification of medieval society into its estates, as another scholar of medieval political thought has written, is that

> it was precisely the hallmark of a member of a particular estate that he could not move out of his own estate ... each member of society should fulfil the functions which were allotted to him, because this was held to have been the effluence of the divine ordering of things. It was the principle of vocation ... according to which every individual had been called (vocatus) to fulfil specific tasks .... What mattered was not the individual, was not the man, but ... the office which that individual occupied.[32]

The individual 'exists', therefore, only insofar as he is an 'actor' in a social 'role'. Society is thinkable only as a theatre, and life as a performance. Yet in that case, strictly speaking, an actual theatre would be inconceivable. And, in fact, feudal society knows that theatre only in its religious form, as the perennial re-enactment of roles prescribed for all eternity. The rebirth of the stage can take place only when the system of roles that constitutes this status society begins to give way, and the solidity of political bonds comes undone in the course of the long crisis of the fourteenth century. Absolutism – again we see the necessity of this historiographical category – has its origin in the attempt to halt this process. The feudal hierarchy whose molecular organization was in a state of extreme disarray hoped to restore itself by concentrating power in the hands of the sovereign.[33] This utopian late-medieval project, so perfectly comprehensible in the framework of the Elizabethan world picture, had an ephemeral life, but it found an interesting dramatic incarnation in the 'dark' or 'problem' plays of the first years of the seventeenth century, plays which from a historical point of view it would be preferable to call de-problematizing plays.

The 'de-problematizing' play *par excellence* is Shakespeare's *Measure for Measure* (1604), which enriches and perfects the structure established the preceding year by John Marston in *The Malcontent*. This structure hinges on four elements, the nature of the protagonist, his relationship to the plot, the characteristics of the minor characters, and the final scene. The four elements define as many ideological junctures in the Elizabethan world picture, and they reappear in tragic structure only to be brought into question. It will be useful, therefore, to examine the 'programmatic' functioning of the Elizabethan world picture in order to perceive more clearly how tragedy constitutes itself as its negation. Beginning with the figure of the protagonist, the legitimate holder of supreme authority, Shakespeare's Duke or Marston's Altofront, we notice that his fundamental characteristic is *not to be subject to the passions*. This separates him from the other characters, who are notably weaker in this respect, and designates him as the sovereign of the Elizabethan utopia, dedicated to the public weal in so far as devoid of personal interests. To return to our earlier terms, he is subject to reason and not to will, while – for the lesson to be as clear as possible – selfish passion overwhelms both Angelo, the deputy of legitimate power, and Mendozo, its usurper. He who restores this power, then, is a figure of integrity, so whole that he can be divided without risk: into the Duke/Friar, or Altofront/Malevole. What in the tragic hero becomes sorrowful laceration and impotence is here subterfuge and canniness, the *arcanum imperii* of disguise that even Elyot could still recall to his 'governors' the better to know their subjects. Dressed up as a friar, the Duke of Vienna wanders about his city and oversees. 'I perceive your Grace, like a pow'r divine, / Hath look'd upon my passes', Angelo exclaims at the end of *Measure for Measure* (V, i, 369–70). This superior vision of authority is a crucial formal element. Tragic heroes are always conspicuously blind, and in Jacobean drama, the idea that any character can 'see' the dramatic development in its entirety is completely lost, with the result that the only one to possess a comprehensive vision of events is the audience. But in a hierarchical society, this radical reversal of what ideally would be a descending order of comprehension, in which the higher one's position, the more one sees,[34] carries with it some explosive consequences. For ultimately, those who possess the most general vision may plausibly claim the most general power, and the pre-revolutionary exaltation of the Country over the Court will be based precisely on the betrayal of the general interest by the latter.[35] The Shakespeare of the 'problem plays' seems concerned to pre-empt such consequences. By means of the Duke, the London public has its own 'representative' on stage, who can, moreover, do that which is denied the public and intervene in events. But the Duke is not merely a figure for the audience; he is also and above all the director of *Measure for Measure*, bringing characters on stage, sending them off, telling them what to do and say, suggesting tricks and devices, substitutions and disguises. The plot of *Measure for Measure* is nothing other than a comedy written by the Duke, whose object – as he clearly explains early on (I, iii) – is to reimpose his authority on Vienna and restore the force of its institutions. With the sovereign as 'director', his intrigue as 'play', the goal of the problem plays is to reconstitute a theatrical world 'from above'. The close of *The Malcontent* is exemplary in this respect.

> *Malevole* (*To* Pietro *and* Aurelia)
> You o'er joyed spirits, wipe your long-wet eyes.
> Hence with this man! (*Kicks out* Mendoza.) An
> eagle takes not flies. –
> (*To* Pietro *and* Aurelia.) You to your vows. –
> (*To* Macquerelle.) And
> thou unto the suburbs. –
> (*To* Bilioso.) You to my worst friend I would hardly give:
> Thou art a perfect old knave. – (*To* Celso *and the* Captain.)
> All-pleased, live
> You two unto my breast. – (*To* Maria.) Thou to my heart.
> The rest of idle actors idly part;
> And as for me, I here assume my right,
> To which I hope all's pleas'd. To all, good night.[36]

According to a strategy that reappears in *Measure for Measure*, the sovereign here redistributes the social roles. The world has once again been made a theatre – and for this reason, the performance can end, declaring the theatre as such henceforward gratuitous. Unlike in the case of tragedy, the

finale here is truly an apex, a conclusion. This is so even at a strictly
temporal level, on account of the functional position that it occupies in the
plot sequence. Here the finale is not just the last ring in the chain of events,
but an act that sends its repercussions backwards,and more than simply
'putting an end' to the plot, it negates its character as an irreversible
temporal sequence, as *history*. Whereas tragedy is dominated by the
perception that there is no going back which is epitomized in the act of
dying (both Desdemona and the Duchess of Malfi 'return to life' for a
moment to give the illusion that everything can start all over again, but
then they expire for good), in the scene of the 'problem' plays, the criminal
acts that the villains thought they were committing are revealed never to
have happened, and those who were believed dead rise again, to the joy of
all present. Thus is dramatically realized the ideal of every restoration
culture: to abolish the irreversibility of history and render the past
everlasting. Social relations, no longer fraudulent and productive of uncontrollable events, are reformulated in a transparent and spatial – that is,
static – form.

It remains to speak of the others, who, seemingly menaced by a quite
different dramatic fate, prove instead to have been pliant, compliant wax in
the hands of a benevolent wizard. Except for the villain, these characters
are marked by the two attributes of the ideal subject, loyalty and passivity.
We meet women who seven years later still love the men who rejected
them and even refused to see them afterwards; jailors who succumb to the
magnetism emanating from a friar; sisters who never entertain the slightest
thought of revenge for a murdered brother; fortress commanders who
remain stubbornly faithful to their legitimate but dispossessed lord. Each
and every one is present to perform in the drama conceived by the
sovereign, on whom is conferred (as in a famous speech of James I in
Parliament) 'power to exalt low things, and abase high things, to make of
their subjects like men at the Chesse'.[37] Thus the sovereign achieves his
real theatrical triumph not over such characters, but over the villain,
Angelo in *Measure for Measure* or Bertram in *All's Well That Ends Well*. The
form of his humiliation is identical in both cases: he is forced to accept the
woman to whom he is bound by law or troth and to renounce the woman
to whom he has been drawn by passion. He is constrained to marry the
former because, imagining he was committing adultery, he has in fact
made love to his wife or his legitimate betrothed. The substitution-trick
dramatizes two important facts. First, it denies all autonomy to the sphere
of private relationships, rendered transparent to the eyes of the sovereign
and the audience. What the villain had tried to keep jealously hidden is on
the contrary pitilessly exposed and ridiculed. Second, Angelo and Bertram
are both aware that they have been mere 'actors' in the sovereign's design.
The role they have physically impersonated imprisons them in its fixity,
dissolves whatever individual aspirations they have entertained, and

reconfirms the basic principle of *status society*: that man is what his sovereign makes him. Thus, everything once again finds its place and its sense – exemplarily, in the context of matrimony. The problem plays exalt the abilities of the king, wise, astute, powerful, only to reduce him in the end to a justice of the peace. Nor should this seem strange, for what was the good king of the Elizabethan utopia but the administrator of traditional justice? The problem plays conclude therefore with scenes of judgement, where the rite of punishment and retribution is perfectly enacted. It must also be noted that Shakespeare's intelligence goes still further in designating the sovereign as the figure who can realize the desired compromise between the *political constitution* of society and the first yearnings for independence on the part of *civil society*. In *Measure for Measure*, in contrast to Angelo's intransigent legalism, the Duke validates with his own authority the 'private contracts' between individuals, even though they are formally deprived of any legal sanction. In *All's Well*, the King exalts the value of merit and scientific ability over the rigid aristocratic hauteur of Bertram. The sovereign reconstitutes a network of social relationships that, precisely because they possess so solid a political base, can be open and tolerant towards a 'newness' that is ready and willing to be inserted within the old framework. The 'mixed' form of tragicomedy embodies in its dramatic structure that compromise between the sphere of the state and civil society that was one of the great Elizabethan aspirations.[38]

Let us resume our examination of tragic structure, in which the sovereign-protagonist of the 'problem' plays is transformed into the considerably more complex figure of the tragic hero. And to begin, let us look at two of the most widely known interpretations of the tragic hero. The first we find in Hegel's *Aesthetics*, where, speaking precisely of Shakespeare, Hegel locates the novelty of 'modern' tragedy in its capacity to construct 'firm and consistent characters who come to ruin simply because of this decisive adherence to themselves and their aims', figures 'without ethical justification, but upheld solely by the formal inevitability of their personality'.[39] This fidelity to his own individuality makes the tragic hero the partial, one-sided character *par excellence*: one in whom *all universality has been lost*.

The ethical powers, just like the agents, are differentiated in their domain and their individual appearance. Now, if ... these thus differentiated powers are summoned into appearance as active ... then their harmony is cancelled and they come on the scene in *opposition* to one another in reciprocal independence .... Therefore what is superseded in the tragic dénouement is only the *one-sided* particular which had not been able to adapt itself to this harmony, and now (and this is the tragic thing in this

61

action), unable to renounce itself and its intention, finds itself condemned to total destruction.[40]

Against this, let us now consider another critical text that also puts the essence of tragedy in the figure of the tragic hero, Lucien Goldmann's *The Hidden God*. Goldmann stands on its head the Hegelian conception of the tragic hero, who now comes on stage to counterpose 'against a world composed of fragmentary and mutually exclusive elements a demand for totality that inevitably becomes a demand for the reconciliation of opposites. For the tragic mind, authentic values are synonymous with totality.'[41] If in Hegel the tragic hero yields to partiality, in Goldmann he stands committed to universal values. The Shakespearean tragic hero, I believe, represents the point at which the two hypotheses meet: not that he manages to unite them, so much as they succeed in dividing him. Opposed and irreconcilable forces, they make of him an irreparably *split* character, like Claudius, 'to double business bound', or Hamlet in his 'distraction', or Antony wandering between Rome and Egypt, or Othello 'perplex'd in the extreme'. This is, in its best summation, the conflict that lays unremitting hold of the regicide Macbeth.

It is pointless to interpret the scission that characterizes the tragic hero as a psychological datum, like the modern 'madness'. This is so because – quite apart from the fact that, as Michel Foucault has shown, the Renaissance conception of 'madness' is far removed from our own – a statement such as 'The tragic hero is a madman' defines a man whereas we are interested in defining a dramatic function. We might begin to define the tragic hero as that element of the work in which two contrary tensions meet and fight it out to the finish. And those two forces, which Hegel and Goldmann call 'particularity' and 'totality', we have called will and reason. As we have seen in *Gorboduc* and *King Lear*, their separation, along with their consequent conflict, is the necessary premiss of tragedy. It is likewise the case with the tragic hero, who exists to emphasize and intensify in his person the overall significance of tragic structure. (Note that only Shakespeare succeeds in perfectly fusing the scission that constitutes tragic structure with that constituting the tragic hero, pointing to their common origin.) Yet, to take a further step, if the tragic split is duplicated within the hero we may finally discard the popular but erroneous conception that tragedy esentially consists in a conflict between characters. This conception, too, finds its source in Hegel's *Aesthetics*, where one reads:

> What we see in front of us are certain ends individualized in living characters and very conflicting situations, and we see them in their self-assertion and display, in their reciprocal influence and design .... The individual does not remain shut into an independence of his own but

finds himself brought into opposition and conflicts with others .... Collision is the prominent point on which the whole turns.[42]

Hegel's suggestions were developed a century later in the first work of George Lukacs: 'Drama is the poetry of the will ... the purest expression of the will is struggle ... all the manifestations of the will could be reduced to struggle.' And again: 'The [dramatic] conflict must be such as to allow man to realize the highest or maximum value of his life – that is, precisely that part of himself in which his entire life is condensed with the greatest force ... tragic man is the only human type whose life is symbolized by a single adventure.'[43] As the last passage makes clear, the notion of the drama as conflict cannot be separated from the definition of the tragic hero as a unitary character. Mutually supportive of one another, the two affirmations concur to form a single argument. The argument is valid in certain cases – the tragedies of Corneille, the history plays of Shakespeare himself – but not for Shakespearean tragedy, it in no way constitutes the essence of the drama. The best example in this respect is *Hamlet*, where the outcome of the clash between Claudius and Hamlet is the reign of Fortinbras, whom we have seen for a few minutes, of whom we are given varying opinions, and who has passed by Elsinore on his return to Norway by pure chance. The result of the conflict is thus blatently *accidental*. Hamlet himself gives it no weight and liquidates the problem of the succession in a sentence. Why? Precisely because the problem of the tragic hero is not one of acting to affirm his own individual ends, any more than the significance of tragic structure lies in the supremacy of one specific end over the others. The political dimension of tragedy does not consist in illuminating the displacements of power, as happens in the long procession of sovereigns in the histories and even in *Julius Caesar*; it lies rather in posing the question of whether a *cultural foundation* of power is still possible, and in answering it in the negative. In the histories, sovereign power is a given that no one puts in question, and hence the dramatic interest is concentrated in the development and issue of the clash that occurs over it. In the tragedies, sovereign power has instead become an insoluble *problem*: forced to face this fact, the hero can no longer believe in his struggle for power, and abandons it as a meaningless enterprise. But let us try to specify this further through the example of him who, on the eve of what ought to be 'the conflict in which his entire life is condensed', discourses on the battlements of a castle and declares himself 'a-weary of the sun'.

In reading the story of Macbeth, one cannot but be reminded of Cesare Borgia. What makes the resemblance particularly interesting is that it stops half-way. For though the actions of the Scottish sovereign can be thought to be inspired by the counsels of Machiavelli to the new prince, they in fact depart from them on a crucial point, the question of 'cruelty used well or badly':

We can say that cruelty is used well (if it is permissible to talk in this way of what is evil) when it is employed once for all, and one's safety depends on it, and then it is not persisted in but as far as possible turned to the good of one's subjects. Cruelty badly used is that which, although infrequent to start with, as time goes on rather than disappearing, becomes more evident. Those who use the first method can, with divine and human assistance, find some means of consolidating their position, as did Agathocles; the others cannot possibly stay in power.[44]

Macbeth is unable to follow in the first path: he hesitates, and allowing his enemies to reorganize, is lost. And he hesitates because he is divided – because he acted according to Machiavelli, while continuing to *think* like Hooker.[45] It is indicative how Macbeth speaks and makes use of his regicide – or rather, how he does not speak and make use of it. In his eyes, it is the action that must never be 'seen', never be entitled to cultural recognition. 'Stars, hide your fires, / Let not light see my black and deep desires; / The eye wink at the hand; yet let that be / Which the eye fears, when it is done, to see' (I, iv, 50–3); 'That my keen knife see not the wound it makes' (I, v, 52); 'I am afraid to think what I have done; / Look on't again I dare not' (II, ii, 48–9). Political murder, which in Machiavelli may be profitably reflected upon and even more profitably put to use as a warning to enemies, becomes in *Macbeth* the unthinkable and unprofitable deed par excellence. Though one must commit it on the way to power, one cannot discourse on it or accept it into the universe of culture. Macbeth's dilemma is that coexisting in him are the imperative of power *and* the imperative of culture, will and reason together. He cannot yet unburden the exercise of power – power as such – from the need for its cultural legitimation. This co-presence of irreconcilable drives deprives his life of a unified meaning: 'It is a tale / Told by an idiot, full of sound and fury, / Signifying nothing' (V, v, 26–8). That is to say: only a madman or imbecile (in effect, those like Edgar or Malcolm who step in claiming to 'conclude' the tragedy) can think that Macbeth's story can be 'told', ordered on the basis of comprehensible meanings. Such a combination of narrative and value-judgement has become impossible, and what remains is only 'sound', the word without force, and 'fury', force without sense. This is, in miniature, the lesson of tragic structure as a whole.

Macbeth epitomizes a whole group of Shakespearean characters who yield to that 'vicious mole of nature' of which Hamlet complains in his first two soliloquies. Claudius yields to it, tempted by the crown and Gertrude; and Lear, in the face of old age; and Antony, in the face of Cleopatra; and Othello, after Iago has dismantled the rigid defences of this Venetian culture. Just as tragedy is born from the dominating irruption of will over reason, so too the tragic hero is moved by a passion that compels him to act despite and against the cultural values that continue to inspire him. So consistent is this paradigm that in *Hamlet* Shakespeare is able to confirm it by diametrically reversing the problem. If for four centuries the tragedy of the prince of Denmark has baffled its spectators and readers, perhaps not the least reason is that *Hamlet* is a work *with the wrong protagonist.* If Claudius were its centre of gravity, everything would run far more smoothly and to pattern. Instead the protagonist is Hamlet, and nothing runs smoothly at all. It is impossible to understand Hamlet by assimilating him to Macbeth or Othello, for he represents the other principle on which the tragic hero may be constructed. The opposition is so fundamental that, unlike what happens in every other tragedy, Shakespeare does not pit Hamlet against a Macduff, or a Caesar, or an Edmund – all univocal, unified characters – but against *another tragic hero*: against Claudius, which is, in the end, merely Danish for Macbeth.

The great and notorious mystery surrounding Hamlet is that he fails to act. The reason for Hamlet's inaction, we should say, is that within the tragic universe there is never a reason for action. One recalls that in *Macbeth* action is speechless fury: one may or may not fall into it, but one cannot in good faith 'convince oneself' to enter it. Therefore when Hamlet says, 'My thoughts be bloody, or be nothing worth!' (IV, iv, 66), he perfectly expresses his dilemma, in so far as he preserves the illusion that 'thoughts' can be 'bloody'. For if reason is incapable of stopping action, it is also, symmetrically, incapable of inciting it. That tie has been severed, and though Hamlet would like to reconnect it, this very ambition, impelling him to reason in even greater depth, irremediably places him further from action.[46] Whereas Macbeth speaks of actions 'which must be acted ere they may be scann'd' (III, iv, 139), Hamlet, once more sheathing the sword he has drawn to kill Claudius, says the opposite: 'That would be scann'd' (III, iii, 75).[47] Macbeth is pulled along by the logic of his first act; Hamlet continually postpones such an act (committed, if at all, by chance, as when he kills Polonius). For Hamlet starts from the conviction (on which his first two soliloquies turn) that everything belonging to the category of 'passion' or 'nature' is for that very reason opposed to the image of the stable, metahistorical absolute sovereign – 'Hyperion to a satyr' – that he sees in his father and feels called upon – 'O cursèd spite' – to reincarnate. Hamlet requires cultural values to provide him with the Form that precedes and directs a passional Nature (just as, to take up a previous comparison, the rational good of Hooker's divine legislator precedes and directs the course of nature and guarantees its meaning). His famous precept to the actors – 'hold as 'twere the mirror up to nature' (III, ii, 22) – does not mean (as even Lukacs believes) 'reflect nature', but rather the opposite: show nature the model to which it must conform. Yet this, we repeat, is now impossible. The form, reason, has lost the power to impose itself on nature: Hamlet's advice is given merely to *actors*, and only in performance (See the 'What's Hecuba to him?' soliloquy in II, ii, 559ff) can the head still rule the heart and an ethics foment a passion.

Hamlet's advice to the players – 'to hold as 'twere the mirror up to nature, to show virtue her feature, scorn her own image, and the very age and body of time his form and pressure' – is filled with nostalgia for a vanished relationship with the world. In effect, what Hamlet asks the players to do is what the Duke in *Measure for Measure* actually does. In Vienna, the theatrical project can be translated into an intervention in the world, an organic restoration of hierarchy and meaning; at Elsinore, it remains a performance, which, moreover, never completed, conveys to the court the opposite meaning of the one Hamlet seeks.[48] The tragic hero cannot be Hooker's legislator, the director of a play with a happy ending. And the world that he can no longer reduce to a theatre opens on to a mode of conduct that both completes and negates the theatre: *the lie*. For if in fact the individual exists socially because he plays a part, then what matters most is his performance. Fidelity is only fidelity to a role, and sincerity simply means a good performance. Othello suspects Desdemona because in her ignorance she isn't preoccupied with conforming to a social type and thus commits 'errors' of conduct; and instead, he believes blindly in Iago, who, conscious of artifice, performs to the rules of art.[49] Not the least of Shakespeare's merits is to have coolly illuminated the extent to which the ideal of the world-as-theatre had become vulnerable once a space of freedom and individual interest had opened up, creating a gap between 'person' and 'function'. To give a newly solid basis to human society, it would be necessary to abandon the ideal of 'fidelity' for that of 'interest' and to transform the social bond from a feudal 'oath' to the 'contract' of natural right philosophy:[50] a cultural shift that overturned the relation between facts and values (and in the realm of literary history replaced tragedy with the novel). But this is truly another story, which Shakespeare quite predates and one vainly tries to read in his works. He may announce the dawn of bourgeois civilization, but not by prefiguring it. On the contrary, he demonstrates inexorably how, obeying the old rules, which are the only ones he knows, the world can only fall apart.

If we place Macbeth and Hamlet against each other, we recognize the two solitary extremes into which the image of the sovereign has been decomposed. In Macbeth, we have force, impelling him to a tyranny well beyond true sovereignty; in Hamlet, we have reason, or a mad obsession with it, keeping him in the role of the 'sweet prince' well to this side of such sovereignty. As the one who, himself in equilibrium, provides the point of equilibrium for the social body, the sovereign is the missing person, the impossible being in Shakespearean tragedy. Only elsewhere does this monarch find his full dramatic incarnation, in another country and another text: in the figure of Segismundo in Calderon's *La vida es sueño*.

Like Machiavelli's centaur, Segismundo holds together man and beast, the Christian philosopher and the commoner dressed in animal skins, mastery of himself and mastery of others. The emergence of such a character had to be preceded by the jesuitical meditation on 'reason of state' and the recognition of a 'technical' validity in Machiavelli's thought that could then be subordinated and brought back to a spiritual end.[51] When in the last scene of the play, Segismundo imprisons the soldier who led the very uprising that brought him to the throne, his gesture shows exactly how the illegality and violence necessary to the conquest of political power can be subsumed, then banished, in the name of the moral ends of that power. 'Force' in Calderon does not have its own independent logic: it can be transformed into an instrument of any project whatsoever. This possibility of mediating and tempering force with reason is what Shakespeare refuses to credit. For him, the 'Christian prince', wholly Christian and wholly a prince, does not exist. In this, Shakespeare is the only dramatist who rises to the level of Machiavelli, elaborating all the consequences of the separation of political praxis from moral evaluation. Not that Shakespeare conceives of this separation in the same fashion as Machiavelli: I said earlier that Macbeth acts like Cesare Borgia but thinks like Hooker, and such is also the position of Shakespeare – the position manifest in his tragic structure, where the axis of actions (the plot) is governed by one logic and the axis of values (the paradigm) by another, without either ever succeeding in over-whelming or expunging the other (as happens, in obviously different directions, in Machiavelli and Hooker). In Shakespeare's intimately paradoxical structure, two mutually exclusive positions appear equally real, and the same world seems governed by two different systems of law.

The clearest manifestation of the paradox occurs when the tragic hero is torn between conflicting claims. The radical character of Shakespeare's position emerges clearly if we compare him to a dramatist such as Corneille, who bases his entire dramaturgy precisely on the soliloquy.[52] Corneille's most typical tragedies – particularly, *Le Cid* and *Horace* – may be described as a succession of duels: first an internal duel, a soliloquy at the end of which the hero has chosen one of the lines of practical and moral conduct between which he was undecided; then, a verbal duel, a dialogue in which the hero displays to his adversary the superior firmness of his own ideal; and finally – off-stage – a physical duel, from which the hero returns victorious. The pattern is elementary, but rich in meaning. We may begin by remarking that the Cornelian hero is always perfectly conscious of the values between which he is rent. His purpose can never be 'dark' like Lear's, nor will he ever be amazed at what he has done or failed to do like Macbeth or Hamlet. That he always chooses (as Starobinski and Doubrovsky have shown) the heroic over the natural, the political over the personal, the 'luminous' over the 'obscure', is already prescribed in the fact that the choice must be expressed in the solar, omnipresent, heroic form of the Cornelian distych. When the dilemma itself is posed in the clear and distinct form of a contrast between values, one easily foresees that the ideally superior value will prevail. Since indeed it always proves so, one might say that, with the initial choice of the hero, the tragedy is already over and done with. What follows – the verbal, then the physical duel – merely repeats the outcome of the opening conflict. Doubrovsky's analysis of Corneille has frequent recourse to the Hegel of the master / servant dialectic in the *Phenomenology*. One might add that Corneille's theatre is governed by the same logic that governs Hegel's philosophy of history: the profound reason why the literal duel can – rather, must – take place off-stage: it is only the material echo, inevitable and redundant, of the ideal conflict. In short, Cornelian action is always an *emanation of reason*. And, insofar as it initiates and determines every successive action, the soliloquy of the divided hero is not so much a verbal act as the sole real action.

With Shakespeare, the soliloquy fills a very different function – not of promoting the action or establishing its implications, but rather of retarding it and making its implications ungraspable. It is the site of doubt and irresolution: of 'the pale cast of thought' with which 'the native hue of resolution / is sicklied o'er' in Hamlet; of the 'words' that 'to the breath of deeds too cold breath gives' in Macbeth. Instead of the lucid Cornelian continuity between word and action, a radical discrepancy, or category difference, makes words impotent and actions mute. This mistrust in the practical force of language – so different from what his culture envisioned – makes Shakespeare's soliloquies the first manifestations of 'poetry' in the modern sense of being emancipated from a rhetoric conceived as the art of convincing. Whereas in the Cornelian soliloquy, the hero prescribed to himself the actions he would then perform, establishing in fact a complete rhetorical circuit, the Shakespearean hero by contrast addresses no one – neither a part of himself, nor another character, nor even the audience. Having no addressee, his words do not even participate in the dramatic context. Though it frequently happens (in *Hamlet*, I, iv, and III, ii, and in *Macbeth*, V, v) that the hero begins a soliloquy in the presence of other characters, these do not hear him, and the soliloquy can end only when the action – a principle now heterogeneous and hostile to his reflections – returns to claim its own rights. When, therefore, an idealist aesthetic excerpts these passages and transforms them into 'poems', the critical operation, however illegitimate, has intuitively understood the dramatically absurd character of the soliloquies. The other characters do not even hear them; they have no connection to the action; it is never clear what is the 'object' of their reflection – indeed the character who pronounces them retains no memory of them, so that Hamlet and Macbeth must begin their entire reasoning afresh every time they soliloquize. And finally, as Tolstoy once observed (in the only reasonable attitude for anybody seeking 'psychological realism' in Shakespeare), it is not Othello or Macbeth or Hamlet speaking in such passages, but 'all his characters speak, not their own, but always one and the same Shakespearean, pretentious, and unnatural language, in which not only they could not speak, but in which no living man ever has spoken or does speak'.[53] A single voice speaks in the soliloquies – or better, a single function: not referential, as in the speeches of Gorboduc's counsellors; nor expressive, as in *self-referential*, forcibly released from all that surrounds it and henceforward painfully absorbed in itself.

It should be clear that this Shakespearean 'poetry' has nothing 'liberating', 'constructive', or 'universal' about it. It is made possible by, and is identical with, the stupefied perception that cultural paradigms, abruptly defaulting, are no longer capable of ordering and guiding the word. A chasm has opened up between signified and referent that, while it provides the imagination with an unexpected semantic freedom, empties reality and history of that meaning which had seemed consubstantial with them.[54] In the tragedies, this is exemplarily revealed in the fact that, from Richard II forward, only the defeated king is allowed (or better, condemned) to accede to speech thus conspicuously poetic: only the king who fails to act 'as the real "God-man", as the *real embodiment* of the Idea'.[55] 'Poetry' is thus born from the disjunction of 'idea' and 'reality': this disjunction in turn becomes the privileged object of poetic reflection which can neither recompose nor resolve it; and finally poetry can be 'spoken' only by one who has lived through an analogous disjunction in his own person – by the sovereign who is unable to unite history and transcendence, action and value, passion and reason, and whose fall therefore epitomizes the collapse of an entire civilization. Poetry is thus synonymous with the organic crisis of a political and cultural order, as we see if, enlarging the field of analysis, we move from the soliloquy to tragic structure as a whole. The latter blatantly violates the function that Elizabethan culture assigned to art and completely departs from its interpretive schemas (by means of which we were able, for instance, to explain *Gorboduc*, but not *King Lear*). Neither Sidney nor Puttenham ever for a moment ceases to abide by a pair of assumptions on which their key works are based: art acquires its right to exist only in so far as it performs an educational function,[56] which in turn is made possible because artistic 'beauty' consists in a *harmonious proportion* that contains within itself the image of the world as (in Sidney's phrase) 'what may be, and should be'.[57] Tragedy evokes proportion and harmony only to dissolve them, in characters as well as in the overall structure. How can an educational function be exercised by a structure that takes for its object the gap between culture and action and for its formal postulate the impossibility of abolishing it? Against the background of English culture, tragedy is that which 'eternally negates': like Goethe's Mephistopheles, it is the midwife of history.

3 'We may go read i'th'stars … if we could find spectacles to read them'

To read Jacobean tragedy with Shakespeare in mind is immediately to notice a vacancy – the tragic hero has disappeared. There is no one in whose person the meaning (or rather the loss of meaning) of the work is concentrated. A new collective protagonist stands in for the sovereign: the court. 'Court is a maze of turnings strange', wrote Thomas Churchyard in 1596, ' a laborinth, of working wits, / A princely seate, subject to change.'[58] It is symptomatic that one of the first deprecations of the court should come from Churchyard, whose denunciations of cupidity, falsity and cruelty are typically applied to a quite different social category: the new (urban, competitive, acquisitive) *civil society*. That he reproduces these accusations in speaking of the court anticipates the image that the Jacobeans will typically bring forward: the court as the exemplary site of an unrestrained conflict of private interests. This is the venal and discredited court of the Stuarts, where the 'crisis of the aristocracy' is degraded to a tragicomedy of intrigue, a hectic and vain assault on the last remnants of power. On stage, those who belong to this court will speak like Iago and act like Edmund. The ambiguous density of Shakespeare's language divides to give rise of two characteristic forms of expression: the *sententia* and the *aside*, on one hand the profession of faith in the guise of a proverb, on the other the cool private undertones of egoism, on one hand public virtue, on the other private vice. If the tragic hero in his soliloquies waged unequal battle with a dubious and elusive meaning, the Jacobean character (except in Webster) never wants for lucid and univocal speech. Thus, in a work from the concluding years of the flowering of Jacobean drama, James Shirley has a character say: 'Alas poor lady, / I half repent me since she is so constant. / But a friend's life weighs down all other love; / Beside, I thus secure my fate. Lorenzo / Threatens my spring. He is my enemy.'[59] Everyone here can perfectly distinguish good from evil, and divide himself accordingly into the two halves that the distinction requires. Social conduct, from being problematic, has become merely tortuous. 'A laborinth of working wits': such will be the characteristic plot of Jacobean drama. 'So who knows policy and her true aspèct / Shall find her ways winding and indirect.'[60] Thus speaks Flamineo in Webster's *The White Devil*, and his maxim is repeatedly borne out in works like *The Revenger's Tragedy* or *Women Beware Women*, where the mortal conflict among characters will never issue in a direct encounter. The aristocratic duel still used, albeit modified, by Shakespeare at the end of *Hamlet, King Lear, Macbeth*, and *Antony and Cleopatra* has been replaced with the courtly intrigue. A character no longer glories in his valour, but rather in his astuteness. Though the tortuousness of individual 'designs' would attest to the superior efficacy of the new form of political dominion, yet there are now *too many* plots, overlapping and undoing one another incessantly. The obsessive lesson of Jacobean drama is that the proliferation of interests and points of view makes them all vulnerable. No one manages to control the plot, or even to understand much about it. The play now lacks a privileged point of observation, a centre such as the tragic hero had previously furnished. In this is manifest the profoundly baroque nature of Jacobean tragedy, perfectly of a piece with what is its most appropriate conclusion, the sudden mockery of slaughter. (Slaughter had already triumphed in *Hamlet*, a work that, were it possible to expunge its protagonist, would effectively offer on all the points mentioned an insuperable model of Jacobean tragedy.) The unique 'solution' of dramatic complications, the only 'meeting place' of the dramatic agents, now consists in the reduction of everything to 'nothing', a word that frequently recurs in this drama. We no longer have even Shakespeare's bloodless heirs to give the illusion of historical continuity, as virtually the entire court expires under our eyes.

In Jacobean tragedy, the structural disappearance of the hero coincides with the political disappearance of the figure of the sovereign. Jacobean princes are almost always 'dukes' of small cities, and their power makes no universal claims and no longer poses the Shakespearean problem of its cultural foundation. Thus divested of all prominence or exemplarity, they become much more like the other characters, from whom they are only separated by a merely quantitative difference. As our remarks on the plot have already suggested, it is as though the barriers of status had fallen and every character were endowed with the same language. Yet the equality that emerges from this metamorphosis is highly paradoxical, for the principle that governs such a process proves to be the destructive impulse *par excellence*: lust, the sexual desire or passion to which everyone – duke and merchant, cardinal and professional killer, brother and sister, procuress and duchess – equally succumbs. 'L'amour', says Corneille in *Le Cid*, 'est un tyran qui n'épargne personne'.[61] Like Cornelian love, Jacobean lust spares no one and thereby renders everyone equal. This very fact makes it an agent of destruction[62] in a social hierarchy based on the diametrically opposed principle of *inequality*. The opposition between a principle of passion and a principle of status, between lust and wealth, subtends the enitre corpus of Jacobean drama. The incest in Ford's *'Tis Pity She's a Whore* (anticipated in *Women Beware Women* and, more obscurely, *The Duchess of Malfi*) may be thought to be its extreme and conclusive incarnation, ironically predicted by the father of Giovanni and Annabella when he declares: 'I would not have her marry wealth, but love.'[63] Incest is that form of desire which makes impossible the matrimonial exchange that, in a society in which power is still connected with physical persons, reinforces and perpetuates the network of wealth. But the conflict between lust and wealth had already, in play after play, claimed illustrious victims: the Duke of Bracciano and Vittoria Corombona, the Duchess of Malfi and Isabella in *The Changeling*, the entire court in *The Revenger's Tragedy* and *Women Beware Women* – all of them follow a single itinerary to destruction that they embark upon as soon as they let desire lead them.

All of them follow a single itinerary because lust is an obsession. In *The Atheist's Tragedy*, Levidulcia speaks of her 'affection' in these terms: 'I would unbrace and entertain / The air to cool it.' Lust appears external and objective, a burden that overwhelms its bearer. A few lines later Levidulcia says: 'Lust is a spirit which whosoe'er doth raise, / The next man that encounters boldly lays.'[64] Lust has become the very name of spectral obsession, a transformation that irrevocably dispels the ribald epicureanism that could still prompt Viscount Conway to exclaim, 'what is a gentleman but his pleasure?'[65] In the heavy Jacobean atmosphere, such pleasure, lacking entirely the essential dimension of freedom, becomes a repetition compulsion. On this account, it is preferable to define lust as 'passion' rather than 'desire', for it is clearly something that one passively undergoes. In Jacobean drama, a single glance suffices to bring about one's capture. Characters don't fall in love by 'seeing', in the passive act of *being dazzled*. Examples abound: the Duke with Bianca and Livia with Leantio in *Women Beware Women*; Alsemero and Deflores with Isabella in *The Changeling*; Lussurioso with Castiza in *The Revenger's Tragedy*; Levidulcia with Sebastiano and then with Fresco in *The Atheist's Tragedy*. Lust changes from an enjoyment into a sign of destiny – or rather, into destiny *tout court*. In the first lines of *'Tis Pity*, the Friar says to Giovanni, 'Death waits on thy lust' (I, i, 59). To which Giovanni replies, 'my fate's my god'. A destiny, a curse, a supreme example of *allegorical deception*, lust promises pleasure, but procures its opposite. In its name, the parable prefigured in the notorious ambiguities of the verb 'to die' (to climax / to expire) is brought to completion.

> *Giovanni* One other kiss, my sister.
> *Anabella*   What means this?
> *Giovanni* To save thy fame, and kill thee in a kiss. *Stabs her*
>   Thus die, and die by me, and by my hand.
>
> ('TIS PITY, V, v, 83–5)

'What means this?' Anabella's perturbation echoes that of Tourneur's Duke, who, as he realizes he is kissing a poisoned skull, lamely cries, 'Oh! what's this? Oh!'[66] At the moment of death, lust reveals itself for what it has always been, a destiny that derides its victims. And at this moment, also, allegory triumphs in its definitive gesture of overturning meanings. The lover becomes a killer; the apparently faithful servant proves a mortal enemy; what seemed vital and attractive (the beautiful skull in *The Revenger's Tragedy*) is shown to be dead and lethal. One woman is murdered by her husband as she kisses the portrait he himself has poisoned; another by a cardinal as she kisses his Bible in token of fidelity. Signifieds are reversed and (in another typically allegorical metamorphosis) fixed once for all in death, the only signified that is truly stable and universal. The characteristic emphasis is carried in Bosola's words: 'Though we are eaten up of lice, and worms, / And though continually we bear about us / A rotten and dead body, we delight / To hide it in rich tissue.'[67] An ephemeral parenthesis, life is nothing more than a wait for the ultimate and irrevocable transformation, the negation of every mask: the skull. The skull of Yorick, which after thirty years shows up in the hands of Hamlet; the skull of Vindice's wife, which he transforms into an instrument of revenge; the unidentified skulls on which Charlemont and Castabella go to sleep; the skull menacingly displayed to Flamineo by Bracciano's ghost. The skull of which Walter Benjamin has penetratingly written:

> in allegory, the observer is confronted with the *facies hippocratica* of history as a petrified, primordial language. Everything about history that, from the very beginning, has been untimely, sorrowful, unsuccessful, is expressed in a face – or rather in a death's head .... The greater the significance, the greater the subjection to death, because death digs most deeply the jagged line of demarcation between physical nature and significance. But if nature has always been subject to the power of death, it is also true that it has always been allegorical. Significance and death both come to fruition in historical development, just as they are closely linked as seeds in the creature's graceless state of sin.[68]

'But if nature has always been subject to the power of death, it is also true that it has always been allegorical.' Benjamin's argument finds its dramatic translation in the Rocambolesque peripety of Jacobean theatre, whose victims – by arrangement of those who have ensnared them – discover in their last moments both the 'truth' of the real state of affairs and the 'mendacity' of what it had appeared to be. As he begins the process of killing the Duke, for instance, Tourneur's Vindice shocks him with the revelation that neither his murderer nor the instrument of his death (the poisoned skull) are what they seemed: and then, sword in hand, compels him to watch the adultery by which, at that very moment, he is about to be betrayed. The deceptiveness of life, clarified only by slow death, coincides exactly with the operation of 'allegorical nature' in Benjamin. It is no accident that Puttenham defines allegory as 'the figure of [false semblant or dissimulation]', having just reminded us: '*Qui nescit dissimulare nescit regnare.*'[69] The Jacobean villain's supreme euphoria comes with his success in elaborating an 'allegorical' scheme to entrap his enemy. His rhetorical voluptuousness is nicely caught in the words of D'Amville concerning the stone with which he has murdered his brother: 'Upon this ground I'll build my manor house, / And this shall be the chiefest corner-stone' (*Atheist's Tragedy*, II, iv, 99–100). Yet such success is typically short-lived, for allegory always ends by revenging itself on whosoever aspired to keep it under his control. Though in Tourneur the villain's 'manor-house' remains intact and impenetrable almost to the end (so much so that some rather clumsy expedients – an involuntary confession, an axe that slips from the executioner's hands – are required to bring it down), the later developments of Jacobean drama offer more satisfying solutions. Contrary to what happens in Tourneur, the proliferation of plots in later tragedies allows no one to take control over events. The allegorical construction of one character becomes only an element already taken into account in the conflicting construction of another, and where one character proposes to write *finis* to 'his' tragedy, another is already prepared to begin his own. As in Benjamin's argument, allegory is not a subjective deception to which someone might be imagined to hold the semantic key, but the objectively deceptive condition of the nature of history by which everyone is ultimately betrayed. This is borne out if we compare the two supremely allegorical masques that respectively conclude *The Spanish Tragedy* and, three decades later, *Women Beware Women*. In Kyd's tragedy, Hieronimo arranges for everyone's role to be replicated in the masque where it is given its moral explanation and judgement. If the masque is the 'figure of dissimulation' permitting Hieronimo and Bel-Imperia to be avenged, it is also at the same time the symbolic re-elaboration of the whole tragic course of events on which it confers a luminous and unequivocal comprehensibility. In Middleton's tragedy, Livia too elaborated a scheme of murder and, putting it into action, assigns every character the role he has already played in the four preceding acts. But this time the actors betray their parts and – before the Duke who, mildly annoyed, deplores these departures from the programme, and then, distracted by the performance, casually drinks from a cup brimming with poison – the masque concludes with the murderous pyrotechnics of Cupids launching envenomed arrows and nymphs releasing lethal vapours. The clear, distinct allegory of Kyd (and of the entire Christian Middle Ages) has given way to the obscure, elusive allegory examined by Benjamin. Like the principal theme of lust, the plot too undergoes this transformation, which it remains for us to follow in the main 'character' of the Jacobean stage as well.

The plot of Jacobean drama requires two newly prominent, complementary functions: one in charge of *mediating* between various conflicting designs in an attempt to avoid catastrophe, the other in charge of *executing* a given such design without hesitation or delay. In Shakespeare, these tasks were assigned to minor and often ridiculous characters – Polonius, Rosencrantz and Guildenstern, Macbeth's hired killers. With the Jacobeans, these go-betweens and assassins (both functions often united in a single figure) occupy centre stage – Flamineo, Bosola, Livia, Deflores, in part even Vindice. The displacement of the dramatic centre of gravity toward persons of lower rank adds another item to the discredit that proceeds to accumulate on the Jacobean ruling class, who are implicitly not only degenerate, but cowardly as well, unable to look their own actions in the face. Macbeth does not hire a killer to murder Duncan, and Othello knows he must strangle Desdemona with his own hands, but the petty Jacobean lord ingloriously discharges all responsibility for his projects onto someone else – whom he will later blame, moreover, for having followed his orders (Ferdinand with Bosola, or Isabella with Deflores). Thus these servile figures are pushed to a 'central' position in the plot, as much as such a position is possible – think of the grand but brief pacification effected by Livia in the third act of *Women Beware Women* – and they become the only characters who from time to time possess a comprehensive knowledge of events. Their supremacy, however, is ambiguous, connected to and even dependent on their lack of autonomy, on their being mere instruments in the hands of others: 'I am your creature', Bosola tells Ferdinand (*Duchess*, I, i, 296). As Flamineo observes, they are constrained to an incessant 'varying of shapes' if they are to be 'great men's apes' (*White Devil*, IV, ii, 224–5). They are constrained never to be 'themselves', but always something else, artificial and deceitful: constrained to strut and fret on stage as nothing more than personified allegories. 'What the bondsman does is really the action of the lord', writes Hegel: 'this action of the second [consciousness] is the first's own action.'[70] At the heart of Jacobean tragedy we find a consciousness devoid of autonomy, an agency devoid of freedom. It is not surprising that these figures impersonate the essence of melancholy: 'I have lived / Riotously ill, like some that live in court, / And sometimes when my face was full of smiles, / Have felt the maze of conscience in my breast. / Oft gay and honoured robes these tortures try: / We think caged birds sing when indeed they cry' (*White Devil*, V, iv, 118–23). This is the lament of inauthentic existence that, as Hegel was right to say, finds its most nearly complete objectification in the servant. And this inauthenticity does not find (as Goldmann's theory would have it) its counterweight in some authentic value, however defeated it might in actuality be. The maze in Flamineo's breast never comes to light, and when his *confrère* Bosola, now dismissed from the service of power, is 'free' to act, an error causes him to kill the 'good' half of himself in the person of Antonio. Jacobean tragedy does not in the least intend to seek a different basis for human society, but only to follow the trajectory of inauthenticity all the way to its inevitable self-dissolution. It is a drama whose subject is not questing, but only straying.

The curse of allegory that in various ways hangs over the Jacobean court finds perhaps its best 'spokesman' in John Webster, where the curse radically invests the domain of language itself. 'When I look into the fish-ponds, in my garden, / Methinks I see a thing, arm'd with a rake / That seems to strike at me' (*Duchess*, V, v, 5–7). The Cardinal's words are a splendid example of Webster's rhetoric: the uncertainty of appearances, the vagueness of 'a thing' oddly matched with the precision of the 'rake' it is armed with, the whole uncanny vision located in the familiar waters of 'the fish-ponds in my garden'. Suddenly, and in the most unexpected place, there appears a sign, an equivocal sign. Its equivocation, moreover, is not that of the classical oracle, the cool ambiguity of Apollo that, if it deceives, does so to reveal in the end its true and single meaning. In Webster, meaning does not deceive, but rather dissolves: into appearance ('methinks'), indeterminacy ('a thing'), and inexplicable detail ('arm'd with a rake'). Nor is the problem even how to interpret such signs, but, more basically, to determine whether or not they are in fact signs. Where does the melancholic's *imagination* (a key word in Webster) end and the manifestation of a transcendental reality begin? Webster's characters waver between the need to find metaphysical 'confirmation' in the form of a transcendent signified and a discouraged scepticism about its actual existence and comprehensibility. For instance, though the horoscope Antonio has cast at the birth of his son predicts for the child a violent death, it is Antonio who dies violently, while his son inherits his dukedom. Or again, as he reads the horoscope, his nose bleeds onto the monogram of his handkerchief: 'One that were superstitious', he notes, 'would count / This ominous: when it merely comes by chance' (*Duchess*, II, ii, 127–8). Yet in saying this, he is distracted and drops the horoscope, which, picked up by Bosola, betrays the Duchess. In the end, then, blood has indeed been an ominous sign, but for the Duchess and Antonio rather than their son. This semantic uncertainty and imprecision is typical of Webster as a whole. There is supposed to be some relationship between human existence and the stars, but what it is, or how one might comprehend it, remains unclear. Ghosts apparently exist, but they may be mere projections of the imagination. St Gregory's description of hellfire should be beyond disputing for the Cardinal, who instead, 'puzzled', finds it contradictory. At one point in *The White Devil*, Flamineo recites a lengthy apologue, glosses it, confesses that the comparison may not hold 'in every particle', and then once more proceeds to trust in it and apply it to the situation at hand (IV, iii, 218f). The specific curse on Webster's characters is that they can never dispense with speech, with sense-making, with the rhetorical amplification of their experience. This one discovers he is cuckold because an 'emblem' is thrown in at his window; that one arranges a murder by staging dreams and riddles. Characters die with a metaphor in their mouths: Marcello, Flamineo, Julia, the Duchess, the Cardinal, Bosola. Yet so much 'poetry' (of all the Jacobeans, Webster is the one who in this respect most recalls Shakespeare), though it never abandons the character, never enlightens his way. Instead it maintains him in an uncertain and equivocal state that makes him the resigned victim of the trap of others. 'Fate's a spaniel', Flamineo says (*White Devil*, V, vi, 179), always at our heels, nor will we ever suceed in getting away from it. Pursued by spirits – 'haunted', as they say to one another – these courtiers go round in circles in the vain attempt to escape that 'thing' they are so hard put to define. Their fate is no longer Macbeth's tale told by an idiot or Hamlet's vicious mole of nature, but a spaniel – or at least seems to them such. Their world survives without vitality, exhausted by the search for an illusory *ubi consistam* in the midst of countless deceptive signs. This is a world whose deepest desire is for oblivion. Flamineo says before he dies, 'To prate were idle. I remember nothing' (*White Devil*, V, vi, 206). And the Cardinal: 'And now, I pray, let me / Be laid by, and never thought of' (*Duchess*, V, v, 90). The palace of the prince is truly haunted, and the inflexible allegorical destiny suspended above every aspect of it (love and ambition, masters and servants, actions and words) makes it a site at once dilapidated and threatening. To the imagination of the Jacobeans, this was a court that, incapable of being set to rights, had to be dispersed, exorcised. A few years later ....

Notes

1. ANDREW MARVELL, 'An Horatian Ode Upon Cromwell's Return from Ireland', *Poems of Andrew Marvell*, Hugh MacDonald, (ed), (Cambridge, Mass., 1952), 53–6.

2. 'The outbreak of war itself', writes Lawrence Stone, 'is relatively easy to explain; what is hard is to puzzle out why most of the established institutions of State and Church – Crown, Court, central administration, army, and episcopacy – collapsed so ignominiously two years before.' Recapitulating the four principal causes of the revolution, he adds: 'Last but not least was the growing crisis of confidence in the integrity and moral worth of the holders of high administrative office, whether courtiers or nobles or bishops or judges or even kings' (*Causes of the English Revolution: 1529–1642* (London 1972), pp. 48, 116). In his summary of the controversy among English historians of the revolution, Mario Tronti writes:

> Of so many interpretive approaches, the hypothesis of a power vacuum works best. Stone and Trevor-Roper are basically agreed on this point: one lays stress on the subjective crisis of the body of politicians who administered power and society, the other underscores the crisis of the objective structures of power in society. In either case, the origin of the revolution, rather than in the offensive of new social forces wanting change, lies in the crisis of the old forces, in the vacancy of their power, in the political space

that after a long and slow erosion of the barriers raised to defend it, suddenly opened up

('Hobbes e Cromwell', in *Stato e Rivoluzione in Inghilterra*, Milan 1977, pp. 235–6).

The same schema may be found in the attempts to reconstruct the cultural antecedents of the revolution. Here, for example, is Christopher Hill: 'The most striking feature … of the intellectual life of pre-revolutionary England is its confusion and ferment …. In retrospect Renaissance and Reformation, the discovery of America and the new astronomy, had been far more successful in undermining old assumptions and prejudices than in substituting new truths' (*Intellectual Origins of the English Revolution*, Oxford 1965, pp. 7–8).

3. See CARL SCHMITT, *Die Diktatur* (Berlin 1968), pp. 25–8; FRIEDRICH MEINECKE, *Die Idee Der Staatsräson* (Munich and Berlin 1925), pp. 70–80; and PERRY ANDERSON, *Lineages of the Absolutist State* (London 1974), pp. 49–51.

4. *The Modern World-System* (New York 1974), pp. 146–7.

5. *Hamlet oder Hekuba* (Dusseldorf and Cologne), p. 67.

6. *Either/Or* (Princeton 1971), vol. 1, pp. 141, 147.

7. The inexorable dialectic that conjoins the absolute sovereign and the tyrant is described by Marx in his reflections on Hegel's *Philosophy of Right*. 'Hegel says only that the *real*, i.e., the *individual*, *will* is the *power of the crown* …. Insofar as this moment of "ultimate decision" or "absolute self-determination" is separated from the "universality" of the content and the particularity of counsel, it is the *real will* in the form of *caprice*. In other words, *"caprice* is the power of the crown", or "the power of the crown is caprice"' ('Critique of Hegel's Doctrine of the State', in *Early Writings* (New York, 1975), p. 76). By a different route, Walter Benjamin reaches similar conclusions: 'In the baroque because the tyrant and the martyr are but the two faces of the monarch. They are the necessarily exreme incarnations of the princely essence. As far as the tyrant is concerned, this is clear enough. The theory of sovereignty which takes as its example the special case in which dictatorial powers are unfolded, positively demands the completion of the image of the sovereign, as tyrant' (*The Origin of German Tragic Drama* (London 1977), p. 69).

8. THOMAS SACKVILLE and THOMAS NORTON, *Gorboduc*, I, ii, 218–20. The text is taken from the first volume of *Drama of the English Renaissance*, Russell A. Fraser and Norman Rabkin (eds), 2 vols (New York 1976).

9. *Politische Theologie: Vier Kapitel zur Lehre von der Souveränität* (Munich 1934), p. 11.

10. 'When a concrete result is to be produced, the dictator must intervene in the causal sequence of events with concrete measures. He takes action … he exercises an executive power, in contrast to the simple passing of a resolution or delivering of a legal decision, the *deliberate et consultare* …. In the dicatorship, therefore, the aim or end, freed of legal restrictions and determined only by the necessity of producing a concrete state of affairs, triumphs over other considerations' (Schmitt, *Die Diktatur*, pp. 11–12).

11. *The Governaunce of Kynges and Prynces* (The Pynson Edition, 1511). Reason for the Elizabethans was a term that bridged the two fields of knowledge and ethics. It was the faculty that allowed man to understand the universe as an organic whole regulated by laws that delimited the individual's sphere of action as well. Will was subordinated to it, just as the individual – as a particular will – was himself subject to the organism of which he was a part. The conflict between

these two faculties can therefore become truly explosive with the appearance of an individual (such as the absolute sovereign) who is no longer subject to any law.

12. *The Boke Named The Governour* [1531], (London 1907), p. 242.

13. WILLIAM BALDWIN, *The Mirror for Magistrates* [1559], Lily B. Campbell, ed., (1938), p. 111. The quotation is taken from the third line of 'Howe kyng Richarde the seconde was for his euyll goueraunce deposed from his seat, and miserably murdered in prison'.

14. RICHARD HOOKER, *The Laws of Ecclesiastical Polity* (London 1888), Book I, p. 76.

15. *The Mirrour of Policie* (anonymous translation of Guillaume de la Perrière, *Le Miroir politique*), London 1598, B.

16. *Mirrour of Policie*, Eiiij retro.

17. See for example the passage from Thomas Starkey's *Dialogue between Cardinal Pole and Thomas Lupset* cited and discussed in E.M.W. TILLYARD, *The Elizabethan World Picture* (London 1943), pp. 90–1.

18. *Shakespeare and the Nature of Man* (Lowell Lectures, 1942, 2nd edn., New York 1961).

19. *Classical and Christian Ideas of World Harmony: Prolegomena to an Interpretation of the Word 'Stimmung'*, Anna Granville Hatcher (ed.), (Baltimore 1963). The original version appeared in Traditio II (1944) and III (1945).

20. *The Elizabethan World Picture*, pp. 2, 5. Two passages from Shakespeare are frequently adduced in support of this conceptualization: Ulysses' speech on *degree* (at once supreme power and principle of inequality of station) in *Troilus and Cressida*, and Agrippa's apologue in *Coriolanus*. It is true in these cases, of course, that Shakespeare becomes the spokesman for the Elizabethan world picture; but both speeches prove to be totally ineffective: Agrippa fails to placate the plebeians, and Ulysses does not re-establish the principle of hierarchy in the Greek army. If these passages demonstrate anything, then, it is not the force of Elizabethan ideology in Shakespeare, but rather its weakness.

21. The relationship between Lear and his daughters anticipates the advice of a manual from the most abject years of English absolutism, *The Mirrour of Complements* (1635). In the speeches recommended for addressing a king, two points already evident in Shakespeare stand out. In the presence of the king, the supplicant forfeits all rights, and to prove it, makes the monarch the arbiter of his fate ('the greatest honour I can possibly attain, is to dye worthily in some action at your service'; 'a fit occasion to maintain [my most humble service] with the peril of my life and bloud', pp. 2, 3). He also forfeits his rights in the domain of language, which he employs not to convince, but only to attest the social gap between sender and receiver ('Sir, if words were able to expresse the duty in which I holde myselfe obliged'; 'I should much forget myselfe, if I thought my vowes alone sufficient to deserve the favour of your most princely grave', pp. 1, 2).

22. All quotations from Shakespeare's plays have been taken from *The Riverside Shakespeare*, G. Blakemore Evans (ed.), 1974.

23. *Origin*, p. 70.

24. '[The] heroes [of Greek tragedians] seem to us always more superficial in their speeches than in their actions; the myth, we might say, never finds an adequate objective correlative in the spoken word. The structure of the scenes and the concrete images convey a deeper wisdom than the poet was able to put into words and concepts. (The same may be claimed for Shakespeare, whose Hamlet speaks more superficially than he acts ...)' (FRIEDRICH NIETZSCHE, *The Birth of Tragedy*, Garden City, NY, 1956, p. 103). Nietzsche's position, accepted also by Benjamin (*Origin*, pp. 108–9), requires two qualifications, even leaving aside his sybylline pronouncement on Hamlet. For one thing, the inadequacy of word to action of which he speaks does not apply only to the hero, but also to the dramatic structure as a whole, including all the other characters as well as the chorus. And second, what Nietzsche calls 'superficiality' and Benjamin 'silence' cannot be seen as an effect of the violence of mythic events (in which alone, therefore, the true kernel of the tragedy would reside), but as a constitutive element of tragic structure as such. I shall return to this shortly, but to broach the distinction involved with the most famous example, let us say that it is possible to treat even the myth of Oedipus in non-tragic form: what makes it tragic is only the specific form in which it is structured.

25. GEORGE STEINER, *The Death of Tragedy* (London 1961), p. 11. The same point is made in LILY B. CAMPBELL, *Tudor Conceptions of History and Tragedy in 'A Mirror for Magistrates'*, Berkeley 1936, p. 17.

26. Anonymous, *Arden of Feversham* (Fraser and Rabkin), vol. 1, iii, 168.

27. THOMAS KYD, *The Spanish Tragedy* (Fraser and Rabkin), vol. 1, II, i, 92–3.

28. ELYOT, *The Gouenour*, p. 41; PHILIP SIDNEY, *An Apologie for Poetrie* (1585?) (London 1929), p. 45; GEORGE PUTTENHAM, *The Arte of English Poesis* (1589) (Kent, Ohio 1970), p. 49.

29. *Aesthetics*, tr. T.M. Knowx (Oxford 1975), p. 1210.

30. THOMAS HEYWOOD, 'The Author to his Booke', prefatory poem to *An Apology for Actors*, Richard H. Perkinson (ed.), (New York 1941), 1–4, 12.

31. C.B. MACPHERSON, *The Political Theory of Possessive Individualism: Hobbes to Locke* (Oxford 1962), p. 49.

32. WALTER ULLMANN, *The Individual and Society in the Middle Ages* (Baltimore 1966), pp. 40, 42, 44.

33. With the generalized commutation of dues into money rents, the cellular unity of political and economic oppression of the peasantry was gravely weakened, and threatened to become dissociated (end of this road was 'free labour' and the 'wage contract'). The class power of the feudal lords was thus directly at stake with the gradual disappearance of serfdom. The result was a *displacement* of politico-legal coercion upwards towards a centralized, militarized summit – the Absolutist State. Diluted at village level, it became concentrated at 'national' level. The result was a reinforced apparatus of royal power.

(ANDERSON, *Lineages*, P. 19).

Immanuel Wallerstein's judgement is similar:

In the heyday of western feudalism, when the state was weakest, the landowner, the lord of the manor thrived .... Lords of the manor then would never welcome the strengthening of the central machinery if they were not in a weakened condition in which they found it more difficult to resist the claims of central authority and more ready to welcome the benefits of imposed order. Such a situation was that posed by the economic difficulties of the fourteenth and fifteenth centuries, and the decline of seigniorial revenue.

(The Modern World-System, p. 28).

The new function of the sovereign as a hedge against social disintegration is faithfully reflected in the acitivities of legislation and coercion that Hooker assigns to God (*Laws*, pp. 64–8, 81). Even natural laws are conceived as 'the edicts of His law', so many means to avoid the universal dissolution that would ensue if individual elements of the cosmos went each its own way (p. 66).

34. ELYOT (*The Gouernour*, p. 5) establishes a strict correspondence between *understanding* and *estate*: 'they whiche excelle other in this influence of understandynge ... oughte to be set in a more highe place than the residue where they may se and also be sene; that by the beames of theyr excellent witte ... other of inferiour understandynge may be directed to the way of vertue and commodious liuynge'.

35. 'The term "country" suggested that the men whom it designated should be regarded as persons of public spirit, unmoved by private interest, untainted by court influence and corruption, representing the highest good of their local communities and the nation in whose interests they, and they only, acted' (P. Zagorin, 'The Court and the Country', *English Historical Review* (1962), i. 309; cited in LAWRENCE STONE, *The Crises of the Aristocracy: 1558–1641* (Oxford 1965), p. 502).

36. JOHN MARSTON, *The Malcontent*, M.L. Wine (ed.), (Lincoln, Nebraska), 1964, V, vi, 154–62.

37. James I, speech of 1609, collected in *The Political Works of James I*, Charles Howard McIlwain, ed., (Cambridge, Mass), 1918, p. 308. Besides the theatre, the game of chess is the other great social metaphor of the Elizabethans, and it is easy to see why. In chess, each piece is defined by a certain number of unalterable possibilities of movement different from those of the others – each piece in short is bound to its station. Furthermore (as is clear in Middleton's great success, *A Game at Chess*), each side in chess – each 'realm' – has a supreme and indisputable leader in the figure of the king.

38. To my central claim that the political sphere of the state is essential to tragedy, Marlowe's plays would constitute a conspicuous qualification. I can only glance at the problem here and say that Barabas and Faustus, to take the best examples, are unique on the Elizabethan stage as exponents (if peculiar ones) of civil society: on one hand, the great accumulator of wealth, on the other the great intellectual. The tragic conflict arises from the fact that prosperity and greatness both depend nonetheless on a superior power, despotic in nature, that denies them full liberty and finally destroys them. It would not be farfetched to call *The Jew of Malta* and *Doctor Faustus* 'tragedies of the monopolist', given that they illuminate with notable rigour the nexus of fear and antagonism that links this historical figure to absolute power.

39. *Aesthetics*, pp. 1229–30.

40. Ibid., pp. 1195–97.

41. London 1964, p. 57.

42. *Aesthetics*, pp. 1159–60, 1168.

43. *Il dramma moderno*, Milan 1976, pp. 24–5, 26, 48.

44. NICCOLÒ MACHIAVELLI, *The Prince* (Harmondsworth 1961), pp. 65–6.

45. And just as Hooker cannot understand Machiavelli, so Macbeth will never understand what it was that impelled him to action. On the only occasion he even makes a suggestion, he loses himself in a metaphor that explains nothing: 'I have no spur / To prick the sides of my intent, but only / Vaulting ambition, which o'erleaps itself / And falls on th'other' (I, vii, 25–8). Not only does the metaphor, reductive of the act Macbeth is about to commit, reduce its agent to the mute, non-human status of a horse to be pricked, but also it does not even claim 'ambition' as a 'cause' of action, only at best a 'spur' to it. The act that initiates the tragedy never is assigned a knowable cause, and the obscure motivation here reappears in Lear's 'darker purpose', Cleopatra's inexplicable flight at Actium, the destructive pleasure of Iago, and , in a special sense, Hamlet's inaction.

The presence of an unknowable element seems essential to tragic structure, and taking up the conclusions of the preceding section, I would argue that such an element is always situated on the plane of actions, and that it is unknowable because this plane, whose fullest expression is the sovereign acting in his unlimited independence, is suddenly dominated by fallen nature, which also has its highest expression in the sphere of royalty, specifically in the figure of the tyrant. By definition devoid of laws, fallen nature is unknowable. It can be represented, in the sense of re-presented, but never comprehended in the Elizabethan acceptance of the word: never, that is, inserted in the great system of causes and effects that is the world as constructed by the divine lawgiver. If at the centre of tragic structure, then, we encounter a 'realistic' element like the Machiavellianism of Macbeth, this, instead of reinforcing the cognitive power of the period, rather brings into relief its unknowability, its full petrifaction. Tragedy takes for its object not cognition, but its impossibility.

46. By the fifth act, up until just before being killed, Hamlet no longer thinks of revenging himself or unmasking the usurper. He recalls his original project only when Laertes tells him that he has 'not half an hour's life' – not as part of some uncontrollable vital instinct (whether of ambition or revenge or whatever), but as a man henceforth dead.

47. It is perhaps not chance that the two expressions occur practically at the same juncture in the drama, when it is a matter of choosing once and for all the line of action to follow: Macbeth decides to remain in that 'blood' of which he has spoken a few lines earlier, Hamlet to prolong his uncle's 'sickly days'.

48. What the court sees in *The Murder of Gonzago* is that a nephew of the king (like Hamlet in respect to Claudius), dressed in black (again like Hamlet), kills the legitimate sovereign (such as it holds Claudius to be). Blind to Claudius's usurpation, it sees instead Hamlet brazenly threatening his uncle.

49. The treatise writers of the time lose no occasion to praise the studied rhetorical preparation over the spontaneous production of discourse. Thus, Elyot in *The Gouernour* (pp. 42–3): 'The utilitie that a noble man shall happe to reason in counsaile, or shall speke in a great audience, or to strange ambassadours of great princes, he shall nat be constrayned to spake wordes sodayne and disordered, but shall bestowe them aptly and in their places. Wherefore the moste noble

emperour Octauius is highly commended, for that he neuer spake in the Senate, or to the people of Rome, but in oration prepared and purposely made.'

50. Christopher Hill has provided an extraordinary analysis of the historical transition in *Society and Puritanism in Pre-Revolutionary England*(New York 1964), pp. 382–419.

51. On Botero and Baccalini and their conception of the role of the prince, see MEINECKE, *Staaträson*, pp. 81–112, and especially pp. 6–8.

52. What follows is largely based on the arguments of JEAN STAROBINSKI, 'Sur Corneille', (in *L'Oeil vivant*, Paris 1961); and SERGE DOUBROVSKY, *Corneille et La Dialectique du Héros* (Paris 1963).

53. LEO TOLSTOY, *Tolstoy on Shakespeare* (New York 1907), p. 53.

54. On this problem see MICHEL FOUCAULT, *The Order of Things* (London 1970), chapters 1–3; and JURIJ M. LOTMAN, 'Different Cultures, Different Codes', *Times Literary Supplement*, 12 October, 1973, pp. 1213–15.

55. MARX, *Critique of Hegel's Doctrine of the State*, p. 81.

56. Sidney's 'defence' of poetry consists precisely in the claim made for its moral and cognitive character. Urged on almost every page, this claim is particularly clear in the argument in which the poet ('the peerelesse Poet') is declared superior from a cognitive point of view to both the philosopher and the historian because 'hee coupleth the generall notion with the particular example'. And since the 'final end' of learning is 'to knowe, and by knowing to lift vp the mind from the dungeon of the body, to the enjoying of his owne diuine essence', then 'the ending end of all earthly learning, being vertuous action, those skilles that most serue to bring forth that, haue a most iust title to bee Princes ouer all the rest' (*Apologie*, pp. 33, 29–30). Thus the circle is closed, and poetry is victoriously defended in the name of her 'force in teaching'.

57. 'It is said by such as professe the Mathematicall sciences, that all things stand by proportion, and that without it nothing could stand to be good or beautiful. The Doctors of our Theologie to the same effect, but in other termes, say: that God made the world by number, measure and weight … Poeticall proportion … holdeth of the Musical, because as we sayd before Poesie is a skill to speake and write harmonically' (PUTTENHAM, *English Poesie*, pp. 78–9). To a large extent Puttenham's work is a systematic collection of prescription on how to obtain this poetical proportion, with particular attention to the symmetry of versification and to the 'decencie', or moderation, of figurative language.

58. *A Pleasant Discourse of Court and Wars* (London 1596), A iv.

59. *The Traitor*, John Stewart Carter (ed.), (Lincoln Nebraska, 1965), II, ii, 112–6.

60. JOHN WEBSTER, *The White Devil* (Fraser and Rabkin), vol. 2, I, ii, 358–9.

61. PIERRE CORNEILLE, *Le Cid*, in *Theatre Complet*, Pierre Lièvre and Roger Caillois (eds.) (Paris 1966), I, ii, 23.

62. 'A strange affection, brother, when I think on't! / I wonder how thou cam'st by it.-Ev'n as easily / As man comes by destruction' (THOMAS MIDDLETON, *Women Beware Women*, Roma Gill, (ed.), (London and Tonbridge 1968), II, i, 1–3).

63. JOHN FORD, *'Tis Pity She's a Whore* (Fraser and Rabkin), vol. 2, I, iii, 11.

64. CYRIL TOURNEUR, *The Atheist's Tragedy*, Irving Ribner, (ed), (Cambridge, Mass, 1964), II, iii, 43–4, 65–6.

65. Cited in LAWRENCE STONE, *Crisis of the Aristocracy*, p. 27.

66. CYRIL TOURNEUR, *The Revenger's Tragedy* (Fraser and Rabkin), vol. 2, III, v, 44.

67. JOHN WEBSTER, *The Duchess of Malfi* (Fraser and Rabkin), vol. 2, II, i, 62–5.

68. BENJAMIN, *Origin*, p. 166.

69. PUTTENHAM, *English Poesie*, p. 197.

70. *Phenomenology of Spirit* (Oxford 1977), p. 116.

ALESSANDRO SERPIERI   *THE BREAKDOWN OF MEDIEVAL HIERARCHY IN* KING LEAR*

Alessandro Serpieri is Professor of English at the University of Florence. The following article on *King Lear* first appeared in an earlier form in Italian in the journal *Il piccolo Hans* in 1978. Although subscribing to a similar intellectual outlook as Moretti, Serpieri is concerned much more with the semiotic aspects of literary texts. It is Serpieri's contention that what he has elsewhere called 'the literary sign' (*Alternative Shakespeares*, p. 119) accumulates meaning through 'a wide network of syntactic and semantic relations manifest in the text itself by its very textual situation' (ibid). The literary sign acts as a point of convergence for a range of meanings which play across the text, but also meanings which are in the strict sense of the term extra-textual. Since drama combines linguistic and non-linguistic forms of signification in and through performance, a semiotic reading must take account of what Serpieri calls 'the cultural pragmatics of its historical context' (ibid., p. 122) as well as the generic requirements of particular texts, and the conventions governing their performance. His concern, therefore is to combine a semiotic analysis, that is to say a formal reading of the text's signifying practices, but also to situate that within the wider cultural framework of the text's reception.

In this short article I shall be examining the first scene of *King Lear* with the aim of offering a reinterpretation of the play from a semiotic standpoint. It

*This article was read in a much shorter form at the first International Conference of Semiotic Studies (Milan, June 1974), and was published in the proceedings of the congress by Mouton (The Hague). The present version is an elaboration of the original material and appeared in *Il piccolo Hans*, **19**, July/Sept. 1978,trans. Sandra Payne.

should be borne in mind that the opening scene of *Lear* finds its origins –
and thus both the basic narrative structure and its development – in myth,
legend and folktale. Indeed, Freud himself, in his well-known essay 'The
Theme of the Three Caskets',[1] pointed out that the structure of the scene in
question is closely related both to the myth of the Judgement of Paris and to
that of Psyche, as well as to the fairy tale of Cinderella and to episodes from
classical epic poetry. The common factor in all these is a man's choice
between three women: the choice falls upon the most beautiful of the three
who inevitably remains silent during the contest (or hides – Freud equating
concealment and dumbness). As Freud evinces, this is an archetypal
narrative scheme, one which man's imagination (through the 'replacement
by an opposite') has adopted as a defence against the ineluctability of
death. Although the favoured contender thus represents Death (the motif
of dumbness or concealment being symbolic of death), she is immediately
transformed into the archetypal maiden or into the Goddess of Love; and it
thus follows that even though man is fated to die he is still able to free
himself from this inevitability by converting fate into free will (the *choice*)
through the workings of this imagination.

In the play the three women are daughters, as befits the king who is an
old man, close to death. Having said this, we should emphasize that Freud
does not touch upon Lear's error, nor upon the fact that he bungles his
choice and that he will only find his tragic apotheosis when he enters with
Cordelia's body in his arms at the play's end. Freud's analysis of the
mythical, anthropological and psychoanalytical models underlying the text
naturally stops short of an investigation into the grammar, rhetoric and
epistemology of the play: an attempt at this will be made here.

. To go back to the beginning: as Shakespeare was building upon the
foundations of an inherited narrative model, he could not modify the
fndamental narrative features of this model to any great extent. The only
alteration to the basic scheme which is of any import (and this, as we shall
see, was not Shakespeare's own) is simply, here again, the replacement by
an opposite. For tragedy to ensue, Lear must bungle his choice; and his
error will not only generate all the successive reversals but will be
exemplary within the cultural model. The motif of the error itself was also,
in the same way, inherited, as it reached Shakespeare through the source
material of the play: Holinshed's Chronicles and an anonymous play *The
True Chronicle History of King Leir*. In these works we come across the
well-worn allegory of the unfortunate consequences deriving from the
division of a kingdom (we should not forget that *Gorboduc*, one of the first
and most influential of Elizabethan tragedies, is explicitly based on the
same subject). This allegory was extremely popular in the Elizabethan
period, as its political and didactic implications echoed a widespread
anxiety: national unity had only recently been attained after centuries of
feudal strife and civil war, and was still considered both precarious and

essential to the development of the emerging bourgeois, mercantile and colonial social model.

Dominated by the anthropological and political structure, Shakespeare could very easily have slipped, from the first scene onwards, either into trite allegory or into the pathetic recounting of the tale of an old fool and his stubborn daughter. Instead, he avoids both these traps and, though beset by inevitable narrative constraints, creates a memorable scene of great theatrical worth, reinventing and rewriting a script forced upon him by myth and political allegory.

To appreciate Shakespeare's achievement, care must be taken to read this first scene (which generates the whole play) not only in terms of its psychological features, but as a semiological system. Right from the start, the semiotics of the play are dominated by its rhetoric and grammar. The rhetoric of the first scene is based on the opposition between the (false) *hyperbole* of Goneril and Regan and the (true) *reticence* of Cordelia, its grammar on the opposition between a series of *comparatives* of superiority (and of superlatives) and a series of negations.

Significantly, the first scene does not open with the main plot involving Lear and his three daughters, but with the subplot, which runs closely parallel to it, and deals with Gloucester and his two sons. The opening speech, delivered by Kent, refers however to the main plot: 'I thought the King had *more* affected the Duke of Albany than Cornwall' (I, i, 1–2). Gloucester answers that this no longer seems to be so, as the fairness of the division of his kingdom, already announced by Lear, rules out any such preference: 'It always did seem so to us. But now in the division of the kingdom it appears not which of the Dukes he values *most*, for qualities are so weighed that curiosity in neither can make choice of either's moiety' (I, i, 3–6).

The conversation then passes immediately to the subplot as Gloucester introduces his illegitimate son Edmund to Kent. He makes embarrassed jokes about the irregular nature of Edmund's birth and admits he has often felt ashamed of him (l. 9: 'I have so often blushed to acknowledge him'). He refers to him as 'whoreson', although he realizes that he 'must be acknowledged'. In spite of his obvious embarrassment, Gloucester, who in his kindness is ideologically just as 'blind' as Lear (and whose blindness will soon become a theatrical reality), denies that he has discriminated against Edmund in favour of his legitimate son, Edgar. He does so by a negation of the comparative which would have favoured Edgar: 'But I have a son, sir, by order of law, some years elder than this, who yet is *no dearer* in my account' (I, i, 18–19).

In this way he denies the discrimination which in fact exists and, in doing so, anticipates Lear who will also confuse the emotional plane with the social plane of hierarchical values. On the emotional plane Edmund may well be Edgar's equal in Gloucester's affections, but on the social plane the discrimination against him is clearly absolute, as is demonstrated by the last remark made by Gloucester before the entry of Lear himself: 'He hath been out nine years, and away he shall again. The King is coming' (I, i, 31–32).

So Edmund is exiled by a social order which does not admit bastards. Considered in terms of the system of signs operative in that society, Edmund is in danger of *not existing*. He will have to leave the country once more, despite the fact that Gloucester loves him. Shakespeare's prologue to the entry of Lear, short and simple as it is, establishes the terms which are essential to the play's interpretation. The morphological paradigm of *comparison* is immediately linked with the theme of social *discrimination*. Whoever is excluded from the medieval hierarchy of signs *is nothing*; and whoever thinks (as does Lear himself) that he may give up his position in the system with impunity and maintain the identity derived from that position will lose his reason and *will be nothing*. The only way of staying within the system of medieval hierarchy is by means of *comparison* between its various levels which are defined according to the codes / rules governing the symbolic system.

In his long opening speech, Lear takes the first step on the road towards eventual madness: he expresses his intention of abdicating, and announces that he will confer the *greatest* power (which is equivalent on the map of his kingdom to the *greatest* extent of territory) to the daughter who declares the *greatest* affection for him. This constitutes the opening gambit in that absurd contest whose hidden motivation is to be found in the axiological model of an entire civilization. Let us examine the beginning of Lear's speech:

> Meantime we shall express our *darker* purpose
> Give me the map there. Know that we have divided
> In three our kingdom; and 'tis our fast intent
> To shake all cares and business from our age,
> Conferring them on younger strengths, while we
> Unburdened crawl towards death. Our son of Cornwall –
> And you, our *no less* loving son of Albany …

(I, i, 35–41)

The first thing we notice is that Lear immediately makes use of a comparative, *darker*, which though morphologically incongruous, furnishes us with the key to his 'error'. What has become of the second term of the comparison? And, moreover, what is the meaning of the qualification? 'Our *most secret* purpose', probably; and yet we know, right from the beginning of the scene (from what transpires between Kent and Gloucester) that Lear's manifest purpose is anything but secret – indeed it is common knowledge. This morphological and semantic incongruity would seem to indicate that the expression must be coherent on other levels: for instance, on the *formal* level of the king's obsessive use of comparison (while remaining himself the superlative at the apex of the hierarchical pyramid): or, again, on the *connotative* level of 'darker' – Lear's purpose is truly obscure and serves as a proof of his symbolic blindness. Indeed, within the *seme* 'dark' his *inclination for death* is conveyed. Lear's approach to death is in fact soon afterwards explicitly evoked (' ... while we/*Unburdened crawl towards death*'), but the terms which qualify this approach, both adjectival ('unburdened') and verbal ('crawl') will, during the course of the play, be gradually *overdetermined* – although the 'blind hero', in uttering them, does not realise their irony. 'Unburdened', besides its contextual meaning of *freedom from responsibility and the duties of government*, also implies *possessing nothing*: and Lear will, of course, meet his end possessing nothing. He will, moreover, 'crawl' to his death – 'crawl', too, having prophetic overtones. On the tempest-driven heath, rejected by society, the mad outcast Lear will experience the animality of man when he has lost all token of his identity (see III, iv, 99–107).

The play's themes have thus already been connotatively established. But Lear – who uses the *plurale maestatis* during his emphatic and assertive address – is nevertheless still labouring under a delusion: that of a king who wishes to remain king even as he sets about divesting himself of the trappings of regality. He looks about himself and sees everybody in terms of a scale of comparatives (see, for instance, '... our *no less* loving son of Albany'), of which he is the unchallenged head, and formally opens the contest which will necessarily involve a process of discrimination:

> ...Tell me, my daughters,
> Since now we will divest us both of rule,
> Interest of territory, cares of state,
> Which of you shall we say doth love us *most*,
> That we our *largest* bounty may extend
> Where nature doth with merit challenge. Goneril,
> Our eldest born, speak first.

$$(I, i, 47-53)$$

In giving up his position as king – his position as 'absolute superlative' within the pyramidally structured feudal system – Lear feels the need for a competition to establish his formal evaluation of comparatives. Indeed he states this need explicitly (the logical formulation with which it is expressed 'Tell me, my daughters / ... *Which* of you ... ' is worthy of notice), and in this way he hopes to obtain the guarantee of an *absolute* on the affective plane (his role as father), by means of which he will be able to recognize himself and thereby retain the absolute primacy as 'sign' which he is about to renounce within the power structure. Lear therefore attempts the impossible – he aims to assimilate the non-hierarchical, *qualitative* system of love to the hierarchical, *quantitative* system of power. Such an attempt can only lead to the pretence of love, to love's perversion and its degeneration: in this context *more* love for her father, on the part of each contestant, can only mean discrimination and jealousy – and thus (*more*) hatred for her sisters. The required sign is bound to be a lie, a simulacrum: the only alternative is a refusal to give the sign – and this will be Cordelia's reply.

Lear, in this way, will only achieve the reduction of love to a commodity and, in doing so, will obtain a counterfeit guarantee of his identity, a pretence of pre-eminence which is destined to crumble away when he experiences the breakdown of this identity – that is, his nullity as a 'sign'.

Goneril and Regan accept Lear's conditions and pretend to commute the power system into a love system by climbing a ladder of hyperbolic comparatives which supposedly provides confirmation of the superlative (father, king, demigod) that Lear desires. Goneril declares:

Sir, I love you *more* than word can wield the matter,
Dearer than eyesight, space, and liberty,
Beyond what can be valued rich or rare,
No less than life, with grace, health, beauty, honour,
As much as child e'er loved or father found;
A love that makes breath poor and speech unable;
Beyond all manner of '*so much*' I love you.

(I, i, 54–60)

At this point Cordelia, in an aside, already opts for silence: 'What shall Cordelia speak? Love and be silent' (l. 62). Goneril's hyperbolic scaling of the heights of comparison has rendered any further amplification grammatically and semantically impossible, and has left no room for hyperbole or comparison on the part of the sisters who are to follow her. Regan, however, uses subtler methods than those of Goneril. She has recourse to a rhetorical and logical procedure which outdoes Goneril's superabundant series of comparatives, while refraining from the use of any comparative herself. By now a comparative would be overexplicit, worn to a cliché: what *more* could she have said than Goneril's 'Beyond all manner of "so much"'? So she declares:

I am made of that self mettle *as* my sister
And price me at her worth. In my true heart
I find she names my very deed of love;
Only she comes *too short*, that I profess
Myself an enemy to all other joys
Which the most precious square of sense possesses,

And find I am alone felicitate
In your dear highness' love.

(I, i, 62–75)

She begins with an assertion of equality with Goneril's comparatives which have already had the desired effect on Lear. She then makes a judgement which both belittles Goneril's love and magnifies her own, by hinting at a 'more' which is not actually expressed: 'Only she comes *too short.*' In this way Goneril's comparatives are made to shrink to insufficiency when compared with the greater, unexpressed comparative of Regan.

Once again, just as she did after Goneril's declaration, Cordelia inserts as an aside, 'Then poor Cordelia! / And yet not so, since I am sure my love's / *More ponderous* than my tongue' (ll. 75-7). Cordelia, too, uses a comparative of superiority, but only to bring herself to silence, thus moving in exactly the opposite direction to her sisters.

After rewarding Regan to the same extent as Goneril ('*No less* in space, validity, and pleasure', l. 80), Lear calls on his favourite daughter ('Now, our joy, / Although our last and least … '), explicitly offering her more and thus inviting her to 'win' more by saying more:

…what can you say to draw
A third *more opulent* than your sisters'? Speak!

(I, i, 84–5)

It is at this point that Lear's hyperbolic frenzy (previously manifested marginally in the superlatives directed towards Goneril, 'Our *eldest* born', l. 54, and towards Regan, 'Our *dearest* Regan', l. 68), a frenzy which calls for falsehood within that symbolic and hierarchical system of which the king is the maximum exponent, is balked by a barrier of negation, of reticence and silence. As is often the case in Shakespearean tragedy, the chosen rhetorical axis, after exhibiting one of its aspects, then shows the other which is antonymic to the first. *More* is at this point displaced by *less*, which de-escalates until it reaches *nothing*. In the competition set by Lear, the affirmative only takes on meaning to the extent that it falsifies itself through comparison and discriminates against others. Cordelia cannot, therefore, reply in the positive, which would otherwise be the only grammatical sign permitted by the qualitative system of love. She replies with a pure negative, which, incidentally, rejects the competition itself, and counters Lear's amazement and indignation by explicitly rejecting any form of comparison:

Cordelia	Nothing, my lord.
Lear	Nothing?

Cordelia	Nothing.
Lear	Nothing will come of nothing. Speak again.
Cordelia	Unhappy that I am, I cannot heave
	My heart into my mouth. I love your majesty
	According to my bond, *no more nor less.*

(I, i, 87–93)

Cordelia accepts neither the contest nor the bartering of love for power. She only recognizes the interchange of love, which is not a matter of more or less but is founded upon equality. The tragic irony of the play lies in the fact that both Lear and Gloucester (in the subplot) are blind to the realities of the power they represent, and they waste whatever power remains to them in discriminating against and expelling from the social system precisely those people who reject the logic of might: Cordelia and Edgar.

When considered within certain long-established anthropological and tribal canons, Lear can be seen to represent the semi-divine figure of the king/father/god who bestows or withholds fertility; many are the instances in which he is connoted in this sense throughout the play. It is on this level that the old king repudiates his daughter who has dared to 'unmake' his system, expelling her not only from the chessboard of power, but from life itself:

Let it be so! Thy truth then be thy dower!
For by the sacred radiance of the sun,
The mysteries of Hecate and the night,
By all the operation of the orbs
From whom we do exist and cease to be,
Here I disclaim all my paternal care,
Propinquity and property of blood,
And as a stranger to my heart and me
Hold thee from this for ever ...

(I, i, 108–16)

The curse is pronounced in the name of darkness and death to the detriment of Cordelia – but it will rebound upon Lear himself and express his own annihilation. Lear then goes on to announce the paradox that although he *is no longer* king, he *will be* king ('Only we shall retain/the name and all th'addition to a king', ll. 134–5), and as a sign of his identity he retains a personal escort of a hundred knights.

Kent then intercedes on Cordelia's behalf and qualifies Lear as 'mad' and 'old', omitting his royal title:

...Be Kent unmannerly
When Lear is mad. What would'st thou do old man?

(I, i, 145–6)

91

Lear's only reaction (and his last regal action) is to eliminate Kent from
the social system by banishing him. So Kent, a member of the nobility, who
had been one of those nearest the top of the pyramid of power, becomes in
one fell swoop a nameless 'trunk' as Lear sentences him:

> ...If on the tenth day following
> Thy banished *trunk* be found in our dominions
> The moment is thy death. Away!

> (I, i, 176–8)

Kent does not simply drop within the social scale. He is socially
annihilated. He becomes nothing more than a carcass and, losing his
human connotations, is reduced to mere *animality*. The rejection of
comparison implies the rejection of a whole system of signs. It involves a
leap into *nothingness*, the loss of identity. This is made clear beyond any
doubt by Lear's final curse against Cordelia which 'cancels out' her very
birth. The entire play is thus effectively enclosed between life and death,
between the symbolic system and the non-system of madness, between the
panoply of rank and the anonymity of nakedness – this last exemplified by
the naked Edgar disguised as a madman. The tragic web of comparatives,
spun in the first scene, reaches its conclusion in a perfectly circular scheme,
that of *epanalepsis*:

> ...*Better* thou
> Hadst not been born than not t'have pleased me *better*.

> (I, i, 233–4)

For the whole of the remainder of the play, Lear will himself experience
the same social annihilation – as the Fool is the first to point out to him: 'I
am a Fool; thou art *nothing*' (I, iv, 190–1). The escort of a hundred knights,
which Lear had kept for himself as the symbol of a power already
relinquished, is progressively reduced by Goneril and Regan, first to fifty,
then to twenty-five, and finally to *nothing*, in a process which is ironically
inverse to the crescendo of false comparatives with which they had outbid
one another in the first scene in order to obtain power. In the sphere of
family relationships the situation is also reversed. The daughters of the
patriarch-king take on the role of strict mothers to the childish and
capricious old man: and yet the logic of their behaviour is the same as that
of Lear when he was king. The play should not be interpreted in terms of
ingratitude and natural piety. It is not concerned with the individual *per se*,
but with the dramatic functions of the individual within the system
operative in the play (which is medieval in type, although it is vaguely set
in a pre-Christian age), a system that is struggling to survive according to
the laws of a more than individual logic.

The king (no longer king), who was once the summit of the feudal pyramid, undergoes the experience (which necessarily *is* madness), of what a man becomes once he is expelled from the axiological order – an empty shell. He discovers that even a king, once he has lost his place in the great semiotic network of differential degree becomes *nothing* (a theme word which, from Cordelia's first 'nothing' in the opening scene, informs the whole play with all the variations of its meaning). In III, iv, Lear reaches the end of his journey towards madness and the void. The decisive moment is his meeting with Edgar, at night on the storm-wracked heath. Edgar too has been excluded from society by Gloucester, and has disguised himself as a madman. In him Lear 'sees' that as soon as man is disconnected from society, deprived of the illusory trappings which confer his social 'identity' upon him, he becomes nothing but a 'bare, forked animal'. It is at this point that Lear's frenzied comparisons crumble away into meaninglessness:

> Thou wert *better* in a grave than to answer with thy uncovered body this extremity of the skies. Is man *no more* than this? Consider him well. Thou owst the worm no silk, the beast no hide, the sheep no wool, the cat no perfume. Ha! Here's three on's are sophisticated; thou art the thing itself; unaccommodated man is *no more* but such a poor, bare, forked animal as thou art. Off, off, you lendings! Come; unbutton here.
>
> (III, iv, 103–112)

He too rids himself of his garments and, in doing so, finally abandons society and embraces the state of total madness, the result of the loss of all orientation in a jungle of signs which has excluded him as a now meaningless element.

Shakespeare's *King Lear* is, in effect, a tragic parable of the breakdown of the medieval system of signs which still precariously held the world view together in the Elizabethan age. The 'great chain of being' which underwrote the meaning of every element in terms of its position on a scale stretching up to the empyrean and down to the sublunary world (human, animal, vegetable and mineral) was, very evidently, beginning to fall apart. The key to the old world view had been the bestowing of identity to things on the basis of their status within an undisputed and global ontological model of reality. This whole way of thought is challenged by the creation of the figure of a king thrust out from the great chessboard of being towards madness and nothingness. The world becomes a stage full of fools, as Lear comes to recognize:

> When we are born we cry that we are come
> To this great stage of fools.
>
> (IV, vi, 184–5)

The medieval semiotic process is now being threatened and emptied of meaning by the codes and values of the Baroque era: the 'noise' of madness rises, as it were, from the emptiness, the 'gap' between the signifying systems of one world view and the other. On this interpretation, *King Lear* is a presentation in dramatic terms of the final disintegration of a society held together by what Jury Lotman terms 'a high degree of *signicity*'. This is Lotman's brilliant definition of medieval society:

> The sign was important because of its capacity to substitute. This immediately revealed the twofold nature of the sign – the substituted item was considered the content and the item substituted for it the expression. This was why the substitute-item was unable to have an autonomous value. The value given it depended in the hierarchical status of its content within the general model of the world... And, as the real existence of the human being depended on his or her relationship with the structure of which he or she was a sign, the arguments over precedence in processions, meetings or banquets were pertinent to the existence of each participant. Losing your place meant ceasing to exist.
>
> (LOTMAN, 1973: 44–6)[2]

Lear loses his place and acquires a full knowledge of his own annihilation. To paraphrase another concept formulated by Lotman, in Shakespeare the two-layer system of medieval symbolism (essence above and expression below) had not yet been replaced by the syntagmatic system; in the latter the meaning of human existence is determined not by an upward-aspiring hierarchy but by insertion into a given plane of relationships. Lear losses his bearings in the darkness of unrelieved crisis. He finds truth only in madness, which represents the upheaval of the semiosis he has rejected. Because of this there can be no final message, but only an escape into negation (see Lear's 'No, no, no, no!' and 'Never, never, never, never, never!' in v, iii, 8 and 307) and, at last, into death. Lear's ultimate negation, which rejects society, rejects with it man's precarious hold on corporeal existence – rejects, that is, life itself (he answers the blind Gloucester's request to kiss his hand with *disgust*: 'Let me wipe it first; it smells of mortality', IV, vi, 132). At the end, it is the negation of the whole of history, as is clear from Lear's last speech to Cordelia:

> No, no, no, no! Come, let's away to prison.
> We two alone will sing like birds i'the cage;
> When thou dost ask me blessing I'll kneel down
> And ask of thee forgiveness; so we'll live,
> And pray, and sing, and tell old tales, and laugh
> At gilded butterflies, and hear poor rogues

Talk of court news; and we'll talk with them too –
Who loses and who wins, who's in, who's out -
And take upon's the mystery of things
As if we were God's spies; and we'll wear out,
In a walled prison, packs and sects of great ones
That ebb and flow by the moon.

(V, iii, 8–19)

It is, in a sense, an abdication from history into the prison he invokes as a refuge: a rejection of competition and the logic of might which is implicit in the power game. His only salvation seems to be that of the sending and receiving of verbal messages – in *speech* – as is revealed on the lexical plane by the evident presence of the paradigm: *sing, ask, pray, sing, tell, hear, talk, talk*. Here we may discern the shadowy figures of a subsequent Shakepearean father-and-daughter relationship, that of Prospero and Miranda in their island prison in *The Tempest*. But the salvation offered by speech is only an illusion, in *King Lear* cut off by the tragic ending, and in *The Tempest* scotched by Prospero's realization that the spell cast by words cannot offer a valid alternative. Speech is merely another illusion, a game whose players are empty shells, or masks, and whose magic aims to exorcize life itself and to abscond from man's drama. The only valid form of 'exorcism' would be that of creating new models, new codes and new responsibilities. But that could not be Shakespeare's solution. He could only expose the great epistemological crisis of his age by showing how all the 'received' (medieval) signs and systems were collapsing into blanks. The *nothing* of the play turns out to be death. In fact, the only 'resolution' which is held out in *King Lear* is that of absolute negation. And so we go back to the beginning, to that death – rejected, misunderstood, desired, in turn -which is to be found in the ambiguous myth sequence investigated by Freud. The choice of the three caskets/women is the choice (read fate) of Eros (read Thanatos) which finally leads Shakespeare's tragic hero beyond history.

Notes

1. See S.FREUD, 'The Theme of the Three Caskets', in *Vol. 14 Art and Literature*, Penguin Freud Library, trans. James Strachey, ed. Albert Dickson (Penguin, 1985), pp. 235–47.
2. See J.M. LOTMAN, 'Il problema del segno e del sistema segnico della cultura russa prima del XX secolo' in *Ricerche semiotiche*, ed. J.M. Lotman and BA. Uspenskij, (Torino:Einaudi, 1973), pp. 44–6.

3 Marxism and Materialism

WALTER COHEN   *ARISTOCRATIC FAILURE**

Walter Cohen is currently Professor of Comparative Literature at Cornell University. His book *Drama of a Nation: Public Theater in England and Spain* was published by Cornell University Press in 1985. The following extract, from a chapter entitled 'Aristocratic Failure' expands those issues raised by Moretti and Serpieri, but extends them into the arena of performance, and 'history'. Beginning from a classical Marxist position, Cohen suggests that tragedy emerges, and is given a historical specificity in Shakespeare, as a dramatic and theatrical form which is peculiar to a transitional phase, that of the decline of feudalism and the rise of modern capitalism. He takes the view that in the tragedies beginning with *Julius Caesar*, but especially in those from 1604–08, the interrelationship between aristocracy, emergent bourgeoisie, and the poor, helps to foreground 'both irreconcilable, destructive social conflict, and the creative nobility of the hero's unsuccessful struggles'. In this respect the tragedies disclose a series of conflicting 'voices' which can be assigned to particular social classes. Cohen holds on to the early Marxist notion of 'ideology' as false consciousness, a distortion of the real social relations operating in this society, and he detects at the core of Shakespearean tragedy an irreducible humanism overlayed by historical conflict. Moreover, Cohen begins from a position which accepts the explanatory force of 'totality' in his attempt to produce an alternative account of the place and function of the Elizabethan and Jacobean theatres, 'and the elucidation of the drama's subversive political efficacy during the seventeenth century and radical potential today' (*Drama of a Nation*, p. 22). Cohen is well aware of the current concerns in the realm of critical theory, particularly the challenge to the continuity of historical

---

*Reprinted from *Drama of a Nation: Public Theater in Renaissance England and Spain* (Ithaca: Cornell University Press, 1985), pp. 302-22.

narrative, and he proposes, through a scholarly comparative study of the theatrical traditions of two distinct cultures, English and Spanish, a drawing together of historical scholarship and theory.

In Shakespeare's career, tragedy absolutely and unambiguously replaced English history. The two tragedies and nine history plays of the 1590s gave way to a sequence of nine tragedies between 1599 and 1608. In that period Shakespeare set *Julius Caesar, Antony and Cleopatra* (1607), and *Coriolanus* (1608) in the Roman world and both *Troilus and Cressida* (1602) and *Timon of Athens* (1607) in the Greek. Even *King Lear* (1605) is nominally classical, a pattern that continues into the late romances as well. Yet closer scrutiny inevitably modifies this perspective. First, Shakespeare's main concern with antiquity apparently occurred only after 1605. More important, at the other public theaters the national history play remained at least as prominent as tragedy up to that time. Perhaps, then, the 1599 order had only relative impact until reinforced by Jacobean theatrical centralization a few years later. Perhaps, too, the earlier switch by Shakespeare reflected the caution of his company in avoiding the wrath of the authorities, although such a hypothesis is not easily reconciled with the Chamberlain's Men's reckless agreement to perform *Richard II* on the eve of Essex's Rebellion.

Shakespeare's decision may also have owed something to the opening of the Globe. Its Bankside location, combined with its greater physical attractiveness, enabled the Chamberlain's Men to draw a section of their audience from the fashionable areas of London more easily than had been possible at the older Middlesex theaters. Perhaps partly with this consideration in mind, Shakespeare offered, in *Julius Caesar*, a more overtly neoclassical play than had been his custom. The success of that tragedy, as well as the problems it raised, might then have led to *Hamlet* (1601).

Whatever the merit of these speculations *Julius Caesar* did function as a generic shifter, inaugurating Shakespeare's tragic period and with it new possibilities of representation. At the other end of that period, *Coriolanus* realizes some of these possibilities. The opening of the play pits the oppressed plebeians against the Roman senators, 'who make edicts for usury, to support usurers; repeal daily any wholesome act established against the rich, and provide more piercing statutes daily to chain up and restrain the poor'.[1] The plebeians may here be echoing the popular protests of 1607, in which Levellers and Diggers first appeared.[2] Although Shakespeare hardly advocates the overthrow of patrician rule he at least shows the legitimacy of lower-class grievances. Coriolanus, both the noblest and the most arrogant member of the aristocracy, lives and dies in relation to this struggle. That the resolution of the crises of early republican Rome depends on his exclusion[3] reveals the radical difference between *Coriolanus* and a play such as Corneille's *Horace*. For the French dramatist, the recourse to classical Rome provided a means of approaching his own nation; for Shakespeare, it offered a way of establishing critical distance. In England the closest generic analogue to Corneille's play, the proper vehicle for depicting the potential harmony between class and state or between upper class and lower, was the national history play.

Jonson's *Sejanus*, a failure at the public theater, produces a somewhat different subversive effect from *Coriolanus's*. The true tragic complement to dramatic satire in general and, of course, to Jonson's comedies in particular, it replaces Juvenal by Tacitus as part of its abandonment of the exclusively social for the exclusively political. As in the comedies, Jonson pursues loosely didactic ends, attacking dictatorship and informers while insisting that principled action will prove victorious. Yet the plot shows this belief in the ability of human freedom to shape society to be illusory. The ineffectual good characters prove easy prey for the villainous protagonist, who in turn can be defeated only by another consummate villain. Thus Jonson represents politics as a sordid power struggle. Since the lower classes are objects of contempt, Jonson's aristocratic spokesman has no potential allies, human or divine, at the end of the play. For the survivors of the tyranny, the final note is not hope but paranoia.[4]

Chapman's *Caesar and Pompey* (1605), perhaps never performed, is also troubled by unconscious ideological contradictions. Though nominally a tragedy, it ends somewhat incongruously with a sense of Cato's triumph. Yet the Senecan Stoicism that motivates the hero is a philosophy of defeat. As the climax approaches, Cato's passionate concern for the destiny of Rome and the welfare of its populace, whom Chapman, in defiance of historical fact, aligns with the Republicans, fades into insignificance before the stirring scene of one man's pursuit of personal freedom in life and in death. So as not to detract from the rather narrowly aristocratic moral, the simultaneous political dimension of suicide so prominent in *Julius Caesar* must here be suppressed. Thus the important national issues raised by both Jonson and Chapman prove insoluble at the political level. The virtuous characters, essentially helpless victims of circumstance, can retain their moral stature only as private, aristocratic individuals incapable of influencing the course of events. The ideological distortions in both works arise from the playwrights' unwillingness to face the obvious, but admittedly depressing, implications of the historical material they dramatize. The plays, in other words, reveal more, and more of significance, about the authors and their society than Jonson and Chapman apparently intended.

Related difficulties beset *Timon of Athens*. Both literally and figuratively, money rules Athens, shaping government policy, social class and human relations. Timon, disillusioned by the city's previous exploitation of his neofeudal extravagant hospitality, curses all humanity , attributing to gold the absolute power to invert traditional values, to make 'Black white, foul fair, wrong right, / Base noble, old young, coward valiant' – a rhetorical formulation of moral outrage typical of the time.[5] Also a feudal figure of sorts, Alcibiades responds to his banishment by the Senate with a vow to destroy Athens. This parallel between main plot and subplot gives rise to the central interpretive problem of the play, however. Although the selective vengeance for which Alcibiades ultimately settles seems juster than Timon's universal misanthropy, Timon is surely right in insisting on the irredeemable depravity of Athens. Since the practices of Alcibiades' and Timon's enemies quite clearly conform to the norms of the entire society, Alcibiades' final victory carries with it no likelihood of the profound changes necessary for a return to a precapitalist economy. This ideological impasse is manifested in the fractured form of the play.[6] *Antony and Cleopatra*, however, does not try to have it both ways. The dichotomies of the play issue in no reconciliation; the verbal paradoxes that in *Macbeth* (1606) reflect the hero's, rather than the world's, disorder are never resolved. The suicide with which Cleopatra caps her career removes her from a new world in which she, like Antony, has no real place. In this respect the lovers' deaths constitute a judgement on the processes of history.[7] The play faces directly what remains oblique in *Sejanus, Caesar and Pompey*, or even *Timon of Athens*.

Both *Sejanus* in particular and the classicizing tendencies of all these plays in general suggest the similarity of tragedy to satiric comedy. The setting for tragedy, as for satire, is a new mode of production. Again like satire, tragedy derives its critical perspective on capitalism from a rootedness in a prior mode of production, Finally, it too reveals a disjunction between social action and moral judgement, the most extreme divergences coinciding with the widest range of social representation. In Shakespeare's career, the turn to tragedy responds in part to the interconnected rise of satire and of the private theaters. The imprint of satiric comedy may be discerned at least in *Hamlet, Troilus and Cressida, Othello* (1604), *King Lear*, and *Timon of Athens*.

Yet it would be misleading to overstress the similarities between tragedy and satiric comedy. Shakespearean tragedy does not consistently, and certainly does not structurally, offer approbation for social mastery. Audience response to the vitality of a belated Vice figure like Iago or Edmund, whose ancestry derives significantly from the popular theatrical tradition, is qualitatively different from the admiration elicited by the adroitness of more neoclassical characters such as Volpone, Subtle, and Face. Nor does Shakespearean tragedy merely complement dramatic satire. It also attempts to incorporate the latter form, in ideological sympathy as well as in social breadth. It is not concerned only with political adaptation. These asymmetries are partly consequences of distinct institutional affiliations. The widest-ranging satiric comedy was generally a product of a transitional balance between public and private theater, in the years from 1609 to 1614. Shakespearean tragedy dates from the previous decade and was composed exclusively for a public theater that was in the process of absorbing the secondary influences of the private stage. Partly as a result, it was more indebted to the tradition of popular dramaturgy.

The strength of that tradition, combined with Shakespeare's critical commitment throughout his career to aristocratic rule in general and monarchical power in particular,[8] helps account for the relative continuity between the national history play and tragedy. Well before 1600, the institutional configuration of the theater, reinforced for Shakespeare by his own modest social origins, opened the way to a judgement of the absolutist state according to its ability to live up to the full popular, humanist and bourgeois dimensions of its claims. Since, however, that state's actual social basis lay elsewhere, even the history plays offer a critical perspective on the triumph of the monarchy over the separatist feudal nobility. In his entire career Shakespeare presents many admirable aristocrats but few good rulers.

In this sense his tragic period is the climactic dramatic representation of the failings of absolutism. From his history plays, Shakespeare retains a sense of the dynamism of history, the overriding importance of national unity, and the grandeur of human aspiration.[9] *King Lear* and *Macbeth* are even set in the British Isles. On the other hand, the change of subject – from the triumph of a people to the death of a single, often isolated noble figure – suggests a declining belief in the correlation between individual action and the larger movements of social and political transformation. At the beginning of this period, for instance, *Julius Caesar* and *Hamlet* portray the heroic defeat of the finest representatives of the aristocracy by those other members of their class who embody the more typical and despicable features of power. Yet neither these plays nor *Troilus and Cressida*, the last of the Elizabethan tragedies, offers a consistent perspective on the social or ideological significance of such struggles.[10]

In *Hamlet*, for example, even before the truth about Claudius becomes known, Hamlet's inwardness is a matter of conscience, a rejection of the external and hollow rites of the Danish court. As the prince contemptuously retorts to Guildenstern later on, 'You would play upon me, you would seem to know my stops, you would pluck out the heart of my mystery, you would sound me from my lowest note to the top of my compass; ... Call me what instrument you will, though you fret me, you cannot play upon me.'[11] At the end of the play, Horatio accepts the responsibility of faithfully reporting Hamlet's story to the world:

> So shall you hear
> Of carnal, bloody, and unnatural acts,
> Of accidental judgements, casual slaughters,

Of deaths put on by cunning and forc'd
    cause,
And, in this upshot, purposes mistook
Fall'n on th' inventors' heads. All this can I
Truly deliver.

(V, ii, 385–91)

Accurate though this account may be, it utterly fails to capture the depth of
Hamlet's experience, a depth available only to the audience. Yet even to the
audience, and even to those members of it who could see in Hamlet's
identification with Wittenberg a synthesis of Renaissance and Reformation,
the precise ideological significance of *Hamlet* remains somewhat
obscure.[12]

After 1603, in the Jacobean tragedies, Shakespeare shifts his focus subtly
but crucially. Most of his protagonists in the plays of the next five years are
victims, if not always of the rise of capitalism, then at least of some
dimensions of bourgeois ideology. The private theaters, in addition to
fostering satire, may have impressed upon Shakespeare, by their very
existence and by the kind of appeal they made, the growing divisions in
English society. These divisions provide the basis of Shakespearean
tragedy. They constitute the necessary, though by no means the sufficient,
conditions of its formation. Even this qualification is by itself inadequate,
however, it is not possible to demonstrate a break in English history during
1599 sufficiently sharp to motivate so major a generic re-orientation. The
conflicts in society began earlier. On the other hand, the struggles between
Parliament and the crown increased toward the end of the 1590s and
continued thereafter, conspiracies and rebellions against the state
punctuated the first years of the new century, and the accession of James
immediately intensified preexistent antagonisms while engendering new
ones. Shakespeare's histories coincide with a period of war and depression,
his tragedies with an era of peace and prosperity. The conflicts that
underlie Shakespearean tragedy, like the oppositions on which satiric
comedy turns, are not military or economic, but social.

At this point the implications of the rejection of national history in favor
of tragedy emerge. In mediated fashion, the earlier form pits feudalism
against absolutism; the later, absolutism against capitalism. Shakespeare's
general failure to treat the two stages of the transition at once does not
constitute a defect, a distorting incompleteness of vision, however.
Virtually nowhere in western Europe did capitalism directly succeed
feudalism: the absolutist state regularly intervened. But again, and as the
dramatic forms themselves imply, that state was not a neutral entity.
Because the struggle between the feudal nobility and the centralizing
monarchy occurred within a single class, its outcome, from the point of
view of that class, was not necessarily tragic. It could therefore be treated

in the national history play. But the antagonism between absolutism and capitalism involved two classes and hence more fundamental issues. As Marx suggested in a celebrated passage,

> The *ancien régime* had a *tragic* history, so long as it was the established power in the world while liberty was a personal fancy; in short, so long as it believed and had to believe in its own validity. So long as the *ancien régime*, as an existing world order, struggled against a new world which was just coming into existence, there was on its side a historical error but no personal error. Its deadline was, therefore, tragic.[13]

Awareness of the shattering force of the new economic and social relations could easily have caused Shakespeare to retreat to a relatively uncritical defense of absolutism, to commit, in other words, the 'historical error'. But the confrontation with bourgeois ideology instead led him to recognize that the standard justifications of absolutism were equally ideological.[14] Shakespearean tragedy thus is a synthetic achievement that at times almost transcends the dual and complementary impasses of the two main kinds of late-sixteenth-century serious drama. It retains the critical freedom of earlier tragedy but without a corresponding political or social impoverishment. This political and social richness, a legacy of the history play, is in turn sufficiently freed from its nationalist constraints. The inherent limits discernible even in *1 and 2 Henry IV* no longer strictly apply. Subjecting the moral claims of the traditional order to a more searching analysis than at any other time in his career, Shakespeare is particularly sentitive to the nobility's treatment of the lower classes. The hard-won reaffirmation of aristocratic values in these plays, insofar as it occurs at all, is accompanied not only by the death of the main character, but also by the painful acknowledgement of his unfitness to rule. Between 1604 and 1608, then, Shakespeare exploits the ideological opportunities presented by his new form. Every one of the tragedies draws at least partially on the tripartite interrelationships of aristocracy, bourgeoisie, and urban and rural poor, emphasizing both irreconcilable, destructive social conflict and the creative nobility of the hero's unsuccessful struggles.[15]

As the earlier discussion of the shift to classical tragedy may have suggested, *Timon of Athens* offers the clearest account of the antagonism between aristocratic and bourgeois ideology, *Coriolanus* the most direct representation of the opposition between upper class and lower. Similar claims about the other Jacobean tragedies may well seem excessively allegorical, however. The social conflicts of early-seventeenth-century England are not so much the subject of the plays as the crucial force behind them. But of course other forces also intervene, and often in the formation of a single character. For instance, in *Othello*, significantly the earliest of these works, Iago somewhat inconsistently combines the Vice's perverse pleasure in amoral destruction with a cynical self-interest and reductive materialism that, from a certain point of view, are the harbingers of a new economic system.[16] *Macbeth* turns on a related internal tension, but this time one that is at the center of the character's consciousness as well as of the play as a whole. In murdering Duncan, a man who is at once his kinsman, his guest, and his lord, Macbeth violates specifically feudal social relations, not, of course, in the name of economic calculation, but in allegiance to an amoral ambition whose superficial rationality leads inexorably away from personal fulfilment and toward a meaningless nihilism.[17] And in *Antony and Cleopatra* the irresolvable dichotomies point to the same underlying problematic. Furthermore, the absence of the cataclysmic feel of the two earlier tragedies, combined with the supersession of the protagonists by the pragmatic and businesslike Caesar, perhaps indicates a resigned acceptance of change previously resisted, but ultimately unavoidable.

Lower-class expression is also polyvocal in these tragedies. It falls loosely into two overlapping categories, an indebtedness to the practices of popular dramaturgy and an explicit portrayal of popular concerns and grievances. The first is perhaps most important when it involves the assimilation of popular elements into a major character, such as Hamlet or Iago. But of course the popular heritage also plays a significant structural role in the persons of comic, lower-class figures who directly or indirectly comment on the main plot. From the tragedies alone the list would include the gravediggers in *Hamlet*, Thersites in *Troilus and Cressida*, the Porter in *Macbeth*, Apemantus in *Timon of Athens*, and the simple countryman who brings the heroine the asp in *Antony and Cleopatra*.[18] This first popular dimension, however, is evidently less prominent in the classical tragedies and especially in the works from after 1605. In a sense, then, the unusually overt and extended presentation of lower-class ideology in *Coriolanus* compensates for the decline of a traditional mode of popular dramaturgy. Finally, as will later become clear, *King Lear* achieves the fullest synthesis among the tragedies not only of these two appropriations of popular culture, but also of the dual social oppositions, between upper class and lower and between aristocratic and bourgeois ideology.

A comparable national perspective often informs Spanish heroic drama of this period. In another respect, however, a focus on Shakespearean tragedy leads to an overemphasis on the differences between the English and Spanish stages. From 1599 to 1608, the vast majority of pieces performed in the private theaters were comedies. As noted above, however, tragedy did indeed supersede the national history play not only in Shakespeare's career, but in the public theater as a whole. Thus the generic differences between the two national dramas after 1600 remain undeniable. The social and theatrical changes in Spain during the first two decades of the seventeenth century were less pronounced than those that had occurred in England by 1608. In particular, the relative absence of a conflict between modes of production reduced the ideological space for tragedy.[19] Peninsular heroic drama does not consistently reveal the failure of the aristocracy to adapt to a new political situation, much less jettison the Spanish people as an object of representation. The national history play, like romantic comedy, continued to flourish long after the turn of the century.

Indeed, Tirso de Molina's celebrated *La prudencia en la mujer* (probably 1622)[20] represents something like the apotheosis of the genre. At least ambiguously feminist in perspective,[21] it may be seen as a nontragic reworking of some of the major issues of *Bamba*, with a woman replacing a peasant as guardian of the state. The potential interchangeability of sexual oppression and class oppression, or at least the association between the two, generally characterizes early-seventeenth-century serious drama in both countries. More particularly, *La prudencia en la mujer*, drawing its subject from the political conflicts of the late Middle Ages – its historical setting is virtually contemporaneous with that of *Edward II* – ties its feminist concerns to a national and dynastic focus. It turns on the struggle between aristocracy and monarchy, between class and state. Tirso's allegiances are unambiguously with the latter. In all these respects the work is perhaps the closest Spanish analogue not to Shakespearean tragedy, but to the Shakespearean national history play. A national and dynastic perspective also shapes the second part of Castro's *Las mocedaes del Cid* (1610?–15?).[22] Both plays, however, present unusually sordid views of the high aristocracy. The struggle between the nobility and the crown recurs at the end of the century in Bances Candamo's *El escalvo en grillos de oro* (1692),[23] although the plot is set in imperial Rome rather than Spain and its composition for a court audience further narrows the frame of reference.

Yet these elements of continuity and the corresponding absence of tragedy should not obscure the real break with earlier serious drama that occurred after 1600 in response to the growing national crisis. The Spanish equivalent to Shakespearean tragedy took the form of a symptomatic moral belt tightening, an aggressive effort to cope with the unfamiliar experience of defeat, an extreme reconsolidation of aristocratic ideology, a reassertion of the values that had accompanied earlier success, and hence a return to the past for a stylized and exaggerated code of honor.[24] A fundamental issue throughout seventeenth-century Spanish drama,[25] the honor code, though traceable to primitive Germanic society, is rooted in the material and ideological conditions of the feudal aristocracy, the operative component of which was the complementary combination of military vocation and freedom from manual labor. Its hierarchical assumptions were an international inheritance of the European ruling class in the Renaissance. During this period, it served to perpetuate sexual inequality

far less in the Protestant North than in Catholic, and especially
Mediterranean Catholic, nations. The unusual importance of honor in
Spain was also a consequence of the atypically strong survival of feudal
relations, at least by western European standards, as well as of the legacy
of Moorish influences. The Reconquest and the subsequent subjugation of
the New World, both agents of that survival, also contributed to the
diffusion of the concept of honor to classes beneath the nobility.[26]

Most recent discussion of this phenomenon, though properly attuned to
the formative role of the Middle Ages, has nonetheless tended to ignore
these particular influences and to concentrate instead on the problem of the
conversos (Jews forced to accept Catholicism) and the resulting societal
obsession with *limpieza de sangre* (purity of blood).[27] It is easy enough to see
how attention to the racial and religious purity of blood might reinforce
pride in the social purity of blood. But *limpieza de sangre* could also work
against hierarchical principles, becoming a vehicle for an egalitarian notion
of honor of sorts and as such a mystified ideological weapon of the poor
against the rich.[28] Given the general context of the Inquisition and the
Counter-Reformation, this was possible because the nobility in the towns
intermarried with men and women of Jewish descent more frequently than
did the rural masses, because it was easier to trace the lineage of an
aristocrat than of a peasant, and because wealthy Jews had traditionally
served as fiscal agents of the state and thus as direct oppressors of the
lower classes. Yet the effectiveness of *limpieza de sangre* was fairly limited
when directed against the higher and more powerful circles of the
aristrocracy. It is nonetheless far preferable to see the concern with purity
of blood as an issue in its own right that sometimes became an adjunct of
class struggle than to reverse the relationship, as some contemporary
scholars do, and to transform depictions of social conflict into covert
allusions to racial antagonism.[29]

As a defining feature of early-seventeenth-century Spanish heroic drama,
the code of honor did not entail an abandonment of affairs of the nation.
But it did deflect attention from the destiny of the state in general and the
conflict between feudalism and absolutism in particular toward a
demonstration of the efficacy of an ideal norm of aristocratic conduct in
protecting the nation and its ruling class. Perhaps the central form of
political drama was the *comedia de privanza* (play about royal favor),
cultivated assiduously during the first third of the century and
intermittently thereafter. *La prudencia en la mujer* and *El esclavo en grillos de
oro* both belong ambiguously to this subgenre, which often has a tragic
outcome. In general, however, *comedias de privanza* concentrate on the
emotional and personal side of the relationship between king and favorite
rather than on its larger political significance.[30]

An extreme example of the attenuation of national concerns is provided
by Alarcon's *Ganar amigos* (1619-21),[31] in which the *privado*'s extraordinary

spiritual nobility leads him to increasing peril in a society incapable of understanding the selfless motives underlying his behavior. As the title suggests, however, his conduct simultaneously wins him friends, who are furthermore impelled by his example and by the complications of the plot to adopt for themselves the protagonist's exalted standard of honor, in order to restore him to his former felicity. The play concludes with the aristocracy and the crown at a higher moral plane than before. Yet the most desirable female marries a rapist, the hero ends up with a woman of questionable character, and the second most honorable figure in the play is left unwed. Since this resolution is entirely a consequence of the code of honor,[32] *Ganar amigos* unwittingly reveals, against Alarcon's obvious intention, that the exercise of honor even by the entire aristocracy does not completely answer to that class's needs. In this respect the play has affinities with the tragedies of Jonson and Chapman.

Although national and dynastic issues are more prominent in the famous first part of Castro's *Las mocedades del Cid* (1612?–15?),[33] even here there is no absolute equation of aristocratic honor and the triumph of Spain. Honor dominates the central love plot and is intermeshed with affairs of state through the acts of military prowess by which the Cid wins over first the king and then Ximena. But it has almost nothing to do with matters of royal succession or with the conduct of the heir, Prince Sancho, and his sister Urraca. The continuation of the play moves this background activity to center stage. In *Le Cid*, Corneille excises it entirely as part of a general process of narrowing and intensification: his adaptation, after all, is by definition no longer a national history play.[34] But at the same time, he fully integrates honor and politics. *Le Cid* works toward the accommodation of private feudal values to the needs of the absolutist state. The absence of a comparably complete fusion in *Las mocedades del Cid* is an indication both of the comparative weakness of Habsburg absolutist pressure on the nobility and of the limited potency of aristocratic honor as a solution to the crisis of Spain.

It would be wrong, however, to stress such unresolved contradictions while ignoring the at least superficially successful achievement of reconciliation and related preservation of a conservative social order. The early-seventeenth-century Spanish nobility, as depicted in the public theater, retains much of its traditional vocation as a class. Its ideals and behavior, however exclusive, continued to possess a corporatist dimension. The heroine of *La prudencia en la mujer* is identified with humble shepherds, who come to her aid at the climactic moment of the play. In *Ganar amigos* a servant shows himself the moral equal of most of the aristocracy and accompanies this demonstration with a diatribe against class-based definitions of honor that is ideologically of a piece with the critical treatment of the protagonist in *La verdad sospechosa*. *Las mocedades del Cid* is profoundly indebted to the *romances* and hence to a popular conception of national history.[35] This interclass perspective aligns Spanish heroic drama with Shakespearean tragedy.

Yet the fullest utilization of popular culture on the Spanish stage occurs in peasant honor drama, a form that finds an important analogue in English bourgeois tragedy. The fundamental role of *romances* in such plays as Lope's *Peribañez y el comendador de Ocaña* (1604–14)[36] and Luis Velez de Guevara's *La serrana de la Vera* (1613)[37] is paralleled in Heywood's *A Woman Killed with Kindness* (1603).[38] The relics of pagan festival preserved in many of the peasant plays[39] may be compared to the Morris dance in Dekker, John Ford, and William Rowley's *The Witch of Edmonton* (1621). Popular parody or qualification of the serious plot occurs briefly in *A Yorkshire Tragedy* (1606) and in *Arden of Feversham* (1591), and more profoundly, especially in the character of Nicholas, in *A Woman Killed with Kindness*.[40] There is something of this sort in Lope's *El mejor alcalde el rey* (1620–23) and more, in Nuno, in Calderon's *El alcalde de Zalamea* (1636?, early 1649s?). But the true peasant *gracioso* is almost a contradiction in terms.[41] At any rate, the popular dimension of the Spanish plays is carried above all by the protagonists themselves. Relatedly, the vast majority of bourgeois tragedies and peasant dramas have national settings. In addition, most of the English works and a number of the Spanish plays – Lope's *Fuente Ovejuna* (probably 1612–14) and *El mejor alcalde el rey* among them – are based on actual events.

The resemblances between the two forms extend to ideology as well. A pervasively religious context, common in the Spanish plays and perhaps most evident in *Peribáñez*, regularly emerges at the conclusion of the English works. In the latter it is associated with a rapid sequence of repentance, pardon, and promise of salvation that blunts the tragic force of the action,[42] just as happens in *La serrana de la Vera* through the universally acknowledged justness of the heroine's punishment.[43] The apparent generic contrast between all these tragedies and most of the peasant drama is thus somewhat blurred. Again, the comfortable rural domesticity that provides the backdrop for the plays involves an implicit association of wealth, concentrated in landed private property, with moral virtue.[44] One thinks especially of Frankford in Heywood's tragedy, Old Carter in the *Witch of Edmonton*, Peribáñez, Pedro Crespo in *El alcalde de Zalamea*, Juan Labrador in Lope's *El villano en su rincón* (1611), and the titular figure in Francisco de Rojas Zorrilla's (?) *Del rey abajo, ninguno o El labrador más honrado, García del Castañar* (1631?–44?).[45] But for a number of these characters, the highest satisfaction of their middling, private existence derives from married love, the threat to which causes them extreme misery. Several of the plays accordingly reveal a transformation of extreme aristocratic and masculine notions of honor into what for the time represented a far more humane system of morality, implicitly based on a conviction of at least relative sexual and social equality.

Strictly speaking, however, most of the protagonists in Spanish peasant drama or English bourgeois tragedy do not belong to the bourgeoisie. This is evident enough with the peasant heroes, whose birth is either humble or, in *El mejor alcalde el rey and Del rey abajo, ninguno*, aristocratic – an incongruity that owes something to the geographical vagaries of peninsular history. Similarly, the main characters of the English plays are consistently members of the gentry: *A Yorkshire Tragedy* scarely extends beyond that class. Yet not only were the gentry integrally linked to the rise of capitalism; the themes and attitudes that shape the plays of both countries possess in retrospect a distinctively bourgeois quality. Although one would of course not want to push this argument too far with the Spanish plays, it is surely symptomatic that Lukács, after twice referring to Pedro Crespo as a peasant, goes on to describe *El alcalde de Zalamea* as one 'of the important bourgeois dramas'.[46] Even Noël Salomon who labors under no such misconception, remarks: 'in the opening in a still feudal horizon, this aspiration of the peasant to issue forth on the free sea of dignity already causes us to catch a glimpse of the distant brightness of equality of the bourgeois type'.[47] Yet the plays also reveal the problematic quality of this consciousness. The placidity of everyday life in all of them is interrupted by sudden bursts of violence that are often engendered by sexual conflict and that produce significant formal and ideological contradictions.

The subject may be best approached, however, by reversing direction and considering the major contrasts between peasant drama and bourgeois tragedy. The latter category comprises only a miniscule percentage of the plays performed on the English Renaissance stage. Peasant dramas, on the other hand, are not only far more numerous, but also far more influential: *Peribáñez, Fuente Ovejuana*, and *El alcalde de Zalamea* – admittedly, ideologically heterodox specimens – have won a place in European culture as a whole. This distinction ultimately depends on the difference between two modes of production. Bourgeois tragedy is rooted in early English capitalism. There is some interesting juxtaposition of classes in *A Woman Killed with Kindness* and *The Witch of Edmonton*. *Arden of Feversham* briefly but suggestively dramatizes the social conflict over the land that helped lead to the initial formation of the British working class. But all the plays reveal a social narrowness inseparable from the historical immaturity of the English bourgeoisie and of English capitalism as late as the early seventeenth century. They take on neither national politics nor class struggle. The deepening conflict between absolutism and capitalism, like the incipient one between capitalist and proletarian, is beyond their range. Bourgeois tragedy is static: it conceives of the bourgeoisie neither as a rising force in conflict with the traditional order nor as an established class challenged from below. Almost despite itself, it points beyond the present to what could not yet be thought, at a time when aristocratic ideology remained hegemonic.

The limits of bourgeois self-consciousness, pervasively evident in these plays, especially take the form of an uncertain relationship between the represented action and the conventional values by which it is judged. In *Arden of Feversham*, the homiletic conclusion seems strangely inadequate to the passions and inner conflicts that motivate the characters. The multiple plots of *A Woman Killed with Kindness* and *The Witch of Edmonton* raise similar difficulties. Although the two plots of Heywood's play result in a generalization and fertile ambiguity of meaning,[48] they also reveal the dramatist's reluctance to choose between the behavior of different social classes, a desire to subsume real oppositions into a specious unity, and, most important, a sense that the central bourgeois values lack sufficient generalizing forces in themselves, that they require an aristocratic buttress. Similarly, in *The Witch of Edmonton*, although the crimes in both plots seem to have social causes, the audience is actually presented with two different worlds. One, relatively realistic, involves the gentry and yeomanry; the other, pervaded by superstition, folklore, and witchcraft, concerns the peasantry. Human freedom is insisted upon, but, unlike the drama and literature of later centuries, the play can demonstrate the seriousness of everyday life only by diabolical intervention.[49] In *Othello*, on the other hand, Shakespeare superimposes these two perspectives by introducing Iago's apparently demonic powers into a domestic tragedy. The play's famous double time – a sign of ideological ambivalence – socializes this metaphysical dimension. Whereas the compressed temporality lends intensity to the action, allusions to a more leisurely chronology anchor the tragedy in a more realistic social world. Finally, and perhaps most telling, the main plot of *A Woman Killed with Kindness* simultaneously asserts the equality and inequality of man and woman, of husband and wife.

The continued domination of the nobility that lies behind these evasions is in the Spanish peasant drama, by contrast, a crucial source of strength. The wealthy protagonists, like the aristocracy, exploit lower-class labor and in this sense are miniature analogues, rather than antagonists, of the traditional rulers of the countryside. Yet their real historical models, by their very success and the further expectations it aroused, did come repeatedly into conflict with the nobility. Their struggle, then turned on the basic coercive relationship of feudal society between lord and peasant. This irreconcilable contradiction distinguishes peasant drama from bourgeois tragedy, and indeed from nearly all other Renaissance drama and popular culture as well.[50] An unexpansionist, political quiescent bourgeoisie did not automatically find itself opposed to a feudal nobility: neither class depended on the exploitation of the other. But much of the peasantry, as a normal and inevitable part of its daily life, had a portion of its surplus product appropriated by the aristocracy. The centrality of this experience made it possible for peasant drama to retain a national dimension, evoking not only the monarchy and its wars, but also the intraclass conflict between the aristocracy and the absolutist state. A few of the plays, moreover, did so indirectly enough to avoid the inherent ideological constraints of the national history play. For these reasons, though peasant drama is rooted in less modern relations of production than is domestic tragedy, its resonance for the social conflicts of the contemporary industrialized West remains far greater.

The triumph of the peasant play about 1610 probably depended not only on the general social conditions already outlined, but also on more immediate events and relationships, in all of which Lope, the founder of the form, may have had a personal stake. These included the expulsion of the *moriscos* between 1609 and 1614, which gave added ideological weight to the assertion of *limpieza de sangre*; temporary intraaristocratic conflicts; and declining respect for the military orders. A less specific impulse was the long-term struggle between the peasantry and the troops that, against its will, were quartered in its villages.[51] But the plays also grew out of a long prior generic evolution, a gradual process of popularization, a movement from pastoral to peasantry, a transfer of attention from aristocratic desires to peasant needs. The increasing intrusion of reasonably authentic aspects of peasant life into pastoral drama produced an important modification in the ideological function of the form. To be sure, the theatrical image of rural retreat, especially in a play like *El villano en su rincón*, remained for the nobility a fantasy of freedom from the combined pressures of court and city. The apparent intensification of the honor code may even have reinforced this meaning. But like that code, the idealization of the peasantry seems to have been a means of returning to the sources of the Spanish people, to a lost vitality that could be recovered, surprisingly enough, only in agricultural labor. For the aristocracy, then, peasant drama may have come to constitute a fantasy of precapitalist work.

But in *Peribáñez* the ideological impetus has changed even more radically. Motifs formerly used to ridicule the peasantry are refashioned to add to the dignity of the class, the devices of pastoral, for instance, now applying to Peribáñez and his wife Casilda. More important, in a manner adumbrated by *Bamba*, the very literary resources of aristocratic culture are called into question. Peribáñez can say of Casilda:

El olivar más cargado
de aceitunas me parece
menos hermoso, y el prado
que por el mayo florece,
sólo del alba pisado
    (The olive-grove most laden / with olives and the meadow / that flowers
in May, / trampled only by the dawn, / seem to me less beautiful.
                        [1146–50]).

But the comendador, his belated, upper-class rival for her affections, must fall back on:

Hermosa labradora,
más bella, más lucida
que ya del sol vestida
la colorada aurora;
sierra de blanca nieve
que los rayos de amor vencer se atreve
(Beautiful peasant, / more beautiful more shining / than the colored dawn / already dressed in sunlight; mountain of white snow, / which the rays of love dare to conquer.

[1522–7]).

Peribáñez knows and loves Casilda and compares her to the earth; the comendador knows the language of love and compares her to the sky. Again, when describing an encounter with Casilda, the comendador says:

yo, con los humildes ojos,
mostraba que sus enojos
me daban golpes mortales.
(I, with humble eyes, showed that her anger gave me mortal blows.

[2, 3, 1253–5]).

The appropriation here of a Petrarchan love conceit bears a complex relationship to reality. In portraying himself as the servant or victim of Casilda, the aristocratic lover inverts the actual social situation. Yet this reversal neatly establishes the proper ethical order, since the comendador's language expresses his moral inferiority.[52]

Nonetheless, modern critics tend to minimize the significance of class conflict both in this work and in the peasant drama in general.[53] Of course most of the plays find means of softening or evading the issue. In *Del rey abajo, ninguno*, for instance, not only does the peasant hero turn out to be of noble birth, his enemy, whom he had assumed and feared was the king, also proves to be simply another aristocrat. *El mejor alcalde el rey* removes political autonomy from the peasantry, reserving all power for the wise, just, and disguised monarch – a familiar popular motif.[54] The profound sexual and social rebellion of *La serrana de la Vera* is ideologically censored, at least in part, from the point of view of traditional morality.[55] A concluding peasant acquiescence that violates the emotional force of *El villano en su rincon* resolves the relatively plotless but genuine ideological conflict between rural retirement and courtly concerns. More generally, the transfer of social and economic struggles to the arena of sexual relations, despite having certain historical analogues and despite expressing

111

authentic feminist concerns, helps avoid the full tragic implications of irreconcilable antagonism.

But in at least three plays – *Fuente Ovejuna*, *Peribáñez*, and *El alcalde de Zalamea* – even most of these limited qualifications do not apply. Not only can royal intervention at the ends of these works be interpreted equally well as reactionary corporatism and progressive affirmation; the role of the monarchy is essentially limited to the acceptance of a fait accompli. *Fuente Ovejuna* may be left for separate, more extended treatment. In *Peribáñez* the king abandons his plan to punish the hero when he hears Peribanez's defense of private vengeance. But he retains an aristocratic sense of surprise that a peasant could act on such noble values. And in *El alcalde de Zalamea*, though the monarch agrees with Pedro Crespo about the guilt of the offending captain, he denies Zalamea's jurisdictional rights until presented with the captain's corpse. It is hard to imagine how a fully sympathetic portrayal of the peasantry literally getting away with murder at the expense of the aristocracy with the crown confined to ambivalent acquiescence, could have served to reinforce the social status quo.

Yet the monarchist resolutions of the plots cannot be lightly dismissed. Salomon's solution to the problem does justice to their prominence. These peasant plays, he argues,

> are an attempt to 'comprehend' (embrace) some of the internal conflicts of monarcho-seigneurial society and to master the tangling up of its contradictions by a sort of ideological miracle. Thanks to monarchist sentiment and thanks to the appearance of the royal figure in the denouement, the accumulated problems disappear in an absence of problems or, more exactly, these pass away through having received their solution and remain not open but closed as if by decree. Finally, the unanimity about the king, which emerged from these 'comedias', made it possible to blur the existing disagreements in the interior of monarcho-seigneurial society and gave the spectators the illusion that it was prefected, coherent, definitive.[56]

Thus as in much Renaissance drama, the form is designed to reconcile the irreconcilable. But peasant plays, unlike most domestic tragedy, for instance, present a conflict between what is said at the end and what is shown throughout. What is said points to integration; what is shown, to revolution. Similarly, Shakespeare's tragedies portray violent upheaval, only to end either without reconciliation, or with a plot resolution that violates the logic of prior events, or at least with a concluding statement inadequate to the experience of the play. Despite the generic difference, Spanish peasant drama should ultimately be compared with Shakespearean, rather than bourgeois, tragedy. Each group of plays represents the most profound legacy of the popular tradition in its nation to the public theater. In the absence of that institution no combination of social conditions with literary and dramaturgical heritage could have produced such works. The formal resolution of social conflict in Shakespearean tragedy and in the Spanish peasant play may be understood as the full dramatic realization of the inherent contradiction between artisanal base and absolutist superstructure in the public theater.

Notes

1. SHAKESPEARE, *Coriolanus*, ed. Harry Levin, in *William Shakespeare: The Complete Works*, gen.ed. Harbage (Baltimore: Penguin, 1969), 1, ii, 77–80.

2. CHRISTOPHER HILL, 'The Many-Headed Monster,' in *Change and Continuity in Seventeenth Century England* (Cambridge: Harvard University Press, 1975), p.182.

3. See ANSELM SCHLÖSSER, 'Reflections upon Shakespeare's *Coriolanus'*, *Philologica Pragensia* 6 (1963): 11–21; SIEGEL, *Shakespeare in his Time and Ours*, (Notre Dame : Indiana, 1968) pp. 149–55.

4. JONAS A.BARISH, introduction to Jonson, *Sejanus His Fall*, ed. Barish (New Haven: Yale University Press, 1965), pp. 1–24.

5. SHAKESPEARE, *Timon of Athens*, ed. Charlton Hinman, in *William Shakespeare*, gen. ed. Harbage, IV, iii 29–30. For expressions like Timon's, see THOMAS LODGE, *An Alarum against Vsurers* (London, 1584), sig. B1ᵛ and C1ᵛ; THOMAS BELL, *The Speculation of Vsurie* (London, 1596), sig. A2¹.

6. See E.C. PETTET, '*Timon of Athens*: The Disruption of Feudal Morality', *Review of English Studies* 23 (1947): 321–36; KENNETH MUIR, '*Timon of Athens* and the Cash-Nexus', *Modern Quarterly Miscellany* 1 (1947): 57–76; LEONARD GOLDSTEIN, 'Alcibiades' Revolt in *Timon of Athens'*, *Zeitschrift für Anglistik und Amerikanistik* 15 (1967): 257–78: Seigel pp. 155–62.

7. See JOHN F. DANBY, *Poets on Fortune's Hill: Studies in Sidney, Shakespeare, Beaumont and Fletcher* (Port Washington, N.Y.: Kennikat Press, 1952), pp. 128–51; DIPAK NANDY, 'The Realism of *Antony and Cleopatra'*, in *Shakespeare in a Changing World*, ed. Arnold Kettle (New York: International Publishers, 1964), pp. 172–94.

8. Marxist critics who take the opposite position, emphasizing the progressive, bourgeois, or radical and democratic humanist essence of Shakespeare of the state he supported, or of both,or who at least place primacy on his ideological independence of any class position, include, but are not limited to: A.L. MORTON, 'Shakespeare's Historical Outlook'. *Shakespeare Jahrbuch* (Weimar) 100/101 (1964/65): 216: MIKLÓS SZENCZI, 'The Nature of Shakespeare's Realism', *Shakespeare Jahrbuch* (Weimar) 102 (1966): 50; HEINEMANN, 'Shakespearean Contradictions and Social Change', *Science and Society* 41 (1977): 7–16; ANNETTE T. RUBINSTEIN, 'Bourgeois Equality in Shakespeare', *Science and Society* 41 (1977): 25–35; WEIMANN, 'The Soul of the Age: Towards a Historical Approach to Shakespeare,' in *Shakespeare in a Changing World*, ed. Kettle, pp. 17–42; idem, *Drama und Wirklichkeit in der Shakespearezeit: Ein Beitrag zur Entwicklungsgeschichte des elisabethanischen Theaters* (Halle [Saale]: Veb Max

Niemeyer Verlag, 1958), e.g., p. 310. Some of these positions are challenged by MICHAEL B. FOLSOM, 'Shakespeare the Marxist', *Studies on the Left* 5, no. 4 (1965): 106–19.

9. For a similar point, see A.A. SMIRNOV, 'Shakespeare, the Renaissance and the Age of Barroco', in *Shakespeare in the Soviet Union*, ed. Roman Samarin and Alexander Nikolyukin, trans. Avril Pyman (Moscow: Progress Publishers, 1966), pp. 58–83.

10. For a view of *Troilus and Cressida* as a critique of capitalism, see RAYMOND SOUTHHALL, *Literature and the Rise of Capitalism: Critical Essays Mainly on the 16th and 17th Centuries* (London: Lawrence and Wishart, 1973), pp. 70–85.

11. SHAKESPEARE, *Hamlet*, ed. Harold Jenkins (London: Methuen, 1982), III, ii, 355-63. The subsequent reference is cited in the text.

12. THOMAS METSCHER, 'Shakespeare in the Context of Renaissance Europe', *Science and Society* **41** (1977): 20–2.

13. KARL MARX, 'Contribution to the Critique of Hegel's *Philosophy of Right*: Introduction', in *The Marx–Engels Reader*, ed. Robert C. Tucker (New York: Norton, 1972), pp. 14–15.

14. TERRY EAGLETON, *Criticism and Ideology: A Study in Marxist Literary Theory* (London: NLB, 1976), p. 96.

15. GEORG LUKÁCS, *The Historical, Novel*, trans. Hannah and Stanley Mitchell (Boston: Beacon, 1963), pp. 99, 122, discusses the nobility of struggle in tragedy. KENNETH MUIR, 'Shakespeare and Politics', in *Shakespeare in a Changing World*, ed. Kettle, pp. 65–83, reviews changes in Shakespeare's attitudes. On this subject, see also Morton, pp. 219–20, 224–26.

16. On *Othello* see G.M. MATTHEWS, '*Othello* and the Dignity of Man', in *Shakespeare in a Changing World*, ed. Kettle, pp. 123–45; GEORG MURI, '*Othello*', *Shakespeare Jahrbuch* (Weimar) **104** (1968): 85–108.

17. On *Macbeth* see J.K. WALTON, '*Macbeth*', in *Shakespeare in a Changing World*, ed. Kettle, pp. 102–22.

18. ROBERT WEIMANN, *Shakespeare and the Popular Tradition in the Theatre: Studies in the Social Dimension of Dramatic Form and Function*, ed. Robert Schwartz (Baltimore: Johns Hopkins University Press, 1978), pp. 215–46, especially 238–9.

19. For alternative explanations, see RAYMOND R. MacCURDY, 'Lope de Vega y la pretendida inhabihdad española para la tragedia: Resumen crítico', in *Homenaje a William L. Fichter*, ed. Kossoff and Amor y Vazquez, pp. 525–35; idem, *The Tragic Fall: Don Alvaro de Luna and Other Favorites in Spanish Golden Age Drama*, North Carolina Studies in the Romance Languages and Literatures, no. 197 (Chapel Hill: University of North Carolina Department of Romance Languages, 1978), pp. 17–37.

20. MacCURDY, introduction to his edition of '*El burlador de Sevilla y convidado de piedra*' and '*La prudencia en la mujer*', by Tirso de Molina (New York: Dell, 1965), p.26.

21. But see McKENDRICK, *Women and Society in the Spanish Drama of the Golden Age* (London: CUP. 1974), pp. 199, 201–3, 204, 207.

22. COURTNEY BRUERTON, 'The Chronology of the *Comedias* of Guillén de Castro', *Hispanic Review* 12 (1944): 150. See STURGIS E. LEAVITT, 'Una comedia sin

paralelo: *Las Hazanas del Cid*, de Guillén de Castro', in *Homenaje a William L. Fichter*, ed. Kossoff and Amor y Vázquez, pp. 429–38.

23. E.M. WILSON and DUNCAN MOIR, *The Golden Age: Drama 1492–1700, Vol. 6 in A Literary History of Spain* (London: Ernest Benn. 1971), p.141.

24. For the change in Lope's treatment of honor in this direction after 1600 see DONALD R. LARSON, *The Honor Plays of Lope de Vega* (Cambridge: Harvard University Press, 1977), p. 161.

25. General discussions of honor on the *Siglo de Oro* stage include RAMÓN MENÉNDEZ PIDAL, 'Del honor en el teatre español', in *De Cervantes y Lope de Vega* (Buenos Aires: Espasa-Calpe, 1940), pp. 153-84; ARNOLD REICHENBERGER, 'The Uniqueness of the "Comedia"', *Hispanic Review* **27** (1959): 307-9: C.A. JONES 'Spanish Honour as Historical Phenomenon, Convention, and Artistic Motive', *Hispanic Review* **3** (1965): 32-9.

26. J.H. ELLIOT, *Imperial Spain, 1469-1716* (New York: St. Martin's Press, 1964), pp. 215, 229, 303-4.

27. See, for example, AMÉRICO CASTRO, 'El drama de la honra en la literature dramatica', in *De la edad conflictiva*, vol. 1. *El drama de la honra en España y en su literatura*, 2d ed. (Madrid: Taurus, 1963), pp. 59–107; ANTONIE A. VAN BERYSTERVELDT. *Répercussions du souci de la purete de sang sur la conception de l'honneur dans la 'comedia nueva' espagnole* (Leiden: Brill, 1966): JOSEPH H. SILVERMAN, 'Some Aspects of Literature and Life in the Golden Age of Spain', in *Estudios de literature espanola ofrecidos a Marcos A Morinigo* (Madrid: Insula, 1971), pp. 133-70.

28. For the two dimensions of honor outlined here, see GUSTAVO CORREA 'El doble aspecto de la honra en el teatro del siglo xvii', *Hispanic Reverse* **26** (1958): 99-107. The egalitarian and democratic aspects of Spanish society are emphasized, indeed overemphasized by CARMEN OLGA BRENES, *El sentimiento democratico en el teatro de Juan Ruiz de Alarcon* (Valencia: Editorial Castalia, 1960), pp. 13-32, 45-58.

29. The argument here follows ELLIOTT, pp. 213-17, and SALOMON, pp. 114-25, against the position represented by the scholars cited in n.68 above.

30. LEICESTER BRADNER, 'The Theme of *Privanza* in Spanish and English Drama, 1590-1625', in *Homenajo a William L. Fichter*, ed. Kossoff and Amor y Vazquez, p.106; MACCURDY, *The Tragic Fall, passim*.

31. Date: SISTER MARY AUSTIN CAUVIN. O.P. 'The *Comedia de Privanzo* in the Seventeenth Century', Ph.D. diss., University of Pennsylvania, 1957, p.432, n.7. For the relative lack of political interest in *Ganar amagos*, see p. 431.

32. CAUVIN, p.439.

33. BRUERTON, p.150.

34. For a recent comparison of the two plays, see WILLIAM E. WILSON, *Guillén de Castro* (New York: Twayne, 1973), pp. 77–82.

35. See MENÉDEZ PIDAL, *La epopeya castellana a través de la literature española*, 2d edn (1910; rpt. Madrid: Espasa-Calpe, 1959), pp. 191-20).

36. For the continuing debate on the date, see ALONSO ZAMORA VICENTE (ed), '*Peribáñez y el comendador de Ocaña' y 'La dama boba'*, by Lope de Vega (Madrid: Clásicos Castellanos, 1963), pp. vii–xiv. Subsequent references to *Peribáñez* are to

this edition and are cited in the text. For the function of the romance, see Salomon, pp. 334, 555-8.

37. SALOMON, p.22; *Romance:* Menédez Pidal, *La epopeya castellana*, p.201.

38. MICHEL GRIVELET, *Thomas Heywood et le drame domestique élizabéthain* (Paris: Didier, 1957), pp. 203-4.

39. Salomon, p.663.

40. ARTHUR BROWN, 'Thomas Heywood's Dramatic Art', in *Essays on Shakespeare and Elizabethan Drama in Honor of Hardin Craig*, ed. Richard Hosley (Columbia: University of Missouri Press, 1962), p.336.

41. SALOMON, pp. 160-3, who perhaps overstates the case.

42. Cf. T.S. ELIOT, *Selected Essays* (New York): Harcourt, Brace and World, 1950), p.158.

43. See MCKENDRICK, pp. 115-18.

44. For the Spanish plays see Salomon, pp. 236-307, 755-78.

45. The range of dates, relevant only if the play is by Rojas, indicates his first known association with court literary circles, on the one hand, and the closing of the theaters, on the other. Rojas died in 1648. See JEAN TESTAS, introduction to his edition of *Del rey abojo, ninguno o El labrador más honrado, García del Castañar*, by Francisco de Rojas Zorrilla (Madrid: Editorial Castalia, 1971), pp. 17-27.

46. LUKÁCS, *Historical Novel*, pp. 104, 119, and, for the quoted phrase, 129.

47. SALOMON, p. 832.

48. GRIVELET, *Thomas Heywood*. p. 206; idem, 'The Simplicity of Thomas Heywood', *Shakespeare Survey* **14** (1961): 65.

49. Cf. the title of an older work in the field: OTELIA CROMWELL, *Thomas Heywood: A Study in the Elizabethan Drama of Everyday Life* (1928; rpt.n.p.: Archon Books, 1969).

50. PETER BURKE, *Popular Culture in Early Modern Europe* (New York: Harper and Row. 1978), p.159.

51. SALOMON, pp. 819-28, 863, 890-7. The subsequent discussion is indebted to this work.

52. On these issues, as well as on the play in general, see AUBRUN and JOSÉ F. MONTESINOS prologo to their edition of *Peribáñez* (Paris: Hachette, 1943). pp. xv-Xlviii: JOSÉ MANUEL BLECUA, 'Análisis de la comedia', in his edition of *Peribáñez* (Zaragoza: Editorial Ebro, 1944), pp. 9-22; WILSON, *Spanish and English Literature of the 16th and 17th centuries: Studies in Discretion, Illusion and Mutability* (Cambridge: Cambridge University Press, 1980), pp. 130-54; R.G. SANCHEZ, 'El contenido irónico-teatral en el *Peribáñez* de Lope Vega', *Clavileño* 5 (1954); 17-25; CORREA, 'El doble aspecto de honor en *Peribáñez y el comendador de Ocaña*', *Hispanic Review* **26** (1958): 188-99; ALISON TURNER, 'The Dramatic Function of Imagery and Symbolism in *Peribáñez* and *El caballero de Olmedo*', *Symposium* **20** (1966): 174-86.

53. The most extreme example of this position is JOSE ANTONIO MARAVALL, *Teatro y literatura en la sociedad barroca* (Madrid: Seminarios y Ediciones, 1973), pp. 57-145. But see also EVA R. PRICE, 'The Peasant Plays of Lope de Vega', *Modern Language*

Forum **20** (1937): 214-19; R.D.F. PRING-MILL, introduction to his edition of *Lope de Vega (Five Plays)*, trans. Jill Booty (New York: Hill and Wang, 1961), pp. xx–xxvi; R.O. JONES, 'Poets and Peasants', in *Homenaje a William L. Fichter*, ed. Kossoff and Amor y Vázquez, pp. 341-55.

54. BURKE, p. 152.

55. See DUVIGNAUD, p.197, for a general application of this paradigm to English and Spanish Renaissance drama.

56. SALOMON, pp. 910-11.

ROBERT WEIMANN   *SHAKESPEARE'S THEATER: TRADITION AND EXPERIMENT**

Robert Weimann is Professor of Literature at the Academy of Arts in what was until recently the German Democratic Republic, in Berlin. The book from which the following extract is taken, first appeared in a slightly different form in German in 1967 as *Tradition des Volkstheaters: Soziologie, Dramaturgie, Gestaltung*, (Berlin, 1967). It was revised, and subsequently translated by Robert Schwarz, and was published by Johns Hopkins University Press in 1978 as *Shakespeare and The Popular Tradition in the Theater*. Weimann's book, and his approach, is not to be confused with S.L.Bethell's much earlier *Shakespeare and The Popular Dramatic Tradition* (London, 1944) which seeks to apply modern perceptions of the 'popular' to Shakespearean texts. Rather, Weimann takes a line similar to that of Marxist historiographers, such as Mikhail Bakhtin, in seeking to excavate through the means of painstaking scholarly research the connections in the Shakespearean theatre between aesthetics and politics. His approach is also to be distinguished from what is now labelled the 'old historicism' of critics such as E.M.W. Tillyard, in its concern to penetrate the ideological surfaces of texts such as Shakespeare's tragedies, and to recover a 'popular voice' overlayed by the dominant structures of political power. Weimann views the Elizabethan theatre as an amalgam of

---

*Reprinted from *Shakespeare and the Popular Tradition in the Theater,* trans. Robert Schwartz (Baltimore: John Hopkins University Press), pp. 208–37.

traditional and experimental impulses. But he also explores theatrical representation, including the physical conditions of performance itself, as a means of figuring forth the symbolic forms through which Renaissance society articulated its own political concerns – the illusion of reality that Weimann associates with the 'locus' or 'place' occupied by figures of power in these plays – and a popular voice endlessly questioning such power from a position on the stage in closer proximity to the audience: 'the platea'. Weimann takes his terminology from medieval drama which distinguished between the 'platea' or 'place', close to the audience, resembling a platform area, and the 'locus' or scaffold. Weimann argues that these divisions correspond to the unlocalized acting area, and to the 'throne on the pageant stage' (p.74). In the chapter entitled 'Shakespeare's Theater: Tradition and Experiment' Weimann's careful research into the history of the theatre informs his criticism of the plays themselves.

1 The platform stage

The many links between Elizabethan drama and society must be kept in mind when we consider the physical shape and theatrical conventions of Shakespeare's stage. Like the origin of the Elizabethan public theater, its mode of production must be seen in light of the social and cultural synthesis that characterized the highly transitional balance of class forces in the late Tudor period. No longer based on a corporate social structure (like the German Shrovetide play or the Parisian *confrères*), the Elizabethan theater was a national institution in which native popular traditions were enlarged and enriched in many ways by a variety of elements, most notably, Renaissance ideology. It was precisely because the London theater was *not* exclusively a courtly, academic, or guild theater that there developed a stage and a mode of production the theatrical possibilities of which were as diverse as the models and sources from which it drew. Among these were not only the traditional scaffold and innyard stages used by itinerant players, and the medieval pageant wagons, which could also have been arranged for performance-in-the round, but also contemporary *tableaux vivants*, and thus, indirectly, Renaissance visual arts.

Recent research into Elizabethan stage conditions has revealed the limitations of all reductive approaches to Shakespeare's theater and refuted the late Romantic conception of a simple and unsophisticated wooden stage. The so-called 'thatch-and-groundling' approach has gradually lost favor since G.R.Kernodle cast new light on the public theater by pointing out its debt to the tradition of the *tableaux vivants* and the Dutch *Rederijk* theater.[1] Similarly, more recent research by C.Walter Hodges, Richard Southern, Richard Hosley, Glynne Wickham, and others reveals not one standard public theater, but a variety of theatrical institutions.

The most important of the many revisons of the older reconstruction of the Elizabethan stage (as designed, for example, by J.Q.Adams) concerns the existence of an 'inner stage', an acting area recessed into the rear stage wall and separated from the main stage by a curtain. Theater historians like A.H.Thorndike and, of course, Adams placed many of Shakespeare's indoor scenes on this inner stage, assuming that it would have facilitated an uninterrupted performance and would have supported the illusionary effect of important scenes and scene changes. Detailed study of the thirty extant plays that were performed in Shakepeare's *Globe* theater between 1599 and 1608 does not, however, support this assumption. In twenty plays with indoor scenes there is no indication that an inner stage was, or even could have been, used. In only nine of the plays does the text indicate the discovery of a character (and in only three cases a group of two or three figures) concealed by a curtain. In each of these cases, however, the 'discovery' serves a tableau effect and not a fully mimetic illusion of speech and action. The space needed would not have been more than four feet in depth; and so, if the rear wall in the *Globe* theater was anything like the wall in van Buchel's sketch of the *Swan* theater, the effects indicated in these nine plays could have been achieved by using a doorway.[2]

George F. Reynolds' pioneering study of stage practices in the popular *Red Bull* supports this reconsideration of the 'inner stage'. In the *Red Bull*, curtained movable scaffolds or a scaffoldlike house may have been used instead of an inner stage: 'perhaps the "rear stage" was not a real and permanent structural part of the stage but itself only a removable structure, more non-committal in its outward appearance than shop or tent, but just as easily brought in and removed'.[3] This suggestion, reinforced by practical theatrical experiments by Bernard Miles and others,[4] has made possible entirely new visualizations of important Shakespearean scenes, such as Hodges' convincing reconstruction of the death scene in *Antony and Cleopatra* (IV, xiv).[5]

The implications of this revised attitude toward the 'inner stage' are quite far reaching and lead almost as a matter of course to a reconsideration of traditional notions about the 'upper stage'. A little more than a generation ago scholars like E.K.Chambers and W.J.Lawrence had reconstructed the upper stage as part of the upper gallery forming a roof over the inner stage. J.C.Adams placed no fewer than five of the twenty-six scenes in *King Lear*, and an average of about one-fifth of the scenes in Shakespeare's other plays, on this upper stage (in a chamber that could be separated from the gallery).[6] Later and more detailed studies by Reynolds, Hosley, T.J. King, and others indicate, however, a far smaller number of upper stage scenes: of 419 scenes in twenty-two of the plays performed by

Shakespeare's troupe, only eleven are undoubtedly upper stage scenes.[7] But, as in the *Red Bull*, the balcony was not essential in these scenes to insure nonstop acting for the sake of illusion. As Reynolds points out, the balcony 'was never used to fill in pauses in action on the front stage'.[8] And even in the rare cases in which the upper stage was used – as a city wall, a balcony or a window – the scene enacted there was short, with little movement, and so closely connected with what was happening on the front stage that speakers generally stood at the edge or railing and not in the interior (which certainly made their speeches more audible).

Similarly, King demonstrates that out of 276 plays considered only forty-five required 'an acting place above the stage'. But even then 'above' or 'aloft' usually served as 'an observation post from which one or two actors comment on, or converse with, actors down on the main stage.' Consequently, this 'above' acting area 'should … be considered as an auxiliary to the main stage rather than a distinct and separate "upper stage" '. As Richard Hosley suggests, then, since the same space was used by spectators and was obviously of minor importance if used only about once in a play, the term 'upper stage' seems 'rather inappropriate and in some respects misleading'.[9]

To this date interest in the workings of the upper or the disputed inner stage has made it easy for critics to underestimate the importance and diversity of the front stage, The rapid movement and short scenes so characteristic of Shakespeare's plays were not so much enhanced by movement between inner, upper, and front acting areas as by a continuation of traditional platform stage conventions. The front stage was much more flexible and changeable than has been suggested in the past, for as an acting area it was basically neutral, free of illusion, recognized, even in performance, to be a stage. Scenes were changed and props were shifted in full view of all; and this front, or rather main, stage was used almost without interruption – for indoor as well as outdoor scenes. Such a flexible use of the main stage, surrounded on three or perhaps even four sides by spectators, reflects the constant efforts of the Elizabethan dramatist and actor to keep the play in close touch with the audience's response.

If the inner and upper stages were neither as developed nor essential to the course of the action as had formerly been assumed, it is reasonable that greater attention should be paid to the platform stage. It is easier to understand now why the main acting area was so very large – even by modern standards. Henslowe's contract for the building of the stage at the *Fortune* theater gives the following measurements:'in length Fortie and Three foote of lawfull assize and in breadth to extende to the middle of the yarde of the saide howse'. The platform stage was so large that it could easily have accommodated most of the various scenes that have at one time or another been attributed to the inner or upper stage. This implies, of course, that the platform stage was not a homogeneous acting area, but may have used front, middle, rear, or other specific locations to produce a variety of theatrical effects – effects that can best be understood when related to the continuing interplay of *locus* and 'place', *mimesis* and ritual, in the tradition of the popular theater.

In order fully to judge the scenic function of the main stage we must re-examine its original relation to the rear stage wall. As the sketch of the *Swan* theater seems to show, the entire tiring-house facade was probably not connected to the galleries or circular building at all. The circular building and the tiring-house seem to have been separate structures, probably separate in origin.[10] The circular building corresponded to the medieval round theater or the arena used for bear-baiting and other popular amusements, but the scaffold set up inside this arena and the tiring-house belonging to it may well have had their origins in the booth stages known to have existed all over Europe.[11] These booth stages were furnished with a scaffold-like rear structure which, on the continent, developed into the imposing and often richly decorated facade of the Dutch *Rederijk* theater. Of course such a modern approach to the origins of the Elizabethan stage remains in many ways as hypothetical as the older theories it seeks to revise; but even though reasonable counter-arguments can be made, this new construction is supported by facts as well as by practical experiments in the staging of Renaissance drama that have greatly enhanced our understanding of Shakespeare's plays.

Since downstage acting brought the actor so far into the midst of his audience, it is conceivable that the pit, or the yard, which had no chairs or benches, might also have been used as an acting area. If only for its sensational effect, it is reasonable to suppose (as Hodges does) that some amount of acting was done in the yard.[12] But while Hodges only suggests the possibility that messengers and riders on horseback may have entered in this way, precedents in the older theater have already demonstrated the theatrical effect achieved when an actor entered in the midst of the audience. This was the case in the mysteries, where 'Erode ragis in the pagond and in the strete also', and in moralities, where the Vice appeared in the yard or sported with those around him. Appearances of this sort may indeed have been sensational, but they possessed more than what Hodges called a 'stunt value'. Underlying this mode of acting were traditional architectural configurations and conventions of stagecraft with which Shakespeare was almost certainly familiar. (For such a familiarity it was not absolutely necessary for him to have seen the Herod scenes in Coventry, but as J.Q.Adams pointed out, it is most likely that he did.)[13]

Acting in the pit is known to have taken place in *Henry VIII*, where the porter pushes through the spectators to make room for a procession (V,iv).[14] And while critics such as J.W.Saunders conjecture an appearance in the yard in Act II, scene i of *Romeo and Juliet* and Act V, scene ii of

Antony and Cleopatra, Allardyce Nicoll made the more general suggestion that the stage direction direction 'pass over the stage,' found in numerous texts, does not, as was hitherto assumed, mean to move between the doors in the rear stage wall, but from the pit, across the stage, and back into the pit. The starting and finishing points of this passage over the stage might then be the 'ingressi' clearly marked in the Swan drawing, and might well have been connected to the rear stage structure.[15]

Although this last suggestion cannot be conclusively proved, when juxtaposed with the other revisions discussed here it confirms the likelihood that the architecture and stagecraft of the Elizabethan public theater were closer in appearance and structure to the native popular theater than critics have been willing to admit. A corollary to this view would posit that the origin of the English picture-frame stage is not to be found in the doubtful inner stage of Shakespeare's theater, but must be sought in the aristocratic theater of the Italian Renaissance court which made its mark on coterie and court stages in England and the stage settings created by Inigo Jones and later Restoration producers. This, and not the Elizabethan inner stage, explains the advent of the modern proscenium stage, its painted backdrops and visual effects.[16]

In explaining the variability of the platform stage, even as it was modified by humanist and Renaissance influences, it is best to recur to the traditonal interplay between *platea* and *locus*, between neutral, undifferentiated 'place' and symbolic location. Such an interplay accommodates action that is both non-illusionistic and near the audience (corresponding to the 'place') and a more illusionistic, localized action sometimes taking place in a discovery space, scaffold, tent, or other *loci* (corresponding to the medieval *sedes*). Between these extremes lay the broad and very flexible range of dramatic possibilities so skillfully developed by the popular Renaissance dramatist.

While Inigo Jones' lavish Italianate scenery was designed to catch the eye and present what was clearly an idealized imitation of nature, the customs of the traditional popular theater presupposed a collaboration between dramatist and audience in the creation and visualization of dramatic setting. In accordance with this, the relationship between the production and the reception of plays in the popular theater was very close indeed. The proximity of actor and audience was not only a physical condition, it was at once the foundation and the expression of a specific artistic endeavour. Unlike the theater of the subsequent three hundred years, the actor – audience relationship was not subordinate, but a dynamic and essential element of dramaturgy. For the Elizabethan playgoer the drama was more than a play taking place on a stage separated from the audience; it was an event in progress in which good listening and watching were 'rewarded by a sense of feeling part of the performance'.[17]

In Shakespeare's youth the popular actor, especially the comedian with his extemporal wit, performed not so much *for* an audience as *with* a community of spectators who provided him with inspiration and, as it were, acted as a chorus. Such was the case with Richard Tarlton: 'it was his custome for to sing extempore of theames given him'.[18] The spectator who challenged the actor had the weight of the audience behind him; collectively, they were collaborators in and judges of an elementary theatrical process. The audience was both the challenger and the challenged; even when pelted with apples Tarlton countered with a suitable couplet, just as he answered criticisms from the audience or from his partner in dialogue with nimble wit and wordplay.[19]

The separation of the audience into groups based on rank was not traditional: it was new in Tarlton's and even in Shakespeare's day. As late as in *Henry VIII* (V, iv) the actual audience was identified with the undifferentiated mass of curious spectators who had come to watch the christening of Elizabeth in front of Henry VIII's palace – an indiscriminate fusion of the audience that Beaumont and Fletcher and other coterie dramatists would have frowned upon. In this way the fictive spectators and the actual audience merged and became a vital link between play and real life:

> (*The palace yard.*
> *Noise and tumult within. Enter Porter and his Man.*)

Porter	... You must be seeing christenings? Do you look for ale and
	cakes here, you rude rascals?
Man	Pray, sir, be patient; 'tis as much impossible,
	Unless we sweep 'em from the door with cannon
	To scatter 'em as 'tis to make 'em sleeps,
	On May-day morning; which will never be
	We may as well push against Paul's as stir 'em.
Porter	How got they in, and be hang'd?
Man	Alas, I know not: how gets the tide in?

(V, iv, 8–16)

Probably speaking from the pit, the Porter draws the audience into the play by pushing them aside to make room for the procession. 'An army cannot rule 'em', he says to the audience, who by now must have felt a heightened sense of both their relation to the subject of the play and their power as a mass of people unified in a dramatic role that had powerful correlatives in Tudor and, of course, Stuart history.

The traditional readiness and ability of the audience to be drawn into the play which is indicated here is as noteworthy as the willingness of author and actor to speak directly to the audience and to acknowledge basic agreement with its tastes and ideas. These links between the world of the play and the audience's world of experience are further extended in prologue, chorus, and song. Directly and indirectly reinforcing the play–audience relationship, these links illuminate the similarities and differences between dramatic illusion and Elizabethan reality. The world is seen as a stage, the stage, in turn, as an image of the world; and this link between art and society presupposes and fosters a sense of both unity and tension between actor and audience: the play, the product of theatrical activity, and the process of doing it (as well as the process of being involved through watching and listening) have a profound effect on each other. The gain in terms of consciousness does not involve a loss for the reality of its objects.[20]

It was this precariously balanced sense of community in the theatrical experience that gave the popular Renaissance drama its unique mode of production. We can search in vain for the equivalent of the modern stage manager in Shakespeare's theater. The prompter and keeper of the scripts did not have sufficient authority to fill such a position properly; if he was in charge of rehearsals at all, he was certainly not in complete control. The real decisions – choice of plays, procurement of costumes, distribution of roles, etc. – must have been arrived at by agreement within the troupe of actors and shareholders. The Chamberlain's (later the King's) Men were organized along cooperative lines, and even though important decisions could be made by one acting on behalf of the majority,' the ultimate authority was vested solely in the actor–sharers as a group'.[21] The principle of joint ownership and joint responsibility accorded fully with the implications and spirit of the Elizabethan theatrical experience. The success and prolonged harmony of Shakespeare's troupe and its most distinguished members testified to the practicability of a collective theatrical and business venture. Too little attention has been paid to the connection between the organization of Shakespeare's troupe and the dramaturgy and artistic principles that made its plays the greatest and most successful experiment in the history of the modern theater.

Most characteristic of this kind of theatrical world was not the virtuoso display of individual talent, but the individual's renunciation of the need to assert himself, and hence the employment of his talent in cooperation with the needs and possibilities of 'everyone working in the theatre on the joint venture of production'.[22] Naturally, the 'ability of dramatist and actor to devote themselves to their joint work, which corresponded to the spectators' ability to participate creatively, presupposes common thought and common feeling';[23] in the words of Alfred Harbage, 'Shakespeare wanted to say what his audience wanted him to say'. Such was the delicate balance between dramatist, actor, and audience. Shakespeare never disingenuously catered to the audience or relied on purely sensational effects in production primarily because of 'his sense of identity with and responsibility to those thousands of other men who honored him with their trust'.[24] To this audience Shakespeare spoke directly, for they were the 'gentles all' to whom he referred in the Prologue to *Henry V* in the inspiring speech of the Chorus:

> And let us, ciphers to this great accompt,
> On your imaginary forces work.

Here the great dramatist and the actor modestly subordinate themselves to the process of consciousness shared by the audience; and through this communal form of experience, where hopefully with 'humble patience' the play may be 'Gently' heard and 'kindly' judged, the world of the play swells to encompass the most complex realities of political experience. 'Suppose that you have seen ... O! do but think ... Follow, Follow! Grapple your minds ... Work, work your thoughts ... Behold ...' (Chorus, III). Even the slowest and least literate in the audience should be able to follow along:' Vouchsafe to those that have not read the story / That I may prompt them ...' (Chorus, V). Thus Shakespeare deliberately raises the level of awareness of his unread spectators; and in this sense he is truly 'Shakespeare, the plebeian driller', as Tatham wrote in his 1641 poem to Richard Brome.[25] At any rate, Shakespeare fulfills the end of what Ben Jonson described as a kind of 'spearshaking' art ('à la Pallas Athena'); for Shakespeare here is recalled in his own unique role of popular educator:

> In each of which, he seems to shake a Lance,
> As brandish't at the eyes of Ignorance.

The social consciousness behind the Shakespearean vision was not destructively aimed against plebeian narrow-mindedness and inconstancy, but usually served as a means of conquering or challenging the kind of 'Ignorance' that was the source of both.[26]

2 Role and actor : the language of locality and 'place'

The general absence of scenery on the large acting area of the Elizabethan platform stage placed rigorous demands on the dramatist's use of language, the actor's use of gesture, and the audience's attentiveness and imagination. Through language the dramatist created atmosphere and locale, establishing the physical as well as the poetic disposition of scene, character and plot.[27] Coupled with his 'word scenery' were rhyme, rhythm, and gesture, the integration of which fostered an extremely effective unity of physical action and poetic expression. As Otto Ludwig pointed out, Shakespeare divided a situation 'into gestures of thought, speech, position and intonation ... the language moves visibly, so to speak, the sound itself may be comical .... Everything must be visible, audible, tangible, the thought sensation, the sensation word, the word form and form movement'.[28]

While the Elizabethan theater did not strive to create a visual illusion of actuality, it did attempt to imitate nature, albeit in poetically heightened terms. A platform stage capable of sustaining both illusionistic and nonillusionistic effects was indispensible to the interplay between realistic and stylized modes of expression, and between a new consistency of *mimesis* and traditional audience awareness. Once the tensions between these various theatrical modes were subsumed within flexible platform dramaturgy, an astonishing variety and richness of language naturally followed.

Such was the case in what has been called the 'extraordinary variety'[29] and variability of the Shakespearean monologue. When, for example, an angry and distracted Lear challenges the forces of nature – 'You cataracts and hurricanes, spout'– he uses a stylized and elevated diction. His apostrophe to lightning and thunder is grandiose and rhetorical:

> You sulph'rous and thought-executing fires,
> Vaunt-couriers of oak-cleaving thunderbolts,
> Singe my white head. And thou, all-shaking thunder,
> Strike flat the thick rotundity o'th' world;
> Crack nature's moulds, all germens spill at once,
> That makes ingrateful man.
>
> (III, ii, 4–9)

But this is immediately followed by a most ordinary kind of prose:

> O nuncle, court holy water in a dry house is
> better than this rain-water out o'door.
>
> (III, ii, 10–11)

The contrast between elevated metaphor and simple, everyday speech here sharpens the effect of both. But the difference in meter, assonance, and style produces more than a formal contrast; for it signalizes the distance between two basically different themes and two widely divergent attitudes. No sooner has the raging King adjured the 'all-shaking thunder' to flatten the earth and 'Crack nature's moulds' than 'natural' common sense comes to the fore in the person of the pragmatic Fool, who would rather compromise principles than face the torrent.

The range of speech serves here to characterize two fundamentally different attitudes which correspond to different patterns of theatrical activity and different conventions of character. But even within Lear's own speech we find a similar range of expressive modes. Whereas here he uses

elevated rhetoric to command the elements, when he awakes to find
Cordelia in Act IV his tone and speech change:

> Where have I been? Where am I? Fair daylight?
> I know not what to say.
> I will not swear these are my hands. Let's see.
> I feel this pin prick.
>
> (IV, vii, 52–6)

These words are especially moving when compared with Lear's previously
exalted speech. Similar, if not such striking, examples can be found in the
language of almost all of the tragic heroes. The rhetorical and stylized
language of Macbeth, Othello, Cleopatra, and Hamlet is mixed with
everyday syntax and diction in remarks like Macbeth's 'I have done the
deed', or 'I am afraid to think what I have done' (II, ii, 14, and 51), Othello's
'Soft you; a word or two before you go' (V, ii, 341), Cleopatra's 'Will it eat
me?' or 'What should I stay' – (V, ii, 269, 311), and Hamlet's frequent use of
popular images and proverbs.

This extremely effective alternation between rhetorical and mundane
language, stylization and directness, presupposed and helped to
perpetuate specific stage conditions such as those offered by the large and
variable platform. A downstage position, for instance, allowed for a
smoother transition from dialogue to monologue[30] and facilitated the
delivery of wordplay and proverbs directly to the audience – a mode of
delivery with obvious precedents in the popular theater. Such transitions
abound in Shakespeare's plays, as, for example, in Hamlet's conversation
with his mother (III, iv):

> *Queen* O Hamlet, thou hast cleft my heart in twain.
> *Hamlet* O throw away the worser part of it,
> And live the purer with the other half.
> Good night, but go not to my uncle's bed, …
> For use almost can change the stamp of nature,
> And either curb the devil, or throw him out,
> With wondrous potency: once more, good night,
> And when you are desirious to be blessed,
> I'll blessing beg of you. For this same lord,
>
> (*pointing to Polonius*)
>
> I do repent; but heaven hath pleased it so,
> To punish me with this, and this with me,
> That I must be their scourge and minister.
> I will bestow him and will answer well
> The death I gave him; so again, good night.
> I must be cruel only to be kind.

> Thus bad begins, and worse remains behind…
>
> (*he makes to go, but returns.*)
>
> One word more, good lady.
>
> *Queen* What shall I do?[31]

This passage begins as genuine dialogue that leads to Hamlet's first 'Good night' (167), which being repeated a second and a third time indicates that the passages in between suspend the convention of dialogue in favor of a more generalized, chorus-like kind of monologue (168–70; 173–5; 178–9). Because of its content – the significance and the consequences of Hamlet's thoughts and actions – this chorus-like speech must be clearly differentiated from the surrounding dialogue; and indeed the closing couplets accentuate both its departure from the illusion of conversation and the fact that its content is basically a summary and an interpretation of past, present, and future action. The manner of delivery and the prophetic content so broaden the nature of Hamlet's speech that it supersedes the immediate context of dialogue and functionally becomes a direct address to the audience, in this case, something like a chorus. The change from one convention of speech to another does not come unannounced, however; for the *self-expressive* statements that transcend the illusion of one-to-one conversation follow *the dramatic representation* of leave-taking. In moving beyond the limitations of the illusion of conversation, and so in moving away, physically and psychologically, from his partner in dialogue, Hamlet also distances himself from the illusionistic modes of causality and locality and assumes a theatrically more neutral position from which he, as it were, collaborates with the audience. But, again, the traditional patterns of audience address are integrated into the dialogue with its *mimesis* of verbal exchange and leave-taking. Thus, an old popular stage convention is impressed into the service of a new kind of realism. The final return to dialogue -' One word more, good lady' – may indeed be interpreted psychologically by the modern producer as being motivated by Hamlet's forgetfulness or altered intention (an interpretation that is not unjustified on one level), but such an interpretation is surely one-sided in light of the potentialities of downstage acting.[32]

A second example illustrates even more strikingly the interchange of contrasting forms of speech. Speaking to the blind Gloucester, Lear asks

> What, art mad? A man may see how this world goes with
> no eyes … Thou hast seen a farmer's dog bark at a beggar?
>
> *Gloucester* Ay, sir.
>
> *Lear* And the creature run from the cur? There thou mightst
> behold the great image of authority: a dog's obey'd in office.
> Thou rascal beadle, hold thy bloody hand!
> Why dost thou lash that whore? Strip thy own back;

Thou hotly lusts to use her in that kind
For which thou whip'st her. The usurer hangs the cozener.
Through tatter'd clothes small vices do appear;
Robes and furr'd gowns hide all. Plate sin with gold,
And the strong lance of justice hurtless breaks;
Arm it in rags, a pigmy's straw does pierce it.
None does offend, none – I say none; I'll able 'em.
Take that of me, my friend, who have the power
To seal th'accuser's lips. Get thee glass eyes,
And, like a scurvy politician, seem
To see the things thou dost not. Now, now, now, now!
Pull off my boots. Harder, harder – so.

(IV,vi)

When read in its entirety, this passage can be seen to fall into three parts: first, a dialogue, couched in everyday language in which question and answer heighten the sense of conversation:

	What, art mad? … Thou has seen a farmer's dog bark at a beggar?
Gloucester	Ay, sir.

This prose passage leads to a monologuelike statement (160–72) elevated in meter and rhetoric the intensity and vision of which are supported by the convention of Lear's madness:

Thou rascal beadle, hold thy bloody hand!
Why dost thou lash that whore? Strip thy own back;

This iambic verse, which breaks the illusion of dialogue, leads back ultimately to dialogue via the completely unstylized, unrhetorical, and unmetrical,'Now, now, now, now!' As in Act III, scene iv of *Hamlet*, theatrical convention and poetic vision coalesce in a dialogue accompanied by physical acting which attains an almost naturalistic precision. The unity of 'word' and 'action' is complete. On the surface a trivial detail, the gesture precipitated by the remark 'Pull off my boots…' is actually a remarkably profound piece of stage business. Since the visionary ideas just expressed by Lear exist outside the world of 'Robes and furr'd gowns', the rebirth of his dignity demands that he abandon all the accoutrements of royal prestige, which he does: 'Harder, harder – so.' As in the first example, the poetically heightened, non-illusionistic lines of the body of the speech are framed by a more illusionistic type of dialogue, which so carries the action forward the detail and generality, the concrete and the universal, experience and vision are inextricably fused. The result is no 'confusion' nor is it, as T.S.Eliot also thought, 'fundamentally objectionable'. Rather, such fusion of 'naturalism' and 'convention' serves to enhance a sense of movement and complexity in the work as a whole.

The sheer scope of Lear's and Hamlet's language – in content, style and rhythm – illustrates the symbiotic relationship between Shakespeare's verbal art and a flexible stage that could localize the scene in dialogue but could just as easily neutralize it once again in monologue or aside. The dramatic change from locality to neutral 'place' and back to locality again corresponds to a verbal change from the dramatic illusion of conversation to a non-illusionistic, audience-directed generalizing monologue, and back to dialogue. Such facility in alternating forms of speech is inconceivable without an equally flexible stage.

This, however, gives only a very general (and certainly oversimplified) idea of the dramatic function of the monologuelike speech. A more detailed look at the passage from *Hamlet* (III, iv, 178–9) shows how it functions, as similar speeches in Shakespeare often do, to underline 'an important state of affairs, bringing it to the fore with more volume of sound and emphasis'.[33] This 'volume of sound' does not necessarily reflect the content of the speech, nor does it result from the acoustics of the hall; rather it derives from a stage position similar to that from which the chorus-like statement of the Scrivener and Buckingham's self-contemplation in III, vi and V, i of *Richard III* are delivered. The summarizing effect of Hamlet's words is unmistakably underlined by the demonstrative use of 'Thus';[34] and the non-illusionistic status of the comment only intensifies the universality of the idea and hence the possible wordplay on 'kind'.

Quite different means are used in Lear's speech, but they serve a similar purpose. His visionary lines ('Thou rascal beadle...') dissolve the illusion of conversation with Gloucester; since they are abstract – generalized – they are addressed less to a partner in dialogue than to a general listener (perhaps even to an individual in the audience singled out by an icy stare or accusing finger).[35] In momentarily turning away from his partner in dialogue and the on-stage action, Lear effectively engages the audience in generalized issues that are central to the play's meaning, issues the immediacy of which are not only visualized dramatically but experienced realistically as the role dissolves and the man behind the actor speaks directly to his fellow man in the audience. In the final analysis Shakespeare not only strengthens a realistic approach to the world, but to the world of art as well.

In an earlier section of this book it was pointed out that in a ritual context *mimesis* is not only consecrative but also productive, since the blurring of differences between religion and knowledge (between belief and activity) makes miming a way of coping with the practical world. But even completely outside of the ritual context, as, for example, in Lear's and

Hamlet's speeches, *mimesis* not only serves a remarkably similar function, but does so in terms of a similar process of blurring two different kinds of knowing. Here it is not ritual and cognition that are reconciled, but rather the fictive world of the play and the real experience of the audience that are integrated by the alternating modes of dramatic and extradramatic speech. What primitive mimetic magic and Elizabethan *mimesis* have in common is the fact that both rely (in the former intuitively and in the latter empirically) on the acceptance as fundamentally real actions and words that define a supraindividual, or communal reality.

Because of the variety of sources and influences that pervaded Elizabethan dramaturgy, monologue – like dialogue and the aside – was a changing and changeable form of speech that was capable of many different effects depending on the immediate dramatic context. Obviously monologue served both illusionistic and non-illusionistic, naturalistic and stylized functions.[36] It could be used in aside or in the direct address of the prologue, or it could become a form of soliloquy or the kind of thinking out loud in which a character in 'solitude renders an account to himself of his innermost thoughts and feelings'.[37] In light of the rich and diverse dramatic functions of Shakespeare's language, it is difficult to separate monologue and dialogue too dogmatically. We can say, however, that as a general rule the localization and neutralization of scene and action in downstage acting reflects, respectively, a dissociation from or identification with the audience, and that the structure and style of speech are largely determined by this relationship.

The two extremes of this relationship could, for example, be viewed as the difference between speech delivered by elevated persons from the throne (localized, illusionistic) and the speech of the clowns (neutral, non-illusionistic). Logically, in light of stage action and social convention, the speaker from the throne was raised physically above those around him and did not function on a level of direct audience contact. Claudius' great speech from the throne (*Hamlet* 1, ii) and Timon's speech at the banquet (*Timon of Athens* 1,ii) do not in any way directly address the audience. Neither speech contains asides, wordplay, couplets, or many proverbs. In terms of theatrical history this mode of presentation corresponded to the use of the scaffold as *locus* where – as in the *Ludus Conventriae*, for example – the ruling and high-born characters sat: a physical social correlative that had already resulted in a more self-contained kind of staging in the circular theater.

But downstage, somewhere in between the socially and spatially elevated Claudius and Timon and the audience, stood characters less inclined to accept the assumptions – social, ideological, and dramatic – of the localized action. These characters, by means of asides, wordplay, proverbs, and direct audience address offered a special perspective to the audience. In the banquet scene of *Timon* this in between position is occupied by Apemantus. During Claudius' speech the position is held by Hamlet, who, through the use of aside, establishes a close initial bond with the audience. A similar in-between-world, albeit different in terms of stagecraft, is established by the gravediggers in *Hamlet*, and the porters in *Macbeth* and *Henry VIII*, and, of course, such clowns as Launce, whose direct address to the audience is couched in ordinary language filled with proverbs and wordplay, and punctuated with phrases like 'Look you',' I'll show you', and 'You shall judge'.

Between the two extremes – the illusion of conversation from a localized setting and non-illusionistic direct address from a neutral 'place' – there existed many forms of transition. These involved an infinitely variable conception of dramaturgy based on what Anne Righter called that 'equilibrium of involvement and distance characteristic of the Shakespearean attitude towards the audience'.[38] The balance achieved by Shakespeare was especially remarkable in light of the general affinity of Renaissance dramatists for the self-contained play. Shakespeare did, of course, move in this direction, but without abandoning the popular heritage. In *Hamlet* there are still signs of direct address (IV, iv, 47), but these are admittedly quite rare. More characteristic of a play like *Hamlet* is an indirect audience contact that operates through an awareness of the theatrical medium itself. Such is the case when Hamlet compares his own inactivity with the effusions of the player moved to tears by the emotion of his role. Here Hamlet judges himself not as a prince but as an actor:

> ... what would he do
> Had he the motive and the cue for passion
> That I have? he would drown the stage with tears,
> And cleave the general ear with horrid speech,
> Make mad the guilty, and appal the free,
> Confound the ignorant, and amaze indeed
> The very faculties of eyes and ears; yet I,
> A dull and muddy-mettled rascal, peak
> Like John-a-dreams, unpregnant of my cause,
> And can say nothing ...
>
> (II, ii, 563–72, ED. J.D.WILSON)

Without departing from this role or deviating from the action, Hamlet here suggests, through this imagery, a full awareness of the effect he would like his speech to have on the spectators in the theater: of stirring up and sharpening their 'very faculties of eyes and ears', the full capacity of their physical as well as their moral sensibilities.

Built into Hamlet's complex audience contact, and fundamental to Launce's direct address, was a principle of popular dramaturgy that was already well-developed in Tarlton's day. When Tarlton had his face slapped while playing the role of the Chief Justice in *The Famous Victories*, as an actor he reacted with a double awareness; for to himself and to his audience he was simultaneously Tarlton and the judge: the slap administered to the judge was clearly understood as a slap to Tarlton as well. It is on the basis of this double action, which utilized both the *platea*-like and the localized dimensions of the platform stage, that Tarlton's subsequent reaction may be said to anticipate somewhat the interplay between role and actor and between actor–role and audience already seen in *Hamlet*. Perhaps it is not fortuitous that Hamlet so often appears in a most uncourtly light. It is as if the plebeian *ohm*, or measure, of the popular tradition in acting re-emerges once more in an expression of the *actor's* true self – the self behind the role of prince – when Hamlet compares himself to 'John-a-dreams', a popular figure 'usually associated by editors with John a Droynes, a country bumpkin' and probably identical to 'some forgotten nursery character like Little Johnny Head-in-air'.[39]

Considering the universalizing and humanizing effect of Shakespeare's dramaturgy within a play world and upon a real world beset alike by rigid class barriers, the links between his verbal art and his stagecraft seem more significant than any purely formal synthesis that might have been achieved. The profound interaction of poetic imagination and theatrical technique, renewed and refined at almost every level, serves, in Shakespeare, as a mode and a medium of perceiving and comprehending the world as a temporal, spatial, and social experience. The interplay of poetry and theater itself helps to constitute the universalizing pattern of Shakespeare's drama. It helps to provide a basis for a mode of drama by which image and meaning, the particular and the general, the representation and the vision of objects are complementary aspects of the theatrical product. But this product results from, and consummates, a theatrical process from the actor (and the citizen) to the role and the spectators and back again to the actor and the citizens in the audience, all participating in a common cultural and social activity.

Such a view of the dialectic of the 'production' and 'reception' of poetic drama involves, as a matter of course, a critical position from which several questions follow – questions that should be asked now, even in the concluding chapter, to suggest some of the more explicit answers. For instance, the 'effect which interferes with the illusion'[40] has been observed ever since German critics like Kilian and Schücking took up this question: but it has rarely been viewed in a larger context of history and value. Obviously, this effect can no longer be considered to be the 'primitive' result of a 'naive technique',[41] even when we have to concede that occasionally it is only the 'author's instructions to the audience'[42] that are involved. Is direct and indirect audience contact, as many English and American scholars would hold, the latent manifestation of a submerged 'homiletic comment', an element of 'homiletic showmanship'?[43] Is

Shakespeare's 'multi-consciousness' an expression of that 'balance of opposites which constitute the universe of Christianity'?[44] To ask these questions in the present context is simply to express the need for a more complex sense of method and approach. The answer, at its most general and provisional level, will, I suggest, have to be looked for where historical analysis and value judgment can be made to relate so that neither the charge of primitivism nor any metaphysical eulogy, neither the bias of the theater of illusion nor a more modern preoccupation with distance and alienation, can serve as altogether adequate points of departure.

3 *Figurenposition*: the correlation of position and expression

Shakespeare used popular audience contact and related elements of traditional platform stagecraft to such varying degrees and in such variable ways that it is difficult to formulate even general observations about the nature and function of popular conventions in his plays. A number of Shakespeare's characters stand out, however, because they draw so clearly from popular tradition or present new ways in which traditional practices were adapted to new dramatic forms and functions. This group of characters, who share little in common with respect to social class, psychology, and length or importance of role, can be considered as a group provided we shift our attention from the more speculative concerns of character analysis to a more objective understanding of *Figurenposition* – the actor's position on the stage, and the speech, action, and degree of stylization associated with that position.

An admittedly incomplete list of these characters would include Launce and his friend Speed, most of the other Shakespearean clowns, the porters in *Macbeth* and *Henry VIII*, the gravediggers in *Hamlet*, Bottom in *A Midsummer Night's Dream*, the nurse in *Romeo and Juliet*, Richard Gloucester, Iago, the Fool, and, partly, Edmund in *King Lear*, Falstaff, Thersites, Apemantus, and – with some reservations – Aaron in *Titus Andronicus*, the Bastard Falconbridge in *King John*, and Autolycus in *The Winter's Tale*. Also belonging to this group are characters whose status within court groupings is temporarily changed or weakened as a result of real or feigned madness (Edgar, Lear, Hamlet, and, to a lesser extent, Ophelia). Taken together, these characters can be identified with a stage position that functions to greater and lesser degrees (and not exclusively, of course) as a means of achieving a special role and meaning within the play.

As an example, Apemantus' stage position during the banquet scene in *Timon of Athens* (I, ii) illustrates some of the potentialities of downstage acting on the Elizabethan platform stage. According to the stage direction 'A great banquet served in',[45] the banqueting table is set up and decked out probably at about the centre of the stage. Timon, Alcibiades, and the Senators enter, and 'Then comes, dropping after all, Apemantus...'. The men of elevated degree sit down at the main table in the middle of the stage, but, at Timon's instruction, the grumbling Apemantus is given a table by himself downstage from the banquet table. The action that follows takes place, as the text indicates, on two levels: Timon and his guests delivering high-sounding speeches from the illusionistic area around the banqueting table (a true *locus*), Apemantus speaking usually in such a way that the audience, whom he faces, can hear, but those behind him cannot. Such a reconstruction of the scene in performance explains the flexibility and variability of conventions of speech immediately apparent from the text.

Timon	I take no heed of thee;...prithee let my meat make thee silent.
Apemantus	I scorn thy meat; 'twould choke me, for I should ne'er flatter thee. O you gods, what a number of men eats Timon, and he sees 'em not! It grieves me to see so many dip their meat in one man's blood; and all the madness is, he cheers them up too. I wonder men dare trust themselves with men. Methinks they should invite them without knives: Good for their meat, and safer for their lives. There's much example for't; the fellow that sits next him, now parts bread with him, pledges the breath of him in a divided draught, is the readiest man to kill him: 't has been proved. If I were a huge man, I should fear to drink at meals, Lest they should spy my windpipe's dangerous notes. Great men should drink with harness on their throats.
Timon	My lord, in heart; and let the health go round.
Second Lord	Let it flow this way, my good lord.
Apemantus	Flow this way? A brave fellow. He keeps his tides well. Those healths will make thee and thy state look ill, Timon. Here's that which is too weak to be a sinner, Honest water, which ne'er left man i'th'mire. This and my food are equals; there's no odds. Feasts are too proud to give thanks to the gods....
First Lord	Might we but have that happiness, my lord, that you would once use our hearts, whereby we might express some part of our zeals, we should think ourselves for ever perfect.
Timon	O, no doubt, my good friends, but the gods themselves have provided that I shall have much help from you: how had you been my friends else?... O, what a precious comfort 'tis to have so many like brothers commanding

	one another's fortunes! O joy, e'en made away ere't can be born! Mine eyes cannot hold out water, methinks. To forget their faults, I drink to you.
Apemantus	Thou weep'st to make them drink, Timon.
Second Lord	Joy had the like conception in our eyes, And at that instant like a babe sprung up.
Apemantus	Ho, ho! I laugh to think that babe a bastard.
Third Lord	I promise you, my lord, you moved me much.
Apemantus	Much!

(I, ii, 35–111)

Dissociating himself from the feasters at the banquet table, Apemantus neutralizes his own position and so reviews the *locus*-centred action from a perspective something like, but not identical with, that of the traditional 'place' from which he seems to say to the audience, 'Look at them, and at what their feasting really means'. His frequent use of proverb and wordplay, inverting and ironically heightening the meaning of what is said at the banquet table accords nicely with his superior awareness, his choruslike function, and his position on the stage that recalls, in some way, the old Vice (he retains the Vice's scornful 'Ho, ho!'). Yet the dramatic effect of this choruslike link between the world of the play and the world of the audience is by no means unsophisticated. Apemantus' keen-edged remarks comment critically on the pomp, the ceremony, and the high-sounding words of the feasters without destroying the theatrical effect of the banquet itself. Thus, two perspectives are presented in such a way that neither alters or obscures the essential integrity of the other. The dual perspective that results acknowledges the sensuous attraction of a dazzling theatrical occasion, but also penetrates the showy surface; for there is in it 'a huge zest-for-life and the moral strength to see through its glitter, its hypocrisies, its shame and its rewards'.[46]

The process of drawing the audience into the play has become inseparable from the development of a complementary perspective that helps refine basic issues and restructure basic positions; at the same time, the process of differentiating between truth and appearance has become part of the dramatic mode itself. Dramatic images of central conflicts achieve a greater depth when subjected both to mimetic representation and self-expressive enactment; for through this mode the audience is drawn into the tensions between the feast and reality, between words and their meaning, flattery and criticism, enchantment and disenchantment. Of course Apemantus cannot simply tell the audience what to think; his vicious bitterness can hardly be taken at face value. He can, however, through his well-articulated counterperspective, expand the audience's awareness and establish new, perhaps deeper and more comprehensive dramatic tensions that in their turn expand the meaning of the play as a whole.[47]

Actually, Shakespeare seldom kept up this kind of complementary perspective from a *platea* level of acting for very long. Even in *Timon of Athens* Apemantus' downstage position is only temporary; and his choral function obviously suffers when his physical proximity to the audience disssolves in more illusionistic acting. But another example can perhaps illustrate that Shakespeare developed the interplay of *platea* and *locus* positions with great freedom and flexibility by going beyond the more direct modes of correlating the two. In Act V, scene ii of *Troilus and Cressida*, Cressida's meeting with Diomedes is watched from a distance by Troilus and Ulysses, who likewise are being watched by Thersites, as indicated by the direction, '*Enter Troilus and Ulysses, at a distance; after them Thersites*'.[48] The primary level of *mimesis* – Cressida's dialogue with Diomedes – is seen and commented upon by Troilus, but the second level of acting – Troilus' dialogue with Ulysses, which is closer in perspective to the audience than the first but still a *locus*-oriented dialogue – is seen and commented upon by Thersites. Thersites observes not only Cressida's faithlessness, but Troilus' disillusioned response as well. Although all three levels of acting are in turn watched by the spectators, the last is certainly the closest to the audience in terms of speech, stage position, and the scope of action that is seen. Not only does Thersites view most nearly what the audience views (from a neutral 'place'), he communicates his impressions not in dialogue or through the illusion of soliloquy, but in unpretentious direct address:

Diomedes	How, now, my charge!
Cressida	Now, my sweet guardian! Hark, a word with you.
Troilus	Yea, so familiar! (*whispers*)
Ulysses	She will sing any man at first sight.
Thersites	And any man may sing her, if he can take her clef; she's noted.

(V, ii, 7–12)

Thersites acts from a more nearly neutralized place where he can watch and hear the others but cannot be watched or heard by them. His wordplay here further underlines his unique position since it sarcastically sounds a realistic 'note' that sharply contrasts Troilus' bewildered idealism. After summing up Cressida's exit with a couplet – 'A proof of strength she could not publish more, / Unless she said "My mind is now turn'd whore" '(V,ii, 113–14) – Thersites witnesses the following interchange between Troilus and Ulysses:

Troilus	Let it not believed for womanhood!
	Think we had mothers. Do not give advantage
	To stubborn critics, apt without a theme

	For depravation, to square the general sex
	By Cressid's rule; rather think this not Cressid.
Ulysses	What hath she done, prince, that can soil our mothers?
Troilus	Nothing at all, unless that this were she.
Thersites	Will 'a swagger himself out on's own eyes?
Troilus	This she? No; this is Diomed's Cressida.

(129–37)

Troilus would gladly close his eyes to what he has just seen, but Thersites' comment keeps the audience from doing the same by quashing any sentimental response to, let alone identification with, Troilus' wishful thinking. Like Apemantus and the Vice figure before him, Thersites is a *provocateur* of truth, not a moral judge. And like the characters whose madness, feigned or real, forces dormant truths to the surface, his debunking and skeptical commentary serves to offer viable alternatives to the main or state view of things. In this sense, characters like Apemantus and Thersites help point out that the ideas and values held by the main characters are relative to their particular position in the play,[49] while by projection the audience realizes that this is equally true of the counter-perspectives offered by the plebeian intermediaries who occupy a *platea*-like position. This basic recognition of the relationship between character and circumstance, like so much else in Shakespeare, is a profoundly original observation that must be seen in connection with the dramatist's awareness of the tensions between society and the individual, the general, and the particular, from which an essential element of Shakespeare's universality derived.

Although *Love's Labour's Lost* offers unique problems as one of Shakespeare's most stylized works (both formally and linguistically), Act IV, scene iii is remarkable for its clever dramatic treatment of the complexities and potentialities of yet another form of *Figurenposition*. The scene opens not with dialogue but with one of the most boldly punning monologues in Shakespeare's plays. In it, Berowne reveals the true nature of his feelings and brings the audience up to date as to his own activities, but his position is still relatively removed from the audience's perspective. When the King enters, however, Berowne hides; and this is where the sheer comedy of his *Figurenposition* really starts. As the King begins to read, Berowne's new role as eavesdropper necessarily establishes a fundamental link with the audience, a perspective from which he can and does distance himself from the illusion of the represented *locus* (in much the same way as Apemantus and Thersites). When Longaville enters and the King hides, not only does the King, now an eavesdropper also, move closer to the audience in perspective, but Berowne, since he is watching the King watch Longaville, moves closer still to the audience. At this point the scene must have looked something like the scene from *Troilus and Cressida* discussed above. But everyone's perspective is changed once again when Dumaine enters, since Longaville assumes the King's perspective (watching but unaware of being watched), the King Berowne's (watching, aware that a watcher is being watched, but unaware that he himself is being watched), and Berowne another perspective closer still to the audience (so aware of the watcher/watched regression that he speaks freely to those who watch him from the audience). What results is a series of comments spoken in aside whose status relative to the two spatial and verbal extremes – Dumaine's monologue and Berowne's perspective so close to the audience – even the most clear-headed observer could have confused. We might suppose, if this is true, that Shakespeare was not only parodying the inconstancy of the 'scholars' (on the level of plot and theme), the ludicrousness of excessive sonneteering (on the level of language), but also, on the level of structure and stagecraft, the traditional interplay between *locus* and *platea*, representation and self-expression.

In light of this effect, it seems possible to reinterpret Berowne's gleeful comment:

> All hid, all hid, an old infant play,
> Like a demie God, here sit I in the skie,
> And wretched fooles secrets heedfully ore-eye.

(F$_1$ IV, iii, 78–80)

From the scenic circumstance it is clear that the first line refers, as most editors acknowledge, to some childern's game like hide-and-go-seek. But since the first line is not separated grammatically from the second and third (although the punctuation in modern editions has been changed to suggest that it is) it is possible that the word 'play' in the first line is also a pun on 'dramatic performance'. 'An old infant play', then, could refer to the older, but less artistically developed mystery plays (see *OED* 'Infant': 'In its earliest stage, newly existing, ungrown, undeveloped, nascent ...') in which a demigod (a pun on the fact that the actor who played *Deus* was indeed mortal) sat in the 'heavens' looking down upon and judging the actors.[50]

More interesting still is the probability that Berowne, in his successive changes of perspective, moved from a mere 'aside' position to a position closer to the audience and above the other actors to accord with his direct address, 'here sit I in the skie'. Perhaps a good way to visualize his movement would be to picture Berowne climbing one of the downstage columns, such as the ones indicated in the *Swan* drawing, or some other downstage scaffold structure – although an upstage balcony might have come closer in appearance to the conventional 'heavens' associated with the hut-roof area and so heightened the parody of the traditional representation of God in heaven.

But however the scene is reconstructed (and these are only a few of many possibilities) it remains remarkable because it reveals an interest in and a thorough understanding of the potentialities of a stagecraft that hinges on deliberately varied degrees of dissociation from illusionistic action, all within the context of perhaps the most stylized, rhetorical, and intellectually self-conscious play of Shakespeare's career. That Shakespeare used this clever device so early in his career supports and in part explains his more dramatically effective use of similar perspectives in his later works.

The downstage position of Apemantus, Thersites, and in his own uniquely involved way, Berowne, is achieved by the interplay of theatrical and verbal conventions which we have called, for lack of a satisfactory English term, *Figurenposition*. This *Figureposition* should not be understood only in the sense of the actor's physical position on the stage, but also in the more general sense that an actor may generate a unique stage presence that establishes a special relationship between himself and his fellow actors, the play, or the audience, even when direct address has been abandoned. Hamlet's behavior during the scene in Gertrude's closet already discussed above, for example, is certainly continuous with the action of the play and does not require a second level of acting like that in the banquet scene in *Timon of Athens*. Yet in terms of speech patterns Hamlet and Apemantus have much in common; notably, their emphatic use of couplets, wordplay, and similar illusion-breaking speech patterns, his position relative to his fellow actors remains extremely flexible, and he can fall back on conventions of both *locus* and *platea* stagecraft. His *Figurenposition* is therefore defined verbally as well as spatially, as we see in his first lines, which immediately hint at a unique perspective.

King	… But now, my cousin Hamlet, and my son -
Hamlet	[*Aside*] A little more than kin, and less than kind.
King	How is it that the clouds still hang on you?
Hamlet	Not so, my lord; I am too much in the sun.
Queen	Good Hamlet, cast thy nighted colour off,
	And let thine eye look like a friend on Denmark.

(I, ii, 64–9)

Hamlet's riddling first line flatly rejects Claudius' assumptions about their relationship, while the second – both a proverb and a pun – is a further clever departure from the King's meaning and point of view. These early breaks with the conventional form and content of continuous dialogue complement Hamlet's unusual relationship with the court already suggested by his entrance after courtiers of lesser degree and by the dark clothes of mourning that only he still wears. Certainly by his speech, but probably also spatially, Hamlet stands apart from his peers as well as his fellow actors through a *Figurenposition* that, while not at all impairing the range of his relations to the play world, establishes a functional link between himself and the audience (almost certainly reinforced by a downstage position).

Still, Hamlet's position on the stage is so complex that the 'aside' added by the modern editor hardly does it justice. To begin with, there is really no essential difference between Hamlet's first line, designated 'aside' and his second, which can be considered an impertinent reply – 'impertinent' in the sense that I have used the word in regard to the Vice's speech. The wordplay in Hamlet's second line reflects and maintains the same dissociation from the *locus* of the court and the same degree of contact with the audience as the first. The functional unity of both lines is much more important than any purely technical differentiation that the modern director or editor might be inclined to make between the literal aside and the impertinent answer. The punning phrase, 'I am too much in the sun', links up, of course, with Claudius' question, but after the fashion of the Vice who had a fondness for taking symbolic or metaphoric expressions literally and so inverting them by wordplay. What is misleading about the term 'aside' as it refers to the first line, then, is that it suggests that Hamlet and the rest of the court are initially more closely integrated than we might have cause to assume, since 'aside' implies that Hamlet is standing with the group and merely turns his head for a moment to make this one remark. This simply skirts the issue by subordinating Hamlet's ambiguous relationship with the court to a single dramatic gesture.

The ritual identification between actor and audience was, to be sure, a thing of the past in Shakespeare's day; and so although Hamlet's rapport with the audience may be linked to the self-introduction characteristic of the figures who traditionally acted on the *platea*, by the time Shakespeare made use of it, it had taken on entirely new forms and served entirely new functions. What has been termed the 'extra-dramatic moment' in the Renaissance theater,[51] then, was the product of both tradition and the new Renaissance conception of drama, by which means the connection between action and character became much more effective. Apemantus not only *stands apart* in space, he is, as a character with values, ideas and attitudes, *different* from Timon and his friends. Thersites is not only a sarcastic commentator, he is a character whose fundamental assumptions – like those of Falstaff or Iago – exist outside of the heroic, courtly, or romantic ethos of the main or state action.

In the same way Hamlet's speech patterns and his related *Figurenposition* reveal not only surface differences with his peers, but a more basic kind of contradiction between his position, his character, and theirs . Their difference is first suggested in a highly original form of self introduction in which traditional *platea*-conventions are transformed into something strange and new. Compared with Hamlet's opening lines (I, ii, 65, 67), the impertinent mode is almost discontinued after the opening 'Seems'; the principle of inversion, however, is not surrendered but, as it were, turned inward. Almost unprovoked, he snatches the word 'seems' from the lips of the Queen, only to give it an entirely nonpertinent, that is, egocentric meaning and function within the negative terms of his self-definition.

> *Hamlet* Seems, madam! Nay, it is; I know not seems.
> 'Tis not alone my inky cloak, good mother,
> Nor customary suits of solemn black,
> Nor windy suspiration of forc'd breath,
> No, nor the fruitful river in the eye,
> Nor the dejected haviour of the visage,
> Together with all forms, moods, shapes of grief,
> That can denote me truly. These, indeed, seem;
> For they are actions that a man might play;
> But I have that within which passes show -
> These but the trappings and the suits of woe.
>
> (1, ii, 78–86)

The attributes of his appearance ('inky cloak', 'solemn black') are still self-expressed, still self-introduced, but with a difference: they are mentioned only to be dismissed as some outward and insufficient definition of self. They are mere attributes of a potential *role* that cannot 'denote me truly'. Hamlet's self-introduction is designed to dissociate himself from 'actions that a man might *play*'. Rejecting 'seems' and 'play' as modes of his existence, the actor makes his own role problematic. The function of illusion is questioned from within, though not destroyed from without. In other words, the traditional dialectic between representation (playing, seeming) and self-embodiment ('that within which passes show') is used and almost deliberately quoted, but all within the symbolic frame of reference of Renaissance *mimesis*: Hamlet's special *Figurenposition*, his being apart from the *locus* (and the 'illusion') of court society, has a real (theatrical) as well as an imaginative (characterizing) significance. And so, spatial position assumes a moral function: the actor's rejection of illusion is turned into the character's honesty 'which passes show'.

Thus, traditional forms of dramaturgy are turned into modern modes of characterization; the paradox being that Hamlet, who knows no 'seems' has to develop his *platea*-like *Figurenposition* within the 'seems' that is, the illusionistic frame of the Renaissance play. So he is made to use the most traditional conventions of a *platea*-like embodiment – here, the verbal modes of his antic disposition – as a deliberate 'show', a psychological illusion, a strategy for discovery and survival. Hamlet's madness has a function in the play only because he *seems* mad. The resulting contradictions are obvious; but by not suiting the action to the words

Hamlet reveals his dilemma to be both one of the theater and one of character. The complexity of the interplay between the two aspects is the measure of the dramatist's achievement in combining innovation and tradition. The continuing contradiction between role and self-expression (which is the virtual *Leitmotiv* of his self-introduction) serves as a basic and most powerful impulse for bringing forth and maintaining the effectiveness of the links between stagecraft and verbal art.

Figurenposition, then, involves a variety of factors and cannot be defined dogmatically in terms of the function of any one set of verbal conventions. No single proverb, pun, instance of wordplay, or use of the aside can be isolated from other elements of plot, character, and language in order to argue the existence of a traditional actor – audience relationship. But if the aside and related verbal conventions go together they usually do more than simply pass on information to the audience. Besides filling the audience in on what has happened, what will happen, or what is being comtemplated at the moment, devices like the aside are capable of generating powerful ironies, particularly in the building up of character – where a character's thoughts or how much he knows about his own circumstance (what Bertrand Evans called 'artistically graded awareness') can create dramatic tensions in light of what the audience has already seen or heard. When, to some degree or other, verbal conventions such as these break the dramatic illusion and create the so-called 'extra-dramatic moment', the effect achieved can be a complex one involving conventions of both acting and characterization, that is, spatial and sometimes moral positions.[52]

And yet, this says very little about the functional relationship between the aside and the kinds of speech considered here: the couplet, the proverb, and wordplay. As our examples suggest, these frequently serve functions similar to earlier forms of exposition and self-introduction. But unlike traditional direct address, Shakespeare's couplets, proverbs, and wordplay are, for the most part, well-integrated into the dialogue, even when they should not necessarily be read as the expression, say, of a poetic spirit or a lively personality. We must recognize, then, that between non-representational speech and psychological realism there is a vast and often misunderstood threshold where the traditional and the modern mix rather freely; and only after the full extent and significance of this mixture is understood can we even approach passages like the Fool's puzzling prophecy in *King Lear* and the more perplexing aspects of Hamlet's 'antic disposition'.

The transitional role of the couplet or wordplay between realistic dialogue and the convention of audience contact is difficult to establish when what is said relates directly to the action of the play. Hamlet's couplet in III, iv, 178–9, for example, is essentially a veiled prophecy, while just prior to this he aptly sums up his double role as 'scourge and

minister'. A statement likewise related to the course of the action that
follows is Hamlet's famous couplet at the end of the first act:

> Let us go in together;
> And still your fingers on your lips, I pray.
> The time is out of joint. O cursed spite,
> That ever I was born to set it right!
> Nay, come, let's go together.   (*Exeunt*)
>
>   (I, v, 187–91)

Although the couplet usually comes at the very end of the scene, giving it
additional emphasis and so underlining its meaning, this couplet is
followed by one more line. Hamlet, on his way out, abandons the illusion
of dialogue after his repeated request for secrecy. (The couplet that follows
is too generalized and too far removed from the context of the preceding
conversation to have been directed solely at his companions). But the
couplet itself is followed by a return to genuine dialogue. Hamlet's last line
clearly refers to the previous 'Let us go in together'; and so it is obvious
that Horatio and the others have been waiting while Hamlet delivered the
couplet and now stand aside to let him exit first. Hamlet rejects this
perfectly appropriate court etiquette, however, and repeats, 'let's go
together'.

What is of interest is the way in which Shakespeare integrates the
couplet into dialogue. Here he breaks with the convention of the
concluding couplet only in order to end the scene in a representational
mode that allows him to re-emphasize an important aspect of Hamlet's
character. Whereas Hamlet in his first and succeeding scenes clearly
dissociated himself from the court (and such courtiers as Polonius and
Osric), here he just as clearly reassociates himself with his friends and
those of lesser degree. Hamlet's rejection of etiquette seems important
enough to warrant a return to dialogue in the last line, which return, in its
own way, recalls his final resumption of dialogue with his mother – 'One
word more, good lady' – following several chorus-like reflections likewise
in couplet form. In both scenes the attempt to integrate the hero in a more
self-contained mode of drama and the endeavour to delineate his
character as an image of human personality go together, but they do not
preclude the continuity, in a new context, of *platea*-derived popular
conventions and attitudes.

Usually a couplet occurring at the end of a scene does in fact conclude
it; and often enough the speaker of the couplet is the last actor to leave the
stage, sometimes even with a clear 'Away!' (*Troilus and Cressida* III, ii, 205).
It is true that the couplet spoken at this point has the effect of summing up
or emphasizing important ideas, that it made last lines easier to hear as
the actor retreated toward the rear doors, and that structurally it signalized

the break between scenes. But although these functions became more important in Shakespeare's day, quite different functions rooted in traditional platform stagecraft were still at work beneath the surface. In pursuing this point we must remember that in the pre-Shakespearean popular theatre illusion was achieved only in the course of a scene and could not be assumed at the very beginning. On a platform stage surrounded by spectators seated on the stage itself, the fiction of location has to be built up at the beginning of the scene and more or less abandoned at the end, when the illusion dissolved and the stage returned to the reality of the communal occasion in the playhouse. Since the actors who turned the 'word scenery' and related gestures into a locality left that *locus* at the end of the scene, the locality itself – having been created solely by words and the physical presence of the actors – vanished, faded away into air, 'into thin air', like 'the baseless fabric of this vision' (*The Tempest* IV, i, 148 and 151). The end of a scene, therefore, was a return to the beginning. And it is in light of such renewed neutrality on the stage that the *platea* position of figures like Richard III, Hamlet, Iago, Thersites, and Prospero allowed a special relationship with the audience throughout most of the play.

The actor delivering a concluding couplet in the presence of others – as Hamlet did – spoke from a *Figurenposition* functionally very much like the aside; for he established audience contact without departing from his role. (This kind of aside spoken upon leaving the stage or ending a scene was so common that special terms have been coined for it, such as 'exit aside' or 'end-of-scene aside'.)[53] The frequency of the concluding couplet corresponds to the no less frequent aside at the beginning of a scene. This is logical if the traditonal theatrical process of gradually building illusions on the platform stage is kept in mind. Although less effective dramatically, 'since they postpone the establishment of a relationship through dialogue',[54] the aside spoken by the actor entering for the first time or the aside at the beginning of a scene must have served equally traditional functions of *platea*-derived staging. Since locality did not exist at the beginning of the scene and could not be sustained *per se* beyond the end of the scene, the introductory and concluding *Figurenpositionen* tended to be physically or dramatically close to the audience. It was already traditional for the Vice figure to open the scene or play with an extended self-introduction that had no representational significance whatsoever.

Kyd, Marlowe, and Shakespeare dispensed to a considerable degree with this unveiled opening and closing audience contact. Marlowe went so far as to begin *in medias res* the introductory monologue in *The Jew of Malta*; Shakespeare often opened scenes in the middle of a dialogue. But traditional stagecraft still exerted a strong influence, and the non-dialogue opening (like Berowne's opening of Act IV, scene iii in *Love's Labour's Lost* discussed above) remained always an important element of construction.

Since for reasons of characterization or social or dramatic decorum not all characters were allowed the forms of speech that correspond to a *platea* mode of performance, it is not surprising that some types of figures concluded scenes more frequently than others. Although there is no hard and fast rule about this we could note, for example, that Thersites, who is definitely in touch with the audience, concludes scenes with marked frequency. Since he speaks in prose Thersites does not conclude with couplets, but his comments at the end of four scenes (III, iii, V, i, V, ii, V, iv) fulfill what is obviously a comparable function; sarcastic summary or evaluation of what has happened, spoken after the actors engaged in dialogue have left the stage. In *Timon of Athens*, concluding lines are likewise significant, not only because Timon, Alcibiades, and a Senator share the task of ending scenes with Apemantus (I, ii), the steward Flavius (II, ii, IV, ii), the servant Flaminius (III, iii), and a soldier (V, iii), but because these lesser characters are often only marginally integrated into the action of the play, and as such are well-suited to dismissing the illusion of *locus* and marking the return to the actual platform stage.

Similar observations can be made about the use of other forms of speech, such as the proverb. If M.P.Tilley's dictionary of proverbs is used as a basis for analysis, their distribution can be found to back up the relationship between *Figurenposition* and dramatic speech postulated here. *Hamlet*, for example, contains more proverbs than any other Shakespearean play; and it is noteworthy that Hamlet himself speaks seventy-one of the one hundred and four found in it. Likewise, the Fool in *King Lear* (who we must remember drops out of the play at the end of Act III) delivers twenty-one proverbs, Lear twenty-five, and Kent fourteen. This can be contrasted with Goneril's six, Edmund's two and Regan's three. In *Twelfth Night* Feste speaks twenty-nine proverbs and Sir Toby eighteen, while Malvolio is given a mere five. Thus, the use of proverbs functions as an effective means of characterization. In the case of Goneril, Regan, Malvolio, and other similar characters, the relative absence of proverbial speech suggests the 'new age of scientific inquiry and industrial development',[55] whose representatives, for better or worse, discard the form and content of popular wisdom.

As in the case of Iago and Richard III, the new mode of characterization and the traditional *Figurenposition* can be combined and made to enhance each other. But they can also create awkward tensions, as, for example, those between Edmund as we first see him (the bastard making scornful and inverting comments to the audience) and Duke Edmund as he appears later in the play (no longer in touch with the audience). From the point of view of stagecraft Edmund fulfills a variety of functions, like the very different Duke in *Measure for Measure*, when the downstage position takes on original, no longer traditional, functions. Thus, insofar as the popular legacy ceases to have an effect in such experimental transformations and is used in a way no longer consonant with its original context, Shakespeare's achievement consists in having combined the new poetic realism with modified and experimental versions of traditional stage practices.

Turned in on themselves and imprisoned by their own egotism, Malvolio, Regan, and Goneril represent a new individualism. They are so far removed, not only in moral outlook but also in physical space, from the plebeian audience and its collective understanding of the world and of art that they occupy a *Figurenposition* that permits knavish speech and self-revealing aside but not that type of proverb and wordplay that is rooted in the common experience and inherited traditions of the people. In fact, they are not given any forms of speech that recall the festive element and ritual origins of audience contact. Unlike Thersites, Apemantus, the servants, and the fools, their outlook, regardless of how brilliantly it is presented, does not permit any sustained downstage position. That is one reason why they do not conclude the play. For Shakespeare it is not these representatives of egotism, but rather lovers and cheerful characters or those who are sad but wise who generally have the last word and sustain the audience rapport into and beyond the play's ending.[56]

Notes

1. C.W. HODGES, 'The Lantern of Taste', *Shakespeare Survey* **12** (1959): 8. Cf. G.R. KERNODLE, *From Art to Theatre: Form and Convention in the Renaissance* (Chicago, 1944), pp.130–53. Cf.L.B. WRIGHT, *Shakespeare's Theatre and the Dramatic Tradition* (Washington, 1958), p.14: 'one cannot escape the conclusion that usage varied and that stage construction in the theatres may have differed in some important details'. For a discussion of the flexibility of Shakespeare's theatre, see J.L. STYAN, *Shakespeare's Stagecraft* (Cambridge, 1967), pp.7ff.

2. RICHARD HOSLEY, 'The Discovery-Space in Shakespeare's Globe', *Shakespeare Survey* **12** (1959):35–46.

3. G.F. REYNOLDS, *The Staging of Elizabethan Plays at the Red Bull Theater*: 1605–1625 (London, 1940), p.188; cf.pp. 131–63. E.K.Chambers had already postulated the existence of a 'curtained structure' in the Swan theatre, but had not enlarged upon his theory (*The Elizabethan Stage*, vol. 3, Oxford, 1923, p.86, hereafter cited as El.St.). C.W. Hodges (n.5 below) and LESLIE HOTSON (for example, in *Shakespeare's Wooden O*, London, 1960, pp.56–7)have gone far beyond this. Doubt about the existence of the rear had led to various reinterpretations of individual scenes (for example, RICHARD HOSLEY, 'The Staging of Desdemona's Bed', *Shakespeare Quarterly* **14** 1963: 57–65) and to the reconstruction of plays with the aid of concealed stages or tents (for example, L.J.Ross, 'The Use of a "Fit-Up" Booth in *Othello*', *Shakespeare Quarterly* **12** (1961): 359–70). The existence of similar structures in plays by Jonson and Chapman has also been postulated; cf. W.A. ARMSTRONG, 'The Enigmatic Elizabethan Stage', *English* **13** (1961): 216–20.

4. BERNARD MILES and JOSEPHINE WILSON, 'Three Festivals at the Mermaid Theatre', *Shakespeare Quarterly* 5(1954): 310:'We have learnt that it is impossible to play scenes on the so-called "inner stage", or even far upstage at all'.

5. C.W.HODGES, *The Globe Restored: A Study of the Elizabethan Theatre* (London, 1953), pp. 58–9. A.M.NAGLER (*Shakespeare's Stage* [reprint ed., New Haven, 1964]) characterizes the rentlike structure as an 'auxiliary stage, a potential scene of action' (p.26) and refers to the medieval example of the fixed-roof *pinaculum* in Vigil Raber's sketch of the play at Bozen, 1514 (p.49).

6. J.C. ADAMS, *The Globe Playhouse: Its Design and Equipment* (Cambridge, Mass.,1943), p.294; also the same author's 'The Original Staging of King Lear', in J.Q. *Adams Memorial Studies*, ed. James McManaway et al. (Washington, 1948), pp. 315–35.

7. G.F. REYNOLDS, 'Was there a "Tarras" in Shakespeare's Globe?' *Shakespeare Survey* 4 (1951): 100, n.9.

8. REYNOLDS, *The Staging of Elizabethan Plays* ..., p. 190.

9. T.J.KING, *Shakespearean Staging*: 1599–1642 (Cambridge, Mass., 1971), p.31.Cf. RICHARD HOSLEY, 'The Gallery over the Stage in the Public Payhouses of Shakespeare's Time', *Shakespeare Quarterly* 8 (1957): p.21, and the same author's 'Shakespeare's Use of a Gallery over the Stage', *Shakespeare Survey* 10 (1957): 77.

10. Cf. the graphic demonstration in GLYNNE WICKHAM, *Early English Stages: 1300–1600*, vol.2 (London, 1959), pp. 161–3. Henslowe's specifications require a 'Stadge and Tyreinge howse to be made, erected & settupp *within the saide fframe*' (italics mine; cf. Chambers, El.St.,2:137).

11. See RICHARD SOUTHERN, *The Open Stage* (London, 1953), pp. 15–21, and the drawing by Hodges in appendix A of *The Globe Restored*, pp. 170–7, which was preceded by the publication of 'Unworthy Scaffolds: Theory for the Reconstruction of Elizabethan Playhouses', *Shakespeare Survey* 3 (1951): 83–94.

12. *The Globe Restored*, p. 49.

13. J.Q. ADAMS, ed., *Chief Pre-Shakespearean Dramas* (Boston, 1924), p. 158, n. l.

14. Cf.J.W.SAUNDERS, 'Vaulting the Rails', *Shakespeare Survey* 7 (1954): 69–81.

15. ALLARDYCE NICOLL, 'Passing Over the Stage', *Shakespeare Survey* 12 (1959): 47–55. This has been confirmed by RICHARD SOUTHERN in *The Staging of Plays Before Shakespeare* (London, 1973),pp.569–70, where he suggests that there were small steps at the corner of the stage to facilitate entrance from and exit to the yard. Still, the evidence is not conclusive; 'passing over the stage' may indeed refer to no more than the movement of an actor around the platform from door to door. Since this book was written, work on the Elizabethan stage has continued to grow at an unprecedented rate. For some of the most stimulating contributions, see the collection of essays in *Renaissance Drama* 4 (1972), or the series *The Elizabethan Theatre* (ed.David Galloway, Toronto, 1969 ff). For what is perhaps the most rewarding discussion of some of the basic issues, see P.C.Kolin's Report on the 1971 MLA Conference on Renaissance Drama, paneled by Bernard Beckerman, Richard Hosley, and T.J.King (*Research Opportunities in Renaissance Drama* 15–16, 1972–73: 3–14). There are some new emphases and trends toward a consciousness of, for instance, the dramatic and 'emblematic' significance of the theatrical 'discovery', or, again, a new awareness, as formulated by Bernard Beckerman or Norman Rabkin, of the critical and social implications of historical research into the physical stage. (See, among many others, *Reinterpretations of*

Walter Cohen and Robert Weimann

Elizabethan Drama, Selected papers from the English Institute, ed. Norman
Rabkin, New York, 1969). But many questions remain unanswered and some
previous answers are increasingly questioned, as in Richard Hosley's mounting
objections to the 'liberal position' of C.W.Hodges and George Reynolds on the
use of curtained booths. See Hosley's well founded emphasis on plays like
Hamlet as 'an "arras" or "hanging" play, a purely open stage play' (Kolin's
Report, p.6). Here as elsewhere it may be said that 'extensive investigations of
the severely limited evidence have won us few widely and easily accepted
solutions'. See P.C. KOLIN and R.Q. WATT in the introduction to what is the most
useful recent 'Bibliography of Scholarship on the Elizabethan Stage Since
Chambers', *Research Opportunities in Renaissance Drama* **15–16** (1972–73):33–59.
There is a shorter but selective bibliography, together with a summary, by
MICHAEL JAMIESON, 'Shakespeare in the Theatre', *Shakespeare: Select Bibliographical
Guides*, ed. Stanley Wells (London, 1973). For a somewhat fuller synthesis see
ANDREW GURR, *The Shakespearean Stage: 1574–1642* (Cambridge, 1970).

16. For a classic statement of the older theory, see A.H. THORNDIKE, *Shakespeare's
Theater* (New York, 1916), p. 77. On the following, cf. Rudolf Stamm, *Geschichte
des Englischen Theaters* (Bern, 1951), pp. 51, 101, 110, for an extremely balanced
statement of the problems involved.

17. J.W. SAUNDERS, 'Vaulting the Rails', *Shakespeare Survey* 7 (1954), p. 79.

18. *Tarlton's Jests and News out of Purgatory* (London, 1844), p. 27.

19. Ibid., pp. 14, 22–23, 44. Cf the jest, 'How Tarlton and one in the gallery fell out'.

20. Cf ANNE RIGHTER, *Shakespeare and the Idea of the Play* (London, 1962), *passim*.

21. ALFRED HARBAGE, 'The Role of the Shakespearean Producer', *Shakespeare Jahrbuch*
91 (1955), p. 163. Cf JOHN RUSSEL BROWN, *Free Shakespeare* (London, 1974).
especially pp. 48–57, where the significance of such performances without
directors and designers is explored. See BERNARD BECKERMAN (*Shakespeare at the
Globe: 1599–1609*, New York, 1962, p. 24): 'From a common creative act arose the
plays that Shakespeare penned and the productions that his friends presented.
The record of this partnership is contained in the extant scripts, not merely in
stage directions or in dialogue, but in the very substance of the dramatist's craft,
the structure of the incidents'.

22. See STAMM, *Geschichte des englischen Theaters*, p. 55.

23. Ibid. Cf JACKSON I. COPE, *The Theater and the Dream: From Metaphor to Form in
Renaissance Drama* (Baltimore/London, 1973), especially the prologue,'The
Rediscovery of Anti-Form in Renaissance Drama', pp 1–13. (I have reviewed and
commented on this suggestive book in *Zeitschrift für Anglistik* **24** 1976: 78–80.)

24. ALFRED HARBAGE, *Shakespeare and the Rival Traditions* (New York, 1952), pp 296,
307, 298.

25. Quoted from HARBAGE, ibid, p. 305.

26. Indeed, as Alexander Anikst stresses, Shakespeare was no partisan of popular
rule ('Shakespeare – volkstumlicher Schriftsteller', *Shakespearowski Sbornik*,
Moscow, 1958, p. 43). Cf Anselm Schlosser's 'Zur Frage" Volk und Mob "bei
Shakespeare', ZAA 4 (1956): 148–71, and Brents Stirling's important study of *The
Populace in Shakespeare* (New York, 1949). LORENTZ ECKHOFF, *Shakespeare,
Spokesman of the Third Estate* (Oxford, 1954), is an exceedingly problematic book.
Above quotation from Ben Jonson in E.K. CHAMBERS, *William Shakespeare: A
Study of Facts and Problems*, vol 2 (Oxford, 1930), p. 209.

Shakespearean Tragedy

27. Cf ANTON MÜLLER- BELLINGHAUSEN, 'Die Workulisse bei Shakespeare', *Shakespeare Jahrbuch* **91** (1955): 182–95, among others.

28. RUDOLF STAMM, 'Dichtung und Theater in Shakespeares Werk', *Shakespeare Jahrbuch* **98** (1962): 12; cf. the same author's *Zwischen Vision und Wirklichkeit* (Bern/Munich, 1964), pp. 9–27.

29. WOLFGANG CLEMEN, *Shakespeare's Soliloquies*, Pres. Address of the Mod. Hum. Research Assoc., (1964), pp. 1, 8, 24; *Shakespeares Monologe* (Göttingen, 1964), p. 5 Cf also KENNETH MUIR, 'Shakespeare's Soliloquies', *Ocidente* **67** (1964): 45–48; as well as the older studies by M.L. Arnold (1911) and Hermann Poepperling (Dissertation, 1912); cf NEVILL COGHILL, *Shakespeare's Professional Skills* (Cambridge, 1964), pp. 128–63.

30. Cf B.L. JOSEPH, *Elizabethan Acting* (London, 1952) pp. 122, 132; J.L. STYAN, 'The Actor at the Foot of Shakespeare's Platform', *Shakespeare Survey* **12** (1959): 56–63.

31. J.D. Wilson's text, 'The New Shakespeare', (reprint ed, Cambridge, 1961) is quoted, with the exception of the emendation (which follows other editors) 'curb' (1.169) and the folio reading 'thus' (instead of Wilson this from Q2, 1.179).

32. Behind John Dover Wilson's highly detailed stage directions as M.C. Bradbrook noted, stand 'traces of nineteenth century realist staging' (*Elizabethan Stage Conditions: A Study of their Place in the Interpretation* of Shakespeare's Plays, 1931 Hamden, Conn., 1962, p. 136).

33. WOLFGANG CLEMEN, *Kommentar zu Shakespeares Richard III* (Göttingen, 1957), p. 35.

34. Even before Shakespeare such a 'thus' is frequently associated with some form of audience address; cf BERNARD SPIVACK, *Shakespeare and the Allegory of Evil* (New York, 1958), p. 190. This corresponds to the Scrivener's 'such' or 'Here's' and similar verbal gestures which are used to present and to comment on the play in performance.

35. That the actor of Lear actually spoke to a particular spectator cannot, of course, be proved: but that Shakespeare's audience was familiar with such a tradition is evident from the unmistakable precedents in late Moralities and interludes. In the popular *King Cambises*, Ambidexter says: 'I care not if I be maried befor to-morrow at noone, / If mariage be a thing that so may be had. / How say you, maid?...' (950ff.). J.Q. Adams' stage direction, 'To one in the audience', is undoubtedly correct. An original instance occurs in Heywood's *The Play of the Weather*: '*Mery-reporte*. My Lord, there standeth a sewter even here behynde, / ... He wolde hundte a sow or twayne out of thys sorte. / *Here he poynteth to the women* (Adams, (ed), 245ff.).

36. *Elizabethan Acting*, pp 123ff, 149. The far-reaching generalization ('we have not to do with true dialogue, but with a sequence of alternate declamation', p. 131) contradicts what is, to my mind, a correct interpretation, 'that the style must have varied ... according to the needs of individual scenes. But even the fact that 'Elizabethan acting varied in accordance with the style of the words to be spoken' (p. 151) does not derive, finally, from conventions of rhetoric, but rather from the scenic and dramatic 'mingle-mangle' of the popular theater, which also, of course, admits of rhetoric. Beckerman (pp. 113–21) offers a convincing total picture and a just critique of the exaggerated claims for rhetoric. See LEONARD GOLDSTEIN, 'On the Transition From Formal to Naturalistic Acting in the Elizabethan and Post-Elizabethan Theatre', *Bull. New York Public Library* **62**

(1958): 330–49. A similar tendency 'from formalism to illusion' is asserted by W.G. McCollum ('Formalism and Illusion in Shakespearean Drama, 1595–1598', *Quarterly Journal of Speech* **31**. 1945:446 ff.), Clifford Leech (*Shakespeare's Tragedies*, London, 1950, p. 56), and others.

37. Eugen Kilian, 'Der Shakespearesche Monolog und seine Spielweise', *Shakespeare Jahrbuch* **39** (1903): xviii.

38. Righter, p. 205.

39. Cf *Hamlet*, ed. Dover Wilson p. 276.

40. L.L. Schücking, *Die Charakterprobleme bei Shakespeare* (Leipzig, 1932), p. 19.

41. Kilian, p. xxxix.

42. Schücking. pp 25–6

43. *Shakespeare and the Allegory of Evil*, pp 286, 302, 303, 339, 341; Spivack also speaks, with reference to the Vice's relationship to the audience , of 'homiletic logic' (p 168) and even of 'homiletic bravura' and 'homiletic jest' (p 405). Cf. above chapter IV, n. 82.

44. S.L. Bethell, *Shakespeare and the Popular Dramatic Tradition* (London, 1944) p. 81.

45. *The Life of Timon of Athens*, ed. J.V. Maxwell, 'The New Shakespeare' (Cambridge, 1957).

46. A.P. Rossiter, *English Drama from Early Times to the Elizabethans* (London , 1950), p. 75.

47. Clemen, *Kommentar zu Shakespeares Richard III*, p. 151.

48. Quoted from *Troilus and Cressida*, ed. Alice Walker, 'The New Shakespeare' (Cambridge, 1957)

49. Cf L.C. Knights, 'Shakespeare's Politics: With Some Reflections on the Nature of Tradition', *Proceedings of the British Academy* (1957):117.

50. The etymology of 'infant' further enhances the possible depth of the pun since the Latin substantive use of *infans* – 'unable to speak' – might be a perfect description of the silent *tableau vivant* effect achieved in some medieval pageantry and dramaturgy. This, at any rate would support the already playful oxymoron, 'old infant' : old in the history of the theater, infant , as the etymology suggests, in terms of the mode of performance. (Here I wish to thank my editor, to whom I owe this note as well as the interpretation of Berowne's *Figurenpositions*.)

51. See Doris Fenton, *The Extra-Dramatic Moment in Elizabethan plays before 1616* (Philadelphia, 1930), pp. 113ff.

52. On the myriad dramatic functions of the aside (interest , characterization, irony, transmission of information, etc.), cf. Wolfgang Riehle, *Das Beiseitesprechen bei Shakespeare: Ein Beitrag zur Dramaturgie des elisabethanischen Dramas*, Dissertation (Munich, 1964), especially pp. 111ff.

53. Riehle, p. 26.

54. Ibid p. 27.

55. J.F. Danby, *Shakespeare's Doctrine of Nature: A Study of King Lear* (London, 1961), p. 46.

56. The audience rapport of Gloucester, Iago, and, in part, Edmund derives from other premises. They are, like their predecessor the knavish Vice, the theatrical managers of their own intrigues and dramatic inversions. They continue to challenge the status quo, not so much from any personal motivation (although Shakespeare, somewhat perfunctorily, supplies that too) but rather for the sake of challenge and negation. They are great perverters of state, marriage, and filial love, re-enacting the *Geist, der stets verneint* – the Mephistophelean spirit which persistently destroys. In this sense, their audience contact is profoundly in the popular tradition. Their natural ambivalence as well as their insuperable vitality stem to a degree from the exuberance with which they freely exploit the vantage points of both platform and *locus*, ritual and representation.

4 New Historicism

STEPHEN GREENBLATT *THE IMPROVISATION OF POWER**

Stephen Greenblatt is Professor of English Literature at the University of California at Berkeley. His book *Renaissance Self-fashioning from More to Shakespeare*, published by the University of Chicago Press in 1980, inaugurated the movement known as 'New Historicism'. Greenblatt's starting position is the post-structuralist perception of the human subject as discontinuous, moulded in and through variable relationships of power. Although this position can be traced back to the work of Michel Foucault, it also draws eclectically upon Marxist and Freudian models. One area of contention concerns the extent to which literature and drama simply figure forth relations of power or whether they permit some possibility of resistance, or even subversion. Greenblatt refuses to be drawn into any theory of grand narratives, but his reading of Foucault is an extraordinarily subtle one which does not at all rule out resistance as a position within the specific relations of power. Indeed, he takes as his starting point the Foucauldian assertion that 'Power is not something that is acquired, seized or shared, something one holds on to or allows to slip away; power is exercised from innumerable points, in the interplay of non-egalitarian and mobile relations' (Michael Foucault, *The History of Sexuality, Vol. 1*, Harmondsworth, 1981, p.94). Greenblatt undertakes to investigate in precise historical detail the interplay of these 'non-egalitarian and mobile relations', exploring the effects that power exerts in and through particular fields of discourse. But Greenblatt goes further than that in his investigation of the conditions which follow from the perception that 'improvisation is made possible by the subversive perception of another's truth as an ideological construct', but that this might also involve violence and anxiety of various kinds. In the following extract Greenblatt explores the

---

*Reprinted from *Renaissance Self-fashioning from More to Shakespeare* (Chicago: Chicago University Press, 1980), pp. 222–54.

opposition between the human and the bestial as a structuring agency, nothing its operations in a text such as Shakespeare's *Othello*.

Spenser and Marlowe are, from the perspective of this study, mighty opposites, poised in antagonism as radical as that of More and Tyndale in the 1530s. If Spenser sees human identity as conferred by loving service to legitimate authority, to the yoked power of god and the state, Marlowe sees identity established at those moments in which order – political, theological, sexual – is violated. If repetition for Spenser is an aspect of the patient labor of civility, for Marlowe it is the means of constituting oneself in an anonymous void. If Spenser's heroes strive for balance and control, Marlowe's strive to shatter the restraints upon their desires. If in Spenser there is fear of the excess that threatens to engulf order and seems to leave an ineradicable taint on temperance itself, in Marlowe there is fear of the order that threatens to extinguish excess and seems to have always already turned rebellion into a tribute to authority. If Spenser writes for an aristocratic and upper-middle-class audience in a self-consciously archaizing manner, thereby participating in the decorative revival of feudal trappings that characterized Elizabethan courtly ritual,[1] Marlowe writes for the new public theater in a blank verse that must have seemed, after the jog-trot fourteeners of the preceding decades, like reality itself. If Spenser holds up his 'other world' to the gaze of power and says, 'Behold! This rich beauty is your own face', Marlowe presents *his* and says, 'Behold! This tragic-comic, magnificent deformity is how you appear in my rich art'. If Spenser's art constantly questions its own status in order to protect power from such questioning, Marlowe undermines power in order to raise his art to the status of a self-regarding, self-justifying absolute.

There is not, of course, anything in Spenser or Marlowe comparable to the violent polemical exhange between More and Tyndale, but there is at least one resonant moment of conjunction that will serve to exemplify the opposition I have just sketched here. In book 1, canto 7 of *The Faerie Queene*, dismayed by the news that Redcrosse has been overthrown by the giant Orgoglio, Una providentially encounters Prince Arthur, the embodiment of Magnificence – the virtue, according to the letter of Ralegh, that 'is the perfection of all the rest, and containeth in it them all'. This is Arthur's first appearance in the poem, and there follows an elaborate description of his gorgeous armor, a description that includes the following stanza on his helmet's crest:

Vpon the top of all his loftie crest,
A bunch of haires discolourd diuersly,
With sprincled pearle, and gold full richly drest,
Did shake, and seem'd to daunce for iollity,

Like to an almond tree ymounted hye
On top of greene *Selinis* all alone,
With blossomes braue bedecked daintily;
Whose tender locks do tremble euery one
At euery little breath, that vnder heauen is blowne.

(1. 7. 32)

As early as the late eighteenth century, a reader records his surprise to find
this passage almost verbatim in part 2 of *Tamburlaine*.[2] It occurs in the scene
in which Tamburlaine is drawn on stage in his chariot by the captive kings,
'with bits in their mouths', the stage direction tells us, 'reins in his left
hand, in his right hand a whip, with which he scourgeth them'. Exulting in
his triumphant power, Tamburlaine baits his captives, hands over the
weeping royal concubines to satisfy the lust of his common soldiers, and –
his own erotic satisfaction – imagines his future conquests:

Through the streets with troops of conquered kings,
I'll ride in golden armour like the Sun,
And in my helm a triple plume shall spring,
Spangled with Diamonds dancing in the air,
To note me Emperor of the three-fold world,
Like to an almond tree ymounted high,
Upon the lofty and celestial mount,
Of ever green *Selinus* quaintly decked
With blooms more white than *Hericina's* brows,
Whose tender blossoms tremble every one,
At every little breath that thorough heaven is blown.

(4, 3, 4094–4113)

What is sung by Spenser in praise of Arthur is sung by Tamburlaine in
praise of himself; the chivalric accoutrement, an emblem of Arthur's
magnanimous knighthood, is here part of Tamburlaine's paean to his own
power lust. Lines that for Spenser belong to the supreme figure of civility,
the chief upholder of the Order of Maidenhead, the worshipful servant of
Gloriana, for Marlowe belong to the fantasy life of the Scythian Scourge of
God. Marlowe's scene is self-consciously emblematic, as if it were a
theatrical improvisation in the Spenserean manner, but now with the hero's
place taken by a character who, in his sadistic excess, most closely
resembles Orgoglio.[3] And even as we are struck by the radical difference,
we are haunted by the vertiginous possibility of an underlying sameness.
What if Arthur and Tamburlaine are not separate and opposed? What if
they are two faces of the same thing, embodiments of the identical power?
Tamburlaine's is the face Arthur shows to his enemies or, alternatively,
Arthur's is the face Tamburlaine shows to his followers. To the Irish kern

Spenser's Prince of Magnanimity looks like the Scourge of God; to the English courtier, Marlowe's grotesque conqueror looks like the Faerie Queene.

How shall we characterize the power that possesses both faces and can pass from one to the other? In a famous passage in *The Prince*, Machiavelli writes that a prince must know well how to use both the beast and the man, and hence the ancients depicted Achilles and other heroes as educated by Chiron the centaur. This discussion is an early instance of the celebration of psychic mobility that has continued to characterize discussions of Western consciousness to the present time. Thus in his influential study of modernization in the Middle East, *The Passing of Traditional Society*, the sociologist Daniel Lerner defines the West as a 'mobile society', a society characterized not only by certain enlightened and rational public practices but also by the inculcation in its people of a '*mobile sensibility*' so adaptive to change that re-arrangement of the self-system is its distinctive mode'.[4] While traditional society, Professor Lerner argues, functions on the basis of a 'highly constrictive personality' (51), one that resists change and is incapable of grasping the situation of another, the mobile personality of Western society is 'distinguished by a high capacity for identification with new aspects of his environment', for he 'comes equipped with the mechanisms needed to incorporate new demands upon himself that arise outside of his habitual experience' (49). Those mechanisms Professor Lerner subsumes under the single term *empathy*, which he defines as 'the capacity to see oneself in the other fellow's situation' (50). In the West, this capacity was fostered first by the physical mobility initiated by the Age of Exploration, then confirmed and broadened by the mass media. 'These', he writes, 'have peopled the daily world of their audience with sustained, even intimate, experience of the lives of others. "Ma Perkins", "The Goldbergs", "I Love Lucy" – all these bring us friends we never met, but whose joys and sorrows we intensely "share"' (53). And the international diffusion of the mass media means a concomitant diffusion of psychic mobility and hence of modernization: 'In our time, indeed, the spread of empathy around the world is accelerating' (52).

To test the rate of the acceleration, Professor Lerner devised a set of questions that he and his assistants put to a cross-section of the inhabitants of the Middle East, to porters and cobblers, as well as grocers and physicians. The questions began, 'If you were made editor of a newspaper, what kind of a paper would you run?' and I confess myself in complete sympathy with that class of respondents who, like one shepherd interviewed in a village near Ankara, gasped 'My God! How can you say such a thing? ... A poor villager ... master of the whole world' (24). Professor Lerner invariably interprets such answers as indicative of a constrictive personality incapable of empathy, but in fact the Turkish shepherd, with his Tamburlainian language, reintroduces the great missing term in the analysis of modernization, and that term is *power*. For my own part, I would like in this chapter to delineate the Renaissance origins of the 'mobile sensibility' and, having done so, to shift the ground from 'I Love Lucy' to *Othello* in order to demonstrate that what Professor Lerner calls 'empathy', Shakespeare calls 'Iago'.

To help us return from the contemporary Middle East to the early seventeenth century, let us dwell for a moment on Professor Lerner's own concept of Renaissance origins: 'Take the factor of physical mobility', he writes, 'which initiated Western take-off in an age when the earth was underpopulated in terms of the world man–land ration. Land was to be had, more or less, for the finding. The great explorers took over vast real estate by planting a flag; these were slowly filled with new populations over generations' (65). It didn't exactly happen this way. Land does not become 'real estate' quite so easily, and the underpopulation was not found but created by those great explorers. Demographers of Mesoamerica now estimate, for example, that the population of Hispaniola in 1492 was 7–8 million, perhaps as high as 11 million. Reduction to that attractive man–land ratio was startlingly sudden; by 1501, enslavement, disruption of agriculture and, above all, European disease had reduced the population to some 700,000; by 1512, to 28,000.[5] The unimaginable massiveness of the death rate did not, of course, go unnoticed; European observers took it as a sign of God's determination to cast down the idolaters and open the New World to Christianity.

With the passage from the sociologist's bland world of ceremonial flag-planting in an empty landscape to violent displacement and insidious death, we have already moved toward Shakespeare's tragedy, and we move still closer if we glance at an incident recounted in 1525 by Peter Martyr in the Seventh Decade of *De orbe novo*. Faced with a serious labor shortage in the gold mines as a result of the decimation of the native population, the Spanish in Hispaniola began to raid neighbouring islands. Two ships reached an outlying island in the Lucayas (now called the Bahamas) where they were received with awe and trust. The Spanish learned through their interpreters that the natives believed that after death their souls were first purged of their sins in icy northern mountains, then borne to a paradisal island in the south, whose beneficent, lame prince offered them innumerable pleasures: 'the soul enjoys eternal delights, among the dancings and songs of young maidens, and among the embracements of their children, and whatsoever they loved heretofore; they babble also there, that such as grow old, wax young again, so that all are of like years full of joy and mirth'.[6] When the Spanish understood these imaginations, writes Martyr, they proceeded to persuade the natives 'that they came from those places, where they should see their parents, and childern, and all their kindred and friends that were dead: and should enjoy all kind of delights, together with the embracements and fruition of beloved things' (625). Thus deceived, the entire population of the island passed 'singing and rejoicing', Martyr says, onto the ships and were taken to the gold mines of Hispaniola. The Spanish , however, reaped less profit than they had anticipated; when they grasped what had happened to them, the Lucayans, like certain German Jewish communities during the Crusades, undertook mass suicide: 'becoming desperate, they either slew themselves, or choosing to famish, gave up their faint spirits, being persuaded by no reason, or violence, to take food' (625).

Martyr, it appears, feels ambivalent about the story. He is certain that God disapproves of such treachery, since many of those who perpetrated the fraud subsequently die violent deaths; on the other hand, he opposes those who would free enslaved natives, since bitter experience has shown that even those Indians who have apparently been converted to Christianity will, given the slightest opportunity, revert to 'their ancient and native vices' and turn savagely against those who had instructed them 'with fatherly charity' (627). But, for our purposes, Martyr's ambivalence is less important than the power of his story to evoke a crucial Renaissance mode of behavior that links Lerner's 'empathy' and Shakespeare's 'Iago': I shall call that mode *improvisation*, by which I mean the ability both to capitalize on the unforeseen and to transform given materials into one's own scenario. The spur-of-the-moment quality of improvisation is not as critical here as the opportunistic grasp of that which seems fixed and established. Indeed, as Castiglione and others in the Renaissance well understood, the impromptu character of an improvisation is itself often a calculated mask, the product of careful preparation.[7] Conversely, all plots, literary and behavioral, inevitably have their origin in a moment prior to formal coherence, a moment of experimental, aleatory impulse in which the available, received materials are curved toward a novel shape. We cannot locate a point of pure premeditation or pure randomness. What is essential is the Europeans' ability again and again to insinuate themselves into the preexisting political, religious, even psychic structures of the natives and to turn those structures to their advantage. The process is familiar to us by now as the most tawdry business fraud, so familiar that we assume a virtually universal diffusion of the necessary improvisational talent, but that assumption is almost certainly misleading. There are periods and cultures in which the ability to insert oneself into the consciousness of another is of relatively slight importance, the object of limited concern; others in which it is a major preoccupation, the object of cultivation and fear. Professor Lerner is right to insist that his ability is a characteristically (though not exclusively) Western mode, present to varying degrees in the classical and medieval world and greatly strengthened from the Renaissance onward; he misleads only in insisting further that it is an act of imaginative generosity, a sympathetic appreciation of the situation of the other fellow. For when he speaks confidently of the 'spread of empathy around the world' we must understand that he is speaking of the exercise of Western power, power that is creative as well as destructive, but that is scarcely ever wholly disinterested and benign.

To return to the Lucayan story, we may ask ourselves what conditions exist in Renaissance culture that make such an improvisation possible. It depends first upon the ability and willingness to play a role, to transform oneself, if only for a brief period and with mental reservations, into another. This necessitates the acceptance of disguise, the ability to effect a divorce, in Ascham's phrase, between the tongue and the heart. Such role-playing in turn depends upon the transformation of another's reality into a manipulable fiction. The Spanish had to perceive the Indians' religious beliefs as illusions, 'imaginations' as Martyr's English translator calls them. Lucayan society, Martyr observes, is based upon a principle of reverent obedience fostered by a set of religious fables that 'are delivered by word of mouth and tradition from the Elders to the younger, for a most sacred and true history, insomuch as he who but seemed to think otherwise, should be thrust out of the society of men' (623). The Lucayan king performs the supreme sacral functions and partakes fully in the veneration accorded to the idols, so that if he were to command one of his subjects to cast himself down from a precipice, the subject would immediately comply. The king uses this absolute power to ensure the just distribution, to families according to need, of the tribe's food, all of which is stored communally in royal granaries: 'They had the golden age, *mine and thine*, the seeds of discord, were far removed from them' (618). Martyr then perceives the social function of Lucayan religious concepts, the native apparatus for their transmission and reproduction, and the punitive apparatus for the enforcement of belief. In short, he grasps Lucayan religion as an ideology, and it is this perception that licenses the transformation of 'sacred and true history' into 'crafty and subtle imaginations' (625) that may be exploited.

If improvisation is made possible by the subversive perception of another's truth as an ideological construct, that construct must at the same time be grasped in terms that bear a certain structural resemblance to one's own set of beliefs. An ideology that is perceived as entirely alien would permit no point of histrionic entry; it could be destroyed but not performed. Thus the Lucayan religion, in Martyr's account, is an anamorphic representation of Catholicism: there are 'images' carried forth with solemn pomp on the 'holy day of adoration'; worshippers kneel reverently before these images, sing 'hymns', and make offerings, 'which at night the nobles divide among them, as our priests do the cakes or wafers which women offer' (622); there are 'holy relics' about which the chief priest, standing in his 'pulpit', preaches, and, as we have seen, there is absolution for sin, purgatory, and eternal delight in paradise. The

European account of the native religion must have borne some likeness to what the Lucayans actually believed; why else would they have danced, singing and rejoicing, onto the Spanish ships? But it is equally important that the religion is conceived as analogous to Catholicism, close enough to permit improvisation, yet sufficiently distanced to protect European beliefs from the violence of fictionalization. The Spanish were not compelled to perceive their own religion as a manipulable human construct; on the contrary, the compulsion of their own creed was presumably strengthened by their contemptuous exploitation of an analogous symbolic structure.

This absence of reciprocity is an aspect of the total economy of the mode of improvisation that I have sketched here. For what we may see in the Lucayan story is an early manifestation of an exercise of power that was subsequently to become vastly important and remains a potent force in our lives; the ownership of another's labor conceived as involving no supposedly 'natural' reciprocal obligation (as in feudalism) but rather functioning by concealing the very fact of ownership from the exploited who believe that they are acting freely and in their own interest. Of course, once the ships reached Hispaniola, this concealed ownership gave way to direct enslavement; the Spanish were not capable of continuing the improvisation into the very mines. And it is this failure to sustain the illusion that led to the ultimate failure of the enterprise, for, of course, the Spanish did not want dead Indians but live mineworkers. It would take other, subtler minds, in the Renaissance and beyond, to perfect the means to sustain indefinitely an indirect enslavement.

I have called improvisation a central Renaissance mode of behavior, but the example on which I have focused is located on a geographical margin and might only seem to bear out Immanuel Wallerstein's theory that Western Europe in the sixteenth century increasingly established its ownership of the labor and resources of those located in areas defined as peripheral.[8] But I would argue that the phenomenon I have described is found in a wide variety of forms closer to home. It may be glimpsed, to suggest two significant instances, in the relation of Tudor power to Catholic symbolism and the characteristic form of rhetorical education.

The Anglican Church and the monarch who was its Supreme Head did not, as radical Protestants demanded, eradicate Catholic ritual but rather improvised within it in an attempt to assume its power. Thus, for example, in the Accession Day celebration of 1590, we are told that the queen, sitting in the Tilt gallery:

> ... did suddenly hear a music so sweet and so secret, as every one thereat greatly marvelled. And hearkening to that excellent melody, the earth as it were opening, there appears as Pavilion, made of white Taffeta, being in proportion like unto the scared Temple of the Virgins Vestal. This Temple seemed to consist upon pillars of porphyry, arched like unto a

Church, within it were many lamps burning. Also, on the one side an Altar covered with cloth of gold; and thereupon two wax candles burning in rich candlesticks; upon the Altar also were laid certain Princely presents, which after by three Virgins were presented unto her Majesty.[9]

This secular epiphany permits us to identify two of the characteristic operations of improvisation:displacement and absorption. By displacement I mean the process whereby a prior symbolic structure is compelled to coexist with other centres of attention that do not necessarily conflict with the original structure but are not swept up in its gravitational pull; indeed, as here, the sacred may find itself serving as an adornment, a backdrop, an occasion for a quite secular phenomenon. By absorption I mean the process whereby a symbolic structure is taken into the ego so completely that it ceases to exist as an external phenomenon; in the Accession Day ceremony, instead of the secular prince humbling herself before the sacred, the sacred seems only to enhance the ruler's identity, to express her power.[10]

Both displacement and absorption are possible here because the religious symbolism was already charged with the celebration of power. What we are witnessing is a shift in the institution that controls and profits from the interpretation of such symbolism, a shift mediated in this instance by the classical scholarship of Renaissance humanism. The invocation of the Temple of the Vestal Virgins is the sign of that transformation of belief into ideology that we have already examined; the Roman mythology, deftly keyed to England's Virgin Queen, helps to fictionalize Catholic ritual sufficiently for it to be displaced and absorbed.

This enzymatic function of humanism leads directly to our second instance of domestic improvisation, for the cornerstone of the humanist project was a rhetorical education. In *The Tudor Play of Mind*, Joel Altman has recently demonstrated the central importance for English Renaissance culture of the *argumentum in utramque partem*, the cultivation of the scholar's power to speak equally persuasively for diametrically opposed positions. The practice permeated intellectual life in the early sixteenth century and was, Altman convincingly argues, one of the formative influences on the early drama.[11] It is in the spirit of such rhetorical mobility that Erasmus praises More, as we have seen, for his ability to play the man of all hours with all men and that Roper recalls the young More's dazzling improvisations in Cardinal Morton's Christmas plays.

The hagiographical bias of Roper's and most subsequent writing on More has concealed the extent to which this improvisational gift is closely allied to a control of power in the law courts and the royal service: the mystification of manipulation as disinterested empathy begins as early as the sixteenth century. As a corrective, we need only recall More's controversial works, such as *The Confutation of Tyndale's Answer*, whose recurrent method is through improvisation to transform the heretic's faith into a fiction, then absorb it into a new symbolic structure that will ridicule or consume it. Thus Tyndale had written:

> Sin we through fragility never so oft, yet as soon as we repent and come into the right way again, and unto the testament which God hath made in Christ's blood: our sins vanish away as smoke in the wind, and as darkness at the coming of light, or as thou cast a little blood or milk into the main sea.

More responds by maliciously improvising on Tyndale's text:

> Neither purgatory need to be feared when we go hence, not penance need to be done while we be here, but sin and be sorry and sit and make merry, and then sin again and then repent a little and run to the ale and wash away the sin, think once on God's promise and then do what we list. For hoping sure in that, kill we ten men on a day, we cast but a little blood into the main sea.

Having thus made a part of his own, More continues by labeling Tyndale's argument about penance as 'but a piece of his poetry' – an explicit instance of that fictionalization we have witnessed elsewhere – and concludes:

> Go me to Martin Luther ... While that friar lieth with his nun and woteth well he doth nought [i.e.,knows he does evil], and saith still he doth well:let Tyndale tell me what repenting is that. He repenteth every morning, and to bed again every night; thinketh on God's promise first, and then go sin again upon trust of God's testament, and then he calleth it casting of a little milk into the main sea.[12]

Improvisation here obviously does not intend to deceive its original object but to work upon a third party, the reader, who might be wavering between the reformers and the Catholic Church. If the heretic speaks of sin redeemed by God's testament as milk, More returns that milk to sin, then surpasses the simple reversal by transforming it to semen, while he turns the sea that imaged for Tyndale the boundlessness of divine forgiveness into the sexual insatiability of Luther's nun.

These perversions of the reformer's text are greatly facilitated by the fact that the text was already immersed in an intensely charged set of metaphorical transformations – that is, More seizes upon the brilliant instability of Tyndale's prose with its own nervous passage from Christ's blood to sin conceived progressively as smoke, darkness, blood, and finally milk. More's artful improvisation makes it seem that murder and lust lay just beneath the surface of the original discourse, as a kind of dark subtext, and he is able to do so more plausibly because both violence and sexual anxiety are in fact powerful underlying forces in Tyndale's prose as in More's. That is, once again, there is a haunting structural homology between the improviser and his other.

I would hope that by now *Othello* seems virtually to force itself upon us as the supreme symbolic expression of the cultural mode I have been describing, for violence, sexual anxiety, and improvisation are the materials out of which the drama is constructed. To be sure, there are many other explorations of these materials in Shakespeare – one thinks of Richard III wooing Anne[13] or, in comedy, of Rosalind playfully taking advantage of the disguise that exile has forced upon her – but none so intense and radical. In Iago's first soliloquy, Shakespeare goes out of his way to emphasize the improvised nature of the villain's plot:

> Cassio's a proper man, let me see now,
> To get this place, and to make up my will,
> A double knavery ... how, how? ... let me see,
> After some time, to abuse Othello's ear,
> That he is too familiar with his wife:
> He has a person and a smooth dispose,
> To be suspected, fram'd to make women false:
> The Moor a free and open nature too,
> That thinks men honest that but seems to be so:
> And will as tenderly be led by the nose ...
> As asses are.
> I ha't, it is engender'd; Hell and night
> Must bring this monstrous birth to the world's light.
>
> (I, iii, 390–402)[14]

We will try shortly to cast some light on why Iago conceives of his activity here as sexual; for the moment, we need only to observe all of the marks of the impromptu and provisional, extending to the ambiguity of the third-person pronoun: 'to abuse Othello's ear / That he is too familiar with his wife'. This ambiguity is felicitous; indeed, though scarcely visible at this point, it is the dark essence of Iago's whole enterprise which is, as we shall see, to play upon Othello's buried perception of his own sexual relations with Desdemona as adulterous.[15]

What I have called the marks of the impromptu extend to Iago's other speeches and actions through the course of the whole play. In act 2, he declares of his conspiracy, ''tis here, but yet confus'd; / Knavery's plain face is never seen till us'd', and this half-willed confusion continues through the agile, hectic maneuvers of the last act until the moment of exposure and silence. To all but Roderigo, of course, Iago presents himself as incapable of improvisation, except in the limited and seemingly benign form of banter and jig.[16] And even here, he is careful, when Desdemona asks him to improvise her praise, to declare himself unfit for the task:

> I am about it, but indeed my invention
> Comes from my pate as birdlime does from frieze,
> It plucks out brain and all: but my Muse labours,
> And thus she is deliver'd.

(II, i, 125–8)

Lurking in the homely denial of ability is the image of his invention as birdlime, and hence a covert celebration of this power to ensnare others. Like Jonson's Mosca, Iago is fully aware of himself as an improviser and revels in his ability to manipulate his victims, to lead them by the nose like asses, to possess their labor without their ever being capable of grasping the relation in which they are enmeshed. Such is the relation Iago establishes with virtually every character in the play, from Othello and Desdemona to such minor figures as Montano and Bianca. For the Spanish colonialists, improvisation could only bring the Lucayans into open enslavement; for Iago, it is the key to a mastery whose emblem is the 'duteous and knee-crooking knave' who dotes 'on his own obsequious bondage' (1.i.45–6), a mastery invisible to the servant, a mastery, that is, whose character is essentially ideological. Iago's attitude toward Othello is nonetheless colonial: though he finds himself in a subordinate position, the ensign regards his black general as 'an erring barbarian' whose 'free and open nature' is a fertile field for exploitation. However galling it may be to him, Iago's subordination is a kind of protection, for it conceals his power and enables him to play upon the ambivalence of Othello's relation to Christian society: the Moor at once represents the institution and the alien, the conqueror and the infidel. Iago can conceal his malicious intentions toward 'the thick-lips' behind the mask of dutiful service and hence prolong his improvisation as the Spaniards could not. To be sure, the play suggests, Iago must ultimately destroy the beings he exploits and hence undermine the profitable economy of his own relations, but that destruction may be long deferred, deferred in fact for precisely the length of the play.[17]

If Iago then holds over others a possession that must constantly efface the signs of its own power, how can it be established, let alone maintained? We will find a clue, I think, in what we have been calling the process of fictionalization that transforms a fixed symbolic structure into a flexible construct ripe for improvisational entry. This process is at work in Shakespeare's play, where we may more accurately identify it as *submission to narrative self-fashioning*. When in Cyprus Othello and Desdemona have been ecstatically reunited, Iago astonishes Roderigo by informing him that Desdemona is in love with Cassio. He has no evidence, of course – indeed

we have earlier seen him 'engender' the whole plot entirely out of this
fantasy – but he proceeds to lay before his gull all of the circumstances that
make this adultery plausible: 'mark me, with what violence she first lov'd
the Moor, but for bragging, and telling her fantastical lies; and she will love
him still for prating?' (II, i, 221–3). Desdemona cannot long take pleasure in
her outlandish match : 'When the blood is made dull with the act of sport,
there should be again to inflame it, and give satiety a fresh appetite,
loveliness in favour, sympathy in years, manners and beauties' (II, i,
225–9). The elegant Cassio is the obvious choice: 'Didst thou not see her
paddle with the palm of his hand?' Iago asks. To Roderigo's objection that
this was 'but courtesy', Iago replies, 'Lechery, by this hand: an index and
prologue to the history of lust and foul thoughts' (II, i, 251–5). The
metaphor makes explicit what Iago has been doing all along: constructing a
narrative into which he inscribes ('by this hand') those around him. He
does not need a profound or even reasonably accurate understanding of
his victims; he would rather deal in probable impossibilities than
improbable possibilities. And it is eminently probable that a young,
beautiful Venetian gentlewoman would tire of her old, outlandish husband
and turn instead to the handsome, young lieutenant: it is, after all, one of
the master plots of comedy.

What Iago as inventor of comic narrative needs is a sharp eye for the
surfaces of social existence, a sense, as Bergson says, of the mechanical
encrusted upon the living, a reductive grasp of human possibilities. These
he has in extraordinarily full measure.[18] 'The wine she drinks is made of
grapes', he says in response to Roderigo's idealization of Desdemona, and
so reduced, she can be assimilated to Iago's grasp of the usual run of
humanity. Similarly, in a spirit of ironic connoisseurship, he observes
Cassio's courtly gestures, 'If such tricks as these strip you out of your
lieutenantry, it had been better you had not kiss'd your three fingers so oft,
which now again you are most apt to play the sir in: good, well kiss'd, an
excellent courtesy' (II, i, 171–5). He is watching a comedy of manners.
Above all, Iago is sensitive to habitual and self-limiting forms of discourse,
to Cassio's reaction when he has had a drink or when someone mentions
Bianca, to Othello's rhetorical extremism, to Desdemona's persistence and
tone when she pleads for a friend; and, of course, he is demonically
sensitive to the way individuals interpret discourse, to the signals they
ignore and those to which they respond.

We should add that Iago includes himself in this ceaseless narrative
invention; indeed, as we have seen from the start, a successful
improvisational career depends upon role-playing, which is in turn allied
to the capacity, as Professor Lerner defines empathy, 'to see oneself in the
other fellow's situation'. This capacity requires above all a sense that
one is not forever fixed in a single, divinely sanctioned identity, a
sense Iago expresses to Roderigo in a parodically sententious theory

of self-fashioning: ' our bodies are gardens, to the which our wills are gardeners, so that if we will plant nettles, or sow lettuce, set hyssop, and weed up thyme; supply it with one gender of herbs, or distract it with many; either to have it sterile with idleness, or manur'd with industry, why, the power, and corrigible authority of this, lies in our wills' (I, iii, 320–6). Confident in his shaping power, Iago has the role-player's ability to imagine his nonexistence so that he can exist for a moment in another and as another. In the opening scene he gives voice to this hypothetical self-cancellation in a line of eerie simplicity: 'Were I the Moor, I would not be Iago' (I, i, 57). The simplicity is far more apparent than real. Is the 'I' in both halves of the line the same? Does it designate a hard, impacted self-interest prior to social identity, or are there two distinct, even opposing selves? Were I the Moor, I would not be Iago, because the 'I' always loves itself and the creature I know as Iago hates the Moor he serves or, alternatively, because as the Moor I would be other than I am now, free of the tormenting appetite and revulsion that characterize the servant's relation to his master and that constitute my identity as Iago. I would be radically the same / I would be radically different; the rapacious ego underlines all institutional structures / the rapacious ego is constituted by institutional structures.[19]

What is most disturbing in Iago's comically banal and fathomless expression – as for that matter, in Professor Lerner's definition of empathy – is that the imagined self-loss conceals its opposites: a ruthless displacement and absorption of the other. Empathy, as German *Einfühlung* suggests, may be a feeling of oneself into an object, but that object may have to be drained of its own substance before it will serve as an appropriate vessel. Certainly in *Othello*, where all relations are embedded in power and sexuality, there is no realm where the subject and object can merge in the unproblematic accord affirmed by the theorists of empathy.[20] As Iago himself proclaims, his momentary identification with the Moor is a strategic aspect of his malevolent hypocrisy:

> In following him, I follow but myself.
> Heaven is my judge, not I for love and duty,
> But seeming so, for my peculiar end.
>
> (I, i, 58–60)

Exactly what that 'peculiar end' is remains opaque. Even the general term 'self-interest' is suspect: Iago begins his speech in a declaration of self-interest -' I follow him to serve my turn upon him'- and ends in a declaration of self-division: 'I am not what I am'.[21] We tend, to be sure, to hear the latter as 'I am not what I seem', hence as a simple confirmation of his public deception. But 'I am not what I am' goes beyond social feigning: not only does Iago mask himself in society as the honest ancient, but in private he tries out a bewildering succession of brief narratives that critics have attempted, with notorious results, to translate into motives. These inner narratives – shared, that is, only with the audience – continually promise to disclose what lies behind the public deception, to illuminate what Iago calls 'the native act and figure' of his heart, and continually fail to do so; or rather, they reveal that his heart is precisely a series of acts and figures, each referring to something else, something just out of our grasp. 'I am not what I am' suggests that this elusiveness is permanent, that even self-interest, whose transcendental guarantee is the divine 'I am what I am', is a mask.[22] Iago's constant recourse to narrative then is both the affirmation of absolute self-interest and the affirmation of absolute vacancy; the oscillation between the two imcompatable positions suggests in Iago the principle of narrativity itself, cut off from original motive and final disclosure. The only termination possible in his case is not revelation but silence.

The question remains why anyone would submit, even unconsciously, to Iago's narrative fashioning. Why would anyone submit to another's narrative at all? For an answer we may recall the pressures on all the figures we have considered in this study and return to our observation that there is a structural resemblance between even a hostile improvisation and its object. In *Othello* the characters have always already experienced submission to narrativity. This is clearest and most important in the case of Othello himself. When Brabantio brings before the Signiory the charge that his daughter has been seduced by witchcraft, Othello promises to deliver 'a round unvarnish'd tale ... / Of my whole course of love'(I,iii, 90–1), and at the heart of this tale is the telling of tales:

> Her father lov'd me, oft invited me,
> Still question'd me the story of my life,
> From year to year, the battles, sieges, fortunes,
> That I have pass'd:
> I ran it through, even from my boyish days,
> To the very moment that he bade me tell it.

> (I, iii, 128–33)

The telling of the story of one's life – the conception of one's life as a story[23] – is a response to public inquiry: to the demands of the Senate, sitting in judgement or, at the least, to the presence of an inquiring community. When, as recorded in the fourteenth-century documents Le Roy Ladurie has brilliantly studied, the peasants of the Languedoc village of Montaillou are examined by the Inquisition, they respond with a narrative performance: 'About 14 years ago, in Lent, towards vespers, I took two sides of salted pork to the house of Guillaume Benet of Montaillou, to have them smoked. There I found Guillemette Benet warming herself by the fire, together with another woman; I put the salted meat in the kitchen and left'.²⁴ And when the Carthaginian queen calls upon her guest to 'tell us all things from the first beginning, Grecian guile, your people's trials, and then your journeyings', Aeneas responds, as he must, with a narrative of the destiny decreed by the gods.²⁵ So too Othello before the Senate or earlier in Brabantio's house responds to questioning with what he calls his 'travel's history' or, in the Folio reading, as if noting the genre, his 'traveller's history'. This history, it should be noted, is not only of events in distant lands and among strange peoples: 'I ran it through', Othello declares, from childhood 'To the very moment that he bade me tell it'. We are on the brink of a Borges-like narrative that is forever constituting itself out of the materials of the present instant, a narrative in which the storyteller is constantly swallowed up by the story. That is, Othello is pressing up against the condition of all discursive representations of identity. He comes dangerously close to recognizing his status as a text, and it is precisely this recognition that the play as a whole will reveal to be insupportable. But, at this point, Othello is still convinced that the text is his own, and he imagines only that he is recounting a lover's performance.

In the 45th sonnet of Sidney's *Astrophil and Stella*, Astrophil complains that while Stella is indifferent to the sufferings she has caused him, she weeps piteous tears at a fable of some unknown lovers. He concludes,

Then think my dear, that you in me do read
Of Lovers' ruin some sad Tragedy:
I am not I, pity the tale of me.

In *Othello* it is Iago who echoes that last line – 'I am not what I am', the motto of the improviser, the manipulator of signs that bear no resemblance to what they profess to signify – but it is Othello himself who is fully implicated in the situation of the Sidney sonnet: that one can win pity for oneself only by becoming a tale of oneself, and hence by ceasing to be oneself. Of course, Othello thinks that he has triumphed through his narrative self-fashioning:

she thank'd me,
And bade me, if I had a friend that lov'd her,
I should but teach him how to tell my story,
And that would woo her. Upon this hint I spake:
She lov'd me for the dangers I had pass'd,
And I lov'd her that she did pity them.

(I, iii, 163–8)

But Iago knows that an identity that has been fashioned as a story can be unfashioned, refashioned, inscribed anew in a different narrative: it is the fate of stories to be consumed or, as we say more politely, interpreted. And even Othello, in his moment of triumph, has a dim intimation of this fate: a half-dozen lines after he has recalled 'the Cannibals, that each other eat', he remarks complacently, but with an unmistakable undertone of anxiety, that Desdemona would come 'and with a greedy ear/Devour up my discourse' (I,iii,149–50).

Paradoxically, in this image of rapacious appetite Othello is recording Desdemona's *submission* to his story, what she calls the consecration of her soul and fortunes 'to his honours, and his valiant parts' (I, iii, 253). What he has both experienced and narrated, she can only embrace as narration:

> my story being done,
> She gave me for my pains a world of sighs;
> She swore i'faith 'twas strange, 'twas passing strange;
> 'Twas pitiful, 'twas wondrous pitiful;
> She wish'd she had not heard it, yet she wish'd
> That heaven had made her such a man.

(I, iii, 158–63)[26]

It is, of course, characteristic of early modern culture that male submission to narrative is conceived as active, entailing the fashioning of one's own story (albeit within the prevailing conventions), and female submission as passive, entailing the entrance into marriage in which, to recall Tyndale's definition, the 'weak vessel' is put 'under the obedience of her husband, to rule her lusts and wanton appetites'. As we have seen, Tyndale explains that Sara, 'before she was married, was Abraham's sister, and equal with him; but, as soon as she was married, was in subjection, and became without comparison inferior; for so is the nature of wedlock, by the ordinance of God'.[27] At least for the world of Renaissance patriarchs, this account is fanciful in its glimpse of an original equality; most women must have entered marriage, like Desdemona, directly from paternal domination. 'I do perceive here a divided duty', she tells her father before the Venetian Senate, 'you are lord of all my duty'.

> but here's my husband:
> And so much duty as my mother show'd
> To you, preferring you before her father,
> So much I challenge, that I may profess,
> Due to the Moor my lord.

(I, iii, 185–9)[28]

She does not question the woman's obligation to obey, invoking instead only the traditional right to transfer her duty. Yet though Desdemona

proclaims throughout the play her submission to her husband –
'Commend me to my kind lord', she gasps in her dying words – that
submission does not accord wholly with the male dream of female
passivity. She was, Brabantio tells us,

> A maiden never bold of spirit,
> So still and quiet, that her motion
> Blush'd at her self,
>
> (I, iii, 94–6)

yet even this self-abnegation in its very extremity unsettles what we may
assume was her father's expectation:

> So opposite to marriage, that she shunn'd
> The wealthy curled darlings of our nation.
>
> (I, ii, 67–8)

And, of course, her marriage choice is, for Brabantio, an act of astonishing
disobedience, explicable only as the somnambulistic behaviour of one
bewitched or drugged. He views her elopement not as a transfer of
obedience but as theft or treason or a reckless escape from what he calls his
'guardage'. Both he and Iago remind Othello that her marriage suggests
not submission but deception:

> She did deceive her father, marrying you;
> And when she seem'd to shake and fear your looks,
> She lov'd them most.
>
> (III, iii, 210–11)[29]

As the sly reference to Othello's 'looks' suggests, the scandal of
Desdemona's marriage consists not only in her failure to receive her
father's prior consent but in her husband's blackness. That blackness – the
sign of all that the society finds frightening and dangerous – is the indelible
witness to Othello's permanent status as an outsider, no matter how highly
the state may value his services or how sincerely he has embraced its
values.[30] The safe passage of the female from father to husband is
irreparably disrupted, marked as an escape: 'O heaven', Brabantio cries,
'how got she out?' (I.i.169).

Desdemona's relation to her lord Othello should, of course, lay to rest
any doubts about her proper submission, but it is not only Brabantio's
opposition and Othello's blackness that raise such doubts, even in the
midst of her intensest declarations of love. There is rather a quality in that
love itself that unsettles the orthodox schema of hierarchical obedience and
makes Othello perceive her submission to his discourse as a devouring of

it. We may perceive this quality most clearly in the exquisite moment of the lovers' reunion on Cyprus:

Othello   It gives me wonder great as my content
To see you here before me: O my soul's joy,
If after every tempest come such calmness,
May the winds blow, till they have waken'd death,
And let the labouring bark climb hills of seas,
Olympus-high, and duck again as low
As hell's from heaven. If it were now to die,
'Twere now to be most happy, for I fear
My soul hath her content so absolute,
That not another comfort, like to this
Succeeds in unknown fate.
Desdemona   The heavens forbid
But that our loves and comforts should increase,
Even as our days do grow.
Othello   Amen to that, sweet powers!
I cannot speak enough of this content,
It stops me here, it is too much of joy.

(II, i, 183–97)[31]

Christian orthodoxy in both Catholic and Protestant Europe could envision a fervent mutual love between husband and wife, the love expressed most profoundly by Saint Paul in words that are cited and commented upon in virtually every discussion of marriage:

So men are bound to love their own wives as their own bodies. He that loveth his own wife, loveth himself. For never did any man hate his own flesh, but nourisheth and cherisheth it, even as the Lord doth the congregation: for we are members of his body, of his flesh and of his bones. For this cause shall a man leave father and mother, and shall be joined unto his wife, and they two shall be one flesh. This mystery is great, but I speak of Christ and of the congregation.[32]

Building upon this passage and upon its source in *Genesis*, commentators could write, like the Reformer Thomas Becon, that marriage is a 'high, holy, and blessed order of life, ordained not of man, but of God, yea and that not in this sinful world, but in paradise that most joyful garden of pleasure'. But like the Pauline text itself, all such discussions of married love begin and end by affirming the larger order of authority and submission within which marriage takes its rightful place. The family, as William Gouge puts it, 'is a little Church, and a little Commonwealth … whereby trial may be made of such as are fit for any place of authority, or of subjection in Church or Commonwealth'.[33]

In Othello's ecstatic words, the proper sentiments of Christian husband sit alongside something else: a violent oscillation between heaven and hell, a momentary possession of the soul's absolute content, an archaic sense of monumental scale, a dark fear – equally archaic, perhaps – of 'unknown fate'. Nothing *conflicts* openly with Christian orthodoxy, but the erotic intensity that informs almost every word is experienced in tension with it. This tension is less a manifestation of some atavistic 'blackness' specific to Othello than a manifestation of the colonial power of Christian doctrine over sexuality, a power visible at this point precisely in its inherent limitation.[34] That is, we glimpse in this brief moment the *boundary* of the orthodox, the strain of its control, the potential disruption of its hegemony by passion. This scene, let us stress, does not depict rebellion or even complaint – Desdemona invokes 'the heavens' and Othello answers 'Amen to that, sweet powers!' Yet the plural here eludes, if only slightly, a serene affirmation of orthodoxy: the powers in their heavens do not refer unmistakably to the Christian God, but rather are the nameless transcendent forces that protect and enhance erotic love. To perceive the difference, we might recall that if Augustine argues, against the gnostics, that God had intended Adam and Eve to procreate in paradise, he insists at the same time that our first parents would have experienced sexual intercourse without the excitement of the flesh. How then could Adam have had an erection? Just as there are persons, Augustine writes, 'who can move their ears, either one at a time, or both together' and others who have 'such command of their bowels, that they can break wind continuously at pleasure, so as to produce the effect of singing', so, before the Fall, Adam would have had fully rational, willed control of the organ of generation and thus would have needed no erotic arousal. 'Without the seductive stimulus of passion, with calmness of mind and with no corrupting of the integrity of the body the husband would lie upon the bosom of his wife', and in this placid union, the semen could reach the womb 'with the integrity of the female genital organ being preserved, just as now, with that same integrity being safe, the menstrual flow of blood can be emitted from the womb of a virgin'.[35] Augustine grants that even Adam and Eve, who alone could have done so, failed to experience this 'passionless generation' since they were expelled from paradise before they had a chance to try it. Nevertheless, the ideal of Edenic placidity, untried but intended by God for mankind, remains as a reproach to all fallen sexuality, an exposure of its inherent violence.[36]

The rich and disturbing pathos of the lovers' passionate reunion in *Othello* derives then not only from our awareness that Othello's premonition is tragically accurate, but from a rent, a moving ambivalence, in his experience of the ecstatic moment itself. The 'calmness' of which he speaks may express gratified desire, but, as the repeated invocation of death suggests, it may equally express the longing for a final *release* from desire, from the dangerous violence, the sense of extremes, the laborious climbing and falling out of control that is experienced in the tempest. To be sure, Othello *welcomes* this tempest, with its charge of erotic feeling, but he does so for the sake of the ultimate consummation that the experience can call into being: 'If after every tempest come such calmness ... . 'That which men most fear to look upon in the storm – death – is for Othello that which makes the storm endurable. If the death he invokes may figure not the release from desire but its fulfilment – for *death* is a common Renaissance term for orgasm – this fulfilment is characteristically poised between an anxious sense of self-dissolution and a craving for decisive closure. If Othello's words suggest an ecstatic acceptance of sexuality, an absolute content, they suggest simultaneously that for him sexuality is a menacing voyage to reach a longed-for heaven; it is one of the dangers to be passed. Othello embraces the erotic as a supreme form of romantic narrative, a tale of risk and violence issuing forth at last in a happy and final tranquillity.

Desdemona's response is in an entirely different key:

> The heavens forbid
> But that our loves and comforts should increase,
> Even as our days do grow.

This is spoken to allay Othello's fear, but may it not instead augment it? For if Othello characteristically responds to his experience by shaping it as a story, Desdemona's reply denies the possibility of such narrative control and offers instead a vision, of unabating increase.Othello says 'Amen' to this vision, but it arouses in him a feeling at once of overflowing and inadequacy:

> I cannot speak enough of this content,
> It stops me here, it is too much of joy.

Desdemona has once again devoured up his discourse, and she has done so precisely in bringing him comfort and content.[37] Rather than simply confirming male authority, her submission eroticizes everything to which it responds, from the 'disastrous chances' and 'moving accidents' Othello relates, to his simplest demands,[38] to his very mistreatment of her:

> my love doth so approve him,
> That even his stubbornness, his checks and frowns, –
> Prithee unpin me, – have grace and favour in them.
>
> (IV, iii, 19–21)[39]

The other women in the play, Bianca and Emilia, both have moments of disobedience to the men who possess and abuse them – in the case of Emilia, it is a heroic disobedience for which she pays with her life.[40] Desdemona performs no such acts of defiance, but her erotic submission, conjoined with Iago's murderous cunning, far more effectively, if unintentionally, subverts her husband's carefully fashioned identity.

We will examine more fully the tragic process of this subversion, but it is important to grasp first that Othello's loss of himself – a loss depicted discursively in his incoherent ravings – arises not only from the fatal conjunction of Desdemona's love and Iago's hate, but from the nature of that identity, from what we have called his submission to narrative self-fashioning. We may invoke in this connection Lacan's observation that the source of the subject's frustration in psychoanalysis is ultimately neither the silence nor the reply of the analyst:

> Is it not rather a matter of frustration inherent in the very discourse of the subject? does the subject not become engaged in an ever-growing dispossession of that being of his, concerning which – by dint of sincere portraits which leave its idea no less incoherent, of rectifications which do not prevent his statue from tottering, of narcissistic embraces which become like a puff of air in animating it – he ends up by recognizing that this being has neven been anything more than his construct in the Imaginary and that this construct disappoints all of his certitudes? For in this labor which he undertakes to reconstruct this construct for *another*, he finds again the fundamental alienation which made him construct it *like another one*, and which has always destined it to be stripped from him *by another*.[41]

Shakespeare's military hero, it may be objected, is particularly far removed from this introspective project, a project that would seem, in any case, to have little bearing upon any Renaissance text. Yet I think it is no accident that nearly every phrase of Lacan's critique of psychoanalysis seems a brilliant reading of *Othello*, for I would propose that there is a deep resemblance between the construction of the self in analysis – at least as Lacan conceives it – and Othello's self-fashioning. The resemblance is grounded in the dependence of even the innermost self upon a language that is always necessarily given from without and upon representation before an audience. I do not know if such are the conditions of human identity, apart from its expression in psychoanalysis, but they are unmistakably the conditions of theatrical identity, where existence is conferred upon a character by the playwright's language and the actor's performance. And in *Othello* these governing circumstances of the medium itself are reproduced and intensified in the hero's situation: his identity depends upon a constant performance, as we have seen, of his 'story', a loss of his own origins, an embrace and perpetual reiteration of the norms of another culture. It is this dependence that gives Othello, the warrior and alien, a relation to Christian values that is the existential equivalent of a religious vocation; he cannot allow himself the moderately flexible adherence that most ordinary men have toward their own formal beliefs. Christianity is the alienating yet constitutive force in Othello's identity, and if we seek a discursive mode in the play that is the social equivalent of the experience Lacan depicts, we will find it in *confession*. Othello himself invokes before the Venetian Senate the absolute integrity of confession, conceived, it appears, not as the formal auricular rite of penitence but as a generalized self-scrutiny in God's presence:

> as faithful as to heaven
> I do confess the vices of my blood,
> So justly to your grave ears I'll present
> How I did thrive in this fair lady's love,
> And she in mine.
>
> (I, iii, 123–36)[42]

The buried identification here between the vices of the blood and mutual thriving in love is fully exhumed by the close of the play when confession has become a virtually obsessional theme.[43] Theological and juridical confession are fused in Othello's mind when, determined first to exact a deathbed confession, he comes to take Desdemona's life:

> If you bethink youself of any crime,
> Unreconcil'd as yet to heaven and grace,
> Solicit for it straight ....
> Therefore confess thee freely of thy sin,
> For to deny each article with oath
> Cannot remove, nor choke the strong conceit,
> That I do groan withal: thou art to die.
>
> (V, ii, 26–8, 54–7)

The sin that Othello wishes Desdemona to confess is adultery, and her refusal to do so frustrates the achievement of what in theology was called 'a good, complete confession'.[44] He feels the outrage of the thwarted system that needs to imagine itself merciful, sacramental, when it disciplines:

> thou dost stone thy heart,
> And makest me call what I intend to do
> A murder, which I thought a sacrifice.
>
> (V, ii, 64–6)

We are at last in a position to locate the precise nature of the symbolic structure into which Iago inserts himself in his brilliant improvisation: this structure is the centuries-old Christian doctrine of sexuality, policed socially and psychically, as we have already seen, by confession. To Iago, the Renaissance skeptic, this system has a somewhat archaic ring, as if it were an earlier stage of development which his own modern sensibility had cast off.[45] Like the Lucayan religion to the conquistadors, the orthodox doctrine that governs Othello's sexual attitudes – his simultaneous idealization and mistrust of women – seems to Iago sufficiently close to be recognizable, sufficiently distant to be manipulable. We watch him manipulate it directly at the beginning of act 4, when he leads Othello through a brutally comic parody of the late medieval confessional manuals with their casuistical attempts to define the precise moment at which venial temptation passes over into mortal sin:

> *Iago*   To kiss in private?
> *Othello*   An unauthoriz'd kiss.
> *Iago*   Or to be naked with her friend abed,
> An hour, or more, not meaning any harm?
> *Othello*   Naked abed, Iago, and not mean harm?
> It is hypocrisy against the devil:
> They that mean virtuously, and yet do so,
> The devil their virtue tempts, and they tempt heaven.
> *Iago*   So they do nothing, 'tis a venial slip.
>
> (IV, i, 2–9)

Iago in effect assumes an extreme version of the laxist position in such manuals in order to impel Othello toward the rigorist version that viewed adultery as one of the most horrible of mortal sins, more detestable, in the words of the *Eruditorium penitentiale*, 'than homicide or plunder', and hence formerly deemed punishable, as several authorities remind us, by death.[46] Early Protestantism did not soften this position. Indeed, in the mid-sixteenth century, Tyndale's erstwhile collaborator, George Joye, called for a return to the Old Testament penalty for adulterers. 'God's law', he writes 'is to punish adultery with death for the tranquillity and commonwealth of His church'. This is not an excessive or vindictive course; on the contrary,'to take away and to cut off putrified and corrupt members from the whole body, lest they poison and destroy the body, is the law of love'.[47] When Christian magistrates leave adultery unpunished, they invite more betrayals and risk the ruin of the realm, for as Protestants in particular repeatedly observe, the family is an essential component of an interlocking social and theological network. Hence adultery is a sin with the gravest of repercussions; in the words of the great Cambridge Puritan William Perkins, it 'destroyeth the Seminary of the Church, which is *a godly seed* in the family, and it breaketh the covenant between the parties and God; it robs another of the precious ornament of chastity, which is a gift of the Holy Ghost; it dishonours their bodies and maketh them temples of the devil; and the Adulterer maketh his family a Stews'.[48] It is in the bitter spirit of these convictions that Othello enacts the grotesque comedy of treating his wife as a strumpet and the tragedy of executing her in the name of justice, lest she betray more men.

But we still must ask how Iago manages to persuade Othello that Desdemona has commited adultery, for all of the cheap tricks Iago plays seem somehow inadequate to produce the unshakeable conviction of his wife's defilement that seizes Othello's soul and drives him mad. After all, as Iago taunts Othello, he cannot achieve the point of vantage of God whom the Venetian women let 'see the pranks/They dare not show their husbands' (III, iii, 206–7)

> Would you, the supervisor, grossly gape on,
> Behold her topp'd?

(III, iii, 401–2)

How then, without 'ocular proof' and in the face of both love and common sense, is Othello so thoroughly persuaded? To answer this, we must recall the syntactic ambiguity we noted earlier – to abuse Othello's ear, /That he is too familiar with his wife – and turn to a still darker aspect of Orthodox Christian doctrine, an aspect central both to the confessional system and to Protestant self-scrutiny. *Omnis amator feruentior est adulter*, goes the Stoic epigram, and Saint Jerome does not hesitate to draw the inevitable inference: 'An adulterer is he who is too ardent a lover of his wife'.[49] Jerome quotes Seneca: 'All love of another's wife is shameful; so too, too much love of your own. A wise man ought to love his wife with judgement, not affection. Let him control his impulses and not to be borne headlong into copulation. Nothing is fouler than to love a wife like an adultress … Let them show themselves to their wives not as lovers, but as husbands'.[50] The words echo through more than a thousand years of Christian writing on marriage, and, in the decisive form given them by Augustine and his commentators, remain essentially unchallenged by the leading continental Reformers of the sixteenth and early seventeenth century, by Tudor ecclesiastical authorities, and even by Elizabethan and Jacobean Puritans who sharply opposed so many conservative Anglican doctrines. There is, to be sure, in all shades of Protestantism an attack on the Catholic doctrine of celibacy and a celebration of married love, a celebration that includes acknowledgement of the legitimate role of sexual pleasure. But for Reformer as for Catholic, this acknowledgement is hedged about with warnings, and restrictions. The 'man who shows no modesty or comeliness in conjugal intercourse', writes Calvin, 'is

committing adultery with his wife', and the *King's Book*, attributed to
Henry VIII, informs its readers that in lawful matrimony a man may break
the Seventh Commandment 'and live unchaste with his own wife, if he do
unmeasurably or inordinately serve his or her fleshly appetite or lust'.[51]

In the Augustinian conception, as elaborated by Raymond of Penaforte,
William of Rennes, and others, there are four motives for conjugal
intercourse: to conceive offspring; to render the marital debt to one's
partner so that he or she might avoid incontinency; to avoid fornication
oneself; and to satisfy desire. The first two motives are without sin and
excuse intercourse; the third is a venial sin; the fourth – to satisfy desire – is
mortal. Among the many causes that underlie this institutional hostility to
desire is the tenacious existence, in various forms, of the belief that
pleasure constitutes a legitimate release from dogma and constraint. Thus
when asked by the Inquisition about her happy past liaison with the
heretical priest of Montaillou, the young Grazide Lizier replies with naive
frankness, 'in those days it pleased me, and it pleased the priest, that he
should know me carnally, and be known by me; and so I did not think I
was sinning, and neither did he'.[52] 'With Pierre Clergue', she explains, 'I
liked it. And so it could not displease God. It was not a sin' (157). For the
peasant girl, apparently, pleasure was the guarantee of innocence: 'But
now, with him, it does not please me any more. And so now, if he knew me
carnally, I should think it a sin' (151). A comparable attitude, derived not
from peasant culture but from the troubadours, evidently lies behind the
more sophisticated courtship of Romeo: 'Thus from my lips, by thine my
sin is purged'.[53]

It should not surprise us that churchmen, Catholic and Protestant alike,
would seek to crush such dangerous notions, nor that they would extend
their surveillance and discipline to married couples and warn that
excessive pleasure in the marriage bed is at least a potential violation of the
Seventh Commandment. 'Nothing is more vile', says Raymond's
influential *summa*, 'than to love your wife in adulterous fashion'.[54] The
conjugal act may be without sin, writes the rigorist Nicolaus of Ausimo,
but only if 'in the performance of this act there is no enjoyment of
pleasure'.[55] Few *summas* and no marriage manuals take so extreme a
position, but virtually all are in agreement that the active *pursuit* of pleasure
in sexuality is damnable, for as Jacobus Ungarelli writes in the sixteenth
century, those who undertake intercourse for pleasure 'exclude God from
their minds, act as brute beasts, lack reason, and if they begin marriage for
this reason, are given over to the power of the devil'.[56]

Confessors then must determine if the married penitent has a legitimate
excuse for intercourse and if the act has been performed with due regard
for 'matrimonial chastity', while Protestants who have rejected auricular
confession must similarly scrutinize their own behaviour for signs that
their pleasure has been too 'spacious'.[57] 'Lust is more spacious than love',

writes Alexander Niccoles in the early seventeenth century; it 'hath no mean, no bound ... more deep, more dangerous than the Sea, and less restrained, for the Sea hath bounds, but it (lust) hath none'.[58] Such unbounded love is a kind of idolatry, an encroachment upon a Christian's debt of loving obedience to God, and it ultimately destroys the marital relationship as well. Immoderate love, another Puritan divine warns, 'will either be blown down by some storm or tempest of displeasure, or fall of itself, or else degenerate into jealousy, the most devouring and fretting canker that can harbour in a married person's breast'.[59]

These anxieties, rich in implication for *Othello*, are frequently tempered in Protestant writings by a recognition of the joyful ardor of young married couples, but there remains a constant fear of excess, and, as Ambrose observed centuries earlier, even the most plausible excuse for sexual passion is shameful in the old: 'Youths generally assert the desire for generation. How much more shameful for the old to do what is shameful for the young to confess'.[60] Othello himself seems eager to ward off this shame; he denies before the Senate that he seeks

> To please the palate of my appetite,
> Nor to comply with heat, the young affects
> In me defunct ....
>
> (I, iii, 262–4)[61]

But Desdemona makes no such disclaimer; indeed her declaration of passion is frankly, though by no means exclusively, sexual:

> That I did love the Moor, to live with him,
> My downright violence, and scorn of fortunes,
> May trumpet to the world: my heart's subdued
> Even to the utmost pleasure of my lord.
>
> (I, iii, 248–51)[62]

This moment of erotic intensity, this frank acceptance of pleasure and submission to her spouse's pleasure, is, I would argue, as much as Iago's slander the cause of Desdemona'a death, for it awakens the deep current of sexual anxiety in Othello, anxiety that with Iago's help expresses itself in quite orthodox fashion as the perception of adultery.[63] Othello unleases upon Cassio – 'Michael Cassio,/ That came a-wooing with you' (III, iii, 71–72) – the fear of pollution, defilement, brutish violence that is bound up with his own experience of sexual pleasure, while he must destroy Desdemona both for her excessive experience of pleasure and for awakening such sensations in himself. Like Guyon in the Bower of Bliss, Othello transforms his complicity in erotic excess and his fear of engulfment into a 'purifying' saving violence:

> Like to the Pontic sea,
> Whose icy current and compulsive course
> Ne'er feels retiring ebb, but keeps due on
> To the Propontic and the Hellespont,
> Even so my bloody thoughts, with violent pace,
> Shall ne'er look back, ne'er ebb to humble love,
> Till that a capable and wide revenge
> Swallow them up.

(III, iii, 460–7)

His insupportable sexual experience has been, as it were, displaced and absorbed by the act of revenge which can swallow up not only the guilty lovers but – as the syntax suggests – his own 'bloody thoughts'.

Such is the achievement of Iago's improvisation on the religious sexual doctrine in which Othello believes; true to that doctrine, pleasure itself becomes for Othello pollution, a defilement of his property in Desdemona and in himself.[64] It is at the level of this dark, sexual revulsion that Iago has access to Othello, access assured, as we should expect, by the fact that beneath his cynical modernity and professed self-love Iago reproduces in himself the same psychic structure. He is as intensely preoccupied with adultery, while his anxiety about his own sexuality may be gauged from the fact that he conceives his very invention, as the images of engendering suggest, as a kind of demonic semen that will bring forth monsters.[65] Indeed Iago's discourse – his assaults on women, on the irrationality of Eros, on the brutishness of the sexual act – reiterates virtually to the letter the orthodox terms of Ungarelli's attack on those who seek pleasure in intercourse.

The improvisational process we have been discussing depends for its success upon the concealment of its symbolic center, but as the end approaches this center becomes increasingly visible. When, approaching the marriage bed on which Desdemona has spread the wedding sheets, Othello rages, 'Thy bed, lust stain'd, shall with lust's blood be spotted' (V, i, 36), he comes close to revealing his tormenting identification of marital sexuality – limited perhaps to the night he took Desdemona's virginity – and adultery.[66] The orthodox element of this identification is directly observed:

> this sorrow's heavenly:
> It strikes when it does love –

(V, ii, 21–2)

and on her marriage bed/deathbed Desdemona seems at last to pluck out the heart of the mystery:

Othello   Think on thy sins.
Desdemona   They are loves I bear to you.
Othello   And for that thou diest.
Desdemona   That death's unnatural, that kills for loving.

(V, ii, 39–42)

The play reveals at this point not the unfathomable darkness of human motives but their terrible transparency, and the horror of the revelation is its utter inability to deflect violence. Othello's identity is entirely caught up in the narrative structure that drives him to turn Desdemona into a being incapable of pleasure, a piece of 'monumental alabaster', so that he will at last be able to love her without the taint of adultery:

Be thus, when thou art dead, and I will kill thee,
And love thee after.

(V, iii 18–19)

It is as if Othello had found in a necrophilic fantasy the secret solution to the intolerable demands of the rigorist sexual ethic, and the relation that Cassio has not slept with Desdemona leads only to a doubling of this solution, for the adulterous sexual pleasure that Othello had projected upon his lieutenant now rebounds upon himself.[67] Even with the exposure of Iago's treachery, then, there is for Othello no escape – rather a still deeper submission to narrative, a reaffirmation of the self as story, but now split suicidally between the defender of the faith and the circumcised enemy who must be destroyed. Lodovico's bizarrely punning response to Othello's final speech – 'O bloody period!' insists precisely upon the fact that it was a speech, that his life fashioned as a text is ended as a text.

To an envious contemporary like Robert Greene, Shakespeare seems a kind of green-room Iago, appropriating for himself the labors of others. In *Othello* Shakespeare seems to acknowledge, represent, and explore his affinity to the malicious improviser, but, of course, his relation to the theater and to his culture is far more complex than such an affinity could suggest. There are characters who can embrace a mobility of desire – one of whose emblems is the male actor playing a female character dressed up as a male – that neither Iago, nor Othello, nor Desdemona can endure. Destructive violence is not Shakespeare's only version of these materials, and even in *Othello*, Iago is not the playwright's only representation of himself. Still at the least we must grant Robert Greene that it would have seemed fatal to be imitated by Shakespeare. He possessed a limitless talent for entering into the consciousness of another, perceiving its deepest structures as a manipulable fiction, reinscribing it into his own narrative form.[68] If in the late plays, he experiments with controlled disruptions of narrative,

moments of eddying and ecstasy, these invariably give way to
reaffirmations of self-fashioning through story.

   Montaigne, who shares many of Shakespeare's most radical perceptions,
invents in effect a brilliant mode of *non-narrative* self-fashioning: 'I cannot
keep my subject still. It goes along befuddled and staggering, with a
natural drunkenness. I take it in this condition, just as it is at the moment I
give my attention to it'.[69] Shakespeare by contrast remains throughout his
career the supreme purveyor of 'empathy', the fashioner of narrative selves,
the master improviser. Where Montaigne withdrew to his study,
Shakespeare became the presiding genius of a popular, urban art form with
the capacity to foster psychic mobility in the service of Elizabethan power;
he became the principal maker of what we may see as the prototype of the
mass media Professor Lerner so admires.

   Finally, we may ask, is this service to power a function of the theater
itself or of Shakespeare's relation to his medium? The answer, predictably,
is both. The theater is widely perceived in the period as the concrete
manifestation of the histrionic quality of life, and, more specifically, of
power – the power of the prince who stands as an actor upon a stage before
the eyes of the nation, the power of God who enacts His will in the Theater
of the World. The stage justifies itself against recurrent charges of
immorality by invoking this normative function: it is the expression of
those rules that govern a properly ordered society and displays visibly the
punishment, in laughter and violence, that is meted out upon those who
violate the rules. Most playwrights pay at least professional homage to
these values; they honor the institutions that enable them to earn their keep
and give voice to the ideology that holds together both their 'mystery' and
the society at large.

   In Marlowe, as we have seen, we encounter a playwright at odds with
this ideology. If the theater normally reflects and flatters the royal sense of
itself as national performance, Marlowe struggles to expose the underlying
motives of any performance of power. If the theater normally affirms God's
providence, Marlowe explores the tragic needs and interest that are served
by all such affirmations. If the Elizabethan stage functions as one of the
public uses of spectacle to impose normative ethical patterns on the urban
masses, Marlowe enacts a relentless challenge to those patterns and
undermines employment of rhetoric and violence in their service.

   Shakespeare approaches his culture not, like Marlowe, as rebel and
blasphemer, but rather as dutiful servant, content to improvise a part of his
own within its orthodoxy. And if after centuries, that improvisation has
been revealed to us as embodying an almost boundless challenge to the
culture's every tenet, a devastation of every source, the author of *Othello*
would have understood that such a revelation scarcely matters. After all,
the heart of a successful improvisation lies in concealment, not exposure;
and besides, as we have seen, even a hostile improvisation reproduces the

relations of power that it hopes to displace and absorb. This is not to dismiss the power of hatred or the significance of distinctions – it matters a great deal whether Othello or Iago, the Lucayans or the Spaniards prevail – only to suggest the boundaries that define the possibility of any improvisational contact, even contact characterized by hidden malice.

I would not want to argue, in any event, that Shakespeare's relation to his culture is defined by hidden malice. Such a case can no doubt be made for many of the plays – stranger things have been said – but it will sound forced and unconvincing, just as the case for Shakespeare as an unwavering, unquestioning apologist for Tudor ideology sounds forced and unconvincing. The solution here is not, I suggest, that the truth lies somewhere in between. Rather the truth itself is radically unstable and yet constantly stabilized, as unstable as those male authorities that affirm themselves only to be undermined by subversive women and then to be reconstituted in a different guise. If any reductive generalization about Shakespeare's relation to his culture seems dubious, it is because his plays offer no single timeless affirmation or denial of legitimate authority and no central, unwavering authorial presence. Shakespeare's language and themes are caught up, like the medium itself, in unsettling repetitions, committed to the shifting voices and audiences, with their shifting aesthetic assumptions and historical imperatives, that govern a living theater.

Criticism can legitimately show – as I hope my discussion of *Othello* does – that Shakespeare relentlessly *explores* the relations of power in a given culture. That more than exploration is involved is much harder to demonstrate convincingly. If there are intimations in Shakespeare of a release from the complex narrative orders in which everyone is inscribed, these intimations do not arise from bristling resistance or strident denunciation – the mood of a Jaques or Timon. They arise paradoxically from a peculiarly intense *submission* whose downright violence undermines everything it was meant to shore up, the submission depicted not in Othello or Iago but in Desdemona. As both the play and its culture suggest, the arousal of intense, purposeless pleasure is only superficially a confirmation of existing values, established selves.[70] In Shakespeare's narrative art, liberation from the massive power structures that determine social and psychic reality is glimpsed in an *excessive* aesthetic delight, an erotic embrace of those very structures – the embrace of a Desdemona whose love is more deeply unsettling than even an Iago's empathy.

Notes

1. On the feudal revival, see ARTHUR B. FERGUSON, *The Indian Summer of English*

Chivalry (Durham, N.C.: Duke University Press, 1960), FRANCES A. YATES, 'Elizabethan Chivalry: The Romance of the Accession Day Tilts', in *Astraea: The Imperial Theme in the Sixteenth Century* (London: Rout ledge, 1975), pp. 88–111, and ROY STRONG, *The Cult of Elizabeth: Elizabethan Portraiture and Pageantry* (London: Thames and Hudson, 1977).

2. John Steevens, cited in SPENSER, *Variorum* 1 : 252.

3. It is not certain who borrowed from whom, though I think the dominant view, that Marlowe borrowed from Spenser, is quite likely. For the parallels between Spenser and Marlowe, see also CHARLES CRAWFORD, 'Edmund Spenser', 'Locrine', and 'Selimus', *Notes and Queries* (9th ser.) 7 (1901), pp. 61–63, 101–3, 142–4, 203–5, 261–3, 324–5, 384–6.

4. DANIEL LERNER, *The Passing of Traditional Society: Modernizing the Middle East* (New York: Free Press, 1958; rev. ed 1964), p.49.

5. The figures are from SHERBURNE COOK and WOODROW W. BORAH, *Essays in Population History: Mexico and the Caribbean* (Berkeley: University of California Press, 1971), pp. 376–411.

6. PETER MARTYR (PIETRO MARTIRE D'ANGHIERA), *De Orbe Novo*, trans. M. Lok, p.623. The Seventh Decade was finished in the middle of 1525. On Peter Martyr, see HENRY R. WAGNER, 'Peter Martyr and his works', *Proceedings of the American Antiquarian Society* 56 (1946), pp. 238–88. There is a rather pallid modern translation of *De Orbe Novo* by Francis A. MacNutt (New York: Putnam's, 1912).

7. It is the essence of *sprezzatura* to create the impression of a spontaneous improvisation by means of careful rehearsals. Similarly, the early English drama often strove for this effect; see, for example, *Fulgens and Lucres* where the seemingly incidental conversation of 'A' and 'B' is fully scripted.

8. IMMANUEL WALLERSTEIN, *The Modern World System: Capitalist Agriculture and The Origins of the European World Economy in The Sixteenth Century*, (New York, 1974).

9. ROY STRONG, *The Cult of Elizabeth: Elizabethan Portraiture and Pageantry*, p. 153.

10. As an example of the operation of displacement in the visual arts, one may consider Breughel's *Christ Bearing the Cross*, where the mourning figures from Van der Weyden's great *Descent from the Cross* are pushed out to the margin of the canvas and the swirling, festive crowd all but obscures Christ. Similarly, for absorption we may invoke Durer's self-portrait of 1500, where the rigidly frontalized, verticalized, hieratic figure has taken into itself the Christ Pantocrator.

11. JOEL B. ALTMAN, *The Tudor Play of Mind*. See also JACKSON I. COPE, *The Theater and the Dream: From Metaphor to Form in Renaissance Drama* (Baltimore: The Johns Hopkins University Press, 1973), especially Chapters 4–6. Cope argues brilliantly for the central importance of improvisation in the drama of the Renaissance, but for him improvisation is in the service finally of 'a real coherence' of 'the eternal order' of the myths of renewal (p.210). One passes, by means of an apparent randomness, a chaotic flux, to a buried but all-powerful form. Improvisation is the mask of providence, and Cope concludes his study with a discussion of *The Tempest* as a 'mythic play' of natural resurrection and Christian doctrine. I would argue that the final effect of improvisation in Shakespeare is the reverse: we always begin with a notion of the inescapability of form, a sense that there are no surprises, that narrative triumphs over the apparent disruptions, that even the disruptions serve narrative by confirming the presence of the artist as a version of the presence of God. And through

improvisation we pass, only partially and tentatively, to sense that in the very acts of homage to the great formal structures, there open up small but constant glimpses of the limitations of those structures, of their insecurities, of the possibility of their collapse.

12. *Confutation*, 8:1, pp. 90–2. My attention was drawn to this passage by Professor Louis L. Martz who discussed it in a lecture at the Folger conference. 'Thomas More: The Man and His Age'. On More's 'art of improvisation' see MARTZ, 'The Tower Works', in *St Thomas More: Action and Contemplation*, pp. 63–5.

13. Richard III virtually declares himself an improviser: 'I clothe my naked villainy/With odd old ends stol'n forth of holy writ' (I,iii, 335–6). He gives a fine demonstration of his agility when he turns Margaret's curse back on herself. Behind this trick perhaps is the fact that there were in the popular culture of the Renaissance formulaic curses and satirical jigs into which any names could be fitted; see CHARLES READ BASKERVILL, *The Elizabethan Jig and Related Song Drama* (Chicago: University of Chicago Press, 1929), pp. 66–7.

14. All citations of *Othello* are to the Arden edition, ed. M.R. RIDLEY (Cambridge, Mass: Harvard University Press, 1958). Iago's description of Cassio, 'a finder out of occasions' (II, I, 240–1), is a far more apt description of himself as an improviser.

15. This interpretation is argued powerfully in an unpublished essay, 'On the Language of Sexual Pathology in *Othello*', by Edward Snow of George Mason University. A similar case is made by Arthur Kirsch in a sensitive psychoanalytic study, 'The Polarization of Erotic Love in *Othello*' (*Modern Language Review* 73 (1978), pp. 721–40). Kirsch suggests that what becomes insupportable for Othello is 'the fulsomeness of his own sexual instincts and, as his verbal and physical decomposition suggest, his jealous rage against Cassio is ultimately a rage against himself which reaches back to the elemental and destructive triadic fantasies which at one stage in childhood govern the mind of every human being' (p.737).

16. Iago's performance here, which Desdemona unnervingly characterizes as 'lame and impotent', is one of the ways in which he is linked to the playwright or at least to the Vice-like 'presenter' of a play; see BERNARD SPIVACK, *Shakespeare and the Allegory of Evil: The History of a Metaphor in Relation to His Major Villains* (New York: Columbia University Press, 1958).

17. One might argue that Shakespeare, like Marx, sees the exploiter as doomed by the fact that he must reduce his victim to nothingness, but where Marx derives a revolutionary optimism from this process, Shakespeare derives the tragic mood of the play's end.

18. For Iago's 'corrosive habit of abstraction', see MAYNARD MACK, 'The Jacobean Shakespeare: Some Observations on the Construction of the Tragedies', in *Stratford-upon-Avon Studies: Jacobean Theatre* 1 (1960), p. 18. For Iago as a 'portrait of the artist', see STANLEY EDGAR HYMAN, *Iago: Some Approaches to the Illusion of His Motivation* (New York: Atheneum, 1970), pp.61–100.

19. The vertigo intensifies if we add the sly preceding line: 'It is as sure as you are Roderigo, / Were I the Moor, I would not be Iago'. One imagines that Roderigo would unconsciously touch himself as this point to make sure that he is Roderigo.
    Iago is a master of the vertiginous confounding of self and other, being and seeming:

Men should be what they seem,
Or those that be not, would they might seem none.

(III, iii, 130–1)

He's that he is, I may not breathe my censure,
What he might be, if, as he might, he is not,
I would to heaven he were!

(IV, i, 267–9)

20. See, for example, Theodor Lipps:

> The specific characteristic of esthetic pleasure has now been defined. It consists in this: that it is the enjoyment of an object, which however, so far as it is the object of *enjoyment*, is not an object, but myself. Or, it is the enjoyment of the ego, which however, so far as it is esthetically enjoyed, is not myself but objective.
>   Now, all this is included in the concept empathy. It constitutes the very meaning of this concept. Empathy is the fact here established, that the object is myself and by the very same token this self of mine is the object. Empathy is the fact that the antithesis between myself and the object disappears, or rather does not yet exist.
>
> ('Empathy, Inner Imitation, and Sense-Feelings', in *A Modern Book of Esthetics,* ed. Melvin Rader, New York: Holt, Rinehart and Winston, 1960, p.376)

  To establish this 'fact', Lipps must posit a wholly esthetic dimension and what he calls an 'ideal', as opposed to a 'practical self'. In *Othello* there is no realm of the purely esthetic, no space defined by the intersection of negative capability and the willing suspension of disbelief, and no separation of an 'ideal' from a 'practical' self.

21. To complicate matters further, both declarations occur in a cunning performance for his dupe Roderigo; that is, Iago is saying what he presumes Roderigo wants to believe.

22. Thus Iago invokes heaven as the judge of his self-interested hypocrisy, for *self* and *interest* as stable entities both rely ultimately upon an absolute Being.

23. Elsewhere too, Othello speaks as if aware of himself as a character: 'Were it my cue to fight', he tells the incensed Brabantio and his own followers, 'I should have known it,/ Without a prompter' (I, ii, 83–4). His acceptance of the commission to fight the Turks is likewise couched in an inflated diction that suggests he is responding to a cue:

> The tyrant custom, most grave senators,
> Hath made the flinty and steel couch of war
> My thrice-driven bed of down: I do agnize
> A natural and prompt alacrity
> I find in hardness, and would undertake
> This present wars against the Ottomites.

(I, iii, 229–34)

24. EMMANUEL LE ROY LADURIE, *Montaillou: The Promised Land of Error,* trans. Barbara Bray (New York:Braziller, 1978), pp. 8–9. In a review essay, Natalie Zemon Davis calls attention to the narrative structure of the testimony, a structure she attributes not to the pressure of the Inquisition but to the form of village culture: 'Some of these details were probably remembered over the decades – good memories are part of oral culture – but most form a reconstructed past: from a

Stephen Greenblatt

general memory of an event, a narrative is created that tells with verisimilitude how the events could have unfolded. The past is a story' ('Les Conteurs de Montaillou', *Annales: Economies, Sociétés, Civilisations* **34** 1979, p.70).

On narrativity as a mode, see LOUIS MARIN, *Utopiques: jeux d'espaces;* SVETLANA ALPERS, 'Describe or Narrate? A Problem in Realistic Representation', *New Literary History* 7 (1976–7), pp.15–41; LEO BERSANI, 'The Other Freud', *Humanities in Society* 1 (1978, pp. 35–49.

25. *The Aeneid of Virgil*, trans. Allen Mandelbaum (New York:Bantam Books, 1972), bk 1, lines 1049–51.

26. I very reluctantly accept the Quarto's *sighs* for the Folio's *kisses;* the latter need not, as editors sometimes claim, suggest an improbable immodesty but rather may express Othello's perception of Desdemona's nature, hence what her love has given him. Moreover, the frank eroticism of *kisses* is in keeping with Desdemona's own speeches; it is Othello who emphasizes a pity that she voices nowhere in the play itself. On the other hand, *sighs* admits a simpler reading and by no means excludes the erotic.

There is another interpretive problem in this speech that should be noted: the last two lines are usually taken as a continuation of Desdemona's actual response, as recalled by Othello. But they may equally be his interpretation of her feelings, in which case they may say far more about Othello than about Desdemona. A competent actor could suggest either possibility. There is a further ambiguity in the *her* of 'made her such a man': I hear *her* as accusative, but the dative cannot be ruled out.

27. WILLIAM TYNDALE, *Obedience*, p. 171.

28. Both the Folio and the Second Quarto read 'You are the Lord of duty', but the paradox of an absolute duty that must nevertheless be divided is suggestive.

29. Iago is improvising on two earlier remarks of Brabantio:

> and she, in spite of nature,
> Of years, of country, credit, everything,
> To fall in love with what she fear'd to look on?
>
> (I, iii, 96–8)

and

> Look to her, Moor, have a quick eye to see:
> She has deceiv'd her father, may do thee.
>
> (I, iii, 292–3)

In a society deeply troubled by clandestine marriage, the circumstances of Desdemona's union already brand her as faithless, even at the moment Othello stakes his life upon her faith, while, quite apart from these circumstances, it would seem for the male psyche depicted in the play that the very act of leaving her father borders obscurely on sexual betrayal.

30. See GEORGE K. HUNTER, 'Othello and Colour Prejudice', *Proceedings of the British Academy 1967* **53** (1968), pp. 139–63; LESLIE A. FIEDLER, *The Stranger in Shakespeare* (New York: Stein & Day, 1972), Chapter 3.

A measure of the complex significance of Othello's blackness may be taken from a glance at the competing interpretive possibilities of Desdemona's 'I saw Othello's visage in his mind' (1, iii, 252):

'Do not be surprised that I have married an older black man who looks to you grotesque and terrifying. I have married not a face, a complexion, but a mind: a resolute, Christian mind'.

'I saw Othello's valuation of himself, his internal image, the picture he has in his mind of his own face. I saw how much he had a stake in his narrative sense of himself, how much his whole existence depended upon this sense, and I was deeply drawn to this "visage"'.

'I saw Othello's visage – his blackness, his otherness – in his mind as well as his complexion: there is a unity in his being, I am subdued to precisely this quality in him'.

31. Ridley, in the Arden edition, adheres to the Quarto's 'calmness' at line 185. Most editors prefer the Folio's 'calms'.

32. Ephesians 5.28–32, as cited in the marriage liturgy (*The Book of Common Prayer 1559*, ed. John Booty [Charlottesville: University of Virginia Press, 1976], p.297). The passage is quoted by ARTHUR KIRSCH, 'The Polarization of Erotic Love in *Othello*', p.721, who draws conclusions closely parallel to some of my own, though he differs in emphases and methodology.

33. Becon and Gouge are cited in WILLIAM and MALLEVILLE HALLER, 'The Puritan Art of Love', *Huntington Library Quarterly* 5 (1941–2), pp.44–45, 46.

34. From its inception, Christianity competed fiercely with other sexual conceptions and practices. For a detailed and moving study of one episode in this struggle, see LE ROY LADURIE'S *Montaillou*. Michel Foucault has attempted the beginnings of a modern history of the subject in *La volonté de savoir*.

35. *The City of God*, trans. Marcus Dods (New York; Modern Library, 1950), bk 14, Chapter 24, pp. 473–5.

36. For the inherent violence of sexuality, see LUCRETIUS, *The Nature of the Universe*, trans. Ronald Latham (Baltimore: Penguin, 1951):

Lovers' passion is storm-tossed, even in the moment of fruition, by waves of delusion and incertitude. They cannot make up their mind what to enjoy first with eye or hand. They clasp the object of their longing so tightly that the embrace is painful. They kiss so fiercely that teeth are driven into lips. All this because their pleasure is not pure, but they are goaded by an underlying impulse to hurt the thing, whatever it may be, that gives rise to these budding shoots of madness.

(pp. 163–4).

37. Richard Onorato has called my attention to the way Iago, who is watching this scene, subsequently uses the word *content*: 'nothing can, nor shall content my soul', he tells himself, 'Till I am even with him, wife, for wife' (II, i, 293–4). Later, when under his influence Othello has bade 'farewell content' (III, iii, 354), Iago proffers the consoling words, 'Pray be content' (III, iii, 457).

38. When Othello asks Desdemona to leave him a little to himself, she replies, 'Shall I deny you? no, farewell, my lord' (III, iii, 87).

39. 'Prithee unpin me' requires that the actress, as she speaks these words, call attention to Desdemona's erotic submission to Othello's violence.

40. As Gabrielle Jackson pointed out to me, Emilia feels that she must explain her refusal to observe her husband's commands to be silent and go home:

> Good gentlemen, let me have leave to speak,
> 'Tis proper I obey him but not now:
> Perchance, Iago, I will ne'er go home.

(V, ii, 196–8)

The moment is felt as liberating gesture and redeems her earlier, compliant theft of the handkerchief, but it is both too late and fatal. The play does not hold out the wife's disobedience as a way of averting tragedy.

41. JACQUES LACAN, *The Language of the Self: The Function of Language in Psychoanalysis*, trans. Anthony Wilden (Baltimore: The Johns Hopkins University Press, 1968), p. 11.

42. In effect, Othello invokes larger and larger spheres of self-fashioning: Othello to Desdemona, Othello to Desdemona and Brabantio, Othello to the Senate, Othello to heaven. We might add that the narrative element in formal auricular confession may have been heightened by the fact that confessors were instructed not to interrupt the penitent but to let him begin with a full and circumstantial account.

43. The word *confession* and its variants (*confess'd, confessions*) is repeated eighteen times in the course of the play, more often than in any other play in the canon.

44. See THOMAS N. TENTLER, *Sin and Confession on the Eve of the Reformation*, and Chapter 2.

45. This is a frequent response in the literature of colonialism; we have encountered it in Spenser's *View of the Present State of Ireland*, where he sees the Irish as living in certain respects as the English did before the civilizing influence of the Norman Conquest.

46. TENTLER, p.229. The *Eruditorium penitentiale* points out that in cases of necessity it is possible to kill or steal justifiably, 'but no one may fornicate knowingly without committing a mortal sin'. Tentler observes, 'This kind of thinking is an exaggeration even of medieval puritanism'. Yet it is also true that the climate of religious opinion allowed and perhaps even encouraged such exaggerations.

      Cf. FRANCIS DILLINGHAM, *Christian Oeconomy or Household Government* (London:John Tapp, 1609): 'Julius Caesar made a law that if the husband or the wife found either in adultery, it should be lawful for the husband to kill the wife or the wife the husband. Death then by the light of nature is fit punishment for adulterers and adulteresses' (p. 13).

47. GEORGE JOYE, *A Contrarye (to a certayne manis) Consultacion: That Adulterers ought to be punyshed wyth deathe,. Wyth the solucions of his argumentes for the contrarye* (London: n.p., 1559?), pp.G4 v, A4 v.

> The sacred integrity therefore of this Christ's holy church, the inviolable honour of holy matrimony ordained of God, the preservation of the private and public peace, all honesty, godly zeal to virtue, to the salvation of our souls and to God's glory should constrain every Christian heart to counsel, to exhort and to excite all Christian magistrates to cut off this contagious canker of adultery from among us, lest in further creeping ... it daily corrupteth the whole body of this noble realm so that it else be at last so incurable that ... neither the vice nor yet the just remedy will be suffered.

(A6^V)

189

The death penalty for adulterers was briefly adopted by the Puritan Parliament in the seventeenth century; see KEITH THOMAS, 'The Puritans and Adultery: the Act of 1650 Reconsidered' in *Puritans and Revolutionaries: Essays in Seventeenth-Century History*, ed. Donald Pennington and Keith Thomas (Oxford: At the Clarendon Press, 1978), pp. 257–82.

48. WILLIAM PERKINS, *A Godly and Learned Exposition of Christ's Sermon in the Mount* (Cambridge: Thomas Pierson, 1608), p. 111. See ROBERT V. SCHNUCKER, 'La position puritaine à l'égard de l'adultère', *Annales: Economies, Societes, Civilisation* 27 (1972), pp. 1379–88.

49. Quoted, with a mass of supporting material, in JOHN T. NOONAN, JR *Contraception: A History of Its Treatment by the Catholic Theologians and Canonists* (Cambridge, Mass: Harvard University Press, 1966), p.80. The Stoic marital doctrine, Noonan observes, 'joined the Stoic distrust of pleasure and the Stoic insistence on purpose' (p.47); early Christians embraced the doctrine and hardened its formulation in combating the gnostic sects.

50. NOONAN, p.47.

51. JOHN CALVIN, *Institutes of the Christian Religion*, bk 2 Chapter 8, section 44, quoted in LAWRENCE STONE, *The Family, Sex and Marriage in England 1500–1800*, p.499; *The King's Book or a Necessary Doctrine and Erudition for Any Christian Man* (1543), ed. T.A. Lacey (London: Society for Promoting Christian Knowledge, 1932), pp. 111–12. See likewise JOHN ROGERS, *The Glasse of Godly Loue* (1569), ed. Frederick J. Furnivall, New Shakespeare Society, ser.6, no.2 (London: N. Trubner, 1876), p.185:

Also there ought to be a temperance between man and wife, for God hath ordained marriage for a remedy or medicine, to assuage the heart of the burning flesh, and for procreation, and not beastly for to fulfil the whole lusts of the devilish mind and wicked flesh; for, though ye have a promise that the act in marriage is not sin ... yet if ye take excess, or use it beastly, vilely or inordinately, your mistemperance makes that ill which is good (being rightly used), and that which is clean, ye defile through your abusing of it.

In the seventeeth century, William Perkins informs his readers that the 'holy manner' in marital intercourse involves moderation, 'for even in wedlock, excess in lusts is not better than plain adultery before God'. 'This is the judgement of the ancient Church,' notes Perkins, citing Ambrose and Augustine, 'that Intemperance, that is, immoderate desire even between man and wife, is fornication' (*Christian Oeconomie*, trans. Thomas Pickering [London: Felix Kyngstone, 1609], pp. 113–14).

52. LE ROY LADURIE, *Montaillou*, p. 151. In fact the priest, who was, in Le Roy Ladurie's words, 'an energetic lover and incorrigible Don Juan' (p.154), held a somewhat different position. 'One woman's just like another', he told Grazide's mother. 'The sin is the same, whether she is married or not. Which is as much as to say that there is no sin about it at all' (p.157). Le Roy Ladurie interprets his views on love as follows: 'Starting from the Cathar proposition that "any sexual act, even between married persons, is wrong", he applied it to suit himself. Because everything was forbidden, one act was no worse than another' (pp. 158–9).

53. I, v, 107. Le Roy Ladurie quotes from the *Brevaire d'amour*. 'a lady who sleeps with a true lover is purified of all sins ... the joy of love makes the act innocent, for it proceeds from a pure heart' (p.159).

See Friar Laurence's warnings to Romeo about excessive love:

These violent delights have violent ends
And in their triumph die, like fire and powder,
Which, as they kiss, consume ...
Therefore love moderately: long love doth so.

(II, vi, 9–14)

54. TENTLER, p.174.

55. TENTLER, p.181: *'hoc est in executione ipsius actus nulla voluptatis delectatione teneatur'.*

56. TENTLER, p.183. According to the *King's Book*, over those who have violated married chastity, 'the Devil hath power, as the angel Raphael said unto Thobit, They that marry in such wise that they exclude God out of their hearts, and give themselves unto their own carnal lusts, as it were an horse or a mule, which have no reason; upon such persons the Devil hath power' (p.112).

For a humanist's version of these notions, see the following aphorisms from JUAN LUIS VIVES'S *Introductio ad Sapientam:*

The pleasure of the body is, like the body itself, vile and brutal.
Sensual delectation bores the soul and benumbs the intellect.
Sensual delectation is like robbery, it vilifies the soul. this is the reason why even the most corrupted man seeks secrecy and abhors witnesses.
Sensual pleasure is fleeting and momentaneous, totally beyond any control and always mixed with frustration.
Nothing debilitates more the vigor of our intellect than sexual pleasure.
(CARLOS G. NORENA, *Juan Luis Vives*, The Hague: Martinus Nijhoff, 1970, P.211).

For an attenuated modern version, see the first televised speech delivered from the Sistine Chapel on 27 August 1978 by Pope John Paul I, the pope prayed that families 'may be defended from the destructive attitude of sheer pleasure-seeking, which snuffs out life' (*S.F. Chronicle*, 28 August 1978, p.1).

57. In the early seventeenth century, Samuel Hieron counsels married couples to recite the following prayer before going to bed: 'Allay in us all sensual and brutish love, purifying and sanctifying our affections one towards another, that we may in nothing dishonour this honourable state, nor pollute the bed of marriage ... but may use this thine ordinance in the holy sort, that carnal lusts may be slaked and subdued, nor increased or inflamed thereby' (*A Helpe Unto Devotion*, 3d ed [London:H.L., 1611]. p.411).

58. *A Discourse of Marriage and Wiving* (London, 1620), quoted in RONALD MUSHAT FRYE,'The Teachings of Classical Puritanism on Conjugal Love', *Studies in the Renaissance* 2 (1955), pp. 156–7.

59. WILLIAM WHATELY, *A Bride-bush* (London, 1619), quoted in Frye, p.156.

60. NOONAN, p.79.

61. A major textual crux, and I have taken the liberty, for the sake of clarity and brevity, to depart from Ridley's reading which is as follows:

the young affects
In my defunct, and proper satisfaction.

As Ridley says, 'after all the discussion, Othello's meaning is moderately clear. He is too mature to be subjugated by physical desire'; but he goes on to read *proper* as 'justifiable' where I would read it as 'my own'. Ridley's *moderately* should be emphasized.

62. Yet another crux: the Quarto reads 'very quality' instead of 'utmost pleasure'. I find the latter more powerful and persuasive, particularly in the context of Desdemona's further mention (1.255) of 'The rites for which I love him'.
   Iago twice echoes Desdemona's declaration: 'It was a violent commencement in her, and thou shalt see an answerable sequestration' (I.iii.342–3), and again 'Mark me with what violence she first loved the Moor' (II, i, 221).

63. Desdemona is, in effect, a kind of mirror reversal of Cordelia: where the latter is doomed in the first act of the play by her refusal to declare her love, the former is doomed precisely for such a declaration.
   Professor Spivack, along with most critics of the play, sees Iago as the enemy of the religious bond in marriage (pp.49–50); I would argue that it is precisely the nature of his bond, as defined by rigorists, that torments Othello.

64. On 'property' see KENNETH BURKE, *A Grammar of Motives* (Berkeley: University of California Press, 1969):

   Iago may be considered 'con-substantial' with Othello in that he represents the principles of jealousy implicit in Othello's delight in Desdemona as a private spiritual possession. Iago, to arouse Othello, must talk a language that Othello knows as well as he, a language implicit in the nature of Othello's love as the idealization of his private property in Desdemona. This language is the dialectical opposite of Othello's; but it so thoroughly shares a common ground with Othello's language that its insinuations are never for one moment irrelevant to Othello's thinking. Iago must be cautious in leading Othello to believe them as true: but Othello never for a moment doubts them as *values*

   (p.414).

   As so often happens, I discovered that Burke's brilliant sketch had anticipated the shape of much of my argument. Burke has an essay on the ritual structure of the play in *Hudson Review* 4 (1951), pp. 165–203.

65. I have read two powerful unpublished essays that analyze the male sexual anxieties in the play at a level prior to or beneath the social and doctrinal one discussed here: EDWARD SNOW, 'On the Language of Sexual Pathology in *Othello*' and C.L. BARBER,'"I'll pour this pestilence into his ear", *Othello* as a Development from *Hamlet*.'

66. In act 4, Othello had first thought of poisoning Desdemona and then was persuaded by Iago to 'strangle her in her bed, even the bed she hath contaminated' (IV, i, 203–4). The blood he fantasizes about later may be simply an expression of violence (as he had earlier declared, 'I will chop her into messes' [4.i.196]), but it is tempting to see it as a projection of the blood that marked her loss of virginity and hence, in his disturbed formulation, as 'lust's blood'. For a sensitive exploration of the anxiety over virginity, staining, and impotence in *Othello*, see STANLEY CAVELL, 'Epistemology and Tragedy: A Reading of *Othello*', *Daedalus* 108 (1979), pp. 27–43.

67. Like Oedipus, Othello cannot escape the fact that it is he who has committed the crime and must be punished.

We should, in all fairness, call attention to the fact that Othello in the end views his wife as 'chaste', but the language in which he does so reinforces the orthodox condemnation of pleasure:

> cold, cold my girl,
> Even like thy chastity.

(V, ii, 176–7)

Indeed the identification of the coldness of death with marital chastity seems to me a *confirmation* of the necrophilic fantasy.

68. Shakespeare's talent for entering into the consciousness of others and giving supreme expression to incompatible perspectives has been a major preoccupation of criticism since Coleridge and Keats. For a recent exploration, see NORMAN RABKIN's concept of 'complementarity': *Shakespeare and the Common Understanding* (New York: Free Press, 1967).

   In *The Anxiety of Influence* (New York: Oxford University Press, 1973), Harold Bloom remarks, 'Shakespeare is the largest instance in the language of a phenomenon that stands outside the concern of this book: the absolute absorption of the precursor' (p.11).

69. 'Of Repentance', in *The Complete Essays of Montaigne*, trans. Donald M. Frame (Stanford: Stanford University Press, 1958), pp.610–11. It is hardly irrelevant for our purposes that Montaigne describes this method in an essay in which he rejects the confessional system.

70. On pleasure and the threat to established order, see GEORGES BATAILLE, *Death and Sensuality: A Study of Eroticism and the Taboo* (New York: Walker & Co., 1962), and Mikhail Bakhtin, *Rabelais and His World*, trans. Helene Iswolsky (Cambridge, Mass: MIT Press, 1968).

   See also BERBERT MARCUSE, *Eros and Civilization* (New York: Random House, 1955); MICHEL FOUCAULT, *Discipline and Punish*; LEO BERSANI, *A Future for Asyanax:Character and Desire in Literature* (Boston: Little, Brown and Co., 1976).

5 Cultural Materialism

JONATHAN DOLLIMORE   KING LEAR (C. 1605–06) AND ESSENTIALIST HUMANISM*

Jonathan Dollimore is Reader in the School of English and American Studies at the University of Sussex. His book *Radical Tragedy: Religion, Ideology and Power in the Drama of Shakespeare and His Contemporaries* was published in 1984 by Harvester Press and republished in a second edition with a new Introduction in 1989. Dollimore begins from the position that the drama of Shakespeare and his contemporaries was 'radical' in its capacity to subvert establishment values, both in its own time and subsequently. In addition to considering its contemporary Renaissance concerns, Dollimore also analyses the values which have informed subsequent critical reception of these texts. He does so from a position which shares some of the concerns of Weimann, Cohen and Greenblatt, although he takes his conceptual bearings from a deft amalgam of post-structuralist Marxism, and the kind of cultural analysis pioneered by the late Raymond Williams. This amalgam has come to be known as 'Cultural Materialism', and its most succinct manifesto is a collection of essays edited jointly with Alan Sinfield entitled *Political Shakespeare* (Manchester, 1985). Dollimore brings together materialist theories of the formation of the gendered human subject, of the decentring of man, and a theory of ideology, as means of situating texts in their historical contexts, and of analysing the conditions of their reception. He begins from assumptions about subjectivity which are similar to those of Greenblatt, although his concern is to explore a much more overtly radical line in which literature may be recuperated for an alternative political project. The decentring of man, a concept partly of Foucauldian provenance, with all that that implies, results for Dollimore in the prospect of 'an alternative conception of the relations between history, society and subjectivity .... It is a radical alternative which in the context of

---

*Reprinted from *Radical Tragedy: Religion, Ideology, and Power in the Drama of Shakespeare and his Contemporaries* (Brighton: Harvester Press, 1984), pp. 189–203.

materialist analysis, helps vindicate certain objectives: not essence but potential, not the human condition but cultural difference, not destiny but collectively identified goals' (*Radical Tragedy*, p. 271). The following extract on *King Lear* places the analysis of the play within the context of a discussion of the 'essentialist humanism' which Dollimore's own general thesis challenges.

When he is on the heath King Lear is moved to pity. As unaccommodated man he feels what wretches feel. For the humanist the tragic paradox arises here: debasement gives rise to dignity and at the moment when Lear might be expected to be most brutalised he becomes most human. Through kindness and shared vulnerability human kind redeems itself in a universe where the gods are at best callously just, at worst sadistically vindictive.

In recent years the humanist view of Jacobean tragedies like *Lear* has been dominant, having more or less displaced the explicitly Christian alternative. Perhaps the most important distinction between the two is this: the Christian view locates man centrally in a providential universe;[1] the humanist view likewise centralises man but now he is in a condition of tragic dislocation: instead of integrating (ultimately) with a teleological design created and sustained by God, man grows to consciousness in a universe which thwarts his deepest needs. If he is to be redeemed at all he must redeem himself. The humanist also contests the Christian claim that the suffering of Lear and Cordelia is part of a providential and redemptive design. If that suffering is to be justified at all it is because of what it reveals about man's intrinsic nature – his courage and integrity. By heroically enduring a fate he is powerless to alter, by insisting, moreover, upon *knowing* it, man grows in stature even as he is being destroyed. Thus Clifford Leech, an opponent of the Christian view, tells us that tragic protagonists 'have a quality of mind that somehow atones for the nature of the world in which they and we live. They have, in a greater or lesser degree, the power to endure and the power to apprehend' (*Shakespeare's Tragedies*, p. 15). Wilbur Sanders in an influential study argues for an ultimately optimistic Shakespeare who had no truck with Christian doctrine or conventional Christian conceptions of the absolute but nevertheless affirmed that 'the principle of health – grace – is not in heaven, but in nature, and especially in human nature, and it cannot finally be rooted out'. Ultimately this faith in nature and human nature involves and entails 'a faith in a universal moral order which cannot finally be defeated' (*The Dramatist and the Received Idea*, pp. 336–7).

Here as so often with the humanist view there is a strong residue of the more explicit Christian metaphysic and language which it seeks to eschew; comparable with Sanders' use of 'grace' is Leech's use of 'atone'. Moreover both indicate the humanist preoccupation with the universal counterpart of essentialist subjectivity – either ultimately affirmed (Sanders) or recognised as an ultimate tragic absence (Leech).[2] The humanist reading of Lear has been authoritatively summarised by G.K. Hunter (he calls it the 'modern' view of the play):

[it] is seen as the greatest of tragedies because it not only strips and reduces and assaults human dignity, but because it also shows with the greatest force and detail the process of restoration by which humanity can recover from degradation … [Lear's] retreat into the isolated darkness of his own mind is also a descent into the seed-bed of a new life; for *the individual mind is seen here as the place from which a man's most important qualities and relationships draw the whole of their potential source.*

(*Dramatic Identities and Cultural Tradition*, pp. 252–2, my italics)

What follows is an exploration of the political dimension of *Lear*. It argues that the humanist view of that play is as inappropriate as the Christian alternative which it has generally displaced – inappropriate not least because it shares the essentialism of the latter. I do not mean to argue again the case against the Christian view since, even though it is still sometimes advanced, it has been effectively discredited by writers as diverse as Barbara Everett, William R. Elton and Cedric Watts.[3] The principal reason why the humanist view seems equally misguided, and not dissimilar, is this: it mystifies suffering and invests man with a quasi-transcendent identity whereas the play does neither of these things. In fact, the play repudiates the essentialism which the humanist reading of it presupposes. However, I do not intend to replace the humanist reading with one which rehearses yet again all the critical clichés about the nihilistic and chaotic 'vision' of Jacobean tragedy. In *Lear*, as in *Troilus*, man is decentred not through misanthropy but in order to make visible social process and its forms of ideological misrecognition.

Redemption and endurance: two sides of essentialist humanism

'Pity' is a recurring word in *Lear*. Philip Brockbank, in a recent and sensitive humanist reading of the play, says: 'Lear dies "with pity" (IV, vii, 53) and that access of pity, which in the play attends the dissolution of the senses and of the self, is a condition for the renewal of human life ' ('Upon Such Sacrifices', p. 133). Lear, at least when he is on the heath, is indeed moved to pity, but what does it mean to say that such pity is 'a condition for renewal of human life'? Exactly whose life is renewed? In this connection there is one remark of Lear's which begs our attention; it is made when he first witnesses 'You houseless poverty' (III, iv, 26): 'Oh, I have ta'en / Too little care of this!' Too little: Lear bitterly reproaches himself because hitherto he has been aware of yet ignored the suffering of his deprived subjects. (The distracted use of the abstract – 'You houseless poverty' – subtly suggests that Lear's disregard has been of a general rather than a local poverty.) He has ignored it not through callous indifference but simply *because he has not experienced it.*

King Lear suggests here a simple yet profound truth. Far from endorsing the idea that man can redeem himself in and through an access of pity, we might be moved to recognise that, on the contrary, in a world where pity is the prerequisite for compassionate action, where a king has to share the suffering of his subjects in order to 'care', the majority will remain poor, naked and wretched. The point of course is that princes only see the hovels of wretches during progresses (walkabouts?), in flight or in fairy tale. Even in fiction the wheel of fortune rarely brings them that low. Here, as so often in Jacobean drama, the fictiveness of the genre or scene intrudes; by acknowledging its status as fiction it abdicates the authority of idealist mimesis and indicates the better the reality it signifies; resembling in this Brecht's alienation effect, it stresses artifice not in the service of formalism but of realism. So, far from transcending in the name of an essential humanity the gulf which separates the privileged from the deprived, the play insists on it. And what clinches this is the exchange between Poor Tom (Edgar) and Gloucester. The latter has just arrived at the hovel; given the circumstances, his concern over the company kept by the king is faintly ludicrous but very telling: 'What, hath your Grace no better company?' (III, iv, 138; cf. Cordelia at IV, vii, 38–9). Tom tells Gloucester that he is cold. Gloucester, *uncomprehending rather than callous*, tells him he will keep warm if he goes back into the hovel (true of course, relatively speaking). That this comes from one of the 'kindest' people in the play prevents us from dismissing the remark as individual unkindness: judging is less important than seeing how unkindness is built into social consciousness. That Gloucester is unknowingly talking to his son in this exchange simply underscores the arbitrariness, the woeful inadequacy of what passes for kindness; it is, relatively, a very precious thing but as a basis for human kind's self-redemption it is a non-starter. Insofar as Lear identifies with suffering it is at the point when he is powerless to do anything about it. This is not accidental: the society of *Lear* is structured in such a way that to wait for shared experience to generate justice is to leave it too late. Justice, we might say, is too important to be trusted to empathy.

Like Lear, Gloucester has to undergo intense suffering before he can identify with the deprived. When he does so he expresses more than compassion. He perceives, crucially, the limitation of a society that depends on empathy alone for its justice. Thus he equates his earlier self with the 'lust-dieted man … *that will not see/Because he does not feel*' (IV, i, 69–71, my italics). Moreover he is led to a conception of social justice (albeit dubiously administered by the 'Heavens', 68) whereby 'distribution should undo excess, And each man have enough' (IV, i, 72–3).

By contrast, Lear experiences pity mainly as an inseparable aspect of his own grief: 'I am mightily abus'd. I should e'en die with pity / To see another thus' (IV, vii, 53–4). His compassion emerges from grief only to be obliterated by grief. He is angered, horrified, confused and, above all dislocated. Understandably then he does not empathise with Tom so much as assimilate him to his own derangement. Indeed, Lear hardly communicates with anyone, especially on the heath; most of his utterances are demented mumbling interspersed with brief insight. Moreover, his preoccupation with vengeance ultimately displaces his transitory pity; reverting from the charitable reconciliation of V, iii to vengeance once again, we see him, minutes before his death, boasting of having killed the 'slave' that was hanging Cordelia.

But what of Cordelia herself? She more than anyone else has been seen to embody and symbolise pity. But is it a pity which significantly alters anything? To see her death as *intrinsically* redemptive is simply to mystify both her and death.[4] Pity, like kindness, seems in *Lear* to be precious yet ineffectual. Far from being redemptive it is the authentic but residual expression of a scheme of values all but obliterated by a catastrophic upheaval in the power structure of this society. Moreover the failure of those values is in part due to the fact that they are (or were) an ideological ratification of the very power structure which eventually destroys them.

In *Lear*, as we shall see in the next section, there is a repudiation of stoicism similar to that found in Marston's *Antonio's Revenge*. Yet repeatedly the sceptical treatment, sometimes the outright rejection, of stoicism in these plays is overlooked; often in fact it is used to validate another kind of humanism. For convenience I call the kind outlined so far ethical humanism and this other one existential humanism. The two involve different emphases rather than different ideologies. That of the latter is on essential heroism and existential integrity, that of the former on essential humanity, the universal human condition. Thus, according to Barbara Everett (in another explicitly anti-Christian analysis):

> In the storm scene Lear is at his most powerful and, despite moral considerations, at his noblest; the image of man hopelessly confronting a hostile universe and withstanding it only by his inherent powers of rage, endurance and perpetual questioning, is perhaps the most purely 'tragic' in Shakespeare.
>
> ('The New *King Lear*', p. 333)

Significantly, existential humanism forms the basis even of J. W. Lever's *The Tragedy of State*, one of the most astute studies of Jacobean tragedy to date. On the one hand Lever is surely right in insisting that these plays 'are not primarily treatments of characters with a so-called "fatal flaw", whose downfall is brought about by the decree of just if inscrutable powers ... the fundamental flaw is not in them but in the world they inhabit: in the political state, the social order it upholds, and likewise, by projection, in the cosmic state of shifting arbitrary phenomena called "Fortune" '(p. 10). By the same criteria it is surely wrong to assert (on the same page) that: 'What really matters is the quality of [the heroes'] response to intolerable situations. This is a drama of adversity and stance ... The rational man who remains master of himself is by the same token the ultimate master of his fate.' In Lever's analysis Seneca is the ultimate influence on a drama (including *King Lear*) which celebrates man's capacity inwardly to transcend oppression (p. 9).

If the Christian mystifies suffering by presenting it as intrinsic to God's redemptive and providential design for man, the humanist does likewise by representing suffering as the mysterious ground for man's *self-*redemption; both in effect mystify suffering by having as their common focus an essentialist conception of what it is to be human: in virtue of his spiritual essence (Christian), essential humanity (ethical humanist), or essential self (existential humanist), man is seen to achieve a paradoxical transcendence: in individual extinction is his apothesis. Alternatively we might say that in a mystifying closure of the historical real the categories of idealist culture are recuperated. This suggests why both ethical and existential humanism are in fact quasi-religious: both reject the providential and 'dogmatic' elements of Christianity while retaining its fundamental relation between suffering, affirmation and regeneration. Moreover they, like Christianity, tend to fatalise social dislocation; its causes are displaced from the realm of the human; questions about them are raised but only rhetorically, thus confirming man's impotence to alleviate the human condition. This clears the stage for what really matters: man's responsive suffering and what it reveals in the process about his essential nature. Recognisable here is the fate of existentialism when merged with literary criticism as a surrogate or displaced theology; when, specifically, it was co-opted to the task most symptomatic of that displacement, namely the obsession with defining tragedy. It will be recalled that for the existentialist existence precedes essence, or so said Sartre, who later tried to develop this philosophy in the context of Marxism. In literary criticism the social implications of existentialism, such as they were, were easily ignored, the emphasis being instead on a modernist angst and man's thwarted spiritual potential. This is another sense in which existential humanism is merely a mutation of Christianity and not at all a radical alternative; although it might reluctantly have to acknowledge that neither Absolute nor Essence exist, it still relates man to them on a principle of Augustinian privation: man understands his world only through the grid of their absence.

King Lear: a materialist reading

More important than Lear's pity is his 'madness' – less divine furor than a
process of collapse which reminds us just how precarious is the
psychological equilibrium which we call sanity, and just how dependent
upon an identity which is social rather than essential. What makes Lear the
person he is – or rather was — is not kingly essence (divine right), but,
among other things, his authority and his family. On the heath he
represents the process whereby man has been stripped of his stoic and
(Christian) humanist conceptions of self. Consider what Seneca has to say
of affliction and philosophy:

> Whether we are caught in the grasp of an inexorable law of fate, whether
> it is God who as lord of the universe has ordered all things, or whether
> the affairs of mankind are tossed and buffeted haphazardly by chance, it
> is philosophy that has the duty of protecting us.
>
> *(Letters*, p. 64)

Lear, in his affliction, attempts to philosophise with Tom who he is
convinced is a 'Noble philosopher', a 'good Athenian' (II, iv, 168, 176). It
adds up to nothing more than the incoherent ramblings of one half-crazed
by just that suffering which philosophy, according to the stoic, guards
against. It is an ironic subversion of neo-stoic essentialism, one which
recalls Bacon's essay 'Of Adversity', where he quotes Seneca: '*It is true
greatness to have in one the frailty of a man, and the security of a god*' only to
add, dryly: 'This would have done better in poesy, where transcendences
are more allowed' (*Essays*, p. 15). As I have already shown (chapter 4),
Bacon believed that poesy implies idealist mimesis – that is, an illusionist
evasion of those historical and empirical realities which, says Bacon,
'buckle and bow the mind unto the nature of things' (*Advancement*, p. 83).
He seems to have remained unaware that Jacobean drama was just as
subversive of poesy (in this sense) as he was, not only with regard to
providentialism but now its corollary, essentialism. Plays like *Lear* precisely
disallow 'transcendences'; in this at least they confirm Edmund's
contention that 'men / Are as the time is' (V, iii, 31–2). Montaigne made a
similar point with admirable terseness: 'I am no philosopher: Evils
oppresse me according as they waigh' (*Essay*, III, 189). The Fool tells Lear
that he is 'an O without a figure' (I, iv, 192); both here and seconds later he
anticipates his master's eventual radical decentredness, the consequence of
having separated 'The name, and all th' addition' of a king from his real
'power' (I, i 129, 135): 'Who is it that can tell me who I am?' cries Lear;
'Lear's shadow' replies the Fool.

    After he has seen Lear go mad, Gloucester offers this inversion of
stoicism:

> Better I were distract
> So should my thoughts be sever'd from my griefs,
> And woes by wrong imagination lose
> The knowledge of themselves.

(IV, vi, 281–4)

For Lear dispossession and displacement entail not redemptive suffering but a kind of suffering recognition – implicated perhaps with confession, depending on how culpable we take this king to have been with regard to 'the great *image* of authority' which he now briefly demystifies: 'a dog's obey'd in office' (IV, vi, 157, my italics). Lear does acknowledge blame, though deludedly believing the power which made him blameworthy is still his: 'Take that of me, my friend, who have the power/To seal th' accuser's lips' (IV, vi, 169–70). His admission that authority is a function of 'office' and 'power', not intrinsic worth, has its corollary: power itself is in control of 'justice' (1. 166) rather than vice versa:

> The usurer hangs the cozener.
> Through tatter'd clothes small vices do appear;
> Robes and furr'd gowns hide all. Plate sin with gold
> And the strong lance of justice hurtless breaks;
> Arm it in rags, a pigmy's straw doth pierce it.

(IV, vi, 163–7)

Scenes like this one remind us that *King Lear* is, above all, a play about power, property and inheritance. Referring to Goneril, the distraught Lear cries: 'Ingratitude thou marble–hearted fiend, / More hideous when thou show'st thee in a child / Than the sea-monster' (I, iv, 259–61). Here, as throughout the play, we see the cherished norms of human kindness shown to have no 'natural' sanction at all. A catastrophic redistribution of power and property – and, eventually, a civil war – disclose the awful truth that these two things are somehow prior to the laws of human kindness rather than vice versa (likewise, as we have just seen, with power in relation to justice). Human values are not antecedent to these material realities but are, on the contrary, in-formed by them.[5]

Even allowing for his conservative tendency to perceive all change as a change for the worse, Gloucester's account of widespread social discord must surely be taken as at least based on fact: 'These late eclipses in the sun and moon portend no good to us ... Love cools, friendship falls off, brothers divide, in cities, mutinies; in countries, discord; in palaces, treason ... there's son against father; the King falls from bias of nature: there's father against child' (I, ii, 100–11). ''Tis strange', concludes the troubled Gloucester and exits, leaving Edmund to make things somewhat less so.

Significantly, Edmund does not deny the extent of the discord, only Gloucester's mystified sense of its cause. In an earlier soliloquy Edmund has already repudiated 'the plague of custom .. The curiosity of nations' which label him bastard (I, ii, 3–4). Like Montaigne he insists that universal law is merely municipal law (above, p. 16). Here he goes further, repudiating the ideological process whereby the latter is misrecognised as the former; he rejects, that is, a way of thinking which represents the contingent as the necessary and thereby further represents human identity and the social order as metaphysically determined (and therefore unalterable): 'When we are sick in fortune, often the surfeits of our own behavior, we make guilty of our disasters the sun, the moon, and stars; as if we were villains on necessity, fools by heavenly compulsion ... by a divine thrusting on' (I, ii, 122–32). Closely related to this refusal of the classical ideological effect is the way Edmund also denaturalises the theatrical effect: 'Pat! He comes like the catastrophe of the old comedy. My cue is villainous melancholy' (I, ii, 128). Yet this revolutionary scepticism is discredited by the purpose to which it is put. How are we to take this? Are we to assume that Edmund is simply evil and therefore so is his philosophy? I want to argue that we need not. To begin with we have to bear in mind a crucial fact: Edmund's scepticism is made to serve an existing system of values; although he falls prey to, he does not introduce his society to its obsession with power, property and inheritance; it is already the material and ideological basis of that society. As such it informs the consciousness of Lear and Gloucester as much as Cornwall and Regan; consider Lear first, then Gloucester.

Lear's behaviour in the opening scene presupposes first, his absolute power, second, the knowledge that his being king constitutes that power, third, his refusal to tolerate what he perceives as a contradiction of that power. Therefore what Lear demands of Cordelia – authentic familial kindness – is precluded by the very terms of the demand; that is, by the extent to which the occasion as well as his relationship to her is saturated with the ideological imperatives of power. For her part Cordelia's real transgression is not unkindness as such, but speaking in a way which threatens to show too clearly how the laws of human kindness operate in the service of property, contractual, and power relations:

> I love your Majesty
> According to my bond ...
> I
> Return those duties back as are right fit ...
> Why have my sisters husbands, if they say
> They love you [i.e. Lear] all?

(I, i, 91–2; 95–6; 98–9)

Presumably Cordelia does not intend it to be so, but this is the patriarchal order in danger of being shorn of its ideological legitimation – here, specifically, a legitimation taking ceremonial form. (Ironically yet predictably, the 'untender' [1.105] dimension of that order is displaced on to Cordelia.) Likewise with the whole issue of dowries. Prior to Lear's disowning of Cordelia, the realities of property marriage are more or less transmuted by the language of love and generosity, the ceremony of good government. But in the act of renouncing her, Lear brutally foregrounds the imperatives of power and property relations: 'Here I disclaim all my paternal care, / Propinquity and property of blood' (I, ii, 112–3; cf. II. 196–7). Kenneth Muir glosses 'property' as 'closest blood relation' (ed. *King Lear*, p. 11). Given the context of this scene it must also mean 'ownership' – father owning daughter – with brutal connotations of the master/slave relationship as in the following passage from *King John*: 'I am too high-born to be *propertied* / To be a ... serving man' (V, ii, 79–81). Even kinship then – indeed especially kinship – is in-formed by the ideology of property relations, the contentious issue of primogeniture being, in this play, only its most obvious manifestation. Later we witness Lear's correlation between the quantity of retainers Goneril will allow him and the quality of her love. Regan offers twenty-five retainers, upon which Lear tells Goneril: 'I'll go with thee. / Thy fifty yet doth double five and twenty. / And thou art twice her love' (II, iv, 257–9).

Gloucester's unconscious acceptance of this underlying ideology is conveyed at several points but nowhere more effectively than in Act II scene i; even as he is coming to terms with Edgar's supposed treachery he is installing Edmund in his place, offering in *exchange* for Edmund's 'natural' behaviour, property:

> of my land
> Loyal and natural boy, I'll work the means
> To make thee capable.
>
> (II, i, 83–5)

Thus the one thing which the kind Gloucester and the vicious Cornwall have in common is that each offers to reward Edmund's 'loyalty' in exactly the same way (cf. III, v, 16–18). All this would be ludicrous if it were not so painful: as their world disintegrates Lear and Gloucester cling even more tenaciously to the only values they know, which are precisely the values which precipitated the disintegration. Hence even as society is being torn apart by conflict, the ideological structure which has generated that conflict is being reinforced by it.

When Edmund in the forged letter represents Edgar complaining of 'the oppression of aged tyranny' which commands 'not as it hath power, but as it is suffered' (I, ii, 47–8), he exploits the same personal anxiety in

Gloucester which Cordelia unintentionally triggers in Lear. Both fathers represent a challenge to their patriarchal authority by offspring as unnatural behaviour, an abdication of familial duty. The trouble is they do this in a society where 'nature' as ideological concept is fast losing its power to police disruptive elements – for example: 'That nature which contemns its origin / Cannot be border'd certain in itself' (IV, ii, 32–3). No longer are origin, identity and action a 'natural' ideological unity, and the disintegration of that unity reveals something of fundamental importance: when, as here (also, e.g. at I, ii, 1–22) nature is represented as socially disruptive, yet elsewhere as the source of social stability (e.g. at II, iv, 176–80), we see an ideological construct beginning to incorporate and therby render visible the very conflicts and contradictions in the social order which it hitherto effaced. In this respect the play activates a contradiction intrinsic to any 'naturalised' version of the Christian metaphysic; to abandon or blur the distinction between matter and spirit while retaining the basic premises of that metaphysic is eventually to construe evil as at once utterly alien to the human condition (unnatural) yet disturbingly and mysteriously inherent within it (natural) and to be purged accordingly. If deep personal anxiety is thus symptomatic of more general social dislocation it is also what guarantees the general reaction formation to that dislocation: those in power react to crisis by entrenching themselves the deeper within the ideology and social organisation responsible for it.

At strategic points in the play we see how the minor characters have also internalised the dominant ideology. Two instances must suffice. The first occurs in Act II scene ii where Kent insults Oswald. He does so almost entirely in terms of the latter's lack of material wealth, his mean estate and consequent dependence upon service. Oswald is, says Kent, a 'beggarly, three-suited, hundred-pound, filthy, worsted-stocking … superserviceable … one-trunk-inheriting slave' (II, ii, 15 ff; as Muir points out, servants were apparently given three suits a year, while gentlemen wore silk as opposed to worsted stockings). The second example involves the way that for the Gentleman attending Cordelia even pity (or more accurately 'Sorrow') is conceived as a kind of passive female commodity (IV, iii, 16–23).[6]

We can now see the significance of Edmund's scepticism and its eventual relationship to this dominant ideology of property and power. Edmund's sceptical independence is itself constituted by a contradiction: his illegitimate exclusion from society gives him an insight into the ideological basis of that society even as it renders him vulnerable to and dependent upon it. In this respect Edmund resembles the malcontents already encountered in previous chapters: exclusion from society gives rise both to the malcontent's sense of its worthlessness and his awareness that identity itself is dependent upon it. Similarly, Edmund, in liberating himself from the myth of innate inferiority, does not thereby liberate himself from his society's obsession with power, property and inheritance; if anything that obsession becomes the more urgent: 'Legitimate Edgar, I *must* have your land' (I, ii, 16, my italics). He sees through one level of ideological legitimation only to remain the more thoroughly enmeshed with it at a deeper level.

Edmund embodies the process whereby, because of the contradictory conditions of its inception, a revolutionary (emergent) insight is folded back into a dominant ideology. Witnessing his fate we are reminded of how, historically, the misuse of revolutionary insight has tended to be in proportion to its truthfulness, and of how as this very fact is obscured, the insight becomes entirely identified with (or as) its misappropriation. Machiavellianism, Gramsci has reminded us, is just one case in point (*Selections from Prison Notebooks*, p. 136).

The refusal of closure

Lionel Trilling has remarked that 'the captains and kings and lovers and clowns of Shakespeare are alive and complete before they die' (*The Opposing Self*, p. 38). Few remarks could be less true of *King Lear*. The notion of man as tragic victim somehow alive and complete in death is precisely the kind of essentialist mystification which the play refuses. It offers instead a decentring of the tragic subject which in turn becomes the focus of a more general exploration of human consciousness in relation to social being – one which discloses human values to be not antecedent to, but rather in-formed by, material conditions. *Lear* actually refuses then that autonomy of value which humanist critics so often insist that it ultimately affirms. Nicholas Brooke, for example, in one of the best close analyses of the play that we have, concludes by declaring: 'all moral structures, whether of natural order or Christian redemption, are invalidated by the naked fact of experience', yet manages in the concluding sentence of the study to resurrect from this unaccommodated 'naked experience' a redemptive autonomy of value, one almost mystically inviolable: 'Large orders collapse; but values remain, and are independent of them' (*Shakespeare: King Lear*, pp. 59–60). But surely in *Lear*, as in most of human history, 'values' are shown to be terrifyingly dependent upon whatever 'large orders' actually exist; in civil war especially – which after all is what *Lear* is about – the two collapse together.

In the closing moments of *Lear* those who have survived the catastrophe actually attempt to recuperate their society in just those terms which the play has subjected to sceptical interrogation. There is invoked, first, a concept of innate nobility in contradistinction to innate evil and, second, its corollary: a metaphysically ordained justice. Thus Edgar's defeat of

Edmund is interpreted as a defeat of an evil nature by a noble one. Also nobility is seen to be like truth – it will out: 'Methought thy very gait did prophesy / A royal nobleness' (V. iii, 175–7). Goneril is 'reduced' to her treachery ('read thine own evil', l 156), while Edmund not only acknowledges defeat but also repents, submitting to Edgar's nobility (ll. 165–6) and acknowledging his own contrary nature (ll. 242–3). Next, Edgar invokes a notion of divine justice which holds out the possibility of rendering their world intelligible once more; speaking to Edmund of Gloucester, he says:

> The gods are just, and of our pleasant vices
> Make instruments to plague us:
> The dark and vicious place where thee he got
> Cost him his eyes.

> (V, iii, 170–3)

Thus is responsibility displaced; but perhaps Edgar is meant to wince as he says it since the problem of course is that he is making his society supernaturally intelligible at the cost of rendering the concept of divine justice so punitive and 'poetic' as to be, humanly speaking, almost unintelligible. Nevertheless Albany persists with the same process of recuperation by glossing thus the deaths of Goneril and Regan: 'This judgement of the heavens, that makes us tremble, / Touches us not with pity' (V. iii, 230–1). But when he cries 'The Gods defend her!' – i.e. Cordelia – instead of the process being finally consolidated we witness, even before he has finished speaking, Lear re-entering with Cordelia dead in his arms. Albany has one last desperate bid for recuperation, still within the old punitive / poetic terms:

> All friends shall taste
> The wages of their virture, and all foes
> The cup of their deservings.

> (V, iii, 302–4)

Seconds later Lear dies. The timing of these two deaths must surely be seen as cruelly, precisely subversive: instead of complying with the demands of formal closure – the convention which would confirm the attempt at recuperation – the play concludes with two events which sabotage the prospect of both closure and recuperation.

Notes

1. Thus Irving Ribner (for example) argues that the play 'affirms justice in the world, which it sees as a harmonious system ruled by a benevolent God', *Patterns in Shakespearean Tragedy* (London 1962), p.117.

2. Other critics who embrace, invoke or imply the categories of essentialist humanism include the following: A.C. BRADLEY, *Shakespearean Tragedy* (London 1904), lectures 7 and 8; ISRAEL KNOX, *The Aesthetic Theories of Kant, Hegel and Shopenhauer* (New York: Humanities Press 1958), p. 117; ROBERT ORNSTEIN, *The Moral Vision of Jacobean Tragedy* (Univ. of Wisconsin Press 1965), p. 264; KENNETH MUIR (ed.), *King Lear* (London: Methuen 1964), especially p. lv; GRIGORI KOZINTSEV, *King Lear: the Space of Tragedy* (trans. Mary Mackintosh, London: Heinemann 1977), pp. 250–1. For the essentialist view, with a pseudo-Nietzschean twist, see MICHAEL LONG, *The Unnatural Scene* (London: Methuen 1977), pp. 191–3.

   Jan Kott suggests the way that the absurdist view exists in the shadow of a failed Christianity and a failed humanism – a sense of paralysis in the face of the failure (*Shakespeare Our Contemporary*, pp. 104, 108, 116–17).

3. BARBARA EVERETT, 'The New King Lear'; WILLIAM R. ELTON, *King Lear and the Gods*; CEDRIC WATTS, 'Shakespearean Themes: The Dying God and the Universal Wolf'.

4. For John Danby, Cordelia is redemption incarnate; but can she really be seen as 'allegorically the root of individual and social sanity; tropologically Charity "that suffereth long and is kind", analogically the redemptive principle itself'? (*Shakespeare's Doctrine of Nature*, p. 125; cf. p. 133).

5. In-form rather than determine: in this play material factors do not determine values in a crude sense; rather, the latter are shown to be dependent upon the former in a way which radically disqualifies the idealist contention that the reverse is true, namely, that these values not only survive the 'evil' but do so in a way which indicates their ultimate independence of it.

6. By contrast compare Derek Traversi who finds in the imagery of this passage a 'sense of value, of richness and fertility… an indication of redemption… the poetical transformation of natural emotion into its spiritual distillation' (*An Approach to Shakespeare*, II, 164).

6 Feminism

CATHERINE BELSEY   *FINDING A PLACE**

Catherine Belsey is Professor of English at the University College of Cardiff, and is director of the Centre for Contemporary Critical and Cultural Theory there. Her book *The Subject of Tragedy: Identity and Difference in Renaissance Drama* was published in 1985, and like Dollimore she is concerned to view Shakespearean texts within the larger perspective of other dramatic and non-dramatic texts of the period. Beginning from what was originally a Saussurean concept, that of 'difference', Belsey seeks to show how this mechanism through which meanings are produced serves to establish the *relation* between masculine and feminine identity. Her particular area of concern is the space which Renaissance culture allotted to woman, and the ways in which the identity derived from that positioning was constituted in Renaissance dramatic and non-dramatic texts. The following extract is from the chapter entitled 'Finding a Place', and ranges across a series of texts icluding Shakespeare's *Antony and Cleopatra*. Like Dollimore, Belsey is concerned to identify sites of resistance in these texts, moments when texts disclose their own discontinuity, and to this extent her materialist feminist approach radically challenges a traditional aesthetics preoccupied with harmony, continuity, and wholeness. Moreover, like Dollimore, Belsey also challenges essentialist humanism as the theory which underpins the concept of the autonomous human subject, insisting that *identity* itself is constructed in and through *difference*. Moreover, Belsey forsakes that critical activity which has come to be know as 'practical criticism' for one which regards literary texts both as symptomatic of social and cultural relations generally, and also as a means of constituting resistances to specific forms of oppression. To this extent 'tragedy' is both a subject,

---

*Reprinted from *The Subject of Tragedy* (London: Routledge, 1985), pp. 192–216.

that is to say the object of a scholarly enquiry, *and* it is a form in which individual gendered identities (*subjects*) are constructed.

1 Women as subjects

In the absolutist version of marriage women are objects of exchange and the guarantee of dynastic continuity; in the liberal version they are autonomous subjects freely exercising their power to choose a husband and becoming partners in the affective family which is the seminary of good citizens. Such liberalism was rare but not unthinkable in the pre-revolutionary period, and in the drama it is possible to see the new concepts emerging. It is also possible to see, in the period before liberalism becomes synonymous with common sense, explorations of some of the flaws in that ideal, some of the limitations of the liberal concept of marriage.

Women as subjects find a place – in the home, in the bosom of the family. This, of course, is precisely where they were before, but this time the place is (to varying degrees) chosen – on the basis of romantic love. The degree of choice is one of the areas of uncertainty in the texts of the period. The Duchess of Malfi, who takes the initiative and woos Antonio, is rare in the seventeenth century. Indeed, even in the twentieth century the Duchess's behaviour has seemed so scandalous that the majority of recent critical discussions of the play have taken it for granted that her 'wantonness' and 'wilfulness' in so challenging convention are to blame for the tragic events the play depicts. More commonly the plays, like the domestic conduct books, inadvertently betray an uneasy alliance between liberalism and patriarchy, showing women as free to choose to the extent that they are free to acquiesce. The position of the woman in the family is stabilized in a form which is now familiar as one of negotiator between the father and the children, an authoritative parent who nonetheless softens the discipline imposed by the father. 'Mothering' is thus differentiated from 'fathering' as a process of nurturing, caring, protecting.

The price women pay for finding a place is their exclusion from the political. With the installation of liberalism, the emphasis on the parallels between the family and the state decreases. After 1660 the family progressively becomes a privileged, private realm of retreat from a public world increasingly experienced as hostile and alien. Once the family is outside politics, the power relations within the family are excluded from political analysis. The position of women, at the centre of the family, is thus no concern of political theory. In consequence a new and more insidious form of patriarchy, a 'chosen' patriarchy, comes to rule there unchallenged.

Unchallenged, that is, except by women themselves. To have a place in discourse, even a domestic one, to have a subject-position from which to speak, however inadequate, is to be able to protest. In the late seventeenth century we also find an emerging feminism, a mode of resistance which offers an explicit analysis of women's oppression. The depoliticization of the family led to an incoherence in liberalism. As subjects women began to be entitled to a place in a political discourse whose terms included 'freedom', 'rights', 'votes'; as wives they were not. Defined primarily as members of the family, indeed as its centre, women who were 'temporarily' outside its sheltering structure, as widows for instance, could acceptably earn a living, not simply taking part in or carrying on the work of their husbands, but in their own right – as actresses and playwrights, for example. But such women were thereby part of the public, political world, and their existence threw into relief the fact that they were equal citizens with unequal rights.

The history of the installation of women as subjects is not one of steady and deliberate assaults on the territory of patriarchal absolutism. On the contrary, it is a story of startling and radical conceptual and discursive advances followed by hesitations, uncertainties and retreats. First, the advances. Early in the sixteenth century, before the campaign against popery began to entail a suspicion of all aspects of Italian culture, the circulation of humanist discourses in England produced new definitions of good government in the state and in the family. The humanist subject, rational author of his or her own choices, was to be persuaded rather than coerced, and a sound (and persuasive) education was probably enough to guarantee a rational and virtuous adult – of either sex. Medwall's humanist play, *Fulgens and Lucres* (c. 1500) concerns Lucres's choice of a husband. One suitor is a patrician of dubious virtue and the other is a poor and virtuous scholar. Lucres's wise and worthy father, Fulgens, is proud of his daughter's judgement and discretion as well as of her beauty (ll. 258ff.). When the suitors present themselves to him he at once refers them to Lucres. He is prepared to discuss their qualities with her, and to give her advice, but the decision is hers: 'I am not the man / That wyll take from her the liberte / Of her own choice' (ll. 336–8). Lucres accepts this freedom and asks her father for his counsel. But the text makes it clear that her choice is unconstrained, and at the same time prudent and rational. She defines the terms of the debate between her suitors, reprimands them if they threaten to exceed the bounds of propriety, weighs her father's advice judiciously, and finally makes the proper decision – in favour of poverty with virtue. The play thus affirms marriage as the location of liberal and affective values rather than as a guarantee of dynastic continuity.

More important, Lucres is seen as the author of meaning. The play is primarily, of course, a debate on the nature of true nobility and only secondarily a romantic comedy. Nobility, it concludes, is not a matter of birth but of virtue and of service to the state. But it is Lucres who authorizes this definition for a courtly audience which, presumably, at this date contained many who were not already fully persuaded of these humanist values. The figures identified as A and B, whose discussion opens and concludes the play, consider whether it has ended satisfactorily. A would have preferred another conclusion, but B puts him right:

> Ye, thou art a maister mery man! –
> Thou shall be wyse I wot nere whan.
>   Is not the question
> Of noblenes now fully defynde
> As it may be so by a womans mynde?
>   What woldyst thou have more?

(ll. 881–6)

Determined anti-feminists in the audience might take these words ironically, but B goes on to explain the moral of the play in a manner which contains no trace of irony, and we are therefore left with the remarkable possibility that the play offers 'a woman's mind' as the guarantee of meaning in an instance so central to the concerns of humanism as the definition of true nobility.

Fulgens and Lucres, as far as it is possible to judge, was distinctly radical in its own time. The dramatic descendants of Lucres are obviously Shakespeare's comic heroines, and most notably Portia, who speaks with wisdom and authority to resolve the legal and moral dilemmas defined in *The Merchant of Venice*. But the differences are instructive too. Portia, like the other heroines of Shakespeare's romantic comedies, is invested with authority by her auditors within the fiction on condition that she changes her clothes and speaks with the voice of a man. In Shakespearean comedy women literally 'personate masculine virtue', with the effect of bringing about reconciliation and integration, but it is on the grounds of their discursive and subjective discontinuity that they are presented as able to do so.[1] Moreover, Portia is not free to choose among her suitors, but is subject to the will of her father, whose binding wisdom is shown in the casket scenes to reach from beyond the grave. A century later than *Fulgens and Lucres*, *The Merchant of Venice* is nonetheless rather less radical in its treatment of women as subjects. The comparison offers an instance of the irregular and contradictory nature of textual history. *Fulgens and Lucres* presents its startling case with a freshness and clarity unblurred by subsequent decades of discursive uncertainty about women's subjectivity. *The Merchant of Venice*, on the other hand, reproduces some of the theoretical hesitation within which it is situated.

Another possible descendant of Lucres is the heroine of *Godly Queen Hester*, a play of uncertain date and unknown author, not printed until 1561 but conjecturally attributed by W.W. Greg to the second half of the 1520s (*Godly Queen Hester*, p. x.). If Greg is right about the date, we are entitled to find here vestiges of the same humanism which informs the earlier text. The play follows fairly closely the biblical story of Esther, who persuaded her husband to put a stop to the persecution of the Jews by his minister, Haman. The title page presents Hester as a model for women of duty and humility and it is made quite clear that she owes her husband obedience, but it is explicitly her eloquence which induces Assuerus to choose her as his queen.

When 'many maidens' are brought before him so that he may choose a wife, Assuerus admires their beauty but pays particular attention to those whose appearance suggests qualities of wisdom and constancy. Mardocheus proffers Hester as pure, meek, demure, but also 'In learninge and litterature, profoundely seene, / In wisdome, eke semblant to Saba the Quene' – and thus fit to be the wife of a prince (ll. 258–9). The king at once determines to put to the test 'her lernynge and her language' (l. 264), and asks her to tell him what virtues are appropriate to a queen. Hester replies that the king of course has control, but he might sometimes choose to listen to his queen, 'more for love than for awe' (l. 277). If the king goes to war the queen must rule in his place: she must therefore share his virtues (ll. 282–93). There is nothing in Hester's definition of the qualities of a wife which conflicts with the most absolutist pronouncements of the domestic conduct books of a later period; what is remarkable is that it is her fluency and her wisdom which identify her as the right person to be queen. What is even more remarkable is that the pronouns in the king's reply are plural:

> Then I doute not, but the wysdome of us two
> Knytte both to gether in parfytte charyte
> All thynges in thys realme shall cumpas so,
> By truth and justice, law and equitye,
> That we shall quenche all vice and deformitie.
>
> (ll. 296–300)

Hester promptly urges Assuerus to ensure that the poor of the realm are better fed: they are too weak with hunger to be able to serve him adequately (ll. 304–26). When the persecution of her people begins, Hester's excellent case on their behalf ensures the king's protection and Haman is hanged.

Here again it is evidently possible in the sixteenth century to conceive of a woman as a unified, rational being, the virtuous author of her own eloquence. In the later drama perhaps only Paulina in *The Winter's Tale* is shown as a woman who equally consistently and effectively propels a king towards the good.

Nearly a hundred years after the conjectural date of *Godly Queen Hester,* *The Duchess of Malfi* (1613–14) stands as a perfect fable of emergent liberalism. The text valorizes women's equality to the point where the Duchess woos Antonio, repudiating the hierarchy of birth in favour of individual virtue; it also celebrates the family, identifying it as a private realm of warmth and fruitfulness separate from the turbulent world of politics, though vulnerable to it. Act III scene ii shows the Duchess alone with Antonio and Cariola (who as a loyal servant is a member of the seventeenth-century family). Their exchanges are intimate, affectionate and playful. Indeed, it is this spirit of play which causes Cariola and Antonio to steal out of the room while the Duchess brushes her hair, and which is brutally dissipated by the entry of Ferdinand, the personification of patriarchal absolutism.

In a ballad of 1630, "Tis Not Otherwise: Or the Praise of a Married Life', a young man rejoices in the moral improvements and physical comforts marriage has brought him. The birth of a child intensifies his happiness:

> The babe doth grow, and quickly speaks,
>   this doth increase my joy,
> To heare it tattle, laugh and squeake,
>   I smile and hug the boy:
> I watch it play with great delight,
>   and hush it when it cryes,
> And never wish it in my sight,
>   then *'tis not otherwise.*
>
> (H. Rollins p. 360 (ed.), *Old English Ballads 1553–1625*
> (Cambridge: CUP 1920), p. 360)

The ballad evokes the opening scene of domestic intimacy in *The Winter's Tale*, Lady Macduff's playful exchanges with her son (*Macbeth,* IV, ii), or Antonio's reluctant repudiation of the pleasures of the nuclear family:

> Say a man never marry, nor have children,
> What takes that from him? only the bare name
> Of being a father, or the weak delight
> To see the little wanton ride a-cock-horse
> Upon a painted stick, or hear him chatter
> Like a taught starling.
>
> (*The Duchess of Malfi*, I, i, 398–493)

These pleasures, the play makes clear, are to be Antonio's destiny after all. On the other hand, the first act of tyranny of Ferdinand and the Cardinal is to divide the family by divorcing the Duchess and Antonio and separating their children. The Duchess's final words to Cariola identify her as a nurturing, loving mother:

> I pray thee, look thou giv'st my little boy
> Some syrup for his cold, and let the girl
> Say her prayers, ere she sleep.

(IV, ii, 203–5)

Motherhood, caring, the child-orientated, affective family unit: there is a direct line of descent from the new seventeenth-century definitions of familial relationships to the current representation of happy families in advertisements for margarine and breakfast cereals. What threatens the affective nuclear family is frequently an external tryranny, here the patriarchal absolutism of Ferdinand and the Cardinal, representatives of the family in its other meaning, whose behaviour – the divorce, the banishment, the imprisonment of the Duchess – identifies them with the newly differentiated public world of state power, law and politics. In this too the play anticipates the system of differences which gives meaning to the discourse of liberalism. The terms of the liberal analysis are a series of oppositions between the individual and society, private and public, family and state, in which the first is always understood to be threatened by the encroachment of the second. Moreover, it is the second which is 'political'. Politics is thus devalued by contrast with the true fulfilment available within the enclave of the family. Domestic relationships are defined as affective rather than political in a discourse which works to suppress recognition of the power relations which structure the family, and by this means liberalism opens a gap for the accommodation of an uncontested, because unidentified, patriarchy. In consequence the affective ideal which is so glowingly defined in *The Duchess of Malfi* collapses into the sad history of collaboration between liberalism and sexism which defines the western family from the seventeenth century to the present.

2 Advice and consent

The Duchess of Malfi marks one discursive limit of the sexual politics of the early seventeenth century. Other plays of the period which confront similar issues identify more sharply the problems which tended to impede the installation of women as subjects. Among these is the question of the freedom of choice of a marriage partner. Liberalism depends on consent and this in turn depends on the autonomy of the subject. My choices spring out of what I *am*, and only a speaker entitled to mean these words is truly free to make a deliberate decision. For most of the sixteenth and seventeenth centuries women have only a sporadic, precarious hold on such autonomy. *The Duchess of Malfi*, like *Fulgens and Lucres*, claims for its heroine the right to choose a husband. More commonly, however, such a right is seen as sharply conditional.

Freedom of choice and the miseries of enforced marriage are a constant and recurring concern in the period. There is some evidence of a debate about the extent of parental control in marriage, but it is a debate in which the two sides are not in practice very sharply polarized. On one side John Stockwood argues for parental choice in *A Bartholmew Fairing for Parentes* (1589), 'shewing that children are not to marie, without the consent of their parentes, in whose power and choise it lieth to provide wives and husbandes for their sonnes and daughters' (title page). But Stockwood insists that parents should not exercise compulsion (p. 81), and he appeals to them to take on the responsibility of finding a suitable partner in a way consistent with the will of God (p. 85). On the other side Daniel Rogers in *Matrimoniall Honour* (1642) proposes a number of ways in which children might go about persuading their parents to give their consent, including seeking the aid of the Church and the magistrate, but he does not advocate open defiance (unless it is only the mother who objects, in which case the child may proceed with a clear conscience) (pp. 80–1). But most of the popular discussions of the matter conclude that on the one hand children should not marry without parental consent, and on the other parents should not withhold consent without powerful and compelling reasons (Henry Bullinger, *The Christian State of Matrimonye* (trans. Miles Coverdale, London 1541), sig. B ii v–D i v; William Perkins, *Christian Oeconomie* (trans. Thomas Pickering, Cambridge 1618), pp. 684–5; Richard Brathwait, Vol. 3 in *Works, The English Gentleman: and The English Gentlewoman; Both in the One Volume Couched* (London 1641) p. 21).

The domestic conduct books thus define an ideal and on the whole evade the problem of what happens when one of the parties refuses to conform to it. The plays, by contrast, since fiction depends on obstacles to the implementation of good sense, dwell in detail on the dangers and difficulties which ensue when parental choice fails to coincide with the wishes of the children. Renaissance comedy inherits this motif from Plautus and Terence, and here the sympathy of the audience is invariably invoked in favour of the children. In tragic treatments of the theme, too (*Romeo and Juliet, The Maid's Tragedy, The Witch of Edmonton, The Second Maiden's Tragedy*, for instance), the audience is usually invited to endorse young love as opposed to aged greed, obstinacy or hypocrisy.

But it is not always clear that the degree of freedom which is very nearly universally approved is allotted equally to men and women. Brathwait takes a very liberal line on freedom of choice in *The English Gentleman*, urging his readers in fairly strong terms to make the decision for themselves (p. 145), but there is no equivalent passage in *The English Gentlewoman*, the companion volume addressed to women. The gender of the person making the choice oscillates wildly in the case of Dod and Cleaver. But at the beginning of the passage in question this text reveals its own patriarchal assumptions very clearly when it suddenly makes it apparent that 'everyone' is in fact male: 'everie one that intendeth to marrie, shoulde choose him a meet, fit, and honest mate: for there lyeth much weight in the wise election, and choise of a wife' (Dod and Cleaver, *A Godlie Forme of Householde Government* (London 1612), p. 99). In the drama too there is perhaps an assumption that freedom does not quite extend to women. It is not, for instance, self-evident that the audience is invited to sympathize with Beatrice-Joanna when she asserts her will against her father's in *The Changeling*, and she herself claims that freedom of choice is confined to men (II, ii, 107–13).

The classic dramatic treatment of the liberal case against parental compulsion is *The Miseries of Enforced Marriage* (1607). This play by George Wilkins was based, like *A Yorkshire Tragedy* (1608), on the Calverley murders, though in the Wilkins version murder is only threatened, and an unexpected happy ending produces general reconciliation and rejoicing. *The Miseries of Enforced Marriage* concerns William Scarborrow who at seventeen establishes a pre-contract of marriage with Clare Harcop. Subsequently his uncle and his guardian threaten to lay waste his property if he refuses to marry Katherine, his guardian's niece. Faced with ruin, William reluctantly agrees, protesting that the marriage makes him an adulterer and his children bastards. Clare kills herself when he writes to tell her he is married. William abandons Katherine and his children in his Yorkshire house, and pursues the career of a prodigal in London, in the company of Sir Francis Ilford. Ironically, William thus lays waste his own property, reducing his brothers and sister as well as his wife and children to poverty. The honest family butler invents a series of schemes to save them all, including a marriage between Willaim's sister and the spendthrift Sir Francis Ilford. Finally William is prevailed upon to repent and is restored to his grateful wife and children. His guardian dies, recognizing the error of enforced marriage, and making William heir to twice his former wealth.

As even a bare summary of the plot suggests, there are oddly incompatible elements in the play. It is made very clear that the uncle and the guardian are villains, even though the law scandalously permits them to behave as they do. It is also clear that they mean well: ironically the object of the marriage they plan for William is to ensure that he settles down and does not squander his inheritance. The play, as the title indicates, demonstrates the evils of well-intentioned authoritarianism and constitutes a plea for freedom of choice. The happy ending, however, is predicated on the acquiescence of two women in the miseries of marriages chosen for them by others. Katherine exceeds even Griselda in the patience with which she submits to the marriage and subsequently to William's desertion and the impoverishment of the family. The marriage is arranged by her uncle and carried out at her first meeting with William. Similarly William's sister co-operates with the scheme to marry her to Ilford to save the Scarborrow fortunes. Deceived into believing that his wife is an heiress, Ilford curses and kicks her when she reveals the truth. She does not protest when he snatches the jewels she is wearing and then deserts her. The couple are reunited without explanation in the final scene, and she declares, 'heeres my husbands hand in mine, / And I rejoyce in him, and he in me' (*The Miseries of Enforced Marriage*, ll. 2825–6).

Narrative closure is thus conditional on the submission of two women and the death of a third. William's 'repentance' might have presented more of a problem had Clare lived. Her convenient suicide makes way for the happy ending. While William's enforced marriage to a patient and obedient wife is defined as 'misery' because it is not freely chosen, not based on love, the sufferings of his wife and his sister, whose marriages are not freely chosen either, are simply dissipated in the promise of future happiness which attends William's repentance and return to the arms of this family. Love, which in men is a passion that cannot be constrained, is evidently in women the fruit of dutiful obedience to arrangements made on their behalf by others. At the centre of a play on the evils of enforced marriage, the exchange of women remains apparently unquestioned.

The sub-plot of *A Woman Killed with Kindness* raises, and fails to resolve, the problem of women as objects of exchange between men. Sir Charles Mountford, in prison for debt, is released by his mortal enemy, Sir Francis Acton, who pays the £500 he owes. Learning that the reason for this generous act is Sir Francis's desire for his sister, Sir Charles, still penniless, determines to pay off the debt of honour he has incurred in 'one rich gift' (X, 124). Susan, dressed like a bride, is to be presented to Sir Francis in place of the money. The sum is constantly reiterated in the discussion between Susan and her brother (xiv, 25, 38, 45, 70).

The play does not simply endorse this procedure. Susan pleads with Sir Charles to save her honour. He calls himself a 'barbarous outlaw', an 'uncivil kern' (xiv, 5), a ruffian (11. 8, 36), more like a stranger than a brother (II. 50–1). His 'cold heart shakes with shame' (I. 49). None the less, he is adamant: 'O sister! only this one way, / With that rich jewel you my debts may pay' (ll. 47–8). 'Shall I', he rhetorically asks,

> die in debt
> To Acton, my grand foe, and you still wear
> The precious jewel that he holds so dear?

(ll. 51–3)

To save her brother's honour Susan agrees to be handed over to Sir Francis, taking with her the knife which she will use to redeem her own.

In the course of the discussion between them Sir Charles makes what he himself identifies as a 'strange assertion': 'Thy honour and my soul are equal in my regard' (ll. 60–1). He too will kill himself after the event (I. 62). Brother and sister are thus presented in symmetrical terms, both losing their honour to Sir Francis, both subsequently to redeem it. Both will die by their own hands. The difference, of course, is that Sir Charles prevails on his sister to be the price of the redemption of his debt to another man. The problem is apparently dissolved when Sir Francis offers to make Susan his wife, but since this too has the effect of cancelling the debt, a parallel is drawn between marriage and prostitution on which the play makes no explicit comment. Susan merely 'yields to fate' (xiv, 148).

In *'Tis Pity She's a Whore*, printed in 1633, freedom of choice is problematized in a rather different way, with the effect of foregrounding the limits of liberalism itself as well as the vestiges of absolutism which remain within it. Florio explicitly rejects the mercenary motive that leads to enforced marriages. His daughter, Annabella, is to be free to choose for herself:

> As for worldly fortune,
> I am, I thank my stars, blessed with enough;
> My care is how to match her to her liking;
> I would not have her marry wealth, but love.
>
> (*'Tis Pity She's a Whore*, I, iii, 8–11)

Annabella chooses freely – and chooses her brother. The liberal concept of freedom of choice depends in practice on the silent exclusion of a whole range of freedoms.

When his daughter becomes pregnant Florio at once selects her a husband, and the weeping Annabella is formally betrothed to Soranzo in a ritual which shows clearly where the power to choose now resides:

> Florio My Lord Soranzo, here
> Give me your hand; for that I *give you this*.
>
> (My italics, III, vii, 50–1)

Confronted by its own limits, liberalism readily falls back into the familiar pattern of enforced marriage.

Evidently love, in Florio's definition free and unconstrained, is in practice free only as long as it is confined to the objects defined as appropriate by the social body. As Ford's play makes clear, these objects do not include a brother or sister. We can easily increase the list of exclusions: parents, children, members of the same sex …. The identification of 'perversion' is one of the means by which the liberal valorization of freedom is prevented from offering any serious impediment to control by the social body of one of its central institutions.

3 Love and marriage

Women find a place in marriage, and the cement of liberal marriage is romantic love. True love is human happiness in its highest, most intense and most ideal form. Authorized by nature (birds do it), love is a harmony of souls and bodies which comes to constitute the proper foundation of family life. Love in this period is differentiated increasingly decisively from lust as having its origins in the mind, the very essense of the humanist subject. The imbrication of two minds, united and yet distinct, legitimates desire and sanctifies the conception of children. As an intimate, private relationship, love is the repudiation of the political, its antithesis.

In *The Duchess of Malfi* marriage is represented as a transcendent union based on romantic love:

Duchess	Bless, heaven, this sacred Gordian, which let
	violence
	Never untwine.
Antonio	And may our sweet affections, like the spheres,
	Be still in motion.
Duchess	Quickening, and make
	The like soft music.
Antonio	That we may imitate the loving palms,
	Blest emblem of a peaceful marriage,
	That ne'er bore fruit divided.
Duchess	What can the church force more?

(I, i, 480–8)

Love emulates both the divine (the music of the spheres) and nature (palm trees). It is the source of procreation (fruit). It springs from the subjectivities of the characters, and the institution of the church can only ratify a condition that themselves have legitimately made indivisible. Love excludes the political: 'All discord, without this circumference, / Is only to be pitied' (I, i, 469–70).

It is in this period that love and marriage become indissolubly linked and love itself becomes fully moralized and spiritualized, not now as a neoplatonic rung on the ladder to the love of God, as it is in the cases of Dante's Beatrice or Petrarch's Laura, but as the wholly human ground of a lifetime of domestic concord. Since then fiction, lyric poetry, the cinema and pop music have so idealized romantic love, so celebrated its joy and

naturalness, that it is an effort to remember that love once had other
attributes. We need a genealogy of romantic love. In the meantime it is
perhaps worth drawing attention, however briefly, to its moral ambiguity
in Chaucer's *Troilus and Criseyde*, for instance, where the palinode
condemns as worthless the passion celebrated in Book III. A similar
ambiguity recurs in Sidney's *Astrophil and Stella* (1582?) where the hero
repeatedly reproaches himself for desiring Stella instead of heaven on the
one hand or worldly honour on the other. *Antony and Cleopatra*, which
defines love in cosmic imagery, also identifies it as 'dotage'. In these
instances love conflicts with duty. But with the development of the
affective nuclear family, love and duty become synonymous. In Chaucer's
Knight's Tale love is arbitrary, destructive, and also the height of folly. The
absurdity of love as well as its delight is the source of much that is comic in
Shakespearean comedy. But in the seventeenth century the capricious,
arbitrary desires of an earlier period are progressively harnessed to a
civilized and civilizing morality and, without losing any of their mystery,
are arrested, fixed, domesticated. It is not until the nineteenth century that
the love of a good woman develops its full redemptive power, but it is
possible to identify the rudiments of this position in his guardian's plans
for William Scarborrow.

True love is, of course, eternal. 'Love is not love / That alters when it
alteration finds.' It is for this reason that true love properly issues in
marriage, and this in turn ensures the stability of the family as a seminary
of good subjects. But the course of its installation as the basis of the family
does not run entirely smooth. One of the paradoxes of eternal love is that
its tragic possibilities are also intensified. In *The Second Maiden's Tragedy*
(1611) the Lady kills herself in order to perpetuate love even beyond the
grave:

> His lust may part me from thee, but death, never;
> Thou canst not lose me there, for, dying thine,
> Thou dost enjoy me still. Kings cannot rob thee.

(III, iii, 144–6)

The conceit here depends, of course, on the retention of the absolutist
concept of women as objects, property to be possessed. A similar eternity
of possession is implicit in the emblematic spectacle of Giovanni, in the
final scene of *'Tis Pity She's a Whore*, keeping the spectators at bay as he
holds Annabella's heart before him on a dagger.

Located in the first instance in the mind, true love also shows an
unstable tendency to efface the sexuality it was its project to authorize.
The identification of love with marriage, and of marriage with what is
private, implies a sexuality which is whispered rather than proclaimed.
Ultimately, moreover, the spiritualization of love leads to a sexual

reticence within marriage itself. Love is differentiated from lust, but the two are yoked by violence together in the marriage bed. The precariousness of their unity issues in the scale of prostitution in the nineteenth century, 'corrected' by the idealization of the sexual in the twentieth. The sexual fix, the fixing of the sexual as a guarantee of moral and physical health, and the fixing of the sexes, a man and a woman (Heath, *The Sexual Fix* (London: Macmillan 1982)), offers in our own time to save the family from the disintegration threatening it from the right (individualism) and from the left (feminism).

In *The Broken Heart*, printed in 1633, the spiritualization of love implies that if true minds are separated there is no solace in the union of bodies. Penthea, contracted to Orgilus, is married against her will to Bassanes. To endure a loveless marriage is to be 'buried in a bride-bed' (II, ii, 38). Orgilus withdraws to contemplate a transcendent, unalterable and curiously sexless passion. When he meets Penthea by accident, his declaration of love is entirely changeless, entirely pure:

> Time can never
> On the white table of unguilty faith
> Write counterfeit dishonour. Turn those eyes,
> The arrows of pure love, upon that fire
> Which once rose to a flame, perfumed with vows
> As sweetly scented as the incense smoking
> On Vesta's altars; virgin tears, like
> The holiest odours, sprinkled dews to feed 'em
> And to increase their fervour.
>
> (II, iii, 25–33)

A reference to the body in his next speech proves to be purely metaphorical (l. 36) and 'intercourse' (l. 39) had no sexual connotations before 1798 (OED). At the end of this episode there is some indication that Orgilus makes an unspecified physical overture, which is at once repulsed (ll. 106–9), but the lovers do not seriously contemplate the possibility of adultery.

The separation of true minds is existential death. Eternally divided from the man she eternally loves, Penthea refuses food until life is extinguished. In revenge for her death Orgilus kills Ithocles, author of the enforced marriage, in the presence of Penthea's corpse, and then chooses for himself a mode of death which parallels hers, opening his veins so that the blood flows out of them. These bodies, visible on the stage, drained of being, constitute emblems of the immobilizing power of a romantic love which is at once unalterable and unable to be fulfilled because it implies a union beyond the mingling of bodies.

In the same play, Calantha, who is betrothed to Ithocles, simply ceases to live when she learns of his death. She arranges the disposition of the

kingdom and places her mother's wedding ring on the finger of the dead
man: 'Thus I new-marry him whose wife I am. / Death shall not separate
us' (V, iii, 66–7). Her death has no visible external cause: she dies of a
broken heart. Love, life and marriage have become in effect synonymous,
all three centred in the heart which breaks when the marriage-union is
broken.

Meanwhile, by an odd loop of reasoning, spiritualized marriage becomes
intelligible as an essential state of being which transcends the letter of the
law. Romantic love, free and unconstrained, does not necessarily confine
itself to couples who are legally at liberty to marry. When a legal marriage
is loveless, and thus no marriage at all (cf. Milton, *The Complete Works* (vol.
2, ed. E. Surluck, London : OUP 1959), p. 456 Halkett, (*Milton and the Idea
Of Matrimony* (New Haven : Yale University Press 1970) : p. 8), the
same force which stabilizes the institution of marriage can paradoxically be
invoked to authorize and stabilize an adulterous union of minds and
bodies. By the second half of the seventeenth century marriage has become
a plural term, defining an affective relationship as readily as a legal one.
Dryden's *All for Love* (1677) is an extraordinary instance of this redefinition
of marriage.

The play is a rewriting for the Restoration stage of Shakespeare's *Antony
and Cleopatra*, and the distance between the two texts is a measure of the
transformation of love in the course of the seventeenth century. The
relationship between Dryden's Antony and Cleopatra is oddly domestic.
All the imagery which in the earlier text defines Cleopatra as demonic is
silently erased; the emphasis on the physical nature of her sexuality is
eliminated; and the discursive instability produced as she simultaneously
embraces and refuses the feminine disappears. The lies, evasions and
caprices which cause the catastrophe in 1607 are all attributed seventy
years later to Alexas the eunuch. Dryden's Cleopatra is transparently
honest, unable to sustain a deceit. As a place begins to be found for
women, the uncertainty and instability defining women's sexuality is
transferred to the forms of sexuality which transgress the newly established
system of differences, modes of sexual deviance which seem not to have
elicited much interest in the earlier period. Alexas as a eunuch is neither a
man nor a woman, and is therefore unstable.

In the later version Cleopatra's love for Antony is eternal: she never
loved Caesar. The tragedy is that death threatens not a precarious, arbitrary
and dangerous sexual passion, but a long and happy union open to
destruction only by forces outside itself:

Think we have had a clear and glorious day,
And heav'n did kindly to delay the storm
Just till our close of ev'ning. Ten years' love,
And not a moment lost, but all improved

To th'utmost joys – what ages we have lived!
And now to die each other's.

(*All for Love*, V, 389–94)

In Shakespeare's play Antony's political obligations are compelling. He is 'a third of the world' and the audience glimpses some of the implications of the collapse of empire which is the consequence of his 'dotage'. Antony's dismissal of politics – 'Kingdoms are clay' (*Antony and Cleopatra*,I, i, 35) – is repudiated at his next appearance (I, ii, 112–14), and this oscillation between love and politics structures the play. Dryden's Antony also oscillates, but between personal loyalties – to his friend, Ventidius, his wife, Octavia, and to Cleopatra. The private is valorized at the expense of the public, and political obligation is relegated, apparently without irony, to the inferior status it still holds in the discourse of liberalism. Ventidius urges Antony to go from Cleopatra.

Go? Whither? Go from all that's excellent?
Faith, honor, virtue, all good things forbid
That I should go from her who sets my love
Above the price of kingdoms. Give, you gods,
Give to your boy, your Caesar,
This rattle of a globe to play withal,
This gewgaw world, and put him cheaply off;
I'll not be pleased with less than Cleopatra.

(*All for Love*, II, 439–46)

The play is subtitled, 'The World Well Lost'.

Moralized, tamed, unchanging, love is inseparable from the marriage of true minds. The project of the play, according to Dryden's Preface, was to present 'famous patterns of unlawful love', adultery 'founded on vice' (*All for Love*, pp. 12, 13). But true love cannot be contrary to the spirit of the law, though it may contradict the letter. Sexual passion founded on vice is now by definition something quite different. Dryden's Cleopatra who represents 'faith, honor, virtue', is in effect if not in name married to Antony, and the text increasingly defines her position in these terms. 'Nature', she declares, 'meant me / A wife, a silly, harmless, household dove': it is fortune which has made her a mistress (IV, 91–4). Death will remove fortune's impediment:

I have not loved a Roman not to know
What should become his wife – his wife, my Charmion!
For 'tis to that high title I aspire,
And now I'll not die less. Let dull Octavia
Survive, to mourn him dead; my nobler fate

Shall knit our spousals with a tie too strong
For Roman laws to break.

(V, 412–18)

The conflicting claims of Octavia and Cleopatra are the claims of two
wives. Octavia loves Antony too – but not enough. Her patience is not
infinite and she is finally unable to forgive Antony for preferring
Cleopatra (IV, 414–28). Her retreat is the triumph of true, transcendent
conjugal love.

Love is a necessary ingredient of Restoration heroic drama, and here it is
above all the civilizing power of love which is taken for granted. Virtuous
heroes need the complementary love of a virtuous woman to tame their
fiery courage, harness their restless energies and integrate them into civil
society. Masculinity is strong and resolute: feminine tranquillity and moral
sensibility soften the ruthlessness of the masculine world. A new set of
stereotypes defines women as the opposite but indispensable sex.
Gradually a space has been specified for women at the centre of the private
realm of love and harmony which is marriage. The disruptive elements of
female sexuality have been banished, along with the discursive instability
which defined it, to find a place among whores, hysterics or sexual
deviants: true love is more, domestic, constant. Good women are partners
in the formation of the affective family, where the absolutist ideal of patient
submission has been transformed into active, forgiving, reconciling love. It
is the constancy of good women which is the source of stability within the
family. Men – like Antony – are necessarily caught up in public affairs;
their wives guarantee them a still haven from a restless world. Women
have become identified as the agents of conjugal love.

Thus, for instance, in Catherine Trotter's play, *The Fatal Friendship* (1698),
the hero, after his second and bigamous marriage, turns back to his first
wife for solace – and receives it. Gramont, married to Felicia in secret
because of their poverty, finds that he is unable to ransom his friend, rescue
his son from pirates or protect his wife from destitution. To save his family
and his friend he bigamously marries the wealthy Lamira, but cannot bring
himself to consummate his marriage. Appalled by what he has done and
failed to do, he returns in desperation to Felicia:

Her nature's calm, by no rough passions tossed,
A harbour from this tempest, upon her gentle bosom
All the disorders of my soul will cease,
Or I despair ever to find my peace.

(III, i)

Shown as more patient than Octavia, but more active than Griselda, Felicia
induces Gramont not to kill himself but to live for her sake. He dies in

another cause, but his death turns out to be the means of saving his family, since his wealthy father repents his former harshness and takes in the deserving Felicia, promising to ransom the child from the pirates. The family thus triumphs, preserved not by the wife's submission, as in the Griselda story, but by her active constancy.

Marriage is a partnership, but partnership does not ensure equality. On the contrary, when two oxen are yoked together, the bigger and stronger of them naturally bears a greater part of the burden (Speght, *A Mouzell for Melastomus* (London 1617), p. 12). Thus, while the new meaning of marriage offers women a position as subjects, it does not fundamentally challenge patriarchy. Indeed it reinforces it to the extent that true love becomes the solvent of inequality, the source of women's pliability and the guarantee of marital concord. This is made explicit, though without any obvious element of irony, in *Women Beware Women* (1621?). Wives, Isabella proposes, are slaves whose subjection is made 'happy' by love:

> They do but buy their thraldoms, and bring great portions
> To men to keep 'em in subjection –
> As if a fearful prisoner should bribe
> The keeper to be good to him, yet lies in still,
> And glad of a good usage, a good look sometimes.
> By 'r Lady, no misery surmounts a woman's:
> Men buy their slaves, but women buy their masters.
> Yet honesty and love makes all this happy,
> And, next to angels', the most blest estate.
>
> (I, ii, 170–8)

Love makes slavery blessed. Patriarchal power relations have not changed very much in a marriage where the wife is 'to bee governed with love, not overruled by tyranny', as Robert Wilkinson put it in 1615 (Halkett, op. cit., p. 84). In a period just before the collaboration of liberalism and patriarchy had naturalized the affective nuclear family, Dod and Cleaver spelt out more clearly, in a passage where 'we', the writers and readers, are evidently men, the advantages for 'us' of this arrangement:

> And if wee have regarde unto commoditie and profite, there is nothing that giveth so much as doth a good wife, no not horses, oxen, servants or farmes: for a mans wife is the fellow and comforter of all cares and thoughts, and doe more faithful and true service unto him, then either maid-servant or man-servant, which doe serve men for feare, or else for wages: but thy wife will be led onely by love, and therefore she doth every thing better then all other.
>
> (1612: pp. 152–3)

The argument was evidently a common one. Bathsua Makin was to take it up rather sharply in her essay defending women's education: 'Had God intended women onely as a finer sort of cattle, he would not have made them reasonable' (Bathsua Makin, *An Essay to Revive the Antient Education of Gentlewoman* [London 1673], p. 23).

According to Dod and Cleaver, a woman's place is further up in the hierarchy of values than horses, oxen or servants, and she works harder than any of them – for love. A century later a similar point was made, though from an alternative perspective, by a woman. Mary Astell's *Some Reflections upon Marriage* first appeared anonymously in 1700 (though in many respects it might have been written at any time since then). By the third edition in 1706 it included a preface (an appendix in later editions) which acknowledged that the author was a woman. The voice in the body of the text, however, is ostensibly masculine. None the less, in the following extract the third-person pronouns invite the reader to take up a position in relation to the argument which differs radically from that offered by Dod and Cleaver. The passage identifies what a husband wants from marriage:

> He wants one to manage his family, an house-keeper, one
> whose interest it will be not to wrong him, and in whom therefore he can
> put greater confidence than in any he can hire for money. One who may
> breed his children, taking all the care and trouble of their education, to
> preserve his name and family. One whose beauty, wit, or good humour
> and agreeable conversation, will entertain him at home when he has
> been contradicted and disappointed abroad; who will do him that justice
> the ill-natur'd world denies him; that is, in any one's language but his
> own, soothe his pride and flatter his vanity, by having always so much
> good sense as to be on his side, to conclude him in the right, when others
> are so ignorant, or so rude, as to deny it. Who will not be blind to his
> merit nor contradict his will and pleasure, but make it her business, her
> very ambition to content him; whose softness and gentle compliance will
> calm his passions; to whom he may safely disclose his troublesome
> thoughts; and in her breast discharge his cares; whose duty, submission
> and observance, will heal those wounds other people's opposition or
> neglect have given him. In a word, one whom he can entirely govern,
> and consequently may form her to his will and liking, who must be his
> for life, and therefore cannot quit his service, let him treat her how he
> will.
>
> (Astell, 1730: pp. 24–5)

Half way through the passage 'his' (the husband's) 'language' is differentiated from anyone else's, so that the reader is invited to reinterpret ironically all that has gone before. In consequence, when the final sentence offers a summary 'in a word', in a language shared by reader and writer, it is clear that the perspective that has been offered is feminine – and feminist.

Notes

1. For a discussion of the disruption of sexual difference in the Comedies see, CATHERINE BELSEY, 'Disrupting sexual difference : meaning and gender in the comedies', John Drakakis ed. *Alternative Shakespeares*, (London, 1985) pp. 166–90

MARILYN FRENCH   *THE LATE TRAGEDIES**

Marilyn French is an internationally acclaimed feminist novelist who was formerly a Professor of English at the University of Harvard. Her book *Shakespeare's Division of Experience* was published by Jonathan Cape in 1982, and was regarded then as a significant contribution to feminist studies of Shakespeare which had already begun both in Britain and America. As in the case of Catherine Belsey, feminist criticism generally concerns itself with the ways in which social and cultural structures shape masculine and feminine identities. Marilyn French, in her book acknowledges a *difference* between masculine and feminine identity, according it a structural significance, but she resists firmly the view that that difference is in any way fully dialectical. The result is that the theoretical position from which she works insists upon an *essential* difference between male and female, and hence resists the full consequences of post-structuralist analyses of the gendered human subject. French identifies 'the masculine principle' as 'the pole of power ... the pole of the individual who dedicates his life to a suprapersonal goal', while the 'feminine principle' is 'the pole of sex and pleasure ... the pole of people destined for oblivion who dedicate their lives to personal satisfaction' (*Shakespeare's Division of Experience*, p. 24). She also identifies a third position, what she calls 'the inlaw feminine principle' defined as 'the benevolent aspects of nature "purified" of their malevolent side'. (ibid). There is still much of value in this analysis, although the more rigorous drawing together of feminism and materialism has radically recontextualised these categories.

*Reprinted from *Shakespeare's Division of Experience* (London: Abacus, 1982), pp. 219–51

The following extract from the chapter entitled 'The Late Tragedies' identifies aesthetic form with one or other of these gender principles, and postulates dramatic conflict as a result of a collision between different principles.

Although it may sometimes appear in a 'masculine' form, that is, linear, highly plotted, Shakespearean comedy is a feminine mode. It is concerned with an entire society rather than an isolated individual; it moves towards harmonious integration of all elements of that society, and the promise of continuation through marriage and implicit new birth. The marriages with which most Shakespearean comedies end are syntheses of the gender principles, but are dedicated to the ends of the feminine principles – felicity and procreation.

In the problem plays, which are written in a mixed mode, the gender principles are at war. In *Hamlet*, the Prince, representing the inlaw feminine principle, declares internal war against the outlaw feminine (and all women), and against the pretensions of the masculine principle. The other three problem plays show the masculine principle devaluing, repudiating, or attempting to repress one or another part of the feminine principle. The survival of inlaw values is tenuous in all of these plays, and in fact does not occur in two of them – *Hamlet*, and *Troilus and Cressida*.

The tragedies after *Hamlet* are generally in a masculine mode. (*Antony and Cleopatra* is in a class by itself.) They are linear in structure, focus on a major character, always a male, who lives out an individual life and dies, like all individual humans. However, although a single male protagonist dominates the foreground in a way no single character does in comedy, he shares the focus with the background, his culture. In all the tragedies, the culture (or some aspect of it) is nearly equal in importance with the hero.[1]

This is not true of comedy, which may seem strange since comedy is more concerned with society than tragedy is, and more concerned with society than with the individual. But precisely because of that concern, comedy presents a generalized, universal picture of society. It offers a set of diverse elements that make up *any* society, that are discordant in some way, and creates a perspective broad enough to contain, to tolerate all of them. The societies depicted in the various comedies are not *essentially* different from each other. The cultures of Othello, Lear, Macbeth, and Antony are: they are particularized. We have a sense of Macbeth's Scotland and Lear's England in a way we do not of Messina or Illyria. The background of the comedies, be it Navarre or Arden, is simply a space large and free enough to allow the characters to be themselves. The background of the tragedies is a place; it comes complete with its own demands, its own character, a set of values that impose themselves on those who live in it. And the protagonist of tragedy invariably expresses those values; he grows out of them, is part of them, whether or not he finds himself at some point in opposition to them.

228

Although each culture that figures in the tragedies is different, they all have certain common features. The worlds of Othello, Lear and Macbeth, as well as the other tragic heroes, are utterly 'masculine'; they are dominated by men who place supreme value on the qualities of the masculine principle and to varying degrees, slight, deny, or are ignorant of the value and importance of its complement. The kind of blindness to or rejection of 'feminine' values varies from tragedy to tragedy, but reaches its extremest form in the last two plays, *Coriolanus*, and *Timon of Athens*.

Because the tragedies concentrate on 'masculine' values, which are dominant in the world at large in our own time as well as in Shakespeare's, and because the male heroes of the plays (who incarnate the values of their culture) are also to some degree antipathetic to that culture, what occurs in the dramas is a war, a conflict between an individual and a cultural encapsulation of the same value. It is internecine war, and amounts to a trial of a value in much the same way that *Measure for Measure* is a trial of sex. Thus, the tragedies are among the most radical criticisms ever written of the values of Western society.

Because the tragedies concentrate on 'masculine' values, they have been considered, by generations of critics, more serious and more realistic than the comedies. They are neither. They deal with much the same material, the same concerns, and use many of the same techniques and devices. There is use of folktale, supernatural elements, and disguise in both genres. The difference is that in tragedy, not only acts, but even words are irrevocable. If in comedy, a serious act or speech is saved by the disguise convention, the bed trick, or a fairy potion, in tragedy, acts or words that need not necessarily lead to irrevocable consequences always do. The tragedies seem more realistic because they deal with the masculine principle, that is, they deal with structures, power, possession, and action, all of which are palpable, substantial, whereas the comedies deal with feelings, attitudes, reflections – the fluid and generative and nonsubstantial dimensions of human life. Indeed, so difficult is it (especially in our period – a time when emotion and pleasure are viewed with great disdain and contempt) to discuss the inlaw feminine principle that critics are forced to resort to terms like 'irrational', 'mythic', or 'divine' to describe it, making it sound mysterious and unearthly in a way it is not.[2] There is nothing whatever irrational about the inlaw feminine principle (except cutting it off from its roots in the outlaw aspect); it only *seems* irrational to people whose notion of rationality is a narrow and sterile view of life as logical, linear, and self-interested. It is fortunate that most of us live more broadly than we think.

In both comedy and tragedy, the characters may be easy or uneasy, satisfied or unsatisfied, happy or unhappy in their society. Comedy concentrates on ways in which they can be assimilated. They may discover their true identity (their ordained place in society), or their emotional center (true love). By removing themselves from the power world to a place apart or 'green world' (which is a metaphor for rejecting 'masculine' standards, or ignoring them;

229

turning one's back on power and structure and looking instead at feeling and sensation), and by learning to reject a value – for example, Jaques' melancholy, Sir Toby's dissipation, Katharina's shrewishness – without rejecting the person: in other words, by tolerance, the characters discover a way to live together and an enriched, enlarged world.

In tragedy, the concentration on the individual automatically creates distance between the hero and his society. The anguish implicit in tragedy is rooted in the paradox of being part of a culture, even expressing to a high degree some of its values, and yet increasingly rejecting or being rejected by it. Tragedy presents a tearing away like the original act of birth; in the course of that wrenching separation, the protagonists discover their true natures, their basic identities. But this is not necessarily pleasant: much of our lives is spent in hiding our 'true' identities, from ourselves and sometimes even from others – although the latter is very difficult. This situation is true of all the tragedies, including *Hamlet*. Hamlet incarnates the schizophrenia of his world: he worships the inlaw feminine principle and respects to the point of awe, legitimacy, the masculine principle. From the first moment we see him, he stands – or sits – looking gloomily, then with disgust, then with horror, at the other side of things, rampant sexuality, the pretensions of power, the trivial or serious corruption found in human action. But he himself is capable of just such action, and he is not free of his melancholy until he indulges in it. Lear's progress is from centrality in his world to a place outside it; in all his phases he provides ground for radical criticism of it. Antony, Macbeth, Coriolanus, and Timon are living expressions of a quality highly valued in their cultures, which they carry to a more intense or different development than is permitted within that culture. Othello and to some degree Macbeth are victims of their own cultures, which is why we are able to feel sympathy (and in Othello's case, condescension, to judge from many critics) for them.

In all the plays, we are looking at the full-plumed masculine principle, Bertram made more serious, intense, profound, or deeply feeling, at powerful males who own rights, privilege, possession, and transcendence of the 'feminine' who have few or no worldly boundaries placed upon them. In most, there is none can call their power to account; for harmonious society to exist, they must therefore do so themselves. Their failure or inability to do so provides the story that unfolds.

Othello

Nowhere in Shakespeare are relations between males and females more searchingly, painfully probed. *Othello* is the last play in which this occurs; with it, the concerns that are central in *Comedy of Errors, Taming, Much Ado*, and *All's Well* are finally laid to rest.

The dominant culture of the play is that of Venice, which is shown here as similar to the Venice of *Merchant*, but in a more positive light. Venice is worldly, powerful, moneyed, and mannered. It is not just a place but an influence, and its mores are implanted in all the characters, even in those who, like Othello and Cassio, are not native Venetians. Venice is civilization, a civilization the characters carry with them to primitive, wild, wartorn Cyprus.[3] The graft is as uneasy as the overlay of civility on any basic human core.

The scenes in Venice present the masculine principle in two aspects. The Senate scene shows it at its finest, possessed of honor, lawfulness, decorum, knowledge, and power, yet 'feminine' in its protective and consolatory inclinations. The city is dominated by reason, and the council scene (I, iii) exemplifies reason in action, whether the issue is a set of conflicting reports of an enemy's movements or a father's hysterical attack. Reason is a form of control, and it is control above all that is the ideal of this culture. Control is essential to a culture which views natural humanity as depraved and vicious: thus Hamlet values Horatio, and Polonius lectures Laertes. It is also essential to a culture which views natural humanity as bestial and voracious, which is closer to the view of this play. The shocked Lodovico laments:

> Is this the noble Moor whom our full Senate
> Call all in all sufficient? Is this the nature
> Whom passion could not shake? whose solid virtue
> The shot of accident nor dart of chance
> Could neither graze nor pierce?
>
> (IV, i, 264–8)

Control over others is power. Control over self is invulnerability, transcendence over nature and the contingencies of natural life. In 'Venetian' cultures, control is an absolute good. But belief in the existence of control is belief that reason, which leads to control, can be separated from and dominate feeling.

From a Venetian perspective, self-control is desirable in all people, necessary in males, and most valuable in soldiers, who must frequently undergo physical discomfort and danger. Othello must sleep on 'the flinty and steel couch of war' (I, iii, 230), and survive 'disastrous chances' (I, iii, 134) of battle, accident, and capture. Othello shows a strong self-control from his first appearance in the play. He is ideally calm, reasonable, and rooted in a sense of legitimacy. He does not fear Brabantio; he knows his lineage to be more royal than and as wealthy as that of the Venetians. He remains calm and in control even when suddenly encompassed by naked swords. Attacked in the Senate, he speaks mildly, moderately, and brilliantly, never responding to Brabantio's wild charges. Although when during his wedding night, a melee breaks out in Cyprus, he warns that 'passion, having my best judgment collided , / Assays to lead the way' (II, iii, 206–7), he remains calm throughout the disruption. Othello represents an ideal control.

Iago too is controlled, although his self-control is used for dissembling, as he announces in the first scene and repeats frequently. Loss of self-control makes Brabantio appear a fool in the council scene; it causes Cassio to lose his lieutenantship. Important as this quality is, every major male figure loses self-control at some point in the play *except Iago.*

The values of Venice are shared by all of the characters. The values most important in this play are power (of various sorts), control (which means believing in the possibility of the supremacy of reason over emotion, and thus in the control, or repression, of emotion), and possession.

There is, however, inevitably in a culture that respects control, an 'underside' to the Venetian culture. It is Venice unclothed, lacking ermine robes and gold seals of office. This sphere has the same values as the world of senator and aristocrat, but its members lack some of the cushions legitimacy grants. It is occupied by males with lesser legitimacy, but it is foreign to no male figure. It is rawer and cruder than Venice; the assumptions which can be sugared over, or spread with velvet in aristocratic circles, are glaringly open here. And it is this sphere that we see first as the play opens.

It is the world of the streets, the locker room, the pool hall. It is dominated by concern about money, and by male competition, which may take the form of envy or hatred. The opening scene (as well as all of Iago's scenes with Roderigo) presents its terms, as Iago bilks Roderigo of his money, and spits hatred at Cassio and Othello.

The aristocratic Venetians do nothing like this. They don't have to. Those with wealth do not have to con a man of his purse – they have subtler means, means they have legitimated by law. Those with political power do not have savagely to manipulate one man: they can impersonally manipulate an entire army. Although Shakespeare does not explicitly identify the two worlds (one senses, indeed, that he would prefer to believe them different), their kinship is demonstrated when members of the aristocratic world – Othello, Cassio, and Brabantio – accede to the terms of the second, and even use those terms themselves.

Because both of these spheres are based in a desire to transcend nature, in control, both are profoundly misogynistic. Their fear and contempt for the feminine principle is expressed not just in contemptuous treatment of women, but in disdain for 'feminine' qualities like loyalty, obedience, and above all, emotion. Women are seen largely as functions, and trivialized; there is general belief in male right to own women and control them. In this kind of thinking, there is disdain for bonds that do not advance one (in a linear way) in the world, for any subordination of self, and for sex.

There is a third sphere in the play, although its character is not as firmly delineated as the two Venetian spheres. This is Cyprus, which can be reached only by immersing oneself in nature, risking drowning. It is a space, rather than place, and thus like the 'places apart' found in comedy. It is a space where those things normally kept in control and hidden can – and do – grow and appear in the light. In Cyprus, where there is, symbolically, no real civilization, only that brought by the Venetians, a man may be his own judge and jury and executioner, a woman may be inconstant, and the underlying assumptions of a culture may be glaringly displayed. And, most important, in Cyprus, the conventions of civilization which permit revocability are lacking. In reversal of the comedic device of using equivocating language to suggest the ambivalence of human affairs and to permit revocability, *Othello* shows words as deeds, and as irrevocable as murder.

The character who symbolizes the upper crust of Venice, despite his different nativity, is Othello; the character who bears the lower burden is Iago. But they are two crusts of one pie, and thus do not just intersect, but share the same base, like the imprintings on two sides of a coin.

Iago is unadulteratedly 'masculine'. He believes in control, reason, power, possession, and individualism; he holds any manifestation of the feminine principle in contempt. It is significant that Iago opens the play: it is his terms that dictate its events throughout. The language of that opening is indicative: Roderigo speaks of money; Iago says 'Abhor me', and Roderigo speaks of hate. Iago replies 'despise me', and proceeds to attack Cassio. He claims his rival is 'almost damn'd in a fair wife', and knows no more of war than a 'spinster' or 'toged consul'. Essentially, Iago is calling Cassio a sissy, effeminate, as containing 'feminine' qualities.[4] He blames Othello for choosing his lieutenant by 'affection' (which is sometimes glossed to mean 'favoritism', although the OED lists no such meaning for Shakespeare's period, which contains pejorative connotations not present in Shakespeare's term) rather than by 'old gradation' – seniority, a coded hierarchy. The conversation moves to assertion of self, individuality at the expense of a social whole, and again Iago shows contempt for loyalty, subordination of self, service based on love, and equates such qualities with bestiality: a duteous servant is his 'master's ass', and earns but 'provender' for his pains.

What Iago lacks are the rewards of masculinity – wealth and status; his actions at the opening seem designed to gain these. He does bilk Roderigo of his fortune, and in time, he does supplant Cassio. But these achievements do not seem to satisfy him; they seem utterly insignificant. Like Richard III, Iago is cut off by his nature from the feminine principle. He not only scorns 'feminine' qualities, but wishes to destroy them in others. He is not such an anomaly as he has been made out. His character is not unlike that of some historical figures who have gone into the world carrying the banner of a religious or political cause, wiping out pleasure, mercy, and sexual love.

Iago is totally rational – and I use that word as critics use it who call the feminine principle *irrational* – and his means is his end.[5] Control is his absolute good, but it gets him nothing: he goes round and round, at every step inventing new reasons to exercise control. In the hollowness of those without satisfying ends, he wills the destruction of those who have them; he wants to 'poison the delight' of those who, like Cassio, have a 'daily beauty' in their lives.[6] The only thing that makes Iago unbelievable is that he does this in the name of his own individuality, and not in the name of some 'higher' cause.

Iago's weapons are his unremitting hatred of the feminine principle and his brilliance at articulating that hatred. This hatred appears in the first scene (thus completing the statement of values that dictates the events) when Iago cries out to Brabantio. He first describes Desdemona as if she were one more possession: 'look to your house, your daughter, and your bags'; 'sir, y'are robbed' (I, i, 80–5). Then he presents the marriage of Desdemona and Othello in these ugly images: 'an old black ram / Is tupping your white ewe'; 'You'll have your daughter cover'd with a Barbary horse, you'll have your nephews neigh to you; you'll have coursers for cousins, and gennets for germans'; Othello and Desdemona, he says, are 'making the beast with two backs' (I, i 88–9; 111–13; 116).

Iago consistently uses animal images – that is, images from nature – to describe sexuality and generation. He goes always directly to the heart of things, even if they are prejudices. Roderigo and Brabantio use political terms to describe what has occurred. Brabantio too sees his daughter as his possession: 'She is … stol'n from me' (I, iii, 60). Roderigo says that Desdemona has made a 'gross revolt'; Brabantio calls it 'treason of the blood'. Both men mean not only a revolt against her father's lawful possession and control, but also a revolt against the 'laws of nature', as she moves to the 'gross clasps of a lascivious Moor'.

Both kinds of descriptions of what Desdemona has done are 'masculine', and both betray the values of this culture. But Iago's way of speaking moves the case from the particular to the general. He casts filth not just on the coupling of Desdemona and Othello, but on coupling itself. All sexuality is 'making the beast with two backs', if one has contempt for sex and sees it as bestial.[7]

Othello at first appears to be his ensign's opposite. That he is noble and that Shakespeare intended him to seem so appears to me to be unquestionable. His demeanor is authoritative and calm, his language intelligent and beautiful, and only rarely inflated. He appears in a particularly shining way because he appears *after* Iago. Iago's revelations about his own character 'blacken' him instantly; his hatred for the Moor serves to exalt the general, and to 'whiten' him. And in all the early scenes, Othello is steadily admirable, Iago steadily despicable. On the surface, the two present a clear contrast. Underneath, however, another current moves. For Othello, magnificent as he is, is also as egotistical as his ensign; moreover, his gentility and magniloquence tend to dull. Although it does not happen in the play, Othello could become tedious, boring; Iago is never that. The point is that Iago has the energy and wit and delight in himself that Shakespeare associates with the unleashed masculine principle. Hateful as he is, Iago is fun (in the way Richard III is fun) to listen to.

Othello's values are those of aristocratic Venice; Iago's are those of its underside. Iago has contempt for the feminine principle, for women, and feeling, and sex. Othello, without his awareness, shares this contempt. The first clue to this is his behavior in the Senate chamber. Othello swears that 'as truly as to heaven / I do confess the vices of my blood, / So justly to your grave ears I'll present / How I did thrive in this fair lady's love' (I, iii, 122–5). The comparison seems inept, but Othello is never inept. Unconsciously, he is associating love with vice. In his effort to persuade the Senate that his commission will take priority over his marriage, he uses terms that could be Iago's: if he neglects his work for love, he says, 'Let housewives make a skillet of my helm' (I, iii, 272). In response to the order to leave immediately, before the consummation of his marriage, he says 'With all my heart'. He accepts the commission for Cyprus with 'a natural and prompt alacrity'. He seems to have no regret whatever about leaving Desdemona. When she demurs and asks to go with him, he seconds her, but assures the Senate that he wants her 'not / To please the palate of my appetite ... but to be free and bounteous to her mind' (I, iii, 261; 262; 265). We might assume from this that Othello has a weak or undemanding sensual nature – indeed, one critic has so concluded – but this is the same man who later tells Desdemona she is 'so lovely fair and smell'st so sweet / That the sense aches at thee' (IV, ii, 68–9).[8]

Othello's denial of the erotic element in love is related to Iago's denial of the loving element in eros. Both denials emerge from a need to separate love (the inlaw aspect) from sex (the outlaw). Both attempt to control sexuality, Othello by idealizing it, Iago by demeaning it: 'But we have reason to cool our raging motions, our carnal stings, our unbitted lusts; whereof I take this that you call love to be a sect or scion' (I, iii, 329–32). Both men assume that love and lust are related; Othello tries to purify the lustfulness from love, and Iago tries to rationalize the love out of lust.

Othello is almost as 'masculine' as Iago. He too believes in control, reason, and the assertion of individuality. (Consider his statements: 'Were it my cue to fight, I should have known it / Without a prompter' (I, ii, 83–4); 'She lov'd me for the dangers I had passed, / And I lov'd her that she did pity them' (I, iii, 167–8). Both show a strong ego sense.) He respects power and hierarchy. Dignified and self-respecting as he is before the Senate, he acknowledges it his superior; decent and humane as he is with his inferiors, he never forgets his authority over them.[9] In addition, he shares Iago's sense of the degradation sexuality constitutes, but whereas Iago would engage in sex and then hurl contempt at the woman, assuming boys will be boys, Othello attempts to idealize sex out of existence.

However, misogynistic cultures, because they need the women they despise, always contain a safety pocket. They open a very narrow gate, through which pass those women considered purified from taint, and thus elevated. Othello, Cassio, and the play itself exalt one woman, Desdemona, as being above the common run. Cassio describes Desdemona in terms that any mortal would have trouble living up to: she 'paragons description'; she is so divine that even nature gives her homage. (Othello too is exalted in this section of II, i. The exaltation, coupled with the suspense attending his arrival, emphasizes his greatness. Thus the pair seems, at the moment of their meeting, two superhumans matched.) Between Cassio's hyperbolic comments about Desdemona before Othello's arrival, and Othello's hyperbolic description of his feelings about Desdemona after he arrives, is a short, odd section. It is a dialogue that would be unnecessary and irrelevant to the play if Shakespeare were not focusing on the subject of attitudes towards women.

Iago begins by castigating Emilia, and immediately extends his criticism to women in general. Desdemona challenges him on this, clearly (if implicitly) believing herself worthy, and wishing to hear some words describing worthy women. Iago dredges up a set of ancient attacks on women. Women are dissemblers; by nature they are angry, argumentative, and sexual; they pretend to competence (huswifery), and sainthood. To Desdemona's challenge he replies with a set of verses which emphasize one thing and only one thing: female (dissembling) sexuality. When she challenges him further, he admits that there may be deserving women (the very phrase betrays the assumptions of the culture), and what they deserve is to 'suckle fools and chronicle small beer' (II, i, 160). For Iago, women are body, child-bearers and nurturers, and housewives, none of which functions warrants any respect.

The language of Othello on his arrival is beautiful and extreme. Beside it, Desdemona's sounds pedestrian.[10] In his ecstasy, he wishes for death because 'I fear / My soul hath her content so absolute / That not another comfort like to this / Succeeds in unknown fate' (II, i, 190–3). He is, of course, ironically, quite accurate, but his negligence of, or ignoring of, the sexual consummation still to come is most untypical and therefore significant. Desdemona's language is matter-of-fact and plain. She is not an enraptured idealist, but simply a happy woman expecting a happy life.

These two attitudes – one exalting, one degrading, neither able to deal with the reality – towards women, and particularly towards Desdemona, are contrasted again in II, iii, 15–29, in the dialogue of Cassio and Iago about Desdemona and sex, but they come into direct confrontation in III, iii. And in this scene, it is Othello, not Iago, who associates vulnerability to feeling with bestiality. To Iago's warning against jealousy, he responds 'Exchange me for a goat' if ever he suffers from such an emotion. Iago's campaign is careful. First he impugns Cassio, then warns Othello against jealousy. His warning alone is enough to shake Othello a little; beneath his calm and assured exterior there is a sense of some kind of unworthiness. But he dismisses it: 'she had eyes, and chose me'.

Because male legitimacy is based on pretence, it is always shaky. Like Brabantio and others of his culture, Othello believes in his possession and right to command his wife: inconstancy would be a 'revolt'. But beneath this belief always lurks the suspicion that one person cannot really own another.[11] Thus the grounds on which the entire Renaissance concept of marriage is erected are shaky, and Othello is feeling the tremor.

Iago's next step is a slide onto the dangerous ground of Desdemona. He begins with a commonplace misogynistic statement – Venetian women (all of them, of course) are inconstant. Then he moves closer to home: she deceived her father, why not you? This has special force because Brabantio himself has hurled the warning – about his own daughter – at Othello. Iago adds: she even deceived you, for when she seemed frightened of you, she was most in love with you.

Just these assertions are enough to dash Othello, to undermine all his exalted love. Since for Desdemona to be worthy of his love she must be better than the common run of women, the mere suggestion that she is not the utter paragon of virtue and honesty she has been made out is sufficient to tarnish her.[12] Since she obviously could not be superhuman, Iago's suggestion that she is not has the strong force of truth: honest Iago, indeed. And seeing how the mere intimation that she *can* deceive shakes Othello, understanding that such a suspicion will lead to doubts as to whether she is really free from moral taint (with women, that means sexuality), Iago has a clear path for his next step. He trains Othello to see sex, women, and love as he does.

He accomplishes this through language, which is his greatest gift: Iago is literally a poet of hate and disgust. And in this play, language is action. Iago destroys Othello and Desdemona without lifting a finger; he uses his tongue alone. And it is a brilliant one.

Nevertheless, it would be impossible for Iago to seduce Othello if Othello did not already share Iago's value structure.[13] Othello is not dense or blind, he is not a noble savage. He is a male who lives and thrives in a masculine occupation in a 'masculine' culture, the assumptions of which he shares.[14]

There are two kinds of women, one being superhuman, totally virtuous. (Even Iago believes there are such things as virtuous women: see II, iii

360–1; IV, i, 46–7.) The other kind is a dissembler, a deceiver, because of sexuality; she is thus subhuman, bestial, capable of any degradation. And the two kinds are absolutely mutually exclusive. One can cross into the subhuman camp at any time, but once in it, one can never return. So Othello, perceiving taint in Desdemona for the first time, is deeply shaken. Her later, frightened deception about the handkerchief will clinch the case against her.

But Othello is a deeply feeling person. Unlike Iago, he is capable of dedicating himself to something or someone outside himself. Thus his fury against Desdemona is nothing like Iago's contemptuous treatment of Emilia. Desdemona has betrayed Othello in the deepest part of his being, 'there, where I have garner'd up my heart, / Where either I must live or bear no life; / The fountain from which my current runs / Or else dries up' (IV, ii, 57–60). When he stops loving Desdemona, 'chaos is come again'.

Yet in I, ii, Othello tells Iago that he would not have confined his 'unhoused free condition' except that he loves Desdemona. He does not seem to have suffered from 'chaos' in the years before he loved; he did not 'bear no life' before he met her.

Desdemona has seduced Othello into placing faith and trust in that unfixable, uncontrollable feminine principle; her love for him has seduced him into allowing himself to love. By submitting to the feminine principle, Othello turns his back on his training. While Iago is contemptuous of the qualities of the feminine principle, Othello feels ignorant of them. He apologizes to the Senate for his lack of polish; he thinks Desdemona may have turned against him because he is old, or black, or lacks the 'soft parts of conversation' (III, iii, 264). In loving her he has opened the deepest parts of himself, allowed himself to feel, although he is unused to the 'melting mood'. He has freely accepted vulnerability and subordination to another. And it is Othello's ignorance of the inlaw aspect, an ignorance that in a person of mature years has to be based in fear and distrust, that makes him so vulnerable to Iago's certainty that with women, distrust, mistrust, is the only reasonable, the only rational position.

In truth, the mere suggestion that Desdemona is unfaithful is enough to send Othello into a renunciatory paroxysm that goes beyond just love and marriage and women: he renounces his career as well. It is tempting to read that passage as self-dramatization, but it is of a piece with his character generally. Othello does dramatize his emotions – consider his speech just before he kills Desdemona. He is a passionate man. And loss of faith, once he has placed it, leads to loss of the will to live. In this way, he is related to Hamlet.[15] (So is Iago, in another way.)

We are, I think, meant to find Othello a bit of an innocent, regardless of his age. He sees himself thus and so does Iago at one moment. He is emotionally deep but inexperienced, like Hamlet and (perhaps) Troilus; he is as idealistic as they are as well. His blackness is partly an emblem for this sort of difference from wily Venetians and courtly Florentines. For Othello, as for Hamlet and Troilus, the altar on which he has first placed his devotion must remain fixed, constant, else chaos is come again.

Chaos comes swiftly and it comes through language. It is the vividness and ugliness of the sexual images Iago is able to conjure that leads Othello to hell. 'Would you, the supervisor, grossly gape on? Behold her topp'd?' (III, iii, 345). Othello replies, 'Death and damnation!' The vividness of Iago's account of Cassio's talking in his sleep is enough to lead Othello to swear 'I'll tear her all to pieces', and to abjure all his 'fond love'.

An essential part of the exchanges of Othello and Iago is the pervasive animal imagery. It can signify subordination, as in Iago's early characterization of a loyal servant as an ass; in Iago's hectoring of Brabantio, it is applied to copulation and generation. It next appears – again in Iago's mouth – when Roderigo claims he will die from love. Iago scoffs: 'Ere I would say I would drown myself for the love of a guinea hen, I would change my humanity with a baboon' (I, iii, 314–6). He then proceeds to outline what he considers to be the proper relations among human faculties; his ideas are classical and Catholic, items of accepted philosophical and theological doctrine.[16] One could read his speech and shrug about devils who can quote Scripture. But it is far more likely that Shakespeare was suggesting that the values that motivate and characterize an Iago are *accepted and respected values in the Western world.* Only his apparent ignorance of love makes his statement seem that of a villain; like Troilus, Iago identifies love as appetite (in II, i, 225–35).

Iago's associations are clear: sex, subservience, and affection are parts of the feminine principle, and are therefore not within the pale of the human because they are tied to nature, beasts, and deservedly enslaved classes, which include women.

But Othello, once his idealism is undermined (indeed his idealism is a shift made to allow love in the face of his real beliefs), shares Iago's ideas. Like the ensign, he equates love with appetite, marriage with possession, and considers less than total possession of a wife 'toadlike' (III, iii, 270).[17] Iago whets him with images of Desdemona and Cassio as goats, monkeys, and wolves. Othello falls into a fit, then mutters, 'A horned man's a monster and a beast' (IV, i, 62). 'Goats and monkeys!' (IV, i, 263), his uncontrolled outburst at the end of his tormented speech to Lodovico, proves that Iago's poison poured in his ears has done its work.

Once Iago has poisoned sexuality itself in Othello's mind, there is nothing to be done. Desdemona as idealized woman and his exalted notion of love are dead for him whether he kills the real woman or not. If Desdemona, that paragon, is tainted, so are all women. In his rage at the destruction of his illusion, Othello treats both Desdemona and Emilia as whores. (Thus, at the end of the play, Iago calls Emilia 'whore' when she tells the truth about the handkerchief.) And since Desdemona is clearly sexual – physically as well as emotionally and intellectually in love with Othello – she *is* tainted (whether unfaithful or not) once Iago has taught Othello to see sex as he does.

Nevertheless, Othello could simply turn away from Desdemona; he could divorce her; he could talk to her about the charges; he could … a thousand things. But he must kill her because of the prime value of his culture, his own prime value as well: control. As I said earlier, there are only two forms of control – domestication and killing. Desdemona seems unable to be domesticated, so she must be killed. Trust of the fluid feminine principle is difficult precisely because it cannot be controlled; its very nature is defined by that. Division into inlaw and outlaw aspects is a way of trying to control it, but it does not work very well. Othello must kill Desdemona because he loves her so much that if he did not kill her, he would slide into accepting her infidelity, to giving up control over her entirely.

Although he attempts, in his words over her sleeping body, to ceremonialize her murder, invoking justice and 'more men' as his reasons, he cannot accomplish this. Desdemona's crime is worse than his, and this justifies his. Wakened and asked to confess her sins, Desdemona says 'They are loves I bear to you' (V, ii, 40). She too sees love as sin. The murder in *Othello* is the murder of a vision of human love purified from the taint of a sexuality seen as bestial, vicious, and chaotic.[18]

That Shakespeare himself was thinking in terms like those I have described is demonstrated by his portraits of the three women in the play. They come from three moral levels: the 'divine' Desdemona from the superhuman; Emilia from the realistic world; and Bianca from the subhuman, since she is a prostitute and thus, in the moral universe of Shakespeare's plays (and elsewhere as well), not deserving of human consideration or rights. Yet all three of these women are finally treated in the same way. Moreover, Shakespeare placed words in their mouths that show he was aware of the political situation of women and their personal identities apart from men.

Desdemona, the angel who has not yet experienced mistreatment, accepts her culture's dictum that she must be obedient to males. Her first words in the play express her sense of duty to father and husband, a 'divided duty' (I, iii, 181). The last words she speaks before she is aware of a change in Othello are: 'Be as your fancies teach you; / What e're you be, I am obedient' (III, iii, 88–9). She cannot even conceive of infidelity to a husband; she does not struggle against Othello when he commences to abuse her. To the end she remains submissive, begging Othello to let her live one more night, one more half-hour. Her last words, placing the blame for her death on herself, are self-denying in the extreme: they are the words of a martyr. With Cordelia and Hermione, Desdemona represents the inlaw feminine principle at its most superhuman.

Yet Shakespeare also takes pains to show her human, whole, and possessed of will. She confesses, in the Senate chamber, to 'violence, and storm of fortunes' (I, iii, 249). It is she who protests the separation of the newlyweds; she asserts she wants to live with Othello because she wants 'the rites for why I love him' (I, iii, 257). And it is she who cries out to the senators in dismay, 'To-night, my lord?' (I, iii, 278), after the order to leave immediately. She has defied and deceived her father; like Helena, she would lose her virginity to her own liking.

Desdemona is sexual. Her innocence resides not in her freedom from sexual 'taint' (as does the Virgin Mary's), but in her ignorance of the bestiality others see implicit in it. She is chaste and constant by nature: she cannot conceive of infidelity; she cannot imagine that love can end; and she is ignorant of male ways of talking and thinking about sex. To the degree that she represents part of Othello's psyche, she embodies that part which exalts and idealizes love, separating it from bestial sex. But Shakespeare is at some pains to emphasize that Desdemona herself has no need of such moral schizophrenia, that in her wholeness she finds no need to redeem or idealize sex.

Desdemona has no sexual guilt because she feels no need to transcend sex. She does not claim she wants to go to Cyprus to be 'free and bounteous' to Othello's mind: nor is she hesitant to assert publicly that she has sexual desires. She can jest with Iago about women without embarrassment. Although she knows that sex is sin, her own sexual acts have been sanctified by ceremony into 'rites'. She teases Othello about Cassio with the tenacity of a cajoling child; she lies about the handkerchief like a wary child. And yet when Othello strikes her publicly, she stands her ground with adult dignity: 'I have not deserv'd this' (IV, i, 224).

In short, until the 'brothel' scene, she is a sensitive and confident young woman, straitly kept, kept a dependent child, but retaining spirit nevertheless. She is whole, sexual, given to be happy. But the men in the play see her differently.

For Brabantio, she has the passivity and silence proper in women: 'a maiden, never bold; / Of spirit so still and quiet that her motion / Blush'd at itself'* (I, iii, 95–6). He thinks she is unsexual, 'opposite to marriage' (I, ii, 67). Thus her elopement with Othello is doubly 'unnatural': she has chosen a man of a color different from her own, and she has betrayed that she does possess sexual desires.

Roderigo idealizes Desdemona as holy, 'full of most bles'd condition' (II, i, 249–50). Cassio exalts her even more than Othello does, as divine, a paragon, 'our great captain's captain'. For Othello, Desdemona is not fully a separate being but part of himself, the completion of himself.

---

*Not Evans' reading, but Pope's emendation. Folio and Quarto read 'herself'.

But honest Iago sees her only as 'fram'd as fruitful / As the free elements' (II, iii, 341–2). It is ironic that of all the men, he sees Desdemona the most accurately.

Desdemona perceives herself the way Othello perceives her – as part of him, as not existing without him; his rejection of her in IV, ii stuns her into stupefaction. She tells Iago that the removal of Othello's love will kill her 'but never taint my love' (IV, ii, 161). And as she dies, she puts the blame for her murder on herself. (Interestingly, Othello sneers that she dies in sin, lying; over and again, the inflexibility of the masculine principle leads to a devaluation of the feminine.)[19]

Yet even this ideal figure complains bitterly, after Othello strikes her, of his injustice. And she sighs, 'O, these men, these men!' (IV, iii, 60). And that she is shown as near-ideal and seen by most of the male characters as fully an ideal, does not keep her from being called a 'land-carrack' (slang for prostitute) by Iago. Or from being treated like a whore by her husband.

Bianca echoes, with sad resignation, Desdemona's happy statement of subordination to her man: 'Tis very good; I must be circumstanc'd' (III, iv, 201) she replies to Cassio's order to leave lest Othello see him 'woman'd' (III, iv, 195). Cassio's abrupt contempt for her jealousy provides a brief but pointed contrast to the main action. Women may get jealous as well as men; but they have no power, and their jealousy is dismissed with scorn.

Bianca appears after an amused, contemptuous conversation about her between Iago and Cassio. Cassio attacks her, using animal imagery, until she retorts jealously. He retreats, and Bianca leaves in anger. Nevertheless, she is still supplicant: 'An' you'll come to supper tonight, you may' (IV, i, 159–60).

It is emblematic that Iago and Cassio are discussing Bianca when Othello thinks they are discussing Desdemona. In this male world, all women are the same. Like Othello, Cassio exalts Desdemona; nevertheless, he shares his culture's misogyny, saying to Desdemona after Iago's satire on women, 'he speaks home' (II, i, 165). And he has contempt for the woman whose body he uses. Even her most genuine love and fidelity cannot protect Desdemona from the language, the attitudes, and finally the oppression of the male view of women.

Othello treats Emelia as a bawd when he castigates Desdemona as whore; Iago treats his wife with curt contempt.[20] None of the women imagines independence of men, but Emilia is aware of her own and other women's autonomous being. And she is the spokeswoman for the females of the play. She is worldly, a little cynical, resigned. She murmurs bitterly about male dominance: 'I nothing but to please his fantasy' (III, iii, 299) she says of her relation to Iago. She is bitter: men 'are all but stomachs and we all but food; / They eat us hungerly, and when they are full / They belch us' (III, iv, 104–6).

In IV, iii, Emilia delivers a little sermon on the relations of husbands and wives. In context it seems almost irrelevant, since it is a defense of adultery in wives and Desdemona has not performed this act. It is a piece of moralizing, similar to other passages in Shakespeare in which the lower orders comment on the exemplary implications of the behavior of the upper classes. Here, Emilia suggests that the behavior of husbands and their treatment of their wives necessarily have consequences, and that inconstancy is, after all, a 'small vice' (IV, iii, 69). She assumes that women are human – merely human, but at least human – and like men are subject to affection, temptation, and anger.

One effect of Emilia's speech is to counter the attitudes of the males in the play. Whether they idealize women or degrade them all into whores, like Iago, who says, 'knowing what I am, I know what she shall be' (IV, i, 73), or whether they do both simultaneously, the thing they do not do is see women as human beings. Shakespeare does, in this play.

But on another level, Emilia's speech broadens the implications of the action. Desdemona has not been unfaithful to Othello: that is insisted upon by the play. We overhear her conversations with Cassio; we overhear her shocked conversation with Emilia; we are clearly asked to give the last drop of pity to her and to her maid as they die. In the comedies, an accusation of infidelity is tantamount to actual infidelity on the mythic level of the play. It does not function this way here. Shakespeare took too many pains to inform us at every step of the line, not only of Iago's plot, but also of Desdemona's innocence. But he clearly wishes to consider the broader issue: if Desdemona had been inconstant, would she have deserved death? Does Othello have the right to kill her if she is guilty? He does not deal with these questions in *Othello*, because this play is about male attitudes towards women – and each other – and thus Desdemona must stand as a symbol of what men destroy. He does consider it in *Cymbeline*. But Emilia's defense of inconstancy in women brings up the question. Suppose Desdemona *had* been inconstant? Would the audience wish her dead? And Emilia's speech is a long, long way from the speech given by Luciana to Adriana in *Comedy of Errors:* a lifetime away.

Othello is a profound examination of male modes of thought and behavior, especially with regard to women and 'feminine' qualities. Iago is honest: he speaks the ordinary wisdom of the male world. The consequences of the values he shares with the other males of the play destroy the 'feminine' values held by Desdemona, above all, but also Othello, Emilia, Cassio, Roderigo.

And Iago never changes. He remains. He endures without cracking, the only character in the play who never shows a sign of emotion or passion or the weakness he despises, although his behavior clearly has to be motivated by passion. He talks about lust, but never shows any sign of it.

The prime exponent of reason and control stands firm even as the world around him collapses, even knowing that he caused its collapse. Although tortures are promised, things that will make him speak word again, this brilliant verbal manipulator, this poet for whom silence is indeed punishment, stands alive at the end of the play, surrounded by bodies, and is, in our imagination, triumphant. Well, the truth is, he is.

King Lear

King Lear stands alone in the Shakespearean canon. Plunging deeply into the terrifying darkness of not-knowing that lies below the morals and accepted truths of any period, *King Lear* risks everything. It dares a late-night meeting in a blind alley with the most feared killers of mental and emotional well-being : nihilism and absurdity.[21] The meeting occurs, the killers win. For some, like Sam Johnson, that is devastating. Less courageous souls than he sweeten the play with promises of salvation. But it is not necessary to do this to find affirmation in the play. The tragedy pits the merely human – feeling, suffering, seeing, seeking for significance – against a Goliath of incertitude. Incertitude wins, as it must in any honest contest, but the contest is grand, ennobling and enlarging the human even as it is vanquished. Indeed, humanness is ultimately defined by the suffering and the effort of this struggle.

In *Lear*, Shakespeare momentarily pushes aside the gender principles to examine the original terms of their division, the split between the human and nature.[22] With steady courage, the playwright looks at human existence, and probes two opposing but equal needs – the need to accept human rootedness, participation in nature and subordination to it; and the need to distinguish between nature and the human, thus defining the latter.

The play is pervaded by natural imagery and recurrent use of terms like *Nature, nature, natural,* and *unnatural*. References to nature are wide-ranging in tone and import; so too are images drawn from natural phenomena: no one association or definition dominates the play.[23] *Nature* means *natura* and also *human nature*; at times it refers to physical, at times to psychological dimensions of a human. It is used to refer to vividness and animation, the elan of life; at other times it refers to the bonds of kinship and hierarchy, seen as implicit in 'natural' law as Hooker described it. This last definition is circular: what is 'natural' is what acts according to 'laws of nature' which ordain certain behaviors ('offices of nature'[II, iv, 178]) as 'natural' for humans according to their age, gender, and status. The word *unnatural* is flung many times, usually by parents to and about their children when the latter are perceived as not abiding by those 'laws'.

Thus, the term is deeply ambiguous. Gloucester uses the phrase 'wisdom of nature':

> Though the wisdom of nature can reason it thus and thus, yet nature finds itself scourg'd by the sequent effects. Love cools, friendship falls off, brothers divide. In cities, mutinies; in countries, discord; in palaces, treason; and the bond crack'd 'twixt son and father.
>
> (I, ii, 104–9)

The Earl could mean wisdom or knowledge about nature, including human nature. He could also mean wisdom arising from powers of reason which, as Hooker suggested, arise out of nature itself. In this case, human wisdom is in harmony with 'natural law' because that wisdom arises from nature as it exists in humans. Thus, if nature is 'scourg'd by the sequent effects', something is terribly wrong with the whole conception. If 'natural' reason leads to injury of human 'nature', that reason itself is under suspicion.

In general, the way nature references are used imports less about the nature of nature than about the character of the user. So, Edmund uses it much as we would use *life-force* – energy, talent, and the right to existence and growth such qualities deserve. He opposes this to the 'plague of custom' and the 'curiosity of nations' (I, ii, 3, 4), thus setting up an antagonism between the power and 'natural' right of the individual, and the traditional and hierarchical legitimacy of a class. For Lear, up through III, ii, nature is divine justice modeled of course on earthly justice, and therefore the King's subject and ally. He calls on nature to revenge him on Goneril by making her barren or giving her a 'child of spleen' (I, iv, 282). Albany shares this belief of Lear in divine justice, although he terms it 'the heavens', a term Lear too uses: 'All the stor'd vengeances of heaven fall / On her ingrateful top!' (II, iv, 162–3). However, Lear is calling on nature in the speech in which this passage occurs. And, in fact, the continuing belief that nature is an agent of divine justice, which occurs in Edgar's and Albany's speeches through most of the play, functions after a time to diminish them. What kind of justice is it that would decree Gloucester to be blinded, regardless of his moral obtuseness? To find the hand of providence in the events of human life, one must be moralistic, pietistic, in a particularly narrow way.

There are other uses of the term. Kent claims Oswald was made by a tailor rather than by nature, which is appropriate to Kent's rather unthinking and pugnacious, if loyal, character. And Cordelia speaks directly to the benevolent and fruitful powers of earth, asking nature to reveal its 'blest secrets', its 'unpublish'd virtues' (IV, iv, 15, 16) to help cure the mad King. Cordelia, one moral pole in the play, asks help of the 'inlaw' qualities of 'feminine' nature; Edmund, to some degree representing the 'outlaw' qualities, speaks to the life-force – powerful, sexual, and full of energy. Lear in the early acts, Albany, and Edgar conflate nature with divinity, which is to say they endow it with a moral character. Albany and Edgar see divine justice as an absolute set of standards; Lear's notion is more profoundly investigated.

In the beginning, the King believes in his own rightness and his own power in an absolute way.[24] Thus he identifies divine justice (manifested through natural phenomena) with his own will. Such an identification underlies his trade during nature's storm, a storm that he at first perceives as a divine warning to his immoral daughters and others 'unwhipt of justice' (III, ii, 53). It is 'the great gods, / That keep this dreadful pudder o'er our heads' (III, ii, 49–50). When he goes so far as to command nature, to bid 'the wind blow the earth into the sea' (III, i, 5), or orders earth to crack its molds, or reproaches it for joining with his daughters to oppress him, Lear, 'in his little world of man' (III, i, 10), is as hybristic as Canute.[25]

The indifference of nature to Lear's claims is partly responsible for his breaking in this scene. But even as he calls on the storm to punish the guilty, *he* is the person the storm is punishing. He realizes, gradually (if rather swiftly), that he is a subject here, not a king, a 'poor, inform, weak and despis'd old man' (III, ii, 20). He realizes that he has sinned, even if he is more sinned against. Part of Lear's change is a result of his loss of certitude, of a sense of absolute rightness. He recalls later, near Dover, that he discovered something 'when the rain came to wet me once, and the wind to make me chatter, when the thunder would not peace at my bidding, there I found 'em, there I smelt 'em out' (IV, vi, 100–3). In the beginning of the play, when Lear disinherits Cordelia and banishes Kent, he is absolute not only in power but in his sense of rightness. He begins to falter during his arguments with Goneril, not yet because he has become aware of his lack of power (he still threatens terrible revenge, still tries to command the elements), but because he cannot make his daughters see the *rightness* of his position. They do not seem to be aware of what is self-evident to the King; they shrug off indifferently a matter he sees as his natural and inalienable right. For the first time – presumably – in his long life, his will is challenged.

In fact, all three of his daughters challenge his will. Cordelia refuses to bow to his impossible demand in I, i; Goneril and Regan deny him what he has asserted as his right, afterwards. He begins to move outside the hothouse of certitude: 'I did her wrong', he mutters. When the storm too ignores the rightness of his cause, defies his commands, when he finds himself exiled from all but the disinherited of the earth, wet, hungry, and cold, he cracks entirely. But what is destroyed is not the man, Lear, but the King, Lear.

Starting from a position of political – thus social and moral – preeminence, Lear topples into a class of outsiders, the dispossessed, the illegitimate every complex civilization contains. The cracking of the 'masculine' mold in which Lear was formed and has lived is painful for him and pathetic to watch, but it does not in the end leave him with the 'nothing' so continually threatened by him and to him, in the play. Toppling from power does not strip him of his manhood; it confers humanhood upon him. Man's life is not cheap as beast's if pity touches it, nor can tears 'stain' his humanness.

Thus, the first three acts begin to create a definition of humanness by stripping away certain qualities often associated with it. Humanness is *not* power, because human power is limited, it is not privilege and right because those are only temporarily given and may at any time be challenged or denied: they are dependent upon power, not moral laws. The masculine principle, which is always identified with the human, is actually a shield against it, a protection, ermine hiding naked flesh. Attempting to strip his body to the naked skin it is, Lear does not become nothing; he becomes merely human, suddenly able to examine right and rightness from the underside, the perspective of the illegitimate. Thus a tendency perceivable in the earliest plays comes to fruition and full development in this tragedy.

The viewpoint of the illegitimate, found in the early plays mainly in clowns and women, becomes, through Lear's change, the dominant point of view in the play. From this position, the world's arrangements are not only unkind and unjust, but absurd, delusory. The poor go naked and hungry while the rich surfeit; a daughter kicks her poor old father; even the dogs bark at a beggar. 'Is there any cause in nature that make these hard hearts?' (III, vi, 77–8). By the time he appears in the fields outside Dover, Lear has mulled over and seen through all human pretensions of authority and justice and found them to be merely a matter of power, of *costume*. The assumption of the early comedies, that identity is largely a matter of discovering one's true place in society and accepting it, is here completely refuted. One's given place in society is an accident, and if it is a high one, a mask for the truth of one's participation in nature. The presumption of possession of justice or authority is merely a question of being in possession of the mantle society agrees to defer to as covering nakedness.

That which is stripped away in the first acts of the play as being of the essence of humanness is presented mainly in the first two scenes. As always, the opening scene is a focusing one. The first two speeches appear to deal with affection – Lear's for Albany and Cornwall. But the language is both abstract and quantitative: 'It appears not which of the Dukes he values most, for equalities are so weigh'd, that curiosity in neither can make choice of either's moi'ty. ' What is under discussion is affection that can be weighed, measured, apportioned like land, like the kingdom. This established, the scene moves to Edmund. This is sometimes played with

Edmund standing apart, unable to overhear the dialogue of Gloucester and Kent, as is indicated by the stage directions in some editions. Nevertheless, the use of *this* rather than *that* in 'Is not this your son, my lord' and 'this young fellow's mother', as well as Gloucester's question of Edmund, asked without a summons, imply that Edmund is present during the entire conversation.

Gloucester's language in this segment shows a clear differentiation in moral responsibility for sex. He admits he is responsble for Edmund: he has 'blush'd to acknowledge' the boy but is 'braz'd to it'. But the boy's mother is not in the same way responsible for the child; rather the existence of the child is a definition of *her*. Edmund is a *whore*son because his mother 'had a son for her cradle ere she had a husband for her bed'. Gloucester is urbane and complacent: Edmund's mother, he recalls, was 'fair, there was good sport at his making'.

This is a crass and insensitive way of speaking, indeed of thinking and feeling about one's child and his mother. But Gloucester's insensitivity is much compounded if he speaks thus in the child's presence. In either case, Gloucester is hardened to love and is insensitive to others. Finally, he quantifies love, claiming to love his sons equally.

Lear appears, royal, arrogant, commanding, absolute. Within a few lines, he reinforces the impression made by the opening lines of the play. But he speaks quantitatively not of his love for Albany and Cornwall, but of theirs *for him*. He commands his daughters to quantify their love for him, as well.[26] But he asks: which *'shall we say* doth love us most?'. He receives his answers as he asked for them: in words alone. (In this play, unlike *Othello*, language is not identical with act, but is rather extremely cut off from it. This is inevitable in a play which questions the very foundations of human civilization, in which there is no absolute center in which language and act, tongue and heart, appearance and reality, are utterly atoned. In *Othello*, there is a single and absolute truth: Desdemona is constant.) After they challenge him and defy his power, Lear is not able to take physical revenge on his daughters, but he does so hideously in language.[27] But his real hate is as ineffectual as their pretended love: both live only in words.

There is nothing inherently 'evil' (as some critics suggest) about quantification. It is a structuring, a codification of feeling; it transplants a 'feminine' quality into the 'masculine' sphere. This cannot be accomplished without some change in the quality, unless one is able to translate feeling into poetry. But the 'masculine' is an essential human mode insofar as it structures experience; if it is not an ideal way, or even an absolutely trustworthy way of communicating feeling, it is a legitimate way, so long as it is not taken as absolute, or as the most trustworthy mode. Sensitivity to others is that – seeing, feeling the emotion of the self and of others.

Cordelia, incapable of poetry and incapable of deceit, translates her feeling for her father directly into 'masculine' language, claiming to love him in accordance with the bond between them. Although Lear should know how his favorite daughter feels about him, he takes her word for the thing itself, and banishes her disinherited. Lear identifies word and act. He is old and has been King since he was a boy: for him, statements have been tantamount to realities. What the King says, the court agrees with; what the King orders is performed. 'They flatter'd me like a dog, and told me I had the white hairs in my beard ere the black ones were there' (IV, vi, 96–8).

Lear has never seen himself as anything but King. Thus he confuses personal power with power-in-the-world, that is, lovableness with power. He confuses language with action, power with right, justice with will. He has never, actually or imaginatively, experienced powerlessness; thus he has never seen himself in terms of the feminine principle, as a mere denizen of earth, but only in terms of the masculine, as a wielder of power-in-the world. Given his age, his ignorance is both arrogant and wilfully blind. Where has he been all these years? How has he managed not to *see*?

Lear, however, is not alone. He represents an entire class in Western culture, and a mainstream in Western thinking. For this reason, it seems to me narrowing and fruitless to dissect him in search of his 'fatal flaw'. All ways of thinking contain their own blindnesses. Lear's flaw is a flaw in our society, in all societies where there is a tradition of privilege. And all people who believe in traditional privilege and inherent right exhibit the kind of blindness and arrogance we see in Lear.

When such qualities are exacerbated by rashness, however, they become dangerous indeed. Goneril and Regan will have to tame the King if they are to hold the power he has supposedly given them. He has always been rash: 'I know his heart' (I, iv, 330) Goneril says, and there is no reason to doubt her. She has one like his, although she is not rash. She and Regan spring from and incarnate one side of Lear, much as he tries to disown them.[28] The sisters value power and authority, and believe in their own right to hold them; they respect control and 'reason', and are utterly reasonable except in one thing – Edmund. Their reason stands in the face of Lear's passion, quietly, coolly denying it legitimacy.

But there is more to Lear. At the outset, we know this only indirectly. We know it because Kent and Cordelia, and later, Gloucester, show love for the King. Moreover, Lear has been able, at some time prior to the opening of the play, to *see* Cordelia, to perceive her essential nature. Merely to perceive goodness, generosity of spirit, and love means to be in some way in tune with them, to possess the capacity for them. Cordelia is stubborn. She stands for what she stands for; she refuses to bow to her father's approach to experience. He believes himself entitled to absolute love as well as absolute power, whereas she knows that the former at least is conditional. She grants him what he asks for, if not what he wants – a quantification, along masculine lines, of her feeling for him. It is absurd to find a moral flaw in her.[29] Lear is asking what he has no right to ask: even absolute power is subject to limits. Cordelia is the moral center of the play, its touchstone: she must stand fast.[30]

The consequences of Lear's mistaking the nature of both love and power are predictable. Everyone close to him knows the truth – not just the three sisters, but Kent, Gloucester, and the Fool. Even France, a relative newcomer, senses it. Lear is wrong on every count: Albany and Cornwall do not love him equally; Kent is not trying to challenge his power; his daughters' love cannot be quantified or structured into words. He banishes his loving daughter and his truest subject; he banishes love because it will not and cannot bow to power.

Everything in the play hangs on the first two scenes, not just the plot but the values as well. These scenes are in a different mode from the rest of the play – ritualistic, mythic, like fairy tale. They present an imaginative embodiment of the values of the masculine principle operating in full grandeur and power: from this set of attitudes, all the rest flows inevitably.

To pounce on Lear's guilt or flaw, to see the drama as one of sin leading to punishment, penitence, and (a very questionable) salvation, seems to me to diminish him in a way the play itself refuses to do. For we love Lear not because he is right, or even because he is more sinned against than sinning, but because of the depth of his passion, and the scope of his awareness once it is opened. The same thing is true of Hamlet: the depth of his feeling sweeps us up in him to the point where we do not question his behavior, we overlook certain savage and rash acts. And Othello too, in the depth of his dramatized feeling, takes us with him to the point where half the pity we feel over the murder of Desdemona is for him, not her. The same thing is true of Macbeth; why else do we care about him, if not for the depth and strength of his feelings? The reason – passion critics have the wrong playwright; their standards would make Iago Shakespeare's prime hero.

Lear's blindness to the limits of power, his arrogance in the face of love, is all our blindness, all our arrogance. His roarings about the indifference of nature to human concerns, about human injustice and the illegitimacy of authority, are all our roarings. No one deserves to suffer because they think as their culture thinks: but we all do.

Lear is seduced by a set of cultural assumptions, and by his own act, abandoned by those same assumptions. The same thing happens to Gloucester, and to him too, by words – by Edmund's brilliant, Iago-like speech, by the forged letter. How can it be that Gloucester does not know his sons better, that he does not deal directly with Edgar? At the root of such blindness lies power itself.

Lear is so unaware of the difference between political and personal power that he imagines he will be treated like a king after he has divested himself of the kingship. Gloucester is so jealous of his power, so frightened of losing it, that he is easily tricked; he panics. But like Lear, Gloucester has two sides. One is like Edmund, who will later treat his father with a callousness that is a savage imitation of Gloucester's callousness towards him. Edmund's furious hate for his father is similar to Gloucester's furious (and instantaneous) hatred for Edgar. The other side is like Edgar, the legitimate son, who is capable of compassion and pity, and who, in a parallel course to his father and Lear, grows and learns in the course of the tragedy.

Several elements in the play extend its implications, broaden its scope, so that it becomes not just the story of a king who disinherited himself by not understanding the nature of love, but suggests the consequences of such cultural tendencies for the society as a whole. Among these elements are Edgar's avatars, which will be discussed later, and the entire socioeconomic theme. Mere exposure to naked nature arouses pity in Lear's heart for his Fool; sending the man into the hovel first, he suddenly feels pity for a whole class of humans, the 'poor naked wretches' of the earth. Gloucester has a similar awakening right after he is blinded and set on the road to Dover: he tells a poor man who tries to help him:

> That I am wretched
> Makes thee the happier; heavens, deal so still!
> Let the superfluous and lust-dieted man,
> That slaves your ordinance, that will not see
> Because he does not feel, feel your pow'r quickly;
> So distribution should undo excess,
> And each man have enough.
>
> (IV, i, 65–71)

Lear's speeches outside Dover are a final heartbroken recognition that human arrangements supposedly based on 'natural law' – which imposes hierarchy and legitimacy – and supposedly sanctified by political and religious ceremony, are in fact nothing more than power grabbing and the imposition of an unequal standard of judgment. Dressed in a natural crown, every inch a king now, Lear acknowledges that he is not 'ague-proof', that power can vanquish mortality as little as it can command the elements, and that costume alone divides what the world calls good and evil. Without the ability to see, which both the mad King and the blind Gloucester now have, without sensitivity, power can tolerate love only as possession, and cannot create justice. (Thus too Othello, who listens to Iago's 'reason' but not to Desdemona's unspoken love, which is evident to the eye, to the senses, to the emotions.)

By the time Lear is captured by Cordelia's followers, a set of qualities has been rejected as being essentially human: power-in-the-world, hierarchy, status, legitimacy, right, law and order, control and 'reason'. The rejection of so many items that are part of the masculine principle, however, is not a rejection of that principle itself. Indeed, the masculine principle *cannot be rejected*. Its association with humanness is profound: human minds work through structure and permanencies; human civilization is based on these. (The feminine principle can be rejected and even largely eradicated; although this results in a nightmare world, and leads to the destruction of a society from the inside, it has been done on earth many times and within recent history.) What is rejected in *Lear* is the *pretense* implicit within 'masculine' standards – the pretense that some people are entitled to rank or property or rights, and others are not.

This challenge to the hierarchical structure of the sixteenth century is offered repeatedly. It is implicit in the many versions of Falls of Princes so popular before as well as during the Renaissance, it is implicit in the pastorals. Shakespeare, however, works not by moralizing about how even the highest fall, or how life is more pleasant on a shepherd's hillside, but by showing the consequences of belief in 'masculine' legitimacy as they might occur in a given society. In *Lear*, this kind of thinking destroys not just the legitimate, but everyone, or nearly everyone; it destroys the inlaw feminine principle along with its outlaw aspect. There is no question of watching the operation of justice; rather what we watch is an inevitable set of events that stand in comment on human arrangements.

There is difficulty in separating reason from passion in the characters. Lear speaks most reason at the height of a mad passion; except for their feelings for Edmund, Goneril and Regan are eminently reasonable.[31] Edmund is reasonable all the way through, given his assumptions at the beginning, until, dying with the realization that he *was* loved, he makes a gesture of love from which he has nothing to gain. Reasonableness, that is, worldly human logic, is the burden of the Fool's messages to Lear, although his behavior – his loyalty and affection – undercuts those messages even as he delivers them. And no one, no one at all, has control, although the blind King of the first scenes, and Goneril and Regan later, imagine they do.

So far, we have itemized that which is not of the essence of humanness. It is necessary now to attempt to define what is essentially human. One thing the play insists upon is human connection with nature, and to define what is human, it is necessary to examine the treatment of nature.

Nature is both benevolent and malevolent, and there is no clear distinction between those aspects. Animal, plant, and element imagery are used to describe the viciousness of Goneril, but also to articulate Lear's sufferings. Moreover, the same animals – especially bear, wolf, and dog – are used to suggest very different things. Thus, Lear says he was flattered like a dog, and Cordelia says, in tears, 'Mine enemy's dog, / Though he had bit me, should have stood that night / Against my fire' (IV, vii, 35–7). Natural imagery is used to express the entire gamut of human experience. It describes human feelings, vices, and situations. Nature oppresses humans and animals, and sustains them – clothing, curing, and feeding them (however loathsomely in Tom's description).

Animals are images of natural amorality, human absurdity, human lowliness, and insignificance.[32] Penury, Edgar says, brings man 'near to beast' (II, iii, 9); Lear concurs: 'Allow not nature more than nature needs, / Man's life is cheap as beast's' (II, iv, 266–7). Yet the King prefers to be 'a comrade with the wolf and owl' (II, iv, 210) rather than bow to his daughters' conditions. The Fool claims that horses, dogs, bears, monkeys, and men all get or deserve confinement, and compares his treatment at the hands of those in power with that of a male dog; he compares Goneril to a *brach*, a bitch dog. Albany compares the relation between parent and child to the trunk and branches of a tree, finding it organic, indissoluble. Lear wonders how life can go on, dogs, horses, and rats breathing, when Cordelia is not.

At the core is Lear's discovery that man is no more than 'a poor bare, fork'd animal', and his attempt to remove his clothes in recognition of this truth: 'Come, unbutton here' (III, iv, 107–8). His last words echo the same awareness: 'Pray you undo this button' (V, iii, 310), thus suggesting that this truth is the enduring one, the ultimate one.

Thus, humans and nature are part of a continuum. Nature is a warehouse for human expression: natural imagery can serve to express any human experience and much human experience is identical to that of other animals and plants. The rain wets the wolf along with the King; a tree is an organic unit like a family.

But the nature that dominates *Lear* is completely different from the friendly green worlds of the comedies. It is harsh and violent, a dimension of cataclysms, of ugly, deformed creatures whose entire existence seems to be devoted to poisoning or maiming life, and hideous animals and plants that serve for loathsome but necessary food. Nature in *Lear* is like that in *Timon*, predatory, cruel, and hostile to human life.

To depict nature as hostile to human life, however, is to suggest that humans are *not* part of nature, that they are a transplant, a foreign body which the planet seeks to reject. The two perceptions – that humans are intrinsically part of nature and that they are foreign to it – work throughout the play until the reuniting of Lear and Cordelia. The two ideas do not clash with each other: they coexist.

Presumably, the pain and peril nature offers humans were responsible for the earliest attempts to control, dominate it. But it is not in efforts to control nature – or delusions of control – that Shakespeare locates the specifically human. It is almost as if the playwright were explicitly challenging the traditional formula.[33] He emphasizes the absurdity of notions of control as Lear tries to command the elements, calls them his *ministers*, and strives against a storm that engenders natural fear in bear, lion, and 'belly-pinch'd wolf' (III, i, 13), in all 'the very wanderers of the dark' (III, ii, 44).

Mad and grand as Lear seems in this scene, he is behaving exactly as he behaved at court, arrogantly assuming that he can control human nature – feeling and behavior. *King Lear* is Shakespeare's most profound repudiation of the morality that has governed the Western world for millenia – a morality of power and control based on the relation of man to nature. The tragedy presents an agonizing picture of the consequences of such a morality.

What Shakespeare offers as the ground of humanness, as that which makes us *not* part of nature, makes us aliens in our home, is a morality based on sensitivity and responsiveness, on seeing and feeling others, on cooperation with nature which, even as it sets us off from the savage nature of the play, decreases our alienation. And power is utterly an impediment to this.

Cordelia's crime in the court is that she is not swayed by the desire for power and possession into falsifying her feelings: she does not feed Lear's delusion of control. Nor does Kent. Both are therefore deprived of power and possession, the real goods of their society, as the Fool continually reminds Lear. But the Fool, in despair, Kent, with firm confidence, and Cordelia, sorrowfully, hold to another good, another truth.

Lear is not the only one who has been blinded by power. Gloucester must be literally blinded before he can emotionally *see*. In order to see, he says, one must feel. But power is a bulwark against feelings. Powerless, Lear learns to see, and to feel, and thus to risk madness.

The turbulence of nature, its dangerous cliffs and storms, recedes from the scene when Cordelia prays to nature to grant her its benison, herbs to cure her disturbed father. Lear and Gloucester meet on a peaceful field, Lear adorned with plants and flowers, crowned with a natural crown, every inch a king. The two men speak 'feelingly', seeing. Cordelia, the incarnation of the inlaw feminine principle, 'redeems nature from the general curse' (IV, vi, 205) by standing for, insisting upon, values that have little to do with control. She offers her tears to water the earth from which 'blest secrets' (IV, iv, 15) grow. And when she is reunited with her father, there is music and radiance, harmony and light, as if the sun had finally come out again.

I said at the outset that in *Lear*, Shakespeare probed beneath the gender divisions to examine the division – man and nature – that lies beneath. This is not to say, however, that gender divisions do not exist in the play. They do, and are extremely important on the subsurface of the tragedy.

On the surface, gender roles are blurred. Goneril is a better soldier than her husband; both she and Regan are assertive, nonnutritive, uncompassionate, interested in power, prowess, and status. Regan performs an act unique in Shakespeare: she kills, in her own person, with a sword. Goneril kills, too, but in a 'woman's' fashion – with poison, and offstage. Both sisters act rather than feel, and move to gain what they want in both the public and personal spheres. They are 'masculine'.

On the other hand, Albany and Edgar are largely 'feminine'. Goneril reproaches Albany for 'milky gentleness' (I, iv, 341), and it is Albany who conceives of a family (or society) as organically linked. He also attempts, somewhat feebly, to create harmony between his wife and her father. Edgar's roles in the play involve considerable nutritive and supportive behavior, and from the time he meets Lear until near the end of the play he is locked into the role of suffering witness. Both men are in some sense illegitimate: Albany because Goneril can dominate him, and thus discount him; Edgar because he is hunted and without resources.

Gloucester and the Fool become 'feminine' as they fall into being total outsiders. (The Fool has always been illegitimate to some degree.) Suffering and social illegitimacy invariably bring out the 'feminine' qualities of people who have any (Coriolanus and Timon, for instance, do not).

At the beginning of the play, Edmund sounds like a representative of the outlaw feminine principle. He seems to want to topple masculine structures; he conceives of 'Nature' as vitality and verve. But he is not really outlaw feminine. He repudiates codes, laws, and hierarchy only because there is no legitimate place for him within them. He rebels, not in hopeless despair and rage about structures that are foreign to his spirit, but in an attempt to usurp a place within them – as, indeed, he does.[34] He is willing to dally with unregulated sexuality. Since he apparently offers affection to Regan as well as Goneril, it is unclear to what degree he loves either sister, although he takes deep pleasure in being loved. What he wants above all, however, is power. The three characters – Edmund, Goneril, and Regan – are not only 'masculine' but there are abusers of both principles. They are willing to kill in unsanctioned ways; they are willing to engage in unsanctioned forms of sex.

Lear moves from 'masculinity' to 'femininity'. In the opening scene, dressed in majesty, he stands on power and banishes love. For the next act and a half, he roars and rages, but begins, little by little, to cry. And then he learns to see, to feel. He opens his mind to others – to the poor, to his Fool's shivering, to the necessities by which all humans are bound. By the time he meets Gloucester on the heath, he has discovered that pomp, status, and authority are charades designed to hide us from ourselves. By the time he and Cordelia are captured, he is no longer concerned with power-in-the-world, or with revenge. He cares only about the quality of life, choosing to sing in the prison that is life, enjoying the day, savoring the 'mystery of things' (V, iii, 16).

Gloucester, a parallel to Lear in terms of values as well as in the plot, also stands on power and banishes love. But his love for Lear and his sense of human decency are strong enough to make him, frightened as he is, challenge power when he believes it has gone beyond the pale. Through his ordeal, he too learns to see 'feelingly', and thus becomes 'feminine', like the King.

Cordelia, of course, represents the inlaw feminine principle at its most saintly, supporting and protecting even when she has been hurt. She is constant and sensitive – she knows her sisters' natures, Edgar does not know Edmund's. Her qualities can 'redeem' Lear's sufferings but they cannot sustain her in the world. Cordelian natures get destroyed.

At the penultimate moment of the play, Lear seems very large indeed. He has seen through the self-delusion of 'masculine' definitions of the human, and has endured his 'feminine' suffering. He remains 'masculine': he does not drown in guilt, he retains will, he retains prowess enough to kill Cordelia's killer. He remains 'feminine' in that he renounces power-in-the-world, and desires only felicity, love, harmony. He has achieved full humanness. But this achievement required Cordelia. His 'madness' in the field outside Dover is not really madness at all: it is thwarted wholeness, perception of the delusions in society without a complementary fullness of pleasure in other things. Without Cordelia, Lear would remain in bitter cynicism.

Thus, the play suggests (again) that a chaste constant woman is necessary to transform a legitimate man into an integrated man. One critic has taken this need of Lear's as another example of incestuous feeling in a Shakespearean father.[35] But this emphasis on chaste constancy in women occurs in plays in which fathers are not very important. It is a requirement in many plays, not just for a father, or a husband, but as the cornerstone of a harmonious society.

Thus, beneath the surface, gender roles are absolute, but only for women. Men's behavior matters: an unpunished Cornwall provides a bad example for his inferiors; Lear's blind insensitivity creates a horror for him and war for his kingdom. Abuse of the masculine principle consists essentially in the refusal of males to center themselves in the feminine principle. This is one reason for the importance of chaste constancy: women must be above reproach so that men may depend upon them utterly, may trust them, may reliably serve the inlaw qualities they represent.

Men's behavior matters. But women's behavior is of the essence. Cordelia 'redeems nature from the general curse / Which *twain* have brought her to' (my italics). That *twain* are, of course, Goneril and Regan. Cordelia redeems nature; Goneril and Regan are responsible for its 'curse'. In the rhetoric of the play, no male is condemned as Goneril is condemned. A woman who refuses to uphold the inlaw feminine principle completely topples the natural order and plunges the world into chaos.

The three major villains – Goneril, Regan, and Edmund – are, if we can quantify such a thing, about equal in cruelty to their parents, about equal in ambition and ruthlessness. Cornwall and Regan blind Gloucester; Edmund orders Cordelia's (and Lear's) murder; and all three are willing to be sexual in an unregulated way. Goneril is unyielding to her father, suggests the blinding of Gloucester, and murders Regan. It is hard to select a *worst* from among them. Yet the judgments passed on the rhetorical level of the play are very unequal.

Gloucester, upon hearing that Edgar is (supposedly) planning to murder him, cries out: 'villain! ... Abhorred villain! unnatural, detested, brutish villain! worse than brutish!' (I, ii, 75–7). Rebellion of a son against a father is both associated with nature (brutish) and separated from nature (unnatural), in line with the double strand of attitudes towards nature that inform the play. Gloucester's next decision is 'I never got him.' The import of all of this is that Edgar is *illegitimate* – by birth (Gloucester's wife was an adulterer), in rank (he is villain, not noble; *villain* is, of course, what Hamlet calls Claudius also), and in his morals (parricide is unnatural).

Except for the comments in the first scene which slur Edmund (as well as his mother) as a *whore*son, he is not vilified by Gloucester, not even when the Earl learns the truth. At the conclusion, Albany charges Edmund with capital treason. This is a questionable charge, since he led Goneril's forces, and she was one of the constituted rulers. But it serves the time. Edgar accuses his brother of being 'a most toad-spotted traitor' (V, iii, 139). All of Edmund's horrors, then, are subsumed in this ethical term: he is a traitor.

Regan receives little verbal abuse within the play. That is reserved for Goneril, and she is abused violently, savagely, long before she does anything that can be called worse than ungrateful, unkind, and unloving. The moment she does not defer to Lear's authority and will, he calls her 'degenerate bastard' (I, iv, 254), 'detested kite' (I, iv, 262), and wishes hideous punishments upon her. He says her visage is 'wolvish' (I, iv, 308), that she is 'serpentlike' and a 'disease' (II, iv, 161, 222) in his flesh. Albany too attacks her: 'Proper deformity shows not in the fiend / So horrid as in woman' (IV, ii, 60–1). 'Howe'er thou art a fiend, / A woman's shape doth shield thee' (IV, ii, 66–7). Finally, as the sisters attack each other, Albany contrasts Goneril and Edmund: Edmund is a traitor; Goneril is a 'gilded serpent', 'monstrous' (V, iii, 84, 160).

All three characters are guilty of similar acts. Why should the judgments on them be so different? Why should Goneril bear the weight of the rhetorical condemnation of the play to such a degree that Bradley questioned whether one could even call her human?[36]

Abuse of the masculine principle was an unethical act for Shakespeare. Abuse consisted mainly in two acts of blindness: one is the forgetting of true ends – protection and fostering of the feminine principle. When true ends are forgotten, power becomes its own end and men are deluded into believing they have control over others, over nature, over their own destinies. The second is blindness to human (natural) arrangements, and thus to confusing the power of position with personal power. This leads to the deluded belief that one has an inherent right to certain prerogatives, when in fact the right to those prerogatives adheres to a particular step in the ladder of legitimacy.

Shakespeare's ideas about the masculine principle make sense. They are comprehensible in logical, realistic terms. So is the cure he urges in play after play – that men assimilate the feminine principle into themselves, remind themselves continually of the qualities power is designed to sustain. This is not true of his ideas – feelings, really – about the feminine principle. The inlaw aspect, separated from its vital, sustaining roots, seems to him almost divine. It is perfection on earth, it is the incarnation of Jesus' message (if not of the messages the churches incarnate). Inherent within it, however, is the fact that it cannot protect itself, that it must *be* protected. If it attempts to use worldly force, it loses its character and its saintliness. When it is seen for what it is, and cherished, it confers harmonious joy and radiance on the world around it.

But when women (and it must be women) do not uphold the inlaw aspect, when they attempt to move into 'masculine' power and control, as do Goneril and Regan, they do not threaten the world in the way males do. They do not arouse fear of tyranny or execution or defeat in battle. Rather they emit a hideous stink of sexual pollution that is felt to be contaminating, soul-destroying, and overwhelmingly powerful for *men*. This is true in the first tetralogy, in *Hamlet, Othello,* and *Lear*. (It is not true in *Coriolanus*, probably because Volumnia attempts to control only her son, not the respublica itself.) Women, locked into the feminine principle, cannot abuse 'masculine' qualities, cannot even have 'masculine' qualities. When they abuse the inlaw aspect, they fall into the outlaw aspect of the feminine principle. Women's misdeeds, regardless of the dimension in which they occur, are always interpreted as *fiendish* (superhumanly evil), as participating in the worst ugliness and terrors of nature, and as sexual – sexuality being seen as loathsome, disgusting.

If on the one hand the thing that divides humans from nature is the set of qualities Cordelia embodies, an inlaw feminine morality, on the other, what divides the human from nature is a pair of negatives. These annul, or regulate, the extremes of the gender principles. On the 'masculine' side, based on the ability to kill, killing is regulated: it may be performed only in sanctified ways, that is, in war, or under the aegis of the state (to which the Church gives its sanction). On the 'feminine' side, based on the ability to give birth, sex is regulated and may be performed only between a married woman and man, marriage being sanctioned by both the state and the Church. But for Shakespeare, a woman who attempts to move into the masculine principle violates the *feminine*. Thus, unregulated sexuality is her sin, whether it is or not.

One of the things that most crucially divides humans from animals is this attitude towards sex. This is not stated in the play; it is implicit, but all the more powerful for that. Only the characters plainly marked evil show any manifestations of sexuality – Goneril, Regan, Edmund, and perhaps Oswald. Edgar, in a moment of mean-minded moralization, asserts that 'the dark and vicious place' where Gloucester conceived Edmund has now justly, in retribution, cost him his eyes. As Tom o' Bedlam, he concentrates most on desire as the vice that now torments him with guilt. The Fool mentions sexual 'vice' continually, although there are no sexual events occurring in the play at the time. Both Lear and Gloucester, confronted with real or apparent betrayal in their children, leap to the conclusion that their wives were adulterers.

Finally, in the field near Dover, looking anew at nature, Lear finds it essentially copulative. If copulation is natural, he reasons, adultery should not be condemned, whores should not be whipped, especially since those whipping them are guilty of desire too. His tone is meditative, even kindly: 'The wren goes to't, and the small gilded fly / Does lecher in my sight', until memory hits him, and he mutters bitterly, 'Gloucester's bastard son / Was kinder to his father than my daughters' (IV, vi, 111–13; 114–15). This memory returns him to human, as opposed to animal, sexuality, and he roars in outraged abhorrence about female sexuality, which he sees as bestial, hypocritical, and demonic: hell, darkness, and 'the sulphurous pit' (IV, vi, 128), which in this context becomes a metaphor for the vagina as well as for eternal damnation.[37]

Sex is not logically connected to the events of the play. The sexuality of Goneril, Regan, and Edmund is not fundamental in their treatment of their fathers. Nevertheless, it is woven deeply into the texture of the play, through image, allusion, and rhetoric, as if it were somehow associated with its events.[38]

Inevitably, then, there is also a strain of misogyny in the play. Misogyny invariably accompanies sexual disgust. Many of the Fool's jokes are misogynistic, Edgar is misogynistic when he reads Goneril's letter to Edmund and exclaims, 'O indistinguish'd space of woman's will!' in a parallel movement to Hamlet's when he generalizes his mother's inconstancy to name woman as frail. This generalization is most emphatic in Lear's outburst in the field. There is no event that triggers his outburst. He cannot know about his daughters' desire for Edmund and the only other sexual irregularity in the tragedy is Gloucester's. Yet he roars: 'Down from the waist they are Centaurs, / Though women all above; / But to the girdle do the gods inherit, / Beneath is all the fiends" (IV, vi, 124–7).

This association of powerful (in a worldly sense) women with a sexuality felt to be abhorrent and terrifying is characteristically Shakespearean. Both Spenser and Sidney create female figures who are openly sexual and have some worldly power, but more often than not, they are comic, if also clearly deviant. Moreover, the association of women and power with filthy sexuality does not pervade their work. Duessa is singular in *The Faerie Queene*. And if the image, the emblem, of Duessa is (at the end) of a woman with filthy clotted underparts, her pollution is not sexual but intellectual: she leads the Redcrosse Knight from the one true God and the one true way into duality, duplicity, and errors of thought and belief.

Sexual abhorrence pervades Shakespeare's work and informs some of his most powerful writing. One could, I suppose, psychologize about the man. But this abhorrence is a cultural fact, and still exists – in the United States, today, it is found mainly among people who were raised in strict patriarchal churches. Discussion of the development and significance of such an attitude is out of place here and will be taken up elsewhere.

Here it must suffice to point to the sexual theme, to the consistently vile natural imagery Lear uses to assault Goneril, and to the rhetorical line of the play which implicitly lays on Goneril the blame for all the disorders of Lear's Britain. The power given Cordelia to redeem, like the power given to Mary, is balanced by the power given Goneril to damn, like the power given to Eve.[39] Since in actuality, women have neither sort of power, we must view these figures as symbolic, as references to parts of the self in disharmony, divided by a faulty conception of experience.

The rhetorical line of *King Lear* is enormously strong, so strong that it prevents any reading other than the moral direction given by it. Robert Lowell, in a Harvard seminar on Shakespeare, once shocked the class into silence by suggesting that maybe Goneril and Regan were right, maybe Lear's knights were rowdy and lecherous drunkards, and *were* disturbing the house. There are items which, if developed or described differently, would paint Goneril, Regan, and Edmund in slightly less vile colors, would offer at least ambivalence. There does seem to be love between Goneril and Edmund; his dying joy at realizing he was loved casts a pathetic light on his life until then. Oswald is as loyal to Goneril as Kent is to Lear.[40]

Lear at the opening is arrogant, rash, and wilful; it is clear Cordelia has been his favorite, but he banishes her. How, then, has he treated Goneril and Regan all these years? Can their dislike for him be extenuated? Gloucester turns swiftly against Edgar, on minimal proof: what kind of father has he been all these years? Kent is loyal, but he is also pugnacious and trigger-happy. Lear's threats, offered at the slightest resistance to his will, are out of bounds.

But these questions are not permitted within the terms of the play. They cannot even be built subtly into a production of the play without violating its text. The rhetoric of *Lear*, unlike that of *Richard III*, does not rest with one major figure who damns himself, and a lamenting chorus of women who damn him also. It is woven in, line by line, and its import is unmistakable. Except for Lear and Gloucester, who err and suffer and grow, who provide the human level of the play, the remaining characters are divided almost instantly into the utterly good and the utterly evil.

What differentiates man from nature is his attempt to regulate both men and nature, the extremes of the two gender principles. Edgar, disguised as Tom o' Bedlam, *becomes* Tom o' Bedlam. A shivering, naked wretch, he is the bare forked animal of Lear's sudden recognition. But, part of nature, he is apart from nature. His physical sufferings are less than his psychological torment. Tom's catalogue of sins defines man as the guilty animal. And of the vices he lists, the one most emphasized is sexuality – desire and fornication, seen as filth. The second most emphasized is 'pride', the kind of pride that believes ermine, civet, or a feathered hat confer on man a superiority not only to nature but other men as well, transform one into a controlling god.

These 'vices' are also the foci of Lear's brilliant rage in the field outside Dover. Lear himself is, of all the characters, most guilty of the kind of pride that is really blindness; an unspecified 'they', women in general, are guilty of the sin of sexuality. But because the point of view of the play resides with Lear, because we see him suffer (his suffering and Gloucester's merge to become one single human agony), his 'sin' seems somehow less onerous than that of women, of Goneril and Regan, of nature itself.

It is vice that sets the human off from the animal. Inlaw feminine virtues like Cordelia's are in harmony with nature, are privy to nature's blest secrets. But humans, not animals are proud. Of all the animals, only humans flatter. In an effort to control (manipulate) the powerful, flatterers blind them as Lear was blinded. And only humans murder (as opposed to kill). In *Lear* and *Macbeth*, the ability to murder is seen as distinctively human. In a line reminiscent of *Macbeth*, the Captain accepts Edmund's commission to murder Cordelia and Lear with these words: 'I cannot draw a cart, nor eat dried oats, / If it be man's work, I'll do't' (V, iii, 38–9).

A few final words about Edgar. He is a complex figure and difficult to grasp. But his complexities are all on the surface; he is not profoundly complex, like Lear. Edmund calls him 'noble', and we accept the judgment, although he is a rather narrowly moralistic character.

As himself, in the opening of the play, he is easily duped by his brother, whom he seems to trust. He does *not* trust his father: it does not occur to him to try to speak to the Earl, to repair the damage. He is accurate in his estimate of his parent, at least.

He races to exile, like many characters in the comedies, but unlike them, he finds no Arden but a barren, frozen nature. His physical misery is exacerbated by his psychological misery, as he becomes Tom o' Bedlam. The exiles of Lear and Gloucester are also to nature, but lead the two older men to illumination about themselves and the world's arrangements. Edgar's leads him to a hell of guilt which illuminates little or nothing about himself, but rather offers an embroidery, a restatement of the themes of the play. His 'mad' ravings present the guilt-ridden psychological dimension of the abuses performed by other characters. Thus, as mad Tom, Edgar is not himself but a testifier about the world around him.

But Edgar has many other roles to play. From Tom, the lowest possible member of his society, he becomes a Tom who is possessed of some wit and is able to lead Gloucester. In time he becomes a peasant, in which guise he convinces his father that he has survived a fall from Dover cliff, and overhears Gloucester and Lear in 'mad' conversation. Then he becomes a rustic, in which guise he saves his father and kills Oswald. Finally, he appears as an unknown knight, in which guise he kills Edmund, presently the legitimate Earl of Gloucester. And at the end, Edgar is fully legitimate once more, the new Earl of Gloucester.

Because he is victimized from the outset, he is a contrast to Lear and Gloucester, whose trials come later. Edgar *begins* at the bottom; they begin at the top. But as the powerful plunge swiftly to the bottom, Edgar begins to climb upward. His progress, then, is from illegitimacy to legitimacy, from helpless victimization to power-in-the-world. The implication is that his education in illegitimacy and sorrow will make him worthy of his worldly privilege.

Schematically, this all makes sense. But Edgar makes less sense as a character in the play. Although his main action in the tragedy is to preserve his father, his disguises actually prolong the old man's suffering. There are, of course, good dramatic reasons for this: a reconciliation between Edgar and Gloucester would dramatically undercut that between Cordelia and Lear. The one anagnorisis subsumes the other. Nevertheless, psychologically, Edgar as character is as opaque as the Duke in *Measure for Measure*. He does not function as a son to Gloucester in the scenes in which he leads him. He functions rather as a suffering witness.

And this, it seems to me, is his true role in the drama. He is not so much a character as a composite. He does not have a palpably consistent personality, as most of Shakespeare's disguised characters do – Kent, for instance, is the same man, in disguise or out.

Edgar is a composite of witnesses to events. Like Cornwall's disgusted servants, who watch the behavior of their 'betters' and judge the moral nature of their world accordingly, Edgar watches, thinks, and feels. He sees Lear in the hovel, sees him mad with his Fool, hiding in Gloucester's house. He sees the blinded Earl, recognizes Oswald's – and Goneril's – moral characters, watches the two old men together in the field outside Dover. Finally, he acts, killing Edmund, but his watching is not over. With us, he must endure the bitter finale, the dead Cordelia in the old King's arms, the agony of the 'promised end'.

By the end of the play, Edgar has become a composite figure of illegitimate men in his culture, people who are not blinded by power, who learn to set aside narrow piety in order to see and feel and to support human decency to the limits of their power. He becomes a male parallel to Cordelia. He acts; she is. He does not possess her magical powers of healing, but he is able to fight and to kill. He personifies the quiet, unrecognized will to decency that exists in every people, every nation, as she represents the loving, constant devotion that exists in every nation, every people – in whatever proportions in individuals.

After his restoration to legitimacy, Albany tries to reorder the kingdom, but Edgar ignores this. He is concerned only with the dying King and the suffering he has witnessed (no matter how the last four lines are attributed). Albany's concern with the rule of the kingdom sounds shallow and unfeeling given the situation – the old King in despair hovering over his child's dead body. Of all the characters, Albany is readiest to find divine retribution in the events that have occurred, but we know that he has been least exposed to the horrors, and has participated least in agony. Nevertheless, his response to the sight of Lear and Cordelia diminishes him.

If I were mounting a production of *King Lear*, I would, in this final scene, slowly surround Edgar with figures like those he has impersonated, suggesting the sturdy will to decency and humaneness that is found in every community. Edgar in all his avatars should outnumber Albany at the end of this tragedy.

Macbeth

Macbeth presents another world in which the feminine principle is devalued, but in this case we see the action from the point of view of a legitimate male who gains, in a worldly way, from that devaluation. Iago seems to do the same, but in fact he derives no pleasure from all of Roderigo's money, or from getting Cassio's place. Pleasure is not possible for him. But Macbeth really wants to be king, he has thought about it and seems to have anticipated the succession being placed upon him. And he moves into the kingship with energy and firmness, at first.

This play is not about ambition *per se*; it is about giving up certain things for others, sacrificing seemingly unnecessary values in the course of achieving an ambition. The play is an envisioning of the consequences to a man and to his culture of casting certain values aside. In one way, *Macbeth* is more subtle than *Othello* or *Lear*: Macbeth does not dramatize his feelings as Othello does, or roar them out, as Lear does. His sufferings must be suggested by gesture as well as intonation, and understanding of the play is dependent very much on audience perception of his emotional loss and deprivation.

There is an ambiguity about gender roles in *Macbeth* as there is in *Lear*, but here it is the keynote of the play, the 'myth' from which everything else springs (as in *Lear*, the values implicit in the opening dialogue and the division of the kingdom are the 'myth'; and, as in *Othello*, the opening scene, with its clear contempt for 'feminine' values, provides the 'myth'). This ambiguity is embodied in the Witches, who open the tragedy. Their chant, 'Fair is foul, and foul is fair', is a legend of moral and aesthetic ambiguity, but the Witches themselves incarnate ambiguity of gender. They are female, but have beards; they are aggressive and authoritative, but seem to have power only to create petty mischief. Their persons, their activities, and their song serve to link ambiguity about gender to moral ambiguity.[41]

The reason ambiguity of gender is an element in the play is that Shakespeare did indeed associate certain qualities with the two genders. Perhaps he was shocked, and his imagination triggered by a passage in Holinshed describing women in Scotland fighting with hardiness, courage, and unshrinking bloodthirstiness.[42] But he makes Macbeth's Scotland a world of what seems to be constant war, that is, a 'heroic' culture. In such worlds, the felicities of life must be put aside, and procreation is tenuous: the means by which life is sustained become all important. His sense of such worlds is demonstrated in IV, iii, when Macduff tries to convince Malcolm to raise an army and oppose Macbeth. He tells Malcolm 'Each new morn / New widows howl, new orphans cry.' Ross alludes to depredation of the feminine principle: Scotland 'cannot be called our mother, but our grave.' Malcolm's presence in the country, he says, 'would create new soldiers, make our women fight' (IV, iii, 165–6, 178). In 'heroic' worlds, women must become as men, and the loss such a situation entails to the culture at large is the subject of the tragedy.

The world of Scotland is one of blood and brutality. Indeed, the first human words of the play are 'What bloody man is that?' The answer describes the hero, Macbeth:

Disdaining Fortune, with his brandish'd steel,
Which smok'd with bloody execution,
Like valour's minion carv'd out his passage
Till he fac'd the slave;
Which nev'r shook hands, nor bade farewell to him,
Till he unseam'd him from the nave to th' chops,
And fix'd his head upon our battlements

(I, ii, 17–23)

Such a description might shock and appall an audience, might imply that the hero is not totally admirable, if not for the fact that we hear only praise for Macbeth. He is 'brave Macbeth', 'valour's minion', 'valiant cousin', and 'worthy gentleman'. Most of the praise comes from Duncan, the King, the authority figure. The Sergeant's hideous description of the fighters' motivations: 'Except they meant to bathe in reeking wounds, / Or memorize another Golgotha, / I cannot tell', reaps only more praise and reward. [43]

At the conclusion of this tragedy, we accept without demur the judgment that Macbeth is a butcher. In fact, however, he is no more a butcher at the end than he is at the beginning. Macbeth lives in a culture that values butchery. Throughout the play manhood is equated with the ability to kill. Power is the highest value in Scotland, and in Scottish culture, power is military prowess. Macbeth's crime is not that he is a murderer: he is praised and rewarded for being a murderer. His crime is a failure to make the distinction his culture expects among the objects of his slaughter.

A world that maintains itself by violence must, for the sake of sanity, fence off some segment – family, the block, the neighborhood, the state – within which violence is not the proper mode of action. In this 'civilized' segment of the world, law, custom, hierarchy, and tradition are supposed to supersede the right of might. Although this inner circle is no more 'natural' or 'unnatural' than the outer one (so far as we can judge – some people believe that aggression is profoundly 'natural' to humankind; I believe humans are basically timorous, and that aggression is forcibly taught, learned under duress; neither position, however, can be proven), the play insists that the inner world is bound in accordance with a principle of nature which is equivalent to a divine law.[44]

From the perspective of this study, the inner world is one which harmonizes the two gender principles. Ruled by law, inherited legitimacy, hierarchy, and rights of ownership, the inner world also demands a degree of subordination in all its members. Everyone, including the ruler, must relinquish some worldly power (increasingly as one goes down the social scale) in favor of the good of the whole, if felicity and an environment favorable to procreation is to exist. Those with great power must restrain it; those without power must accept their places gracefully. Without such relinquishment, felicities like friendship, ceremony, orderly succession, peaceful love, hospitality, pleasure, and even the ability to sleep at night become difficult or impossible.[45] An essential condition of this inviolable segment of the world is that the laws bind by themselves. They are not enforceable because enforcement is part of the larger outer sphere, the violent world. If the laws of the inner world must be enforced, that world becomes identical with the outer one. The laws therefore exist only insofar as the members of the group abide by them. Macbeth chooses to break the rules.

The factor responsible for Macbeth's doing so is Lady Macbeth. Although it is clear that Macbeth has, before the opening of the play, considered taking over the kingdom by force, it is also clear from his hesitation that he could easily be dissuaded from killing Duncan. And within the feminine/masculine polarity of morals and roles in Shakespeare's division of experience, it is Lady Macbeth's function so to dissuade him. But Lady Macbeth, a powerful person, is drawn to the role in which worldly power resides. She seems to be, by the world's standards, an exemplary wife.[46] She encourages and supports her husband in good wifely fashion; she does not undermine him; she sees, knows, and understands the terms of the world she lives in, and she accepts them.

Yet at the end of the play, when her husband earns the attribute of 'butcher', she, who has not personally performed acts of violence, is called 'fiend-like'. In Shakespeare's eyes, Macbeth has violated moral law; Lady Macbeth has violated natural law.[47] Her reasoning, in urging Macbeth to the murder, is not unlike that of MacDonwald: he is called *traitor* and *slave*. Both of these terms refer to the ethical world of legitimacy: one suggests resistance to the currently constituted authority; the other insists on illegitimacy. But Lady Macbeth is not so judged; she is seen as supernaturally evil. Her crime is heinous because it violates her social role, which has been erected into a principle of experience; she fails to uphold the feminine principle. For her, as for Goneril, this failure plunges her more deeply into a pit of evil than any man can ever fall.

The imagery of the play is divided into masculine and feminine categories. Blood and royal robes, symbolic of male prowess, authority, and legitimacy, are opposed to procreative and nourishing images of babies, children, the female breast, and milk. Lady Macbeth informs us of her values at her first appearance: Macbeth, she says, is flawed by being 'too full o' th' milk of human kindness' (I, v, 17). Laid against the view of Macbeth the warrior that we have just been given, this is an astonishing perception. It has less to do with Macbeth, however, than with his lady. She who, in Shakespeare's view, should properly encourage this milky side of her husband, resolves instead to align herself with the male principle, in a passage explicitly connecting gender to role and moral value:

> Come, you spirits
> That tend on mortal thoughts, unsex me here,
> And fill me from the crown to the toe topfull
> Of direst cruelty! ... Come to my woman's breasts,
> And take my milk for gall.
>
> (I, v, 40–8)

In her conversation with Macbeth (I, vii), she argues from a perspective that equates manliness with killing. Macbeth protests: 'I dare do all that may become a man; / Who dares do more is none.' She insists: 'When you durst do it, then you were a man; / And to be more than what you were, you would / Be so much more the man.' The 'it' in question is killing; and manliness, for Lady Macbeth, clearly *excludes* compassion and nurturing:

> I have given suck, and know
> How tender 'tis to love the babe that milks me;
> I would, while it was smiling in my face,
> Have pluck'd my nipple from his boneless gums,
> And dash'd the brains out, had I so sworn as you
> Have done to this.
>
> (I, vii, 54–9)

Both agree that manliness is the highest standard of behavior and what they argue about is what the term comprehends.[48] Macbeth's real problem is that he cannot articulate, even to himself, what is wrong with his wife's logic. He floats in vague dread, a sense of wrongness that seems to him to reverberate to the heavens (although his dread is not specifically Christian or religious – he jumps the life to come with ease), but the values he is obliquely conscious of as being in some impalpable way significant have no currency and therefore no vocabulary in his culture. At the end of their conversation, he accepts his wife's definition of manliness; it is, after all, identical to that of his – and her – culture as a whole.

> Bring forth men-children only!
> For thy undaunted mettle should compose
> Nothing but males
>
> (I, vii, 72–4)

Still, he continues to feel uneasy, and Lady Macbeth, gazing down at the sleeping Duncan,has an intimation that there is something unpleasant about killing a father. Their trepidations heighten our sense that the inner circle, the place where murder is illegitimate, is indeed sacred.

And once the deed is done, Shakespeare suggests that the entire character of the world is changed. When the texture of the inner circle is identical to that of the outer one, the connection between means and ends is broken. Instead of procreation and felicity, the end of power becomes more power alone, consolidation and extension of power: thus, life becomes hell.[49] The porter announces the change, knowing he is in hell even though the place is too cold for it.

In Scotland, the feminine has taken to wearing beards and acting aggressively. Lady Macbeth's renunciation of her role leads to the murder of a king, father, guest. These actions lead to a new ambience, a world in which the feminine principle is being wiped out. That this is a 'natural' calamity is suggested by the 'unnatural' events that follow: an attack on a female falcon by a 'mousing owl'; Duncan's horses 'contending 'gainst obedience' and eating each other. Confusion in human gender roles leads in this play to confusion in the hierarchies of nature, as well as to the destruction of one gender principle – Malcolm and Donalbain flee a kingdom where 'there's no mercy left' (II, iii, 146). Duncan's murder is called a 'breach in nature' (II, iii, 113).

That the consequences of Duncan's murder involve the destruction of particularly women and children has been noted by Matthew Proser: 'the content of the speech in which Macbeth plots the destruction of Lady Macduff and her brood is somewhat reminiscent of the suggestive force of Lady Macbeth's portrait of exemplary valor: the idea of the slaughter of innocents is integral to both'.[50] Another critic asserts 'Macbeth's destructive passion at the end of the play is directed against the innocent, especially women and children, those who hold the promise of the future.'[51]

Dame Helen Gardner ties this slaughter to its larger field. She sees Macbeth's anxiety before the murder of Duncan as a fear 'not that he will be cut down by Macduff, but that having murdered his own humanity he will enter a world of appalling loneliness, of meaningless activity, unloved himself and unable to love.... It is not terror of heaven's vengeance that makes him pause, but the terror of moral isolation.'[52] Having killed his own ends, Macbeth inexorably kills them for others, with the same dogged and mindless tenacity that Don John and Iago show.

The victory of the masculine principle over the feminine is a victory of means over ends, and is an empty victory as a result. The severing of connection between means and ends has consequences for the 'victors' as well as for the victims. And it is this that is ideologically important and unusual about *Macbeth*. The Thane and his wife both know there is none can call their power to account. In a world of power, linear reason, and control, there is no reason *not* to kill Duncan. The King has set the succession elsewhere, although it is Macbeth's arm that holds the country up. Lady Macbeth sees this very clearly. Macbeth, however, dreads the consequences he may unleash. 'If it were done when 'tis done' it would be well, but 'bloody instructions' are lessons to others, and boomerang. Beyond that, there are vague reasons for fear.

Macbeth's fears are justified. For with the eradication of pity, compassion, and 'masculine' codes aimed at 'feminine' ends, the felicities that make Macbeth's life worthwhile vanish. When home becomes part of the war zone, life is merely battle. Macbeth's hypocritical lament over the dead Duncan is ironically prophetic.

> Had I but died an hour before this chance,
> I had liv'd a blessed time; for from this instant
> There's nothing serious in mortality:
> All is but toys: renown and grace is dead,

The wine of life is drawn, and the mere lees
Is left this vault to brag of.

(II, iii, 95–100)

There is another irony in the play. Duncan is almost always seen as saintly: the epithet 'gracious' is continually applied to him. He combines 'masculine' authority with 'feminine' meekness, concern with himself with concern for the whole. He is nutritive: he tells Macbeth 'I have begun to plant thee, and will labor / To make thee full of growing' (I, iv, 28–9). He combines the gender principles; he incarnates harmonious unity. When Macbeth considers the violation the murder of such a man would be, he uses masculine and feminine images:

And pity, like a naked new-born babe,
Striding the blast, or heaven's cherubim, hors'd
Upon the sightless couriers of the air,
Shall blow the horrid deed in every eye,
That tears shall drown the wind

(I, vii, 21–5)

Nevertheless, Duncan participates in the unequal value system of his culture. His grateful approval of the hideous slaughter performed in battle, a slaughter designed after all to ensure *his* continued supremacy, bathes him as well as Macbeth and the other warriors in the blood of 'reeking wounds'. Like Macbeth, Duncan is destroyed by the principle to which he grants priority.[53]

The scenes following his murder swiftly and sharply depict a world gone insane from lack of balance. Murder follows murder until the entire country is a death camp. And the terms used by the characters remain sickenly the same. Macbeth eggs on the hired murderers with the same challenge his wife threw to him.

First Murderer   We are men, my liege.
Macbeth   Ay, in the catalogue ye go for men.

(III, i, 90–1)

True men, he claims, would murder an enemy. And so they prove themselves.

During the scene in which Macbeth is terrified by Banquo's ghost, Lady Macbeth several times turns on her husband contemptuously: 'Are you a man? (III, iv, 57) He is, she says, 'quite unmann'd in folly' (III, iv, 72), and scornfully describes his terror as more suitable to 'a woman's story at a winter's fire, / Authoriz'd by her grandam' (III, iv, 64–5). Macbeth insists 'What man dare, I dare', and argues that only if he were to tremble facing a real enemy could he be called 'the baby of a girl'. When the ghost vanishes, he says 'I am a man again' (III, iv, 98, 105).

In worlds dominated by the masculine principle, the feminine principle is partly scorned, but it is also partly feared. It is, after all, the pole of nature and feeling; it is uncontrollable in its spontaneity and its disregard for power. And most important, as the pole of procreation, it embraces the future. Thus, although Fleance is not logically a threat to Macbeth, it is the child Fleance whom the childless King fears. Why should a childless man worry about who will inherit the kingdom? Macbeth's anxiety is psychologically profound: he flails wildly, trying to secure the ends for which power is supposed to exist – which for him at this point have shrunk to the ability to sleep at night.

The very existence of Fleance prevents Macbeth from feeling secure. Moreover in the Witches' evocations for the tormented King, two infants are central. Cleanth Brooks finds the babe to be 'perhaps the most powerful symbol in the tragedy'.[54] The first baby to appear is bloody, symbolizing Macduff, who, born 'unnaturally' – covered with blood from his mother's caesarian delivery – will perform the ritual act of killing the tyrant. (The implications of this are opaque to me. Perhaps Macduff, not being 'tainted' by having arrived in the world through the female vagina, is 'pure' in a special way, and able to destroy the tyrant. Or perhaps, having been born bloody, he has an imperviousness to certain fears, or a lack of certain delicacies, which make him able to defeat Scotland's greatest warrior. The implications of the vision are not essential to the play, but they are to the 'myth' underlying the play.)

The second babe in the vision is clean, born naturally; he is crowned and bears a tree, which may suggest the coming of Birnam Wood to Dunsinane, but more significantly suggests a 'natural' and organic line of succession – all the way to James I of England.

The play reaches its moral climax in IV, ii, with the attack on Lady Macduff and the murder of her child onstage. This horrifying scene is emblematic of the character of a world in which ends have been devalued. The horror and the pity it arouses in the audience are morally exemplary: this is what happens, what it feels like to live in a world in which power can no longer distinguish the elements it was designed to protect. But the moral climax of the play is also its moral turning point.

The next scene shows Macduff, ignorant of what has happened to his family, describing to Malcolm the scene in Scotland. G.W. Knight comments on Lady Macduff's claim that her husband's flight was caused by fear rather than love or wisdom: 'It is partly true .... Macduff is forced to sacrifice the bond of family love.'[55] Wilbur Sanders points out that in his discussion with Malcolm, Macduff actually condones the prostitution of his countrywomen.[56] It is in this scene, too, that the images of Scotland as grave rather than mother, and of women fighting, occur. It is in this scene that the real battle lines of the play are drawn. But the winning streak of the one 'side' of things is broken when Macduff hears the news about his family. 'Dispute it like a man' (IV, iii, 220), Malcolm urges, using the same language we have heard before.[57]

And Macduff, for the first time in the play, expands the meaning of the word *man*: 'But I must also feel it as a man', he says, recalling the blind Gloucester, who without eyes sees how the world goes, sees it 'feelingly'. Macduff refuses either to cry or to bluster: 'O I could play the woman with mine eyes, / And braggart with my tongue' (IV, iii, 230–1). He agrees finally to curtail his mourning, to Malcolm's satisfaction: 'This tune goes manly.'

Thus, the opening scene of the denouement, despite Macduff's definition of a man as one who feels, is still dominated by the same terms in which the play opened. And the play ends as it began, in a totally masculine world. Courage, prowess, the ability to kill, and compassion, nurturance, and mercy, are not equally valuable qualities to be held in a flexible balance. Priority continues to be given to the first set. Siward's son, for instance, who 'only lived but till he was a man', is killed in his first battle. Ross tells old Siward that 'like a man he died'. The old man should have been played by John Wayne. He has only one question: did his son die fighting or fleeing?: 'Had he his hurts before?' (V, ix, 12) This time it is Malcolm who raises a minority voice: 'He's worth more sorrow, / And that I'll spend for him.' The implication of this remark, plus the different tone of the dialogue at the close of this battle – saddened, heavy – compared with that of the triumphant dialogue at the close of the battle scene that opens the play, suggests that feeling will be at least an item in the new governance of Scotland.

But it will still occupy a secondary – or even lower – place. In the dialogue with Malcolm, it is Siward who has the last word: 'He's worth no more.' His mother might not agree. In this world, sons exist to go to war, and women exist to give birth to sons who are born to kill or be killed in battle. The language remains the same right to the end of the play. Macduff's statement to Macbeth that he was not born of woman makes Macbeth as 'effeminate' as Juliet makes Romeo: he tells Macduff the announcement has '*cow'd* my better part of man' (V, vii, 18) (italics mine). And the play concludes with Macduff's entrance bearing the bloody severed head of the butcher in his bloody hands, and his triumphal, 'Hail, King!'

So, although some balance is restored to the kingdom, there is no change in its value structure.[58] What is restored is the sacred inner circle, in which men are expected to refrain from applying the standards of the outer one: what is reasserted is moral schizophrenia.

Such a division may have seemed inescapable to Shakespeare. The world is continually threatened with violence and aggression; indeed, it is (either) because of this that the world grants priority to the masculine principle (or) because the world grants priority to the masculine principle that this happens. In any case, Shakespeare clearly saw the danger to society of such a priority; he examines the cost of allowing power, might, to override every other value. His conclusions are far more profound than some pious or conventional readers will allow.

It is sometimes stated, for instance, that Macbeth kills because of the 'passion' of ambition, which is permitted to overcome his 'reason'. He kills, it is said, 'order and degree': since it is a critical truism that order and degree are good, that passion is evil and reason good, it is clear Macbeth is evil. We hardly need critics to give us this information.[59] A more sympathetic and probing critic has stated that Lady Macbeth denies the existence of 'irrational values' and thus is destroyed by them.[60] But some readers have commented that Macbeth's death is an anticlimax, that he is already dead in the spirit before Macduff meets him.[61] His 'Tomorrow and tomorrow and tomorrow' speech allows no other conclusion.

If passion means emotion, feeling, it is Macbeth's 'passion', insofar as we see it, that makes him dread the murder. He does not kill out of passion, but out of reason. He and his wife have considered the entire political situation, and know that he has the power to seize control. They are correct in their judgment. They are what people today who admire such thinking call 'hardheaded'. What they forget, what Macbeth only intimates, what Heilman suggests by mentioning 'irrational values', is that political considerations are not the only ones that matter. The wholeness of life matters, although humans are given to forget that. And the only rationality that is of benefit to humans is one that is aware of all of the qualities of life.

What happens to Macbeth, long before the final battle, is that he loses all reason for living. He has cut himself off from everything that makes life worth living: 'honour, love, obedience, troops of friends', all life's felicities. Despite the love shown between them in the early scenes,his wife's death barely touches Macbeth. She gave up her part in his life when she renounced the gender principle she was responsible for.

Shakespeare sets the feminine principle, those values to which Judaeo-Christian culture has always given lip service and little real respect, and which Christianity projects into an afterlife, firmly within the mortal span, within everyday experience. We may not repudiate the qualities associated with pleasure and procreation, with nature and giving up of control, without injuring ourselves, perhaps even maiming or destroying ourselves. It is hardly the life to come that we breach: it is life here.

Notes

1. Although I agree with Robert Ornstein (*The Moral Vision of Jacobean Tragedy* [Madison, Wis., 1960], p. 275) that Shakespearean tragedy does not present

heroes sacrificed for the good of the community, and that Jacobean tragedy does not, on the whole, contain a community in the same way that Greek tragedy does, the British literature is not totally detached from communal values. Many Shakespearean heroes are epitomes of some characteristic valued by their cultures; in other words, they are carriers of cultural 'genes', and it is these genes that define them and that eventually destroy them. A culture is a far more abstract thing than a community, and a more complex thing than the communities of Greek drama, but the two are related. To the degree that the hero is a testing ground for a cultural value or set of values, he does *die* for his culture.

2. ROBERT HEILMAN defines Shakespearean tragedy as studies of 'myth in crisis', and he defines myth as an area of life with value that cannot be translated into power, will, or profit. Such a value he terms 'irrational', which is problematic since it suggests that there is something inherently 'rational' about power, will, and profit. See 'The Lear World', *English Institute Essays: 1948*, ed. D.A. Robertson, Jr (New York, 1949). The association of 'feminine' qualities with the divine occurs in all theological interpretations.

3. ALVIN KERNAN describes three circles or worlds in the play: an outer world, representing 'the brute power of nature'; Venice, representing reason, law, and social concord; and Cyprus, which is halfway between the two. Intro., Signet edition (New York, 1963).

4. SAMUEL A. TANNENBAUM sees Iago's Cassio as 'effeminate'. 'The Wronged Iago', *Shakes. Assoc. Bull.* XII, 1 (January 1937): 57–62.

5. Many twentieth-century critics find Iago a rationalist, among them ROBERT HEILMAN, who refers to R.P. Warren's remark that Shakespeare's villains are marked by rationalism. *Magic in the Web* (Lexington, Ky, 1956), and 'The Lear World'. MARK VAN DOREN says Iago has a 'heart that passion cannot rule'. *Shakespeare* (Garden City, N Y, 1953), p. 194. ALVIN KERNAN calls Iago 'icily logical'.

6. MARVIN ROSENBERG, *The Masks of 'Othello'* (Berkeley, Calif., 1961), pp. 170–1, asserts that the ultimate motive for Iago's hatred of Othello, Desdemona, and Cassio is 'his denial of the values they affirm'. Elsewhere, Rosenberg describes Iago as a cool manipulator who asserts the supremacy of will and intelligence and 'their power to efface emotions', and quotes to the same effect KAREN HORNEY's description of a psychological type. 'In Defense of Iago', SQ VI, 2 (1955): 145–58.

7. Iago's misogyny and loathing for sex have been noted by many critics, among them WILLIAM EMPSON, 'Honest in *Othello*', *The Structure of Complex Words* (London, 1951); BERNARD SPIVACK, *Shakespeare and the Allegory of Evil* (New York, 1958); and ROBERT ROGERS, 'Endopsychic Drama in *Othello*', SQ XX (1969): 205–15.

8. Othello has been described as an unsensual lover by THEODORE SPENCER, *Shakespeare and the Nature of Man* (New York, 1942), p. 127. Kernan praises Othello for what he calls self-control, and adds that every major character except Desdemona 'is in some degree touched with sexual corruption'. WOLFGANG CLEMEN, *The Development of Shakespeare's Imagery* (Cambridge, Mass., 1951), p. 124, concludes from the imagery that Othello's approach to experience is primarily sensory.

9. Sometimes Othello is blamed for these qualities. NORMAN COUNCIL claims that he is concerned only with his honor and himself. *When Honour's at the Stake*

(London, 1973), p. 113. A.P. Rossiter accuses Othello of egotism as well as possessiveness and self-pity. *Angel with Horns*, ed. Graham Storey (London, 1961), p. 195. Egotism and self-pity are the burden also of the famous criticism of T.S. Eliot, 'Shakespeare and the Stoicism of Seneca', *Selected Essays* 1917–1932 (London, 1932), and F.R. Leavis, 'Diabolic Intellect and the Noble Hero', *Scrutiny* VI (1937).

Yet as Helen Gardner persuasively argues, the tone of the play does not support such readings, which arise mainly because of twentieth-century distaste for authority, a code of honor, and heroic postures. See *The Noble Moor*, British Academy Lecture, 1956.

10. Desdemona's 'sensible normality' contrasts with the 'emotional exaggeration of Othello', writes S.L. Bethell, *Shakespeare and the Popular Dramatic Tradition* (London, 1944), p. 18.

11. Kenneth Burke writes: 'In ownership as thus conceived [by Othello]...there is...forever lurking the sinister invitation to an ultimate lie, an illusion carried to the edge of metaphysical madness, as private ownership, thus projected into realms for which there are no unquestionably attested securities, is seen to imply also, profoundly, ultimately, estrangement.' '*Othello*: An Essay to Illustrate a Method', *Hudson Review* IV, 2 (1951): 165–203.

12. The accusation made against Othello by Leo Kirschbaum ('The Modern Othello', ELH II 1944: 283–96) is that he tries to transcend the merely human, and thus moves easily into the posture of a god and an agent of divine justice.

13. That Iago and Othello share something has been pointed out by Kirschbaum, Leavis, Frank Kermode, Intro., Riverside Shakespeare (Boston, 1974), and Irving Ribner in the Ribner-Kittredge Intro. to the play (Waltham, Mass., 1963), as well as J.I.M. Stewart, *Character and Motive in Shakespeare* (London, 1949).

14. The 'something' that critics point to that binds Othello and Iago is the misogyny and fear of sex implicit in Western culture. John Holloway suggests this very obliquely when he writes that Iago conjures in Othello the memory of something he has heard or read about women. *The Story of the Night* (London, 1961), p. 46. Iago and Othello are 'binary or double stars revolving about a common axis within a gravitational field'. Brents Stirling, *Unity in Shakespearean Tragedy* (New York, 1956), p. 123. In my reading, the common axis is women = sex, the gravitational field a 'masculine' way of seeing. But Helen Gardner writes that Iago's views represent a 'true view of life'. '*Othello*: A Retrospect', *SS* 21 (1968).

15. Robert Ornstein points out that Othello's anguish shows the profound involvement of the male ego in what I call chaste constancy. *Moral Vision*, p. 221.

16. In fact, of course, misogyny too is both classical and Catholic. Traditional patriarchal thinking disdains both women and the qualities (rightly or wrongly) associated with them.

17. In a way of thinking that exalts transcendence, anything merely human seems bestial, and is most easily expressed in animal imagery. Caroline Spurgeon, *Shakespeare's Imagery* (Boston, 1961), p. 335, shows that the animal imagery comes mainly from Iago, who utters over half of it, and that most of the rest comes from Othello. Other images contribute to the delineation of the characters of the two men. Iago refers frequently to bodily functions and uses technical and commercial – 'masculine' – terms. Othello, the idealist, refers to the cosmos – the elements, the heavens, celestial bodies, winds, and sea. Cf. Wolfgang Clemen,

Shakespeare's Dramatic Art (London, 1972), p. 122, and MIKHAIL MOROZOV, 'The Individuation of Shakespeare's Characters Through Imagery', *SS* 2 (1949).

18. MAYNARD MACK claims Othello faces 'two ways of understanding love: Iago's and Desdemona's', and must choose between 'two systems of valuing and two ways of being'. 'The World of *Hamlet*', *Yale Review* XLI (1952): 502–23. But in fact there are three ways to seeing sex (not love) in the play: Iago's, which reduces it to appetite and commerce, Othello's, which idealizes it into exalted romantic love, and Desdemona's, which blends sex, love, and the everyday into what we may call married love.

19. ALVIN KERNAN states that his murder of Desdemona destroys in Othello 'all the ordering powers of love, of trust, of the bond between the human beings'. S.L. BETHELL writes that Othello 'loses his heaven with his faith in Desdemona'. 'Shakespeare's Imagery: The Diabolic Images in *Othello*', *SS* 5 (1952).

20. MARVIN ROSENBERG remarks that critics do not notice Iago's treatment of Emilia, although it is very significant. 'At best he treats her with sadistic humor, alone with her… he snarls orders at her as if she were an inferior being.' 'In Defense of Iago'.

21. 'To take a donnee so exceptional, to hit upon so unheard-of a set of circumstances and double them, was to call the entire moral order into question, as A.W. Schlegel pointed out', writes HARRY LEVIN, 'The Heights and the Depths: A Scene from *King Lear*', *More Talking of Shakespeare*, ed. John Garrett (London, 1959), p. 91.

22. DEREK TRAVERSI calls *Lear* an allegory of 'man's relation to nature', '*King Lear*', *Stratford Papers on Shakespeare*, ed. B.W. Jackson (Toronto, 1964), p. 195; L.C. KNIGHTS says the play attempts to answer the question: 'What is essential human nature?' *Some Shakespearean Themes* (London, 1959), p. 83; ROBERT HEILMAN believes the play is 'an essay upon nature'. *This Great Stage* (Baton Rouge, La, 1948), p. 11; and H.B. CHARLTON offers an important discussion of the theme of nature in *Shakespearean Tragedy* (Cambridge, 1948).

23. Many uses of the term nature are discussed by JOHN DANBY, *Shakespeare's Doctrine of Nature: A Study of 'King Lear'* (London, 1961), and by ROBERT HEILMAN, *This Great Stage*.

24. WOLFGANG CLEMEN reports that in the early scenes, Lear does not hear others, but speaks what are essentially monologues. *Dramatic Art*, p. 135.

25. L.C. KNIGHTS points out that many of Shakespeare's history plays are concerned with 'rulers who failed because they were isolated within an arbitrary conception of power or privilege', and thus were not 'linked with' the society they ruled. He is describing Coriolanus, but the description fits Lear as well. *Further Explorations* (London , 1965), p. 20. Lear, however, is cut off (as is Coriolanus) not only from his society but from his natural and inevitable place in nature.

26. He continues to quantify until the middle of the play. RUSSELL FRASER remarks that love remains a commodity for the King as late as his choice of returning to Goneril on the grounds that twice the number of retinue equals twice the love. Intro., Signet *Lear* (New York 1963).

27. 'Lear's "disclaiming" of Cordelia at the beginning showed an appalling violence; but that is far outdone by the positively destructive savagery of his curses on Goneril.' S.L. GOLDBERG, *An Essay on 'King Lear'* (Cambridge, 1974), p. 107.

28. W.R. KEAST points to the similarity of the two sisters to one part of their father. 'Imagery and Meaning in the Interpretation of *King Lear*', *Modern Philology* (1949): 45–64.

29. The criticisms that have been directed against Cordelia are dealt with by JOHN DANBY, *Doctrine*, pp. 109–25.

30. ROBERT HEILMAN reads Cordelia's steadfastness as a withdrawal from responsibility resulting from the sin of pride; cf. *Stage*, p. 36.

31. CLEMEN, *Dramatic Art*, p. 135, comments that the three villains of the tragedy use few images, and speak in cool and rational ways.

32. A thoughtful analysis of the function of the animal images is found in H.B. CHARLTON, *Tragedy*, pp. 189–226. Charlton remarks that the world of Lear is barely civilized, that it presents a state in which 'men and beasts are almost indistinguishable', in which 'human nature is palpably a part of nature .... The thin dividing line ... is the consciousness within man of his human nature.'

33. L.C. KNIGHTS paraphrases John Stuart Mill's discussion of nature and the human with agreement: 'Man's progress is a continual triumph over nature.' *Themes*, p. 83.

34. ORNSTEIN (*Moral Vision*, p. 263) points out that despite Edmund's rebellion, what he really wants is honor and legitimacy.

35. BARBARA MELCHIORI, 'Still harping on my daughter', *English Miscellany*, ed. Mario Praz, 11 (1960): 59–74.

36. A.C. BRADLEY writes that Goneril is 'a most hideous human being (if she is one)'. *Shakespearean Tragedy* (London, 1918), p. 300.

37. Sex is the 'subhuman ingredient in mankind.... [It] is used almost exclusively as a symbol of evil, of the animality that is continually put before us as a definition of vicious conduct.' Heilman, *Stage*, p. 100.

38. 'The *cupiditas* which is the root of all evil is carnal more than it is pecuniary. *King Lear* plays in an astonishing way with the idea of sexual intercourse being the root cause of the sufferings, of both Gloucester and Lear; the damage which libidinous mankind inflicts on itself is the main datum on which the Romances are built, and the main effort is to find the Desdemona-figure who is immune from the self-destroying curse of humankind.' PHILIP EDWARDS, *Shakespeare and the Confines of Art* (London, 1968), p. 138. ROBERT H. WEST asserts that the act of procreation comes in this play to seem the devil's, and adds that 'Lear seems in his madness to imply that sex is an insult to mankind and mercilessly alien – or that man is a beast.' 'Sex and Pessimism in *King Lear*', SQ 1 (1960): 55–60.

39. S.L. GOLDBERG offers an important discussion of Cordelia, *An Essay*, pp. 100–88 passim.

40. ARTHUR SEWELL notices the love among the 'villains', and comments, 'The weeds, after all, spring from the same soil as the "sustaining corn".' *Character and Society in Shakespeare* (Oxford, 1951), p. 119.

41. TERENCE HAWKES calls the Witches *epicene*, and adds that this 'exactly suits their function as obscurantist dealers in appearance'. *Shakespeare's Talking Animals* (London, 1973), p. 143. BRENTS STIRLING (*Unity*, p. 139) believes that the Witches' chant and their beards, as well as the behavior of Duncan's horses, demonstrate 'inverted nature', which the critic equates with overturned hierarchy. In the

Intro. to the Signet *Macbeth* (New York, 1963), SYLVAN BARNET writes that it was common for Renaissance literary witches to show petty malice, to have beards and masters, but uncommon for them to speak authoritatively.

Many critics have pointed the ambiguity and paradox of the images, and have linked them to moral ambiguities in the play. 'The normal delimitations of day and night disappear, as do those of manliness and womanliness, prudence and cowardice.' MARION BODWELL SMITH, *Dualities in Shakespeare* (Toronto, 1966), pp. 160–1. Speaking of the Witches, Smith adds (p. 172) 'that women should possess male characteristics, physical or psychological, was considered not merely unnatural and therefore deplorable, along with other "perversions" the reversal of sexual roles was ... taken as evidence of criminal conversation with the Evil One'. J.I.M. STEWART connects the paradox of 'fair and foul' with moral confusion: 'But it is also the victory alone, the snatching honour by unseaming people from the nave to the chops, that is both foul and fair – a monstrous confusion from which Macbeth, imaginative and highly organized as well as a soldier, now emerges, battle-shocked. That night he kills a man for a kingdom.' *Character*, p. 92.

42. 'In those daies also the women ... were of no less courage than the men; for all stout maidens and wives (if they were not with child) marched as well in the field as did the men, and so soone as the armie did set forward, they slue the first living creature that they found, in whose bloud they not onlie bathed their swords, but also tasted thereof with their mouthes.... When they saw their owne bloude run from them in the fight, they waxed never a whit astonished with the matter, but rather doubling their courages, with more eagernesse they assailed their enemies.' 'The Description of Scotland', prefaced to *The Historie of Scotland* (London, 1585), p. 21.

43. Most critics choose to pay attention to Duncan's remarks as bearing the legitimacy and authority of power, and ignore the implications of the tone and imagery of the Sergeant's descriptions. Thus, they accept the early Macbeth as unqualified 'good'. E.E. STOLL finds Macbeth so good that his later deed seems psychologically implausible. *Art and Artifice in Shakespeare* (New York, 1933), pp. 77–86. G. WILSON KNIGHT, *The Imperial Theme* (London, 1931), pp. 125–9, and MATTHEW PROSER, *The Heroic Image in Five Shakespearean Tragedies* (Princeton, N J, 1965), p. 91, both find Macbeth noble and courageous throughout the play because he remains true to his ideals. R.B. HEILMAN writes that the audience is led to sympathize with Macbeth because they are 'secret sharers' in his 'erring humanity', and that the play is a challenge to 'our manly courage'. (This seems to presume an audience of only males.) See 'The Criminal as Tragic Hero', *SS* **19** (1966). But JAN KOTT, who if he does not always see the trees at least sees the woods, blurts out the basic definition of the play: 'A man is he who kills.' *Shakespeare Our Contemporary* (Garden City, N Y, 1964), p. 92.

44. 'Scotland is a family, Duncan its head. A natural law binds all degrees in proper place and allegiance', writes Knight, *Imperial*, p. 126. WILBUR SANDERS, *The Dramatist and the Received Idea* (Cambridge, 1968), p. 267, describes Macbeth as oppressed by the bond of a moral order which he feels to have 'a more than legal validity, to be involved with the great world, the cosmos, the macrocosm ... [to be] rooted in the natural'. L.C. KNIGHTS does not fall back on claims of 'divine' or 'natural' law to authorize his position: he sees bonds among men as a basic condition of humanness. For him, 'evil ... is a violation of those bonds that are essential to the being of man as man'. *Shakespeare's Politics* (Folcroft, Pa, 1957), p. 7. See also MAYNARD MACK, JR, *Killing the King* (New Haven, Conn. 1973), pp. 139 ff.

45. 'Sleep, in Shakespeare, is always regarded as remedial' S.L. BETHELL, *Dramatic Tradition*, p. 53.

46. She is found so by BRADLEY, *Tragedy*, p. 312, and R.G. MOULTON, *Shakespeare as a Dramatic Artist* (Oxford, 1893), p. 156.

47. Many of Shakespeare's readers share this dual standard. From Dr Johnson on, they have used different criteria and different language in discussing Lady Macbeth and Macbeth (Bradley and Moulton are notable exceptions), and the word most frequently used for the lady is *unnatural*. Macbeth is a good man gone wrong; he is judged ethically. Lady Macbeth violates 'nature', and is judged mythically. SMITH, *Dualities*, p. 172, writes that Lady Macbeth reverses the roles 'appropriate to husband and wife, to say nothing of violating her *natural feminine attributes of tenderness and timdity'*. TERENCE EAGLETON, *Shakespeare and Society* (New York, 1967), p. 133n, claims Lady Macbeth desires to be transformed into a woman whose desires as well as actions are *unnatural*. Proser, *Heroic Image*, p. 60, asserts that in Lady Macbeth, 'womanliness, *normally tender, apprehensive, and compassionate*, transforms itself into a cruelty that denies its *usual* characteristics'. (All italics mine.) FRANKLIN DICKEY finds Lady Macbeth more of a villain than her husband, for reasons that remain murky to me. *Not Wisely But Too Well* (San Marino, Calif., 1957), p. 18. A fascinating, unconscious statement of dual standards of judgment occurs in FRANCIS FERGUSSON, *The Human Image in Dramatic Literature* (Garden City, N Y, 1957), p. 120: 'Lady Macbeth fears her husband's *human* nature, as well as her own *female* nature.' (Italics mine.)

    ALEX ARONSON, analyzing the play for Jungian symbols in *Psyche and Symbol in Shakespeare* (Bloomington, Ind., 1972), p. 237, calls Lady Macbeth 'serpentlike', and relates her to Hecate, who is 'emasculating, bewitching, deadly, and stupefying'. He argues further that in myth the male is seen as the bringer of light, form, and order: 'Both in the prehistoric myth and in Shakespeare's tragedies, the symbolism points clearly enough to the victory of the masculine, conscious spirit over the powers of the matriarchate' which are associated with darkness and chaos (p. 256). But the mythic symbology Aronson describes is in direct contradiction to the symbology of *Macbeth*, in which 'feminine' symbols are aligned with concord, order, love, and trust.

48. There are several interesting discussions of the meaning of this word in *Macbeth*. However, in none of them is there any doubt that manliness, properly defined, is indeed the *single highest human standard*, and is identical with virtue. This is explicit in CHARLTON, *Tragedy*, pp. 148ff. It is implicit in E.M. WAITH, 'Manhood and Valor in Two Shakespearean Tragedies', *ELH* **17** (1950), who identifies 'feminizing' and 'womanish' influences with what is 'weak' and 'effeminate'. PROSER, *Heroic Image*, pp. 56–61, like Waith, points to the narrowness of the definition the characters end with, but does not question the primacy of *manliness* in the world of the play. One critic is uncomfortable with these male supremacist notions: TERENCE HAWKES on one hand defines manliness as the ability to speak truly – which leaves women in a peculiar position – but on the other, finds 'non-manly' traits in males 'not altogether unadmirable'. He adds that the play seems to argue that 'to stifle ... "womanly" traits brings about a kind of dehumanization'. *Animals*, p. 128.

49. 'After Duncan's murder the tone of *Macbeth* changes .... In the succeeding portion of the play conscience ceases to function as an agent capable of preventing further crime; nor does it promote repentance.' PROSER, *Heroic Image*, p. 69.

50. *Heroic Image*, p. 58.

51. WILLIAM BLISSET, 'The Secret'st Man of Blood', SQ XIX (1959): 397–408.

52. *The Business of Criticism* (Oxford, 1959), p. 61. JAMES WINNY, *The Player King* (London, 1968), p. 36, claims that both Macbeth and Tarquin destroy parts of themselves; L.C. KNIGHTS points out that many of the histories and tragedies are 'studies of rulers who failed because they were isolated within an arbitrary conception of power or privilege'. *Shakespeare's Politics*, p. 7.

53. FRANCIS FERGUSSON finds Duncan's relation to Macbeth 'competitive' in 'Macbeth as the Imitation of an Action', *English Institute Essays* (New York, 1952), p. 108.

54. *The Well-Wrought Urn* (London, 1968), p. 31. BROOKS sees the baby as an image of compassion and of the future which Macbeth tries vainly to control.

55. *Imperial*, p. 142.

56. *Received idea*, p. 262. Several critics have suggested that all the major characters seem to be touched with guilt. SMITH, *Dualities*, p. 185, describes Macduff in the early portion of the scene with Malcolm as 'incapable of sympathy, scorning Malcolm's tears for Scotland, and calling upon him to act instead of weeping'. In *Wheel of Fire* (London, 1930), pp. 166–7, G.W. KNIGHT suggests 'All the persons seem to share some guilt of the down-pressing enveloping Evil. Even Malcolm is forced to repeat crimes on himself.'

57. Speaking of Malcolm's response to Macduff's sorrow, SANDERS says, 'This is so near to Lady Macbeth's conception of manhood, the masculine ferocity that is really bestiality, that Macduff's quiet vindication of another kind of manhood carries immense conviction.' *Received Idea*, pp. 272–3.

58. CHARLTON, *Tragedy*, p. 147, says the temper of the prevailing moral consciousness can be seen in the secondary characters, notably old Siward. MAYNARD MACK, JR, *Killing*, p. 184, describing the 'hard, somber' ending of the play, writes 'The voice of almost everything human speaks in Macduff's sword, but it is still a sword.' And Ornstein, *Moral Vision*, p. 232, claims that 'though order is restored at … [*Macbeth's*] close, though evil is purged and Macbeth receives the gift of oblivion, there is no sense of repose or reconciliation in its final scenes'.

59. Prominent among the 'order and degree' critics are IRVING RIBNER, *Patterns in Shakespearean Tragedy* (London, 1960), and DEREK TRAVERSI, *An Approach to Shakespeare* (London, 1938). FRANCIS FERGUSSON also thinks *Macbeth* is about passion 'outrunning reason' (*Human Image*, p. 119). FRANKLIN DICKEY argues rather circuitously that passion is evil because it makes a man effeminate because it is 'manly to rule the passions' because passion puts a man under the domination of 'woman', *Not Wisely*, Chapter 2 *passim*.

60. HEILMAN, 'Lear World', p. 53.

61. Notably, HELEN GARDNER, *Business*, p. 61 (n. 52 above), and L.C. KNIGHTS, *Themes*, p. 15. 'The man who breaks the bonds that tie him to other men … is … violating his own nature and thwarting his own deepest needs.'

ELAINE SHOWALTER   REPRESENTING OPHELIA: WOMEN, MADNESS,
AND THE RESPONSIBILITIES OF FEMINIST CRITICISM*

Elaine Showalter is Professor of English at Princeton University. Her
article 'Representing Ophelia: Women, Madness, and the Responsibilities of Feminist Criticism' first appeared in 1985, in a volume of
essays edited by Patricia Parker and Geoffrey Hartman entitled
Shakespeare and the Question of Theory, published by Methuen. Beginning with Lacan's opening statement from his article on *Hamlet*,
Showalter raises a series of fundamental questions concerning *how* a
character such as Ophelia should be represented in the discourse of a
responsible feminist criticism. Her focus is not so much on what
Shakespeare's text of *Hamlet* makes of Ophelia as on the ways in which
various critical and theatrical discourses have dealt with her, and the
consequences which follow from such practices. Showalter's project is
to excavate Ophelia's 'history', that is to say, the history of the
representations of Ophelia. As such, her concern is with cultural
historical factors involving the conditions under which the text is both
represented and interpreted. Whereas Lacan took as the centre of his
discussion the issue of 'mourning' in *Hamlet*, Showalter begins from
the issue of Ophelia's 'madness', and the extent to which the 'symbolic
meanings' which her character generates offer an index of what is
normally taken to be the 'feminine'. In other words, it is her contention
that representation itself is *ideological*, and this charge affects all forms
of critical practice including that of feminism itself.

'As a sort of a come-on, I announced that I would speak today about that
piece of bait named Ophelia, and I'll be as good as my word.' These are the
words which begin the psychoanalytic seminar on *Hamlet* presented in
Paris in 1959 by Jacques Lacan. But despite his promising come-on, Lacan
was *not* as good as his word. He goes on for some 41 pages to speak about
Hamlet, and when he does mention Ophelia, she is merely what Lacan
calls 'the object Ophelia' – that is, the object of Hamlet's male desire. The
etymology of Ophelia, Lacan asserts, is 'O-phallus', and her role in the
drama can only be to function as the exteriorized figuration of what Lacan
predictably and, in view of his own early work with psychotic women,
disappointingly suggests is the phallus as transcendental signifier.[1] To play
such a part obviously makes Ophelia 'essential', as Lacan admits; but only

---

*Reprinted from Patricia Parker and Geoffrey Hartman (eds), *Shakespeare and the
Question of Theory* (London: Methuen 1985), pp. 77–94.

because in his words, 'she is linked forever, for centuries, to the figure of Hamlet'.

The bait-and-switch game that Lacan plays with Ophelia is a cynical but not unusual instance of her deployment in psychiatric and critical texts. For most critics of Shakespeare, Ophelia has been an insignificant minor character in the play, touching in her weakness and madness but chiefly interesting, of course, in what she tells us about Hamlet. And while female readers of Shakespeare have often attempted to champion Ophelia, even feminist critics have done so with a certain embarrassment. As Annette Kolodny ruefully admits: 'it is after all, an imposition of high order to ask the viewer to attend to Ophelia's sufferings in a scene where, before, he's always so comfortably kept his eye fixed on Hamlet'.[2]

Yet when feminist criticism allows Ophelia to upstage Hamlet, it also brings to the foreground the issues in an ongoing theoretical debate about the cultural links between feminity, female sexuality, insanity, and representation. Though she is neglected in criticism, Ophelia is probably the most frequently illustrated and cited of Shakespeare's heroines. Her visibility as a subject in literature, popular culture, and painting, from Redon who paints her drowning, to Bob Dylan, who places her on Desolation Row, to Cannon Mills, which has named a flowery sheet pattern after her, is in inverse relation to her invisibility in Shakespearean critical texts. Why has she been such a potent and obsessive figure in our cultural mythology? Insofar as Hamlet names Ophelia as 'woman' and 'frailty', substituting an ideological view of feminity for a personal one, is she indeed representative of Woman, and does her madness stand for the oppression of women in society as well as in tragedy? Furthermore, since Laertes calls Ophelia a 'document in madness', does she represent the textual archetype of woman *as* madness or madness *as* woman? And finally, how should feminist criticism represent Ophelia in its own discourse? What is our responsibility towards her as character and as woman?

Feminist critics have offered a variety of responses to these questions. Some have maintained that we should represent Ophelia as a lawyer represents a client, that we should become her Horatia, in this harsh world reporting her and her cause aright to the unsatisfied. Carol Neely, for example, describes advocacy – speaking *for* Ophelia – as our proper role: 'As a feminist critic,' she writes, 'I must "tell" Ophelia's story.'[3] But what can we mean by Ophelia's story? The story of her life? The story of her betrayal at the hands of her father, brother, lover, court, society? The story of her rejection and marginalization by male critics of Shakespeare? Shakespeare gives us very little information from which to imagine a past for Ophelia. She appears in only five of the play's twenty scenes; the pre-play course of her love story with Hamlet is known only by a few ambiguous flashbacks. Her tragedy is subordinated in the play; unlike

Hamlet, she does not struggle with moral choices or alternatives. Thus another feminist critic, Lee Edwards, concludes that it is impossible to reconstruct Ophelia's biography from the text: 'We can imagine Hamlet's story without Ophelia, but Ophelia literally has no story without Hamlet.'[4]

If we turn from American to French feminist theory, Ophelia might confirm the impossibility of representing the feminine in patriarchal discourse as other than madness, incoherence, fluidity, or silence. In French theoretical criticism, the feminine or 'Woman' is that which escapes representation in patriarchal language and symbolism; it remains on the side of negativity, absence, and lack. In comparison to Hamlet, Ophelia is certainly a creature of lack. 'I think nothing, my lord', she tells him in the Mousetrap scene, and he cruelly twists her words:

Hamlet: That's a fair thought to lie between maids' legs.
Ophelia: What is, my lord?
Hamlet: Nothing.

(III, ii, 117–19)

In Elizabethan slang, 'nothing' was a term for the female genitalia, as in *Much Ado About Nothing*. To Hamlet, then 'nothing' is what lies between maids' legs, for, in the male visual system of representation and desire, women's sexual organs, in the words of the French psychoanalyst Luce Irigaray, 'represent the horror of having nothing to see'.[5] When Ophelia is mad, Gertrude says that 'Her speech is nothing', mere 'unshaped use'. Ophelia's speech thus represents the horror of having nothing to say in the public terms defined by the court. Deprived of thought, sexuality, language, Ophelia's story becomes the Story of O – the zero, the empty circle or mystery of feminine difference, the cipher of female sexuality to be deciphered by feminist interpretation.[6]

A third approach would be to read Ophelia's story as the female subtext of the tragedy, the repressed story of Hamlet. In this reading, Ophelia represents the strong emotions that the Elizabethans as well as the Freudians thought womanish and unmanly. When Laertes weeps for his dead sister he says of his tears that 'When these are gone, / The woman will be out' – that is to say, that the feminine and shameful part of his nature will be purged. According to David Leverenz, in an important essay called 'The Woman in *Hamlet*', Hamlet's disgust at the feminine passivity in himself is translated into violent revulsion against women, and into his brutal behavior towards Ophelia. Ophelia's suicide, Leverenz argues, then becomes 'a microcosm of the male world's banishment of the female, because "woman" represents everything denied by reasonable men'.[7]

It is perhaps because Hamlet's emotional vulnerability can so readily be conceptualized as feminine that this is the only heroic male role in Shakespeare which has been regularly acted by women, in a tradition from

Sarah Bernhardt to, most recently, Diane Venora,in a production directed by Joseph Papp. Leopold Bloom speculates on this tradition in *Ulysses*, musing on the Hamlet of the actress Mrs Bandman Palmer: 'Male impersonator. Perhaps he was a woman? Why Ophelia committed suicide?'[8]

While all of these approaches have much to recommend them, each also presents critical problems. To liberate Ophelia from the text, or to make her its tragic center, is to re-appropriate her for our own ends; to dissolve her into a female symbolism of absence is to endorse our own marginality; to make her Hamlet's anima is to reduce her to a metaphor of male experience. I would like to propose instead that Ophelia *does* have a story of her own that feminist criticism can tell; it is neither her life story, nor her love story, nor Lacan's story, but rather the *history* of her representation. This essay tries to bring together some of the categories of French feminist thought about the 'feminine' with the empirical energies of American historical and critical research: to yoke French theory and Yankee knowhow.

Tracing the iconography of Ophelia in English and French painting, photography, psychiatry, and literature, as well as in the theatrical production, I will be showing first of all the representational bonds between female insanity and female sexuality. Secondly, I want to demonstrate the two-way transaction between psychiatric theory and cultural representation. As one medical historian has observed, we could provide a manual of female insanity by chronicling the illustrations of Ophelia; this is so because the illustrations of Ophelia have played a major role in the theoretical construction of female insanity.[9] Finally, I want to suggest that the feminist revision of Ophelia comes as much from the actress's freedom as from the critic's interpretation.[10] When Shakespeare's heroines began to be played by women instead of boys, the presence of the female body and female voice, quite apart from details of interpretation, created new meanings and subversive tensions in these roles, and perhaps most importantly with Ophelia. Looking at Ophelia's history on and off the stage, I will point out the contest between male and female representations of Ophelia, cycles of critical repression and feminist reclamation of which contemporary feminist criticism is only the most recent phase. By beginning with these data from cultural history, instead of moving from the grid of literary theory, I hope to conclude with a fuller sense of the responsibilities of feminist criticism, as well as a new perspective on Ophelia.

'Of all the characters in *Hamlet*,' Bridget Lyons has pointed out, 'Ophelia is most persistently presented in terms of symbolic meanings.'[11] Her behavior, her appearance, her gestures, her costume, her props, are freighted with emblematic significance, and for many generations of

Shakespearean critics her part in the play has seemed to be primarily iconographic. Ophelia's symbolic meanings, moreover, are specifically feminine. Whereas for Hamlet madness is metaphysical, linked with culture, for Ophelia it is a product of the female body and female nature, perhaps that nature's purest form. On the Elizabethan stage, the conventions of female insanity were sharply defined. Ophelia dresses in white, decks herself with 'fantastical garlands' of wild flowers, and enters, according to the stage directions of the 'Bad' Quarto, 'distracted' playing on a lute with her 'hair down singing'. Her speeches are marked by extravagant metaphors, lyrical free associations, and 'explosive sexual imagery'.[12] She sings wistful and bawdy ballads, and ends her life by drowning.

All of these conventions carry specific messages about feminity and sexuality. Ophelia's virginal and vacant white is contrasted with Hamlet's scholar's garb, his 'suits of solemn black'. Her flowers suggest the discordant double images of female sexuality as both innocent blossoming and whorish contamination; she is the 'green girl' of pastoral, the virginal 'Rose of May' and the sexually explicit madwoman who, in giving away her wild flowers and herbs, is symbolically deflowering herself. The 'weedy trophies' and phallic 'long purples' which she wears to her death intimate an improper and discordant sexuality that Gertrude's lovely elegy cannot quite obscure.[13] In Elizabethan and Jacobean drama, the stage direction that a woman enters with dishevelled hair indicates that she might either be mad or the victim of a rape; the disordered hair, her offense against decorum, suggests sensuality in each case.[14] The mad Ophelia's bawdy songs and verbal license, while they give her access to 'an entirely different range of experience' from what she is allowed as the dutiful daughter, seem to be her one sanctioned form of self-assertion as a woman, quickly followed, as if in retribution, by her death.[15]

Drowning too was associated with the feminine, with female fluidity as opposed to masculine aridity. In his discussion of the 'Ophelia complex', the phenomenologist Gaston Bachelard traces the symbolic connections between women, water, and death. Drowning, he suggests, becomes the truly feminine death in the dramas of literature and life, one which is a beautiful immersion and submersion in the female element. Water is the profound and organic symbol of the liquid woman whose eyes are so easily drowned in tears, as her body is the repository of blood, amniotic fluid, and milk. A man contemplating this feminine suicide understands it by reaching for what is feminine in himself, like Laertes, by a temporary surrender to his own fluidity – that is, his tears; and he becomes a man again in becoming once more dry – when his tears are stopped.[16]

Clinically speaking, Ophelia's behavior and appearance are characteristic of the malady the Elizabethans would have diagnosed as female love-melancholy, or erotomania. From about 1580, melancholy had become a fashionable disease among young men, especially in London, and Hamlet himself is a prototype of the melancholy hero. Yet the epidemic of melancholy associated with intellectual and imaginative genius 'curiously bypassed women'. Women's melancholy was seen instead as biological, and emotional in origins.[17]

On the stage, Ophelia's madness was presented as the predictable outcome of erotomania. From 1660, when women first appeared on the public stage, to the beginnings of the eighteenth century, the most celebrated of the actresses who played Ophelia were those whom rumor credited with disappointments in love. The greatest triumph was reserved for Susan Mountfort, a former actress at Lincoln's Inn Fields who had gone mad after her lover's betrayal. One night in 1720 she escaped from her keeper, rushed to the theater, and just as the Ophelia of the evening was to enter for her mad scene, 'sprang forward in her place ... with wild eyes and wavering motion'.[18] As a contemporary reported, 'she was in truth *Ophelia herself*, to the amazement of the performers as well as of the audience – nature having made this last effort, her vital powers failed her and she died soon after'.[19] These theatrical legends reinforced the belief of the age that female madness was a part of female nature, less to be imitated by an actress than demonstrated by a deranged woman in a performance of her emotions.

The subversive or violent possibilities of the mad scene were nearly eliminated, however, on the eighteenth-century stage. Late Augustan stereotypes of female love-melancholy were sentimentalized versions which minimized the force of female sexuality, and made female insanity a pretty stimulant to male sensibility. Actresses such as Mrs Lessingham in 1772, and Mary Bolton in 1811, played Ophelia in this decorous style, relying on the familiar images of the white dress, loose hair, and wild flowers to convey a polite feminine distraction, highly suitable for pictorial reproduction, and appropriate for Samuel Johnson's description of Ophelia as young, beautiful harmless, and pious. Even Mrs Siddons in 1785 played the mad scene with stately and classical dignity. For much of the period, in fact, Augustan objections to the levity and indecency of Ophelia's language and behavior led to censorship of the part. Her lines were frequently cut, and the role was often assigned to a singer instead of an actress, making the mode of representation musical rather than visual or verbal.

But whereas the Augustan response to madness was a denial, the romantic response was an embrace.[20] The figure of the madwoman permeates romantic literature, from the gothic novelists to Wordsworth and Scott in such texts as 'The Thorn' and *The Heart of Midlothian*, where she stands for sexual victimization, bereavement, and thrilling emotional extremity. Romantic artists such as Thomas Barker and George Shepheard painted pathetically abandoned Crazy Kates and Crazy Anns, while Henry

Fuseli's 'Mad Kate' is almost demonically possessed, an orphan of the romantic storm.

In the Shakespearean theater, Ophelia's romantic revival began in France rather than England. When Charles Kemble made his Paris debut as Hamlet with an English troupe in 1827, his Ophelia was a young Irish ingenue named Harriet Smithson. Smithson used 'her extensive command of mime to depict in precise gesture the state of Ophelia's confused mind'.[21] In the mad scene, she entered in a long black veil, suggesting the standard imagery of female sexual mystery in the gothic novel, with scattered bedlamish wisps of straw in her hair. Spreading the veil on the ground as she sang, she spread flowers upon it in the shape of a cross, as if to make her father's grave, and mimed a burial, a piece of stage business which remained in vogue for the rest of the century.

The French audiences were stunned. Dumas recalled that 'it was the first time I saw in the theatre real passions, giving life to men and women of flesh and blood'.[22] The 23-year-old Hector Berlioz, who was in the audience on the first night, fell madly in love, and eventually married Harriet Smithson despite his family's frantic opposition. Her image as the mad Ophelia was represented in popular lithographs and exhibited in bookshop and printshop windows. Her costume was imitated by the fashionable, and a coiffure 'à la folle', consisting of a 'black veil with wisps of straw tastefully interwoven' in the hair, was widely copied by the Parisian beau monde, always on the lookout for something new.[23]

Although Smithson never acted Ophelia on the English stage, her intensely visual performance quickly influenced English productions as well; and indeed the romantic Ophelia – a young girl passionately and visibly driven to picturesque madness – became the dominant international acting style for the next 150 years, from Helena Modjeska in Poland in 1871, to the 18-year-old Jean Simmons in the Laurence Olivier film of 1948.

Whereas the romantic Hamlet, in Coleridge's famous dictum, thinks too much, has an 'overbalance of the contemplative faculty' and an overactive intellect, the romantic Ophelia is a girl who *feels* too much, who drowns in feeling. The romantic critics seem to have felt that the less said about Ophelia the better; the point was to *look* at her. Hazlitt, for one, is speechless before her, calling her 'a character almost too exquisitely touching to be dwelt upon'.[24] While the Augustans represent Ophelia as music, the romantics transform her into an *objet d'art*, as if to take literally Claudius's lament, 'poor Ophelia / Divided from herself and her fair judgment, / Without the which we are pictures'.

Smithson's performance is best recaptured in a series of pictures done by Delacroix from 1830 to 1850, which show a strong romantic interest in the relation of female sexuality and insanity.[25] The most innovative and influential of Delacroix's lithographs is *La Mort d'Ophélie* of 1843, the first of three studies. Its sensual languor, with Ophelia half-suspended in the stream as her dress slips from her body, anticipated the fascination with the erotic trance of the hysteric as it would be studied by Jean-Martin Charcot and his students, including Janet and Freud. Delacroix's interest in the drowning Ophelia is also reproduced to the point of obsession in later nineteenth-century painting. The English Pre-Raphaelites painted her again and again, choosing the drowning which is only described in the play, and where no actress's image had preceded them or interfered with their imaginative supremacy.

In the Royal Academy show of 1852, Arthur Hughes' entry shows a tiny waif-like creature – a sort of Tinker Bell Ophelia – in a filmy white gown, perched on a tree trunk by the stream. The overall effect is softened, sexless, and hazy, although the straw in her hair resembles a crown of thorns. Hughes' juxtaposition of childlike feminity and Christian martyrdom was overpowered, however, by John Everett Millais's great painting of Ophelia in the same show. While Millais's Ophelia is sensuous siren as well as victim, the artist rather than the subject dominates the scene. The division of space between Ophelia and the natural details Millais had so painstakingly pursued reduces her to one more visual object; and the painting has such a hard surface, strangely flattened perspective, and brilliant light that it seems cruelly indifferent to the woman's death.

These Pre-Raphaelite images were part of a new and intricate traffic between images of women and madness in late nineteenth-century literature, psychiatry, drama, and art. First of all, superintendents of Victorian lunatic asylums were also enthusiasts of Shakespeare, who turned to his dramas for models of mental aberration that could be applied to their clinical practice. The case study of Ophelia was one that seemed particularly useful as an account of hysteria or mental breakdown in adolescence, a period of sexual instability which the Victorians regarded as risky for women's mental health. As Dr John Charles Bucknill, president of the Medico-Psychological Association, remarked in 1859, 'Ophelia is the very type of a class of cases by no means uncommon. Every mental physician of moderately extensive experience must have seen many Ophelias. It is a copy from nature, after the fashion of the Pre-Raphaelite school.'[26] Dr John Conolly, the celebrated superintendent of the Hanwell Asylum, and founder of the committee to make Stratford a national trust, concurred. In his *Study of Hamlet* in 1863 he noted that even casual visitors to mental institutions could recognize an Ophelia in the wards: 'the same young years, the same faded beauty, the same fantastic dress and interrupted song'.[27] Medical textbooks illustrated their discussions of female patients with sketches of Ophelia-like maidens.

But Conolly also pointed out that the graceful Ophelias who dominated the Victorian stage were quite unlike the women who had become the majority of the inmate population in Victorian public asylums. 'It seems to be supposed,' he protested, 'that it is an easy task to play the part of a crazy girl, and that it is chiefly composed of singing and prettiness. The habitual courtesy, the partial rudeness of mental disorder, are things to be witnessed .... An actress, ambitious of something beyond cold imitation, might find the contemplation of such cases a not unprofitable study.'[28]

Yet when Ellen Terry took up Conolly's challenge, and went to an asylum to observe real madwomen, she found them 'too *theatrical*' to teach her anything.[29] This was because the iconography of the romantic Ophelia had begun to infiltrate reality, to define a style for mad young women seeking to express and communicate their distress. And where the women themselves did not willingly throw themselves into Ophelia-like postures, asylum superintendents, armed with the new technology of photography, imposed the costume, gesture, props, and expression of Ophelia upon them. In England, the camera was introduced to asylum work in the 1850s by Dr Hugh Welch Diamond, who photographed his female patients at the Surrey Asylum and at Bethlem. Diamond was heavily influenced by literary and visual models in his posing of the female subjects. His pictures of madwomen, posed in prayer, or decked with Ophelia-like garlands, were copied for Victorian consumption as touched-up lithographs in professional journals.[30]

Reality, psychiatry, and representational convention were even more confused in the photographic records of hysteria produced in the 1870s by Jean-Martin Charcot. Charcot was the first clinician to install a fully equipped photographic atelier in his Paris hospital, La Salpetriere, to record the performances of his hysterical stars. Charcot's clinic became, as he said, a 'living theatre' of female pathology; his women patients were coached in their performances for the camera, and under hypnosis, were sometimes instructed to play heroines from Shakespeare. Among them, a 15-year old girl named Augustine was featured in the published volumes called *Iconographies* in every posture of *la grande hysterie*. With her white hospital gown and flowing locks, Augustine frequently resembles the reproduction of Ophelia as icon and actress which had been in wide circulation.[31]

But if the Victorian madwoman looks mutely out from men's pictures, and acts a part men had staged and directed, she is very differently represented in the feminist revision of Ophelia initiated by newly powerful and respectable Victorian actresses, and by women critics of Shakespeare. In their efforts to defend Ophelia, they invent a story for her drawn from their own experiences, grievances, and desires.

Probably the most famous of the Victorian feminist revisions of the Ophelia story was Mary Cowden Clarke's *The Girlhood of Shakespeare's Heroines*, published in 1852. Unlike other Victorian moralizing and didactic studies of the female characters of Shakespeare's plays, Clarke's was specifically addressed to the wrongs of women, and especially to the sexual double standard. In a chapter on Ophelia called 'The rose of Elsinore', Clarke tells how the child Ophelia was left behind in the care of a peasant couple when Polonius was called to the court at Paris, and raised in a cottage with a foster sister and brother, Jutha and Ulf. Jutha is seduced and betrayed by a deceitful knight, and Ophelia discovers the bodies of Jutha and her still-born child, lying 'white, rigid, and still' in the deserted parlor of the cottage in the muddle of the night. Ulf, a 'hairy loutish boy', likes to torture flies, to eat songbirds, and to rip the petals off roses, and he is also very eager to give little Ophelia what he calls a bear-hug. Both repelled and masochistically attracted by Ulf, Ophelia is repeatedly cornered by him as she grows up; once she escapes the hug by hitting him with a branch of wild roses; another time, he sneaks into her bedroom 'in his brutish pertinacity to obtain the hug he had promised himself', but just as he bends over her trembling body, Ophelia is saved by the reappearance of her real mother.

A few years later, back at the court, she discovers the hanged body of another friend, who has killed herself after being 'victimized and deserted by the same evil seducer'. Not surprisingly, Ophelia breaks down with brain fever – a staple mental illness of Victorian fiction – and has prophetic hallucinations of a brook beneath willow trees where something bad will happen to her. The warnings of Polonius and Laertes have little to add to this history of female sexual trauma.[32]

On the Victorian stage, it was Ellen Terry, daring and unconventional in her own life, who led the way in acting Ophelia in feminist terms as a consistent psychological study in sexual intimidation, a girl terrified of her father, of her lover, and of life itself. Terry's debut as Ophelia in Henry Irving's production in 1878 was a landmark. According to one reviewer, her Ophelia was 'the terrible spectacle of a normal girl becoming hopelessly imbecile as the result of overwhelming mental agony. Hers was an insanity without wrath or rage, without exaltation or paroxysms.'[33] Her 'poetic and intellectual performance' also inspired other actresses to rebel against the conventions of invisibility and negation associated with the part.

Terry was the first to challenge the tradition of Ophelia's dressing in emblematic white. For the French poets, such as Rimbaud, Hugo, Musset, Mallarmé and Laforgue, whiteness was part of Ophelia's essential feminine symbolism; they call her 'blanche Ophelia' and compare her to a lily, a cloud, or snow. Yet whiteness also made her a transparency, an absence that took on the colors of Hamlet's moods, and that, for the symbolists like Mallarmé, made her a blank page to be written over or on by the male imagination. Although Irving was able to prevent Terry from wearing

black in the mad scene, exclaiming 'My God, Madam, there must be only
one black figure in this play, and that's Hamlet!' (Irving, of course, was
playing Hamlet), nonetheless actresses such as Gertrude Eliot, Helen
Maude, Nora de Silva, and in Russia Vera Komisarjevskaya, gradually won
the right to intensify Ophelia's presence by clothing her in Hamlet's
black.[34]

By the turn of the century, there was both a male and a female discourse
on Ophelia. A.C. Bradley spoke for the Victorian male tradition when he
noted in *Shakespearean Tragedy* (1906) that 'a large number of readers feel a
kind of personal irritation against Ophelia; they seem unable to forgive
her for not having been a heroine'.[35] The feminist counterview was
represented by actresses in such works as Helena Faucit's study of
Shakespeare's female characters, and *The True Ophelia*, written by an
anonymous actress in 1914, which protested against the 'insipid little
creature' of criticism, and advocated a strong and intelligent woman
destroyed by the heartlessness of men.[36] In women's paintings of the *fin de
siècle* as well, Ophelia is depicted as an inspiring, even sanctified emblem
of righteousness.[37]

While the widely read and influential essays of Mary Cowden Clarke are
now mocked as the epitome of naive criticism, these Victorian studies of
the girlhood of Shakespeare's heroines are of course alive and well as
psychoanalytic criticism, which has imagined its own prehistories of
Oedipal conflict and neurotic fixation; and I say this not to mock
psychoanalytic criticism, but to suggest that Clarke's musings on Ophelia
are a pre-Freudian speculation on the traumatic sources of a female sexual
identity. The Freudian interpretation of *Hamlet* concentrated on the hero,
but also had much to do with the re-sexualization of Ophelia. As early as
1900, Freud had traced Hamlet's irresolution to an Oedipus complex, and
Ernest Jones, his leading British disciple, developed this view,influencing
the performances of John Gielgud and Alec Guinness in the 1930s. In his
final version of the study, *Hamlet and Oedipus*, published in 1949, Jones
argued that 'Ophelia should be unmistakably sensual, as she seldom is on
stage. She may be "innocent" and docile, but she is very aware of her
body'.[38]

In the theater and in criticism, this Freudian edict has produced such
extreme readings as that Shakespeare intends us to see Ophelia as a loose
woman, and that she has been sleeping with Hamlet. Rebecca West has
argued that Ophelia was not 'a correct and timid virgin of exquisite
sensibilities', a view she attributes to the popularity of the Millais painting;
but rather 'a disreputable young woman'.[39] In his delightful
autobiography, Laurence Olivier, who made a special pilgrimage to Ernest
Jones when he was preparing his *Hamlet* in the 1930s, recalls that one of his
predecessors as actor-manager had said in response to the earnest question,
'Did Hamlet sleep with Ophelia?' – 'In my company, always.'[40]

The most extreme Freudian interpretation reads *Hamlet* as two parallel male and female psychodramas, the counterpointed stories of the incestuous attachments of Hamlet and Ophelia. As Theodor Lidz presents this view, while Hamlet is neurotically attached to his mother, Ophelia has an unresolved Oedipal attachment to her father. She has fantasies of a lover who will abduct her from or even kill her father, and when this actually happens, her reason is destroyed by guilt as well as by lingering incestuous feelings. According to Lidz, Ophelia breaks down because she fails in the female developmental task of shifting her sexual attachment from her father 'to a man who can bring her fulfillment as a woman'.[41] We see the effects of this Freudian Ophelia on stage productions since the 1950s, where directors have hinted at an incestuous link between Ophelia and her father, or more recently, because this staging conflicts with the usual ironic treatment of Polonius, between Ophelia and Laertes. Trevor Nunn's production with Helen Mirren in 1970, for example, made Ophelia and Laertes flirtatious doubles, almost twins in their matching fur-trimmed doublets, playing duets on the lute with Polonius looking on, like Peter, Paul, and Mary. In other productions of the same period, Marianne Faithfull was a haggard Ophelia equally attracted to Hamlet and Laertes, and, in one of the few performances directed by a woman, Yvonne Nicholson sat on Laertes' lap in the advice scene, and played the part with 'rough sexual bravado'.[42]

Since the 1960s, the Freudian representation of Ophelia has been supplemented by an antipsychiatry that represents Ophelia's madness in more contemporary terms. In contrast to the psychoanalytic representation of Ophelia's sexual unconscious that connected her essential feminity to Freud's essays on female sexuality and hysteria, her madness is now seen in medical and biochemical terms, as schizophrenia. This is so in part because the schizophrenic woman has become the cultural icon of dualistic feminity in the mid-twentieth century as the erotomaniac was in the seventeenth and the hysteric in the nineteenth. It might also be traced to the work of R.D. Laing on female schizophrenia in the 1960s. Laing argued that schizophrenia was an intelligible response to the experience of invalidation within the family network, especially to the conflicting emotional messages and mystifying double binds experienced by daughters. Ophelia, he noted in *The Divided Self*, is an empty space. 'In her madness there is no one there .... There is no integral selfhood expressed through her actions or utterances. Incomprehensible statements are said by nothing. She has already died. There is now only a vacuum where there was once a person.'[43]

Despite his sympathy for Ophelia, Laing's readings silence her, equate her with 'nothing', more completely than any since the Augustans; and they have been translated into performances which only make Ophelia a graphic study of mental pathology. The sickest Ophelias on the contemporary stage have been those in the productions of the pathologist-director Jonathan Miller. In 1974 at the Greenwich Theatre his Ophelia sucked her thumb; by 1981, at the Warehouse in London, she was played by an actress much taller and heavier than the Hamlet (perhaps punningly cast as the young actor Anton Lesser). She began the play with a set of nervous tics and tuggings of hair which by the mad scene had become a full set of schizophrenic routines – head banging, twitching, wincing, grimacing, and drooling.[44]

But since the 1970s too we have had a feminist discourse which has offered a new perspective on Ophelia's madness as protest and rebellion. For many feminist theorists, the madwoman is a heroine, a powerful figure who rebels against the family and the social order; and the hysteric who refuses to speak the language of the patriarchal order, who speaks otherwise, is a sister.[45] In terms of effect on the theater, the most radical application of these ideas was probably realized in Melissa Murray's agitprop play *Ophelia*, written in 1979 for the English women's theater group 'Hormone Imbalance'. In this blank verse retelling of the Hamlet story, Ophelia becomes a lesbian and runs off with a woman servant to join a guerilla commune.[46]

While I've always regretted that I missed this production, I can't proclaim that this defiant ideological gesture, however effective politically or theatrically, is all that feminist criticism desires, or all to which it should aspire. When feminist criticism chooses to deal with representation, rather than with women's writing, it must aim for a maximum interdisciplinary contextualism, in which the complexity of attitudes towards the feminine can be analyzed in their fullest cultural and historical frame. The alternation of strong and weak Ophelias on the stage, virginal and seductive Ophelias in art, inadequate or oppressed Ophelias in criticism, tells us how these representations have overflowed the text, and how they have reflected the ideological character of their times, erupting as debates between dominant and feminist views in periods of gender crisis and redefinition. The representation of Ophelia changes independently of theories of the meaning of the play or the Prince, for it depends on attitudes towards women and madness. The decorous and pious Ophelia of the Augustan age and the postmodern schizophrenic heroine who might have stepped from the pages of Laing can be derived from the same figure; they are both contradictory and complementary images of female sexuality in which madness seems to act as the 'switching-point, the concept which allows the co-existence of both sides of the representation'.[47] There is no 'true' Ophelia for whom feminist criticism must unambiguously speak, but perhaps only a Cubist Ophelia of multiple perspectives, more than the sum of all her parts.

But in exposing the ideology of representation, feminist critics have also the responsibility to acknowledge and to examine the boundaries of our own ideological positions as products of our gender and our time. A degree of humility in an age of critical hubris can be our greatest strength, for it is by occupying this position of historical self-consciousness in both femininism and criticism that we maintain our credibility in representing Ophelia, and that, unlike Lacan, when we promise to speak about her, we make good our word.

Notes

1. JACQUES LACAN, 'Desire and the Interpretations of Desire in *Hamlet*', in *Literature and Psychoanalysis: The Question of Reading: Otherwise*, ed. Shoshana Felman (Baltimore, 1982), pp. 11, 20, 23. Lacan is also wrong about the etymology of Ophelia, which probably derives from the Greek for 'help' or 'succour'. CHARLOTTE M. YONGE suggested a derivation from 'ophis', 'serpent'. See her *History of Christian Names* (1884, republished Chicago, 1966), 346–7. I am indebted to Walter Jackson Bate for this reference.

2. ANNETTE KOLODNY, 'Dancing through the Minefield: Some Observations on the Theory, Practice, and Politics of Feminist Literary Criticism', *Feminist Studies* 6, 1980, p. 7.

3. CAROL NEELY, 'Feminist Modes of Shakespearean Criticism', *Women's Studies* 9, 1981, p. 11.

4. LEE EDWARDS, 'The Labors of Psyche', *Critical Inquiry* 6, 1979, p. 36.

5. LUCE IRIGARAY: see *New French Feminisms*, ed. Elaine Marks and Isabelle de Courtivron (New York, 1982), p. 101. The quotation above, from III, ii, is taken from the Arden Shakespeare, *Hamlet*, ed. Harold Jenkins (London and New York, 1982), p. 295. All quotations from Hamlet are from this text.

6. On images of negation and feminine enclosure, see DAVID WILBERN, 'Shakespeare's Nothing', in *Representing Shakespeare: New Psychoanalytic Essays*, ed. Murray M. Schwartz and Coppelia Kahn (Baltimore, 1981).

7. DAVID LEVERENZ, 'The Woman in *Hamlet*: An Interpersonal View', *Signs* 4, 1978, p. 303.

8. JAMES JOYCE, *Ulysses* (New York, 1961), p. 76.

9. SANDER L. GILMAN, *Seeing the Insane* (New York, 1981), p. 126.

10. See MICHAEL GOLDMAN, *The Actor's Freedom: Toward a Theory of Drama* (New York, 1975), for a stimulating discussion of the interpretative interaction between actor and audience.

11. BRIDGET LYONS, 'The Iconography of Ophelia', *English Literary History* 44, 1977, p. 61.

12. See MAURICE and HANNA CHARNEY, 'The Language of Shakespeare's Madwomen', *Signs* 3, 1977, pp. 451, 457; and CARROLL CAMDEN, 'On Ophelia's Madness', *Shakespeare Quarterly*, 1964, p. 254.

13. See MARGERY GARBER, *Coming of Age in Shakespeare* (London, 1981), pp. 155–7; and Lyons, op. cit. pp. 65, 70–2.

14. On dishevelled hair as a signifier of madness or rape, see CHARNEY AND CHARNEY, op. cit., pp. 452–3, 457; and ALLAN DESSEN, *Elizabethan Stage Conventions* and *Modern Interpreters* (Cambridge, 1984), pp. 36–8. Thanks to Allan Dessen for letting me see advance proofs of his book.

15. CHARNEY AND CHARNEY, op. cit. p. 456.

16. GASTON BACHELARD, *L'Eau et les rêves* (Paris, 1942), pp. 109–25. See also BRIGITTE PEUCKER, 'Droste-Hulshof's Ophelia and the Recovery of Voice', *Journal of English and Germanic Philology*, 1983, pp. 374–91.

17. VIEDA SKULTANS, *English Madness: Ideas on Insanity* 1580–1890 (London, 1977), pp. 79–81. On historical cases of love-melancholy, see MICHAEL MACDONALD, *Mystical Bedlam* (Cambridge, 1982).

18. C.E.L. WINGATE, *Shakespeare's Heroines on the Stage* (New York, 1895), pp. 283–4, 288–9.

19. CHARLES HIATT, *Ellen Terry* (London, 1898), p. 11.

20. MAX BYRD, *Visits to Bedlam: Madness and Literature in the Eighteenth Century* (Columbia, 1974), p. xiv.

21. PETER RABY, *Fair Ophelia: Harriet Smithson Berlioz* (Cambridge,1982). p. 63.

22. Ibid., p. 68.

23. Ibid, pp. 72, 75.

24. Quoted in CAMDEN, op. cit., p. 247.

25. RABY, op. cit., p. 182.

26. J.C. BUCKNILL, *The Psychology of Shakespeare* (London, 1859, reprinted New York, 1970), p. 110. For more extensive discussions of Victorian psychiatry and Ophelia figures, see ELAINE SHOWALTER, *The Female Malady: Women, Madness and English Culture* (New York, 1985).

27. JOHN CONOLLY, *Study of Hamlet* (London, 1863), p. 177.

28. Ibid., pp. 177–8, 180.

29. ELLEN TERRY, *The Story of My Life* (London, 1908), p. 154.

30. Diamond's photographs are reproduced in SANDER L. GALMAN, *The Face of Madness: Hugh W. Diamond and the Origin of Psychiatric Photography* (New York, 1976).

31. See GEORGES DIDI-HUBERMAN, *L'Invention de Phystérie* (Paris, 1982), and STEPHEN HEATH, *The Sexual Fix* (London, 1983), p. 36.

32. MARY COWDEN CLARKE, *The Girlhood of Shakespeare's Heroines* (London, 1852). See also GEORGE C. GROSS, 'Mary Cowden Clarke, The Girlhood of Shakespeare's Heroines, and the Sex Education of Victorian Women', *Victorian Studies* 16, 1972, pp. 37–58, and NINA AUERBACH, *Woman and the Demon* (Cambridge, Mass., 1983), pp. 210–15.

33. HIATT, op. cit., p. 114. See also WINGATE, op. cit., pp. 304–5.

34. TERRY, op. cit., pp 155–6.

35. ANDREW C. BRADLEY, *Shakespearean Tragedy* (London, 1906), p. 160.

36. HELENA FAUCITY MARTIN, *On Some of Shakespeare's Female Characters* (Edinburgh and London, 1891), pp. 4, 18; and *The True Ophelia* (New York, 1914), pp. 15.

37. Among these paintings are the Ophelias of Henrietta Rae and Mrs F. Littler. Sarah Bernhardt sculpted a bas relief of Ophelia for the Women's Pavilion at the Chicago World's Fair in 1893.

38. ERNEST JONES, *Hamlet and Oedipus* (New York, 1949), p. 139.

39. REBECCA WEST, *The Court and the Castle* (New Haven, 1958), p. 18.

40. LAURENCE OLIVIER, *Confessions of an Actor* (Harmondsworth, 1982), pp. 102, 152.

41. THEODOR LIDZ, *Hamlet's Enemy: Madness and Myth in Hamlet* (New York, 1975), pp. 88, 113.

42. RICHARD DAVID, *Shakespeare in the Theatre* (Cambridge, 1978), p. 75. This was the production directed by Buzz Goodbody, a brilliant young feminist radical who killed herself that year. See COLIN CHAMBERS, *Other Spaces: New Theatre and the RSC* (London, 1980), especially pp. 63–7.

43. R.D. LAING, *The Divided Self* (Harmondsworth, 1965), p. 195n.

44. DAVID, op. cit. pp. 82–3; thanks to Marianne DeKoven, Rutgers University, for the description of the 1981 Warehouse production.

45. See, for example, HÉLÈNE CIXOUS and CATHERINE CLEMENT, *La Jeune Née* (Paris, 1975).

46. For an account of this production, see MICHELINE WANDOR, *Understudies: Theatre and Sexual Politics* (London, 1981), p. 47.

47. I am indebted for this formulation to a critique of my earlier draft of this paper by Carl Friedman, at the Wesleyan Center for the Humanities, April 1984.

7 Psychoanalytical Criticism

JULIA KRISTEVA   ROMEO AND JULIET: *LOVE-HATRED IN THE COUPLE**

Julia Kristeva is Professor of Linguistics at the University of Paris VII and a major exponent of post-Lacanian forms of psychoanalytical criticism. The essay 'Romeo and Juliet: Love – hatred in the Couple' is taken from a larger study, *Tales of Love*, translated by Leon S. Roudiez and published by Columbia University Press in 1987. Kristeva argues that 'the state of love is such a disconcerting dynamic and at the same time the supreme guarantee of renewal', as well as 'the privileged site of the passion of signs constituted by their condensation and literary polyvalence' (*Tales of Love*, p. 16). Following Lacan, Kristeva suggests that the Freudian *symptom*, which is a metaphor for the workings of the unconscious, a 'condensation, of fantasy', can now be analysed as 'a screen through which one detects the workings of *significance* (the process of formation and deformation of meaning and the subject)' (ibid., p. 23). Her concern with the figures of Romeo and Juliet thus becomes a concern with 'Transgression love, outlaw love', in so far as the 'law' itself institutes both an 'ego ideal' *and* a form of tyranny against which the lovers resist. She also takes the view that the play is a wholly Shakespearean account 'of death's immanent presence within love'. But, in addition to suggesting that the lovers are 'of the night', and 'remain solitary beings', she also asks the question of who or what is responsible for what happens to Romeo and Juliet. Clearly institutions have a part to play in their eventual fate, but she also asks inquisitively if indeed the responsibility lies with 'love itself, two-faced, sun and night, delightful, tragic tenseness between two sexes'. Kristeva then proceeds to read the text of the play both as a series of symptomatic encounters between the characters *and* at the same time as a symptom of Shakespeare's own psychic life. Also, into the

*Reprinted from Julia Kristeva, *Tales of Love* (trans. Leon S. Roudiez, Columbia University Press 1987), pp. 209–33.

analysis of both writer as text and the text itself, Kristeva inserts, in italics, a topicial analogue from one of her sessions as psychoanalyst, as a means of broadening the appeal of her argument. Indeed, she ends by suggesting that the discourse of analysis and the situation in which the patient transfers her/his unconscious wishes on to the analyst (transference) both 'provide us with a certain amorous imaginary stock for our erotic and social dramas'.

Outside the law

Transgression love, outlaw love, these are the notions that prevail in ordinary consciousness and literary texts as well; Denis de Rougemont in his *Love in the Western World* largely contributed toward imposing the concept in its strongest form: love is adulterous (cf. *Tristram and Isolde*).

Such a patently obvious statement rests upon the incompatibility between idealization and the law, to the extent that compliance with the latter depends on the superego. It is a fact that the lover (especially the woman lover) desires his or her passion to be legal. The reason may be that the law, which is external to the subject, is an area of power and attraction that can merge with the Ego Ideal. Nevertheless, once instituted for the subject, the law reveals its no longer ideal but tyrannical facet, woven with daily constraints and consonant hence repressive stereotypes. Out of this amatory 'we' in a delightful state of destabilization, the law then produces a coherent set, a mainstay of reproduction, of production, or simply of the social contract. Because it has merged with the superegotic practice of law, marriage – a historically and socially determined institution – is antinomic to love. There is, however, no reason not to think of other settings of legality in the matrimonial relationship in which the law would preserve its ideal facet and thus shelter the idealization that is so favorable to our loves, and at the same time trim its superegotic features. Marriage turned into the social mirror that acknowledges our loves, without for that matter setting itself up as an authority checking our desires? Is it a perversion in marriage that one thus imagines to be possible? And what if, as literature testifies more openly than the discourse of analysands, the very essence of the amatory relationship lay in preserving the necessity of the Ideal and its detachment from the Superego? And what if the economic evolution of technical societies allowed one more and more to relegate outside the family those constraints upon which the life of the species depends? It is not that the family might become a place unencumbered by authority. But is not an authority that one might idealize rather than fear, for it is first an ideal and secondarily a constraint, an authority to be loved? Perversely? In utopian fashion?

On secret and the figure 3

The loving couple is outside the law, the law is deadly for it – that, too, is what the story of Romeo and Juliet proclaims, as immortalized in Shakespeare's play. And young people throughout the entire world, whatever their race, religion, or social status, identify with the adolescents of Verona who mistook love for death. No other text affirms as passionately that, in aspiring to sexual union as well as to the legalization of their passion, lovers enjoy only ephemeral happiness. The story of the famous couple is in fact a story of the impossible couple: they spend less time loving each other than getting ready to die. That accursed love, however, has nothing in common with the impossible meeting of lovers in the Song of Songs; where the Bible posited an erotic and metaphysical distance that actually guaranteed the durability of the Jewish couple, here the Renaissance, humanistic, and total merging leads straight to death through the device of an antiquated, tribal law that, from the very beginning, rejects the jouissance of bodies and decrees social incompatibilities. But before turning to this morbid feature, apparently more unusual as one considers the tale of the young lovers, let me first emphasize their happiness. For if the couple is destined for death, Shakespeare seems to tell us, clandestine loves are the paradise of amorous passion.

Breaking the law is the initial condition of amatory exaltation: even though the Capulets and the Montagues hate one another, we are going to love each other. This *challenge* (for Romeo knows perfectly well that both Rosaline and Juliet belong to the enemy family) is protected by *secrecy*.

In Verona and universally, ardent glances are exchanged on the sly, go-betweens one hopes will never be caught. Words that are whispered or disguised within the banality of trivial conversation, go unperceived by others. Slight touches under the watchful eyes of those who suspect nothing, which arouse the senses more than the most obscene embrace might do. There is, in the happiness of secret lovers – as in that unique, elusive scene of the play set in the Capulets' orchard, with Juliet on her balcony, against a backdrop of moon and stars (II, iii) – the intense feeling of being within a hairsbreadth of punishment. Do they joy in the fullness of being together or in the fear of being reproved? The shadow of a third party – relatives, father, husband or wife in the case of adultery – is doubtless more present to the mind during carnal excitement than the innocent seekers of happiness together are willing to admit. Take away the third party and the whole construct often crumbles, lacking a cause for desire, after having lost some of its passional tinge. In fact, without this third party, this commandant of the secret, the man loses his amatory submission to the threatening father. While in her avenging ardor against her own father or husband, the woman recaptures with her secret lover the unsuspected jouissances of maternal fusion. Let us not forget the case of the unfaithful husband who, in his wife, flees what he imagines to be a possessive mother, in order to find in the series of his conquests the assurance of an unfailing autoeroticism. Through such challenge to law, secret lovers come close to madness, they are ready for crime.

It would be inaccurate to call their fire perversion, unless one uses that word in a very broad sense, suggesting that we are all perverts because we are neoteinic, incapable of subsisting solely within the symbolic order, constantly driven to seek the animal sources of a passion that defies the Name to the advantage of loss of self in the flood of pleasure. "Tis but thy name that is my enemy; thou art thyself, though not a Montague. What's Montague? It is nor hand nor foot, nor arm, nor face, nor any other part belonging to a man ...' Juliet complains, burning with the desire to possess a 'part belonging to a man'. 'O be some other name! ... Romeo, doff thy name, and for thy name, which is no part of thee, take all myself' (II, ii, 38 – 49). Lose your symbolic entity to enable me, on the basis of your loved, fragmented body, to become entire, whole, one: out of myself and myself alone there becomes a couple! In other respects, as we shall see when taking up the couple from the viewpoint of hatred, Juliet is mistaken and the name of her lover is not irrevelant to the triggering of their passion; quite the contrary, it determines it.[1] But let us remain within the romance.

The loving death

'The Most Excellent and Lamentable Tragedie of Romeo and *Juliet*' is, as the second quarto edition title page suggests, a deeply ambivalent text, 'excellent and lamentable' since the amatory situation of which it sings is lamentable and excellent. For we are indeed dealing with a *song*, and the lyrical qualities of the play have often been pointed out (the rimed prologue is followed by blank verse; Benvolio and Romeo speak in rimed couplets when they speak of love; Capulet switches to rime when speaking of Juliet's early childhood; Benvolio uses the sonnet form to propose that he seek a new mistress for Romeo in place of Rosaline, etc.). The sonnet is clearly in evidence at the time of the ecstatic encounter between the two lovers and one can imagine how novel the absorption of the sonnet form by the action of the play appeared to an audience captivated by the playwright's art.[2] Probably influenced by Sidney's *Asphodil and Stella*, which depended on a melancholy lover's code with a slightly literary sensitivity (it will be noted that Shakespeare emphasized this tendency by having the play and its developments rely on the sending of messages and their erroneous interpretations),[3] the play nevertheless remains wholly

Shakespearean on account of death's immanent presence within love. All this leads him to accentuate the *present moment*, and, where expression is concerned, an abrupt, resolute, imperative discourse, which shows up as soon as Romeo falls in love with Juliet, in contrast with his previous speech. That is because the time of his love is 'wild': 'The time and my intents are savage-wild, more fierce and more inexorable by far than empty tigers or the roaring sea' (V, iii, 37–9). Filtered by loving, idealizing passion, the presence of death endows death symbolism with a fully gothic character: 'Shall I believe that unsubstantial death is amorous, and that the lean abhorred monster keeps thee here in dark to be his paramour?' (V, iii, 102–5).

Solar or blind love

Only the very first meeting of the lovers seems to be free of the ambiguous compression of time caused by the immanence of death.[4] Their first glances nevertheless infer a mutual dazzlement and produce, in their loving discourse, the metaphor of metaphors, that is, the Sun – clue to the metaphoricalness of the loving discourse, to its nonrepresentability. 'It is the east, and Juliet is the sun! Arise, fair sun, and kill the envious moon ...'

Out of time, out of space, this solar disposition, dazzling with love, as Brian Gibbons points out, impugns even the proper name and identification itself (Romeo says that he 'never will be Romeo'). The time of love would be that of the present moment (no sorrow can 'countervail the exchange of joy that one short minute gives me in her sight' – II, vi, 4–5), and marriage, as continuity, is its opposite. The rhythm of meetings, developments, and mischances is not only the result of that incompatibility between the amorous instant and temporal succession; it also displays how demiurgic passion truly, and thus in fact magically, modifies temporal succession for its subjects. At this point of its trajectory, certain of its solar power, love selects as its target the opposite of the solar metaphor – the nocturnal metaphor. When idealizing, love is solar. Condemned in time, squeezed into the present moment, but just as magnificently trusting of its power, it takes refuge in blindness, in darkness.

> Or, if love be blind, it best agrees with night. Come, civil night, thou sober-suited matron, all in black .... Come, gentle night, come, loving, black-brow'd night, give me my Romeo; and when he shall die, take him and cut him out in little stars, and he will make the face of heaven so fine, that all the world will be in love with night, and pay no worship to the garish sun.
>
> (III, ii, 9–25)

Let me make it clear once again: the shattered, murdered solar metaphor displays Juliet's unconscious desire to break up Romeo's body. Within the somber blindness of such a passion, there nevertheless arises the meaning of another metaphor – the metaphor of Night. As if love drew from two sources, light and darkness, and could maintain its insolent self-confidence only from their alternation – day and night. What is Night? – Woman Night, and it is indeed Juliet who speaks of it; or death Night …. Night, however, is, like its opposite the sun, not only half of real time-space but an essential part of metaphorical meaning germane to love. It is not nothingness, lack of meaning, absurdity. In the polite display of its black tenderness there is an intense longing that is positive with respect to meaning. Let me emphasize the nocturnal motion of metaphor and *amor mortis*: it bears on the irrational aspect of signs and loving subjects, on the nonrepresentable feature on which the renewal of representation depends. Because it is Juliet who reveals that infernal quickening leading to the night of death, a quickening peculiar to amorous feeling, this does not only signify that a woman is, as they say, in direct contact with rhythm. More imaginatively, feminine desire is perhaps more closely umbilicated with death; it may be that the matrical source of life knows how much it is in her power to destroy life (see Lady Macbeth), and moreover it is through the symbolic murder of her own mother that a woman turns herself into a mother. Cradled on the spate of such an unconscious stream, the woman-subject does not control it, but who can? The poet's dramatic assertion involves a 'we' all of us: 'It lies not in our power to love, or hate, for will in us is over-rul'd by fate.'[5] Finally, a certain intrinsic melancholy with Juliet contrasts sharply with Romeo's solar eagerness when she expresses her own luminosity not by means of the sun but by the stars and meteors: 'Yond light is not day-light, I know it, I: It is some meteor that the sun exhales, to be to thee a torch-bearer, and light thee on thy way to Mantua' (III, v, 12–15).

There is nevertheless a comic vein in this tragedy; as if Shakespeare wanted to maintain a belief in vitality beyond the disastrous passion. But what comic strain there is is displayed by the Nurse and Mercutio, for instance (I, ii, 12–57, and I, iv, 53–103), outside the passion of the two lovers properly speaking. Now, even the friendly, reassuring figure presented by the nurse during the early portion of the play seems to betray the vital current of the work and act, after Romeo's banishment, like an opportunist matron, insensitive to Juliet's feelings, and advises her to marry Count Paris. Moreover, are not all comic scenes dominated by fury rather than joyous laughter (thus, Mercutio speaking of Queen Mab, in I, iv, and also his remarks in II, iv)?

Death, like a final orgasm, like a full night, waits for the end of the play. When death appears in the text as such and not simply as insinuation or foreboding, it is a death that mistakes its object. It is the wrong, ironic if you will, death of a rival who did not deserve that much. Neither Tybalt nor Paris, killed by Romeo, can reduce the passion mixed with violence that impels amorous feelings. They leave us dissatisfied, as they leave Romeo himself dissatisfied and disturbed – not guilty but nonplussed because he did not strike the right object. As a consequence of having thrust his sword into two rivals Romeo released the fury that underlies his love, and it will never leave him. 'Away to heaven, respective lenity, and fire-eyed fury be my conduct now! .... O, I am fortune's fool!' (III, i, 124–5, 138). Juliet, too, feels panic-stricken as death is set loose, and the mini-glossolalia of her speech should be noted: 'I am not I, if there be such an I, or those eyes shut, that makes thee answer "I"' (III, ii, 48–9), she tells the Nurse who gives a confused account of Tybalt's murder at Romeo's hands. But it is in truth the young lover of Verona who speaks of her loss of identity in the face of death's incoming tide that henceforth threatens the lover's universe.

A last sign of the passion carried along by its opposite may doubtless be found in the paradoxical imbroglio of the protagonists' death. What artful devices, what misunderstandings indeed are needed in order to produce a Juliet who is rigid but not dead, put to sleep by the potion, and more beautiful than ever in her rigidity. What is this body, erroneously dead and beautiful, if not the image of a contained, padlocked, one could say frigid passion because it was not able to give its violence free rein? She goes back into the night, at the end of the play, joying to penetrate herself with Romeo's dagger. All by herself. Romeo, after he has possessed his rivals, Tybalt and Paris, by means of death, meets his own death, by his own hand, without ever embracing Juliet.

There is something autarkic about night-jouissance for each of the two partners of the amorous couple. The dark cave is their only common space, their sole true community. These lovers of the night remain solitary beings. There you have the most beautiful love dream in the Western world. Love, a solar dream, a thwarted idea? And a nocturnal, solitary reality, a frigid death together. Whose fault is it? The parents? Feudal society? The Church, for it is true that Friar Laurence departs in shame? Or love itself, two-faced, sun and night, delightful, tragic tenseness between two sexes?

Salvation through the couple: Shakespeare and Hamnet

If there is romance, and it is there indeed, it is guaranteed by secrecy and sanctioned by brevity. Let us imagine Romeo and Juliet liberated, living according to different customs, little concerned over the animosity between their kin – and surviving. Or what if, within the same Shakespearean framework, a mediocre dramatist made them survive; Friar John, for instance,might have been able to warn Romeo in time about that most peculiar sleep Friar Laurence induced in Juliet, and the beautiful bride might have awakened in Romeo's arms. What if they had escaped their persecutors, and once the clans' hatred had been appeased they experienced the normal existence of married couples. There would then only be two borderline situations, with obvious combinations and variations possible between the two. Either time's alchemy transforms the criminal, secret passion of the outlaw lovers into the banal, humdrum, lackluster lassitude of a tired and cynical collusion: that is the normal marriage. Or else the married couple continues to be a passionate couple, but covering the entire gamut of sadomasochism that the two partners already heralded in the yet relatively quiet version of the Shakespearean text. Each acting out both sexes in turn they thus create a foursome that feeds on itself through repeated aggression and merging, castration and gratification, resurrection and death. And who, at passionate moments, have recourse to stimulants – temporary partners, sincerely loved but victims still, whom the monstrous couple grinds in its passion of faithfulness to itself, supporting itself by means of its unfaithfulness to others.

Let us imagine the two lecherous lovers of Verona, possible survivors of their dramatic story, as they chose the second path. One might find arguments for such a scenario even in their own lines. But as far as Shakespeare is concerned, he seems to have wished to conform to proprieties, for once; by having them die, he saved the pure couple. He safeguarded the innocence of marriage under the shroud of death; in this text, he did not want to go to the end of the passionate night that belongs to the durable couple. Why not? Shakespeare preserving the idea of marriage that perishes only through the fault of others? Whereas if marriage is wedded to passion, how could it last without some rehabilitation of perversion? Oh Lady Macbeth, oh the foul couples that surround Hamlet. But in that case, does it not mean the end of the beautiful dream, henceforth called 'Oedipal', that all children have: 'Your relatives perhaps, but not mine....' If everything is thus malevolent, perverse, foul, does it not mean the end of the immaculate home, of aseptic marriages – the pillar of the State? Is that not outrageous?

In 1596 Shakespeare had no need for such a subversion. Published in 1597, probably written in 1595 or 1596 when Shakespeare was about thirty, *Romeo and Juliet*, his ninth play, belongs to what has been called his second period, that of his lyrical plays and masterpieces (such as *A Midsummer Night's Dream*), and proved his first great success. Some critics, basing their argument on a reference to an earthquake in the text, date it back to 1591, and this would make it his first play. If one adopts the first hypothesis, which is generally accepted today, it would seem that Shakespeare composed this drama of love – hate exactly when he was thirty-one to thirty-two. Young, without doubt. But a major fact of his biography appears to be more important: his son Hamnet (born in 1585) died in 1596 at age eleven. Already eleven years earlier, after the birth of the twins, Hamnet and Judith, he had left his wife Anne Hathaway and settled down in Stratford. *Romeo and Juliet* reaches us, against that background, as a kind of nostalgic feeling for marriage, henceforth seen as impossible, but ideally maintained in the face of a guilty sorrow caused by the loss of the son. As a youthful fervor attempting to preserve the image of two lovers whom life undertakes to separate. Such an idyllic coloring of the play doubtless betrays the playwright's youth. I might also advance the hypothesis, with no other evidence than possibly cross-checking the unconscious paths of the reader with those of the writer (text and biography), that Hamnet's death triggered within Shakespeare the nostalgia for a couple that would have been in love. In love as precisely William and Anne were not able to be, with Anne older than her husband and giving him a daughter in 1582, after six months of marriage, and twins three years later.

Against the backdrop of his own marriage made commonplace by births, branded by death, Shakespeare, the dreamer and already a relentless blasphemer of matriarchal–matrimonial power, sets up the dream of lovers scalded by the law of hatred but in themselves immortally sublime. Ideal lovers, impossible couple: promising eros and real hatred weave reality. Shakespeare seems to apologize: hatred has come from others. Let us then think of *Romeo and Juliet*, in its idyllic tinge, as a dirge for the son's death. The father's guilt confesses in this play, along with hatred for marriage, the desire to preserve the myth of the enamored lovers. To preserve the idealization of the couple, ephemeral as it may be, to keep from having to enter into the hatred that dwells in marriage and produces death (of the children: Romeo, Juliet, and perhaps Hamnet?). It may be the father's gift to the son's tomb. A gift from William Shakespeare to Hamnet Shakespeare. The law, full of hatred, is intact. To let the sons sleep in peace and whitewash the fathers, it is henceforth endowed with a luminous reverse – the sublime love of young outlaws.

Later, when Shakespeare's father died in 1601, the law collapsed. There then appeared, with the same similarity that linked *Romeo and Juliet* to Hamnet's death, the play *Hamlet*, related this time to the father's death. In *Hamlet*, as an echo to both the son's and the father's deaths but in antithesis to *Romeo and Juliet*, no couple can withstand the onslaught of the corrosive tongue of Shakespeare, who carried revenge for the paternal ghost against the mother, the criminal wife, to the point of making any couple appear hideous.[6] Then, in 1609, the poet's mother died, and Shakespeare published his Sonnets, which extol homosexual love for William H., the Black Lady, William Hamnet, the son, or the father who discovered himself as son, flesh-man, woman-man, or rather a Christlike passion of the body.[7]

But in 1596 that point had not been reached. *Romeo and Juliet* exists as a casting out of Hamnet's death, as an antidote for a failed marriage. Hamnet is dead, nevertheless sublime and untouchable lovers are needed. Nostalgia for amorous happiness? Nostalgia: *nostos* – return; *algos* – pain. A painful return to a past that is dead, however, and leads to a dead person? Accept, dear Hamnet, as a funeral wreath, the immortal image of your parents' passionate love, who, ardent lovers, might have saved you from death or, accursed lovers in the manner of Romeo and Juliet, might have spared you existence. For you, Shakespeare immortalizes love, but your death is the symptom, the evidence that hatred triumphs.

'My only love, my only hate'

One often likens Romeo and Juliet as a couple to Tristram and Isolde, producing the evidence of a love thwarted by social rules; emphasizing how the couple is cursed and destroyed by Christianity, which smothers passion at the heart of marriage; seeking a revelation of the death that rules at the core of amatory jouissance. Shakespeare's text includes, with all that, an even more corrosive element, which his skill with ambiguity and the reversal of values handles with insidious magic in the very height of the most intense glorification of love. Under the guise of sex, it is hatred that prevails, and that comes out most obviously in the very first pages of the text. In the first scene, the two servants' remarks, peppered with puns and obscenities, cause the darkness of sex and inversions of all sorts to hang over this presumably pure romance. One is already prepared for Romeo's remark terming love 'a madness most discreet' (I, i, 192), even saying that 'it is too rough, too rude, too boisterous, and it pricks like thorn' (I, iv, 26 – 6). A little later it will be described by Mercutio – a baneful character who, along with Benvolio, brings about a chain of violence and whose death in the third act forces Romeo to avenge him by killing Tybalt – by means of the allegory of the fairies' midwife, Queen Mab. A gnomelike ghost, fascinating and hideous, ruler of amorous bodies, the dark, drunken, and murderous other side of loving radiance, it is Queen Mab who calls the tune with 'her whip of cricket's bone; the lash, of film' (I, iv, 63).

It is Juliet, however, who finds the most intense expressions to show that this love is supported by hatred. One could possibly see in the words of this noble maiden a simple rhetorical device at once heralding a final death, or an ambiguous language clause, blending opposites, something that is operative at other moments of the play and in Shakespeare's esthetics in general. But more deeply, what is involved is hatred at the very origin of the amorous surge. A hatred that antedates the veil of amorous idealization. Let us note that it is a woman, Juliet, who is most immediately unconscious of it, senses it with a sleepwalker's lucidity. Thus, as early as their first meeting – while Romeo suddenly forgets Rosaline, whose love nevertheless tortured him sorely a short time before, and only admits 'The more is my unrest' when he is told Juliet is the daughter of the enemy family – it is Juliet herself who states frankly, 'My only love sprung from my only hate!' (I, v, 139).

Did not Romeo himself, however, go to the Capulets' feast knowing that he was going to a feast of hatred? Juliet, again: 'Tis but thy name that is my enemy' (II, ii, 38). Or else, at the very height of the amatory monologue that sets in place the passion of waiting and extols the lovers' qualities ('Come, night, come, Romeo, thou day in night ...'), Juliet continues innocently, 'come, gentle night ... and, when he shall die, take him and cut him out in little stars, and he will make the face of heaven so fine, that all the world will be in love with the night ...' (III, ii, 19–24). 'When he shall die, take him and cut him out': it is as if one heard a discreet version of the Japanese *Realm of the Senses*. That feeling goes unnoticed because it is swept along by a hatred that one can look in the eye – the familial, social curse is more respectable and bearable than the unconscious hatred of the lovers for each other. The fact remains that Juliet's jouissance is often stated through the anticipation – the desire? – of Romeo's death. This, long before her drugged sleep deceives Romeo and leads him to suicide, long before she turns that death wish back upon herself at the sight of Romeo's corpse, driving herself to suicide, too: 'Methinks I see thee, now thou art below, as one dead in the bottom of a tomb' (III, v, 55–6).

Such frequent evocations of death are not simply intended to state that there is no room for passion in the world of old people, and, more generally, in marriage – that love must die on the threshold of its legislation, that eros and the law are incompatible. Friar Laurence says it indeed, and this is a leftover from vulgarized Christian asceticism: 'She's not well married that lives married long, but she's best married that dies married young' (IV, v, 77–8).

More deeply, more passionately, we are dealing with the intrinsic presence of hatred in amatory feeling itself. In the object relation, the relation with an *other*, hatred, as Freud said, is more ancient than love.[8] As soon as an other appears different from myself, it becoms alien, repelled, repugnant, abject – hated.[9] Even hallucinating love, as distinct from autoerotic satisfaction, as a precocious feeling of narcissistic fulfillment in which the other is not sharply separated from myself, does not otherwise come up in relation to that other until later, through the capacity for primary idealization. But as soon as the strength of desire that is joined with love sets the integrity of the self ablaze; as soon as it breaks down its solidity through the drive-impelled torrent of passion, hatred – the primary bench mark of object relation – emerges out of repression. Eroticized according to the variants of sadomasochism, or coldly dominant in more lasting relationships that have already exhausted the delights of infidelity, as delusive as it is seductive, hatred is the keynote in the couple's passionate melody. Whether heterosexual or homosexual, the couple is the utopic wager that paradise lost can be made lasting – but perhaps it is merely desired and truly never known? – the paradise of loving understanding between the child and its parents. The child, male or female, hallucinates its merging with a nourishing-mother-and-ideal-father, in short a conglomeration that already condenses two into one. That child, the loving child, in its couple mania, tries to make two where there were three. Man or woman, when he or she aspires to be a couple, the lover goes through the mirage of being the 'husband' or 'wife' or an ideal father: that is the extent to which the idealized object of love dons the finery of that 'father of individual prehistory' Freud talked about, the one who absorbs those delightful primary identifications.[10] In such a coupling with the ideal, shored up by a happy, domesticated fatherhood, man becomes feminized; is there anything more androgynous, or even feminine, than the adolescent madly in love with an adolescent of the opposite sex? One soon notices, however, in the last instance (that is, if the couple truly becomes one, if it lasts), that each of the protagonists, he and she, has married, through the other, his or her mother.

The mother – pedestal of the couple

The man then finds a harbor of narcissistic satisfaction for the eternal child he has succeeded in remaining: an exquisite normalization of regression. The woman calms down temporarily within the restoring support furnished by the mother–husband. This brings about, in a first stage, feminine homosexuality, which has thus become preconscious and seeks satisfaction as such; unless it causes depression as a result of finding herself dispossessed, by a penis-bearing being, of the nourishing values yet phantasmatically attributed to an inaccessible mother. Such a wife, happy because she found a mother in her husband, will then require sound phallic satisfactions, through the intermediary of children or of reiterated social rewards, so that the equilibrium of the couple might continue to prevail.

With man as with woman, meeting up with the partner's mother means finding the pedestal of the couple, thereby perpetuating it. But that life-giving figure paradoxically induces death – unavailingly checked by means of phallic reinforcements. Mother, mortal … Why?

'The earth that's nature's mother is her tomb; what is her burying grave, that is her womb' ((II, iii, 9–10), Friar Laurence sententiously declares. The jubilatory vanishing of identity at the heart of a nostalgic love for a maternal embrace is nevertheless felt by the adult as a loss, even as a mortal danger. The defense mechanisms then react, kneaded by drives and by egotic and superegotic hatred, in order to give back shape, identity, and existence to the *same* swallowed up in the *other*.The alternating love/hatred braids passion's tangle, and its eternal return never produces a 'better' couple than the sadomasochistic one. Better, because it feeds on its internal possibility for libidinal charging and discharging, and this supposes that each partner assumes sexual ambivalence. Does this mean androgynism? Not exactly. For man's 'feminine' is not woman's 'feminine', and the woman's 'masculine' is not the man's 'masculine'. The asymmetrical bond of the two sexes with the phallus, which determines their sexual character, causes them to be four who want to be two within the couple, and thus set the insoluble harmonization of the uneven. To make a couple out of the child–father–mother triad where the third party has become subject only because excluded. Love–hatred is the squaring of that imaginary circle that ideal love should be if I could be father-mother-and-myself united in a Whole.

Juliet, so cold with her mother, sends back, mirrorlike, to her progenitress the icy distance that Lady Capulet maintains with her daughter. Juliet imagining her lover dead; Juliet rebelling against the Nurse, an apparently good mother, when the latter does an about-face and urges her to forget Romeo; Juliet stabbing herself with Romeo's dagger. One should note that 'the hopeful lady of [her father's] earth' (as Capulet himself says, I, ii, 15), who provokes her father to a wrath that is too passionate to be innocent when she refuses the man he has chosen to be her husband (III, v), is possessed by refusal and a presence of mind that must be called phallic, marking a certain violence, a possible aversion. 'My only love sprung from my only hate!'

It is Friar Laurence, moreover, who points to the feminity of Romeo, whose warm masculine friendships, doubtless common at the time, nevertheless reveal that such friendships are built upon the comparison, the commensuration, with the (sexual) power of others, and at best with that of the enemies (privileged objects of passion). For this reason, it is the passional excitement of men belonging to inimical families that leads Romeo to present himself to his first love, Rosaline, to discover the second, Juliet, before penetrating Tybalt and Paris with his sword. It will be noted that Tybalt, the cousin, is the substitute of Capulet, the father, just like Paris, the husband chosen by the same father. Likewise, the ease with which Romeo switches from Rosaline to Juliet may be explained because they both proceed from the same source of hatred, the Capulet family. But the learned priest reveals the other side of this coin, so aggressive and vengeful in its loving passion – a certain 'feminity' in Romeo. 'Art thou a man? Thy form cries out thou art; thy tears are womanish; thy wild acts [the murder of Tybalt] denote the unreasonable fury of a beast .... But, like a misbehaved and sullen wench, thou pout'st upon thy fortune and thy love: take heed, take heed' (III, iii, 109–11, 143–5).

Topicality of the couple

If desire is fickle, thirsting for novelty, unstable by definition, what is it that leads love to dream of an eternal couple? Why faithfulness, the wish for a durable harmony, why in short a marriage of love – not as necessity in a given society but as desire, as libidinal necessity?

It is during their teens, in general, that young men and women dream of faithfulness, of stable couplings. The discovery of sexual pleasure, on the other hand, destabilizes, but it also leads, contrapuntally, to a need for (maternal?) security and nostalgia for recreating the lost paradise of the first dyad. Later, better able to control the castration game constituted by the experience of jouissance, the man flees from being swallowed up by the matrimonial couple in an attempt to secure his phallic power; he does so through the successive mirrors of more or less numerous transgressive conquests that are reassuring because ephemeral and manifold. But a woman rarely acts like Don Juan, or else, when she happens to play that game, it is through the virile expense of a bravura more shocking yet than that of her male homologue and with greater risks of psychic collapse. It is a common-place, and the changes, radical as they may be, that feminism has forced upon our morals have not upset this one aspect of erotic life: women want marriage. According to ethologists, this would be due to a matrical instinct of stability for the sake of nesting the offsprings. From a more psychic point of view, what may perhaps be involved is an unshakable need to secure, once and for all, through the husband, possession of the nourishing mother – the one a woman irremediably loses by having access to the father as normal object of her heterosexual desire. The idea is hence to get married and, in the warm, sheltering stability of the home, to enable her father's little girl not only to become a mother in her turn but also to have a mother, to obtain nourishment from her and joy in her. But actually it is the wife who becomes the man, the husband of that phantasmal mother who is none other than the stable, nourishing husband. She becomes the phallus, if you will, by adopting the mask of domesticated virility: secret, absent-minded, lenient but self-confident ruler of the maternal husband. Does not, for a woman, marrying a mother of whom she, the wife, will be the phallus, constitute the fantasy of the successful couple? Where she might hold the key to the other's jouissance but also be his social delegate, silently and solidly dominating? It is believed that in the fantasy of the good marriage the woman marries a good father; but if the fantasy of goodness is so lasting, it is because a good mother has inserted herself into paternal authority to insure – with primary identification as guarantee of narcissism – a few possibilities of more archaic regression. Without which, where would the 'joys of marriage' come from? They run a great risk of being reduced to the masochistic submission, which is truly quite appealing, of a household servant. An entire chapter of conjugal life unfolds there – a libido soaked up by the housewife's worries....

Contemporary mores, whipped up by the pill and artificial insemination, increasingly dissociate sexuality and reproduction. They will render the eternal couple socially and scientifically useless, and do the same for marriage as a social necessity that insured optimal conditions for the reproduction of the species. The psychic needs for permanent couplings will quite obviously lessen, without for that matter disappearing.

For on the one hand, the faithful couple that the law used to wish for, remains for many a therapeutic erotic necessity in the face of the loss of identity caused by the open multiplicity of pleasures and jouissances. Insuring security by furnishing an identity marker ('you love me therefore I am, in moments of passion, too, also in time of illness...'), the couple is a durable mirror, a repeated recognition. It sustains, as a mother does her infant. Beyond that restoring function, however, can it also take upon itself the calling that would make of it the temple where the eternal flame of desire has been lit? Perversion alone is in control of the situation, binding in self-esteem partners who are tied to such and such a partial object furnished by the other, or to such and such an active–passive, masculine–feminine alternation provided by erotic or existential dramatic art. The great flights of feminine independence have not shattered this law, necessarily reactionary because it is unconscious, which supports and at the same time damages desire in the bosom of the archaic maternal object. The feminist struggle has given a boost to libidinal vitality by means of phallic competition, through the amatory war underlying identification with the other sex. Nevertheless, couples, held in contempt, have come together again, homosexual or heterosexual, mothering or sadomasochistic.

One may surmise, regardless of the evolution of the body sciences and changes in manners that precede and follow, women shall need the couple, especially during the fertile period of their lives, in order to have a certain reliability. Even if it means dissociating part of their sexual lives from the life of that couple. Motherhood – another love that is dissolving and death-bearing, ecstatic and lucid, delightful and painful – needs a support. A mother's mother must be present – a role that, since the collapse of large families or clans in contemporary life, has fallen to the father.

Why should man consent to that function? What might he seek there, a Don Juan urged on by tribal emotions? A more or less incorrigible teenager, he nevertheless imagines himself free, like the poet, to the extent that he cherishes the mother; he remakes her by getting her pregnant in place of the father; or else, matricidally, he rejects her by preferring a rival. But he cannot get out of it. It is his way of settling her accounts, desirable castrator that she is, morbid source of life, mother earth, land of the dead. An account eternally in abeyance, including when he abandons both mother and wife to his clan-stimulated erections in a sequel of women or signs of glory, for the sake of his self-esteem. The beyond of the couple is a beyond of the mother. Those who believe they have reached it do not cease violating her in the language: they are creators of style, of music.... As to the woman, she reaches that beyond as mother-woman, through the community of her children that neutralizes the pregnancy of the couple. In most cases, it is true, the children repress the child-bearer who nevertheless knows the discrete glory of *multiplying herself through her off-springs….*

And the couples of old people, you might ask, the most touching, the most stubborn? Do they not tell another story: that of a withered love, still impish perhaps, but tempered in the chestnut-hued autumn of friendship….

Genny dreams only of slaughter …

There are no more dissimilar persons than Genny, a blonde with a sturdy body of a farmer from the Landes region, and the beautiful Italian whom Shakespeare immortalized under the name of Juliet. And yet, her eternal childhood, her intelligent innocence that masks a mischievous and at times fearsome aggressivity immediately reminded me of the Verona heroine. The connection never ceased to impress me, in spite of Genny's less than idyllic lot, and as you will surely understand it made me smile at my tendency for ready analogies…. Genny complains, at the beginning of her analysis, of the stormy relations that keep brewing between herself and the women around her. A mother whom we have called, just between the two of us (and I shall return to this new and strange 'couple' made up of analysand and analyst), a submarine mother, so deep and invisible her presence was in Genny's life, showed up early in her narrative. Holding the only respectable power in that low-income family, culinary power, the mother is in Genny's eyes an impeccable and disgusting cook, a fat, dirty body that dominates the slender father, a music lover, uprooted from overseas amusement fairs that were his only joy…. Genny symbolically parted with her mother during the first years of her analysis, tearing herself away from her grip by means of pregnancies that brought her a girl and a boy – tangible corroboration that she, too, is a mother, an even better one than the other.

At this point, another person, heralded with considerable mystery and idealizing veneration as early as our first meetings, an essential but also submarine person, walks onstage: the husband. By coincidence, John's profession was the same as mine and Genny was able to tell me everything she had against it, on the basis, of course, of the way her husband practiced it. I already knew that she had married him to 'get away from my family, I am the one who taught him sex and that says it all because, at seventeen, I knew nothing about it'. Child-husband, underage-savior, John constituted, thanks to his family, whose easy circumstances both seduced and annoyed Genny, a home, a sturdiness, a house. Her indecisive husband, whom she had to guide at first, was nevertheless for Genny a sort of good mother. Or at least he completed, through his own clan, the failing image of her mother as source of shame, which was hers during her childhood; John's clan brought the image of an elegant mother-in-law, self-confident, able to impress other women. An ideal mother. But now, as Genny, herself a mother, was also becoming the recognized and appreciated woman that she had found in her husband – what was she to do with such a husband? Seeing furthermore that he was no longer satisfied with his position as a minor and, following his own evolution, assumed the bearing of a master? The compensating couple no longer had a reason for being.

'Kill', such a thought became more and more obsessive with Genny. Kill whom? Him or myself? For the abhorred, desired, gap-filling and burdensome, security-giving and dissolving couple is also the one that the analysand, in her imagination, makes up with her analyst. For better and for worse, with the desire that it last, and the panic-stricken, obsessive fear that it might never end. And what about analysts who, it is said, play the game, make marriages and divorces – to take their place within the couple?

As for Genny, she thinks she wants to kill John. At times, she sees this as a fake desire, sprung out of a movie or a detective novel, and which she does not endorse. At other times, on the contrary, it appears to her as the only reasonable way out. Indeed, how else could she discard the burden she believes her husband henceforth to be? She considers divorce impossible: 'there are the children, and then our parents – mine and John's – would not hear it!' She then contemplates an accident – a murder disguised as an accident…. Genny dreams of nothing but slaughter: she drives John down a ravine; a train runs over him cutting his throat – yes, precisely, with unbelievable accuracy; she has his car booby-trapped, it explodes and blows his body to pieces, 'one finds only unidentifiable fragments …' – 'You mean, perhaps, it was someone else' – 'Oh no, it was John alright', Genny insists, always ready to reject my suggestions. 'Anyway,' she continues, 'very near the place of the accident there was a house with a yard around it, like yours, but with a lake where you were drowning, when the explosion attracted a crowd, and thus you were saved…. So, you see…', Genny concluded, relieved. But I was obstinate: 'Murdering John helped to save the submarine mother.' Ginette, once more, claims she does not see the connection. But suddenly, doubtless in connection with my drowning, she stays almost two months without coming to her sessions. She plays dead: I had taken both John's and her mother's place in her desire to kill the devouring couple. She thus at the same time wanted to give me a wide berth (I was drowning her?) and atone for her murderous desire by a shameful flight.

When she came back it was to tell me that in fact things were going well, and she supposed I had understood that under such circumstances she did not need one. She had an excellent vacation with John, 'insufferable as always, but what do you expect'. And we spent a long time digging out her hatred, through myself, for the mother that she could not afford to hate – the same hatred that Genny had buried in 'her' couple. Love-hatred, passion of the eldest daughter who had been rejected in favor of the next one, the younger sister whom the father preferred and the mother nourished, having weaned Genny in order to do so. All that was left for her to do was to reject the entire family in turn, her despicable clan, and rise above it all, through books. But the intellectual, cut off from her roots, remained nostalgic for her big devouring mother who was to be devoured. She was, in short, addicted to jouissance, the housewife who had confessed to her daughter ('but it is possible that I am making this up', says Genny, doubtfully) the pleasure she felt when she made love with her own father, and how sure she was that such and such an orgasm had produced such and such a child.... Since she had imagined that she could behave with John as if she were his nourishing mother, Genny had become frigid.

Genny's couple foundered for a while under the squalls of a hatred that analysis nevertheless partially deflected toward maternal figures, the analyst's to begin with. Genny left John in order to 'love madly, with a true love', one of her young homosexual friends – Henry, thirsting for friendship, at a low trough of his exhausting hard-core erotic exercises. They lived for a while through the romantic idyll of Romeo and Juliet: with tenderness, courtliness, troubadour-style, androgynal identification. And with the entire range of Genny's anal-clitoridean orgasm, thus identified with a penis-bearing woman, a dirty but total woman. The phallic assumption was left behind when, being sure of having and even being the phallus – 'like Henry, we are all alike' – Genny came out of her social phobia and strove to achieve true professional recognition. She rode to the head of her department and immediately relinquished her passion for Henry without for that matter leaving him. Her mother's death brought her back to the family home – less to John than to the children. 'A woman of two couples, that is what I am, bigamous. In fact, if John were more perverse and Henry more maternal, that would be ideal.'

The name and social rooting provided by the husband constitute a weak dam against the excitive fever marked by 'more' and 'that is not it', which rock the hysterical person. Beyond them – and it is truly a beyond that is involved – the body, center of desire, longs for an ethereal idealization where the mirage of the 'perfect couple' is seen to hover. The ideal for the hysterical person would be a maternal harbor provided with a penis – a perverse mother. For that sake, to imagine herself like that, she is ready for anything, from orgy to pain, from enslavement to death.

The perverse mother: a conglomerate of good mother and almighty father, fused into one monstrous, adorable, fulfilling being. Sexually desired? Not exactly. Genny's erotic life with Henry was more phantasmal than real (for Henry continued to find his best pleasure with men). But because this allows her to let her fantasies run wild – she is a woman equal to the man, a mother with a penis – she holds on to him. The homosexual experience with Henry enabled her to hold a discourse without handicap, daring, obscene – in short, to speak as one is supposed to speak with an analyst, as the analyst is supposed to speak even if he or she remains silent. Were Henry and Genny (another variation on the analyst-analysand couple?) acting out an erotic fantasy frustrated by the couch?

Conversely, the maternal, phobic-obsessive, security-giving, law-full John, had no imaginary. The law without imaginary is the enemy of the couple. It rests on husbands who merely perform their duty, and nothing more; joined with their own frigid mothers, impeccable spouses and housewives, such husbands establish an abode, not a couple. Their sexual performance, often respectable, does not prevent their wives from being depressed, nymphomaniac, or suicidal. And hysterical wives do not make mistakes. Suddenly filled with hatred, these contemporary *bacchantes then rush out to capture their interwoven, indissociable pleasure and love, in the guise of a claim for phallic recognition. Many present-day feminist demands are cast in that mold.*

The androgynal lovehate, the fascinated identification of Genny with Henry was fed by hatred even more strongly than with John. Apart from the fact that, once named, present, acknowledged, hatred was finally revealed as the deep motivation for Genny's jouissance. 'Here lies a submarine, penetrating mother, whom my jouissance and paranoid longing for power wish to equal' – that is the signal given by such a passional householdry. For having lived it to the end, in her body and in words, Genny ends her analysis by choosing to be a woman. 'The true couple, with someone different and made of a piece,it is finally with you that I experienced it,' she told me. 'But in reality John suits me better, if one truly has to, if one must, live with someone. Because we are, each one of us, incomplete, and the couple completes, otherwise it makes no sense. While with Henry there are never two of us, there are two copies of the same, the print and the negative. Obviously, I joy in it, but I lose myself in it, too. I go mad, if you must know: at times, I do not know which sex is mine and which is his. So, I feel like disappearing, killing myself. Not him this time, but myself …. Fortunately there is John, who is willing to put up with my going from one to the other ….'

The sleep of lovers

Even though the death of the Verona lovers is beyond remedy, the spectator has the feeling that it is only sleep. In the denial that makes us dream of the two corpses as being mere sleepers, it is perhaps our thirst for love – magical challenge to death – that speaks out. The risky game with the sleeping drug in the very events of the play already suggests such a confusion. Nevertheless, the final image of the motionless couple perhaps leads us to the promised land constituted by the sleep of lovers. Indeed, the erotic satisfaction of desires is not the soothing primary identification, and in that sense 'love confiscates narcissism'.[11] Sleep is then both a restoration of narcissism, exhausted through desire, and a protective shield that allows amatory representation to take shape. Without the representation of the lovers' union, sleeping in each other's arms, erotic expenditure is a race toward death. The sleep of lovers, moreover, merely refills a stock of imaginative energy that is ready, at the wakening, for new expenditures, new caresses, under the sway of the senses …. Romeo and Juliet, in their sleeping death, are, like our sleep together when we are in love, a stock of fusional images that assuage erotic frenzy for a while before stimulating it again.

The transference situation and analytical discourse also provide us with a certain amorous, imaginary stock for our erotic and social dramas. But without allowing us to fall asleep, analysis sets out to be the lucid wakening of lovers.

Notes

1. As for Romeo, he suspects that the Name is obscene, like an obscene part of the body, and consequently (we may say it, but he cannot) the name is the source of desire: 'In what vile part of this anatomy / Doth my name lodge? tell me, that I may sack / The hateful mansion' (III, iii, 105 – 7).

2. See the Arden edition of the Works of Shakespeare, *Romeo and Juliet*, edited by Brian Gibbons (London: Methuen, 1979).

3. Ibid., p. 41.

4. Perhaps one should also mention the nurse's speech, the good mother, who maintains her trust in time and takes pleasure in evoking Juliet's birth, childhood, and destiny, as well as earthquakes that are casually, innocently suggested.

5. 'It lies not in our power to love or hate, / For will in us is over-rul'd by fate' – CHRISTOPHER MARLOW, *Hero and Leander*, I, 167–8.

6. See A. GREEN, *Hamlet et Hamlet* (Paris: Balland, 1982) and particularly his thesis, which holds that Polonius's children are the King's illegitimate children; it would have been to avenge that unfaithfulness that the Queen killed the father-King and married his brother. A marriage of betrayal and hatred, that generalized Oedipal perspective that Hamlet may have gained over his destiny forces the primal scene itself into the heart of his psychic experience. As a superrepresentable, a primal spectacle, a prime mover of the play that extols the representation of representation.

7. See PHILIPPE SOLLERS, *Femmes* (Paris: Gallimard, 1983), pp. 467–9, where he suggests that interpretation of Shakespeare's 'homosexuality'.

8. See 'Drives [Instincts] and their Vicissitudes', *in Papers on Metapsychology* (1915).

9. In that connection, see my *Powers of Horror* (New York: Columbia University Press, 1982).

10. *Three Essays on the Theory of Sexuality*. See also 1.

11. See *Eros et Anteros*, pp. 195ff.

ANDRÉ GREEN OTHELLO: A TRAGEDY OF CONVERSION : BLACK
MAGIC AND WHITE MAGIC*

André Green is a French psychoanalyst who has also ventured into the
realm of literary criticism. His book The Tragic Effect: The Oedipus
Complex in Tragedy first appeared in French in 1969 but was
subsequently translated by Alan Sheridan and published by
Cambridge University Press in 1979. In his Foreword to this edition,
Frank Kermode ventured to reject some of Green's suggestions about
Othello, although he was forced to admit that, 'I think my understanding of that tragedy is increased, not only by what I accept but
also by what I resist' (The Tragic Effect, p. xii). The following extract
comprised the first two sections of Green's substantial essay on
Othello. His study of particular texts is preceded by a long theoretical
Prologue in which he seeks to establish 'a mysterious bond between
psychoanalysis and the theatre' (ibid., p. 1). He asserts that the theatre
is 'the best embodiment of that "other scene", the unconscious' (ibid.),
and that the 'edge' of the stage represents a kind of frontier between
the unconscious and theatrical representation of its concerns.Theatrical
representation promises the disclosure of material repressed into the
unconscious as part of the emergence of the human subject into full
subjectivity. Green argues that in addition to the manifest text, that is,
the words uttered by the characters, there is also a latent text, a
'notional text implied by the action' (ibid., p. 6). Moreover, he also
insists that 'No reading can be either that of the representation or that
of the text, but only that of a text in performance, in representation'
(ibid., p. 7). He goes on to argue for a pre-Freudian (Aristotelian) and
post-Freudian way 'of listening to the unconscious', and that with the
advent of psychoanalysis a change occurred 'in the relation between
the implicit and the explicit' (ibid., p. 17). And he suggests further that
'The aim of a psychoanalytic reading is the search for the emotional
springs that make the spectacle an affective matrix in which the
spectator sees himself involved and feels himself not only solicited but
welcomed, as if the spectacle were intended for him' (ibid., p. 18). It is
from this position that he embarks on a reading of Othello as a tragedy
concerned with neurosis and psychosis. To some extent Green's
terminology echoes certain concerns of Stephen Greenblatt, but his
notion of jealousy is peculiarly Freudian in its insistence that 'Every
man ... is born of two parents one of whom was the object of his desire

---

*Reprinted from The Tragic Effect: The Oedipus Complex in Tragedy (trans. Alan
Sheridan, Cambridge: Cambridge University Press, 1979), pp. 88–123.

and the other an obstacle to the fulfilment of his desire.' Moreoever, he goes on to answer the question of why we are 'ourselves, interested in the spectacle'.

For the use of Alain Cuny
... e che da me le Donne Italiane imparino, di non si accompagnare con huomo, cui la Natura, e il Cielo, e il modo della vita disgiunge da noi.
(Giraldi Cinthio, quoted by Bradley)

For when the flames of love arise,
Then Self, the gloomy tyrant, dies.
(Muhammad ibn Muhammad (Jalal et Din),
quoted by Freud (Standard Edition, XII, 65))

The psycho-analyst and *Othello*

What is a psycho-analytic reading? Let us not play the innocent and dodge the difficulty by replying: it is a reading by a psycho-analyst. The psycho-analyst reads Shakespeare for two reasons. First, because Shakespeare is a literary genius, whose creation is a rich source of knowledge about man. The enormous impact of his work, in which almost every man feels concerned, indicates that this knowledge is of a fundamental kind. Second, because Shakespeare is an investigator of the human characteristics that throw a bridge between that humanity of which all men are part and the humanity that belongs to the proper field of the psycho-analyst: that of neurosis and psychosis. Just as there is an alienation common to all men and an alienation that affects only some of them, Othello belongs, by good or ill chance, to both registers. Every man feels inevitably involved in jealousy, since he is born of two parents one of whom was the object of his desire and the other an obstacle to the fulfilment of his desire; some men experience insane jealousy, though the clinician observes a whole range of intermediary states between the most ordinary structures, those closest to the common condition of men, and the most mysterious structures, those furthest removed from communicable experience.

So the psycho-analyst approaches *Othello* with curiosity and sympathy. What does he hope to find? Before answering this question, let me deal with some of the possible objections to his approach. The analyst does not arrive before the text in a virginal state. He is pregnant with his knowledge, that is to say, burdened,bound by his prejudice. He cannot attain the emptiness that he must practise whenever he undertakes the analysis of a patient, listening with his 'third ear' to the new sounds of the analytic speech. He cannot do this, because the text that is submitted to him is not the text of a psycho-analytic session. That is a form of speech that is both free in that it has let go its rational moorings, and constrained by the analytic pact to say everthing. So, on the one hand, we have an analyst with an analytic theory – that of Freud on jealousy – and, on the other, a text communicated through written speech, which is no more analysable than its author would be through it. So is not the whole undertaking doomed to failure, especially if the analyst desires to hear only the text and not the author? There is a false dilemma here. If the analysis is true, then the analyst derives true knowledge about man from it. He may set out to verify it, even when the technical conditions of analysis are not fulfilled, as if he were confronted simply by one of the various modes of disguise that he encounters in his practice. It is a frozen disguise, and therefore not accessible to an interrogation capable of providing an answer, even a veiled one. But it is a fixed disguise, that is to say, apprehensible, open to as many readings as are necessary to form an opinion. Meaning is veiled but also unveiled by that very veiling, since the veil clings so closely to what it hides that it reveals its contours exactly.

Did not Freud think that psycho-analytic therapy was itself merely one of the aspects of applied psycho-analysis, psycho-analysis claiming above all to be a theory and method that would lead to general conclusions that went well beyond those derived from the treatment of the neuroses? Through what language can the encounter between a subject (psycho-analyst) and an object (*Othello*, the Shakespearean tragedy) take place? Through language written to be represented. *Othello* is a play written to be performed, to be represented. It implies the existence, therefore, not so much of a reader as of a spectator–listener who has to be involved. The psycho-analyst's reading will therefore be a double reading: a reading of the text and a reading of the representation, that is to say, a search in the organization of the signifiers for whatever it is that affects the spectator–listener through its representation in the representation. In short, the question is, why was the Elizabethan spectator, and why are we ourselves, interested in the spectacle?

This first double reading will, therefore, be confronted by another double reading, that of the Freudian theory of jealousy with that of the phenomenology of the experience of jealousy. It might be thought that one could establish a relation between, on the one hand, the representation and the phenomenological experience of jealousy, both grouped under the banner of the conscious, and, on the other hand, the organization of the signifiers that support the representation by acting on the spectator–listener and the Freudian theory, the last two being placed at the level of their effects on the subject in the register of the unconscious.

Freud deconstructs the conscious experience of jealousy. He proposes its 'construction' at the level of the unconscious. Shakespeare, who describes an insane jealousy in order to make his public share it, succeeds in this, because he set in operation, unknown to himself, a homologous construction.

1 Structure, subject, trial

Synchronic difference and diachronic difference

Of Shakespeare's four major tragedies, *Hamlet, Macbeth, Lear* and *Othello*, the last is the only one with a contemporary setting. Based on a story by Giraldi Cinthio, *Othello* dates from 1604, three years after *Hamlet*, a year before *King Lear*, two years before *Macbeth*. (A comparison between Cinthio's and Shakespeare's plots, interesting as it may be, only brings out Shakespeare's genius in pruning, simplifying, tightening up – for the whole interest of *Othello* derives from the articulation between the elements of action, character and language. Two differences are perhaps worth mentioning. In Cinthio's version, Iago is in love with Desdemona and his villainy is motivated by the fact that his love is not reciprocated. Moreover, the crime is committed jointly by Iago and Othello, who simulate an accident.)

The *Hecatommithi* (published in 1565), from which *Othello* is taken, is a collection of stories recounted by passengers during a sea voyage from Rome to Marseilles in 1527. Shakespeare found the material for a tragedy in an anecdotal narrative, similar to the interludes that are interspersed among the adventures of *Don Quixote* to entertain the reader. This was not the first or the last time that Shakespeare was to use a contemporary plot, but *Othello* is the only tragedy in which he did so.

It is as if the distance that tragedy always requires – a distance that gives the hero his special aura and which is usually produced by setting the scene in the past – was created here by the myth of a distant origin. Certain critics, among them were Oscar Campbell, have noted a certain 'far away and long ago' quality in the character of Othello himself. The last descendant of a race of giants, he is too large-scale a figure for this small world. The play is called *Othello, the Moor of Venice*, thus marking the distance between the hero's native country and the city of the Doges.[1] But this substitution for the diachronic effect of a synchronic effect proves a source of ambiguity.

In my view, there is a very close correspondence between the contemporaneity of the action and the foreign origin of the hero, that ultimate foreignness that complete blackness would represent for a Renaissance world in the process of discovering strange new lands.[2] These links enable us to understand that there is from the very beginning of the play, a context of alienation – the sociological aspect reflects it – whose aim is to establish a difference (which Othello would like to reduce by his admission to Venetian citizenship).[3] The essence of this alienation is

original here, and dependent on place of birth, where in the ancient tragic
forms it was usually established by the evocation of a mythical time or the
exceptional circumstances surrounding the hero's birth.

The two worlds and their representatives

There are in *Othello* two worlds: that of men and that of the gods. The
human world is divided into three classes.

First, there is the 'class of power', that of the state of Venice,
administered by the Doges. This class is jealous of its power and of its
wealth. It serves as a framework to the tragedy, appearing at the beginning
and at the end. But this class, which sits in council and represents 'the
bloody book of law', subtly betrays it to safeguard its own interests. As
often in Shakespeare, the class of power is one not quite on the point of
collapse, but which has lost its self-confidence and is under reprieve. The
Turks are defeated, not by the Republic of Venice, but by the storm. But
Venice has already revealed its weaknesses in the failure of old Brabantio
to get a father's word respected. For if Desdemona's consent is enough to
declare her marriage valid, why defend Cyprus and prevent it from being
seduced by the Turks?

Then there is the 'class of pleasure', to which Desdemona belongs, the
class of love and gallantry, of the flower of Venetian youth. Desdemona in
no way surrenders this world, whatever she says, as is clear in the scene of
her arrival in Cyprus. No doubt she wishes to be associated with Othello's
military exploits, but is it not obvious that she goes on enjoying the
pleasures of the girl she still is, judging by the sport and mirth of the second
act, while her husband is still at sea, perhaps even in danger? Othello and
Iago do not belong to this class. Desdemona – despite her desire to share
Othello's life as a soldier – does not renounce the advantages of her sex,
and Cassio, though a soldier, does not forget that there are times when a
handsome officer is also a gallant. Cassio, too, belongs to the class of
pleasure. Not that he is entirely part of it: he is there as a mediator.

The third class is that which communicates between the first two. It is
the 'class of war', between the power that it serves and the pleasure that it
despises. It is the class of heroes and of men. Othello's tragic situation
stems from the fact that by his marriage he stands between power and
pleasure and is incapable of bringing together these two extremes which,
for him, are as far apart as heaven and earth.

Opposite this speaking world there is the silent world of the gods, who
work away unheard and unseen by men. There is an opposition between
the Moorish gods, who work through magic and sorcery, and the Christian
God, a God of love, of fidelity, but also a subtle, crafty God, whose servants
bear on their faces a thousand contradictory and mysterious expressions
that are a source of deception. Once the transgression has been committed

with the marriage of Desdemona and Othello, made possible by Othello's conversion, this conversion itself turns against him the Moorish gods of his birth, whom he has abandoned, and also turns away from him the Christian God, who wishes to have nothing to do with him. Together they make him pay for this conversion with his life.

No individual figure emerges to represent the class of power. The agents of the law, the Doge in particular, are, quite rightly, a mere expression of the government, as also are the senators, apart from the sorry figure of Brabantio. They display neither strength, virtue nor courage. They react to the Turkish threat rapidly and efficiently, but they do not refer to a heritage in danger, or to a threat to some part of the national territory. Cyprus is a warehouse to be defended, a key position on the trade route to the East. It would seem that Shakespeare intended to contrast the magnificent monstrosity of the Moor, who arouses pity, with the timid mediocrity of the Doge's ambassadors as represented by Lodovico and Gratiano. In the last act, when Roderigo, Cassio and Iago are killing one another and cries for help echo unanswered in the night, Lodovico is concerned more for his own safety than with rising to the situation:

> Two or three groan. It is a heavy night.
> These may be counterfeits: let's think't unsafe
> To come in to the cry without more help.

> (V, i)

It is the same Lodovico who brings the tragedy to an end, as the ambassador of power:

> Myself will straight abroad and to the State
> This heavy act with heavy heart relate.

> (V, ii)

The last word is for the Republic of Venice, its governors and its God.

It is not difficult to establish a relation between the characters of the first act and the 'messengers of Venice' of the last act, passing judgement on Othello's crime. It might be said that Lodovico is to the Doge what Gratiano is to Brabantio. The first two are the representatives of the interests of the state, the second two of the rights of the family. The Doge and Lodovico lay down the law and issue orders, but they do not persuade us of the authenticity of their idea of justice or authority. Brabantio and Gratiano are pitiful figures who would have been quite incapable of preventing either the elopement (in Brabantio's case) or the murder (in Gratiano's). Here, as often in Shakespeare, power is suspended. The fact that this situation recurs so frequently shows that the Shakespearean

universe does not so much stigmatize power for its mistakes as bind it
indissolubly to its decline. Moreover, Shakespeare shows how impossible it
is for any power to maintain itself at the level at which it is expected to
operate. Political power is linked with paternal power under the emblem
of the phallic signifier. It is to this that Othello must come, in this tragedy;
it is here that he must prove himself before Eros by acceding to the
situation of a husband, that is to say, by taking in Desdemona's eyes the
place of the father from whom he took her. And Desdemona, with her own
lips, before the entire Senate, has declared in his favour. He wanted the
father's place: he has it. This is as much as to say that he puts himself in a
position to lose it.

The class of soldiers is represented by two major figures: the valiant
Moor and his ensign Iago. Othello, called to plead his cause before the
senators, describes himself thus:

> Rude am I in my speech,
> And little blest with the soft phrase of peace.
>
> (I, iii)

For Othello, peace is the time of love. It is not so much that he lacks
eloquence, since it was precisely his eloquence that seduced Desdemona,
but it is a soldier's eloquence and it was through the accounts of his
adventures that he won his bride:

> And little of this great world can I speak,
> More than pertains to feats of broil and battle.
>
> (I, iii)

Many commentators have pointed out there is nothing 'rude' about
Othello's style, with its hyperbole and high-flown figures of speech, spiced
with evocations of his African condition that verge on bombast. His
powerlessness when confronted with the experience of jealousy lies in his
use of the traditional language of love. When he questions himself for the
first time about the possible causes of Desdemona's infidelity (III, iii), he
cites his age ('for I am declined / Into the vale of years'), his colour ('Haply,
for I am black') and his manners ('And have not those soft parts of
conversation / That chamberers have'). His vacillation in love corresponds
to a failing in his language.

Iago's misogyny is striking and has been noted by everyone. It is easy
enough to interpret it as stemming from the homosexuality that unites the
members of what Freud called that 'artificial crowd', the army. For the
moment, let us just examine his attitude to women; the first scene of the
second act gives him an opportunity of expressing this in the play of
apologies in which Desdemona invites him to participate for her

amusement. Iago emerges as the soldier for whom all women are tarts, 'Players in your housewifery, and housewives in your beds'. The important point for us is to note the signification of this attitude for Iago himself. For it obeys an imperative: narcissistic mastery in the omnipotent exercise of the means at his disposal in the service of self-interest. This is his false scent; this return of desire, which is expressed only through its negation, will not prevent it from being linked with his unconscious desire, of which I shall say more later. The malignity that has been analysed, though seldom accounted for – critics have been right to say that it is without foundation - is not enough to dispel the mystery of the character and cannot be taken as the ultimate motive of his action.

Cassio is the third element of this triad. We have already placed him, as Desdemona's companion, in the class of pleasure. But he is also a soldier, the Moor's lieutenant, having overtaken Iago, his senior, in obtaining this promotion. He differs profoundly from the other two in manners and upbringing: "tis my breeding / That gives me this bold show of courtesy' (II, i). He has neither the rough manners nor the crude speech of a soldier. Iago calls him 'a great arithmetician', and a 'bookish theoric' (I, i). He is a wit rather than a hardened soldier, a man who knows how to talk to the ladies, a master of all the gallantries that win their hearts. 'Very good; well kiss'd! an excellent courtesy!' remarks Iago, observing him and biding his time. He is the Moor's exact negation and provides an image very close to one of those patrician's sons who were rivals for Desdemona's hand in Venice and to whom she preferred Othello.

Othello, Iago and Cassio constitute the three points of the male triangle, a triangle imposed on the female triangle formed by Desdemona, Emilia and Bianca. Although Desdemona is the central figure in this triangle – as Othello is for the class of soldiers – she assumes her full value only when associated with Emilia, who serves as her lady's companion, and is contrasted with Bianca, the prostitute, with whom Othello identifies her at the end of the tragedy. Thus three images of woman are drawn. Desdemona is the young bride, the young beloved, hardly yet a woman, still close to the masculine part of herself in phallic identification with her husband. Emilia is the married woman, who has lost the early illusions of marriage, the object of the sarcastic remarks of her husband, whom she serves with submission, but to whom she is not bound by fidelity. We do not know whether to believe Iago when he accuses her of having been the mistress of both Othello and Cassio. It may be that this, like others of his remarks, is a calumny – but she herself, at the end of the tragedy, when Desdemona asks her whether she would be unfaithful to her husband, replies unambiguously: 'In troth, I think I should; and undo't when I had done' (IV, iii). What, then, distinguishes Emilia from Bianca, the soldier's girl, a prostitute, perhaps, but a good-hearted girl for all that, who is sincerely in love with Cassio? The fact that she gets money out of it?

Emilia, an honest woman, who is not without generosity, since she is to sacrifice her life to vindicate the truth, says: 'who would not make her husband a cuckold to make him a monarch?' (IV, iii).

Desdemona, at the very beginning of her married life, seems to be confronted here with other types of feminity and, at this point, she has not yet opted decisively for any one of them. She contains within herself the ambiguity of several possible ways.

The subject between two trials

Who is, where is, the subject in Othello? The title seems to provide an answer: Othello is the hero as subject. This is obvious enough but it does not take us far and leaves the real questions unanswered. Is the subject, then, the subject as the subject of the tragedy, jealousy? There is a middle way: these two aspects may be brought together to reveal the subject as jealous hero. But this is to settle the matter rather prematurely, for it is to use words pregnant with meaning that seem rather too self-explanatory. Why is it necessary to dwell on the topic of jealousy at all? Is it not so widespread an experience that anyone may identify with it directly enough to understand on the normal scale what Othello experiences in an exaggerated form?

Let us suspend judgement on jealousy and its signification. Let us note simply that the subject in the structural sense is the trial, the trial as process of the tragedy, as the nodal point of the forces inter-linked in the spectacle. It is the spectacular trial of the destruction after its conquest, or by its conquest, of the love-object whose loss involves the loss of the ego. It is as if this misfortune were a terrible penalty, a punishment laid down by some invisible authority.

If we think back to the four great tragedies, we note that the tragic element in *Hamlet* derives from circumstances that take place before the action of the play, and which confront the hero with obligations that he feels incapable of carrying out – the revenge of his father's murder. In *Macbeth*, the ambition that brings the hero to his downfall is primarily punished for crimes that it did not baulk at. As for *King Lear*, it is a defect of judgement that is expiated so dearly by the old king. There is nothing comparable in *Othello*. Here, everything is as it should be. Othello is a victorious captain whose marriage was also a sort of victorious battle sanctioned by a treaty – the approval of the Doge – and who suddenly falls as by some purely internal mechanism, which can be attributed only to insane passion. The subject, therefore, is the trial of insane jealousy.

But we must take things quite literally. For it is certainly a trial that is involved here. Indeed, the whole play is stretched between two trials: the trial of Desdemona's elopement with which the tragedy opens and the trial of her murder that brings it to an end, with the suicide of the jealous husband. *Othello* is the trial between two trials.

This final slaughter, in which only the deaths of the husband and wife concern us, forces us to seek the reason for this fatality. There is a suggestion here of the fulfilment of an oracle as in Greek tragedy. One sets out in quest of some equivalent that takes its place, like the appearance of the ghost in *Hamlet*, the strident predictions of the witches in *Macbeth*, or some riddling remark thrown out by the Fool in *Lear*. We must be content with less here: with a single sentence, in which Desdemona's father gives full vent to his sorrow and disappointment. His words serve as a curse that is to hang over Othello for the rest of his days.

The transgression, the necessary correlative of the punishment, is here (as always) paternal transgression. The elopement fully justifies the father's anger and ensuing curse. The law has been violated. The law here is respect for the father's trust in admitting the foreigner into his house: 'Her father loved me; oft invited me' (I, iii). But is this law simply the human law of hospitality? Does not such a series of misfortunes indicate an angry God? (Both Charlton and Swinburne mention the comparison with ancient tragedy.) Who would the gods be if they were present? Is it the Christian God from whom Othello forces Desdemona to ask pardon before her death? And who is Othello's God? Is it the God of his conversion? Is it some pagan god of war to whom Othello sacrifices everything? Would it not rather be the gods of Mauritania, whom he never mentions, but who are those of his birth? But who are the Moorish gods, what do they want? We have no means of knowing at first. Let us question the trial, which will tell us. Essentially, this trial will be a witches' trial; the Mauritanian god is a sorcerer's god.

The two trials

The elopement trial and the murder trial have the same object, the same clause, Desdemona. These two trials are won by Othello in somewhat different circumstances. In the elopement trial, he gets the sentence reversed and the secret marriage accepted. In the murder trial, he snatches victory as if from old Brabantio, who would hand him over to the courts, by inflicting his punishment on himself. His suicide, like that of any criminal, baffles justice. Othello gives himself death as he gave himself Desdemona. He was the author of the punishment. He does everything himself, preparing the way to the grave as he prepares the way to the bridal bed, as if all this was of concern only to him. The crime and the suicide are inextricably linked: a part of himself conquered by himself is destroyed to prove that it is conquered, bringing with this conquest the destruction of the conqueror who eternally proves that he is inseparable from his conquest.

The law of Venice recognized Othello's right to elope with Desdemona and to make her his. The law might take her back from him. The law did no more than approve his cause, a necessary approval for whoever wishes to live among his fellow men. But, in preference to life among men, Othello chooses his own law and his own desire, for which he needs no other approval than his own. To accept that the punishment should come from Venice is to accept a third authority between himself and Desdemona; it is to find himself once more face to face with something he wished to tear himself away from. To die for Venice, for Desdemona, yes. To die at the hands of Venice, Venice having taken Desdemona back from him, is to be for ever separated from the love-object. For Othello, the law and desire are one.

Sorcery and oracle

If we began at the end, with the outcome of this second trial, in the presence of the representatives of Venice – Lodovico and Montano, and more particularly Gratiano, the brother of Brabantio, Desdemona's dead father, who is thus represented by his brother – it is because the end often throws light on the beginning. Thus it is by means of a cunning trick – a hidden dagger – that the disarmed and guarded Moor succeeds in killing himself before the eyes of his judges. The effect of deception that is the keynote of the tragedy is even more striking if one remembers that the suicide by stabbing re-enacts Othello's account of how he once punished a Turk, 'a circumcised dog', for having beaten a Venetian and insulted the state. In doing so, Othello, despite the allegiance he has shown to his new masters and to his new God, kills himself by identifying himself with the victim closest to him in race and origin. Also, in the very movement in which he affirms his loyalty to Venice, by carrying out justice on himself, he subtracts himself from its law. The simulacrum here becomes truth.

Deception has once again been effective – again, for it was through deception that he seduced Desdemona. Travellers have leave to lie, but there is nothing to show that Othello lied in the fantastic accounts he tells of his own history. His deception lies elsewhere. While speaking to the father, he sought the ear of his daughter, who was attending to household duties.

> This to hear
> Would Desdemona seriously incline:
> But still the house-affairs would draw her thence;
> Which ever as she could with haste dispatch,

She'd come again, and with a greedy ear
Devour up my discourse: which I observing,
Took once a pliant hour; and found good means
To draw from her a prayer of earnest heart
That I would all my pilgrimage dilate,
Whereof by parcels she had something heard,
But not intentively.

(I, iii)

Brabantio's supervision was deceived only because Othello could not be
suspected of courting his daughter: he had devoted his life to soldiering
and, unlike Desdemona's usual suitors, whom she had rejected, Othello
was no longer a young man. This is why the old man cannot see in this
marriage, as do his peers the Doges, a natural consequence of a very
ordinary situation. He needs other reasons: the Moor has some power, the
Moor uses sorcery. Yet he has had a presentiment of the outcome in his
dreams: 'This accident is not unlike my dream' (I, i), he remarks when he
learns of Desdemona's elopement.

Nevertheless, he goes on to speak of

charms

By which the property of youth and maidenhood
May be abused.

'Thou hast enchanted her,' he tells the Moor:

Judge me the world, if 'tis not gross in sense
That thou has practised on her with foul charms;
Abused her delicate youth with drugs or minerals
That waken motion.

(I, ii)

For the nature of this virgin, brought up in the Christian religion, a
patrician's daughter, could not be deceived without sorcery, without 'some
mixtures powerful o'er the blood'.

The whole action of the tragedy is enveloped in the mystery of unleashed
acts of violence that constantly surprise: the sudden attack of the Turks, the
sudden rising of the storm, the dispersal and almost miraculous shipwreck
of the enemy, the survival of the Venetians, sailing through the storm
unscathed. Over all these events hovers the shadow of the supernatural.
Othello possesses a particular charisma since the deeds of valour associated
with his 'star' may indeed be imputed to some extra-terrestrial power. At
the very beginning of the play, Iago links Othello with demoniacal imagery.
He wakens old Brabantio by yelling up at his windows:

327

> An old black ram
> Is tupping your white ewe.

(I, i)

In this metaphor the erotic and satanic elements remain indeterminate, while two lines later, the latter completely obscures the former and retroactively tips the scales of meaning in one direction:

> Arise, arise!
> Awake the snorting citizens with the bell,
> Or else the Devil will make a grandsire of you

(I, i)

Othello is mentioned even before he appears in that space of phantasy that we do not enter. We seek him in the darkness of the scene that centres around the father's sorrow, as he himself will seek the handkerchief given to Desdemona to seal their union:

> there's magic in the web of it.
> A sibyl, that had number'd in the world
> The Sun to course two hundred compasses,
> In her prophetic fury sew'd the work;
> The worms were hallow'd that did breed the silk;
> And it was dyed in the mummy which the skilful
> Conserved of maidens' hearts.

(III, iv)

We may see in this two-hundred-year-old seamstress the phallic mother who combines in her creation the composition of silk and mortuary dust to make Desdemona's wedding veil – a veil held up between Othello and Desdemona because above all it is evidence of the Moor's desire for his mother. For it was she who gave it to him. On this point Shakespeare assigns a double origin to the precious material. According to the first version (III, iv), an 'Egyptian charmer' gave it to Othello's mother, while according to another passage in the last scene of the play the Moor declares that the handkerchief was given to his mother by his father. In so far as Shakespeare provides no justification for it, the mystery of this double origin must contradict any simplistic explanation such as, for example, that the Moor made it all up in order to frighten Desdemona. The mystery can only be cleared up by elucidating the phantasy that underlies the story. That is why it seems to me to be preferable to leave things as they are and to see in the coexistence of the two versions an invitation to articulate them one upon the other.

Is not the apparent contradiction like a double inscription of Othello's desire? The two versions are separated by Desdemona's death. Alive, she must be possessed of the attributes of a charm that she herself cannot inspire, but which is conferred on her by the handkerchief. She joins the line of women: the sibyl, the 'Egyptian charmer', the mother, all surrounded by a halo of omnipotence conferred on them by a gift such as that possessed by the Egyptian woman who 'could almost read / The thoughts of people', an omnipotence that goes with the handkerchief, its possession being a guarantee of the desire inspired by the love-object. Othello says of this talisman:

> while she [the mother] kept it,
> 'Twould make her amiable and subdue my father
> Entirely to her love; but, if she lost it,
> Or made a gift of it, my father's eye
> Should hold her loathed, and his spirits should hunt
> After new fancies.
>
>   (III, iv)

The father's eye is also the eye that Othello deceives in seducing Desdemona. When Desdemona is dead, Othello appears before the Venetian authorities sitting as an improvised court. It is the father who reappears on this occasion so that Othello may designate him as the one who gave the handkerchief to his mother, in recognition of her desire of the phallus.

The attribution to women of the power to charm, to which Othello is the first to refer, is contrasted later with the fact that it is her husband's wish that Desdemona should radiate beauty and charm. Each of Desdemona's attractions is later transformed, under the effects of jealousy, into a magic power: 'Death and damnation!' (III, iii). There is a devil in Desdemona. One may well wonder whether Othello is not evoking in the language of his new religion the powers of his ancestral faith. And in declaiming that Desdemona is a witch, is he doing any more than re-establishing her, after this loss of the handkerchief, in the series of maternal figures of primitive omnipotence, all-powerful in evil as they were in good? What was excluded from the phallic power reappears at the end of the tragedy only after Desdemona's death, in reference to the paternal speech that was betrayed by conversion to the Christian God. Othello's Name-of-the-Father (Lacan) having been defaced by this renunciation, it falls to another ridiculed father, Desdemona's, at the beginning of the tragedy, to invoke a punishment, however purely moral and ineffective it may be, following the elopement in which Othello is linked without mediator to Desdemona. But this paternal speech will be swamped in the illusory triumph over authority that the Doge's endorsement has made legal by recognizing the validity of the marriage.

For Othello will emerge absolved from the witch trial. In fact, Othello never doubted that he would. He never feared the justice of the Doge, and when he presents himself before the Senate, assembled as a court, he listens quietly to the Doge's promise to Brabantio:

> The bloody book of law
> You shall yourself read in the bitter letter
> After your own sense; yea, though our proper son
> Stood in your action.
>
> (I, iii)

This cannot touch him: he is the pillar of the state, the guarantor of the power of Venice. Iago has already said as much to the spectator:

> For, I do know, the State –
> However this may gall him with some check –
> Cannot with safety cast him.
>
> (I, i)

Othello confirms this when he defies Desdemona's father:

> Let him do his spite:
> My services which I have done the signiory
> Shall out-tongue his complaints.
>
> (I, ii)

In Jacques Lacan's terminology, I should say of Othello that at the moment of the tragedy he is the phallus. Or, as Lacan shows, *having* it implies that one ceases to sustain the belief that one *is* it. And all Othello's misfortunes stem from the fact that *being* a great captain, he will have to pass to the state in which he *has* a wife. The problematic of having her will reappear in everything affected by the question of 'having' or 'not having' the handkerchief.

This power attributed by Brabantio to Othello,this black magic, is simply the phallic power, the effect of Othello's seduction of Desdemona. The identification of the young Venetian woman with the triumphant hero of a thousand perils is thus expressly designated by Shakespeare:

> She wish'd
> That Heaven had made her such a man.
>
> (I, iii)[4]

And Othello says confidently and no doubt truthfully:

This only is the witchcraft I have used.

Brabantio is thunderstruck by his daughter's betrayal. In time, it kills him. Henceforth, all that remains for him is to struggle against the black magic with white magic. His God has betrayed and abandoned him. His peers are concerned more to preserve their wealth than their honour. Having lost, he asks, with cruel irony, that they should move on to the only matter that is of concern to the Doges at that moment: 'on to the State-affairs.' Nevertheless, he throws out a warning that serves as a kind of fate for his victor:

Look to her, Moor, if thou hast eyes to see:
She has deceived her father, and may thee.

(I, iii)

The eye of the betrayed father becomes the evil eye of the challenge, which will bring about the ruin of the wife who loses possession of the talisman. This is the equivalent in *Othello* of the oracle. And, as often in situations in which the oracle speaks, the hero replies with the quiet assurance of a favourable present. Thus the presumptuous Othello replies confidently and trenchantly:

My life upon her faith.

(I, iii)

He will pay for this reply with two lives rather than one, and will lose his faith.

2 Desire

The object of desire: between Desdemona and Othello

It is usual to develop analyses of *Othello* around the trio formed by the object of jealousy, Desdemona, its inducing agent, Iago, and the induced subject, Othello. When one limits oneself to this perspective, one is caught between tautology (jealousy is jealousy, it is inexplicable, it is without foundation) and lack of verisimilitude (*Othello* is a mere melodrama, totally divorced from reality). In the second case, one has no need to explain how a brilliant captain praised for his intelligence loses his head so easily when confronted with so crude a piece of scheming. One swings constantly between two theses, the first that makes Iago the diabolical constructor of the effective machinery in which Othello is caught like a fly in a spider's web, the second in which Othello, predisposed to jealousy, seizes upon the bait offered him by Iago to feed the green-eyed monster that inhabits him. In all these analyses one is struck by the exclusion of one term and the silence on one question. The discussion eliminates the character of Cassio, who is regarded as negligible, hardly more important than Roderigo or Montano, and not a moment's pause is given to the question of the possible foundation of Othello's jealousy: is it conceivable that Desdemona might love Cassio? In this case, the handkerchief plays the role of the decoy or lure, though this is not its only effect. Since Cassio possesses Desdemona's handkerchief only by accident or by someone else's design, and since Desdemona did not give it to him, the love attributed to them by Othello is pure imagination. But this exclusion and this silence are highly suspect. To begin with, one forgets that the play opens with an event that concerns Cassio: his recent promotion, which does not follow the normal course of events, to the rank of the general's lieutenant (*lieu-tenant*, one who takes the place of and replaces, when necessary). This promotion is presented to us solely from the point of view of the jealousy it arouses in the man who has most to lose from it, the ensign Iago, who is Cassio's senior. But the promotion is also evidence of another fact: Othello's predilection for Cassio; and we have no reason to reject the hypothesis of a possible favouritism on the part of the Moor. Indeed, by his behaviour, Cassio appears in no way to conform to the image that one has of the Moor's lieutenant, the man who must replace him on all occasions. On the contrary, he proves to be rather weak, irresolute, naive, effeminate. Certainly this Phoebus is attractive: young, handsome, well-bred, educated, a good talker, gallant, one who wins the hearts of young women by the attentions he pays them. It seems that Othello is hard put to justify this passing over when Iago's emissaries demand an explanation for the appointment. It is said that Othello

Evades them, with a bombast circumstance
Horribly stuff'd with epithets of war.

(I, i)

In the scene in which Iago casts suspicion on Cassio, Othello says that he 'went between us very oft'. That is Cassio's precise situation: he is between Desdemona and Othello. This means that he offers the young Venetian woman all that an education as a gallant has taught a young officer about the courtship of the fair sex and that he offers Othello his professional life as a soldier by way of gaining his affection. When Iago accuses Cassio and Desdemona of having an illicit love affair, we react in protest, indignant at such calumnious treachery. But it would be naive to see this as no more than pure invention. Iago does not invent this hypothesis simply to serve his own ends: he is convinced of it. Or rather, he anticipates it with discreet signs, but he does not create it out of nothing. Cassio, before the Moor, welcomes Desdemona to Cyprus; he does so in such a way that it is difficult to draw the line between admiration felt for the general's wife and a new kind of emotion. 'Divine Desdemona' is hailed like a queen:

> O, behold,
> The riches of the ship is come on shore!
> Ye men of Cyprus, let her have your knees.
> Hail to thee, lady!
>
> (II, i)

And, in Othello's absence, Iago makes the following commentary on their conversation:

> He takes her by the palm: ay, well said, whisper: with as little a web as this will I ensnare as great a fly as Cassio. Ay, smile upon her, do; I will gyve thee in thine own courtship. You say true; 'tis so, indeed: if such tricks as these strip you out of your lieutenantry, it had been better you had not kiss'd your three fingers so oft,which now again you are most apt to play the sir in. Very good; well kiss'd! An excellent courtesy! 'tis so, indeed. Yet again your fingers to your lips? Would they were clyster-pipes for your sake!
>
> (II, i)

Before we accuse him of vulgarity for this last remark, we should rather recognize at this point the mark of homosexuality in Iago's jealousy. The analysis of Desdemona's feelings that Iago gives Roderigo bears the mark of his subjective position, of course. But it is not entirely disqualified on that account. It may also contain a grain of truth – and when he declares, 'Desdemona is directly in love with him [Cassio]', he expands and therefore necessarily distorts what is visible of a courtship that at this stage is no more than light-hearted in its aims and traditional in its methods. Nevertheless, we should examine its development attentively. Will Desdemona's love of Othello last? Would this love at first sight, as Iago experiences it, prove to be no more than a flash in the pan? 'When the blood is made dull with the act of sport, there should be – again to inflame it, and to give satiety a fresh appetite – loveliness in favour, sympathy in years, manners, and beauties; all which the Moor is defective in' (II, i). Now, Cassio has all these things: everything that the Moor is defective in. The probable is not always true and the true not always probable. But is not the scene in which Desdemona should have shown more anxiety for her husband, who was still at sea in the midst of a storm that had not yet calmed, and in which she seems to have been very glad of Cassio's company, a sign of things to come? 'Didst thou not see her paddle with the palm of his hand? didst not mark that?' Iago asks, 'Yes, that I did; but that was courtesy', Roderigo protests. 'Lechery, by this hand .... They met so near with their lips, that their breaths embraced together' (II, i). Iago swears an oath with Roderigo, the spurned suitor, now tricked by his supposed friend, by offering him his hand as a sign of his sincerity. But as he does so his outstretched hand becomes in his phantasy first that of the courteous lieutenant, offered to Desdemona, then Desdemona's fingers penetrating Cassio from behind. Under sarcasm and mockery Iago masks the anticipated pleasure aroused in him by the play of interpenetrating breaths. We should remember Freud's observation about the desire of the jealous man who tears away the veil of the unconscious in order to make himself receptive to the secret of the signs of female seduction, which have been robbed of their signification by social usage. This extra-lucidity concerning the recognition of their erotogenic value, which has been eroded by social practice to such an extent that those who exchange them have lost any sense of their original function, is paid for in full by the *méconnaissance* of the part played in this game by the jealous man who deciphers these signs and interprets them. This prevents him from being the recipient of these acts of homage so that he is assured all the more of finding himself in a space outside his own view, brilliantly occupying the place too discreetly held by the female source of these messages. But we should not see this solely as the effect of projection. Projection also comes into play when he begins to interest us in the spectacle. In any case, there is, for the moment, nothing improbable in Iago's analysis. His description of Cassio – 'a knave very voluble; no further conscionable than in putting on the mere form of civil and humane seeming, for the better compassing of his salt and most hidden-loose affection ... a slipper and subtle knave; a finder-out of occasions ... the knave is handsome, young, and has all those requisites in him that folly and green minds look after' (II, i) – is perhaps exaggerated, in order to revive Roderigo's tottering faith. But it sins not so much by its falseness as by the illusion of insight to which it lays claim. Moreover, when he is alone, Iago shows that his appraisal of the situation is more moderate and that this appraisal is not simply pretence:

> That Cassio loves her, I do well believe it;
> That she loves him, 'tis apt, and of great credit.

> (II, i)

What follows is to show that Desdemona's 'inviting eye' has not failed to have its effect on Cassio, who has aroused Desdemona's affection. The two young people meet in secret, unknown to the general. Desdemona promises to plead Cassio's cause, that is to say, to question Othello's decision as if it were more important to her to save Cassio, whose guilt is acknowledged, than to respect her husband's judgement in an affair that hardly calls for intercessors:

> my lord shall never rest;
> I'll watch him tame, and talk him out of patience;
> His bed shall seem a school, his board a shrift;
> I'll intermingle every thing he does
> With Cassio's suit: therefore be merry, Cassio;
> For thy solicitor shall rather die
> Than give thy cause away.
>
> (III, iii)

It would seem that the critics and commentators have never read or heard those lines in which Othello's wife, the day after her wedding night, swears to her husband's second-in-command to regard his defence as being more important than any other matter, to use every opportunity, including that of conjugal intimacy, to obtain from her husband the rehabilitation of a man whom he has punished. And this is precisely what she does for the 'thrice-gentle Cassio', incurring Othello's displeasure in doing so. Realizing this, she nevertheless makes her situation worse by seeking help from a third party who has power over Othello (Lodovico) in order to make him change his mind. It is, of course, clear enough that the feelings involved here are not conscious or clearly defined in Desdemona. It is a love ignorant of itself, which grows unknown to her who feels it only because it is lived in innocence and purity. It is also a love in which all sexual desire is for the present banished. The desire is there, as desire of the Other, as Iago guesses. And no doubt Desdemona, at the moment of truth, would have perceived it. For how are we to understand, without falling into the platitudes of an explanation by blind self-sacrifice, the lines she speaks shortly before her death:

> 'Tis meet I should be used so, very meet.
> How have I been behaved, that he might stick
> The small'st opinion on my great'st abuse?
>
> (IV, ii)

Later, at the moment of her death, she defends herself, less perhaps to save her life than to convince Othello of her fidelity. What is in question is not so much an infidelity in act as a desire that hits the target by corresponding with Othello's sexual desire at the moment when he encounters his lack, which everything about Cassio reminds him of. To Emilia, who finds her dying, and presses her to reveal the author of her death, Desdemona replies: 'Nobody; I myself.' These words have been interpreted as proof of her unconditional and absolute love for Othello.

This is certainly the case. But the time of this final avoval coincides perhaps with her first avowal. On her last night, Desdemona confides to Emilia, who is preparing her for bed,her true feelings for the Moor:

> my love does so approve him,
> That even his stubbornness, his checks, his frowns, –
> Pr'ythee, unpin me, – have grace and favour in them.

(IV, iii)

As she undresses, she recalls the anger of her father, who refused his blessing to this marriage. She finds pleasure in her husband's abuse. Meeting the truth, she recognizes in Othello's desire the place she has come to occupy, the place of the woman who betrays the husband after betraying the father, who now pays with her husband's hand what she once made her father pay.

My hypothesis of Desdemona's love for Cassio as part of the kernel of truth is not complete, however. It must have as its complement another aspect of things, the aspect which is much more difficult to perceive and is totally obliterated from the spectator's view. Silent, but effective, the whole mainspring of the tragedy lies here: Othello's desire for Cassio. I have already noted that the tragedy begins with Cassio's promotion to the lieutenancy given by Othello himself, which suggests a particular favour on the part of the general. We have seen that all Iago's plotting must be bent to Cassio's cashiering, which lays the foundation of the jealousy, because it causes Desdemona to reveal her desire in defending the disgraced lieutenant. It has not been sufficiently noted how necessary this episode is. It is as if, for the jealousy to work, the object of desire which Cassio represents for Othello should weaken and disappoint. Cassio's devaluation precedes or coincides with Desdemona's devaluation.

It is a strange night, which was to have been a night of celebration for all. A wedding night that the elopement, the trial and the expedition had delayed, a night in which desire should blossom, all obstacles removed. The cause has been heard without the trial taking place, victory achieved without a battle. The night of Cyprus is full of promise:

> Come, my dear love,
> The purchase made, the fruits are to ensue;
> That profit's yet to come 'tween me and you. –
> Good night.

(II, iii)

The soldiers' drunkenness and the brawl that follows are set before us, mingling the din of drinking and singing with the clash of swords, while behind the scenes the encounter of the two bodies of Othello and Desdemona is taking place. And it is this night that the general's favourite chooses to disturb. Cassio permits the worst of crimes – apart from desertion – for a soldier: drunkenness and brawling while on guard. He arouses for Othello the spectre of weakness at the moment when he himself must make love his principal desire. When the lieutenant groans, 'Reputation, reputation, reputation! O, I have lost my reputation! I have lost the immortal part of myself, and what remains is bestial' (II, iii), we must see that these words do not concern him alone. In losing not only his reputation but the Moor's love, he also sullies Othello's reputation by thus revealing that Othello's choice of lieutenant was motivated less perhaps by honour than by partiality.

> Cassio, I love thee;
> But never more be officer of mine.
>
> (II, iii)

Of that love, nothing is left that can sustain the esteem of his men. In demoting Cassio, Othello throws doubt on his own judgement in promoting him so rapidly. By interrupting Othello's revels, Cassio suggests the solider's most unpredictable failing. The demotion of the lieutenant is reflected on to the object who now occupies first place; it passes from Cassio, his second, to Desdemona his half. But as a result of Cassio's demotion, the term that represents Othello as the impeccable, incorruptible general is cancelled out in the opposition between love for his men and the love he has just felt for his wife. This is the message that is brought back to him from the citadel he commands, which should have been sleeping in rediscovered peace and assuaged anxiety. This devaluation of the object of unconscious desire must bring him down so that, dislodged from the pedestal on which he stood, he might rekindle the slumbering feeling he inspired, in now finding himself the object of the compassion and solicitude of the Other. This Other that is his half will be his intercessor. What Desdemona does not know is that she will die for having revived the unbearable desire that Othello felt for Cassio. Iago's machination will have the same result. Henceforth, everything surrounding this unconscious, rejected love is caught up in a struggle to the death: either Othello will triumph and Cassio will disappear from his desire, or Othello will succumb and Cassio will triumph. Of the various possible endings, including the one in which the lieutenant might have been engulfed in the final slaughter, Shakespeare chooses the triumph of Cassio. Othello asks him for forgiveness and Lodovico pronounces the transfer of power:

Your power and your command is taken off,
And Cassio rules in Cyprus.

(V, ii)

This is more than a rehabilitation; it is a crowning that marks the
assumption of the subject and the defeat of the ego.

Othello's desire: between Eros and the death drive

Although commentators realize clearly enough that *Othello* is a tragedy of
jealousy, they have done little to situate the precise context of the birth of
this jealousy. It has been found surprising that Othello, at the moment of
death, should so unexpectedly say of himself that he was 'one not easily
jealous'. This is seen as a monstrous lack of self-knowledge. And yet there
is a grain of truth in the judgement. What we are witnessing is not simply
the contemporaneity of love and jealousy, but rather the contemporaneity
of marriage and jealousy. As long as the love-object is free, it is not
suspected, but as soon as the institutional bond is established, the bond
that re-establishes the knot that unites the father and the mother, then the
persecution-delusion of jealousy is triggered off. Moreover, we are not
surprised that it is during the wedding night that the drama erupts. The
noise of the young couple is muffled by the noise of the brawl in the citadel
and the spectator is himself distracted by the carousing from the other orgy
that is taking place behind the scene, in the nuptial chamber hidden from
sight, where the love-object falls from the altar of idealization, at the
moment when flesh is bound to flesh.

Too little has been said about this conjunction that unites the condition of
soldier and the condition of jealous man in Othello's character. By
separating the external framework from the action, one behaves as if the
former were contingent and one fails to take account of the relations that
unite the situation of the hero dedicated to a soldier's life with that of his
entry into the sphere of love. Everything shows us that Othello is gifted in
the art of war, that he is successful at it and that he has won glory in its
practice; there is nothing to show us that he might have the same talent in
love and reap the same success. Indeed, there are indications that this
warrior, so bound up with his companions in arms, has considerable
difficulty in accepting love and especially in being loved. In the first
instance, Desdemona was a fortified place to be captured. Then she is
subjected to his will, tamed. He cannot reconcile himself to seeing
Desdemona as no more than a woman, his wife; she becomes the woman
who will deprive him of being his wife, of no longer having to be
conquered. When he sets foot in Cyprus, he goes straight to her,
exclaiming: 'O my fair warrior!' This is no doubt the response to her desire,
expressed ever since they were married in Venice, to share Othello's

military life. On this point, a certain complicity unites them. But whereas
Desdemona can play on the two aspects of her desire – the masculine
aspect, which makes her a warrior's companion, and the feminine aspect,
which assures her that she will receive once again from Cassio the homage
due to her as a young patrician of Venice – Othello finds it much more
difficult to move from the field of battle to the infinitely more perilous one
of the marriage-bed.

Who can say what took place during their wedding night? And one may
well wonder what Othello means when, weeping over Desdemona's
corpse, he remarks:

> Cold, cold, my girl!
Even like thy chastity.

(V, ii)

If the Moor thinks that he did not succeed in moving Desdemona, as a
result of his own inability to allow himself to be invaded by love, how
much more plausible the basis of the jealousy then appears. Some other, for
whom this conquest was still to come, would certainly succeed where he
had failed. This other, who has 'all which the Moor is defective in', is
Cassio. The handkerchief testifies to this jouissance that Cassio has been
able to give Desdemona:

> And she did gratify his amorous works
With that recognizance and pledge of love
Which I first gave her; I saw it in his hand.

(V, ii)

Let us not forget the precise signification attached to this magic
handkerchief, whose power is to assure the efficacy of desire.

The fact that once Desdemona has lost the handkerchief she loses all
value in the eyes of Othello reveals, for me, its value as a fetish. Deprived
of her phallic emblem she is no more than a castrated woman – to be
avoided in order to avoid any contact with castration. But that Othello
himself should have lost possession of the handkerchief by giving it to her
was already a great risk – a risk that she transmit it to someone who had
everything that he lacked. This narcissistic quality[5] in Othello's love, which
is so marked at every point by the mapping of the signs of the phallus, is
attested in certain famous lines. When Othello is finally convinced of
Desdemona's infidelity, we learn what he has lost with her:

> O, now, for ever
Farewell the tranquil mind! farewell content!
Farewell the plumed troop, and the big wars,

> That make ambition virtue! O, farewell!
> Farewell the neighing steed, and the shrill trump,
> The spirit-stirring drum, th'ear-piercing fife,
> The royal banner, and all quality,
> Pride, pomp, and circumstance of glorious war!
> And, O you mortal engines, whose rude throats
> Th'immortal Jove's dread clamours counterfeit,
> Farewell! Othello's occupation's gone!

(II, iii)

What he has lost with the love-object is neither the happiness he experiences in Desdemona's arms, nor sexual pleasure, nor jouissance, nor the happiness of being loved, nor the possibility of himself loving. What he has lost is the glory of Eros confused with Mars under the appearance of Jupiter. Othello is made for death. The love for which he deserted death will throw him back into its arms and push him back to that death-dominated space from which he came and which tempts him still. Was this not what he expected at Cyprus, a battle in which he would be able to perish or enhance his glory, or both at once? And how are we to interpret that mysterious storm that engulfs the Turkish fleet and spares the ships of Venice[6] other than as a sign from the gods that his hour has come, and that they are withdrawing from the victorious general the sign of their favour? It will not be given to the valiant Moor to die on the field of dishonour. He chose love and in doing so betrayed death; love betrayed him, making him choose death.

Halfway between that Other that inhabits the strange land of love through which Othello travels with neither map nor weapons, delivered over to Desdemona's spell, and this Same, in which Othello looks at himself as in a mirror in his warrior's armour, there stands the noble, elegant shape of the young Cassio. It is by moving back that we find him here on the path that leads from the female genital object to the narcissistic love that the subject has for himself. Let us examine this for a moment. Is this not how Cassio is presented? We have only to remember the portrait that Iago gives of him, in which his subtleness, his finesse, his manners and his looks are criticized or praised, but in any case envied. But are these not the same qualities that Desdemona possesses? Moreover, Casio is a soldier. He is no hardened old trooper, of course, but he possesses – at least until his disgrace – all the qualities of a true soldier. He is an accomplished man, possessing all the qualities necessary to please, a virility that has achieved refinement. This is, indeed, everything the Moor longs to possess, since it is precisely this that he has been unable to attain, despite his own eminent qualities. And if narcissism is Othello's most impregnable quality, it is understandable that Cassio should attract love as his chief would like to do. This would also explain the appointment, which cannot be suspected of irregularity, but which certainly springs from favouritism. In short, Cassio, while possessing the same charms as Desdemona, preserves the attributes of the soldier in which Othello would like to recognize himself. And being loved by such a figure must be delightful. Hence the identification with the love-object in jealousy, where Othello feels, almost as if he had managed to be its beneficiary, the admiration that Cassio is able to arouse. In this light, Othello's exclamation as he sets eyes on Desdemona in Cyprus – 'O my fair warrior!' – takes on new meaning. As does also the fact that his love for Desdemona has passed through the medium of Desdemona's desire to be herself a man like Othello. This brings together the narcissistic love, in which Othello's desire takes root and his object-love with which Othello finds it so difficult to accommodate himself when it concerns a female, castrated being.

No trace of this love for Cassio, which the psycho-analyst infers, is to be found in Othello's words; but is further proof of its plausibility required? It might be noted that, as soon as the jealousy is triggered off, Cassio assumes much more importance than Othello, since Othello sacrifices his love-object to him. Commentators have found it very surprising that Iago should be so much more easily believed than Desdemona, and have failed to understand how Othello blinds himself so easily to the truth. In the logic of consciousness, this is indeed very surprising. But if one accepts my hypothesis, the tragedy is to be interpreted otherwise. Othello is not so much furious at Desdemona's betrayal, as cruelly wounded by Cassio's. Cassio's infidelity – his drunkenness on guard was an indication of it – is more important to him than Desdemona's. And when Othello is consumed with anger as he witnesses, off-stage, as it were, a scene which he is not supposed to observe, in which Iago tries to provide proof of Cassio's guilt, Shakespeare chooses to arrange things in such a way that this scene takes place between two men, Cassio and Iago. Othello hastens to see Cassio miming the gestures of a woman whom he presumes to be his own wife, yet Othello also sees Cassio lavish these gestures upon the person of Iago; and when Iago tries to win Othello over to his interpretation of events, he invents a story for the Moor's benefit. He recounts to Othello how he overheard certain things that Cassio had said in his sleep:

> I lay with Cassio lately;
> And, being troubled with a raging tooth,
> I could not sleep. There are a kind of men
> So loose of soul, that in their sleeps will mutter
> Of their affairs: one of this kind is Cassio.
> In sleep I heard him say, *Sweet Desdemona,*
> *Let us be wary, let us hide our loves;*
> And then, sir, would he gripe and wring my hand,

Cry O *sweet creature!* and then kiss me hard,
As if he pluck'd up kisses by the roots
That grew upon my lips: then laid his leg
Over my thigh, and sigh'd and kiss'd; and then
Cried *Cursèd fate that gave thee to the Moor!*

(III, iii)

Usually, one simply admires Iago's perversity and one forgets to pay homage to Shakespeare's extraordinary insight. Nowhere is the efficacity of the decoy better shown. In his scheming, Iago has provided Othello with the phantasy before which he recoils. Using the alibi of representing infidelity, it is in fact a homosexual relation that he forces us, with Othello, to see. What the ensign sets before our eyes is a spectacle that serves as a bait of identification, in which Othello can see himself in Iago's place, madly embraced and kissed by Cassio. The wedding night disturbed by the brawling soldiers then takes on a retrospective significance. 'Just like that night ...', Othello might think, shifting his gaze on to what he has been able to learn only through a third party. The thing that eludes this movement of the gaze requires that Othello, at this precise moment, should be looked at in turn by the scene that seizes his attention,more especially as Iago has given the status of impossible verification to his desire for proof:

It is impossible you should see this,
Were they as prime as goats, as hot as monkeys,
As salt as wolves in pride, and fools as gross
As ignorance made drunk.

(III, iii)

This argument convinces him more than any other. Better than any other, it will hit the target.

Othello : O monstrous! monstrous!
Iago : Nay, this was but his dream.
Othello : But this denoted a foregone conclusion:
    'Tis a shrewd doubt, though it be but a dream.

(III, iii)

So much so that when, some scenes later, Iago invites him to hide himself in order to overhear his conversation with Cassio, in which Cassio mimics Bianca's assaults, he offers Othello a means of repeating the phantasy, so that the truth of the desire can emerge, by dramatizing, as in the account of the pseudo-dream, two men in illicit intercourse. Cassio even enacts once more with Iago the embrace that he was supposed to have given him while dreaming. This effectiveness of the phantasy rests on projection – no doubt because the dream and the phantasy are projective work. Projection operates here in its purest, essential state, that is to say, it brings back to the subject, through the medium of the outside – here the scenes of the dialogue between Iago and Cassio – what is abolished inside.

Abolished or, as Lacan would say, foreclosed. This foreclosure is different from other forms of repression; it shows more precisely than Freud himself did that all the representations of desire are so radically barred from the functioning of the subject that the subject receives signs from outside as if they were primary, as if nothing had preceded them in the subject's experience, as if they echoed some effaced, long-inoperative trace and asserted themselves with a quite original self-evidence. This is a subversion of symbolization, which is itself repudiated here, since it declares that the two halves it unites – that which is presented and that which it echoes – are alien to one another. It is as if that moment when the subject was set in motion once more by the signifiers it engenders were also a moment of the emergence of the Other as locus of discourse, of the Other as possessor of the integrality of meaning. It is as if the accumulation of the signifiers had never until that moment signified anything, covered over as it was by a shadow that is dissipated with the brutality of revelation – only to designate the unrepresentable, the unthinkable. And so the subject is crushed, dismantled, its fragments serving the meshing of gears required to constitute the meaning of the Other.

Certainly, in psycho-analysis, the discourse of the jealous man reveals an obsessive concern with the rival bordering on homosexuality. Shakespeare sets this mechanism in operation without being too explicit, without revealing too much. He is content to proceed indirectly, with a resulting gain in effectiveness. These 'pieces of jigsaw' in the functioning of the plot bring us, in the darkness of invisible interpretation, very close to the truth.

At the end of the tragedy, only a moment before Othello's suicide, the ultimate reconciliation takes place:

Cassio : Dear general, I never gave you cause.
Othello : I do believe it, and I ask your pardon.

(V, ii)

These two lines sound very like refound love.

These words of reconciliation are spoken between two deaths: between Desdemona's murder and Othello's suicide, as if death had to win the day. They are words that define Cassio's precise situation between Othello's genital love for Desdemona and Othello's narcissistic love for himself, which leads him to kill himself in order to find his love again. His love! It is an ambiguous formulation that designates both the love-object and the state of being in love, one that enables Othello, through the narcissistic nature of his object-choice, to find himself again in hoping to rejoin Desdemona. (Othello kills Desdemona only when he is convinced that Cassio has been killed by Iago.)

Desdemona can be loved only when dead. Othello never spoke more passionately of Desdemona than at the moment of death, as if death were a conditon of love. After embracing her, he says to the sleeping Desdemona:

> Oh balmy breath that does almost persuade
> Justice to break her sword! One more, one more:
> Be thus when thou art dead, and I will kill thee,
> And love thee after.
>
> (V, ii)

The fact that to die after her, with her, is the realization of their reciprocal attachment is clearly shown in Othello's last words:

> I kiss'd thee ere I kill'd thee; no way but this,
> Killing myself, to die upon a kiss.
>
> (V, ii)

This perfect, point-by-point duplication suggests the relation of the subject to his mirror-image. It is an absolute correspondence, a communicating reciprocity in which death may at last reunite what life has separated. It is not saying much to say that Desdemona is now truly his, since no one can take her from him; it should be added, however, that she is reintegrated in him as a missing half. Desdemona is Othello's and Othello Desdemona's: their relations belong neither to having nor to being, but to something that is common to them and which Freud called the narcissistic investment (cathexis) of the object.

That is why Othello's suicide is the logical act, the reflection on to himself of Desdemona's murder. When, alone with Desdemona's corpse, he has to reply to Emilia, who asks to see him, he says:

> What's best to do?
> If she come in, she'll sure speak to my wife:
> My wife! my wife! what wife! I have no wife.
>
> (V, ii)

Bound to her by mutual possession, he could not accept her alive. He cannot accept her dead, deprived of her as of a part of himself snatched away from him. Alive, she was dead in him as soon as he was acquired. Dead, she lives still, and he must constantly throw her off. This shows – a feature very common among those who commit murder out of jealousy, or suicide – that Othello, like them, has no consciousness of death, either of the death he is about to give or of the death he is to give himself. In killing Desdemona, he renews the moment when he snatched her from the condition in which she was not yet his wife. It would be false to think that Othello's suicide is a consequence of the revelation of Desdemona's innocence. It is the surety for Desdemona's murder. But a difference has emerged here that must be emphasized. When Othello wonders how to kill the object of his love, he rejects the dagger:

> Yet I'll not shed her blood;
> Nor scar that whiter skin of hers than snow,
> And smooth as monumental alabaster.
>
> (V, ii)

Othello wants her in death preserved whole and entire.
She died because she lacked the handkerchief, the sign of her castration; it is this same castration that must be denied with death. Only the breath will be taken from her. It is Othello who holds power over this breath:

> Put out the light, – and then put out thy light. -
> If I quench thee, thou flaming minister,
> I can again thy former light restore,
> Should I repent me; – but, once put out thy light,
> Thou cunning'st pattern of excelling Nature,
> I know not where is that Promethean heat
> That can thy light relume.
>
> (V, ii)

We can see here, in the narcissistic structure, the ever-present seeds of megalomania. How can we fail to suspect in Othello, who is not able to make himself totally, absolutely, unchallengeably master of Desdemona's desire, the desire to have right of life and death over her? Life and death; in other words he wants to have the power to give her life as well as death. His suicide must be understood in the same context. The Moor inflicts death on himself. He does not submit to it; he does not allow sentence and execution to be carried out on him. He makes himself master of his own destiny by an act equivalent to that of giving himself life. He sets out to rejoin his love, by means of the suicide through which he will accede at last to the undivided jouissance of union with Desdemona.

But, whereas suffocation respects unto death the integrity of Desdemona's body, whose perfection remains unimpaired by any wound, Othello kills himself by stabbing as he relates his attack on a Turk, a 'circumcised dog'. He imposes upon himself this suicide by the sword, inflicting upon himself the castration that he abhorred in Desdemona. Thus Desdemona dies immaculate and entire, and Othello joins her after mutilating himself. Each has gone half of the way that separates him from the Other. Henceforth they are similar to the object and to its image in the mirror, though one cannot say which side the decoy is on, and which side the source of desire.

Othello and his double

Confronted by the effects of the tragic, especially when, as in *Othello*, this is a matter of purely internal mechanisms, without the gods showing themselves or speaking, one is bound to ask, 'Why?' Why does death necessarily triumph over love? I have confined myself so far to situating Othello's desire between Eros and the death drive, without giving any explanation for this victory of the forces of death, although we saw what a dependable ally these forces could find in the narcissistic nature of Othello's object-investments. However, we still have to place a fundamental relation that governs others, the Othello–Iago relation.

Many commentators on *Othello* have realized that an analysis of the play must give a preponderant place to Iago. This mysterious character gives rise to very different interpretation. Granville Barker maintained that there was also a tragedy of Iago. It has even been suggested that the play should, by rights,bear the title *Iago* rather than *Othello*, so much does the ensign seem to dominate the course of the action: in turn creator, bringing Othello's jealousy to birth like an alchemist, and interpreter, offering to each individual the image that he demands (Granville Barker). He is compared to Shakespeare's other villains – Richard III and Edmund – but he surpasses them all. In the case of the other two villains, motives can be found for their evil. For Iago, all that can be found seems to be out of all proportion to the perversity he displays. The conclusion usually reached is that Iago is evil in essence rather than by reaction.

At all events, one cannot conceive of Iago in isolation. Some other term must be brought into relation with him in order to clarify the function or truth of the character. But it would be wrong to think that this other term might be contingent or interchangeable. In fact, behind Iago's proteomorphism, which enables him to succeed in his plans, there is something that one may define more specifically. Moreover, for all his cunning, his intrigue does not succeed; although his setting up of the infernal machine cannot be faulted, his plan fails. This failure should be ascribed not to some unforeseen accident, but to the very essence of the plan which, again, must contribute to the triumph of Cassio, which was also the outcome of Othello's secret desire.

For they cannot be imagined separately: Othello–Iago, Iago–Othello. They belong to that gallery of indissociable pairs – Don Juan–Sganarelle, Don Quixote–Sancho Panza – to which Otto Rank drew attention in his study of the double. They are so inseparable that, even when their relations are considered as an opposition, the complementarity that unites them is always preserved. Thus, for Bradley, Iago is everything – devil, spirit of evil – but this means that Othello is nothing, little more than a puppet. For Leavis, on the contrary, Iago is merely a mechanism, a trigger added to an organization that is ready to function of itself, in which Othello is the only agent. How can we reconcile this difference of opinion, without ourselves falling into error? In fact, both theses are equally true and false. Iago is the revealer of Othello's conflict, but not a mere inducing agent. He is much more than the catalyst of Othello's jealousy. He gives body and credence to jealousy by extracting from the depths of his own envy the sympathy that it can assume in the desire of another. And, in another respect, does not Othello, so ready to submit himself to the signs already inscribed in him, drop the tunic of a warrior who makes and unmakes armies only to offer himself to movements and manipulations of which he is a passive toy, in search of a 'pleasure of his own of which he was himself unaware' (S.E., x, 167)? Othello falls into Iago's toils only because he adheres strictly to his desire. But for Iago to be able to conceive the infernal machine, he must have been inspired by the heroic and monstrous elements in Othello's character. In the scene in which Iago plants the seeds of jealousy, it is not only Othello's peace of mind that is disturbed; it is above all that of the audience, in the position of the onlooker called upon as a witness.

Othello and Iago together seal a pact that binds them as closely as two lovers. Do they not end the scene on their knees, facing one another, invoking heaven to look favourably on their plans? Note the invocation of the forces of nature (stars, elements), which refers Othello back to his pagan gods and overshadows the God of his recent conversion:

> Witness, you ever-burning lights above,
> You elements that clip us round about, -
> Witness that here Iago doth give up
> The execution of his wit, hands, heart,
> To wrong'd Othello's service! Let him command,
> And to obey shall be in me remorse,
> What bloody work soe'er.
>
> (III, iii)

And Othello replies:

> I greet thy love,
> Not with vain thanks but with acceptance bounteous.

Having vowed to kill Desdemona and Cassio, Othello invests Iago with this new love:

> Now art thou my lieutenant.

And Iago concludes:

> I am your own for ever.

The modern spectator needs no knowledge of psycho-analytic interpretation to grasp that what he is witnessing here goes well beyond an alliance to carry out a task requiring the collaboration of two parties. What he is participating in is an intimate union, a joining together that becomes the cause of desire, the creation of an object that aims at the destruction of another desire. But it would be rash to see the situation in terms of homosexuality, without explaining what kind of homosexuality is involved. For although Othello several times speaks very highly of Iago, he never expresses himself in terms of desire, but simply praises his lucidity or his honesty. The place of the love-object is occupied by Cassio, a concern shared by Iago and Othello. If we recall that Freud sees in the process of paranoia a regressive path from homosexuality to narcissism, Iago stands before Othello like a mirror that makes his desire all the more unbearable the closer it gets to him. If Cassio has everything the Moor lacks, Iago is everything he is not. I believe that the endless arguments about the respective parts played by Othello and Iago in the jealousy and in its tragic outcome can be solved only if one accepts the identity of Othello and Iago. Othello and Iago are two sides of a single character. Shakespeare does his utmost to present them to us as utterly unlike each other, united by their very contrast.

The opposition is total, like day and night. Origin: Othello is a Moor, therefore a foreigner, Iago (despite his name) is a Florentine. Birth: Othello is a king's son, Iago base of birth. Faith: Othello is a convert and therefore a believer, Iago believes in nothing. Career: Othello is a great captain, Iago an undistinguished subordinate officer. Character: Othello is noble and generous, Iago mean and grasping. Temperament: Othello is passionate, Iago calculating. (Hazlitt was aware of this contrasted opposition.)

When Roderigo reproaches Iago for remaining under Othello's command after being passed over for the lieutenancy, Shakespeare shows the ambiguity of the relations between Iago and Othello in a play on words:

> Were I the Moor, I would not be Iago:
> In following him, I follow but myself.

> (I, i)

What may be meant by this reversal, in the last resort, is that he *is* the Moor and, since therefore he is not Iago, he may be he whom the Moor serves, that is to say, Cassio. But this accession to the object of desire must pass through the channel of him who chooses it. It is not entirely surprising to the psycho-analyst that this answer to Roderigo should end with the line, 'I am not what I am' (I, i), in which 'what I am not, I am' suggests the relation to the Other in the mirror, where that image is not outside where I am, since it is my gaze that constitutes it, but I am only in perceiving that image that I am not.

I have said little so far about Roderigo. He is Shakespeare's invention and might be seen as a mere cog in the machine, a part necessary to the functioning of the plot, a character with no depth and no interest. Nevertheless, he is part of the tragic structure and cannot be dismissed so lightly. What does he amount to? To a simple fool, one might say. His stupidity proves that if love can make heroes lose their heads, so it can with fools. But this analysis is not enough. We must see that Roderigo is the character that Iago chooses for all his basest tricks; it is he who causes the brawl in the citadel, it is he who is given the task of murdering Cassio. But he is one of the poles of the desire of Iago, who tricks him out of his money. Thus he offers himself as a mere instrument in Iago's service. But this same servant will be the cause of Iago's perdition. The proof of Iago's guilt is provided by the note found on Roderigo after his death. So, by this unexpected reversal, the truth emerges through someone even more gulled than Othello–Roderigo, the most child-like of them all.

There is an interplay in the Othello–Iago polarity of black and white complexions. Honesty is on the side of the black, and blackness on the side of the white. This black ram, who used trickery at the beginning of the play, allows himself to be taken in by the appearance of the decoy in a world in which the whites counterfeit innocence and, under cover of their refined manners, use all the falsifications of language, the secret conventions of glances, the equivocation of the gestures of courtesy, to blur the transparency of natural intercourse. Iago succeeds in making Othello believe that he was wrong to leave his native soil and to breathe the air of Venice where the whites are hypocritical, false, affected, treacherous, fickle. Perhaps one should stress the notoriously dissolute character of Venetian morals in this period, something often noted by travellers of the time. This no doubt justifies Iago's words, which may be taken as true:

I know our country disposition well:
In Venice they do let Heaven see the pranks
They dare not show their husbands; their best conscience
Is not to leav't undone, but keep't unknown.

(III, iii)

349

But this complementary narcissistic situation must, if it is to be intelligible, be seen as part of another polarity. After introducing it into psycho-analytic theory, Freud split narcissism into the opposition between Eros and the death drive. Iago is a figure whose link with evil can be solved by no psychological explanation: neither as jealousy of Cassio's promotion, jealousy of the Moor who, he says, seduced his wife, or even, in the last resort, envy and spite at the unreciprocated love he feels for Desdemona. Not even all this, which provides the evil force with the reasons which motivate its action, is enough to explain the Machiavellianism that emanates from Iago. (Iago has been seen as the new man of the Renaissance, the disciple of Machiavelli. His function far exceeds that contemporary interest.) His triumph is contained in two lines that illuminate Othello's conversion to his plan, when Othello says:

Yield up, O love, thy crowned and hearted throne
To tyrannous hate!

(III, iii)

From then on, Othello's marriage will be a marriage with the death that was awaiting him from afar. He deceived death with this marriage, lured on by love. But Iago, that shadowy part of himself, wins in the end, so fulfilling his thanatophoric mission. Othello's and Iago's struggles are complementary and inverted.

What basically unites Othello and Iago is their common *méconnaissance* of their desire for Cassio. Othello does not see the love which underlies his favours to Cassio, or the aspiration – towards that which is outside his grasp – that this love attests. Iago does not realize that his thirst for revenge against a rival more fortunate in all respects is so strongly tainted with passionate desire that he will himself succumb beneath its weight. How else can we understand how Iago, the meticulous choreographer of this satanic ballet, when he holds Cassio at his sword's point, and is determined to kill him, misses this target that he stalks from behind and finds himself at that very moment overcome by some confusion that makes him lower his sword and wound his rival in the thigh, and not kill him (as Othello later wounds Iago without killing him in the last scene). If it had not been an expression of his own desire Iago could not have invented the story of Cassio's 'dream', the phantasy of the night spent with Cassio that he insinuates into Othello's mind. The deception that motivates it does not diminish its power. For although he 'sets the scene' for Othello at this same moment, Iago is so caught up in his invention that he forgets to arouse the lack of the Other, imagining himself enjoying the scene in which he cherishes the hope of Cassio's demotion and Desdemona's disgrace. Similarly, when he deliberately creates misunderstanding by getting Cassio to talk about Bianca while Othello imagines that he is talking about

Desdemona, in the scene that is acted out before him, it is he, Iago, who is won over just as much as Othello, by this masquerade that he has maliciously set up. For, in an earlier scene, he was the chagrined observer of the courteous exchanges between Desdemona and Cassio.

It has been pointed out that jealousy is not the monopoly of Othello in the tragedy. Iago, too, suspects his wife of having been unfaithful with Cassio and Othello, as if Iago was suggesting at the beginning of the play the jealousy that is still to emerge in the Moor, who has as yet no suspicion of his own jealous nature. In fact, Iago's feelings are closer to envy than to jealousy. Should we not, indeed, draw a distinction between jealousy and envy? In *Envy and Gratitude*, Melanie Klein differentiates betwen them. Whereas jealousy involves a preponderance of projection and admits the existence of a third party who enjoys the attributes of which the jealous individual is deprived, envy involves a desire for destructive introjection aimed at the direct degradation of the object of desire, without any intermediary, in the context of a dual relation. There is a further distinction between them, over and above the one drawn by Melanie Klein: jealousy is a desire addressed to the object, while envy is primarily an aspect of narcissism. While Othello is jealous (despite the narcissistic form of his object-investment), Iago is consumed by a thirst for mastery directed more at the desire than at its object, to which Othello is, for a time, still attached. Yet as soon as he attains his end of promotion to the lieutenancy and binds himself to Othello, his narcissistic mastery begins to crack. Swearing his fidelity to the Moor seems to make Iago's betrayal coincide with what betrays the Moor himself, his unavowed desire for Cassio.

It is as if there had been formed a 'set to partners' whose pattern of movement is not grasped by those who dance its figures. At the beginning of the tragedy, Iago speaks the language of envy, but advocates the domestication of desire in the cult of self – 'I never found a man that knew how to love himself' (I, iii). But Othello, preoccupied with his recent marriage, pushes into the background whatever belongs to the order of his more permanent satisfactions, those provided by the links binding him to his men. As soon as Cassio's fall is encompassed, it revives in Othello an unconscious homosexual love, but since this love is unacceptable it can be expressed only through the debasement and defilement of Desdemona. From now on, Cassio surreptitiously enters into Iago's desire, after the successful implantation of jealousy, undermining the security given by his feeling of having captured the Moor, though at the beginning of the play the ensign was more concerned to speak contemptuously of his more fortunate rival. So one comes to see that there is also a tragedy of Iago that is the exact replication of that of Othello. Shakespeare must be taken literally when he makes Othello say: 'By heaven, he echoes me!' (III, iii)

It is through this voice that the return of the foreclosed repressed is uttered. The words of old Brabantio surface and reappear with the self-evidence of a fulfilled prophecy. Othello had erased every trace of this utterance, and now it reappears in the mouth of Iago, bright and edged, like the two-handed sword of the day of judgement:

> She did deceive her father, marrying you;
> And, when she seem'd to shake and fear your looks,
> She loved them most.

(III, iii)

From this moment on, Othello recognizes in Iago his double and other half. The death drive expressed through Iago seizes on this paternal speech as a speech of transgression; it only uses the spring of jealousy or of repressed and unacceptable desire in order to reach its true aim – to undo what has been done, to dissolve the ties of artificial bonds, to turn back the marriage partners – through the mutual annihilation of Othello and Desdemona, who had abolished the difference between them – each to the god of his or her race.

Notes

1. There has been a lot of discussion as to Othello's exact degree of blackness. It has been said that, as an African from Mauritania, he is scarcely to be called black; his blackness was defended by BRADLEY in *Shakespearean Tragedy*. See also the opinions of Coleridge and Lamb, and Charlton's vigorous rectification.

2. The building of the first public theatre coincided, to a year (1576/7), with Drake's circumnavigation of the globe. Four years before *Othello*, the East India Company was founded. The mythology concerning these Africans, of which the West had only a recent knowledge at that time, was also conveyed through the chivalric romances of Palmerin (1511-47), which had close links with *Don Quixote*, itself filled with Moorish references (though not translated into English until 1612), and the *Microcosmos* of John Davies (1603). The war between the Republic of Venice and the Turks, which is referred to in *Othello*, was also a point of contact between East and West.

3. This difference seemed so exorbitant that RYMER (1692) and COLERIDGE (1808), among others, rejected it, accusing Shakespeare of extravagance when he made a Negro a general of the Republic at a time when Negroes could have been nothing but slaves.

4. Green notes here the impossibility of conveying the ambiguity of the English line, 'That heaven had made her such a man'. This may be understood in two ways. Either that Desdemona wished that heaven had so arranged things that she had been born such a man (the sense adopted, not without reason, by Jouve), or that heaven had made such a man for her, had intended such a husband for her. There is a clear relation here between being and having, between identification and desire.

5. This has been stressed by many commentators, but above all by LEAVIS.

6. Especially as the strategic weakness of Cyprus is stressed:

> For that it stands not in such warlike brace,
> But altogether lacks th'abilities
> That Rhodes is dress'd in.

(I, iii)

JANET ADELMAN *'ANGER'S MY MEAT': FEEDING, DEPENDENCY, AND AGGRESSION IN* CORIOLANUS*

Janet Adelman is Professor of English at the Unversity of California at Berkeley. Her essay '"Anger's My Meat": Feeding, Dependency, and Aggression in *Coriolanus*' first appeared in *Shakespeare: Patters of Excelling Nature* (ed. David Bevington and Jay L. Halio, Associated University Presses, 1978). Beginning from the relationships that are established within the family of which Coriolanus is a part, Adelman proceeds to show how the hero's dependency upon his mother is channelled outwardly into a 'phallic aggressive pose' which is 'a defense against collapse into the dependent oral mode of the small boy'. For Adelman, Coriolanus seeks constantly to 'authorize' himself, a fantasy that he can sustain only by denying the subject-position which he occupies as his mother's son. Adelman's analysis is loosely Freudian compared with the theoretically rigorous analyses proposed by Kristeva and Green. But her detailed consideration of the way in which the language of *Coriolanus* 'works to define and separate, to limit possibilities' offers an important way into the latent meanings the text generates. For her, the tragedy of the play resides in Coriolanus's resistance to dependency, which, when he finally capitulates, proves to be the source of his undoing. Adelman works from the assumption that the denial of pre-Oedipal dependency itself, and the persistent refusal to recognise its categorical imperatives, results in an impoverishment of human possibilities.

---

*Reprinted from *Representing Shakespeare: new psychoanalytic essays*, ed. Murray M. Schwartz and Coppelia Kahn (Baltimore: Johns Hopkins University Press, 1982), pp. 129-149.

353

Coriolanus was written during a period of rising corn prices and the accompanying fear of famine; rising prices reached a climax in 1608. In May 1607, 'a great number of common persons' – up to five thousand, Stow tells us in his *Annales* – assembled in various Midlands counties, including Shakespeare's own county of Warwickshire, to protest the acceleration of enclosures and the resulting food shortages.[1] It must have been disturbing to property owners to hear that the rioters were well received by local inhabitants, who brought them food and shovels[2] - doubly disturbing if they were aware that this was one of England's first purely popular riots, unlike the riots of the preceding century in that the anger of the common people was not being manipulated by rebellious aristocrats or religious factions.[3] The poor rioters were quickly dispersed, but – if *Coriolanus* is any indication – the fears that they aroused were not. In fact, Shakespeare shapes his material from the start in order to exacerbate these fears in his audience. In Plutarch the people riot because the Senate refuses to control usury; in Shakespeare they riot because they are hungry. Furthermore, the relentlessly vertical imagery of the play reflects the specific threat posed by this contemporary uprising: in a society so hierarchical – that is, so vertical – as theirs, the rioters' threat to level enclosures implied more than the casting down of particular hedges; it seemed to promise a flattening of the whole society.[4] Nor is Shakespeare's exacerbation of these fears merely a dramatist's trick to catch the attention of his audience from the start, or a seventeenth century nod toward political relevance. For the dominant issues of the uprising – the threat of starvation and the consequent attempt to level enclosures – are reflected in not only the political but also the intrapsychic world of *Coriolanus*; taken together, they suggest the concerns that shape the play and particularly the progress of its hero.

The uprising of the people at the start of the play points us toward an underlying fantasy in which political and psychological fears come together in a way that makes each more intense and hence more heartening. For the political leveling promised by the contemporary uprising takes on overtones of sexual threat early in Shakespeare's play:[5] the rising of the people becomes suggestively phallic; and the fear of leveling becomes ultimately a fear of losing one's potency in all spheres. In Menenius's belly fable, the people are 'th'discontented members, the mutinous parts', and 'the mutinous members' (I, i, 110, 148).[6] An audience for which the mutiny of the specifically sexual member was traditionally one of the signs of the Fall, and for which the crowd was traditionally associated with dangerous passion, would be prone to hear in Menenius's characterization a reference to a part other than the great toe (I, i, 154). In this initial fantasy, the hitherto docile sons suddenly threaten to rise up against their fathers, the Senators (I, i, 76); and it is characteristic of *Coriolanus* that the contested issue in this Oedipal rebellion is food.[7] The uprising of the crowd is in fact presented in terms that suggest the transformation of hunger into phallic aggression, a transformation that is, as I shall later argue, central to the character of Coriolanus himself: when the first citizen tells Menenius, 'They say poor suitors have strong breaths: they shall know we have strong arms too' (I, i, 58–60), his image of importunate mouths suddenly armed in rebellion suggests the source of Coriolanus's rebellion no less than his own.

If the specter of a multitude of hungry mouths, ready to rise and demand their own, is the exciting cause of *Coriolanus*, the image of the mother who has not fed her children enough is at its center. One does not need the help of a psychoanalytic approach to notice that Volumnia is not a nourishing mother. Her attitude toward food is nicely summed up when she rejects Menenius's invitation to a consolatory dinner after Coriolanus's banishment: 'Anger's my meat: I sup upon myself / And so shall starve with feeding' (IV, ii, 50–1). We might suspect her of having been as niggardly in providing food for her son as she is of herself, or rather suspect her of insisting that he too be self-sufficient, that he feed only on his own anger; and indeed, he is apparently fed only valiantness by her ('Thy valiantness was mine, thou suck'st it from me' [III, ii, 129]). He certainly has not been fed the milk of human kindness: when Menenius later tells us that 'there is no more mercy in him than there is milk in a male tiger' (V, iv, 28–9), he seems to associate Coriolanus's lack of humanity not only with the absence of any nurturing female element in him but also with the absence of mother's milk itself.[8] Volumnia takes some pride in the creation of her son, and when we first meet her, she tells us exactly how she's done it: by sending him to a cruel war at an age when a mother should not be willing to allow a son out of the protective maternal circle for an hour (I, iii, 5–15). She elaborates her creation as she imagines herself mother to twelve sons and then kills all but one of them off: 'I had rather had eleven die nobly for their country, than one voluptuously surfeit out of action' (I, iii, 24–5). To be noble is to die; to live is to be ignoble and to eat too much.[9] If you are Volumnia's son, the choice is clear.

But the most telling – certainly the most disturbing – revelation of Volumnia's attitude toward feeding comes some twenty lines later, when she is encouraging Virgilia to share her own glee in the thought of Coriolanus's wounds: 'The breasts of Hecuba / When she did suckle Hector, look'd not lovelier / Than Hector's forehead when it spit forth blood / At Grecian sword contemning' (I, iii, 40–3). Blood is more beautiful than milk, the wound than the breast, warfare than peaceful feeding. But this image is more disturbing than these easy comparatives suggest. It does not bode well for Coriolanus that the heroic Hector doesn't stand a chance in Volumnia's imagination: he is transformed immediately from infantile feeding mouth to bleeding wound. For the unspoken mediator between breast and wound is the infant's mouth: in this imagistic transformation, to feed is to be wounded; the mouth becomes the wound, the breast the sword. The metaphoric process suggests the psychological fact that is, I think, at the center of the play: the taking in of food is the primary acknowledgement of one's dependence on the world, and as such, it is the primary token of one's vulnerability. But at the same time as Volumnia's image suggests the vulnerability inherent in feeding, it also suggests a way to fend off that vulnerability. In her image, feeding, incorporating, is transformed into spitting out, an aggressive expelling; the wound once again becomes the mouth that spits 'forth blood / At Grecian sword contemning'. The wound spitting blood thus becomes not a sign of vulnerability but an instrument of attack.

Volumnia's attitudes toward feeding and dependence are echoed perfectly in her son. Coriolanus persistently regards food as poisonous (I, i, 177–8; III, i, 55–6); the only thing he can imagine nourishing is rebellion (III, i, 68–9, 116). Among the patricians, only Menenius is associated with the ordinary consumption of food and wine without an allaying drop of Tiber in it, and his distance from Coriolanus can be measured partly by his pathetic conviction that Coriolanus will be malleable – that he will have a 'suppler' soul (V, i, 55) – after he has had a full meal. But for Coriolanus, as for his mother, nobility consists precisely in *not* eating: he twice imagines starving himself honorably to death before asking for food, or anything else, from the plebeians (II, iii, 112–13; III, iii, 89–91).[10]

Coriolanus incorporates not only his mother's attitude toward food but also the transformations in mode implicit in her image of Hector. These transformations – from feeding to warfare, from vulnerability to aggressive attack, from incorporation to spitting out – are at the center of Coriolanus's character and of our responses to him: for the whole of his masculine identity depends on his transformation of his vulnerability into an instrument of attack, as Menenius suggests when he tells us that each of Coriolanus's wounds 'was an enemy's grave' (II, i, 154–5). Cominius reports that Coriolanus entered his first battle a sexually indefinite thing, a boy or Amazon (II, ii, 91), and found his manhood there: 'When he might act the woman in the scene, / He prov'd best man i'th 'field' (II, ii, 96–7). The rigid masculinity that Coriolanus finds in war becomes a defense against acknowledgment of his neediness; he nearly succeeds in transforming himself from a vulnerable human creature into a grotesquely invulnerable and isolated thing. His body becomes his armor (I, iii, 35; I, iv, 24); he himself becomes a weapon 'who sensibly outdares his senseless sword, / And when it bows, stand'st up' (I, iv, 53–4), or he becomes the sword itself: 'O me alone! Make you a sword of me!' (I, vi, 76) His whole life becomes a kind of phallic exhibitionism, devoted to disproving the possibility that he is vulnerable.[11] In the transformation from oral neediness to phallic aggression, anger becomes his meat as well as his mother's; Volumnia's phrase suggests not only his mode of defending himself against vulnerability but also the source of his anger in the deprivation imposed by his mother. We see the quality of his hunger and its transformation into aggression when, after his expulsion from Rome, he tells Aufidius, 'I have ... / Drawn tuns of blood out of thy country's breast' (IV, v, 99–100). Fighting here, as elsewhere in the play, is a poorly concealed substitute for feeding (see, for example, I, ix, 10–11; IV, v, 191–4, 222–4); and the unsatisfied ravenous attack of the infant on the breast provides the motive force for warfare. The image allows us to understand the ease with which Coriolanus turns his rage toward his own feeding mother, Rome.[12]

Thrust prematurely from dependence on his mother, forced to feed himself on his own anger, Coriolanus refuses to acknowledge any neediness or dependency: for his entire sense of himself depends on his being able to see himself as a self-sufficient creature. The desperation behind his claim to self-sufficiency is revealed by his horror of praise, even the praise of his general.[13] The dependence of his masculinity on warfare in fact makes praise (or flattery, as he must call it) particularly threatening to him on the battlefield: flattery there, where his independence has apparently been triumphant, would imply that he has acted partly to win praise, that he is not self-sufficient after all; it would ultimately imply the undoing of his triumphant masculinity, and the soldier's steel would grow 'soft as the parasite's silk' (I, ix, 45). The juxtaposition of soldier's steel and parasite's soft silk suggests both Coriolanus's dilemma and his solution to it: in order to avoid being the soft, dependent, feeding parasite, he has to maintain his rigidity as soldier's steel; that rigidity would be threatened were he to be 'dieted / In praises sauc'd with lies' (I, ix, 51–2). (The same fears that underlie Coriolanus's use of this image here are brought home to him by Aufidius's charges at the end of the play: that he broke 'his oath and resolution, like / A twist of rotten silk' [V, vi, 95–6]; that he 'whin'd and roar'd away' the victory [V, vi, 98]; that he is a 'boy of tears' [V, vi, 101].)

The complex of ideas that determines Coriolanus's response to praise also determines the rigidity that makes him so disastrous as a political figure. As he contemptuously asks the people for their voices and later gives up his attempt to pacify them, the language in which he imagines his alternatives reveals the extent to which his unwillingness to ask for the people's approval, like his abhorrence of praise, depends on his attitude toward food: 'Better it is to die, better to starve, / Than crave the hire which first we do deserve' (II, iii, 112–13); 'Pent to linger / But with a grain a day, I would not buy / Their mercy at the price of one fair word' (III, iii, 89–91). Asking, craving, flattering with fair words are here not only preconditions but also equivalents of eating: to refuse to ask is to starve; but starvation is preferable to asking because asking, like eating, is an acknowledgment of one's weakness, one's dependence on the outside world. 'The price is, to ask it kindly' (II, iii, 75), but that is the one price Coriolanus cannot pay. When he must face the prospect of revealing his dependence on the populace by asking for their favor, his whole delicately constructed masculine identity threatens to crumble. In order to ask, a harlot's spirit must possess him; his voice must become as small as that of a eunuch or a virgin minding babies; a beggar's tongue must make motion through his lips (III, ii, 111–18). Asking, then, like susceptibility to praise, would undo the process by which he was transformed on the battlefield from boy or woman to man. That he imagines this undoing as a kind of reverse voice change suggests the extent to which his phallic aggressive pose is a defense against collapse into the dependent oral mode of the small boy. And in fact, Coriolanus's own use of language constantly reiterates this defense. Instead of using those linguistic modes that acknowledge dependence, Coriolanus spits out words, using them as weapons.His invective is in the mode of Hector's wound, aggressively spitting forth blood: it is an attempt to deny vulnerability by making the very area of vulnerability into the means of attack.[14]

Coriolanus's abhorrence of praise and flattery, his horror lest the people think that he got his wounds to please them (II, ii, 147–50), his insistence that he be given the consulship as a sign of what he is, not as a reward (I, ix, 26), his refusal to ask – all are attempts to claim that he is *sui generis*. This attitude finds its logical conclusion in his desperate cry as he sees his mother approaching him at the end:

> I'll never
> Be such a gosling to obey instinct, but stand
> As if a man were author of himself
> And knew no other kin.

(V, iii, 34–7)

The gosling obeys instinct and acknowledges his kinship with mankind; but Coriolanus will attempt to stand alone. (Since his manhood depends exactly on this phallic standing alone, he is particularly susceptible to Aufidius's taunt of 'boy' after he has been such a gosling as to obey instinct.) The relationship between Coriolanus's aggressive pose and his attempts to claim that he is *sui generis* is most dramatically realized in the conquest of Corioli; it is here that Coriolanus most nearly realizes his fantasy of standing as if a man were author of himself. For the scene at Corioli represents a glorious transformation of the nightmare of oral vulnerability ('to th'pot' [I, iv, 47], one of his soldiers says as he is swallowed up by the gates) into a phallic adventure that both assures and demonstrates his independence. Coriolanus's battlecry as he storms the gates sexualizes the scene: 'Come on; / If you'll stand fast, we'll beat them to their wives' (I, iv, 40–1). But the dramatic action itself presents the conquest of Corioli as an image not of rape but of triumphant rebirth: after Coriolanus enters the gates of the city, he is proclaimed dead; one of his comrades delivers a eulogy firmly in the past tense ('Thou wast a soldier / Even to Cato's wish' [I, iv, 55–6]); then Coriolanus miraculously reemerges, covered with blood (I, v, 22), and is given a new name. For the assault on Corioli is both a rape and a rebirth: the underlying fantasy is that intercourse is a literal return to the womb, from which one is reborn, one's own author.[15] The fantasy of self-authorship is complete when Coriolanus is given his new name, earned by his own actions.[16]

But despite the boast implicit in his conquest of Corioli, Coriolanus has not in fact succeeded in separating himself from his mother;[17] even the very role through which he claims independence was designed by her – as she never tires of pointing out ('My praises made thee first a soldier' [III, ii, 108]; 'Thou art my warrior: / I holp to frame thee' [V, iii, 62–3]). In fact, Shakespeare underlines Volumnia's point by the placement of two central scenes. In I, iii, before we have seen Coriolanus himself as a soldier, we see Volumnia first describe her image of her son on the battlefield and then enact his role: 'Methinks I see him stamp thus, and call thus: / "Come on you cowards, you were got in fear / Though you were born in Rome"' (I, iii, 32–4). This marvellous moment suggests not only the ways in which Volumnia herself lives through her son, but also the extent to which his role is her creation. For when we see him in the next scene, acting exactly as his mother had predicted, we are left with the impression that he is merely enacting her enactment of the role that she has imagined for him.

That Coriolanus is acting under Volumnia's direction even in the role that seems to ensure his independence of her helps to explain both his bafflement when she suddenly starts to disapprove of the role she has created ('I muse my mother / Does not approve me further' [III, ii, 7–8]) and his eventual capitulation to her demand that he shift roles, here and at the end of the play. For his manhood is secure only when he can play the role that she has designed, and play it with her approval.[18] He asks her, 'Why did you wish me milder? Would you have me / False to my nature? Rather say I play / The man I am' (III, ii, 14–16). But 'I play the man I am' cuts both ways: in his bafflement, Coriolanus would like to suggest that there is no distance between role and self, but he in fact suggests that he plays at being himself, that his manhood is merely a role. Given that Volumnia has created this dilemma, her answer is unnecessarily cruel, but telling: 'You might have been enough the man you are, / With striving less to be so' (III, ii, 19–20). Volumnia is right: it is the intensity and rigidity of Coriolanus's commitment to his masculine role that makes us suspect the intensity of the fears that this role is designed to hide, especially from himself. For the rigidity of the role and the tenuousness of the self that it protects combine to make acknowledged play acting of any kind terrifying for Coriolanus, as though he can maintain the identity of self and role, and hence his integrity, only by denying that he is able to assume a role. Because he cannot acknowledge the possibility of role playing, Coriolanus must respond to his mother's request that he act a new role as a request that he be someone other than Coriolanus. When he finally agrees to take on the role of humble supplicant, he is sure that he will act badly (III, ii, 105–6) and that he will lose his manhood in the process (III, ii, 111–23).

The fragility of the entire structure by which Coriolanus maintains his claim to self-sufficient manhood helps to account for the violence of his hatred of the plebians. For Coriolanus uses the crowd to bolster his own identity: he accuses them of being exactly what he wishes not to be.[19] He does his best to distinguish himself from them by emphasizing his aloneness and their status as multitude as the very grounds of their being.[20] Throughout, he associates his manhood with his isolation, so that 'Alone I did it' becomes a sufficient answer to Aufidius's charge that he is a boy. Hence the very status of the plebeians as crowd reassures him that they are not men but dependent and unmanly things, merely children – a point of view that Menenius seems to confirm when he tells the tribunes: 'Your abilities are too infant-like for doing much alone' (II, i, 36–7). His most potent image of the crowd is as an appropriately infantile common mouth (III, i, 22, 155) disgustingly willing to exhibit its neediness. Coriolanus enters the play identified by the plebeians as the person who is keeping them from eating (I, i, 9–10); indeed, one of his main complaints about the plebeians is that they say they are hungry (I, i, 204–7).[21] Coriolanus himself has been deprived of food and he seems to find it outrageous that others should not be. His position here is like that of the older brother who has fought his way into manhood and who is now confronted by an apparently endless group of siblings – 'my sworn brother the people' (II, iii, 95), he calls them – who still insist on being fed by mother Rome,[22] and whose insistence on their dependency threatens the pose of self-sufficiency by which his equilibrium is perilously maintained. To disclaim his own hunger, Coriolanus must therefore disclaim his kinship with the crowd: 'I would they were barbarians – as they are, / … not Romans – as they are not' (III, i, 236–7). But the formulation of the disclaimer itself reveals the very tensions that it is designed to assuage. Insofar as he wishes the people non-Roman, he acknowledges their Romanness; but this acknowledgment of kinship must immediately be denied by the assertion that they are in fact not Roman. The very insistence on difference reveals the fear of likeness.

But the multitudinous mouth of the crowd is horrifying to Coriolanus, not only insofar as it threatens to reveal his own oral neediness to him, but also insofar as it makes the nature of his vulnerability uncomfortably precise. In this hungry world, everyone seems in danger of being eaten. The crowd suspects the senators of cannibalistic intentions: 'If the wars eat us not up, they will; and there's all the love they bear us' (I, i, 84–5). Since Coriolanus twice dismisses them as ignoble food ('quarry' [I, i, 197]; 'fragments' [I, i, 221]), their fears seem not entirely without basis. But Coriolanus thinks that, without the awe of the Senate, the crowd would 'feed on one another' (I, i, 187). Given their choice, the tribunes would naturally enough prefer that the 'present wars devour' Coriolanus (I, i, 257) instead of the populace. The people's belief that the death of Coriolanus would allow them to have corn at their own price (I, i, 9) is eventually sustained by the plot, insofar as Coriolanus opposes the giving of corn gratis (III, i, 113–17). But at the start of the play, we are not in a position to understand the logic behind their association between killing Coriolanus and an unlimited food supply; and in the context of all the cannibalistic images, the mysterious association seems to point toward a fantasy in which the people, rather than the wars, will devour Coriolanus.[23] Menenius explicates this fantasy:

> *Menenius* : Pray you, who does the wolf love?
> *Sicinius* : The lamb.
> *Menenius* : Ay, to devour him, as the hungry plebeians would the noble
> Martius.
>
> (II, i, 6–9)

And in the third act, as the people begin to find their teeth and rise against Coriolanus, his images of them as mouths begin to reveal not only his contempt for their hunger but also his fear of his own vulnerability, fear of being bitten, digested,pecked at: 'You being their mouths, why rule you not their teeth?' (III, i, 35); 'How shall this bosom multiplied digest / The senate's courtesy?' (III, i, 130–1); 'Thus we debase / The nature of our seats, ... / ... and bring in / The crows to peck the eagles' (III, i, 134–8). The fear of being eaten that lies just below the surface in these images is made explicit when Coriolanus tells Aufidius that the people have 'devour'd' all of him but his name (IV, v, 77).

The crowd, then, is both dependent, unmanly, contemptible – and terrifyingly ready to rise up and devour Coriolanus. Through his portrayal of the crowd, Coriolanus can manage to dismiss the specter of his own hunger and insist on his identity as an isolated and inviolable thing ('a thing / Made by some other deity than nature' [IV, vi, 91–2], as Cominius says). But he cannot dismiss the danger that exposure to their hunger would bring. His absolute horror at the prospect of showing his wounds to win the consulship depends partly, I think, on the complex of ideas that stands behind his characterization of the crowd. In Plutarch, Coriolanus shows his wounds; in Shakespeare, the thought is intolerable to him and, despite many promises that he will, he never does. For the display of his wounds would reveal his kinship with the plebeians in several ways: by revealing that he has worked for hire (II, ii, 149) as they have (that is, that he and his deeds are not *sui generis* after all); by revealing that he is vulnerable, as they are; and by revealing, through the persistent identification of wound and mouth,[24] that he too has a mouth, that he is a dependent creature. Moreover, the exhibition of his wounds to the crowd is impossible for Coriolanus partly because his identity is sustained by exhibitionism of another sort. Coriolanus is right in believing that he must not 'stand naked' (II, ii, 137) before the crowd, asking for their approval; for this standing naked would reverse the sustaining fantasy by which he hoped to 'stand / As if a man were author of himself' (V, iii, 35–6). For the phallic exhibitionism of Coriolanus's life as a soldier has been designed to deny the possibility of kinship with the crowd; it has served to reassure him of his potency and his aggressive independence, and therefore to sustain him against fears of collapse into the dependent mode of infancy. To exhibit the fruits of his soldiership as the emblems not of his self-sufficiency but of his vulnerability and dependence, and to exhibit them precisely to those whose kinship he would most like to deny, would transform his chief means of defense into a proclamation of his weakness: it would threaten to undo the very structure by which he lives. And finally, insofar as he would expose himself as vulnerable and dependent by displaying his wounds, he would invite the oral rage of the crowd to satisfy itself on him. 'If he show us his wounds and tell us his deeds, we are to put our tongues into those wounds and speak for them' (II, iii, 5–8), the Third Citizen says; his grotesque image suggests that the sweet licked by the multitudinous tongue (III, i, 155–6) would be 'sweet' Coriolanus himself (III, ii, 107).[25]

During the first part of the play, Coriolanus uses his opposition to the crowd to define himself and to fend off his vulnerability. But after the exile from Rome, this source of definition fails, and Coriolanus turns toward his old enemy Audifius to confirm himself. For if Coriolanus has throughout defined himself by opposition, he has defined himself by likeness as well: from the beginning, we have watched him create a mirror image of himself in Aufidius. As soon as he hears that the Volsces are in arms, Coriolanus announces the terms of his relationship with Aufidius: 'I sin in envying his nobility; / And were I anything but what I am, / I would wish me only he' (I, i, 229–31). But the noble Aufidius is Coriolanus's own invention, a reflection of his own doubts about what he is, an expression of what he would wish himself to be. Shakespeare takes pains to emphasize the distance between the Aufidius we see and the Aufidius of Coriolanus's imagination. The Aufidius invented by Coriolanus seems designed to reassure Coriolanus of the reality of his own male grandeur by giving him the image of himself; his need to create a man who is his equal is in fact one of the most poignant elements in the play and helps to account for his tragic blindness to his rival's true nature as opportunist and schemer. Immediately after Coriolanus has imagined himself Aufidius, he allows us to see the extent to which he is dependent on Aufidius for his self-definition in a nearly prophetic confession: 'Were half to half the world by th' ears, and he / Upon my party, I'd revolt to make / Only my wars with

him' (I, i, 232–4). Later, the Coriolanus who shrinks violently from the
praise of others eagerly solicits news of Aufidius's opinion of him; and his
oddly touching 'Spoke he of me?' (III, i, 12) reveals the extent to which he
needs to see himself in Aufidius's eyes.[26] As he approaches Antium after
the exile, he pauses to reflect on the strangeness of his actions but succeeds
only in suggesting that the issue driving him from Rome and toward
Aufidius is a 'trick not worth an egg' (IV, iv, 21), as though for the moment
the fact of his union with Aufidius is more important than the
circumstances that drove him to it. His attempt to explain his actions
begins and ends with the image of friends 'who twin, as 'twere, in
love / Unseparable' (IV, iv, 15–16), who 'interjoin their issues' (IV, iv, 22).
The movement of this soliloquy reveals the fantasy of twinship underlying
his relationship with Aufidius both as foe and as friend.

The union with Aufidius is for Coriolanus a union with an alter ego; it
represents a flight from the world of Rome and his mother toward a safe
male world. Devoured in all but name by Rome (IV, v, 77), Coriolanus
enters Antium afraid of being eaten: he fears that the Volscian wives will
slay him with spits (IV, iv, 5) and tells the Third Servingman that he has
dwelt 'i'th'city of kites and crows' (IV,v, 43), a city of scavengers. (That this
city is both the wilderness and Rome itself is suggested by Coriolanus's
echo of his earlier peril, the crows who will peck the eagles [III, i, 138].)
Here, far from Rome, Coriolanus at last allows his hunger and his
vulnerability to be felt, and he is given food. He presents himself to
Aufidius during a great feast, from which he is initially excluded: 'The
feast smells well, but I / Appear not like a guest' (IV, v, 5–6). But here in
Antium, the play moves toward a fantasy in which nourishment may be
safely taken because it is given by a male, by a father-brother-twin rather
than a mother. Coriolanus is finally taken into the feast. In the safe haven
provided by his mirror image, he will not be devoured; instead, he will eat.
Aufidius's servants give us the final development of this fantasy:

> *First Servant* : ... Before Coriolanus he scotched him
>   and notched him like a carbonado.
> *Second Servant* : And had he been cannibally given,
>   he might have broiled and eaten him too.
>
> (IV, v, 191–4)

The scene moves, then, from hunger and the fear of being eaten to an
image of Coriolanus triumphantly eating Aufidius. Since his mother will
not feed him, Coriolanus will find in Aufidius the only nourishment that
can sustain him; and insofar as Aufidius is his alter ego, he, like his mother,
will sup on himself.

When Coriolanus is banished from Rome, he responds with an infantile
fantasy of omnipotent control: 'I banish you!' (III, iii, 123). He then

attempts to ensure the reality of his omnipotence by wishing on his enemies exactly what he already knows to be true of them: 'Let every feeble rumour shake your hearts! / ... Have the power still / To banish your defenders' (III, iii, 125–8). Few curses have ever been so sure of instantaneous fulfillment. Having thus exercised his rage and assured himself of the magical power of his invective, Coriolanus finally makes his claim to true independence: 'There is a world elsewhere!' (III, iii, 135). His encounter with Aufidius is an attempt to create this world, one in his own image; but even the union with Aufidius leads ultimately back to Rome and his mother. For Coriolanus's rage, like his hunger, is properly directed toward his mother; though it is deflected from her and toward the plebeians and Volscians for much of the play, it finally returns to its source. For Rome and his mother are finally one.[27] In exiling Coriolanus, Rome reenacts the role of the mother who cast him out. Although in his loving farewell, his family and friends are wholly distinguished from the beast with many heads, by the time he has returned to Rome they are no more than a poor grain or two that must be consumed in the general fire (V, i, 27). (Even in his loving farewell we hear a note of resentment when he consoles his mother by telling her: 'My hazards still have been your solace' [IV, i, 28].) As he approaches Rome, the devouring populace becomes indistinguishable from his loving mother. But Menenius has already pointed toward the fantasy that identifies them:

> Now the good gods forbid
> That our renowned Rome, whose gratitude
> Towards her deserved children is enroll'd
> In Jove's own book, like an unnatural dam
> Should now eat up her own!
>
> (III, i, 287–91)

The cannibalistic mother who denies food and yet feeds on the victories of her sweet son stands at the darkest center of the play, when Coriolanus's oral vulnerability is fully defined. Here, talion law reigns: the feeding infant himself will be devoured; the loving mother becomes the devourer. In this dark world, love itself is primitive and dangerous: both the First Citizen and Menenius suggest that here to be loved is to be eaten (I, i, 84–5; II, i, 6–9).

Coriolanus's return to Rome is not ultimately a return to his mother; it is rather a last attempt to escape her love and its consequences. If Coriolanus can make himself a new name, forged in the fires of burning Rome (V, i, 14–15), he can construct a new identity independent of his mother: an identity that will demonstrate his indifference to her, his separation from her. For he can stand as author of himself only by destroying his mother. The return to Rome is an act of retaliation against the mother on whom he has been dependent, the mother who has cast him out. But it is at the same time an acting out of the child's fantasy of reversing the roles of parent and child, so that the life of the parent is in the hands of the omnipotent child. The child becomes a god, dispensing life and death (V, iv, 24–5): becomes in effect the author of his mother, so that he can finally stand alone.

But Coriolanus can sustain neither his fantasy of self-authorship nor his attempt to realize a godlike omnipotent power. And the failure of both leaves him so unprotected, so utterly devoid of a sense of self that, for the first time in the play, he feels himself surrounded by dangers.[28] The capitulation of his independent selfhood before his mother's onslaught seems to him to require his death, and he embraces that death with a passivity thoroughly uncharacteristic of him:

> O my mother, mother! O!
> You have won a happy victory to Rome;
> But for your son, believe it, O, believe it,
> Most dangerously you have with him prevail'd,
> If not most mortal to him. But let it come.

(V, iii, 185–9)

Volumnia achieves this happy victory partly because she makes the dangers inherent in his defensive system as terrifying as those it is designed to keep at bay. Her last confrontation with her son is so appallingly effective because she invalidates his defenses by threatening to enact his most central defensive fantasies, thereby making their consequences inescapable to him.

The very appearance of his mother, coming to beg him for the life of her city and hence for her own life, is an enactment of his attempt to become the author of his mother, his desire to have power over her. He has before found her begging intolerable (III, ii, 124–34); when she kneels to him here, making the role reversal of mother and child explicit (V, iii, 56), he reacts with a hysteria which suggests that the acting out of this forbidden wish threatens to dissolve the very structures by which he orders his life:

> What's this?
> Your knees to me? to your corrected son?
> Then let the pebbles on the hungry beach
> Fillip the stars. Then let the mutinous winds
> Strike the proud cedars 'gainst the fiery sun,
> Murd'ring impossibility, to make
> What cannot be, slight work!

(V, iii, 56–62)

At first sight, this speech seems simply to register Coriolanus's horror at the threat to hierarchy implied by the kneeling of parent to child. But if Coriolanus were responding only – or even mainly – to this threat, we would expect the threatened chaos to be imaged as high bowing to low; this is in fact the image we are given when Volumnia first bows to her son as if – as Coriolanus, says – 'Olympus to a molehill should / In supplication nod' (V, iii, 30–1). But Coriolanus does not respond to his mother's kneeling with an image of high bowing to low; instead, he responds with two images of low mutinously striking at high.The chaos imaged here is not so much a derivative of his mother's kneeling as of the potential mutiny that her kneeling seems to imply: for her kneeling releases the possibility of his mutiny against her, a mutiny that he has been suppressing all along by his exaggerated deference to her. His response here reveals again the defensive function of his hatred of the mutinous and leveling populace: the violence of his images suggests that his mother's kneeling has forced him to acknowledge his return to Rome as a rising up of the hungry and mutinous forces within himself. With her usual acumen, Volumnia recognizes the horror of potential mutiny in Coriolanus's response and chooses exactly this moment to assert, once again, his dependence on her: 'Thou art my warrior' (V, iii, 62).

Coriolanus's forbidden wish to have power over his mother was safe as long as it seemed impossible. But now that protective impossibility itself seems murdered, and he is forced to confront the fact that his wish has become a reality. Nor are the hungry and mutinous forces within him content to murder only an abstract 'impossibility': the murderousness of the image is directed ultimately at his mother. And once again, Volumnia makes Coriolanus uncomfortably clear to himself: after she has enacted his terrifying fantasy by kneeling, she makes it impossible for him to believe that her death would be merely an incidental consequence of his plan to burn Rome.[29] For she reveals exactly the extent to which his assault is on both. Her long speech builds to its revelation with magnificent force and logic. She first forces him to see his attack on his country as an attack on a living body by accusing him of coming to tear 'his country's bowels out' (V, iii, 103). Next, she identifies that body as their common source of nurture: 'the country, our dear nurse' (V, iii, 110). Finally, as she announces her intention to commit suicide, she makes absolute the identification of the country with herself. After she has imagined him treading on his country's ruin (V, iii, 116), she warns him:

> Thou shalt no sooner
> March to assault thy country than to tread –
> Trust to't, thou shalt not – on thy mother's womb
> That brought thee to this world.
>
> (V, iii, 122–5)

The ruin on which Coriolanus will tread will be his mother's womb – a warning accompanied by yet another assertion of his dependence on her as she recalls to him the image of himself as a fetus within that womb.

If Coriolanus's mutinous fantasies are no longer impossible, if his mother will indeed die as a result of his actions, then he will have realized his fantasy of living omnipotently without kin, without dependency. In fact this fantasy, his defense throughout, is articulated only here, as he catches sight of his mother (V, iii, 34–7), and its expression is the last stand of his claim to independence. Throughout this scene, Volumnia has simultaneously asserted his dependence on her and made the danger inherent in his defense against that dependence horrifyingly clear; and in the end, it is the combination of her insistence on his dependency and her threat to disown him, to literalize his fantasy of standing alone, that causes him to capitulate. Finally, he cannot 'stand / As if a man were author of himself / And knew no other kin'; he must become a child again, a gosling, and admit his neediness. The presence of his own child, holding Volumnia's hand, strengthens her power over him. For Coriolanus seems to think of his child less as his son than as the embodiment of his own childhood and the child that remains within him; even when we are first told about the son, he seems more a comment on Coriolanus's childhood than on his fatherhood. The identification of father and child is suggested by Coriolanus's response as he sees his wife, mother, and child approaching: 'My wife comes foremost; then the honour'd mould / Wherein this trunk was fram'd, and in her hand / The grandchild to her blood' (V, iii, 22–4). Here Coriolanus does not acknowledge the child as his and his wife's: he first imagines himself in his mother's womb and then imagines his child as an extension of his mother. Even Coriolanus's language to Menenius as he earlier denies his family reveals the same fusion of father and son: 'Wife, mother, child, I know not' (V, ii, 80), he says, in a phrase that suggestively identifies his own mother as the mother of the child and the child he attempts to deny as himself. Volumnia had once before brought Coriolanus to submission by reminding him of himself as a sucking child (III, ii, 129); now virtually her last words enforce his identification with the child that she holds by the hand: 'This fellow had a Volscian to his mother; / His wife is in Corioli, and his child / Like him by chance' (V, iii, 178–80). But at the same time as she reminds him of his dependency, she disowns him by disclaiming her parenthood; she exacerbates his sense of himself as a child, and then threatens to leave him – as he thought he wished – alone. And as his fantasy of self-sufficiency threatens to become a reality, it becomes too frightening to sustain. Just as his child entered the scene holding Volumnia's hand, so Coriolanus again becomes a child, holding his mother's hand.

The ending of this play leaves us with a sense of pain and anxiety; we are not even allowed the feelings of unremitting grief and satiation that console us in most of the other tragedies. The very nature of its hero insists that we keep our distance. Coriolanus is as isolated from us as he is from everyone else; we almost never know what he is thinking, and – even more intolerably – he does not seem to care what we are thinking. Unlike an Othello or an Antony, whose last moments are spent endearingly trying to ensure our good opinion, Coriolanus makes virtually no attempt to affect our judgment of him: he dies as he has tried to live, heroically mantled in his self-sufficiency, alone. Nor is it only our democratic sympathies that put us uncomfortably in the position of the common people throughout much of the play: Coriolanus seems to find our love as irrelevant, as positively demeaning, as theirs; in refusing to show the people his wounds, he is at the same time refusing to show them to us. In refusing to show himself to us, in considering us a many-headed multitude to whose applause he is wholly indifferent, Coriolanus denies us our proper role as spectators to his tragedy. The only spectators Coriolanus allows himself to notice are the gods who look down on this unnatural scene and laugh, who are so far removed from men that they find this human tragedy a comedy. And as spectators, we are in danger of becoming as distant from human concerns as the gods: for Coriolanus's isolation infects the whole play and ultimately infects us as well. There are very few moments of relaxation; there is no one here to love. We are made as rigid and cold as the hero by the lack of anything that absolutely commands our human sympathies, that makes us feel our own status as dependent creatures, part of a community. Even the language does not open out toward us, nor does it create the sense of the merging of meanings, the melting together, that gives us a measure of release in *King Lear* or *Antony and Cleopatra*, where a world of linguistic fusion suggests the dependence of all parts. Instead, the language works to define and separate, to limit possibilities, almost as rigidly as Coriolanus himself does.[30]

Finally, the nature of our involvement in the fantasies embodied in this distant and rigid hero does not permit any resolution: it also separates and limits. For Coriolanus has throughout given free expression to *our* desire to be independent, and we delight in his claim. But when he turns on his mother in Rome, the consequences of his claim to self-sufficiency suddenly become intolerably threatening to us. We want him to acknowledge dependence, to become one of us; but at the same time we do not want to see him give in, because to do so is to force us to give up our own fantasy of omnipotence and independence. Hence at the final confrontation we are divided against ourselves, and no solution is tolerable: neither the burning of Rome nor the capitulation and death of our claims to independence.Nor is the vision of human dependency that the play allows any compensation for the brutal failure of our desire to be self-sustaining. In *Lear* and *Antony and Cleopatra*, dependency is finally shown to be what makes us fully human: however much the characters have tried to deny it, it finally becomes their salvation, and ours, as we reach out to them. But dependency here brings no rewards, no love, no sharing with the audience; it brings only the total collapse of the self, the awful triumph of Volumnia, and Coriolanus's terribly painful cry: 'O mother, mother / What have you done?'

Notes

1. JOHN STOW, *Annales* (London, 1631), p. 890. See SIDNEY SHANKER, 'Some Clues for *Coriolanus*', *Shakespeare Association Bulletin* **24** (1949), 209–13; E.C. PETTET, '*Coriolanus* and the Midlands Insurrection of 1607', *Shakespeare Survey* 3 (1950), 34–42; and BRENTS STIRLING, *The Populace in Shakespeare* (New York: Columbia University Press, 1949), pp. 126–28, for discussions of the uprising and its political consequences in the play.

2. STOW, p. 890.

3. See EDWIN F. GAY, 'The Midland Revolt and the Inquisitions of Depopulation of 1607', *Transactions of the Royal Historical Society*, NS **18** (1904), 195–244, for valuable contemporary commentary on the uprising and analysis of it in comparison with earlier riots of the sixteenth century. See also PETTET, p. 35.

4. The participants in the uprising were commonly called 'levelers' and their activity 'leveling', in startling anticipation of the 1640s. The common use of this term suggests the extent to which their fight against enclosures seemed to threaten hierarchy itself. (See, for example, Stow, p. 890, and Gay, p. 213, n. 2; p. 214, n. 1; p. 216, n. 3; and p. 242.) The vertical imagery is so prominent in the play that it scarcely needs to be pointed out; at its center is Cominius's warning that the tribunes' stirring up of the people is 'the way to lay the city flat, / To bring the roof to the foundation, / And bury all which yet distinctly ranges / In heaps and piles of ruin' (III, i, 201–5). The threat of the people to rise and cast Coriolanus down from the Tarpeian rock, Coriolanus's horror of kneeling to the people or of his mother's kneeling to him, and ultimately the image of the prone Coriolanus with Aufidius standing on him – all take their force partly from the repetition and intensity of the vertical imagery throughout.

5. Shakespeare had in fact just used the word *level* to suggest a sexual leveling at the end of *Antony and Cleopatra*, when Cleopatra laments: 'The soldier's pole is fall'n: young boys and girls / Are level now with men' (IV, xv, 65–6).

6. All references to *Coriolanus* are to the new Arden edition, ed. Philip Brockbank (London: Methuen, 1976).

7. Coriolanus himself occupies an odd position in the psychological myth at the start of the play: though he is a father, we almost always think of him as a son; though the populace considers him prime among the forbidding fathers, he himself seems to regard the patricians as his fathers. His position midway between father and sons suggests the position of an older sibling who has made a protective alliance with the fathers and now fears the unruliness of his younger brothers. Instead of fighting to take possession of the undernourishing mother, he will deny that he has any need for food.

8. Menenius's words point to the rigid and ferocious maleness so prized by Rome. PHYLLIS RACKIN, in an unpublished paper entitled '*Coriolanus*: Shakespeare's

369

Anatomy of *Virtus'* delivered to the special session on feminist criticism of Shakespeare at the 1976 meeting of the Modern Language Association, discusses the denial of female values in the play as a consequence of the Roman overvaluation of valor as the chiefest virtue. Rackin's analysis of the ways in which the traditionally female images of food, harvesting, and love are turned to destructive purposes throughout the play is particularly revealing.

The ideal Roman woman is in fact one who denies her womanhood, as we see not only in Volumnia but in Coriolanus's chilling and beautiful description of Valeria (V, iii, 65–7). (Indeed, Valeria seems to have little place in the intimate family gathering of V, iii; she seems to exist there largely to give Coriolanus an excuse to speak these lines.) The extent to which womanhood is shrunken in roman values is apparent in the relative unimportance of Coriolanus's wife Virgilia; in her, the female values of kindly nurturing have become little more than a penchant for staying at home, keeping silent, and weeping. (Given the extreme restriction of Virgilia's role, one may begin to understand some of the pressures that force a woman to become a Volumnia and live through the creation of her exaggeratedly masculine son. In 'Authoritarian Patterns in Shakespeare's *Coriolanus*', *Literature and Psychology* 9 1959, 49, GORDON ROSS SMITH comments perceptively that, in an authoritarian society, women will either be passive and subservient or will attempt to live out their thwarted ambition via their men.)

At the end of play, Rome sees the consequences of its denial of female values as Coriolanus prepares to deny nature in himself and destroy his homeland. When Volumnia triumphs over his rigid maleness, there is a hint of restitution in the Roman celebration of her as 'our patroness, the life of Rome' (V, v, 1). But like nearly everything else at the end of this play, the promise of restitution is deeply ironic: for Volumnia herself has shown no touch of nature as she willingly sacrifices her son; and the cries of 'welcome, ladies, welcome!' (V, v, 6) suggest an acknowledgment of female values at the moment when the appearance of these values not in Volumnia but in her son must mean his death.

9. The association of nobility with abstinence from food – and of the ignoble lower classes with excessive appetite for food, in connection with their traditional role as the embodiment of appetite – was first demonstrated to me by MAURICE CHARNEY'S impressive catalog of the food images in the play. See 'The Imagery of Food and Eating in *Coriolanus*', in *Essays in Literary History*, ed. Rudolf Kirk and C.F. Main (New Brunswick, NJ: Rutgers University Press, 1960), pp. 37–54.

10. In fact, Coriolanus frequently imagines his death with a kind of glee, as the badge of his noble self-sufficiency. See, for example, III, ii 1–5, 103–4; V, vi, III–12.

11. The extent to which Coriolanus becomes identified with his phallus is suggested by the language in which both Menenius and Aufidius portray his death. For both, it represents a kind of castration: 'He's a limb that has but a disease: / Mortal, to cut it off; to cure it, easy' (III, i, 293–4); 'You'll rejoice / That he is thus cut off' (V, vi, 137–8).For discussions of Coriolanus's phallic identification and its consequences, see ROBERT J. STOLLER, 'Shakespearean Tragedy: *Coriolanus*', *Psychoanalytic Quarterly* 35 (1966), 263–74, and EMMETT WILSON, JR, 'Coriolanus: The Anxious Bridegroom', *American Imago* 25 (1968), 224–41. In 'An Interpretation of Shakespeare's *Coriolanus*', *American Imago* 14 (1957), 407–35, CHARLES K. HOFLING sees Coriolanus as a virtual embodiment of Reich's phallic–narcissistic character. Each of these analysts finds Coriolanus's phallic stance to some extent a defense against passivity (Stoller, pp. 267, 269–70; Wilson, *passim*; Hofling, pp. 421, 424).

12. DAVID B. BARRON sees Coriolanus's oral frustration and his consequent rage as central to his character. See *'Coriolanus*: Portrait of the Artist as Infant', *American Imago* **19** (1962), 171–93.This essay anticipates mine in some of its conclusions and many of its details of interpretation.

13. Most critics find Coriolanus's abhorrence of praise a symptom of his pride and of his desire to consider himself as self-defined and self-sufficient, hence free from the definitions that society would confer on him. See, for example, A.C. BRADLEY, 'Coriolanus', reprinted in *Studies in Shakespeare*, ed. Peter Alexander (London: Oxford University Press, 1964), p. 229; G. WILSON KNIGHT, *The Imperial Theme* (London: Methuen, 1965), p. 169; IRVING RIBNER, *Patterns in Shakespearean Tragedy* (London: Methuen, 1960), p. 190; NORMAN RABKIN, *Shakespeare and the Common Understanding* (New York: Free Press, 1967), p. 131; and JAMES L. CALDERWOOD, '*Coriolanus*: Wordless Meaning and Meaningless Words', *Studies in English Literature 1500–1900* **6** (1966), 218–19.

14. In his discussion of Coriolanus's cathartic vituperation, KENNETH BURKE suggests that invective is rooted in the helpless rage of the infant. See *'Coriolanus* – and the Delights of Faction', *Hudson Review* **19** (1966), 200.

15. To see Corioli as the mother's womb here may seem grotesque; the idea becomes less grotesque if we remember Volumnia's own identification of country with mother's womb just as Coriolanus is about to attack another city (see discussion elsewhere in this chapter). Wilson suggests (pp. 228–9) that the attack on Corioli represents defloration–specifically, that it expresses the equation of coitus with damaging assault and the resultant dread of a retaliatory castration.

16. The force of his new name is partly corroborated by Volumnia, who delights in reminding her son of his dependence on her: she has trouble learning his new name from the start (II, i, 173) and eventually associates it with the pride that keeps him from pity for his family (V, iii, 170–1). But several critics have argued convincingly that the self-sufficiency implicit in Coriolanus's acquisition of his new name is ironically undercut from the beginning by the fact that the naming of any kind is a social act, so that Coriolanus's acceptance of the name conferred on him by Cominius reveals his dependence on external definition just at the moment that he seems most independent. See, for example, RABKIN, pp. 130–2; LAWRENCE DANSON, *Tragic Alphabet: Shakespeare's Drama of Language* (New Haven, Conn.: Yale University Press, 1974), pp. 150–1; and CALDERWOOD, pp. 219–23.

17. The father's role in the process of individuation and the consequent significance of Coriolanus's fatherlessness have been pointed out to me by Dr Malcolm Pines: the father must exist from the start in the potential space between child and mother in order for separation from the mother, and hence individuation, to take place; the absence of Coriolanus's father thus becomes an essential factor in his failure to separate from his mother. Coriolanus's father is in fact extraordinarily absent from the play: he is never mentioned. That Menenius repeatedly is identified as Coriolanus's father at the end of the play (V, i, 3; V, ii, 62, 69; V, iii, 10) merely underscores this absence; insofar as the weak old man is associated with nurture, he might serve Coriolanus more adequately as a mother-substitute than as a father-substitute. The absolute absence of the father here points toward a parthenogenesis fantasy in which the son is literally the creation of the mother alone, a reversal of the more (typical) Shakespeare fantasy of male parthenogenesis (see, for example, *King Lear* or *The Tempest*).

18. Volumnia's place in the creation of her son's role, and the catastrophic results of her disavowal of it here, have been nearly universally recognized. For a

particularly perceptive discussion of the consequences for Coriolanus of his
mother's shift in attitude, see DEREK TRAVERSI, *Shakespeare: The Roman Plays*
(Stanford, Calif.: Stanford University Press, 1963), pp. 247–54. In an interesting
essay, D.W. HARDING suggests Shakespeare's preoccupation during this period
with the disastrous effects on men of their living out of women's fantasies of
manhood. See 'Women's Fantasy of Manhood', *Shakespeare Quarterly* 20 (1969),
252–3. Psychoanalytically oriented critics see Coriolanus as the embodiment of his
mother's masculine strivings, or, more specifically, as her longed-for penis. See, for
example, RALPH BERRY, 'Sexual Imagery in *Coriolanus*', *Studies in English Literature*
13 (1973), 302; HOflING, pp. 415–16; STOLLER, pp. 266–7, 271; and WILSON, p. 239.
   Several critics have noticed the importance of acting and the theatrical
metaphor in the play. See, for example, WILLIAM ROSEN, *Shakespeare and the Craft
of Tragedy* (Cambridge: Harvard University Press, 1960), pp. 171–3, and KENNETH
MUIR, *Shakespeare's Tragic Sequence* (London: Hutchinson, 1972), pp. 184–5.
HAROLD C. GODDARD, in *The Meaning of Shakespeare* (Chicago: University
of Chicago Press, 1951), pp. 216–17, discusses acting specifically in relation to the
role that Volumnia has cast for her son. Berry points to the acting metaphors as a
measure of Coriolanus's inner uncertainty and his fear of losing his manhood if
he shifts roles (pp. 303–6).

19. GODDARD (p. 238), HOflING (p. 420), and SMITH (p. 46), among others, discuss
    Coriolanus's characterization of the crowd as a projection of elements in himself
    that he wishes to deny, though they do not agree on the precise nature of these
    elements.

20. And so does Shakespeare. In Plutarch, Coriolanus is accompanied by a few men
    both when he enters the gates of Corioli and when he is exiled from Rome.
    Shakespeare emphasizes his isolation by giving him no companions on either
    occasion. EUGENE WAITH, in *The Herculean Hero* (New York: Columbia University
    Press, 1962), p. 124, and DANSON (p. 146) emphasize Coriolanus's position as a
    whole man among fragments.

21. BARRON associates Coriolanus's hatred of the people's undisciplined hunger
    with his need to subdue his own impulses; here, as elsewhere, his argument is
    very close to my own (pp. 174, 180).

22. See note 7 above. The likeness of the plebeians to younger siblings who threaten
    Coriolanus's food supply was first suggested to me by David Sundelson in
    conversation.

23. See LEONARD TENNENHOUSE, '*Coriolanus*: History and the Crisis of Semantic
    Order', *Comparative Drama* 10 (1976), 332. In the course of his suggestive essay on
    the semantic, historical, and psychological issues informing the significance of
    the people's voices in *Coriolanus*, Tennenhouse comes very close to the center of
    my argument when he says: 'Coriolanus, the child denied love in the service of
    patrician ideals, is perceived by the mob as the one who denies. The mysterious
    source of the cannibalistic rage directed against him is the recognition by the
    plebeians that he would withhold from them what the patrician mother would
    withhold from her son–nurturance and thus life itself' (p. 335). Although his
    essay came to my attention after most of the present essay was written, this
    statement and the suggestions of Zan Marquis initiated my understanding of
    cannibalism in the play.

24. See, for example, I, iii, 40–3 (discussed early in this chapter) and II, iii, 5–8.
    Exposed, Coriolanus's wounds would become begging mouths, as Julius
    Caesar's do (*Julius Caesar*, III, ii, 225–6).

25. The Third Citizen's image points also toward the possibility that Coriolanus would be inviting homosexual rape by standing naked before the crowd. Dr Anne Hayman has suggested to me that Coriolanus's fear of his unconscious homosexual desires, especially of a passive feminine kind, is central to his character; she sees his fear of the wish for passive femininity as part of his identification with his mother, who shares the same fear. I am indebted to Dr Hayman for her careful reading of this paper and her many helpful comments. (The relationship with Aufidius, though presented in decidedly homosexual terms [see, for example, IV, iv, 12–16, 22; IV, v, 110–19, 123–4], seems to me more significant as an expression of Coriolanus's need for a mirror image of himself than as the expression of his homosexual desires, as I argue later in this chapter.)

26. That Coriolanus's identity is at issue in the turning toward Aufidius is made uncomfortably clear by the scene in which he comes to Antium. Despite the servingmen's comic and belated assertions that they had nearly pierced Coriolanus's disguise (IV, v, 150–64), they clearly had no inkling of his stature before he revealed himself. Furthermore, Coriolanus's gradual unmasking before Aufidius suggests that he wants to be known as himself before he names himself (IV, v, 55–66). The scene is in part a test of the power of Coriolanus's identity to make itself known without external definition: the results are at best ambiguous.

27. DONALD A. STAUFFER, in *Shakespeare's World of Images* (New York: W.W. Norton, 1949), p. 252, points out that Rome is less *patria* than *matria* in this play; he discusses Volumnia as a projection of Rome, particularly in V, iii. Virtually all psychoanalytic critics comment on the identification of Volumnia with Rome; Barron comments specifically that Coriolanus turns the rage of his frustration in nursing toward his own country at the end of the play (p. 175).

28. It is a mark of the extent to which external dangers are for Coriolanus merely a reflection of internal ones that he feels himself in no danger until the collapse of his defensive system. Unlike Coriolanus, we know that he is in danger before its collapse: Aufidius plans to kill him no matter what he does (IV, vii, 24–6, 56–7).

29. RUFUS PUTNEY, in 'Coriolanus and His Mother', *Psychoanalytic Quarterly* 21 (1962), pp. 368–9, 372, finds Coriolanus's inability to deal with his matricidal impulses central to his character; whenever Volumnia threatens him with her death, he capitulates at once.

30. G. WILSON KNIGHT discusses the hard metallic quality of the language of length; he associates it with the self-containment of the hostile walled cities and distinguishes it from the fusions characteristic of *Antony and Cleopatra* (p. 156). In a particularly interesting discussion, Danson associates the rigidity and distinctness of the language with the play's characteristic use of metonymy and synecdoche, which serve to limit and define, in place of metaphor, which serves to fuse diverse worlds (pp. 155–9).

8 Post-Structuralism and Materialism

MALCOLM EVANS *ALBION'S CONFUSION**

Malcolm Evans currently teaches Art and Design at Goldsmiths' College, University of London. His book *Signifying Nothing: Truth's True Contents in Shakespeare's Text* was first published by Harvester Press in 1986, and republished in a second edition with a Postscript in 1989. Evans' own critical position is very firmly within the parameters of a post-structuralist materialism, amalgamating certain aspects of Althusser, Derrida and Foucault. The following excerpt is from a chapter entitled 'Star Wars', and is concerned with the textuality of – among other plays – *King Lear*. Evans' own critical practice is itself a carnivalesque challenge to that of traditional Shakespeare criticism, and he is concerned to detect those moments of carnival excess in Shakespearean texts which disclose the workings of ideology, and which resist aesthetic closure. For Evans, Shakespeare's texts affirm no metaphysical 'truth', rather language and signification are shown to circle around an 'absent centre' which, in the case of *King Lear*, is the 'nothing' which comes of nothing. Evans' emphasis on the festive elements owes much to Bakhtin and, up to a point, to the work of Robert Weimann, in its location of moments of 'egalitarian idealism' in the play. Unlike certain post-modernist critics, Evans holds on firmly to the notion of a narrative of emancipation, even though he avails himself of a Derridian strategy of deconstruction to undermine discourses of domination.

Discourses, as constituted in Foucault's discourse on the topic, are not just 'groups of signs (signifying elements referring to contents or representations)' but 'practices that systematically form the objects of which they speak' (*The Archeology of Knowledge* [trans. A.M. Sheriden,

*Reprinted from *Signifying Nothing: truth's true contents in Shakespeare's text* (Brighton: Harvester Press, 1986), pp. 219–37.

London: Tavistock 1972], p. 49). The 'text' produced in contemporary deconstruction resembles in many ways that which emerges in the Elizabethan dramatic discourse on the theatre, of which *The Spanish Tragedy* and *The Old Wives' Tale* are early, and seminal, instances. But this does not, of course, go to prove the essential and irreducible 'materiality' of writing, a contemporary transformation of the older representation of writing as that which remains itself across time – '*Vox audita perit littera scripta manet*' (William Caxton, *The Prologues and Epilogues* [ed. W. J. B. Crotch, London: Early English Text Society (176) 1928], p. 51).[1] The 'textuality' of these plays, rather than constituting a neutral dimension in which discourses simply collide and fall apart, is itself tied to a discourse, apparent in other sixteenth- and seventeenth-century texts, which is directed towards a representation of the text's own space and the relations and exclusions that operate within it. And this discourse on the text is a particular production of historical crisis in the social formation, addressed to manifestations of that crisis in the 'representations' produced in the text at a time when various discursive 'essences' of the subject, nature and the real are in conflict.

The tortuous self-scrutiny evident in the work of Kyd, Peele and Shakespeare is by no means unique to them or to the stage. Foucault's analysis of Velazquez's *Las Meninas*, for example, shows how a constitutive 'doubleness' could also cut across the visual codes of mimesis in painting to make a portrait of the Infanta Margarita of Spain, her attendants and the artist 'the representation, as it were, of Classical representation, and the definition of the space it opens up to us'. Here, as in *Hamlet*, it is all done with mirrors, in this case one which *should* reflect the spectator who views *Las Meninas* but in fact displays, among the paintings that hang on a wall in the background, the blurred image of Philip IV and his wife Mariana – at once the true objects of the gaze of Velazquez and others in the group whose eyes seem to meet those of the spectator, and the subjects of a canvas, of which only the reverse is visible, on which the painter is working. In the alternating absences of the mirror, which holds 'the palest, the most unreal, the most compromised of all the painting's images', mimesis marks the presence of its necessarily excluded *subject*, in the triple sense of the painter, the one who is represented and the spectator who occupies the position from which it may be viewed as a representation. At the centre of the painting's grouping and dispersal of figures in space there is this 'essential void' produced to permit representation, freed from its multiple subject, to present itself as 'representation in its pure form' (*The Order of Things: An Archeology of the Human Sciences* [London: Tavistock 1970], pp. 3–16).

Foucault also discovers this pursuit of 'pure representation', which can only be a misnomer once the 'represented' disappears, in *Don Quixote* where 'resemblances and signs have dissolved their former alliances', so that 'words wander off on their own, without content, without resemblance to fill their emptiness' and 'lie sleeping between the pages of books'. Quixote himself is literally the 'character' that constitutes him, a 'long, thin graphism, a letter that has just escaped from the open pages of a book' whose being is 'nothing but language, text, printed pages, stories that have already been written down', a fabrication of 'interwoven words … writing itself, wandering through the world among the resemblances of things' (op. cit., pp. 46–8). This degree of conscious 'textuality' is characteristic of a particular historical conjuncture. If the predominantly realist text – *Sarrasine*, for example, in Barthes' S/Z – requires something of a smash-and-grab operation before it will yield its codes, the text's discourse on itself during the decades on either side of 1600 frequently leaves doors and windows open, also the strongroom which, more often than not, contains a picture of an open safe.

The abyss into which things are put in deconstruction's *mise en abîme*, also the 'essential void' in *Las Meninas*, is familiar in the topography of Elizabethan and Jacobean drama. It is the 'nothing' in the depths of *The Old Wives' Tale* which reappears, along with the bad pun on 'wood', the iconography of the man in the moon, and the equation of wood, dream, madness and theatre, in *A Midsummer Night's Dream*. The ballad of Bottom's dream, to be entitled 'Bottom's Dream', is so called 'because it hath no bottome' (IV, 1742). In its infinite unfathomability it contains a plenitude which is an emptiness. The dream bares many traces of carnival – orgiastic gratification in a utopian congress of queen, weaver and ass; a parody of St Paul on divine illumination; a praise of folly.[2] It is at once a description of a mystical plenitude beyond words,[3] and a series of mundane truisms about life in the real world of subjects and property – 'Me-thought I was, and me-thought I had' (1735) – in which each sense is capable only of the offices proper to it, and anyone who tries to explain what it is all about is 'but an Asse' or 'a patch'd foole' (1734–6).

This world, in its way quite normal, is the play's dream of a place where its various 'translations'[4] – a recurring term which signifies *metaphor* as well as changes in appearance or identity – will be arrested, where 'man's hand is not able to taste, his tongue to conceive, nor his heart to report' (1739–40), and things will no longer 'seeme small & undistinguishable, / Like farre off mountaines turned into Clouds' seen 'with parted eye, / When every thing seemes double' (IV, 1712–15). Theseus's language attempts to institute this closure by installing 'coole reason' in a position of dominance at the expense of 'The Lunaticke, the Lover and the Poet' (V, 1798–9). But Hippolyta's language embraces 'translation' and dream, maintaining that dreams shared communally, 'told over' by 'minds transfigur'd so together', grow to 'something of great constancie' (V, 1815–17), a proposition which applies equally to the experiences of lovers in the wood, the fictive 'truth' consolidated and dispersed in the theatre, and cool reason's production of the world. The last word on Theseus, which joins his magisterial gaze with Hippolyta's parted eye, is that he is the creature of the poet purged and rendered supplementary by his 'reason'. Puck's valediction, 'If we shadows have offended ...' (V, 2207), recalls the Duke's own comment on the 'lamentable Comedie' and 'tragic mirth' of *Pyramus and Thisbe* – 'The best in this kind are but shadowes' (2004) – and funnels the proceedings in general into something 'No more yeelding but a dreame' (2112). In the text's representation of itself this is all the work of the poet who, in a more positive sense than that implied by his puppet, Theseus, 'gives to aire nothing, a locall habitation and a name' (V, 1808–9). But this discourse too works through exclusions in claiming for its creator the divine prerogative of a fresh start, and even the most 'self-molesting discourse' can, as Terry Eagleton argues, be referred back to a 'more fundamental realm, that of historical contradictions themselves' (*Walter Benjamin: or Towards a Revolutionary Criticism* (London: New Left Books 1981, p. 109). It is this realm that holds the true materiality of the 'nothings' of *A Midsummer Night's Dream*.

As Theseus condemns Hermia to death, perpetual virginity or marriage to the man of her father's choice, this is done in the name of the law of Athens which, as the Duke claims, 'by no meanes we may extenuate' (I, 129). When the lovers are woken in the wood after their night of confusion, Theseus lifts this nightmare prohibition as quickly and as arbitrarily as it descended while Egeus still pleads 'the Law, the Law' (IV, 1680). The conflict between the letter and the 'material of conduct' which, according to Aristotle, is 'essentially irregular'[5] is here magically dissolved and with it the contradiction between the absolute sovereignty of law and that of the legitimate leader whose word is law – a conflict of discourses on justice and power which engaged the attention of Queen Elizabeth and was to become central to the struggle between Charles I and Parliament.[6] The law of Athens, like Theseus himself, is and is not absolute. Although banished by the advance of the plot, this contradiction finally remains suspended in the peremptory passage of the lovers through experience to maturity and its ensuing atonement of individual contentment and the social order, which itself remains under partial erasure through the possibility that Demetrius at least is still a prisoner of Puck's love-juice.[7] While *Love's Labour's Lost* declines to 'end like an old Play' in that 'Iacke hath not Gill' (IVb, 2835–6), *A Midsummer Night's Dream* promises that 'Iacke shall have Iill, nought shall goe ill' (III, 1504) with an enthusiasm belied only by the fact that the spectator may, to the end, find these emblematic Jacks and Jills as difficult to tell apart as they find each other. In the process the play also suspends the contradiction between the patriarchal trade in young women carried out under the auspices of the family[8] and the spontaneous integrity of a unique and individual 'love', which Swift in 1723 could still describe as 'a ridiculous passion which hath no being but in plays and romances'.[9]

As ever the text is affirming nothing – yielding no more than a dream – and if its shadows offend, it can still hold up the disclaimer of being only a 'Fairy toye', albeit one of considerable sophistication. Through its riot of dreams, translation, madness and play, all interrogating the metaphysical supplementarity of 'representation', the text's discourse on itself may distance and problematize more 'single' self-naturalizing discourses. But it is also in a curious way disabled, not so much transcendent as ideologically *hors de combat*. Carnival inversion was, as Bakhtin argues, rooted in a 'spiritual and ideological dimension', its true festivity ultimately sanctioned by equality and solidarity – 'by the highest aims of human existence, that is, by the world of ideals' (*Rabelais and his World* [trans. Hélène Iswolsky, Cambridge, Mass.: MIT Press 1968], p. 9). Its deconstructions go beyond delirium and indeterminacy to a vision of a better world, already in prospect at its own moment of levelling and familiarity. The encounter of a popular festive tradition with elements of the court masque in *A Midsummer Night's Dream*[10] produces an idealism of a more attenuated and prevaricating kind. The utopian moment now binds stage and audience in the production of dreams which, when told over, may grow to something of great constancy, however powerless to intervene in the less subtle, less self-conscious dreaming of discourses that intensify the contradictions in the social formation rather than suspending them in the tremors of the 'double' sign. Within the opulence of this sign, which projects a constitutive communion of stage and audience, the 'base mechanicals' are ultimately kept in the place they will occupy in the subsequent history of English Literature, as a broken fragment of the language, or that class of people who, however eager to please, still talk and act funny – 'a sound but not in government' (V, 1921). And the emergent puritan bourgeoisie, in the process of excluding itself by choice from the 'unity' both of the little world of the theatre and of 'Merrie England' at large, confronted this discursive opulence and excess not as the forceful utterance of an ideological adversary with which it shared at least a common language but as a space for unproductive idleness and the indulgence of trivial appetites, a way of letting the time pass by.[11]

In *King Lear* the abyss of subjects and signs, complete with its ideological disclosures and abnegations, appears as an *almost* physical presence, conjured up near the cliffs of Dover during the scene in which Lear and Gloucester finally meet again on the 'great stage of Fooles' (V, 2014). When Edgar, in one of the five parts he assumes, describes the view from an imaginary edge his language is in no way essentially different from that in which the play's 'real' landscape is produced on the bare Jacobean stage, and the gap between aspiration and accomplishment in Gloucester's leap, an actor's pratfall with a degree of forward momentum, displays the gulf that exists between a mimetic 'referent' and the linguistic materials required for its production. Like the absence in the mirror of *Las Meninas*, the vertiginous drop into which Edgar's disguised voice can finally 'look no more, / Least my braine turne, and the deficient sight / Topple downe headlong' (IV, vi, 2457–9) doubles as a topography of 'representation' itself. At the foot of the cliff the 'murmuring Surge, / That on th' unnumbred idle Pebble chafes / Cannot be heard so high' (2555–7), its unmotivated noise produced as the sound surplus to sense in the words that call it into being.[12] As this pure signifier moves up from its silence towards solid ground, a signified is progressively distinguishable albeit deformed by simile and metonymy into a vision of choughs and crows 'scarce so grosse as Beetles', fishermen the size of mice, a samphire gatherer 'no bigger than his head' and the 'tall Anchoring Barke, / Diminish'd to her Cocke: her Cocke, a Buoy / Almost too small for sight' (2448–56). At the edge of the cliff the speaking subject is himself again, or at least the 'self' Edgar is pretending to be, but still faced with a prospect of his own invention in which he is already swallowed up and scattered.

Edgar's pretended fear, above the unnumbered pebbles and the surge, that his brain will turn and 'the deficient sight' topple headlong unites the blindness of Gloucester with the madness of Lear as their meeting approaches, and the vertical line of Edgar's cliff reconstitutes the axis of representation in the text as a whole. 'Madness' is produced in the play's language as a signifier cut free of its signified and as voices that disperse the unified subject – 'Pilicock sat on Pilicock hill', 'suum, mun, nonny, Dolphin my Boy, Boy *Sesey*: let him trot by', 'Sa, sa, sa, sa'. In 'Reason in Madnesse', with its obvious parallels in what Gloucester can *see* once he is blinded, meaning begins to emerge as 'matter, and impertinency mixt' (IV, v, 2615–16). In 'reason' the sign and the subject have each coalesced but remain beset by an ineradicable heterogeneity anticipated in Lear's majestic, already top-heavy rhetoric in the ceremonial division of the kingdom and recalled when he wakes in Cordelia's tent:

> Pray do not mocke me:
> I am a very foolish fond old man,
> Fourscore and upward,
> Not an howre more, nor less:
> And to deal plainely,
> I feare I am not in my perfect mind.
> Me thinks I should know you, and know this man,
> Yet I am doubtfull: For I am mainely ignorant
> What place is this
>
> (IV, vii, 2813–21)

Here the language, like that of the lovers woken in the wood in *A Midsummer Night's Dream*,[13] seeks out the place, the subject who speaks and the relations that shape the utterance. A hesitant shuffling of clauses suggests someone who knows language but is speaking for the first time. In both plays the awakening leaves behind a world of dream and madness which is also the text's representation of the theatre. The heath and the cliffs are, like the wood outside Athens, places of transformation that reverse the supplementary mark of the linguistic and theatrical signifier. While Puck is a quick-change artist who supervises the lovers' 'fond Pageant' (III, 1138) for Oberon, the 'King of shadowes' (1388), the king driven out into the storm is already *'Lear's shadow'* (I, iv, 744), the poor player whose accomplices will be the professional Fool and Edgar in the part of Bedlam beggar. The performances within *King Lear* range from the mock-trial of the daughters, in which an extra increment of imagination is required from the audience to amend the joint-stool that represents Goneril, to the 'great stage of Fooles' scene – the densest extended moment of theatrical doubleness when the two principal players meet over Edgar's imaginary abyss.

The view from the cliff-edge, inscribed in the theatrical trope of the supplement,is the absent centre of the play, a regress into the 'nothing' spoken by the Fool (I, iv, 658), given by Cordelia and promised by her father in return – 'Nothing will come of nothing' (I, i, 96). Lear also tells the Fool that 'Nothing can be made out of nothing' (I, iv, 663), but ultimately this is the source of any affirmations the play has to make and the point to which they return. In the main action, as J.F. Danby's classic study of the play shows, the Tudor discourse on the state and family as structures given by a 'nature' which will revenge itself on 'unnatural' subjects confronts an emergent 'nature' in which the fittest survive and individual enterprise stands against traditional duties – 'the plague of custome', as Edmund calls them, and 'the curiosity of Nations' (I, ii, 337–8).[14] In this struggle neither the 'nature' of Hooker and the Chain of Being nor that of Hobbes is victorious. Self-interest finally consumes itself, but the 'nature' Lear and Gloucester invoke to punish their 'unnatural' children is equally indiscriminate in selecting its targets. Both of these essentialist views of what nature decrees are suspended in the text's discourse on the linguistic and theatrical signifier, produced as the 'nothing' or the excess that precedes the essences engaged in the discursive closures of conflicting ideologies. Lear and Gloucester's respective abrogations, of kingship and paternal duty, bring them to a recognition that these are parts to be vigorously *enacted*, not positions written by nature to be taken as read. The 'natural' discourse on power and the subjects it constitutes are suspended over the blindness, madness and fragmentation of Edgar's imaginary abyss, which doubles as the heterogeneity from which 'Lear', 'Gloucester' and the rest are produced as elements in a mimetic action. In parallel with this gesture of casting metaphysics down to the blind spot where its own constitutive blindness becomes visible, any metaphysical value that endures in the play emanates from the Fool who multiplies words, the eloquent silence of the 'poore fool' Cordelia (V, iii, 3277) and the several roles of the antic released when Poor Tom declares '*Edgar* I nothing am' (II, ii, 1272).

'Men are so necessarily mad, that not to be mad would be another form of madness': Foucault, following Pascal's aphorism, postulates a historical 'zero point in the course of madness at which madness itself is an undifferentiated experience, a not yet divided experience of division itself' (*Madness and Civilisation* [London: Tavistock 1957], p. ix). Out of this zero of undifferentiated experience the rational discourse on madness eventually produces, from the late eighteenth century on, 'mental illness' as a device for separating madness from reason in such a way that the separation can be taken as always having been there. And so psychiatry's 'monologue of reason *about* madness' comes to replace a past dialogue which incorporated 'all those stammered, imperfect words without fixed syntax in which the exchange between madness and reason was made' (op. cit., p. x). The Renaissance texts and paintings located closer to the 'zero point' are, according to Foucault, characterized by a 'proliferation of meaning, from a self-multiplication of significance', an imagery 'burdened with supplementary meanings, and forced to express them' and an 'excess of meaning' into which 'dreams, madness, the unreasonable can also slip' (op. cit., pp. 18–19).

Pascal's dictum, adapted to the theatre and carrying the echo of a text still in dialogue with madness, sums up the trope of the supplement from *The Old Wives' Tale* to *The Winter's Tale*, through Shakespeare's Comedies, *Hamlet* and *Macbeth*: 'Men are so necessarily acting, that not to be acting would be another form of acting.' When Edgar assumes madness in the first of his roles, the syntactical arrangement of his words sets up a dialogue in which madness and acting together reply to reason and the self-present real. '*Edgar* I nothing am' speaks rationally of the assumed madness and madly of identity divided to the point where it can no longer recognize significant difference or the logic of self-identity. It also points to the submerging of the actor's identity in the role and the unreality of the one who does the submerging, an 'Edgar' who is essentially no more and no less substantial than Poor Tom. In the Jacobean theatre, as in carnival, such madness, masking and folly were the occasion for a social and semiotic licence. In making 'nothing' of Edgar, Poor Tom relates this licence to the production of the theatrical illusion in a way that mediates his transformation on the level of mimesis to his audience. This layer of mediation, implicit in the 'nothing' that surrounds and permeates the text, brings madness, the theatre and traditional forms of festive upheaval into a particularly sharp conjunction, through which the *locus* conflict between a feudal 'nature' reformulated by the ideologues of the absolutist Tudor state, and the discourses of competitive individualism is played out *behind* allusions to the festive ideal of equality and plenty.

During the 'great stage of Fooles' scene, Lear – dressed in wild flowers and weeds, at once a May King and a Lord of Misrule – turns his 'Reason in Madnesse' to traditional forms of topsy-turvydom and abuse of authority.[15] The blind Gloucester must look with his ears to see that 'a Dogg's obey'd in Office' and that justice and thief are indistinguishable: 'Change places, and handy-dandy, which is the justice, which is the theefe' (IV, v, 2597–603). The inversion is also a levelling, handy-dandy a figure not only of 'nothing' but also of the utopian plenitude associated with carnival and the Land of Cockaygne. Earlier, in the 'Poore naked wretches speech', Lear has already recognized that the real misrule was before he became his shadow, and he has urged a personified morality–play 'Pompe' to 'Take Physicke' and 'Expose thy selfe to feele what wretches feele, / That thou maist shake the superflux to them, / And shew the Heavens more just' (III, iv, 1809–17). This redistribution would not so much *fulfil* as *produce* something akin to divine justice by 'showing' it in the dramatic sense. Through the breaks he has caused in an order he takes to be transcendent and divine, Gloucester too is drawn some way towards inversion and utopia when he 'sees feelingly' the injustice of wealth:

> Let the superfluous, and Lust-dieted man,
> That slaves your ordinance, that will not see
> Because he doo's not feele, feele your powre quickly:
> So distribution should undoo excesse,
> And each man have enough.

> (IV, i, 2252–5)

The festive ideal of equality and plenty that flickers behind these preliminary gestures of shaking off a 'superflux' and 'undoing excess' is expressed more directly in some parts of the Fool's utopian prophecy, which even levels the stage-audience distinction in making the speaker, alive in pre-Christian Britain, momentarily contemporary with his hearers:

> He speke a Prophecie ere I g3o:
> When Priests are more in word, then matter;
> When Brewers marre their Malt with water;
> When Nobles are their Taylors Tutors,
> No Heretiques burn'd but wenches Sutors;
> When every Case in Law, is right;
> No Squire in debt, nor no poore Knight;
> When Slanders do not live in Tongues;
> Nor Cut-purses come not to throngs;
> When Usurers tell their Gold i'th'Field,
> And Baudes, and whores, do Churches build,
> Then shal the Realme of *Albion*, come to great confusion:
> Then comes the time, who lives to see't,

That going shalbe us'd with feet.
This prophecie *Merlin* shall make, for I live before his time.

(III, ii, 1734–49)

Here the basic festive trope which sets hierarchy on its head is compounded by other internal burlesques and inversions.The whole sequence parodies pseudo-Chaucerian verses in Puttenham's *Arte of English Poesie* (1589, pp. 187–8), and its ideal community is itself adulterated, inverted in the first four lines of the prophecy – which are at once anti-utopian and directly critical of Jacobean society. The bathetic climax of this apocalypse which brings the realm to 'great confusion' is that then people will walk on their feet – a tautologous regress, comparable to the meaning of eating grapes according to Touchstone's philosopher, and a mundane truism like those embedded in Bottom's dream ('the eare of man hath not seene, mans hand is not able to taste') – which inverts inversion by setting everything right way up. The parting claim that 'This prophecie *Merlin* shall make' sets the whole speech in quotation marks as a burlesque and scrambles the 'present' of the performance and the 'past' of the action with the intervening 'future' of Merlin in a continuous supplementary time shared by the actor as Fool, and the Fool as actor, with his audience.

Robert Weimann argues that here 'the theme of Utopia is not merely associated with the inversion motif, it is *expressed* structurally in terms of inversion' and that the 'inversion of inversion is high experimental and itself amounts almost to a method of reason in madness' (*Shakespeare and the Popular Tradition in the Theatre* (ed. R. Schwartz, Baltimore: Johns Hopkins U P 1978, pp. 42–3). But this double inversion, multiple when compounded with other supplementary tropes, occurs in any number of late sixteenth- and early seventeenth-century plays, from *The Spanish Tragedy* and *The Old Wives' Tale* on, which combine a self-conscious theatricality with one or more of such terms as madness, dream and festivity. The mangled prophecy is a special case only in that it adds another twist or two to a supplement that occupies the front of the stage and continually punctuates the 'fable' of *King Lear*, from the interventions of the mad king, the actor-madman and the professional Fool on the heath to be meeting on the great stage of fools.

Although elements of social criticism are thrown out by its centripetal motion, this play of presence and absence is, like the vision of Albion's confusion, tightly wound into itself. The text's intensification of festival inversion overtakes any shadow it might retain of the plebeian feast's egalitarian idealism. 'There is little hope,' as Danby rightly points out, 'of enlisting the Fool as a social reformer' (*Shakespeare's Doctrine of Nature: a study of King Lear* [London: Faber 1949], p. 107), and if traces of a popular utopianism are reproduced in the pleas of Lear and Gloucester for 'distribution', they are heavily policed by an Elizabethan discourse on

Christian charity, which has less to do with turning the social order on its head than with confirming its inequalities by alleviating the symptoms that pose the greatest internal threat to the dominant religious ideology.[16] Shaking off superfluities has very little to do with shaking the world to its foundations, and Gloucester's attribution of social injustices to the fact that the lust-dieted man 'will not see, / Because he doo's not *feele*' contains enough political quietism to fuel a thousand practical criticism seminars. The 'powre' that Gloucester calls down to awaken these dormant feelings, 'So distribution should undoo excesse', is not of course that of the class of carnival levellers but the power of the 'Heavens' (IV, i, 2251), where they may all eventually reap the true rewards of deprivation. There is always a temptation for Marxist humanism to pounce on these lines with great alacrity.[17] But if they do go some way towards undermining an adamantly conservative Bard, seen as a souped-up Hooker or the Tillyard tradition's lickspittle apologist for the Tudor Myth and the Chain of Being, they are scant evidence for regarding Shakespeare as a prototype of the fellow-traveller.

The discourse on representation in *King Lear*, which incorporates timeless prophecy, the imaginary abyss of language, and actors acting (actors acting) madness that contains reason, is a particularly convoluted production of the aesthetic ideology of 'nothing', which is also expressed in the airy nothing of *A Midsummer Night's Dream*, the 'baseless fabricke' of *The Tempest*, and the 'nothing' Sidney's poet affirms and from which Puttenham's creates. While the internal distances and inversions of the text it proposes may disclose the contrivance of ideological discourses that present themselves as natural, the 'textuality' that gets in the way of the conflicting doctrines of nature in *King Lear* also traps in its regresses the egalitarian festive ideal. The apparently rational Lear of the play's opening scene is, as Kent claims, in a way already 'mad' (I, i, 155), and when he says 'Nothing will come of nothing' there is reason in this madness too. The historical transformation of festive inversion and abuse evident in the play are powerless in the face of the sort of essentialist discourse they debunk, the coercive language of law, proclamation and political doctrine, which determines the material conditions of the theatre – the legal status of actors, the location of buildings, even the gradual squeezing of an anarchic festive solidarity into this safer, less volatile, heavily censored space. In the Shakespearean text's self-reflexive dimension these material conditions of production reappear in the guise of the theatrical contract – a utopian 'converse' of stage and audience in the process of creation *ex nihilo*. But here the festive and its potential for hatching revolutionary ideologies are, for all the text's prioritizing of supplements, firmly in an *institutionally* supplementary place, a 'nothing' where anything can happen but acting is always in excess of action. Behind this unending handy-dandy the play proceeds to the point where Lear cries 'Howle, howle, howle' (V, iii, 3217) and moves into either madness, reason or Foucault's zero-point where somehow an undifferentiated experience of reason and madness can still be called 'madness'. The concluding, inconclusive prediction of Poor Tom, now the 'nothing' of Edgar again, seems a safe bet in comparison with the projections of the Fool: 'we that are yong, / Shall never see so much, nor live so long' (V, iii, 3301).

If the indeterminate time of the Fool's prophecy could be pushed forward another hundred years, it would reach an attack on the London stage which recalls those of the Puritans at the turn of the seventeenth century but applies to a theatre, no longer broadly popular, that attracted audiences drawn almost exclusively from the gentry and aristocracy. Thirty-eight years after the restoration of Charles II, Jeremy Collier complained about abuse of the clergy and the higher social orders:

> And has our Stage a particular Privilege? Is their *Charter* inlarg'd, and are they on the same Foot of Freedom with the *Slaves* in the *Saturnalia*? Must all Men be handled alike? ... I hope the *Poets* do not intend to revive the old Project of Levelling, and *vote* down the House of Peers.
> (*A Short View of the Immorality and Profaneness of the English Stage* [London, 1698], pp. 175–6)

Collier's correlation of drama, saturnalian inversion and political struggle for the ideal of a greater equality and democracy is clearly alarmist. Held in the asylum of the theatre pursuing nothing, a modified festive topsy-turvydom was relatively harmless. The historical force of the festive ideal was much more in evidence in the aims of peasant revolts in England and Europe in the late Middle Ages and, in the 1640s, of groups like the Levellers, the Diggers and the Ranters, the suppression of whose egalitarian programme and practices during the English revolution formed part of the compromise between the merchant classes and the aristocracy which led to the constitutional monarchy.[18] If the utopian ideal went through one form of transformation and redoubling in the Elizabethan and Jacobean theatre, its main political thrust involved a rejection of the theatre along with other types of traditional festivity and play. In the more radical Puritan programmes distribution would 'undoo excesse' not only in the sense of personal wealth but in terms of removing the need for a delirious 'second life' of imaginary plenitude.

In the articulation of these aspirations the festive tradition was itself overtaken by a specifically Judaeo-Christian millenarianism in which the press and the pulpit had much more to contribute than the theatre, the vernacular Bibles providing the appropriate authority from within the dominant religious ideology in the promise that the first shall be last and the Pauline proclamation of a kingdom of heaven on earth, attainable through the struggle of true believers who have 'turned the world upside down' (Acts 17: 6).[19] The polemicists who attacked the theatre and other forms of 'pastime' did so within a much broader vision than that permitted to the kill-joy hypocrites obsessed with the letter paraded in the stage's travesty of Puritanism. In *The Anatomy of Abuses*, for example, Stubbes mentions the theatre as only one target among many, including a lack of provision for the poor, 'the fraudulent dealing of Marchant men' and the enclosures of common land that 'bee the causes why rich men eate upp poore men, as beastes do eate grasse'[20]

The Tudor enclosures of the commons and engrossment of estates, whose owners also profited from the expropriation of Church property and the legal chicanery through which large numbers of feudal copyholders were ousted from their lands, produced, on the heaths and in the woodland areas that remained open, communities of 'masterless' men and women who, according to Aubrey, lived 'lawless, nobody to govern them … having no dependence on anybody'[21] Out of this dispossessed class sprang the more radical ideologies of the English Revolution and the political will to transform them into action, from the peasant revolts of the early seventeenth century to the mobilizing of the New Model Army, 'a body of masterless men on the move', which was to become the main political power-base of the Levellers.[22] In its preoccupation with heaths and forests the Shakespearean text occasionally produces fragments of their material reality – in the plight of Lear's 'naked wretches', in Corin's predicament when he first meets Rosalind and Celia, or the position of women with no means of subsistence who could be dealt with more economically by the persecution of witches than by a redistribution of wealth. But for the most part its dream displaces these social contradictions, reproducing them on the level of language and representation. While the text's woods and heaths resist self-naturalizing discourses, its material equivalents, threatened by a more pressing form of 'closure', were a site for the production of ideologies intent on making history by means other than 'faire is foule' and 'handy-dandy'. Those who were young in 1606 when Edgar spoke his concluding words in praise of *King Lear* might well have lived to see much more than that play could ever encompass – a year later the Digger insurrection against enclosures in the county in which Shakespeare himself was a property-owner;[23] in 1642 the closing of the theatres, inaugurating the greatest age of English drama; and in 1649, in place of the carnival effigy of a mock-tryant, the official feast of a royal beheading.

Notes

1. Derrida has strategically overlooked this version of the speech-writing duality, emphasizing its phonophile converse.

2. See 1 Corinthians 3: 9, T.N. GREENFIELD 'A Midsummer Night's Dream and The Praise of Folie', Comparative Literature, **20**, 1968, pp. 236–44; BAKHTIN, M., *Rabelais and His World*, trans. H. Iswolsky, (Cambridge Mass., 1968), p. 14.

3. 'Mystical explanations are regarded as profound, the truth is that they do not even go the length of being superficial' (NIETZSCHE, F., *Joyful Wisdom*, trans. T. Common, (New York, 1960) p. 169).

4. See I, 203; III, 936; III, 1054. On metaphor as 'translation', see WILSON, T., *Arte of Rhetorique, 1560*, ed. G. H. Mair (Oxford, 1909) pp. 172–3.

5. *Nichomachean Ethics*, 1137b (ARISTOTLE, 1926, p. 315).

6. CAS PARI, F., *Humanism and The Social Order in Tudor England*, Classics in Education **34**, (New York, 1968) p. 270; HILL, C., *The Century of Revolution 1602–1714* (Wokingham, 1980) pp. 166f.; BELSEY, Catherine, *Critical Practice*, (London, 1981) pp. 169, 179–81.

7. See BROOKS, 1979, p. 85n.

8. On the overwhelming predominance in the late sixteenth century of arranged marriages, see STONE, 1977) pp. 180–95. Puck's 'Country Proverb' on Jack and Jill continues: 'The man shall have his Mare againe, and all shall bee well.'

9. STONE, Lawrence, *The Family, Sex and Marriage in England 1500–1800*, (London, 1977) p. 283.

10. See WELSFORD, E., *The Court Masque*, (Cambridge, 1927) pp. 324f.; OLSON, P. A., 'A Midsummer Night's Dream and The Meaning of Court Marriage', *Journal of English Literary History*, **24** (1957) pp. 95–119.

11. See NORTHBROOKE, J., *Treatise Against Dicing, Dancing, Plays and Interludes, with Other Idle Pastimes...1577* ed. J.P. Collier, (London, 1843) pp. 43–56; STUBBES, P., *The Anatomie of Abuses*, (London, 1595) pp. 102f.; GOSSON, G., *The School of Abuse (1579)*, ed. E. Arber, (London, 1869) pp. 33–44.

12. J.P. COLLIER discovered in these lines 'an assonant grandeur and solemnity almost worthy of our own Alfred Lord Tennyson' (COLLIER, J. P., *A Short View of The Immorality and Profaneness of The English Stage*, (London, 1842) p. 135).

13. IV, 1671–8.

14. See DANBY, J., *Shakespeare's Doctrine of Nature*, (London, 1949), *passim*.

15. I am much indebted in what follows to Weimann's account of *King Lear* (1978, pp. 40–3).

16. See JOSEPH, B . L., *Shakespeare's Eden : The Commonwealth of England 1558–1629*, (London, 1971) pp. 61–3; and MEHL, D., 'King Lear and the Poor Naked Wretches', *Shakespeare Jahrbuch*, (West) (Berlin, 1975) pp. 154–62.

17. See example, KETTLE, A.,'From *Hamlet* to *Lear*', *Shakepeare in a Changing World*, (London, 1964) pp. 166–9.

18. For the recent debate on the extent of Leveller democracy, see MACPHERSON, C.
    B., *The Political Theory of Possessive Individualism : Hobbes to Locke,* (Oxford, 1962)
    p. 122; MORTON, A. L., *The Wared of the Ranters : Religious Radicalism in The English
    Revolution,* (London, 1970) pp. 197–219; ARBLASTER, A., 'Revolution, the Levellers
    and C. B. Macpherson', BARKER, F., *et al., 1642 : Literature and Power in the
    Seventeenth Century,* (Colchester, 1981) pp. 220–37.

19. See HILL, 1972,*passim,* 'Freedom is the man that will turn the world upside
    downe' (WINSTANLEY, G., *Works,* ed. G. H. Sabine, (Ithaca, 1946) p. 316).

20. STUBBES, 1595, pp. 33, 81–3.

21. HILL, C., *The World Turned Upside Down : Radical Ideas During The English
    Revolution,* (London,1972) pp. 32f.

22. Ibid., p. 68.

23. Both HILL (1980, p. 21) and KAMEN, H., *The Iron Century : Social Change in Europe
    1550–1660,* 2nd. ed. (revised) (London, 1976, p. 303) use the term 'Digger' to
    characterize the 1607–08 uprisings in Warwickshire.

TERRY EAGLETON   VALUE: KING LEAR, TIMON OF ATHENS, ANTONY
AND CLEOPATRA*

Terry Eagleton is Warton Professor of English at the University of
Oxford, and was one of the first British scholars to introduce the work
of Macherey and Althusser into the sphere of literary criticism. His
book *William Shakespeare* (Basil Blackwell, 1986) was one of the first
volumes in the *Re-reading Literature* series, of which Eagleton is the
general editor. Eagleton's book is an attempt to offer an overview of
the Shakespeare canon in the light of a range of new radical forms of
materialist criticism, although his own critical orientation is post-
structuralist Marxist. Eagleton divides the Shakespeare canon into a
series of texts which exemplify particular thematic concerns. Thus,
under the heading of 'Language' he groups *Macbeth, Richard II* and *1
Henry IV*; under the heading of 'Desire' he groups certain of the
comedies; under 'Law' he groups selected 'problem' plays; under the
heading 'Nothing' he groups *Othello, Hamlet* and *Coriolanus*. The
following excerpt is the chapter on 'Value' which incorporates *King
Lear, Timon of Athens* and *Antony and Cleopatra*. Like Evans, Eagleton is
concerned with texts as representations although he grounds the play
of meaning in a firm notion of historical necessity. Thus, *King Lear*
generates a rhetoric which devalues language, and so introduces a

*Reprinted from *William Shakespeare* (Oxford: Basil Blackwell, 1986) pp. 76–89.

contradiction into the process of sign production whereby language is urged to surpass material reality at the same time as it is contained by it. The exchange which takes place in *Timon of Athens* effectively devalues the practice of exchange and becomes the Nietzschean *Übermensch* in Timon's refusal to submit himself to a comparison with others; but it is also symptomatic of an aristocratic ethos 'shot through with a lacerating death-wish, as its own desperate futility continually offers to undermine it'. He sees this ethic as informing also *Antony and Cleopatra*, where what is at issue is a Derridian 'excess' which sets up a contradiction with the notion of 'equitable exchange'. Throughout this chapter Eagleton uses the full resources of post-structuralism to argue a case for these plays as symptomatic of a dying aristocratic order. To this extent, his approach connects with that of Malcolm Evans and Walter Cohen.

1

King Lear opens with a bout of severe linguistic inflation, as Goneril and Regan rival each other in lying rhetoric. Goneril pitches her love for Lear beyond all language and value, and so ironically reveals this 'more than all' as just the resounding nothing that it is:

> Sir, I love you more than word can wield the matter;
> Dearer than eyesight, space, and liberty;
> Beyond what can be valued, rich or rare;
> No less than life, with grace, health, beauty, honour;
> As much as child e'er lov'd, or father found;
> A love that makes breath poor and speech unable;
> Beyond all manner of so much I love you.
>
> (I, i, 54–60)

Goneril's love for Lear is indeed beyond value, since it doesn't exist; it is inarticulate not because it transcends meaning but because it has none. By representing her love as the negation of any particular object, she merely succeeds in cancelling it out, just as she uses language only to suggest its utter inadequacy. Goneril, whom Albany will later call 'Thou worse than any name' (V, iii, 156), fails to see that definitions can be creative as well as restrictive, fashioning something from nothing. It is then up to Regan to negate her sister's negativity to imply an even more grandiose all,

claiming, contradictorily, that Goneril has both defined her own love
precisely and fallen woefully short.

Within this stage-managed charade, where 'all' has been so radically
devalued, Cordelia's murmured 'Nothing' is the only sound currency.
Cordelia is characteristically exact to maintain that she can say nothing to
outdo her sisters, for who can trump 'all'? Lear warns her that nothing
will come of this – 'Nothing will come of nothing. Speak again' (I, i, 89) –
but as usual he is mistaken: when meaning has been inflated beyond
measure, nothing *but* nothing, a drastic reduction of signs to cyphers, will
be enough to restabilize the verbal coinage. Only by a fundamental
inversion and undercutting of this whole lunatic language game can the
ground be cleared for a modest 'something' to begin gradually to emerge.
That 'something' is in fact already figured in Cordelia's reply. With
scrupulous precision, she informs Lear that she loves him 'According to
my bond; no more nor less' (I, i, 92), appealing away from the crazed
subjectivism of the King's whimsical demand for love to the web of
impersonal constraints and obligations of kinship. The other side of
reckless inflation is the crass utilitarian exactitude with which Lear
believes human love can be quantified; Cordelia counters the first with a
more authentic precision, and the second, later in the play, with a
forgiveness which is creative excess. Lear himself, of course, cannot see
such precision as anything but paucity of spirit, gripped as he is by a
semiotic crisis which spurs him to shed the substance of power while
retaining 'The name, and all th'addition to a king', voiding the referent
while clutching at the empty signifier. He trusts to the aura of a title, even
as he credits lines drawn on a piece of paper: 'Of all these bounds, even
from this line to this …. We make thee lady.' No map can fully represent
the terrain it signifies, just as Lear has struck his own title abstract,
divorced it from material life.

Lear's paranoid drama, like the Malvolio-taunting scene of *Twelfth
Night*, fashions a verbal nexus to which there is no 'outside', double-
binding Cordelia so that to play her role or refuse it, speak or keep silent,
become equally falsifying. (The Fool will later complain that he is
whipped whether he speaks truth, lies or holds his peace.) France's
gratuitous action of accepting Cordelia even when 'her price is fallen'
makes something of nothing, cutting across Lear's world of precisely
calculated imprecisions, but he can extricate Cordelia from the charade
only in a way which that fiction can nullify as beggarly sentimentalism.
When social reality has become mystified to its core, truth can lie only
beyond its boundaries, as France lies beyond the extreme limit of Britain
(Dover cliff). But such truth can therefore also be neutralized as marginal
aberration. Cordelia consequently disappears into the future of the play,
and truth becomes a simple inversion of whatever Lear affirms: Cordelia,
France comments, is 'most rich, being poor', just as Kent finds that

'Freedom lies hence, and banishment is here.' We shall see later that the truth of a false condition can be articulated only in the discourse of madness, in a language which raises political insanity to the second power, parodying and redoubling it so as to deconstruct it from the inside. There can be no straight talking, no bold gesture of unmasking, which will not be absorbed and reinflected by the nexus of delusion, becoming yet another mask and falsehood in its turn; only the coupling of two negatives can hope to produce a positive.

In severing himself from Cordelia, spokeswoman for the material bonds of kinship, Lear cuts himself off from his own physical life, leaving his consciousness to consume itself in a void. In madness, as in sleepwalking, the mind ranges impotently beyond the body's limits, capable of destroying its substance: Edgar declares that he eats poisonous matter when seized by devils. Lear's mind is so tormented by his daughters' cruelty that his body is impervious to the storm which assails it: 'When the mind's free / The body's delicate; this tempest in my mind / Doth from my senses take all feeling else, / Save what beats there' (III, iv, 11–14). Body and consciousness, once disjointed, are each reduced to a kind of nothing: the former becomes an insentient blank, the latter, unmoulded by material constraint, emptily devours itself. Gloucester, confronted with Lear's agony, yearns to unhinge his own mind and body:

> The King is mad; how stiff is my vile sense,
> That I stand up, and have ingenious feeling
> Of my huge sorrows! Better I were distract;
> So should my thoughts be sever'd from my griefs,
> And woes by wrong imaginations lose
> The knowledge of themselves.
>
> (IV, vi, 279–84)

What Gloucester will finally learn, once blindness has thrust the brute fact of his body into consciousness, is not to give the body the slip but to 'see feelingly', to allow sight (the symbol of a potentially unbridled self) to be constrained from within by the compassionate senses. Gloucester's body becomes his mode of communication with the material world (he 'smell[s] his way to Dover'), more solidly reliable than the verbal trickery of his bastard son. At the extreme outer limit of political society – on Dover cliff – those fictions can be induced by the fruitfully deceitful ministrations of Edgar to keel over into a kind of truth. This painful rediscovery of the body is what Lear must also learn. To regain touch with the harsh materiality of things, to discover that one is nothing in comparison with all one had imagined, is in that very act to become something:

To say 'ay' and 'no' to everything that I said! 'Ay' and 'no' too was no good divinity. When the rain came to wet me once, and the wind to make me chatter; when the thunder would not peace at my bidding; there I found 'em, there I smelt 'em out. Go to, they are not men of their words. They told me I was everything; 'tis a lie – I am not ague-proof.

(IV, vi)

To say 'ay' and 'no' to everything is to say nothing; Lear has 'smelt out' this truth, absorbed it through the stuff of the ambivalently linking, limiting body, whose stringent boundaries the storm has thrown into exposure. To know your own nothingness is to become something, as the Fool is wiser than fools because he knows his own folly and so can see through theirs.

To be purely bodily, like the non-linguistic animals, is to be essentially passive, a prey to the biological determinations of one's nature. Goneril and Regan, despite a ruthless activism which springs from being unbounded by sensuous compassion, are fundamentally passive in this sense, unable after their initial dissembling to falsify what they are. In this sense they are the true sisters of Cordelia, who is likewise unswervingly faithful to her own being. Edmund sees himself as equally fixed by nature ('I should have been that I am, had the maidenliest star in the firmament twinkled on my bastardizing' [I, ii]), but by reflecting sardonically on his own determinants he is able to escape a blind enslavement to them. He is a self-creating opportunist who can manipulate others' appetites to his own advantage precisely because he knows his own so well. Like Iago, he moves primarily at the level of mystifying language, hostile to physical affinities, intent on rupturing the relations between his father and brother. By consciously appropriating what one ineluctably is, it is possible in part to transcend limit; and this is also true of Edgar and Kent, who deliberately embrace the wretchedness and delusion through which Lear is blindly forced, submitting to degrading limit in order finally to surpass it. The play seeks to distinguish the creative passivity of being constrained in the flesh by the needs of others, from the destructive passivity of being a mere function of one's appetites. For consciousness to be wholly bound by the body is to be a bestial slave to limit; to be purely active, however, is to over-reach those physical bonds for the vacuous freedom of an exploitative individualism. Both modes of being are a kind of nothing, and 'something' emerges in the play only elusively, glimpsed fitfully in the dialectic between them. The paradox which *King Lear* explores is that it is 'natural' for the human animal to transcend its own limits, yet this creative tendency to exceed oneself is also the source of destructiveness. Being 'untrue' to their own nature is natural to human beings: what we call culture or history is an open-ended transformation of fixed boundaries, a transcendence of mere appetite or rich surplus over precise measure. But when this process transgresses the body's confines too far, it violates the bonds of sensuous compassion and begins to prey on physical life itself. A hubristic, overweening consciousness must then be called sharply to order, shrunk back violently within the cramped frontiers of creaturely existence. The problem is how to do this without extinguishing that authentic self-exceeding which distinguishes an animal with history from other natural species.

One can pinpoint this difficult dialectic as the problem of respecting a norm or measure while simultaneously going beyond it. Excess may swamp such measure with its own too much, toppling over by a curious logic into less than anything; yet such superfluity is also precisely that which marks off men and women from the inhuman precision of beasts, or indeed of Goneril and Regan. The sisters fail to understand why their father should require a retinue of knights, and looking at Lear's gang of macho ruffians one can see their point. Lear's reply, however, is telling:

> O, reason not the need! Our basest beggars
> Are in the poorest thing superfluous.
> Allow not nature more than nature needs,
> Man's life is cheap as beast's.
>
> (II, iv, 263–6)

There is no *reason* why human beings should delight in more than is strictly necessary for their physical survival; it is just structural to the human animal that demand should outstrip exact need, that culture should be of its nature. It is this capacity for a certain lavish infringement of exact limit which distinguishes humankind, just as the play's first scene reveals the same capacity to lie at the source of what makes humans immeasurably more destructive than any other species. Surplus is radically ambivalent, not least in economic life. Too many material possessions blunt one's capacity for fellow feeling, swaddling one's senses from exposure to the misery of others. If one could truly *feel* that wretchedness, register it sharply on the senses, then one would be moved to share one's surplus with the poor in a fundamental, irreversible redistribution of wealth:

> Take physic, pomp;
> Expose thyself to feel what wretches feel,
> That thou mayst shake the superflux to them,
> And show the heavens more just ...
>
> (III, iv, 34–7)

> Let the superfluous and lust-dieted man
> That slaves your ordinance, that will not see
> Because he does not feel, feel your power quickly;

So distribution should undo excess,
And each man have enough.

(IV, i, 68–72)

Against this image of a destructive surplus is balanced Cordelia's forgiveness of her father, a gratuitous excess of the strict requirements of justice. It is a kind of nothing, a refusal to calculate debt, out of which something may come.

What is superfluous or excessive about human beings, *King Lear* suggests, is nothing less than language itself, which constantly outruns the confines of the body. 'The worse is not,' declares Edgar, 'So long as we can say "This is the worst"' (IV, i, 28–9). By naming an ultimate limit, speech transcends it in that very act, undoing its own pronouncement by its own performance. Language is the edge we have over biology, but it is a mixed blessing. Goneril and Regan's speech is rigorously exact, pared to the purely functional: Goneril tells Edmund to 'spare speech' when she uses him as a messenger. The disguised Kent's language is as parodically plain as Edgar's is elaborately confusing; Oswald's foppish idiom incites Kent (whose reports are said to be 'nor more nor clipp'd, but so') to spurn him as an 'unnecessary letter'. Language, like much else in the play, has a problem in pitching itself at the elusive point between too much and too little – except, perhaps, in the formally precise yet generously affectionate discourse of Cordelia. Cordelia blends largesse and limitation on her first appearance in the play, when she reminds Lear that her love, though freely given, must be properly divided between himself and her future husband; and the same balance is present in her combination of physical rootedness and freedom of spirit. In this sense, she symbolically resolves many of the play's formal antinomies.

The only problem, however, is that she dies. Edgar's closing injunction – 'Speak what we feel, not what we ought to say' – is no trite tag, denoting as it does that organic unity of body and language, that shaping of signs by the senses, of which Cordelia is representative; but the play has also demonstrated that to speak what one feels is no easy business. For if it is structural to human nature to surpass itself, and if language is the very index and medium of this, then there would seem a contradiction at the very core of the linguistic animal which makes it 'natural' for signs to come adrift from things, consciousness to overstep physical bonds, values to get out of hand and norms to be destructively overridden. It is not, after all, simply a matter of reconciling fixed opposites: it is a matter of regulating what would seem an ineradicable contradiction in the material structure of the human creature. *King Lear* is a tragedy because it stares this contradiction full in the face, aware that no poetic symbolism is adequate to resolve it.

2

An obsession with strict exchanges is typical of middle-class utilitarianism; the aristocracy are traditionally more spendthrift. This is certainly true of Timon of Athens, one of the last of Shakespeare's big spenders, whose grotesque generosity to his friends is a subtle form of egotism, triumphantly trumping their own gifts by returning them many-fold. Timon's giving is a way of cancelling and forestalling the bountifulness of others; since he refuses to learn how to receive, he does not know what a genuine gift is. The act of giving is for Timon its own aesthetic thrill; a man who will bestow anything on anybody is as superbly indifferent to particular persons and use values as the most mean-spirited miser. There is a ruthless formalism and abstraction about Timon's big-heartedness which overrides intrinsic merits, scattering his surplus indiscriminately as the fancy takes him. His munificence is thus rather like money itself, perturbing all particular values in its restless expansiveness. As the Poet says of his own unbridled imagination:

> My free drift
> Halts not particularly, but moves itself
> In a wide sea of tax.
>
> (I, i, 48–50)

This gratuitous generosity turns out to be literally self-destructive, as Timon sinks deeper into debt; and the snarling misanthropy which then overtakes him is merely an inverted image of his erstwhile beneficence. To condemn all individuals indiscriminately is just as abstract as to reward them all indifferently. 'All' and 'nothing' turn out once more to be bedfellows rather than antagonists. It is not fortuitous (though some scholars have found it so) that the play should interpolate into its main narrative an apparently unrelated sub-plot centred on Alcibiades' plea for mercy from the Senate for a friend who has killed in hot blood. It is logical that Timon's prodigality should remind Shakespeare of the issues of mercy and justice, measure for measure. The Senate are as formalistic in their insistence that Alcibiades' friend must die as Timon is in his whimsical patronage; the law, as we have seen already, is coolly indifferent to particular individuals, and thus ironically apes Timon's supposed generosity. In contrast to such abstract formalism, mercy draws attention to specific mitigating factors, and Alcibiades acknowledges that these must temper rather than set aside the claims of justice:

> To kill, I grant, is sin's extremest gust;
> But in defence, by mercy, 'tis most just.

> To be in anger is impiety;
> But who is man that is not angry?
> Weigh but the crime with this.

(III, v, 54–8)

The Senate, however, are not impressed, and Alcibiades is banished for his pains, if not for his atrocious verse.

If Timon of Athens does not exactly engage our heartfelt sympathies, Shakespeare's other two aristocratic big spenders, Antony and Cleopatra, are rather more successful. Perhaps the most revealing approach to this play is through the work of W.B. Yeats. Yeats was the self-appointed spokesman of a decaying aristocracy, the Anglo-Irish Ascendency, who sentimentalized the Irish peasantry they exploited; and his apologia for their passing took the form of swaggering defiance, a reckless celebration of heroic vitality against the niggardly calculations of the middle classes. If the aristocracy are on their way out, then they might as well pass away with a bang rather than a whimper, dancing demonically on the edge of their own grave, squandering their energies in proud disdain for petty-bourgeois prudence, and so dying as they have lived. Confronted with imminent death, the aristocracy make an heroic virtue out of sordid necessity; Yeats gathers the tragedy of their decline into the aesthetic artifice of eternity, rejoicing with fine Nietzschean bravado in the teeth of the historically inevitable. Loss becomes gain, the nadir transfigured to the acme, corruption translated to a triumphant artefact. In this aristocratic or *Übermensch* ethic, each individual becomes his or her own autonomous measure, self-generating and self-delighting, not to be compared with others or subdued to a mean. Thom Gunn's poem 'Lerici', also about a profligate aristocrat, puts the point well:

> Byron was worth the sea's pursuit: his touch
> Was masterful to water, audience
> To which he could react until an end.
> Strong swimmers, fishermen, explorers: such
> Dignify death by fruitless violence,
> Squandering all their little left to spend.

If this violent self-expenditure is to be authentic, however, it must keep one cold eye on its own historical hopelessness. The carefree aristocratic affirmation is shot through with a lacerating death-wish, as its own desperate futility continually offers to undermine it.

It is this Nietzschean or Yeatsian ethic which informs *Antony and Cleopatra*, a play which opens with the censorious remark that Antony's dotage 'o'erflows the measure'. The desperate gamble of the Egyptian world is that if you can only overflow the measure extravagantly enough, then you might just struggle free of its calibrating tyranny into a new transcendence. A wild, wilful self-lavishing ('There's beggary in the love that can be reckon'd') may undercut the mean radically enough to transfigure it, so that Antony and Cleopatra can become their own unique norm, a new creation incommensurable with anything beyond themselves. To be utterly dissolute and undone may, by a strange logic, invert itself into victory (Yeats's 'tragic joy'); and the play is full of such dialectical images of processes which, when pressed to their extreme, tip over into their opposites. The relationship of Antony and Cleopatra makes one little room an everywhere, becoming the sole yardstick by which an otherwise blankly senseless world takes on meaning; the stringent proportions of utilitarian Rome are rejected for a quite different scale of value, linked to intensity and superabundance. Cleopatra is the 'lass unparalleled' who 'beggars all description'; Antony's poker-faced description of a crocodile to the thick-witted Lepidus plays on a thing's incapacity to be defined as anything but itself:

> It is shap'd, sir, like itself, and it is as broad as it has breadth; it is just so high as it is, and moves with its own organs. It lives by that which nourisheth it, and the elements once out of it, it transmigrates.
>
> (II, vii)

As with the subjectivist Trojans of *Troilus and Cressida*, no object is inherently valuable, and there are thus no rational grounds on which to choose between them. Antony's rash decision to fight by sea rather than by land is in the classic existentialist sense an *acte gratuit*, performed defiantly for its own sake. It is an effective way of speeding on the death in which all odds will be even.

The play, then, seizes one term of Shakespeare's customary contradiction – surplus, excess – and rather than seeking to reconcile it with its contrary (equitable exchange), lives it with such fanatical intensity that a perverse kind of value is wrested from this very violent disproportioning. What is known as partial and one-sided takes itself as ultimate, in an ambiguously fertile and lethal fiction. This resolute living towards death, which crams each empty moment of time with hectic pleasure, and transforms each passing sensation into an ecstatic work of art, is the last word in political irresponsibility, and knows itself to be such. In *Antony and Cleopatra* the traditionalist social order flmaboyantly burns itself out, rots itself with motion, snatching a final arrogant victory from its own demise. Creative abundance and clogging superfluity become well-nigh impossible to distinguish. Unfit for social order, Antony and Cleopatra illuminate the meagre pragmatism of calculating Rome in the fire of their self-immolation. What the play's stonily realist characters have to say of the ageing lecher Antony and his shrewish strumpet Cleopatra is at once to the point and gloriously irrelevant; the language of politics no longer meshes with the discourse of value, and the play simply dramatizes their contradiction, practises what Brecht called 'complex seeing', without seeking to resolve it. Banished from the political arena, creative superfluity has now pushed free into a dimension of its own, become its own self-delighting principle quite sundered from history. This poetic transcendence is at the same time the measure of its defeat.

What deconstructs political order in the play is desire, and the figure for this is Cleopatra. In predictably patriarchal style, Cleopatra is portrayed as capricious and self-contradictory, undoing all coherence in her exasperating inconsistency. She is, as it were, pure heterogeneity, an 'infinite variety' which eludes any stable position. Less a rounded 'character' than a complex flow of impulse, her joy in the inconsequential mocks Octavius's view of 'centrality', embodying a 'feminine' trust to sensuous experience which threatens to subvert the public world. Both fearful and admiring of this quality, the play seeks to contain it by making Cleopatra at the same time an image of Nature. If woman for patriarchy is guileful artifice (Cleopatra is a consummate actress), she is also, contradictorily, purely natural. It is as though Cleopatra has the amplitude and spontaneity of Nature itself, containing all things within herself (everything 'becomes' her), as Nature houses an infinite variety of contrary impulses. If she has no fixed identity in herself, she is nevertheless the space within which all creation renews itself, in which conflicting moods converge ('to chide, to laugh, to weep') and every passion strives to make itself 'fair and admir'd'. Her disruptive 'feminine' fickleness can thus be offset by a sense that she harmonizes multitudes in her own being. The effect of this is to blur the borderline between the most 'unnatural' whimsy, intrigue and affectation, and the inexhaustible variety and mutability of Nature itself, just as Enobarbus's great hymn of praise to her ('The barge she sat in, like a burnish'd throne …') subtly deconstructs the distinction between Nature and culture, dissolving both into an all-encompassing Eros. If the woman figures a politically subversive desire, she can also come to symbolize, like Nature itself, the great pre-political matrix from which all cultures proceed, and which supposedly transcends their petty particularities. Woman would appear in this sense to be on the side of both anarchy and order, though the order she symbolizes runs 'deeper' than the political.

If Cleopatra transmutes all things into her own substance, changing one quality into another ('vilest things / Become themselves in her'), then she is uneasily reminiscent of those potentially anarchic forces we have seen at work elsewhere in Shakespeare. Yet to be the space where all things are commutable is to be a kind of cohering principle, even if of a dangerously levelling kind, and so can be presented as an image of variety within order. The chief name for this in Shakespeare is Nature, to which he will finally turn for a mystifying 'resolution' of the historical problems which beset him.

TERENCE HAWKES   *A SEA SHELL**

Terence Hawkes is Professor of English at the University College of Cardiff. His most recent book *That Shakespeherian Rag*, was published by Methuen in 1986. The following extract, 'A Sea Shell', is concerned with the work of the critic A.C. Bradley whose own *Shakespearean Tragedy* (1904) has exerted a considerable influence over generations of Shakespearean critics. Using all the resources of modern critical theory, Hawkes proposes that criticism itself is an improvisational and constitutive discourse, and in Bradley's case the development of a particular brand of Shakespeare criticism proceeded hand in hand with the growth of the discipline we now call English Studies. For Hawkes, 'critical process' effectively constructs the object of its enquiry, and the sense it makes of texts is overdetermined by a complex range of social, cultural and personal factors. Such a view challenges radically the proposition that the text is a transparent surface through which we can glimpse 'what the author had in mind', and this extends also to Bradley's treatment of 'character'. But more importantly, it also challenges the traditional notion of 'text' *per se*: 'Text and reading intermingle as the one becomes an aspect, or particular instance, of the other.' This leads to the radical perception that there is a sense in which texts 'read' readers to the point that reading itself becomes a *dialectical* process involving a series of cultural exchanges. Underpinning the critical position which Hawkes adopts is a theoretical commitment to the 'textual' nature of what we have come to call reality, whereby the material world itself, which the text is said to reflect or mediate, can be understood only in and through textual exchange. Hawkes's approach is post-structuralist in every sense of the term, in its questioning of monologic critical narratives and in its radical witty assault upon the text as fully formed object of a parasitic critical gaze.

Harsh words

It was quite a scandal. The authorities objected strongly to his teaching. In their view it was dominated by a rigid foreign 'system' imported from Europe; obscure, mystifying and replete with 'fuliginous jargon'. Its alien metaphysics exercised a fatal influence over the minds of undergraduates,

*Reprinted from *That Shakespeherian Rag* (London: Routledge, 1986), pp. 27–50.

destroying or at least undermining their British commitment to
straightforward empirical observation, and certainly endangering their
chances in the university examinations, where the examiners were known
for their hostility to this kind of abstract vaporizing. Worse, the ideas
involved had clear, and possibly radical, social and political implications.

The Master felt his world begin to crumble. Formerly an enthusiast, even
something of a 'revolutionary' (he had been called a 'heretic' years
before), he now had little tolerance for this new, foreign, politicized
professionalism which was invading his subject. These youngsters took a
specialized and systematic stance far removed from the rather genteel
mode in which he was accustomed to operate. They were not content to
teach, to aim at producing fully rounded gentlemen. They favoured
rigorous training in the subject and, horror of horrors, postgraduate
research, even the establishment of readerships in the field, committed to
the prosecution of new work within it.

The ringleader, a former friend and current colleague, was invulnerable.
But his subordinates were not. Accordingly, they were edged out, firmly
and decisively: in this particular case 'expelled' in the words of one
commentator, 'martyred' in the words of another. Angry letters passed,
tempers were lost, friendships broken. Eventually the young man obtained
another appointment in a new and soon vigorously expanding field. It led,
not without acrimonious comment in the press, to a chair in Scotland. He
became famous.

No doubt this has a familiar ring. However, the full ironies of the story
emerge when we reflect that these events took place just over one hundred
years ago, in Oxford. The subject involved was philosophy, the Master was
Benjamin Jowett, the college Balliol. And most interesting of all, the name
of the 'martyred' young man whose career, apparently blighted, was then
so decisively revived in a new field by everything that happened, was A.C.
Bradley.

Spreading the word

The family name of Bradley echoes across the Victorian period in a vast
sonorous intellectual peal. Andrew Cecil Bradley was born in 1851. His
father, Charles Bradley, was an Evangelical minister, well known as a
member of the so-called Clapham sect. His half-brother, George Granville
Bradley, was head of Marlborough School, then Master of University
College, Oxford and later Dean of Westminster. His sister, Harriet Bradley,
married George Grove, man of parts, editor for a number of years of the
prestigious *Macmillan's Magazine*, whose major achievement was perhaps
the monumental *Grove's Dictionary of Music*. His older brother was F.H.

Bradley, the idealist philosopher whose work became the subject of T.S. Eliot's doctoral thesis, and ostensibly the reason for that poet's momentous crossing of the Atlantic just before the outbreak of the First World War. Between them, the Bradley family can be said to have had a considerable influence on the fledgling academic subject of 'English' which was invented in their lifetime.

Bradley's doubts concerning his father's Evangelical faith, with its belief in the 'unmediated interpretation of the Bible' and the 'literal truth of scripture', are well attested.[1] There is even talk of a 'spiritual crisis' in the sickly youth, resolved only when in 1869 he entered Balliol College, Oxford, where he encountered the teaching of the man who was the mainstay of the group of British idealist philosophers whose work was having such an intense impact: T.H. Green. Green, Bradley is reported to have said, 'saved' his soul – a feat something of whose dimensions forms the substance of Mrs Humphry Ward's novel about Green (whom she named Grey), *Robert Elsmere*.[2] So saved was he that in 1874 he became a fellow of Balliol, where he taught Philosophy.

According to G.K. Hunter, Bradley's debt to Green is 'quite specific'. It consists, in religious terms,of substituting a Broad Church theology for the more direct claims of Evangelicalism, and as a bulwark against the conservative reaction of High Church theology. In political terms, Green represented that peculiar English confection made from Hegel and an uneasy conscience, Liberalism. Significantly, Bradley was made a Fellow of Balliol on the same day as Asquith. To quote Melvin Richter:

> Between 1880 and 1914 few, if any, other philosophers exerted a greater influence upon British thought and public policy than did T.H. Green .... Green converted Philosophical Idealism, which in Germany had so often served as a rationale of conservatism, into something close to a practical programme for the Left Wing of the Liberal Party.
>
> (*The Politics of Conscience: T.H. Green and his Age*, p. 13)

Green's efforts, as a Broad Churchman, to drop the traditional dogmatic and historically based theology of Christianity in favour of a restatement based on idealist metaphysics could be seen as a direct Liberal challenge to authority, but his embracing and 'liberalizing' of Hegel came to seem an uncritical Germanophilia which gradually effected his own estrangement from Jowett.[3] Jowett's native empiricism clashed directly with Green's idealism, particularly as this grew into the basis for a more 'professionalized' approach to philosophy.

Green's battles to establish philosophy as 'an autonomous professional discipline' (as opposed to a branch of the study of Classics) in fact follows an impetus of Jowett's whose reforms sought to enable philosophy to serve the Broad Church movement.[4] Rejecting the old doctrines of authority, as

Richter says, the new subject sought to teach the history and method of thought, to encourage independent thinking, to teach its students how to think, not what. Green, in Richter's words, 'was certainly the first Fellow of his College, and possibly the first in the University, to conceive of himself as a professional philosopher' (ibid., p. 140). Jowett's disapproval was directed towards what he saw as that philosophy's unwarranted systematization and its separation as a discrete subject from other branches of learning. He stopped Green, and Green's pupils, from conducting tutorials, and his deliberately engineered expulsion of Bradley must be seen as part and parcel of what Green called Jowett's desire 'entirely to expel philosophy from Balliol'.[5]

The details of Bradley's exit remain clouded, but Richter speaks darkly of his 'martyrdom', and a sort of apocalyptic air hangs over the episode. Perhaps we can sense in it the dawn of modern academic specialization and the beginning of a new abrasive mode of secular education. Certainly the pupil of the first 'professional philosopher' left Oxford to become one of the first professional teachers of a new subject: English.

He began at the University of Liverpool. Having applied for a chair in Philosophy and Political Economy, he found himself in fact appointed in 1882 as the first holder of a new chair in Modern Literature and History. After an unsuccessful application for the Merton chair of English at Oxford in 1885, Bradley left Liverpool in 1889 to become Professor of English at Glasgow University. It was this appointment that aroused the notice of the journal *Truth* run by the journalist and MP Henry Labouchère. *Truth's* comment carries more than a hint of the competitive pressures that professionalization brings with it:

> The appointment by Lord Lothian of Mr A.C. Bradley to the Chair of English Literature at Glasgow has given deep offence in Scotland, and, most assuredly, it seems to be an arrant job, for there were several gentlemen whose claims were far superior to those of Mr Bradley, which, indeed, rest on a shadowy foundation, for his merits are by no means widely known, whereas some of the other candidates had distinctly made their mark in literature.
>
> (*Truth*, 1 AUGUST 1889, p. 195)

In 1900, at the age of 49, Bradley took what we would now call early retirement and moved to live in London. And then, in the next year, came the event which affected not only his career, but the intellectual life of the English-speaking world and beyond to a considerable degree. He was made Professor of Poetry at Oxford. It was the return, in a sense, of the repressed.

To say that this post generated some of the lectures which we now know as the substance of Bradley's book *Shakespearean Tragedy* (1904) is to

minimize its importance. In fact, it guaranteed the publication of all of them
– together with a number on more disparate subjects, published as *Oxford
Lectures on Poetry* in 1909 – and in so doing established one of the most
influential texts of our century: one which by now ranks as almost
synonymous with the study of 'English' and which, despite earnest efforts to
unseat it, remains a key, and vastly formative work. Bradley's *Shakespearean
Tragedy* is one of those books whose influence extends far beyond the
confines of its ostensible subject, permeating the attitudes to morality,
psychology and politics of hundreds and thousands of English-speaking
people, regardless of whether or not they have ever set eyes on the text. It
has the authority – not unquestioned of course – of the divine scriptures
(ironically the sort of authority which Green taught their author to question)
and, along with works such as *Scouting for Boys* and *Hymns Ancient and
Modern*, exercises the kind of invisible or subliminal influence on our view of
the world that proves deeply and lastingly persuasive. Still in print (a new
edition appeared in 1985), Bradley's *Shakespearean Tragedy* almost functions,
through a system of universal education which has established the study of
Shakespeare as its linchpin, as part of the air we breathe.

The former rebel philosopher, returning in triumph, and translated to
another dimension, thus exacted a peculiar but not unfitting revenge in
Oxford. Through him, it might be said, Philosophy found itself subverted
by Literature. Together with Classics it sank, in terms of broad social
influence, virtually without trace. English became the huge and continuing
success of the academic world, carrying all before it as the requirement for
social and professional advancement; for instance, in the Civil Service. A
famous comic verse of the 1920s celebrates the inextricable links between
the most important names in exactly that mode:

I dreamt last night that Shakespeare's ghost
Sat for a Civil Service post;
The English paper for the year
Had several questions on *King Lear*
Which Shakespeare answered very badly
Because he hadn't read his Bradley.[6]

Words on the page

'His' Bradley: the possessive conveys a paradoxical universalizing
dimension, stressing the necessity and inevitability of the connection,
heightening it, even, and certainly undermining it by means of the comic
reversal. The reversal's humour lies in its blithe unconcern for an inherited
and implicit notion of the mechanics of 'reading'. It proposes, blandly but

mischievously, that we might be able to read history backwards, thus reinforcing a standard 'commonsense' view that in fact we can *only* read it the other way round. Reading, it insists by comically hinting at the reverse, is unfortunately a one-way process.

Bradley would certainly have agreed, and his theory of reading merits a brief examination for the extent to which it can be said to reinforce this notion. In sum, it rests on the idea of language as a transparent and directly expressive medium. Reading takes the reader through the text to make contact with the author's mind whose contents it expresses. It assumes, as a first principle, that the text functions as a reasonably straightforward pathway to that mind, and as a second that there exists a perfect expressive 'fit' between the text and its author's mental processes. The concern of reading is to follow that pathway as closely as possible and so to re-create in the reader's mind the original process of composition, as it occurred in the poet's mind. In a letter to Gilbert Murray (22 September 1901) Bradley makes the point directly: 'Reading or understanding' the poem, he says, will involve the readers in 'making the same process occur in themselves as occurred in the poet's head'.[7] As a result, he argues elsewhere, 'the poem becomes to the reader what it was to the writer. He [the reader] has not merely interpreted the poem, he has recreated it. For the time being his mind has ceased to be his own, and has become the poet's mind.' We should aim, in short, to 'reproduce in ourselves more faintly that which went on in the poet's mind when he wrote'.[8]

Throughout the lectures in *Shakespearean Tragedy*, the final appeal, in the face of abstract, general ideas is always to the concrete reality, and so to the authority of these mysterious processes, presented – whatever else may be claimed – as what actually happens when the critic reads. For instance, speaking about ideas of Fate in the lecture 'The Substance of Shakespearean Tragedy', Bradley notes that, despite the popularity of that notion,

> I must in candour confess that to me it does not often occur while I am reading, or when I have just read, a tragedy of Shakespeare. Wordsworth's lines, for example about
>
> > ... poor humanity's afflicted will
> > Struggling in vain with ruthless destiny
>
> do not represent the impression I receive; much less do images which compare man to a puny creature helpless in the claws of a bird of prey.
> (*Shakespearean Tragedy*, St Martin's Library edn, London, 1957, p. 22)

And then, as if to reinforce the authority of the personal experience at stake, he adds with the full admonitory force of his Evangelical background, the stern injunction, 'The reader should examine himself closely on this matter.'

Whatever the results of such an examination might be, the twin notions that the words on the page directly and accurately convey what the author had in mind, and that an honest and open reading of them if closely examined will yield access to that mind, clearly operate here. The process involves a text conceived as perfectly transparent: indeed, its perfection results from its transparency. When Bradley reads Shakespeare, then, the action moves entirely one way: the reader checks in, receiving his boarding pass. Beyond the page there lights up a kind of super-smooth runway along which the critic's mind energetically bowls, checking at all times that its responses match the instructions of the control tower, until it launches gratefully and with little effort into the stratospheric mind of the master. At this point the safety belts of close examination may be uncoupled, the cabin crew smile reassuringly, and the in-flight movie begins.

Lost for words

Let us suppose that the film is called *Hamlet, Prince of Denmark*. Bradley's famous lectures on this play begin and sustain the close analytic reading for which he is renowned, and the published version of them in fact advertises this as the decisive point of departure: a preface to the book refers to the first two theoretical introductory lectures as a desirable prolegomenon, but advises, with British empirical dispatch, that 'readers who may prefer to enter at once on the discussion of the several plays can do so by beginning at page 70'. And that page strikes a dominant note: the analysis presents the issue head on:

> Suppose you were to describe the plot of *Hamlet* to a person quite ignorant of the play, and suppose you were careful to tell your hearer nothing about Hamlet's character, what impression would your sketch make on him? Would he not exclaim: 'What a sensational story! Why, here are some eight violent deaths, not to speak of adultery, a ghost, a mad woman and a fight in a grave! ...'
>
> (*Shakespearean Tragedy*, p. 70)

However, something quite simple quickly impresses itself upon this querulous exclaiming person: the conclusion, in Bradley's words, that 'the whole story turns upon the peculiar character of the hero'.

In effect, this lecture scrupulously follows the dictum made plain in the introductory lectures, which establishes immediately the essential feature of Bradley's approach: 'The centre of the tragedy ... may be said with equal truth to lie in action issuing from character, or in character issuing in action' (ibid., p. 7). When he adds 'Shakespeare's main interest lay here', Bradley sets the seal on his whole enterprise. Its focus will be on the reading of character; the inner nature of human beings which determines their deeds and their fate. The dictum that, with Shakespeare, 'character is destiny' may be an exaggeration, he tells us, but only the 'exaggeration of a vital truth'.

Bradley's concern with character has been challenged of course by numbers of critics, specifically L.C. Knights, on the grounds of its reductive nature: it reduces Shakespeare's emblematic, poetic dramas to the level of quasi-realistic portrait galleries of interesting human specimens. It turns the plays into second-rate novels. The same interest has been explained and to some extent justified by G.K. Hunter as a manifestation of the influence on Bradley of Green's Hegelianism. If the tragedies, beyond their surface, give evidence of an 'idealist' dimension, of a general philosophy or meaning (for instance, that the defeat of the tragic protagonist is in the interests of a good greater than himself, as Hunter puts it), then the actions and motivations of the characters in the plays must contain the clues to this meaning (as men's actions do in real life) and can properly be subjected to the closest scrutiny for that purpose. As Hunter argues, 'The world of Shakespearean tragedy is then for A.C. Bradley a world of secular men whose lives yet embody and display the deepest mysteries of our existence'.[9] It is in pursuit of those mysteries that 'character' and the moral choices to which it gives rise are so remorselessly, even obsessionally analysed. The plays become a kind of laboratory in which, under carefully simulated 'real life' conditions, the secrets of existence can be probed.

This is the context, then, in which the analysis of *Hamlet* proceeds. Hamlet's character presents the 'central question' at issue (*Shakespearean Tragedy*, p. 72), and of course the play without that character, *Hamlet* without the Prince, has become a symbol of absurdity. The key to the Prince's character lies in the text, and close reading, close 'attention to the text', repeatedly offers itself as the sole and wholly justifying approach.

Yet remarkably the *Hamlet* lectures proceed to focus a good deal of attention on something that at first sight appears hardly central to the text at all: Hamlet's love for Ophelia. The early reviewers of *Shakespearean Tragedy* certainly remarked upon it. On 28 January 1905, writing in the *Westminster Gazette*, John Churton Collins took Bradley sourly to task on the matter:

> The real points of interest and importance in the drama are not so much as touched on and the particularity with which what is touched on is dealt with is almost invariably in an inverse ratio to its interest and

importance. Probably, for example, no intelligent reader of the play has ever had much difficulty in understanding Hamlet's relation to Ophelia – namely, that he was at first passionately in love with her, that then misunderstanding her reserve, and thinking that she was in league with his enemies, he suspected and mistrusted her, but that to the last something of his old love for her remained. This is discussed under nine headings .... Every lecture teems with those irritating superfluities, aggravated it may be added by the unnecessary diffuseness with which they are discussed.[10]

The essence of Bradley's position lies in the notion that the words on the page transparently express character, and that a vital consistency exists between those elements: 'the text does not bear out the idea that [Hamlet] was one-sidedly reflective and indisposed to action ...' (p. 86); 'But consider the text. This shrinking, flower-like youth – how could he possibly have done what we *see* Hamlet do?' (p. 80) What Hamlet does is of a piece, consistent: 'Imagine Coleridge doing any of these things' (p. 87) – and the overall principle of consistency extends not only to Hamlet's character, but makes that character consistent finally with the character of Shakespeare himself: 'The truth probably is that (Hamlet's 'characteristic humour') was the kind of humour most natural to Shakespeare himself, and that here, as in some other traits of the poet's greatest creation, we come into close contact with Shakespeare the man' (p. 122).

Even concrete personal experience, shared, it is presumed, by Bradley and his reader, finds itself adduced to substantiate the notion that the text expresses a consistency of character development. Take, he argues, 'the idea that the gift and the habit of meditative and speculative thought tend to produce irresolution in the affairs of life': 'Can you verify it', he thunders, '... in the lives of the philosophers, or again in the lives of men whom you have personally known to be addicted to such speculation? I cannot' (p. 92). In real life, as in art, character generates text, text manifests character, and a consistent and perfect 'fit' persists between the two.

Consequently, when Bradley moves to the subject of Hamlet's love for Ophelia, a subject whose importance for him is marked by his decision, he tells us, to reserve for 'separate consideration' this 'important but particularly doubtful point' (p. 103), we confidently expect a close analysis of the text, of the words on the page, in illustration of the argument. In the event, we find quite a different spectacle.

Bradley's problem, like Hamlet's, arises from the question of which of the various conflicting accounts of a particular set of events he is to believe. Certainly Hamlet loved Ophelia. The text offers no difficulties on that point. But as to the course or development of that love in the play, no fewer than three distinct possibilities emerge:

(1) What Bradley calls the 'popular' view. This proposes that Hamlet's love for Ophelia never changed, though he was forced to *pretend* that it did, and thus to act 'a part intensely painful to himself' (p. 123). Over her grave, however, the truth 'bursts' from him. Unfortunately, says Bradley, this view fails to take account of certain 'facts and considerations', which he then proceeds to list, to the derision of Churton Collins, under those infamous *nine* headings (pp. 124ff.). They consist of observations such as: 'How is it that in his first soliloquy Hamlet makes no reference whatever to Ophelia?'; 'How is it that in his second soliloquy, on the departure of the Ghost, he again says nothing about her?'; 'Neither is there the faintest allusion to her in any one of the soliloquies of the subsequent Acts .... If the popular theory is true, is not this an astonishing fact?'; 'Is there no significance in the further fact (which by itself would present no difficulty) that in speaking to Horatio Hamlet never alludes to Ophelia, and that at his death he says nothing of her?'; 'How is it that neither in the Nunnery scene nor at the play-scene does Shakespeare insert anything to make the truth plain? Four words like Othello's "O hardness to dissemble" would have sufficed.' In short, in all but three of the nine cases cited, what Bradley terms Hamlet's 'astonishing' *silence* on key issues proves a major factor.

These considerations suggest two alternative versions of the course of Hamlet's love:

(2) Hamlet's love, though never lost, changed irrevocably as a result of Ophelia's rejection of him, being thenceforth 'mingled with suspicion and resentment' (p. 126)

(3) Hamlet's love was not only mingled with suspicion and resentment as a result of *external pressures*, such as Ophelia's rejection of him, but additionally underwent weakening and deadening from *inside himself*, as a result of his characteristic melancholy. This melancholy lay dormant in him from the beginning and woke 'whenever he saw Ophelia' (p. 127). It failed fully to absorb him, or habitually to occupy his mind, but its 'morbid influence' always lay in wait and 'is the cause of those strange facts, that he never alludes to her in his soliloquies, and that he appears not to realize how the death of her father must affect her'.

Of these three versions of the course of Hamlet's love,

(1) That it never changes,
(2) That it changes because of external reasons,
(3) That it changes because of internal reasons,

Bradley argues that the 'facts' force number three upon us. Once again, he appeals to the coherent 'text' of 'real life': 'psychologically it is quite sound, for a frequent symptom of such melancholy as Hamlet's is a more or less complete paralysis, or even perversion, of the emotion of love' (p. 127).

Yet the plain fact remains that the issue of the course of Hamlet's love for Ophelia depends on elements that are *not* in the text, or on words that Hamlet does *not* say: on his *silence*. This sparks the drama that follows. For given Bradley's commitment to close reading, to 'text', to words on the page, how can he handle silence? And so, having put the case for the importance of the 'internal' operations of Hamlet's melancholy, Bradley recoils in the face of the silence which constitutes its badge: 'yet', he says, 'while feeling no doubt that up to a certain point it is true, I confess I am not satisfied that the explanation of Hamlet's silence regarding Ophelia lies in it' (p. 127). And why is this? Because 'scarcely any spectators or readers of *Hamlet* notice this silence at all; that I never noticed it myself till I began to try to solve the problem of Hamlet's relation to Ophelia; and that even now, when I read the play through without pausing to consider particular questions, it scarcely strikes me' (p. 128).

This opens a textual drama of Hamlet-like proportions. What is the status of the silence in the text? All texts manifest silence. How do we decide whether or not a silence signifies? Or does all silence signify?

Bradley here runs full tilt into the central issues of textuality. We who, since Freud, since Saussure, since Marx, Barthes or Derrida, have felt compelled to listen to the sounds silence makes in a text, to respond to what is *not* said as if it were as significant as what is said, can hardly feel superior to Bradley as he wrestles with this matter. We can and should notice that his struggle reveals the nature and limits of the equipment he brings to it. Certainly, his notion of the text as fully expressive of its author's intention proves inadequate:

> it seems at least possible that the explanation of Hamlet's silence may be that Shakespeare, having already a very difficult task to perform in the soliloquies – that of showing the state of mind which caused Hamlet to delay his vengeance – did not choose to make his task more difficult by introducing matter which would not only add to the complexity of the subject but might, from its 'sentimental' interest distract attention from the main point.
>
> (p. 128)

He also suggests that from his theatrical experience, Shakespeare knew that the audience would not notice the silence. But these are counsels of despair. The text has already ceased to be the bearer of coherent, unitary meaning, or the sure base on which a reading can ground itself. Instead, Bradley tells us, 'I am unable to arrive at a conviction as to the meaning of some of [Hamlet's] words and deeds, and I question whether from the mere text of the play a sure interpretation of them can be drawn' (p. 123).

Neither explanation of the issue, he concludes, can be 'more completely convincing to me than the other' and he finds himself 'driven to suspend judgement, and also to suspect that the text admits of no sure interpretation' (p. 128).

Hamlet himself was never more torn, and Bradley's flat conclusion that 'the text admits of no sure interpretation' could effectively stand as a critical epigraph to the play itself. Like the Prince, he finds himself confronted by complex and bewildering contradictions. First, the three versions of Hamlet's love, all derived from the same text, contradict each other in that they claim on the one hand that Hamlet's love never changes, on the other hand that it does. And if change takes place, they suggest that its cause lies on the one hand with external forces and on the other with internal forces. Second, Shakespeare's intentions with regard to Hamlet's silence appear to be contradictory: on the one hand he seems to be offering a complex account of the Prince's motivation by means of his silence; on the other hand the silence, which we fail to notice anyway, seems a way of avoiding complexity.

In short, by noting the text's silences *as part of the text*, Bradley uncovers a vertiginous vista at its centre, a complex self-engendered paradox, in the face of which any readings can only and must always register bafflement. No appeal to 'real life', no urging that the reader should 'examine himself closely', no attempt to make the same process occur in yourself as occurred in the poet's head will discover the unity and coherence, the 'perfection' of fit between text, author's mind and reader's mind that he searches for.

Bradley's disquiet can be imagined. He has encountered a Ghost on the battlements: it brings the alarming news that a text's 'meaning' cannot be limited to the words it uses. The situation wrings from him a further admission, which he subsequently appends to his analysis as he prepares his lecture for the press. It adds an astonishing dimension. If silence speaks in *Hamlet*, does it not do so in every text? Does not this undermine totally the sense of the text as a positively and fully expressive medium? Does not this apply here and now? Reading over his analysis of Hamlet's silence, a shaken Bradley later attaches the disturbing sentence, 'This paragraph states my view imperfectly' (p. 128).

With this, the fat drops neatly into the fire. If your account of a text's imperfection states your view 'imperfectly', then the *mise en abîme* has no end: your statement that the text 'admits of no sure interpretation' must *itself* be unsure, and the distinction between the text and your commentary on the text begins to dissolve as an immanent imperfection unites them both.

The moment captures and highlights Bradley's encounter with, and his entrapment in textuality. His statement about the imperfection of his own paragraph briefly illuminates the condition that haunts all the lectures on Shakespearean tragedy: there is – as Derrida puts it – no *hors-texte*: no firm, no perfect ground beyond the text from which to mount an objective survey of its imperfections. It follows that the opposition which Bradley has effectively gestured at throughout his lectures – 'perfect' text (which wholly states the author's view and leads directly to the author's mind) and 'imperfect' text (which doesn't) – cannot begin to hold. There are no 'perfect' texts. Bradley's momentary recognition of wholesale imperfection reveals the truth. Texts 'perfectly' reflect little enough in his limited sense. Their plurality – which Bradley labels 'imperfection' and which, for instance, in the obsessional 'nailing down' process characteristic of the 'notes' at the end of *Shakespearean Tragedy*, he attempts to eradicate – in fact defines them and makes them what they are.

With this granted, the prior opposition, Poet's mind–Reader's mind, with its presupposition of a 'perfect' one-way 'reading' transmission from one polarity through a transparent text to the other, can hardly hold. And the specific 'named' instance of that which has already been mentioned and on which Bradley's enterprise famously depends

Shakespeare–Bradley

thus immediately becomes vulnerable as the names begin to melt into one another. Certainly the opposition which currently concerns us, Shakespeare's text of *Hamlet* as against Bradley's reading of *Hamlet*, must collapse as a result. As it does so, we can surely say that Bradley's reading of *Hamlet*, with its princely indecision, its soliloquizing puzzlement over contradiction, its rapier wit, its melancholic worrying, its weary ultimate consignment of vast interpretative realms (the 'rest') to silence, virtually becomes part of the play. Text and reading intermingle as the one becomes an aspect, or particular instance, of the other.

Far from contradicting Bradley's notion of reading, this extends its implications to the full. The reader, we remember, should not merely interpret the poem, but 'recreate' it. His mind should accordingly cease to be his own and should 'become the poet's mind'. He should make 'the same process' occur in himself as occurred in 'the poet's head', and should aim to repeat and reproduce the mental acts in which the poem exists. The reader should *become* the poet and should relive part of the poet's life.

And the spectacle that confronts us is finally of Bradley's becoming the Bard, of his text turning into Shakespeare's and as an effect of that, of Shakespeare reading and indeed writing Bradley; exactly the picture conjured by the verse about the Civil Service examination. Seen thus, it stretches the rather limited sense of those terms 'reading' and 'writing' which we inherit from the nineteenth century. Shakespeare's texts, processed as they must be by the political and social forces of our society, force a deployment of responses to themselves on the reader (constructing in him or her for instance a rage for coherence of 'characterisation') which in this case offers to dissolve the Bradley–Shakespeare, reading–writing polarity entirely. To name the one, as we have said, is to name the other. It is almost as if Shakespeare had read, or reached via the text, 'his' Bradley, Bradley's mind, and written down a version of what he found there.

Can we not distinguish Bradley from Shakespeare then? Is Shakespeare's text the same as Bradley's account of it? In a complex social sense, by means of that linkage of names which the comic verse insists on, the answer must of course be yes. For thousands of the products of our education system this is the case: a situation which the verse affirms, through its mockery. If Shakespearean tragedy 'reads' Bradley, it is, quite literally, A.C. Bradley who writes *Shakespearean Tragedy*.

To underline the point, we might bring to mind a curious episode in the middle of the lecture on *King Lear*. Bradley is discussing the author's design for the character of the Fool. Suddenly, from the lecturer's mouth, we hear a startling new voice, that of Shakespeare himself:

> I will have a fool in the most tragic of my tragedies. He shall not play a little part. He shall keep from first to last the company in which you most object to see him, the company of a king. Instead of amusing the king's idle hours, he shall stand by him in the very tempest and whirlwind of passion. Before I have done you shall confess, between laughter and tears, that he is of the very essence of life, that you have known him all your days though you never recognised him till now, and that you would as soon go without Hamlet as miss him.
>
> (p. 259)

As the Professor's accents become indistinguishable from those of the Bard (Bradley has asked us to imagine Shakespeare reeling winsomely home one evening from The Mermaid Tavern), a central aspect of his criticism shows its hand. Who, listening to his lecture, could confidently identify or separate the speakers at this point? No 'perfect' answer is possible.

The sound of silence

Perhaps the ultimate critical act occurs when reader merges into writer, lecturer into subject. And in the case of *Hamlet* it is instructive to grasp the degree to which Bradley's analysis finally generates total integration of this sort. The bare biographical information that Bradley himself suffered from 'unrequited love and fits of melancholy'[11] fails to surprise. He aims to go beyond the text, to gain access to the author's mind. But the text, as I hope to have shown, always refuses to yield up that quarry. Instead, rejecting its presupposed separate identity it asserts a paradoxical unity with its interpreter, returning the reader's mind back again, but dressed up as the author's: Bradley, as it were, in doublet and hose.

Silence in any text offers the perfect occasion for this kind of transaction. As we have seen in the case of *Hamlet*, silence gives back nothing. Or, indiscriminately open to interpretation, it gives back anything and everything. If we wanted a metaphor for the process we might consider the sea shell: held to the ear, it apparently emits the sounds of the sea. But of course the sea shell does no such thing: it produces no sound. In fact the sound we hear may simply be the sound of the circulation of our own blood. Nevertheless, we impose a meaning on the sea shell's silence that appears to extend well beyond ourselves. We say that it speaks to us closely, of its own intimate connection with the sea.

As we watch Bradley place Shakespeare's sea shell text to his ear, we can only guess at the nature of the pressures that have already begun to shape what he is bound to hear. His commitment to a probing of Hamlet's silence accords with a broader contemporary concern, almost ubiquitous at this time, to penetrate silent and unnameable dimensions thought to lie beyond the surfaces of all manner of texts. Conan Doyle's stories of Sherlock Holmes depend on the detective's urgent will to fathom those depths. Oscar Wilde's *The Picture of Dorian Gray* (1891) offers a classic instance of the more sinister deployment of a sense of culpable interiority, and in the specific case of Shakespeare, it is possible to point to Wilde's earlier version of a similar idea in his outrageous peek behind the texts of the Sonnets in *The Portrait of Mr W.H.* (1889) which unveils Willie Hughes to public view. Frank Harris's *The Man Shakespeare* (1909) subsequently proposed a further sensational lifting of the text's facade. The sense of mute and forbidding, not to say forbidden profundities lurking behind bland textual frontages finally and shatteringly surfaced in the trials of Oscar Wilde in 1895, when the text of love itself was forced openly to admit to dark, shameful realms of experience which Victorian Britain had suppressed by a massive silence, commemorated in Lord Alfred Douglas's scandalous reference to the 'love that dare not speak its name'.

An urgent, if not hysterical, public commitment to the naming of that name nevertheless finds expression in the savagery of the sentence passed on Wilde. The Criminal Law Amendment Act under which he was arraigned had reached the statute book only ten years earlier, and the particular clause dealing with his offence had been inserted into it and zealously carried through Parliament by the same Henry Labouchère who had earlier named Bradley in connection with the Glasgow chair. Labouchère's aim, he makes clear, was to force the law and the public to 'take cognizance', as he put it, of activities such as Wilde's. And indeed his lifelong commitment to the boisterous breaking of silence is confirmed by the uncompromising title of his journal, *Truth*, as well as by his general political stance which frequently found a good deal of public support.[12] Conflicting impulses thus seem to confront each other. On the one hand a pressure not to name, to suppress, occlude, obscure: on the other an opposite pressure to nominate, to pierce the veil, to take cognizance.

In 1868, just before entering Oxford, Bradley published a poem in *Macmillan's Magazine*. A conventional, Keatsian piece of juvenilia, it was called, appropriately, 'A Sea Shell':

> Cool lips of shell, sing, Sea-shell, warm and sweet,
>   Of ripples curling on the creamy beach,
>   Of soft waves singing in each other's ear,
> Small wavelets kissing one another's feet,
>   Where flakes of foam make music, a low speech
>   Tenderly sad to hear.
>
> Tell me of half-formed little broken words,
>   Sung by the ripples to the still sea-flowers
>   In silent sleeping tideless deeps of sea;
> For there the flowers have voices like to birds,
>   That sing full-throated in this world of ours
>   On each melodious tree.
>
> Not now, not now, sweet shell, some other day
>   Tell me of sighings on the lonely shore,
>   And seas that sob to birds that scream above;
> Tell me not now of earth grown weak and pray,
>   Nor longing for the things that come no more,
>   Nor any broken love.
>
> To me thy breathing bears another tone,
>   Of fresh cool currents running under sea,
>   And happy laughter of the sunny spray:
> Ah! hearest thou the words that are thine own,
>   Knowest thou the message that they bear to me,
>   The things they seem to say?
>
> Ah, Sea-shell, it is this – 'The soft blue deep,
>   Which thrills with a heart that knows thee and is kind,
>   Sighed for thy sorrow, now it laughs with thee;
> Love is a secret which man cannot keep,
>   Hide it from heaven and the heedless wind,
>   But trust it with the sea!'

Hindsight, or even a less respectable impulse to coherence might urge that the distinction drawn here between the aridity of the land, 'the lonely shore ... earth grown weak and gray' and the welcoming and comforting depths of the sea hints, albeit damply, at the attraction of those silent, beckoning dimensions to be explored by Bradley's idealism in the years to come, and which subsequently make their formative contribution to his general theory of Shakespearean tragedy. Characteristically, he also insists on the text's transparent connection with actuality, claiming that a reader might make contact through it with its author's mind and with an experience that took place in the real world. He puts this point in his proposal to Macmillan in 1871 that a collection of his verse might be made:

> The poems are arranged in chronological order, for the reason that there is so much change in the subjects and treatment that the book would in this way take an almost biographical form, and I confess one of my reasons for wishing to publish them is the belief that those poems which come near the end of the volume might be of service as well as a pleasure to persons who go through some such experience as is there portrayed.[13]

Macmillan declined the offer. But whatever the nature of the experience at stake, lines such as the last stanza's 'Love is a secret which man cannot keep' seem inextricably involved in the contradictory pressures mentioned above. On the one hand they acknowledge the imperatives of revelation, that love's secrets cannot hope to be hidden; on the other they seem to embrace and even to endorse the comforts of silence and suppression offered by the mysterious sea. The overt complexities at issue for Bradley in Hamlet's unspoken love for Ophelia may or may not be prefigured here. But certainly the syncopation of half-silence with half-utterance, telling with not-telling, naming with not-naming in which the poem invests projects it firmly towards a cognate nexus of discordant tendencies: a curious discursive arena, its contours made concrete and overt years later in the Wilde trials, where silence paradoxically partners eloquence in a continuing, unfathomable *pas de deux*.

The tensions accompanying an effort to link idealism's cloudy concerns with a politics of practical reality were perhaps already troubling the young Bradley before he entered Oxford and encountered T.H.Green. The 'spiritual crisis' of his youth may have had additional dimensions, but this was certainly an area in which Green's teaching had 'saved' more than one soul. By the time he became Professor of Poetry, Bradley had digested a version of Green's idealism capable, as we have seen, of fuelling a critical, if not a poetical *modus operandi*.

In fact his lectures mark a moment of significant ideological change. For the years of Bradley's Oxford professorship, after 1901, were also the years which marked the decline of idealism's intellectual dominance of British philosophy. In fact Anthony Quinton goes so far as to nominate 1903, which saw the publication of Bertrand Russell's *Principles of Mathematics* and Moore's *Refutation of Idealism*, as the specific moment of idealism's demise, and thus the end of a hegemony that had begun in 1874. That was the year of Green's critical introduction to his and Grose's edition of Hume's *Treatise of Human Nature*, and of F.H. Bradley's *The Presuppositions of Critical History* and a number of other influential idealist works. The year 1874 also saw A.C. Bradley's initial appointment to a fellowship in Philosophy at Balliol College. Quinton points out that idealism's decline generated the poignant spectacle of ranks of technically unemployable idealists within the philosophical profession. A remarkable number of them dealt with the problem by becoming vice-chancellors. As Quinton observes, 'The Hegelian mode of thought, with its combination of practical realism and theoretical nebulosity, is a remarkably serviceable instrument for the holders of high administrative positions.'[14] In Bradley's case the fact that the beginning of his career as a professional philosopher coincides with the rise of idealism whilst his tenure of the Oxford Professorship of Poetry coincides with its decline suggests a rather more momentous transfer. In his person, we might say, idealism and liberalism do not decline, so much as migrate with their 'combination of practical realism and theoretical nebulosity' to the new field of English studies where, to this day, in Britain at least, they remain alive and well.

Naming names

The act of taking cognizance, of naming, has always, since Adam, promised a bulwark against chaos. It offers to weld language to the world and the world to language and to use that impacted link as an instrument of control. It was said at the beginning of this essay that the Bradley name rang across Victorian Britain in a great reassuring peal. It seems appropriate at its end to note that Andrew Cecil Bradley's name seems nevertheless to have exhibited a peculiar kind of unsettling potency even before it became widely known. It attracted, as we have seen, the makers of comic verses. It also attracted the constructors of clerihews, that odd and very English investment in the textuality of nomenclature. In common with Curzon –

My name is George Nathaniel Curzon
I am a most superior person.
My face is pink, my hair is sleek,
I dine at Blenheim once a week.

– and others, Bradley appears in the so-called *Balliol Rhymes* not once, but twice. And in each case he does so with the distinct suggestion that there exist in his person silent and potentially disturbing domains beyond the quotidian:

> I am MR ANDREW BRADLEY
> When my liver's doing badly
> I take refuge from 'the brute'
> In the blessed Absolute.

If that rhyme refers to his then overt professional standing as an idealist philosopher, the other nods decisively in the direction of his competing, albeit covert commitment to literature. Indeed, it pretends scandalously to expose that commitment and mocks its covert nature:

> I'm BR-DL-Y, and I bury deep
> 'A secret that no man can keep'
> If you won't let the Master know it,
> Or F-RB-S, I'll tell you, – I'm a poet.[15]

Part of the humour here lies, of course, in the fact that Bradley's 'secret', given the slightest of homosexual tinges by the quotation of that line from 'A Sea Shell' which chimes with Douglas's 'love that dare not speak its name', emerges comically deflated as a silent 'poetic' dimension looming, unacknowledged and unspeaking, behind his professional role as philosopher. Its effects were also never less than unsettling. J.W. Mackail, who knew him at the time, tries to name this extra dimension specifically, calling Bradley 'an enigma, a veiled poet or a veiled prophet',[16] but only succeeds in confirming that personal *aporia* which the Master of the college's later campaign forced him to confront, and to take a decision about.

Like all texts, clerihews finally give back only the opacity from which they derive. The kind of nomination in which they deal not only forgoes the goal of perfect transparency, it tries deliberately to undermine the project by means of its calculated investment in terse partiality. Thus the clerihew flagrantly abandons any notion of a balanced classification of unchanging permanent reality at which the usual act of naming aims. Systematically, it both names the truth and obscures it, and thus seems well matched, in Bradley's case, to its subject.

Its reward lies in its resultant capacity to achieve a kind of sudden, albeit minor subversion of expectation. Like all successful satire, the clerihew leads us to the edge of a 'named' world, and by undermining names offers to tip us over it. While that impossible feat can never actually be achieved, the attempt hints at that world's boundary, its edge. The clerihew hones that edge sharply.

If, finally, those with Bradley as their subject offer to take cognizance of silent and unnameable dimensions in him, and, in that endeavour, suggest early pointers to the shape of his encounter with the silences of *Hamlet*, the Balliol clerihew on Jowett exacts the cruellest revenge in his name. For the author of Bradley's martyrdom remains himself impaled on a rhyme that presents perfectly the trap of textuality that lay in wait for his generation:

First come I: my name is Jowett
There's no knowledge but I know it.

– and it continues in its delicious circularity, to delineate exactly the doom awaiting those who fall into its clutches:

I am Master of this College
And what I don't know isn't knowledge.

That last line remains as perfect a statement of silence-effacing self-reflection as any English text has to offer. In it the voice of the sea shell is heard in the land.

Notes

1. MELVIN RICHTER, *The Politics of Conscience: T.H. Green and his Age* (London, 1964), p. 25, and G.K. HUNTER, 'A.C. Bradley's *Shakespearean Tragedy*', *Essays and Studies* 21 (London, John Murray for the English Association, 1968), 103.

2. RICHTER, op. cit., p. 14. Also J.W. MACKAIL, 'Andrew Cecil Bradley 1851–1935', *Proceedings of the British Academy* XXI (1935), 385ff.

3. RICHTER, op. cit., p. 27.

4. Ibid., p. 138.

5. Ibid., p. 153.

6. See KATHERINE COOKE, *A.C. Bradley and his Influence on Twentieth Century Shakespearean Criticism* (Oxford, Clarendon Press, 1972), pp. 191–2 for the text of the verse and a discussion of its provenance.

7. Cit. COOKE, op. cit., p. 184.

8. Cit. ibid., p. 50. The quotations are from different sources.

9. HUNTER, op. cit., p. 112.

10. Cit. COOKE, op. cit., pp. 3–4.

11. FRANCIS WEST, *Gilbert Murray, A Life* (London, 1984), p. 84.

12. See HESKETH PEARSON, *The Life of Oscar Wilde* (London, 1946: Penguin edn, Harmondsworth, 1960), p. 297. Labouchère's comments make his own position quite clear:

Wilde and Taylor were tried on a clause in the Criminal Law Amendment Act which I had inserted in order to render it possible for the law to take cognizance of proceedings like theirs. I took the clause *mutatis mutandis* from the French Code. As I had drafted it the maximum sentence was seven years. The then Home Secretary and Attorney-General, both most experienced men, suggested to me that in such cases convictions are always difficult and that it would be better were the maximum to be two years. Hence the insufficiency of the severest sentence that the law allows.

(Hesketh Pearson, Labby: *The Life and Character of Henry Labouchère* (London, 1936), p. 242). The sentence was two years' hard labour.

13. SIMON NOWELL-SMITH (ed.), *Letters to Macmillan* (London, 1967), pp. 138–9.

14. ANTHONY QUINTON, *Thoughts and Thinkers* (London, 1982), pp. 186–8. The whole chapter, 'Absolute Idealism', 186–206, repays study.

15. Cit. COOKE, op. cit., p. 24.

16. MACKAIL, op. cit., p. 387.

Bibliography

(1) Theory of tragedy

ARISTOTLE, *The Poetics*, trans. John Warrington (London, 1963)

BENJAMIN, WALTER, *The Origins of German Tragic Drama*, trans. John Osborne (London, 1985)

BOAL, AUGUSTO, *Theater of the Oppressed*, trans. C.A. and Maria-Odilia Leal McBride (London, 1979)

BRADLEY, A.C., 'Hegel's Theory of Tragedy', *Oxford Lectures on Poetry* (London, 1909)

DERRIDA, JACQUES, *Dissemination*, trans. Barbara Johnson (London, 1981)

FREUD, SIGMUND, *Art and Literature*, Pelican Freud Library, vol. 14, ed. Albert Dixon (Harmondsworth, 1985)

GIRARD, RENE, *Violence and the Sacred*, trans. Patrick Gregory, (Baltimore and London, 1977)

GOLDMANN, LUCIEN, *The Hidden God: a Study of the Tragic Vision in the 'Pensées' of Pascal and the Tragedies of Racine*, trans. Philip Thody (London, 1976)

GREEN, ANDRÉ, *The Oedipus Complex in Tragedy*, trans. Alan Sheridan (Cambridge, 1979)

HEGEL, G. W. F. *Hegel on Tragedy*, ed. Anne and Henry Paulucci (New York and London, 1962)

LEECH, CLIFFORD, *Tragedy* (London, 1969)

NIEBUHR, REINHOLD, *Beyond Tragedy: Essays on The Christian Interpretation of History* (New York, 1937)

NIETZSCHE, FRIEDRICH, *The Birth of Tragedy and the Genealogy of Morals*, trans. Francis Golffing (New York, 1956)

STEINER, GEORGE, *The Death of Tragedy* (London, 1961)

THOMPSON, GEORGE, *Aeschylus and Athens: a Study in The Social Origins of Drama* (London, 1941)

UNAMUNO, MIGUEL DE, *The Tragic Sense of Life*, trans. J.E. Crawford-Flitch (New York, 1954)

WILLIAMS, RAYMOND, *Modern Tragedy* (London, 1966)

(2) Shakespearean tragedy

AERS, D., HODGE, R. and KRESS, G., *Literature, Language and Society in England 1580–1680* (Dublin, 1981)

BARKER, FRANCIS, *The Tremulous Private Body: Essays on Subjection* (London, 1984)

BELSEY, CATHERINE, *The Subject of Tragedy: Identity and Difference in Renaissance Drama* (London, 1985)

BEVINGTON, DAVID, and HALIO, JAY L. (eds), *Shakespeare: Pattern of Excelling Nature* (New Jersey, 1978)

COHEN, WALTER, *Drama of a Nation: Public Theater in Renaissance England and Spain* (New York and London, 1985)

DOLLIMORE, JONATHAN, *Radical Tragedy: Religion, Ideology and Power in the Drama of Shakespeare and his Contemporaries* (Brighton, 1984; 2nd ed, 1989)

DOLLIMORE, JONATHAN, and SINFIELD, ALAN, *Political Shakespeare: New Essays in Cultural Materialism* (Manchester, 1985)

DRAKAKIS, JOHN, *Alternative Shakespeares* (London, 1985)

——— 'The Engendering of Toads: Patriarchy and the Problem of Subjectivity in Shakespeare's *Othello*', *Shakespeare Jahrbuch*, 124 (Weimar, 1988) ed. Gunther Klotz

DUSINBERRE, JULIET, *Shakespeare and the Nature of Women* (London, 1975)

EAGLETON, TERRY, *William Shakespeare* (Oxford, 1986)

EVANS, MALCOLM, *Signifying Nothing: Truth's True Contents in Shakespeare's Texts* (Brighton, 1986; 2nd ed, 1989)

FRENCH, MARILYN, *Shakespeare's Division of Experience* (London, 1982)

GOLDBERG, JONATHAN, *James I and the Politics of Literature: Jonson, Shakespeare, Donne and their Contemporaries* (Baltimore and London, 1983)

GREENBLATT, STEPHEN, *Renaissance Self-fashioning from More to Shakespeare* (Chicago and London, 1980)

——— *Shakespearean Negotiations: the Circulation of Social Energy in Renaissance England* (Oxford, 1988)

HAWKES, TERENCE, *That Shakespeherian Rag: Essays on a Critical Process* (London, 1986)

HOLDERNESS, GRAHAM, *The Shakespeare Myth* (Manchester, 1988)

HOLDERNESS, G., POTTER, N. and TURNER, J., *Shakespeare: the Play of History* (London, 1988)

HOWARD, JEAN, and O'CONNOR, MARION, *Reproducing Shakespeare: the Text in History and Ideology* (London, 1987)

JARDINE, LISA, *Still Harping on Daughters: Women and Drama in the Age of Shakespeare* (Brighton, 1983)

KAHN, COPPÉLIA, *Man's Estate: Masculine Identity in Shakespeare* (Berkeley, 1981)

KANTOROWICZ, ERNST, *The King's Two Bodies: a Study in Medieval Political Theology* (Princeton, 1957)

KETTLE, ARNOLD. (ed), *Shakespeare in a Changing World* (London, 1964)

KRISTEVA, JULIA, *Tales of Love*, trans. Leon Roudiez (New York, 1987)

LACAN, JACQUES, 'Desire and the Interpretation of desire in Hamlet', Shoshana Felman (ed.), *Literature and Psychoanalysis: the Question of Reading: Otherwise* (Baltimore and London, 1982)

LENZ, C., GREENE, G. and NEELEY, C., *The Woman's Part: Feminist Criticism of Shakespeare* (Chicago, 1980)

LOOMBA, ANIA, *Gender, Race, Renaissance Drama* (Manchester, 1987)

MARCUS, LEAH, *Puzzling Shakespeare: Local Reading and its Discontents* (Berkeley and London, 1988)

MARIENSTRAS, RICHARD, *New Perspectives on the Shakespearean World*, trans. Janet Lloyd (Cambridge, 1985)

MORETTI, FRANCO, *Signs Taken for Wonders: Essays in the Sociology of Literary Forms* (London, 1983)

MULLANEY, *The Place of the Stage: License, Play and Power in Renaissance England* (Chicago and London, 1988)

NEELEY, CAROL THOMAS, *Broken Nuptials in Shakespeare's Plays* (New Haven and London, 1985)

PARKER, P., AND HARTMAN, G. (eds), *Shakespeare and the Question of Theory* (London, 1985)

PATTERSON, ANNABEL, *Shakespeare and the Popular Voice* (Oxford, 1989)

PYE, CHRISTOPHER, *The Regal Phantasm: Shakespeare and the Politics of Spectacle* (London, 1990)

SCHWARTZ, M., and KAHN, C., *Representing Shakespeare: New Psychoanalytic Essays* (Baltimore and London, 1980)

SINFIELD, ALAN, *Literature in Protestant England 1560–1660* (London, 1983)

TENNENHOUSE, LEONARD, *Power on Display: the Politics of Shakespeare's Genres* (New York and London, 1986)

WEIMANN, ROBERT, *Shakespeare and the Popular Tradition in the Theater: Studies in the Social Dimension of Dramatic Form and Function*, trans. Robert Schwartz (Baltimore and London, 1978)

Index

absolutism, 27, 28, 47-48, 100, 101-2, 105, 106, 108
absorption, 161, 166
acting area, 118-25, 148-9
actor–audience relationship, 122-5, 130-3, 136-9, 141, 143, 147, 150, 152
Adams, J.C., 148
Adams, J.Q., 119, 121, 148, 150
Adelman, Janet, 35
  Representing Shakespeare, 353-73
adultery, 175, 176-8, 180-1, 189-90, 243, 259
aesthetics, 4, 5, 6, 8, 25
Alarcon, Juan Ruiz de ,
  Ganar amigos, 105-6
  La verdad sospechosa, 106
allegory, 72-4, 76-7, 85-6
Alpers, Svetlana, 187
Altman, Joel,
  The Tudor Play of Mind, 161, 184
Ambrose, St, 179, 190
anagnorisis, 6
Anderson, Perry, 22, 43, 58
  Lineages, 78, 80
androgynism, 307, 308, 314
Ainkst, Alexander, 149
animal imagery, 234, 239, 242, 252-3, 274, 276
anthropology, 2-3, 14, 16
Arden of Feversham (anon), 55, 107, 108, 109
aristocracy, 96, 100, 102, 104, 109, 395-6
Aristotle, 1, 2, 8, 12, 21, 49
  The Nicomachean Ethics, 40, 387
  Poetics, 5-6, 32, 38-9
Armstrong W.A., 147
Arnold, M.L., 150

Aronson, Alex, 278
asides, 70, 131, 132, 141, 143, 145, 151
Astell, Mary, 226
Aubrey, John, 386
Auerbach, Nina, 294
Augustine, St, 172, 177, 190
  City of God, 188
author function, 19

Bachelard, Gaston, 284, 294
Bacon, Francis, 200
Bakhtin, Mikhail, 117, 193, 374, 378, 387
Baldwin, William
  The Mirror for Magistrates, 50, 55, 79
Bances Candamo, Francisco Antonio de,
  El escalvo en grillos de oro, 104, 105
Barber, C.L., 192
Barker, Thomas, 285
Barnet, Sylvan, 277
Barron, David B., 371, 372
Barthes, Roland, 4, 5, 19
  Image, Music, Text, 38, 42
  The Pleasure of the Text, 38
Baskervill, Charles Read, 185
Bass, Alan, 42, 44
Bataille, Georges, 193
Beaumont, Francis (and John Fletcher)
  The Maid's Tragedy, 215
Beckerman, Bernard, 148, 149
Becon, Thomas, 171, 188
Bell, Thomas, 113
Belsey, Catherine, 18
  The Subject of Tragedy, 27, 32-3, 42, 43, 44, 208-27, 387
Benjamin, Walter, 7, 40, 49, 53, 73, 74, 377
  The Origin of German Tragic Drama, 78, 79, 80, 84